THE STORY OF WORK

THE STORY OF WORK

A New History of Humankind

JAN LUCASSEN

YALE UNIVERSITY PRESS
NEW HAVEN AND LONDON

For information about this and other Yale University Press publications, please contact:
U.S. Office: sales.press@yale.edu yalebooks.com
Europe Office: sales@yaleup.co.uk yalebooks.co.uk

Set in Minion Pro by IDSUK (DataConnection) Ltd
Printed in Great Britain by TJ Books, Padstow, Cornwall

Library of Congress Control Number: 2021935440

ISBN 978-0-300-25679-6

A catalogue record for this book is available from the British Library.

10 9 8 7 6 5 4 3 2

CONTENTS

ILLUSTRATIONS, MAPS AND FIGURES

Plate section

1. Communal hunting: Joseph Lycett, 'Aborigines using fire to hunt kangaroos', c. 1817, from *Views in Australia; or New South Wales and Van Diemen's Land Delineated* (London: J. Souter, 1824). National Library of Australia, PIC MS STRONG ROOM 12/1/4 #R5689.
2. From hunting-gathering to agriculture: later Han tomb chamber decoration, 25–220. Sichuan Provincial Museum, Chengdu, China. Granger Historical Picture Archive / Alamy Stock Photo.
3. Grain harvest in Ancient Egypt (Luxor, 1390–1380 BCE): tomb of Menna, Luxor (Theban Tombs TT69). DEA / G. DAGLI ORTI / Getty Images.
4. Maritime and port work for Rome: sestertius of Emperor Nero, 54–68. Brussels National Library, coin cabinet (photo Johan van Heesch).
5. Working the land in North Africa, 200–25: mosaic in a villa. Archaeological Museum of Cherchell, Algeria. DEA / G. DAGLI ORTI / Getty Images.
6. Glass making, c. 1400: tinted grisaille drawings on green parchment. British Library, Add. Ms. 24189, fol. 16r. © British Library Board. All Rights Reserved / Bridgeman Images.
7. Working Aztec children: page from the Codex Mendoza, 1541.
8. Goa washermen and women: page from the Códice Casanatense, c. 1540. Biblioteca Casanatense. The Códice Casanatense / CC0 1.0.
9. Guild procession: miniature from the *Surname-i Hümayun*, 1582. Topkapı Sarayı Müzesi, Istanbul, Hazine 1344, fols. 338b–39a.
10. Dutchman with his Indonesian slave in Japan: polychromatic woodblock print, published by Yamatoya Publishing House, Nagasaki, c. 1800. IISH, NEHA # Japanese prints, Box 2, no. 12. International Institute of Social History (Amsterdam).

11. Slaves washing for diamonds: etching after T. Webster after J. Mawe, 1815. Photo 12 / Getty Images.

12. Cottage industry, sericulture: 'Rikuchū no kuni yōsan no zu. 6'. Colour woodcut by Hiroshige III, published by Nihonbashi, Tokyo, c. 1877. University of British Columbia. Library. Rare Books and Special Collections. Asian Rare-6 no. L2:1.

13. May Day: 'Labour's May Day dedicated to the workers of the world' propagating the 8-hour working day, by Walter Crane. Coloured edition in German, Austria, 1897. IISH Amsterdam IISG # BG C3/900. International Institute of Social History (Amsterdam).

14. Pay day at the Braat machine-building plant: *Gedenkboek van de N.V. Machinefabriek Braat te Soerabaja 1901–1921* (Batavia, 1921). IISH-NEHA, Amsterdam # Collection NV Machinefabriek Braat (Soerabaja) ARCH03606. International Institute of Social History (Amsterdam).

15. Soviet work propaganda: poster design by Gustav Klutsis, 1932; photographer S. Blochin; publisher Ogiz-Izogiz, Moscow/Leningrad. IISH, Amsterdam, # USSR, 1932 – BG E12/680–1. International Institute of Social History (Amsterdam).

16. China work propaganda: poster design by Jin Zhaofang, July 1954. Serial no. 538, IISH, Amsterdam # China, 1954 – BG E16/627. International Institute of Social History (Amsterdam).

17. Ford assembly line: Ford's 10 millionth Model T, 4 June 1924. Shawshots / Alamy Stock Photo.

18. Control room: fossil fuel power plant in Point Tupper, Nova Scotia, 27 May 2007.

In text

Introduction. *Washing day on the street*, Lindenstraat, Amsterdam, 1951. Photo Ben van Meerendonk. International Institute of Social History (Amsterdam).

Chapter 1. Hadza woman digs for edible tubers. John Warburton-Lee Photography / Alamy Stock Photo.

Chapter 2. Uruk-period (4000–3100 BCE) seal. Yale Babylonian Collection, NBC 2579.

Chapter 3. Victory stele of a king of Akkad (2300 BCE). Louvre Museum, GNU Free Documentation License, CC BY 3.0.

Chapter 4. Women and men mining for silver (Bohemia/Saxony), woodcut by Blasius Freming in Georgius Agricola, *Vom Bergkwerck XII* (Basel: Froben, 1557). International Institute of Social History (Amsterdam).

Chapter 5. Pieter van Laer, *Pigs and Donkeys*, plate 4 from the series *Different Animals*, Italy, 1636. Rijksmuseum (Amsterdam).

Chapter 6. Detail of an illustration of Coster's diamond factory on Zwanenburgerstraat, Amsterdam *Eigen Haard*, 1875. International Institute of Social History (Amsterdam).

Chapter 7. Basti Bagirova at the cotton harvest, Azerbaijan, 1950. De Brug / Djambatan 27b, no. 5469, Photo Hans Luhrs, International Institute of Social History (Amsterdam).

Outlook. Frans Masereel, *The Ideal Producer of the Future*, in *La Feuille*, 27 October 1919. International Institute of Social History (Amsterdam).

Maps

Figures

PREFACE

The idea for this book emerged in the 1990s, in that optimistic period after the fall of the Berlin Wall. State socialism had failed, and with it, apparently, the idea that the exploited worker could only find liberation in a totally 'classless' society. Instead, a new utopian dream began to emerge. This started in the West but was quickly embraced globally, with the same enthusiasm with which Coca-Cola had been welcomed worldwide. From now on, it seemed, we would be able to earn our money as independent entrepreneurs, hiring out our creative talents to the highest bidder. We would have to work perhaps only a few hours a day, or even a week. We would be so successful that, ultimately, we would have time – vast expanses of delicious leisure time. Our life would be defined by consumption, not by production.

In this utopia, crucially, only losers work for someone else; the new, true individuals are the self-employed and the entrepreneurs, and everyone craves a 'portfolio' career. And, while the banking crises of 2008 and, more recently, the global coronavirus pandemic have tempered enthusiasm somewhat, this utopia is still alive and kicking, if only because of the lack of a serious challenger. The entrepreneur is a hero, the ordinary worker a slave.

Such a misconception is widespread because it does not reside only among champions of the 'free' market; it is just as much a source for left-wing utopian thinking, which, of course, does not trumpet independent entrepreneurship but rather glorifies wage labour for the community and, with it, the notion of well-earned free time.

I have become increasingly vexed by this view of conventional working people as either exploited victims or as uninventive and unimaginative dullards. Not that I have anything against the entrepreneurial spirit of the individual. But is work – and by that I refer specifically to wage labour or small businesses absent from the utopian vistas of boundless expansion – a dying occupation? Is the *history* of the work of the ordinary man and woman no longer important to us? And what does this glorification of leisure time and entrepreneurship mean for women's emancipation and the pursuit of equal opportunities for women in the labour market (let alone the valuing of domestic work)?

Undoubtedly, feelings of vexation are related to my own intense pleasure in intellectual wage labour, and to my upbringing in the context of the post-war work ethos – I am, apparently, less touched by the liberating spirit of 1968 than I thought. My encounter with work and its history, shaped, in particular, by contact with India since the mid-1990s, has only strengthened my conviction that it is central to almost every human life on every continent.

In contrast to the utopias heralded by both the right and the left, the daily reality for most of the world's population is still one of working five to six days a week, usually in household and wage labour. And I don't expect that to change anytime soon. Work is not only necessary for all of us, but, on the whole, it also fulfils us. We experience satisfaction from our accomplishments. It meets our basic need for company, both in and outside the home. Work is not an Old Testament curse, a necessary evil that must be avoided at all costs. Work determines our lives and our social contacts, both positively and negatively. Paradise is neither ahead of us nor behind us.

I have never understood why one type of work is rewarded so differently from another. For example, why is a schoolteacher (like my father) paid half, or even less than half, of what a university professor (like me) is paid? Why is a nurse (like my mother) paid less than the doctor next to her or him? All are busy teaching the same youngsters or helping the same patients, all with exactly the same commitment and effort. To mitigate this imbalance, within a household, we pool income, and in society as a whole, we implement income-levelling tax measures. But that does not answer the original question, nor does it eliminate the original injustice: the disparity in rewards for equal effort and commitment.

Vexation may be a good starting point for raising such an issue, but it is not nearly enough of a reason for writing a book – nor is my personal curiosity about work experiences worldwide and in the long term, rather than only in the recent history of the West, as found in most overviews so far. So why do we need this book now?

My sense is that we need to do justice to the experiences of as many working people as possible, then as now, irrespective of cultural, ethnic or social background, because only such an approach can unite us in fellow feeling. Recognizing all the good and all the harm that has and can come from work is crucial in order to make changes to protect and enhance workers' lives for the future in our shrinking world. After all, work is an activity that takes up at least one-third of the global population's time on earth; it therefore needs to be understood and appreciated in the broadest possible context. This also may mitigate the feeling that so many people have that in working nine to five they have in some way failed – that they have not and will not achieve utopia. If this global overview of the most important human experiences of work and its organization in a social context (household, tribe or community, city, state) succeeds in reaching readers then I will be truly satisfied; but, of course, I am aware that it is only then that the real reflection on all these human experiences can begin.

Intellectually, this is an exercise in labour history, but one that goes far beyond the limits that, until recently, this specialism has imposed on itself by focusing on the history of the male factory worker in the most developed parts of the world. In the last twenty-five years, labour historians have begun to ask questions that go much further in time and space. The International Institute of Social History (IISH) in Amsterdam has played a not insignificant role in this, and I am happy that my ideas have been able to develop in that environment.

A book such as this is inspired from many quarters – by the work ethic modelled by my parents, much more than I realize, and by my own work experiences and those of my loved ones. In the last few decades, my thinking on this point has been, without doubt, stimulated and shaped by my colleagues, especially at the IISH (to name just a few: Marcel van der Linden, Lex Heerma van Voss, Gijs Kessler and Karin Hofmeester), but also beyond. I hope those not named will forgive me and find consolation in the references to their work. In addition, a number of colleagues were kind enough to provide comprehensive and often enthusiastic expert commentary on earlier versions, including Wil Roebroeks (Leiden University, especially Chapter 1) and Bert van der Spek (Free University Amsterdam, especially Chapters 3 and 4). Last, but not least: I am very grateful to Jaap Kloosterman, Leo Lucassen and Matthias van Rossum from the IISH, and to my life-long friend Rinus Penninx, as well as a number of anonymous reviewers, for their critical reading of the whole manuscript-in-the-making, as well as Prita Trehan for her valuable comments and Francis Spufford for his encouragement. All this help and inspiration does not, of course, relieve me of my ultimate responsibility for this book. I am most grateful to Julian Loose for his confidence and enthusiastic support, to his colleagues at Yale University Press (Rachael Lonsdale, Katie Urquhart and Rachel Bridgewater), to Anna Yeadell-Moore for her excellent and creative translation and editing, to Marien van der Heijden (IISH) for his advice regarding the illustrations from the Institute's collections, to Marie-José Spreeuwenberg (IISH), and certainly to Aad Blok (IISH) for his enthusiasm and his assistance in the final stages of the book production. Lastly, to my companion Lieske Vorst, who witnessed the conception and growth of this work from the beginning to the end.

I dedicate this work to both the people of the IISH and to the next generations: Maria, Mathies, Geertje and their partners, all dedicated workers; Joaquin, already an accomplished pizza courier, and Caecilia, Joris and Lotte, who are still to start their working lives.

Gouda, 15 December 2020

A NOTE ON HISTORIES, METHODS AND THEORIES OF WORK

The story of work may not be one of straightforward development from then to now, but is the alternative version one of unsystematic diversity? Or is there an internal logic (albeit a complex one) to the narrative? The big names in social science thought so. Adam Smith, Karl Marx and Max Weber all anticipated a kind of engine propelling the changes in labour relations, however differently they thought about its fuel, the cylinder capacity and, in particular, its economy.

What these thinkers have in common is the decisive force that they attribute to the market, from the moment that it burst forth in Western Europe, and especially in the Dutch Republic, in the early modern period.[1] For Smith, the effects of that market were ultimately creative; for Marx, they were devastating. Max Weber opined a 'capitalist spirit', that is, a certain mindset focused on making a profit, a necessary condition for the success of the market economy. This would have been lacking among, for example, the landowning elites of Greek and Roman antiquity. For this reason, Weber – and, in his wake, Karl Polanyi and Moses Finley – considered these ancient societies to be of a fundamentally different order to the one that gradually came into being in Europe after 1500.[2]

According to the aforementioned philosophers and their followers (like the Weber-influenced Marxist Karl Wittfogel[3]), 'more primitive' forms of society existed before the development of the markets for goods, capital and labour. They referred to this as feudalism, slavery or Asian despotism, and in doing so they engaged with a prejudice dating from classical antiquity. According to authors such as Herodotus, the Greeks had an innate desire for freedom, while the Persian nemesis was doomed to a hierarchical society characterized by unfree labour. As a matter of course, this led, in the West – via 'feudalism' – to 'capitalism', and, for some, it steered inevitably towards 'socialism'. The rest of the world would follow the same path, albeit much later and at an accelerated pace.[4]

This conception of the long-term developments in world history has long prevailed and, in a sense, does so because it has been and is shared by both liberal and Marxist thinkers. In the first half of the twentieth century, Alexander Chayanov and Karl Polanyi made theoretically interesting but, ultimately, empirically unconvincing attempts to come up with alternatives[5] – unconvincing primarily because, in their zeal, they tended to seriously exaggerate the importance of the self-sufficiency and anti-market-oriented behaviour of the global population since the Neolithic Revolution. Chayanov did this on the basis of extensive statistics about Russian peasants between around 1880 and 1920; Polanyi and his school by including many more cases – from Mesopotamia to Dahomey – but with considerably less depth than Chayanov.[6]

I will return to these two influential interpretations in more detail later in the book. For now, the reader should know that I have opted for neither; nor is my plan to come up with a grand alternative. My study of the global history of work has taught me first and foremost that these traditional schemes navigate every possible twist and turn. It is also too soon, in my opinion, to formulate exactly what the internal logic of this narrative is.

Why is this so difficult? Why not tread the beaten path?[7] In view of the recent globalization of historiography, what these interpretation schemes have in common is their limited empirical basis and therefore their bias. They take the developments that have occurred around the Mediterranean since classical antiquity as their starting point, pursue them mainly or exclusively in Western Europe and – crucially – then try to fit the rest of world history into this representation. The end result is a characterization of the current North-Atlantic-dominated world as 'modern' and/or 'capitalist'.

No one confronted this Eurocentrism in world history more than the French historian Fernand Braudel. He forced us to acknowledge that capitalism began centuries before the Industrial Revolution, not only in Europe but also in Asia. In his footsteps, the Dutch historian Bas van Bavel recently shifted the boundaries even further back, to medieval Iraq. Van Bavel has distinguished a recurring, centuries-long cycle not only in Mesopotamia but also in Renaissance north Italy, the Dutch Republic and, later, the UK and the US: social revolts–dominant markets and growth–inequality–decline. He posits that our current version of capitalism is in the 'decline' phase and that: 'Capitalism could be defined by the dominance of markets in the exchange and allocation of land, labour and capital. This is a first element, in which the rise of wage labour is a conspicuous one, found at the beginning of each cycle.'[8]

Such thinking increasingly renders the term 'capitalism' identical to the growth and flourishing of markets and, somewhat hesitantly, some authors now tend to equate capitalism more or less with the market economy.[9] Other recent participants in this debate propose its origins as being: in the early Middle Ages (like Van Bavel); between 1400 and 1800; circa 1500 or 1600; between 1600 and 1800; or in the industrialization period of 1850–1920.[10] I conclude that although the concept is used almost universally today, there is no consensus about its content, and therefore about its dating. Likewise, we are seeing the pushing back of the boundaries of 'modernity', to wit the Dutch economy of 1500–1815 has been characterized by some as 'The First Modern Economy'.[11]

In short, the central concepts of capitalism and modernity are now in flux and thus have lost their original analytical function – the drawing of a sharp line in world history.[12] That poses a problem for writing a long-term history like this.[13] It reminds me of Albert Einstein, who remarked in 1916, 'Concepts that have proven useful in ordering things easily achieve such authority over us that we forget their earthly origins and accept them as unalterable givens.'[14] For this reason, I have refrained from giving the terms *capitalism* (and the associated *class* and *class struggle*) and *modern* (versus *traditional*) a central place in this book. Not because I am against Marx,[15] Weber or their followers for ideological reasons, but because I believe that these terms have become so contaminated in the discussions of the last one to one-and-a-half centuries that they have largely lost their analytical power in global labour history. I do, however, wield the terms that are behind them, in particular *market* (internal and external), *labour relations*, *social inequality*, *collective action* and even morally loaded terms such as *exploitation*.

This choice does not mean that, analytically, I must start from scratch. Since the middle of the nineteenth century, a number of authors have written compendiums about the history of labour. I have been gratifyingly inspired by such works, even though most of them are now seriously outdated. They are, almost without exception, either Euro- or Atlanto-centric and most of them rove no further back than a few centuries (very occasionally to the classical antiquity of the Greeks and Romans).[16] As stated regarding Marx and Weber, this is not a reproach; it simply reflects the development of historical science (including archaeology and, even more so, interdisciplinary prehistory). This makes the achievements of Karl Bücher, like Marx and Weber a great German thinker, all the more remarkable. Already more than a century ago, Bücher's intellectual breadth (as well as being an econo-mist, he founded journalism as an academic discipline) was instrumental.[17] Among the many earlier scholars who have inspired me are the influential authors Thorstein Veblen and Hannah Arendt, both of whom thought deeply about the theme of work.[18]

In recent decades, much new and high-quality research has been done, and with a sensible spread over time and space, making it possible to forge a new path.[19] As I see it, all this research has yielded four key results for our view of the development of labour relations.[20] Firstly, I distinguish two important alternatives for market economies: reciprocal relations, dominant among hunter-gatherers but still vibrant today within households every-where, and tributary redistribution societies. Moreover, market economies have emerged not just once but several times in history and at various places in the world, and in many cases they also disappeared again. We therefore encounter related radical changes in labour relations in diverse locations. Secondly, in this context, large-scale wage labour, slave labour and self-employment have arisen multiple times in history and often declined again or even vanished. Thirdly, the remuneration level for wage labour does not necessarily tally with the enforced minimum but shows strong variations and fluctuations. Lastly, these wage fluctuations are not – or are not only – the result of the whims of those in power or of blind market forces, but also of individual and collective actions by wage workers themselves. Opinions about a fair reward for labour and on the corresponding social (in)equality play a crucial role in this regard.

$$\chi$$

A book covering the chronological and geographical span that the present volume does is ipso facto comparative in nature. It must espouse the advan-tages of the comparative method, assuming that humans as working beings demonstrate enough similarities through time and space – or, that their opportunities are limited in the same way – that it is possible to trace them worldwide and from the very beginning.

Theoretically, I agree with the description of another academic discipline – anthropology – that, in my opinion, also applies to the present historical overview. Robert McC. Netting, famous for his work on, among other things, cultural ecology, defines his field as:

an empirical social science of practical reason, grounded in an Enlightenment faith that there are regularities in human behavior and institutions that can be understood as filling human biological and psychological needs under particular circumstances of geography, demography, technology and history. These commonalities can be discerned cross-culturally in groups separated by space and time and displaying a splendid variety of cultural values, religions, kinship systems, and political structures.[21]

'Empirical' also means paying attention to exactly what work involves: descriptions of the daily practices of men and women, and in their own words, or illustrated, when possible.[22]

Likewise, some readers may miss more elaborate theoretical discussions and historiographical debates. I am not opposed to modelling in the historical or social sciences – this book could not have been written without it – rather, I prefer to present the results of my balancing of several proposals that have been posited in the literature over the last two centuries. Those wanting to know more about my ultimate choices are referred to my earlier work and, in particular, to the notes.[23]

Let me emphasize here that global labour history is a highly dynamic field brimming with empirical, methodological and theoretical progress, without which this book would have been impossible. I expect this progress to continue. Despite the length of my bibliography and my efforts to read and summarize as much as I can, I realize only too well how imperfectly I have succeeded in this. Many specialists will be able to identify omissions. The recent secondary literature is vast – but this proves just how alive this subject is.

INTRODUCTION

Today, most people on this planet spend more than half of their waking hours working, including travelling between the workplace and home; and while asleep they recover from the fatigues of their work. Seen that way, the story of work is to a great extent the history of humankind. But what exactly do we mean by work?

The main problem with the countless definitions of work and labour is their one-sidedness. Generally, they emphasize some forms of work while neglecting others. For example, women's work is often overlooked compared to men's, work outside the factory walls compared to that going on inside them, intellectual work measured against manual work, work in the home (when it is recognized at all) contrasted with work outside it (also known as the 'reproductive–productive' contradiction).

And it is really not simple to come up with a definition of work for a book such as this with the ambition to cover the whole of world history. A

Mrs Na van Assendelft van Wijck-Meijer washes her children in the tub in front of her house, Lindenstraat, Amsterdam, 1951.

1

good starting point is the broad definition of work by US sociologists (and father and son) Charles and Chris Tilly:[1]

> Work includes any human effort adding use value to goods and services. However much their performers may enjoy or loathe the effort, conversation, song, decoration, pornography, table setting, gardening, housecleaning, and repair of broken toys, all involve work to the extent that they increase satisfactions their consumers gain from them. Prior to the twentieth century, a vast majority of the world's workers performed the bulk of their work in other settings than salaried jobs as we know them today. Even today, over the world as a whole, most work takes place outside of regular jobs. Only a prejudice bred by Western capitalism and its industrial labor markets fixes on strenuous effort expended for money payment outside the home as 'real work', relegating other efforts to amusement, crime and mere housekeeping.[2]

The great merit of this definition is that it is explicitly not limited to market-related activities. It is worth reiterating the attention the Tillys draw to housekeeping as real work: 'Despite the rise of takeouts, fast foods, and restaurant eating, unpaid preparation of meals probably constitutes the largest single block of time among all types of work, paid or unpaid, that today's Americans do.' If this is true for the birthplace of the Big Mac and Kentucky Fried Chicken, then we can safely apply this observation to the rest of the world and to human history as a whole.[3]

The problem with such universal definitions is that it is never entirely clear which human pursuits *cannot* be defined as labour. The Tillys explicitly exclude three types of activities from their definition: 'purely destructive, expressive, or consumptive acts'.[4] They regard purely destructive labour as anti-work, since it does not *add* use value, rather it *deprives* commodities of value. This would seem to exclude many or all of the activities of, say, soldiering, due to the undeniably destructive aspects of this profession; but military craftsmanship is work, however, not only because, in practice, daily barrack life is non-destructive, but also because the intention of much, if not all, conscious destruction is to add value to other commodities and services.[5] By precluding pure expression and consumption, the Tillys are excluding those activities that, in principle, have no use value for anyone other than the producer himself. Their reasoning is sound. Even the broadest definition of use value does not include, for example, 'solitary weightlifting pursued solely for personal gratification'. This is in contrast to 'weightlifting for the pleasure of sports fans'. With the addition of this social criterion, only a handful of activities fall outside of the Tillys' definition – eating, drinking and sleeping (collectively referred to as 'recuperation') as a means for every person, and therefore every producer, to sustain his mechanism. I regard all human pursuits apart from free time or leisure as work.

A brief note about leisure.[6] A mid-twentieth-century series of studies found that work, or activities directly related to work, represented 25–30 per cent of men's time (in wage labour and commuting), 40 per cent of house-wives' time, and 50 per cent of the time of mothers with a paid job, while sleeping accounted for a third and eating and personal care a tenth of all indi-viduals' time. The hours remaining for leisure time thus varied from around 30 per cent for wage workers (mostly men) to around 15 per cent for house-wives, and a little over 5 per cent for mothers with a paid job.[7] Yet even that time was not necessarily free. The studies found that both men and women spent the majority of their free time engaged in social obligations – club membership, volunteering, paying visits – which, though pleasurable, *are* seen as obligations. Interestingly, research among indigenous Ecuadorians reveals differences with European ideas about obligations and leisure: 'They work steadily when necessary but not in the Western tempo … All their time is used, if not in work then in other "structured activities". However, in their non-work time … they often enjoy drinking and hilarity. The Indian works and saves as if weddings, Christenings, birthdays and fiestas were the main reason for living. … They do not regard such fun-making with the same atti-tudes that Westerners have for leisure.'[8]

American sociologist Nels Anderson believed that, even in the industri-alized world, 'non-work obligations' are distinct from leisure: 'It is in performing such obligations that one gets his status as a good spouse, good parent, good neighbor, good citizen, good friend and so on, all roles in which status must be earned, and the effort may be highly satisfying. The effort may be equally as satisfying as leisure activity.'[9] So, although the Tillys would perhaps place these types of social obligations under their definition of work, I don't want to go that far. We are certainly not talking here about time that one can fill at will. For the vast majority of history, free time consisted of brief play and amusement and, for the happy few, of travelling for pleasure (the so-called grand tour), holidays and hobbies; that is to say, activities carried out purely for pleasure and at one's own expense.[10] The ordinary man or woman in the West only came to experience such things in the course of the twentieth century. To this day, these kinds of activities are never, or rarely, an option for large parts of the global population.

We have strongly held views about the role that work plays in our lives – whether it be our preference for self-employment or salaried work, our ideas about typically male or female work, or what we believe to be fair remuneration for the tasks we perform. These views have developed over time, based on our collective work experiences and, ultimately, they originate from the beginning of our existence as human beings.

We define work not only according to our individual efforts – the pain in our back, the sweat on our brow or our mental fatigue – but also according to those with whom, for whom, or even despite whom, we work. People are not solitary islanders: even Robinson Crusoe found his Friday (and swiftly put him to work as his servant). Human relationships are central to work and will be a major emphasis of this book. Looking at work's long and global history we can see recurring patterns in the way principles of work are ingrained in our intimate social interactions, the ways in which we enjoy or spend the fruits of our labour, and what work means and has meant to us. Are we forced to work for someone else or do we have a choice? What is the reward for our labour and who determines what it should be? Can we put up with pay gaps? Do we work together within a household or with others outside it? Who will take care of us when we cannot or can no longer work? In so many ways work defines us socially. Consequently, the pursuit of fair compensation (via private and collective strategies) is inherent to the social character of work.

From prehistory until today, a number of solutions have been devised for organizing work. Until some 12,000 years ago – that is, for 98 per cent of the history of humankind and until the 'invention' of farming – work was divided among small communities consisting of only a few households. In close mutual cooperation, they collected their food and shared the fruits of their labour among themselves based on *reciprocity*. We can call these reciprocal labour relations[11] between members of a few households that collaborated in bands of hunter-gatherers internal – in contrast to later, external labour relations outside the household or bands of households.

The food surpluses of agrarian societies made large-scale division of labour possible, resulting, after thousands of years, in the earliest cities with specialist division of labour and, ultimately, 5,000 years ago, in the first states.

In these more complex societies, consisting of hundreds or thousands of households, other external labour relations now emerged alongside reciprocal labour relations. These can be broken down into *self-employment* and *tributary labour* – complemented later, after the emergence of markets, by *free wage labour*, *slavery* and *employership*. From that moment, human history can essentially be viewed as an eclectic mix of a handful of different labour relations that existed subsequent to, alongside and in competition with each other.

We have become much more aware of this eclectic mix since the demise of the Soviet Union, when the state socialism or command communism alternative in Eastern Europe declared itself bankrupt – when also, and not coincidentally, intense globalization simultaneously arose. China, Africa and pre-Columbian America all have their own fascinating histories of work. Taken together, these histories indicate much more than any simple, steady line of development from hunter-gatherers to the slaves of antiquity, the serfs of the Middle Ages, the farmers and artisans driven into the factories, via a detour to communism (or not), and, more than 100 million concentration camp labourers later, to the here and now.

Looking at work across time and space enables us to trace the complexity of work's story. (See 'A note on histories, methods and theories of work', pp. xiii–xvii, for the different histories of work and labour relations and a survey of the theoretical field.) Aside from the market economy that we now take for granted are revealed arrangements based on reciprocal relations (founded by our hunter-gatherer ancestors yet still familiar to today's households) and tributary redistribution societies. We can see recurrences in history: large-scale wage labour, slave labour, self-employment, even market economies themselves have appeared multiple times, in various parts of the world, and (sometimes) vanished again. These in turn have given rise to very different relations between people and work, and wildly fluctuating remuneration – not always due to the market, or those in power, but also because of wage workers' individual or collective actions in pursuing fair compensation for work done, addressing – or exacerbating – social inequality.

※

The building blocks of such fundamental structural change in work's history are the experiences and behaviours of the individual working man and woman. Generally, people do not work alone and certainly not only for themselves. In the first place, every *individual* spends the largest part of his life working within or for a *family* or *household*, defined here simply as a group of relatives, who pool their incomes and who, as a rule, live and eat together. The activities of all members can thus be seen as a whole.[12] The members coordinate their activities, and, to that end, we can speak of a group strategy – a 'household living strategy'.[13] This domestic arrangement involves the division of tasks according to skills, gender, age, and a marriage strategy. Taking the idea of the individual person as the core, we can distinguish a first shell – the household – around an individual.

Furthermore, members of different households work together in larger social groups, called *polities* – the second shell. For a long time, these were small, like the bands of hunter-gatherers, but these bands also operated within a larger entity, a group of bands in which, for example, marriage partners were exchanged, necessary for genetic diversity. Later, following the Neolithic Revolution, (city) states became viable. The exchange of goods and services could be organized via tributary redistribution within these complex polities, such as in Ancient Egypt or in the Inca Empire, but gradually also through *markets*.[14] Polities allowing markets establish what their rules of play are, but can also be held hostage by certain players in this market.[15] Then, fickle power relations are possible between actors, who at times lean more on the polity, at others, more on the market.

People work with and for others. This suggests horizontal and vertical labour relations within and beyond the household. *Horizontal* labour relations emerge from working together with equals or co-workers. *Vertical* labour relations define who we work for and under what rules. These rules (implicit or explicit, written or unwritten) determine the type of work, the type and amount of remuneration, working hours, degrees of physical and psychological strain, as well as degrees of freedom and autonomy.[16]

By making a distinction between individuals, households, polities and the market, vertical labour relations in particular can be mapped: who determines which work is to be done and under what rules and conditions? That is the way we usually talk about work relationships and, thus, all members of a given society can be classified by asking the following straightforward questions: are they not working yet or can they no longer work? Do they have so much money that they do not have to work at all? Do they work primarily in a household or small band-like unit; in a tributary-redistributive society in the past where everyone's efforts were focused on the god and his temple; or mainly via the market? And, if via the market, either as a small independent enterprise, as an entrepreneur, as a wage worker, or as a slave?

The sum of all these labour relations is what characterizes a society – so we can speak of hunting-gathering, tributary-redistributive or of market polities.

One of the limitations of labour history to date is that labour relations are mainly restricted to *vertical* oppositions within market societies – between employee and employer, slave and slaveowner, citizen and state. Certainly, this is important and therefore this story will encompass trade unions, strikes, (written and unwritten) employment contracts, as well as work incentives, the ways in which an employer can encourage his workers and even his slaves to perform more and better. Such incentives are, as the Tillys rightly point out, never wholly about money: workers are never motivated solely by wages. To the reward of compensation they add, alliteratively, commitment and coercion to the mix.[17] All three can be used, to different degrees, to talk about anyone who performs work. But although the power relations between employer and employee (free or not) are real and important, the behaviour of a working person is explained by more than just this type of subordination. In all known societies, as a rule, people work together with others (members of the same household, fellow wage workers, fellow slaves and fellow forced labourers) and their mutual, *horizontal*, relationships are an intrinsic part of labour history.

A wide variety of mutual cooperation and opposition is possible, depending on some form of 'contract'. The foundation is the generally silent contract between household members working together – unpaid caring work, or labouring on the family farm. Most readers now will have an individual work contract, but still will have to deal on a daily basis with colleagues in a more or less pleasant way. This was not so different in the past, though there we also often encounter groups of workers who hired themselves out and received piecework pay via cooperative subcontracting.[18] The equally subcontracted but not-at-all cooperative 'sweating' industry continues to demonstrate how abusive such relations can be, yet slaves also worked together and free and unfree workers could cooperate at the same job. All such horizontal work relationships could make life easy or difficult for workers; it is not only dependent on their owner and boss.

In short, both *horizontal cooperation* and *vertical subordination* are key elements in a comprehensive history of work and will be a major theme of this book.[19] The power resources in vertical labour relations, for example those of master versus servant, or plantation owner versus slave, are greater because, ultimately, they can be enforced through the polity. But that does not mean that in everyday practice only vertical labour relations can make or break the pleasure in work.

The relation between effort and remuneration is also a key factor in linking individual working experience with structural change. In the case of hunter-gatherers, the group works together and the yield is, in principle, equally distributed among members; this would not have been much different among the earliest farmers (even until 1,000 years ago in Africa). Ultimately, however, agriculture could yield such large surpluses that some members of the group could specialize in non-agricultural crafts, and a few were then able to appropriate a larger proportion for themselves. Moreover, the group could now also become so large that these *aggrandizers* took on the necessary leadership role.

The distribution of surpluses would take a special form in the emerging cities and city leagues. In these complex societies, formal redistribution systems arose, for example around a temple. All surpluses belonged, in theory, to the temple gods and their servants – that is to say, to the elite, among whom the priests then divided the total. There were, of course, differences in this redistribution, depending on the presumed importance of households in the polity. In such theocratic societies, priests were, after all, more important than farmers. Thus, the uneven redistribution of communal revenue became institutionalized.

In the states – that is, the polities – that emerged from city leagues, elites became increasingly powerful, internally and externally. Internally, they could now claim for the state not only all revenues but also the means of production and, in exchange for remuneration, the services of non-property-owning citizens (for example, as professional soldiers). At the same time, citizens could work for themselves and, in addition, traders and other professionals could acquire production resources and, ultimately, they could also employ wage workers. Externally, the polity could acquire prisoners of war and have them work as slaves. Once available as a production resource, these enslaved and their descendants could also be acquired and put to work by private individuals. In addition to land and goods markets, this also created slave and labour markets.

Given the frequent mismatch since the emergence of states between effort and remuneration – in short, social inequality – a key question is how

8

the victims (and sometimes compassionate outsiders) reacted. After all, the common heritage of mankind stems from the much more egalitarian work relations among hunter-gatherers, which, it cannot be repeated enough, covers 98 per cent of our human history. As will be elaborated in more detail in Chapter 1, the principle of reciprocity is at the basis of human work relations. The many subsequent deviations from this, both in tributary-redistributive and market polities, made ideological adjustments necessary to reconcile working people with the new situation of inequality. Or, they are strived for at least. The alternative, after all, is the destabilization of a polity.[20] In this book we will see individual and collective attempts to deal with this problem.

Individual attempts at improving working conditions (or mitigating or averting a deterioration) by entertaining good relations with the boss or his aides are the rule. Similar behaviour applies to the self-employed and their customers. Failing that come attempts to find a new boss (or for that matter customers), locally or by migration.[21] But working people can also choose other solutions. In practice, this is done by combining different labour relations over time, rather than with a sudden change of strategy. Think of the cottage industry, in which peasants combined agricultural work with weaving cloth. The so-called proletarianization of peasants who became factory workers took many generations, sometimes up to ten. Even slaves, for instance in the Roman Empire and in nineteenth-century Brazil, could try to save their earnings and buy their freedom. This way, they might acquire freedom for themselves or their offspring and continue independently as smallholders or artisans. Russian serfs worked for themselves, on top of enforced work for their landlord but, in many cases, added to their income by wage work in the city.

Collective power, on the other hand, is harnessed through the use of strikes, mutual benefit societies and unions. The manifold options for individuals to strive for improvements in their work and remuneration (or to prevent deterioration) apply also to collective strategies. Wage workers can join a strike or not, stay neutral or cross the picket line. Slaves may abscond, make the best of their situation, start a rebellion or join forces to repel it.

All known labour relations have resulted from these strategies and their various inversions and combinations. Subsequent shifts in the directions of, first, increasingly dominant slavery and second, wage labour, are obviously powered by states. States can, for example, impose slavery, but they can also abolish it again. They can make free wage labour or employer and independent entrepreneurship possible through legislation and regulation, but they can also expunge it, as was the case with communist revolutions in various countries.

Distinguishing between the shifts initiated by the state and those by working people is useful in terms of filleting work's history, and also lends workers an essential agency. However, it also veils the connection between the states and citizens. Polities cannot change the rules with impunity and workers cannot go against polities unsanctioned. The binding force is the prevailing system of rules and ideas about work and labour relations, what we could call the role of work ideology as a binding force in society.

X

This book is structured chronologically and thematically and addresses common themes that recur, to a greater or lesser extent, in each period, of which I distinguish six. The first is by far the longest, from the emergence of *Homo sapiens* (who, based on genetic calculations, split off from Neanderthals 700,000 years ago) to the Neolithic or agricultural revolution. Initially, and this must be our starting point, there was essentially no distinction between human and animal attempts to survive, but through the development of human speech and thus new forms of communication, new forms of collaboration grew. The individual lived within a household, households formed bands, and bands exchanged individuals. All work took place within these units.

Reciprocity would have long been the rule with the Neolithic Revolution from roughly 12,000 years ago. Nevertheless, it offered increased opportunities for obtaining and hoarding food, and thus for the division of labour, which may have led to greater enrichment of some households and, ultimately, to disparities between households. Here, the seed was sown for inequality; alongside cooperation, subordination was now being created too. The differences, however, were still small in the second period distinguished in this book, and Africa demonstrates that there is no causal link between the agricultural revolution and social inequality.

Following the emergence of cities, first in Mesopotamia some 7,000 years ago – extremely late in the evolution of *Homo sapiens* – and a little later in China and India, the division of labour between urban and rural areas and among urban residents was possible. The emergence of city leagues and states from 3000 BCE strengthened this trend. This third period created the full spectrum of labour relations as we have known it ever since. Alongside individuals and households, polities with their institutions became indispensable, starting with the polity (city, temple or state), which collected the surplus production, for example for the god, and then redistributed it (tributary-redistributive labour, as in Ancient Egypt and pre-Columbian America). In the first states, four new types of labour relations appeared: free wage labour, slavery and self-employment (including by tenants), and, finally, employership. From this point, human history can be seen as a competition between different labour relations, with fluctuating relationships between cooperation and subordination. This determines the classification in the fourth, fifth and sixth periods.

Around 500 BCE, a renewal in human transactions took place in three locations in the world, with far-reaching consequences for the already existing labour relations: the advent of currencies. This 'invention', and especially that of small coins for daily use (*deep monetization*), facilitated the expansion of market transactions, especially the payment of wages and spending these wages on purchasing daily food and craft products from the self-employed. Given that these forms of work have become so important, if not self-evident, today, a separate chapter has been devoted to those parts of the world where large-scale wage labour and monetary wage payments developed. Indeed, they were able to thrive in long-term successful (urbanized) states where consolidation was at least as important as expansion and aggression. Examples of this can be found in various parts of Eurasia between 500 BCE and 1500 CE. This forms the fourth period: in particular, the Persian–Greek–Roman–Byzantine–Arab sequence in the west of Eurasia, the Mauryas and successors in South Asia and the Han and Song dynasties in China, as compared with state formation elsewhere, without wage labour, especially in Africa and the Americas.

Some states were so successful, also and especially economically, that they expanded globally in what I categorize as the fifth period, roughly 1500–1800. This was the time of 'globalization', in the current sense of the word.[22] In these centuries, competition between political entities took such forms that the organization of labour in the different parts of the world began to vary widely. To mention the most striking examples: the expansion of free labour in Western Europe with new forms of collaboration, and, conversely, new forms of subordination in the guise of serfdom in Eastern Europe and slavery in Africa and the Americas, but also in South and South East Asia. At the same time, however, both in East Asia and in Western Europe, and

THE STORY OF WORK

apparently independently of each other, there was an intensification of the labour of peasant households with an increase in women's labour, the so-called *Industrious Revolution*.

The sixth and last period (thematically divided between Chapters 6 and 7) starts with the *Industrial Revolution*. The division of work and skills created innumerable new occupations, and subsequently eradicated many others. Robotization is the phase we live in now. This also led, albeit in fits and starts, to a major shift in labour relations. Slowly but surely, the importance for the market of domestic, independent and somewhat faster, unfree labour decreased. This was heralded by the abolition of slavery in Haiti, of the transatlantic slave trade and of serfdom in Eastern Europe, culminating in the establishment of the International Labour Organization (hereafter, ILO) and the Universal Declaration of Human Rights.

The shifts in labour relations outlined in this book (see Figure 1), and certainly the global convergence of labour relations in the last two centuries, should not be seen as a natural phenomenon, but primarily as the result of individual and collective strategies and actions by working people. Consequently, cooperation and subordination regained some balance. This is the history of the labour movement, of workers' parties and of the welfare state – the core of classical labour history. And, moreover, not only did global labour relations converge but also, significantly, labour relations between men and women.

However, as the recent history of Western Europe, Russia and China teaches us, as well as the current global economic crisis, this is not a simple, unilinear development. At the same time as the growth of global prosperity, in particular since the Second World War, inequality between workers has increased. The book concludes by reflecting on future developments. What can longer-term historical patterns underlying current concerns about pressing issues such as migration, robotization and social equality tell us about where work is taking us? How will our essential need to work manifest itself in a fast-changing world? Can we choose what our working lives will look like next?

This book suggests that there are answers to these questions. The long-term experience of humankind shows not only that work is necessary for our survival – even in our era of robotization. Work is more than that: the sense of fulfilment it brings makes it indispensable for our self-esteem and the regard of our peers. The history of humankind may be conceived as straddling two fundamental tensions: our evolutionary history and our existence

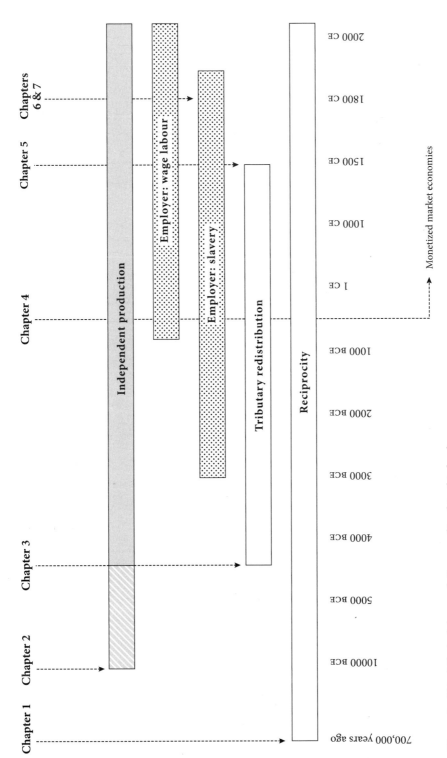

Figure 1. The shifts in labour relations outlined in this book.

as hunter-gatherers until a few thousand years ago determines our basic striving towards fair compensation for our efforts, yet the division of work in more complex societies easily occasions inequality. The story of work makes clear that strong ideologies defending inequality may be lastingly successful, yet globalization points in another direction. Despite the nadirs of unfair remuneration of the last centuries, the universal appeal of fairness seems to be prevailing now. Bringing it into practice without succumbing to the lure of utopias of sorts is the difficult task ahead.

1

HUMANS AT WORK, 700,000–12,000 YEARS AGO

Roughly 700,000 years ago, modern humans and Neanderthals went their separate ways. That is where this book starts – but not without considering the similarities and differences between the work of humans and of other living beings. For most of our history, work consisted of hunting and gathering; then, eventually, 45,000 years ago, the emergence of the specialization of a few artisans led to a greater variety of social relations according to gender and age.

Animals and humans at work

The American pioneer of time and motion studies Frank Bunker Gilbreth remarked, somewhat provocatively, in 1911: 'a human being or a work animal is a power plant, and is subject to nearly all the laws that govern and limit the power plant.'[1] In order to define work more precisely, we must start

A Hadza woman digs for edible tubers. The Hadzabe are one of the few societies in the world that still earn a living from wild resources.

by interrogating exactly what the difference is between a human at work, a working animal and a working machine.

Satisfied with a newly purchased or recently repaired device, we do not hesitate to say, 'it works'. Apparently, machines work, and of course they do, but only because humans *make* them work and only after they have been switched on. Barring the realm of science fiction, machines do not work without human intervention. While this question may have a relatively easy answer, the next one – 'do animals work?' – is less straightforward.

Firstly, we must re-frame the question. What we should be asking is, what is the difference between working *modern humans* and our closest relations, working *primates*?[2] The reflexive answer is that, analogous to machines, animals cannot work without us. Bears would not dance, donkeys would not pull carts and Lipizzaners would not perform without the coerced training or commands of a human being.

Nevertheless, there are several reasons why animals' activities, and in particular those of bonobos and chimpanzees, resemble humans' work more than the work of machines does. Hence, the first sensible step in our narrative must be to study the basics of the work of these primates; it will surely teach us a lot about ourselves. Firstly, our sole activity before the Neolithic Revolution some 12,000 years ago was the daily procurement of food by hunting and gathering. It was the same for most animals. Consequently, if human hunting and gathering is work, then we must accept that animals work as well – independently of human action. Secondly, the compensation of slaves in the form of food, shelter and medical care is comparable to our treatment of draught animals. Slaves and horses work under similar conditions. Reason enough, then, not to dismiss too quickly commonalities between animal and human activities. Let us therefore examine the life of animals in more detail, and in particular that of bonobos and chimpanzees, with a view to understanding the origins and specificities of the work of the first human beings.

While the procurement of food is not only the most necessary but also the most basic type of work that every individual must perform from the age of independence, among primates it is not a strictly individual activity; indeed, it implies the division of labour. The most famous example, of course, is that of honeybees, who live in colonies with a queen, drones and workers.[3] Given the vast evolutionary distance between bees and humans, there is little value in pursuing this example any further. But for the primordial stages of humans, however, we can consult ethology and socio-biology, which study the social behaviour of great apes and especially that of bonobos and the chimpanzees, who, 7 to 10 million years ago, shared the same ancestors as us.[4]

What, then, do we know about the division of labour and, specifically, the distribution of tasks between adult male and female primates? Firstly, in most species there is a difference between male and female tasks, the latter being exclusively responsible for raising young, since only they can suckle. Crucially, others do not take on the not-strictly-biological care tasks from the mother either.[5] Put differently, among most primates, the specifically female task of caring for young does not lead to reciprocity, such as groupmates taking on other tasks, in particular the gathering of food, for mothers.

Among a few species of primates, however, things are a bit more complicated and reciprocal division of labour does indeed occur, especially in hunting. While the, in principle, relatively straightforward supply of plant-based food is a constant concern for every individual, hunting is a laborious and unpredictable activity for great apes.[6] As a rule, hunters are adult males (among apes, in any case, they are much bigger and more powerfully built than the females), with the most skilful and the strongest individuals at the forefront. With efficient cooperation and the necessary luck, these individuals are capable, from time to time, of securing highly prized meat. Once in possession of such food – which is invariably in one piece, susceptible to decay, and too much for the hunter or hunters to consume alone – chimpanzees and capuchin monkeys apparently voluntarily distribute it to other members of the group, on the basis of reciprocity. Who receives what may be based on generosity during previous distributions, or on sexual and emotional services (as in the case of defleaing among monkeys). Fortunate recipients are not exclusively close relatives (this is in contrast to birds, who feed each other during the breeding season).[7]

The Dutch primatologist Frans de Waal takes the leap from social behaviour among apes to that of humans by pointing to parallels between omnivorous, hunting non-human primates and hunting peoples in Paraguay, Southern Africa and Brazil. In the latter case, he follows the American anthropologist and primatologist Katharine Milton, who states:

Unlike our economic system, in which each person typically tries to secure and control as large a share of the available resources as possible, the hunter-gatherer economic system rests on a set of highly formalized expectations regarding cooperation and sharing. ... For instance, no hunter fortunate enough to kill a large game animal assumes that all this food is his or belongs only to his immediate family.[8]

The principle that meat must be shared by everyone in the camp and that it cannot be reserved by the hunter and his family is illustrated in the many monographs about hunter-gatherers.[9]

Sarah Blaffer Hrdy, whose pioneering work *Mothers and Others* (2009) helped modernize our understanding of the evolutionary basis of female behaviour in both non-human and human primates, points to another form of cooperation that emerged later in evolution, long before modern humans – the ability of mothers to entrust the care of their precious, slow-growing children to others, so-called alloparents (including the father). According to her, this could have happened already between 1.8 and 1.5 million years ago.[10] Perhaps a key element in this regard is that humans have a higher birth rate and a longer reproductive lifespan than other large great apes. Humans also have a much shorter weaning period. Consequently, their offspring grow up with more siblings, which, in turn, enhances their social and cognitive abilities. In addition, the use of fire to heat and cook food enables humans' pre- or extra-somatic digestion and contributes to improving their nutrition and health.[11]

Moreover, humans' distinctive menopause led to the 'grandmother hypothesis': 'having an extra pair of hands would have meant that daughters and daughters-in-law could reproduce more quickly'.[12] We see the same pattern among certain African hunter-gatherers, for example the Hadza in modern-day Tanzania. During their first four years, Hadza children spend 31 per cent of their contact hours with individuals other than their mothers. It is unthinkable that the great apes would permit this from their conspecifics or even the mother's male siblings – hence the long interval of four to eight years between births among great apes.[13] This important evolutionary step may have coincided with the emergence of the first human speech. And with speech came a revolutionary improvement in the first stone tools, something only possible when the necessary technical tricks could be transmitted by the earliest forms of language ('yes', 'no', 'here', 'there').[14]

The paleoanthropologist Leslie Aiello has shown that the appearance of the genus *Homo* 2 million years ago, with its larger brain and larger body size, notably among females, greatly influenced female reproduction costs, both during gestation and lactation.[15] She states that 'the resulting high energy costs per offspring could have been considerably reduced by decreasing the interbirth interval'. Clearly, this would have been advantageous early in the evolution of the genus *Homo*, who, at that time, moved to a more dangerous, open environment with, as a consequence, higher numbers of accidental deaths. But, because of the shorter birth interval, a mother would be responsible for dependent weanlings while gestating or nursing a subsequent child. What are the social implications of this? After considering a number of possibilities, Aiello posits the following scenario for solving the problem of high female reproduction costs:

> Where the hunting success of males is sporadic, but success produces large returns, the desired group size would be one that assured a reasonably constant supply of a limited resource. In this context, it does not matter why or how food provided by the male is distributed, as long as it is distributed in the group and the size of that group is such as to insure that male-provided resources supplement those provided by the females to the degree required to support their reproductive energy requirements.[16]

We must add another important element to this: that of the three-generational transfer of food (energy) and knowledge.[17] Because – compared to non-human primates – human foragers, with their diet of nutrient-dense and difficult-to-acquire high-quality food, are characterized by large bodies and brains and, in particular, longevity, they have a specific life pattern. Until the age of 14, they not only produce less energy than they consume, but their net production of energy becomes increasingly negative. Only after the age of 20 does a positive increase in production occur. Between the ages of 30 and 45, they reach the 'overproduction' stage, with human net production peaking at about 1,750 calories per day at roughly 45 years old. Between 60 and 65, they are back in the negative range. This tells us two things: humans need a lot of time to produce energy as efficiently as possible, and, during this period of apprenticeship, they are dependent on older group members – men and women in different age groups. In this period, young people gain knowledge from their elders, codified in myths and rituals (the so-called tribal encyclopaedia).[18] Whereas chimpanzees reach maturity around the age of 12, among *Homo erectus* this was 14, among Neanderthals 15–16 and for *Homo sapiens* around 18–19.[19] The argumentation of Aiello and others therefore supports both human cooperation, as posited by De Waal, and the notion of alloparenting by Hrdy.[20]

In fact, this approach involves comparing the social behaviour of three groups: that of animals alive now, specifically primates (and within this order especially bonobos and chimpanzees); that of hunters/food gatherers now or in the recent past; and that of the whole of humanity prior to the Neolithic Revolution. By starting from a standpoint of comparability, De Waal and Hrdy adopt a position in the historical debate that the theory of evolution is anachronistic.[21] De Waal, especially, speaks out loudly against the nineteenth-century philosopher Herbert Spencer, 'Darwin's bulldog' Thomas Henry Huxley, and their countless followers, who embraced the adage 'survival of the fittest' as the sole basis of society.[22]

Indisputably, humans, like all primates, are capable of competitive and aggressive behaviour, but this is only half the story.[23] Just as important for the evolutionary success of the species is the human capacity for cooperation. This is a direct result of the vulnerability of primates, including man, to predators: 'Security is the first and foremost reason for social life.... We very much rely on one another for survival. It is this reality that ought to be taken as a starting point for any discussion about human society, not the reveries of centuries past, which depicted our ancestors as being as free as birds and lacking any social obligations.'[24]

In terms of the development of human work, it is important to note that the essential principle of reciprocity, and with it the sharing of childcare tasks, has probably been a human quality from the outset. This observation is consistent with the definitional issues raised above. If, prior to the existence of *Homo sapiens*, not only the supply of food – to be defined as 'real' work – but also mutual emotional and sexual services are fixed elements of the behaviour of our species, then the boundary between 'real' work and social obligations is blurred. Consequently, Chris and Charles Tilly's broad definition of 'work' (see Introduction, p. 2) is a good departure point for the whole of world history. The fitness of the individual, and of their descendants, for survival is based not only on a long period of dependency for sustenance, but also on the acquisition of knowledge. Knowledge transfer in the broadest sense and in the long term determines the survival chances of foragers.[25]

Humans are a species that can be understood not only through competition but also and especially through the prism of cooperation. Furthermore, the females of our species do not have to take care of their children exclusively; we allow others, especially grandmothers, to take on this role too. This provides two important starting points for the history of the work of hunter-gatherers, and perhaps also for what we have done since: not only subordination but, crucially, also cooperation.[26] In sum, work by modern humans during at least the first 95 per cent of their existence has been a form of 'reciprocal altruism'.[27]

Hunter-gatherers at work

How did human work develop before the Neolithic? In order to answer this question, we must first reflect on a few million years of human history.[28] Since chimp–human divergence about 7–10 million years ago, hominins have known 2 major evolutionary developments, both occurring in Africa. From 2–2.5 million years ago, we find the genus *Homo*, represented for the last 2 million years by *Homo erectus*. The 2 best-known species within this genus are *Homo neanderthalensis* (Neanderthals), who lived until 39,000 years ago, and the separate branch of *Homo sapiens* (modern humans). These 2 branches split some 700,000 years ago. We all belong to the species *Homo sapiens*, although to a lesser extent a mixing of non-African modern humans with Neanderthals and Denisovans (a branch that split off from the Neanderthals 400,000 years ago) occurred.[29] This rather dull list of human species in fact represents something very exciting: the tripling of brain size; the reduction of height differences between women and men (until then, women were smaller); a substantial reduction in colon capacity in favour of the small intestine; and, related to this, a varied and high-quality diet and a longer lifespan. The end product of all these developments is *Homo sapiens*, with – and this is impor-tant for the theme of work – the most varied diet of all.[30]

Like other hominins before them, modern humans migrated from Africa to other continents.[31] Slowly but surely, they replaced all archaic conspecifics in the Old World. We are not talking here about large numbers; indeed, our lineage was at the edge of extinction 70,000 years ago, and between 40,000 and 10,000 years ago – the moment when the first hunter-gatherers began their successful experiments with agriculture – the world was populated by some 8 million humans.[32]

The definitive crossing of modern humans from Africa to Eurasia took place roughly 50,000 years ago (after a number of ingresses into the Levant from about 160,000 years ago). This was followed by a rapid dispersal across

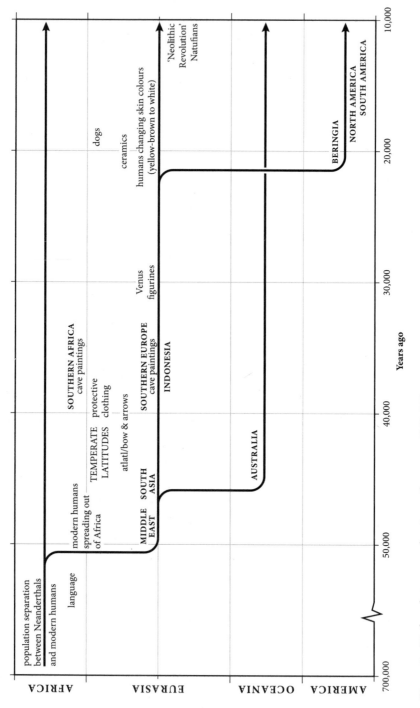

Figure 2. Modern humans as hunter-gatherers until 10,000 years ago.

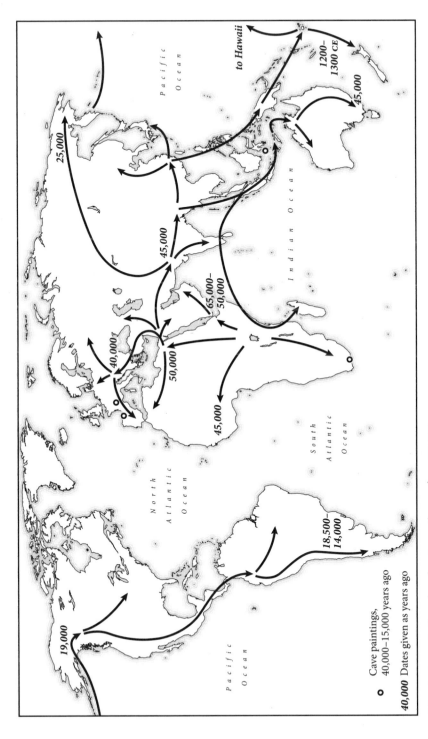

Map 1. Spread of modern hunter-gatherers from 70,000 years ago.

the whole of Eurasia all the way to Australia.[33] South East Asia, reached via the coasts of South Asia, was formed much later (14,000 years ago) when, due to a much higher sea level, a large land mass ('Sunda') became separated from New Guinea and Australia (together the continent 'Sahul') by an island area with straits ('Wallacea': the Philippines, Sulawesi and the Lesser Sundas). Modern humans had certainly reached Australia 47,000 years ago, but onward migration to the Pacific was not yet possible due to a lack of suitable crafts. A little later, the dispersal across temperate Eurasia occurred, both north and north-westwards to Europe and from South Asia eastwards to China. About 19,000 years ago, humans moved from north-east Asia, via the Bering Strait, towards the Americas, where, within the same coastal Pacific biotope, the south of Chile was reached relatively quickly. Thus, our species spread throughout the whole world, with the exception of most of the islands of Oceania. These, then, are the headlines according to current archaeological and genetic insights, which are being adjusted and redefined almost daily.

Throughout the world – and during by far the largest part of their history – modern humans, like their non-human primate ancestors, were almost exclusively engaged with gathering food by picking or digging out plants and their fruits, the gathering of shells, fishing and hunting. Thus, around 700,000 years ago, the ancestors of modern humans in Africa (and the same is also true for Neanderthals in Eurasia) had already undergone a considerable technological evolution in comparison with other primates.[34]

The mode of existence of great apes, and particularly chimpanzees, consists of collecting a diet of predominantly plant foods, sporadically supplemented with communally organized hunting of smaller or young apes and other animals. This often involves both males and females, with strong males doing the actual killing. The appearance of the genus *Homo*, 2.5 million years ago, coincided with the collecting of roots and tubers using digging implements as well as scavenging from the kills of large predators with the help of stone tools for crushing leg bones to extract marrow or skulls to extract the brain. Already 2 million years ago, *Homo erectus* was able to fabricate hand-axes and cleavers.[35] Half a million years ago, hominins developed the skills to hunt living animals, larger in size than the hunters themselves. This implies a good knowledge of animal behaviour. Helpful, if not requisite for that change, around 300,000 years ago, were wooden thrusting and throwing spears and trapping techniques. As will be discussed in the next chapter, the hunt changed dramatically at the end of this period, in the millennia preceding the Neolithic Revolution. But first, we must address the question: what exactly is meant by hunting as a means of subsistence?

Hunting and gathering food in practice

For most people today, it is difficult to imagine what kind of work hunting and gathering food entails concretely. How much time does it take and who does it? How is it organized? There is no comprehensive answer to these questions covering all hunter-gatherers, simply because humans manage to survive in so many different climate zones, from sea coasts to high mountains and from deserts to rainforests.[36] This global distribution and development of different types of work in diverse ecological and climate zones results in a diversification that does not occur in animals without major genetic change and the emergence of new species. In humans, it has become possible as a function of brain development, language and communication. There have been no new human species since the creation of *Homo sapiens*. In evolutionary terms, *Homo sapiens* have made no further progress in their history than a diversification in skin colour and body proportions as a consequence of their migrations to more northerly climes.

One reason why it is not easy to depict and understand the working life of early modern humans as hunter-gatherers is because archaeology can provide only partial, but fortunately increasingly powerful, evidence. Animal parallels are of no help to us here. So, we are still largely reliant on descriptions of recent and extant hunter-gatherers from the last few centuries. The problem with this is that it was not possible to study any of these groups in a 'pure' state, untouched by other, 'more advanced' means of subsistence.[37]

Whereas until 12,000 years ago (10000 BCE) all humans shared a foraging existence, by the time Columbus sighted the Americas, 5 centuries ago, this way of life had been pushed back to Australia, most of North America, north-east Asia and large tracts of South America and Africa. An optimistic count of all pastoral nomads, reindeer herders, fishers and swidden (slash-and-burn) horticulturalists in the early twenty-first century adds up to 250 million individuals. That is 4 per cent of the world's population, the nucleus of which consists of 'hundreds of thousands of descendants a generation or two removed from a foraging way of life'. Only a small number of this nucleus, say a few tens of thousands, persisted in a roughly direct tradition of descent from ancient hunter-gatherers, whereas others descended from farmers or herders who turned to foraging, as seen in South America in order to escape the invading Spaniards.[38]

In the *Cambridge Encyclopedia of Hunters and Gatherers* (*CEHG*, 2004), a meagre eight groups of recent hunter-gatherers are treated in more detail. It is assumed, on historical and especially archaeological grounds, that their ancestors have always followed this way of life.[39] This cannot be ascertained for the dozens of other current or recent hunting and food-gathering peoples in this impressive encyclopaedia, but it is either demonstrable or probable that earlier in their existence they subsisted through farming or cattle raising, as was the case, for example, with the Mikea on Madagascar and for most current hunter-gatherers in South and South East Asia.[40]

But we must proceed cautiously even in relation to the eight aforementioned 'real' groups that, for thousands of years, from generation to generation, have lived as groups of hunter-gatherers. They, too, have undergone demonstrable historical development, particularly in terms of contact with neighbouring farmers and, more recently, with representatives of industrialized nations, such as oil-drilling companies.[41] Notwithstanding these reservations, we will try, by analogy, to reconstruct the work and associated social relationships of hunter-gatherers in prehistory.

The compilers of the *CEHG* use the following definition of hunter-gatherers: 'Foraging refers to subsistence based on hunting of wild animals, gathering of wild plant food, and fishing, with no domestication of plants, and no domesticated animals except the dog.'[42] And as core social elements they add: 'The basic unit of social organization of most (but not all) hunting and gathering peoples is the band, a small-scale nomadic group of fifteen to fifty people related by kinship.' Their members share the following features: they are relatively egalitarian; they are mobile according to a pattern of concentration in larger groups and dispersion in smaller groups during part of the year; and their land tenure system is based on a common property regime, a kinship-based collective, ruled by reciprocity.

Egalitarianism, sharing, generosity and reciprocity are not performed indiscriminately but primarily within the band; they also do not exclude a wide range of boundary-maintaining measures. We may suppose this is as true for hominins, including early *Homo sapiens*, as it is for other primates and for extant hunter-gatherers, who show variations in the ways they manage access to land and resources: 'Sharing is not a product of an evolutionary stage or a subsistence mode, it is the outcome of a decision-making process. There are costs and benefits to sharing resources and it is clear that hunter-gatherers balance these in making decisions to share food or to admit outsiders to their territory.'[43]

Taking these characteristics of the way of life of hunter-gatherers as our foundation, let us now examine the actual work of hunting and gathering food. Below, we will probe the possibilities for specialization in other activities, including the division of labour between men and women, the relationship between work and free time and, finally, social relationships within the group (the internal labour relations within households and the 'band'), and those between different bands, who exchange goods, services and people (marriage candidates).

Despite the many differences between hunter-gatherers in the various ecological and climate zones, there are, nevertheless, recognizable patterns. Perhaps most striking is the need for cooperation in the hunting of large game.[44] Before humans learned to use the hunting dog, it was all about the ability to run. Thanks to our gluteal muscles and our ability to sweat, we humans are good long-distance runners, and that is useful for hunting game, as the South African anthropologist Louis Liebenberg discovered when he took part in hunting parties with the San in Botswana. The hunters he was allowed to join were not even that young, almost 40 years old, but they still managed to run behind an antelope during the hottest part of the day (42 degrees Celsius) for between 23 and 40 kilometres, and to run until the animal gave up and could be captured. Their average speed varied between 4 and 6.5 kilometres per hour, but there is a documented case of 10 kilometres per hour over a distance of 35 kilometres.[45] As mentioned, this was a hunting party with a number of men, and this cooperation is crucial.

Take the hunting of bison by nomadic bands in North America.[46] For at least 2,000 years, they employed the 'impoundment' method. A closer look at the Nitsitapii or Blackfoot Indians reveals concretely what kind of work this entails. From at least the fourteenth century CE, this group occupied the northern Great Plains in units of 80 to 160 persons, living in 10 to 20 *tipis*, each tipi housing 2 able-bodied men, as many women and 4 children or elderly. In the spring, these hunters and gatherers built a bison pound, a corral towards which a herd was enticed by a young man imitating a bleating calf. The main hunting team hid close to the pound behind lines of rocks or brush piles. As the herd entered this funnel, the whole band jumped up, waving robes and shouting, causing the herd to stampede into the corral, where the men waited to kill anything from a few dozen to two hundred bison with clubs and bows and arrows. Teams of six able-bodied adults worked on each carcass. While stomach contents and organs were eaten fresh, most of the flesh was dried in thin strips. This dried flesh and rendered fat combined with dried berries was called *pemmican*. Packed and stored in hide bags, it could be used by the band until the next big spring hunt, but external trade in this food has also been documented.

Before their adoption of the horse a few centuries ago, the action radius of these bison hunters was necessarily small. After the big hunt, bands aggregated in early summer at rendezvous of several thousand people and dispersed into sheltered stream valleys in autumn. The berries in the pemmican required a different type of work from the Blackfoot – that is, the harvesting of plant foods by the women; and not only berries, but also camas bulbs and prairie turnips, which they cultivated. Women also created the tipi-camp, cooked, clothed and sheltered everyone and, importantly, women performed the rituals.

But it wasn't just game hunting that required intensive cooperation; the same was true of fishing. The Itenm'i of the Kamchatka Peninsula, who settled there no later than 3,000 years ago, were semi-sedentary fishers, hunters and gatherers with seasonal fishing as their core subsistence activity.[47] Salmon was intensively fished by all able-bodied members of a group (the size of which varied from a few dozen to over two hundred) who trekked to the river estuaries from May to October when the annual runs of fish occurred. Groups of men of the same kin built fishing weirs, where they used different sorts of nets and spears to catch the fish. Women processed and preserved the catch; assisted by the elderly and children, they hung the fish out to dry, and it was also fermented. Dried fish was the main staple, while fermented salmon was a delicacy for feasting. Fish skin was used to make footwear. In addition to these communal fishing activities, women collected molluscs, berries (raspberry, currant, dog-nose), nuts, grasses and roots. They made clothes, footwear, basketry and nets and they cared for the young. Meanwhile, men hunted furbearers like sables and foxes, as well as seals; they provided fuel, made sledges and canoes, and prepared food for humans and dogs. The important position of women is reflected in things such as the customary bride-service (a groom lived for a period with the bride's parents prior to the wedding) and shamanism. Only women or transvestites wearing women's clothes and doing women's work could be shamans, who worked with drums and hallucinogens prepared from amanita mushrooms.

In both examples, and this applies to hunter-gatherers worldwide, *cooperation* is the keyword, and this is especially true for hunting. But how do you become a successful hunter-gatherer? You must learn it, and the apprenticeship is long.[48] Above, we have already seen how long it takes for humans to achieve net productivity – only from the age of 14, and even then they are not mature. To give a brief idea of the techniques that a hunter-gatherer must learn, let us consider a common kangaroo-hunting technique in Central Australia, which takes place at midday, when the animals are 'shading' under brush or small trees:

> The hunter observes the way the animal is facing and positions himself so that he is directly in front of the shading animal. He begins to approach the animal, standing fully erect, nude so no clothing will move in the wind, with arms rigidly positioned relative to his body. He slips one leg at a time forward so there is no change in his silhouette as seen by the animal. As the animal begins to get nervous it will jump slightly to one side or the other to get an oblique angle view. The well-practiced hunter knows this little trick and is waiting for it so that when the animal jumps, so does the hunter, so that he comes down again directly aligned with the animal's line of sight but much closer to the animal. This deadly dance continues until the hunter is close enough to quickly use the atlatl to spear the kangaroo.

I borrow this observation from arguably the most influential archaeologist of the twentieth century, Lewis Binford, who stresses the deep and detailed knowledge necessary for successful hunting, adding: 'With an AK47 you don't have to know so much!'[49]

A comparison of anthropological material[50] has generated the following schema for the 'training' of hunter-gatherer children: Observation of tool-making and hunting, practice and listening to hunting stories are much more important than demonstration and teaching. At an early age, adults provide children with toy or small hunting weapons. Then, between the ages of 5 and 7, children begin to accompany adults on hunting trips, and around the age of 12–13 they also begin to go on hunting trips with peers, or are introduced to more hunting strategies. Late in adolescence they learn strategies to catch larger game.

The great danger of the above description is that it causes us to perceive the very long human history before 12,000 years ago as one in which little technical progress was made. That is clearly not the case. Hominins did not sit still and then suddenly become hyperactive in the Neolithic. Even before this time, major technical and organizational leaps were made. Recently, it has been shown that at least 300,000 to 400,000 years ago, off-site fire making by humans occurred in both Europe and the Near East, consequently changing and varying landscapes and their means of existence. Significantly, this occurred 'in the same time range as the greatest increase in relative brain size documented in the hominin fossil record'.[51] Even the Neanderthals, who cared for their sick and elderly, had a level of 'cognitive sophistication' and an appreciation of symbolism, attested by the stone circles built 180,000 years ago and jewellery made from eagle talons dated 130,000 years ago.[52]

Two developments in East Africa matter in particular. First, the development of speech, maybe 70,000 years ago, and, subsequently, between 50,000 and 40,000 years ago, what has been characterized in East Africa, the Near East and a little later in southern Europe as the 'Great Leap Forward'.[53] Standardized stone tools were developed, but also what we might dub art- and showpieces, such as 'jewels' made from the shell of ostrich eggs. The first needles, awls, engraving tools, harpoons and rope also date from this period. The cave paintings and the statues and musical instruments in France, Spain, Indonesia and South Africa belong to this nexus as well.[54] This is also the period that the entire ancient world in the tropical and temperate zones became inhabited, initially by *Homo sapiens*, who would soon be the last remaining subspecies of hominins. Meanwhile, archaeology has not sat still for the past few decades, and instead of one Great Leap Forward, archaeologists now prefer to talk in terms of several leaps.[55]

The invention of ballistic weapons, in particular the step from the long-established thrusting and hand-thrown spear to the atlatl or spear-thrower and the bow and arrow, was useful for the successful hunting of large game. The invention of the bow and arrow (or atlatl and arrow), sharpened with microliths, may also have played a role in the dispersal of *Homo sapiens* beyond Europe.

Another good example of important pre-Neolithic 'inventions' is the poisoning of arrows in Southern Africa and, in Asia, the training of dogs for hunting, probably between 20,000 and 12,000 years ago. But less spectacular innovations also deserve our attention. The development of techniques for preserving food for longer are particularly important. The world's leading theorist on egalitarian hunter-gatherer societies, James Woodburn, has introduced the distinction between hunter-gatherers who belong to 'immediate-return' societies, which usually obtain an immediate return on their labour, and 'delayed-return' societies, which manage their economies on a more long-term basis. This distinction is somewhat reminiscent of that between foragers and collectors introduced by Lewis Binford.[56] Strongly guided by the landscape, foragers constantly move their base camp, while collectors have a fixed base camp (possibly varying between summer and winter) and from there move around in a large landscape (comparable with shepherds much later, see below). Regarding delayed-return societies and collectors, think of, for example, all kinds of techniques for wind-drying and smoking food in the polar and subpolar regions. A good example is the Jomon culture in Japan (14500–500 BCE), where, from early on, hunter-gatherers were making pottery (important for food storage, allowing more sedentary work arrangements) and lacquerware, grinding the edges of stone axes, eating smoked food and decorating their things. In short, these were early sedentary lives without agriculture, but with important technological advances and with the maintenance of social equality.[57]

Ceramics originated earlier, and not in Japan. We know of clay figurines from some 25,000 years ago, like the famous Venuses from Central Europe, and the first fired pots in China 20,000 years ago, thus already among hunter-gatherers, who were soon shaping deer antlers into tools. These pots 'were used for cooking during the relatively harsh conditions of the Late Glacial maximum. This method was a critical improvement over the old technique of cooking over hides over fire'. Four thousand years later, this new invention would spread to Japan and a little later also to Siberia.[58]

Technological development did not stagnate among those peoples who clung to hunting and gathering as the main means of existence, even after the Neolithic Revolution had taken place elsewhere. In Australia, 4,000–3,000 years ago, hafted tool types and seed-grinding techniques appeared as developments of existing technologies.[59] We also know of the autonomous development of techniques for gathering plants in South America.[60] And, of course, these types of innovations also came into contact with farmers. The autonomous developments as well as contact among hunter-gatherers and farmers/shepherds in Siberia is a good example of this dynamic.[61]

The division of labour between women, men and children

Based on the proposition that the earliest hominins already had to share the burden of a costly reproductive system among the sexes, we must now ask ourselves what the division of labour between women, men and children would have looked like in the period under scrutiny. The answer will remain opaque as long as we rely almost exclusively on anthropological descriptions of extant or recent hunter-gatherers – the material is appealing, but difficult to project back in time.[62] Currently, we have little more than a single study about skeletal activity-related morphology. Let us, therefore, venture to reconstruct the division of labour between men and women – the foundation of all labour relations.

Summarizing all the evidence on modern hunter-gatherers, anthropologist Karen Endicott concludes: 'nowhere can it be said that women and men live in a state of perfect equality' and cases of wife-beating and rape among hunter-gatherers have also been documented. Nevertheless, according to her, the women of hunter-gatherer societies have a higher status than women in most of the world's contemporary societies. She underscores this general conclusion with some remarkable observations. She writes of actual hunting and gathering activities that: 'The stereotype of man the hunter, woman the gatherer accurately describes only how many forager peoples divide daily work responsibilities. In reality, many hunter-gatherer men also gather vegetable foods and women procure animal foods, though the latter is not always called hunting.'[63]

This would have been encouraged by regular shortages of large game due to overhunting, with the consequence that the hunting of small game and other food types became more important. Among modern humans, gathering became more central as the reproductive core than among Neanderthals. This means, on the one hand, fewer risks for food gatherers and, on the other, that a division of labour became possible whereby every member of the band could be assigned a task. The gathering of seeds, nuts and tubers also involved processing with the help of grind- and millstones and thus a further division of labour.[64]

As for other, non-food-getting tasks, these are divided variously. Whereas men and women tend to perform jobs ancillary to their food-getting work, other tasks like construction work vary from society to society. Finally, although women tend to be the primary caregivers for infants and very young children, fathers help to varying degrees.

The many travel descriptions and ethnographic studies of the nineteenth and twentieth centuries are perhaps most revealing about recent hunter-gatherers in Australia, the Aboriginal peoples. Among this group, there is often a distinct gender division of labour, in which men hunt the larger and more prestigious game, while women take care of the foraging (including the capture of small animals), food preparation and child-rearing. This can lead to inequality, as the anthropologists of that continent never tire of emphasizing.[65] They also offer many exceptions to this rule. For example, the gender division of labour among the Kimberley peoples of Fitzroy Valley in Western Australia has been described as 'complementary':

While women more commonly foraged (e.g. bush potato, tomato, banana onion, bush honey), they also hunted small game (like the goanna lizard), and while men commonly hunted, they also foraged (bush honey). The preparation and cooking of food was sometimes shared, although senior women generally assumed responsibility for these tasks ... [w]omen (particularly those between twenty and sixty), often accompanied by dependent children and grandchildren, spent considerable periods of time acquiring bush foods.[66]

We are told that the gender-based division of labour among the Ngarrindjeri of south-eastern Australia was less marked and more equitable in relation to the collection and processing of food than elsewhere in Aboriginal Australia.[67] Men hunted and collected a great number and range of food types (especially birds, mammals, marsupials, reptiles and fish) and expended more time and energy in the food quest than did women, yet women's gathering (for example, seeds, berries, vegetables, plants, shellfish) was more specialized and much food-getting was collaborative. Similar 'exceptions' to the 'rule' are reported from the Cape York peoples in North Queensland (Australia) where, comparatively, relations between the sexes are relatively egalitarian.[68]

Strong cooperation between men and women when hunting is recorded among the Ju/'hoansi of Botswana and Namibia.[69] Two-thirds of their diet was vegetal, consisting in particular of mongongo (or manketti) nuts and fruits, gathered by women. Meat was of secondary importance, although much desired, and its procurement the result of great skill, strength and knowledge by both men and women. While men hunted, their wives often assisted them in tracking and, of course, in the final preparation and processing of the kill. This cooperation between men and women may be related to the fact that the core composition of the groups of fifteen to fifty persons tended to be several siblings of both sexes, with their 'in-marrying' spouses. Men often joined the wife's family group upon marriage. This division of tasks among men and women is confirmed by women's economic and decision-making power.

Similar cooperation was found until recently between men and women at hunt among the Mbuti Batwa of the Ituri forest in north-eastern Congo.[70] Their principal subsistence activity was collective net hunting. Roughly 10 nets of 1 metre high and 30–50 metres wide were joined together in a large semicircle. Women beat the bush and chased the prey towards the nets while the men handled the nets and killed the animals entangled in them. Women then transported the animals to the camp.

Intensive cooperation between men and women hunting in the nineteenth century could still be found among the Yámana of Tierra del Fuego (or people with a Yámana-like way of life), who inhabited the Beagle Channel region from 6,200 years ago.[71] Yámana people were typically sea hunters, especially in winter. Seals and porpoises were approached by boat and harpooned. Local groups usually comprised between fifteen and twenty canoes. Daily pursuits like sea hunting required intimate man–woman cooperation, since the woman manoeuvred the canoe to give her husband the best possible shot. Every activity related to the canoe except its construction was the woman's responsibility. She gave orders to her crew. Remarriage among widows and widowers had everything to do with preserving the vital balance of the 'canoe-holds'.[72]

At the extreme of the recent anthropological spectrum are women who go hunting alone, like the Agta of eastern Luzon. Some Agta groups allow women to hunt the wild Philippine bearded pig, deer, monkey and smaller game. Both men and women fish in the rivers and along the Pacific shoreline, using wire spears and goggles. The fish, caught by men and women two to three times a day, provide the bulk of the protein intake. Children may begin 'play' fishing at the age of 4 and begin hunting with parents or older siblings around the age of 10. Recently, archaeological and historical evidence has also come to light, for example, of the women's guild of elephant hunters in the early modern Kingdom of Dahomey, and women as big-game hunters in the Andean highlands pre-8,000 years ago and among other early populations throughout the Americas.[73]

From all these observations of hunter-gatherers over recent centuries we can conclude that both men and women played a key role in obtaining food. Women seem to have had a more important role in the task of preparing food, and it goes without saying that they spent a great deal of time looking after their babies and toddlers, at least until they were about 4 years old. Moreover, we should not underestimate the role of 'alloparents', although here too women seem to be better represented than men, or at least grandmothers better than grandfathers.

The big question, of course, is whether we can simply transpose all these observations onto their peers from 12,000 plus years ago. Archaeological evidence for gendered task differentiation is not easily available.[74] Excavations of hunter-gatherer settlements from 8,000–5,000 years ago at La Paloma, on the central Peruvian coast, indicate that men and women did the same kind of heavy work: 'both men and women developed larger upper body muscles, possibly from hauling nets. Both had lower arthritis from carrying heavy loads'.[75] These findings appear to undermine the antiquated and simplistic opposition of man the hunter and woman the gatherer. Nevertheless, old skeletal material from hunter-gatherers shows that men experienced much more damage to their elbow tendons than women, suggesting that they mainly did the throwing during the hunt and thus were vulnerable to 'thrower's elbow'.[76]

Beyond hunting and gathering

Although hunting and gathering were indispensable and, therefore, the most important activities undertaken by our ancestors, that is not to say that they did nothing else before the introduction of agriculture. Other activities presented themselves, and there was also room for free time. Finally, then, we must delve deeper into social relationships, insofar as they are directly significant for a better understanding of the work of hunter-gatherers.

Professional specialization

Initially, the spread of modern humans across the globe was extensive: the constant colonizing of new areas and crossing of climate zones led to work other than gathering and preparing food and defending against natural enemies. In order to survive in the colder Northern Hemisphere, which humans moved into from 45,000 years ago, fire, clothing[77] (which animals don't have) and housing[78] (which some animals have but not generally outside the natural protection of caves) were necessary.

As we have seen, the use of fire was important not just on-site for heating the body and food preparation and off-site for increasing variegation and thus the productivity of landscapes, but it also had social implications.[79] Fire is 'cosy' and improves sociability. It also extends the duration of the day and opens up opportunities to tell and transfer stories, myths and rituals. This is in contrast to daytime conversations, which are more practical in nature.

Whereas, as far as we know, the use of fire had no consequences for professional specialization, the production of clothing and shelter probably did. The oldest eyed needles, used for sewing animal skins, date from 37,000 years ago, and the use of strings and hence of weaving from 26,000 years ago. It is remarkable that the Venus figurines that date from the same period clearly wear woven hats and have fibre accoutrements. It is possible to conclude from this that weaving was invented and originally practised by women.[80]

We can assume, however, that we are not talking here about full-time occupations. To the extent that these specialists were not able to take care of their own nutrition, they could easily obtain food via redistribution.[81] If we follow the famous American anthropologist Marshall D. Sahlins, then there are other reasons why there was little space for specialization among the earliest hunter-gatherers, not least because this mode of existence involved people constantly running around after their food, making possessions a burden. In Sahlins' highly classical formulation: 'Mobility and property are in contradiction.'[82]

He does, nevertheless, take into account that modern ethnography overlooks another, perhaps unexpected form of specialization: artistry.[83] Although already advanced, the visual arts appear to have developed to an almost perfect level of technology some 35,000–40,000 years ago. This is apparent from the special skills that are visible from the oldest cave paintings from this time, which were found in French and Spanish caves, such as those of Chauvet, Lascaux and Altamira, but also now in Indonesia, and not much later South Africa. Perhaps even more surprising is the fact that these skills have been maintained for hundreds of consecutive generations. Underlying this persistent level of high artistic skill must have been 'a compelling form of teaching'.[84] Others point to the crucial importance of coexistence in sufficiently large numbers of several generations.[85] Patrick Manning calls this 'basic format' in institutional evolution the emergence of 'workshops'.[86]

Some groups will also have been involved in the exchange of valuable goods, however tenuous these flows may have been by our standards. We are talking primarily in this period about the transport of exotics as a consequence of group mobility rather than trade in our sense of the word, which only developed late in the Neolithic.[87] We can turn again to the Ngarrindjeri of south-eastern Australia and their well-developed material culture for an example of this type of 'exchange'.[88] They practised a greater degree of specialization in economic activities than elsewhere on the continent, linked to both seasonal preservation of vegetables, fish and meat and to regional variations in resource availability, and sometimes associated with particular clans. There was no full-time specialization, but key roles included those of song composer, sorcerer, healer, fur and cloak preparer and basket maker. Well-established trade routes brought red ochre and native tobacco from afar. No wonder that a lively exchange system operated within and beyond Ngarrindjeri territory, featuring cloaks, rugs, nets, lines and animal and fish oils. This involved trading expeditions and barter and more formalized, enduring, culturally important ritual exchange partnerships between individuals and their families.

Interregional exchange in prehistory derives from finds of flint objects outside their natural area of origin. They will have initially got there through 'down-the-line exchange' via social networks. This does not necessarily indicate a certain form of division of labour between different population groups. The extent to which this had a profound influence on the total pattern of activities of these people is not known, let alone whether it led to other social relationships. What do we know, for example, about the division of labour that must have existed among the people or peoples who lived at the factory sites of the Rohri Hills in Sind in the south of what today is Pakistan? These sites indicate specialized procurement of high-quality flint, used until as late as the first millennium BCE.[89]

Also relevant in this regard is the mutual barter between hunter-gatherer communities. Among the Andaman Islanders, internal exchange was conducted between bands of forest dwellers, each consisting of twenty to fifty persons, hunting pigs with bows during the wet season, and coastal dwellers, hunting sea turtles with either nets or harpoons. The 'pig hunters' exchanged clay paint, ceramic clay, honey, bow and arrow wood, canoe logs and betel nuts for the 'turtle hunters'' metal (gathered along the shore), shells for ornaments, ropes and string and edible wild lime. The bands took turns hosting exchange ceremonies. Moreover, marriages were arranged by elders (married women often collectively influenced major camp decisions) between turtle hunters and pig hunters. Apart from hunting, both men and women performed all other daily activities, including childcare, cooking and gathering most foodstuffs and materials.[90]

Work and leisure: The original affluent society?

Our ideas about the relationship between work and leisure time are based almost exclusively on anthropological observations of the few remaining representatives of this mode of existence from the second and third quarters of the previous century. Hence, Sahlins thought that, though strenuous at times, the way of life of hunter-gatherers involved plenty of leisure time as their adults provided the group's food by working two or three days a week. In a provocative article, originally published in 1968, Sahlins dubbed these and other hunter-gatherers 'the original affluent society' and their history as 'the Zen road to affluence' before market economies. Then, means were 'unchanging but on the whole adequate', while human material wants were finite and few and thus easily satisfied by desiring little. Of course, the standard of living was low in comparison to later periods. Market economies are the opposite; consequently, Sahlins says, 'man's wants are great, not to say infinite, whereas his means are limited, although improvable: thus, the gap between means and ends can be narrowed by industrial productivity, at least to the point that "urgent goods" become plentiful'.[91] The latter is a reference to John Kenneth Galbraith's famous interpretation of post-war American society, entitled *The Affluent Society*, which had been published ten years earlier.

The innumerable technical and societal changes that have taken place in the long human history before the Neolithic Revolution – indeed, the logic of the Neolithic Revolution itself – seem to contradict Sahlins' opposition of unchanging and improvable technical means. He also seems to forget the necessity of spreading risk by means of the dominant sharing norm and by maintaining extensive networks, both patrilineal and matrilineal.[92] The American anthropologist Robert L. Kelly's criticism of Sahlins' basic idea that finite wants and few desires equated to 'plenty of leisure time' for hunter-gatherers is fundamental. He attacks the prevailing 'generalized foraging model' of Sahlins and his peers by contrasting it with the great variation within hunter-gatherer economies – and with that, the great variation in the amount of time spent foraging, depending on the environment. Simply put, 'Zen economy has an ecological master'.[93]

One of the problems when reconstructing the time spent on leisure is the definition of work. Kelly points out, for example, that definitions of work – in essence, what people do away from home – were often unintentionally derived from the situation in the West. Or, when studying hunter-gatherers, that what was considered work was 'only the time spent in the bush searching for and procuring food, not the labor needed to process food resources in camp'.[94]

Perhaps Sahlins' idea applied most to children and adolescents. A word, then, about the term 'adult'. The anthropological literature reports almost unanimously that hunter-gatherers still enjoyed great freedom before marriage and were not supposed to cooperate as full members of the band. We can therefore assume a degree of resistance about embarking on this next life phase.[95] For girls, this might be related to the fact that their menarche occurred quite late, only around the age of 16. Consequently, they married between the ages of 15 and 20. Boys married five years later and this, in combination with relatively short workdays, could have been why so many healthy, active teenagers were found among the !Kung bushmen of the Kalahari, moving from camp to camp while their older relatives provided food for them. Children took on the important role of babysitter.[96]

Contrast this with the hard-working elders, in particular grandmothers. After all, despite an average life expectancy of 30 years, the chance of 15-year-olds reaching 45 was 60 per cent, and 8 per cent of the population was 60 or older – some as old as 72, the age to which the body of modern humans is 'designed to last'.[97]

How much effort and time did it take for adult hunter-gatherers to scrape together their food? In the 1960s, it was calculated that, on average, !Kung San or Ju/'hoansi women from Botswana and Namibia, who performed the foraging tasks, walked 2,400 kilometres annually, or 6.6 kilometres a day.[98] At the same time, they carried equipment, 7 to 10 kilos of plant food on the return leg, and very often a child as well. The typical mother carried her child some 7,800 kilometres annually, or 5.4 kilometres a day, during the first 4 years of its life. A similar pattern arises from descriptions of the Aché of eastern Paraguay. The men engage in 7 strenuous hours of hunting per day, while the women forage a mean of 2 hours per day and, carrying heavy loads, spend an additional 2 hours per day moving camp. Women's remaining time is expended on high-quality childcare.[99] That, of course, means caring for those children who were still alive, because infant mortality was enormous, also due to the infanticide of those babies deemed as having little chance of surviving such a hard life.[100]

Similar work hours were observed among the /Gui and //Gana, who have been living in central Botswana for possibly the last 2,000 years. Before sedentary life started in 1979, within an area of, probably, on average 300 square kilometres, these hunter-gatherers had a range of about 50 kilometres. Hunting, done by men, involved 3 to 5 days a week for anything from 5 to 12 hours. These activities yielded 20 per cent of the total food intake; the rest was composed of plant foods gathered by women, who collected tubers, nuts, berries, melons, truffles and lilies for between 1 and 5 hours almost every day.[101]

Apparently much more supportive of Sahlins is the reconstruction of the work effort of the Cuiva, who straddle the border between Colombia and Venezuela, which does not exceed 15–20 hours a week; the majority spend 15–16 hours a day in their hammocks.[102] However, age-matched physical fitness, expressed as maximal oxygen uptake and analogous to strength testing, averages a full third higher for modern hunter-gatherers than for modern North Americans.[103] If this is true for hunter-gatherers in general, then the hammock-dwelling variant must definitely have been a minority among them.

More anthropologists have attempted to come up with statistics for the hours that hunter-gatherers spent working every day.[104] According to the more inclusive definitions, both adult men and women spent between 6 and 8 hours per day on 'work'. Although according to Hrdy, all primates are 'social opportunists' and their care behaviour is highly flexible, I think we have to add 1 hour for childcare by a male 'alloparent' to this reckoning.[105] In addition to foraging and food processing and preparation, women spend time on childcare.[106] Recuperation in the form of sleep may have taken 7 hours or a maximum of 9 if there was the opportunity to take a nap for 2 hours during the day.[107]

The remaining time – 9 hours for men and a few less for women – is hard to divide between social obligations and leisure, but the descriptions of the way these hours were spent points strongly to social obligations,[108] at least if we consider visiting and entertaining visitors, dancing and gambling as activities that individual band members could not and would not abstain from. If nothing else, this networking functioned as a kind of insurance policy. The cooperative nature of foraging, but also, to a certain extent, of childcare, would be an extra argument for this choice. The difference between the time men and women devote to social obligations is partially an illusion, as intensive childcare by mothers and other women may go hand in hand with social obligations in some cases. Even if someone else was taking care of her child, the mother was always close by. Among the Efé Batwa of the Democratic Republic of the Congo, babies spend 60 per cent of their time with other women, and it has been calculated that they change hands 8 times per hour. But they are still held most by their mother, who also breast-feeds them for years – although she is not necessarily the only woman to do this.[109] Regardless of the care that babies and small children receive, they also provide constant entertainment for the whole band in which they grow up.

This division of time among humans differs substantially from that of most non-human primate species, who spend 50 to 60 per cent of their day searching for food and eating, and 30 to 40 per cent resting, leaving some 5 to 15 per cent for social activities.[110] Converted into hours, this means that human hunter-gatherers have become much more efficient at foraging, while simultaneously depending more on social activities or obligations, which can also be seen as tools of survival.[111]

Secondly, many anthropologists believe that hunter-gatherers do not experience work as a burden, but rather as a pleasurable task that is, more-over, interrupted or followed by extended rest periods. If this seems very subjective, then the fact that the Yir Yoront of North Queensland (Australia) do not have separate words for working and playing indicates an entirely different perspective than expressed by the English language, in which labour can mean both strenuous work and giving birth.[112]

Social relations

The very low population densities of this period – a result of the mobile character of these hunting-gathering societies and their habitation in small groups or bands – implied a particular form of society. All specialists agree that social equality is much greater within such bands of hunter-gatherers than among agriculturalists.[113] This is often explained by mobility leading to a minimum of material property, small living groups, reciprocal access to food, lack of concern about storage and conflict-resolution mobility.[114]

From an evolutionary perspective, the British anthropologist and evolutionary psychologist Robin Dunbar argues that, according to the 'social brain hypothesis', the large brain size of later hominins has enabled their transition from a 'dispersed (or fission-fusion) social system', characteristic of great ape societies, to strong group cohesion.[115] An enlarged brain (or, more precisely, an enlarged neocortex) enables *Homo sapiens* in particular to live in extended communities. Dunbar defines (regional) groups or communities as a set of individuals who occupy a common range and whose relationships are known explicitly, sometimes referred to as 'the cognitive group size'.[116] To achieve a stable sex ratio, a sufficiently diverse gene pool (translated into incest taboos), and thus sufficiently healthy offspring, such a group must have an average of a least 500 individuals, or 20 bands each with 25 members.[117] But opposite the biological minimum, there is a social maximum and, remarkably, the two do not differ substantially.

Enlarged group size has both benefits and costs. The benefits are the capacity for mutual assistance, for specialization, for teaching and learning and for more extensive trading or exchange networks in ecologically more risky habitats. The costs of bonding or of the maintenance of group size with social cohesiveness through time should not be underestimated. As Dunbar eloquently explains:

> Living in groups (sociality) creates tensions and frustrations simply by virtue of the fact that individuals are forced together in a relatively confined space where they must inevitably get in each other's way. In addition, as group size increases, individuals are forced to forage further afield in order to meet their daily nutrient requirements, thereby imposing real ecological costs measured in terms of travel time and the additional food intake required to fuel the extra travel. Increased group size may also result in a significant increase in the opportunity for harassment and aggression that may add further centrifugal forces.

In short, social skills 'can be used for exploitative, as well as cohesive functions'.[118] Exploiting one's fellow group members is called 'free riding'. This taking of the long-term benefits of sociality without paying all the short-term costs threatens the implicit social contract and may, ultimately, threaten the persistence of social groups. In order to control free riders, they must be prevented from finding new naïve individuals. This problem of free riding is more serious in large, dispersed communities, and that is why *Homo sapiens* resorted to religion as 'a very powerful stick to use in enforcing social conformity (and hence the war against free-riders)'.[119]

As we have seen, in reality, hunter-gatherer bands form the primary working unit most of the time, and do not meet members of other bands belonging to the same group. On the rare occasions they do, it is to exchange marriage partners or precious goods. In fact, this exchange of brides and grooms between bands is important for our theme of 'work', because it means that one working party loses an able-bodied member while another gains one. Especially interesting is the new member's process of adaptation, both as part of the couple and of the band. Anthropologists have painstakingly described and analysed marriage patterns, post-marital residence, and descent and inheritance rules. Since at least the 1930s, scholars thought that patrilineal/patrilocal bands were the rule also in prehistory, which means that sons stay with their parents and that after marriage their bride must leave her parents' family and band and join his.[120] This means not only a transfer of workforce, but also of labour relations, as henceforth the groom's parents and eventually the groom himself could tell the newcomer what to do. This would be the result of the 'natural' dominance of men, and it would permit men to be familiar with their own area, of which they have a mental map of resource geography, to ensure success in hunting.

On the basis of the variety of hunting roles of men and women, described above, but also of detailed statistics made more recently of extant marriage patterns among hunter-gatherers, alternative theories have been proposed. Some, like Hrdy, are radical and tend to invert things, but her statistical basis is inconsistent with the much more extensive and meticulous data of Robert L. Kelly.[121] Fortunately, we do not have to rely on anthropological research alone. As discussed above, it is clear that alloparenting must have developed much earlier in the evolution of hominins. It cannot be excluded that a matrilinear society also prevailed at the time.[122]

It remains interesting, therefore, to reflect on Hrdy's idea that, initially, matrilocality would have fostered fatherly care behaviour. All men have the aptitude for this, she says, but it can only really develop in an immediate, biological way through actual contact with the newborn. In her own environment, the mother would feel safe enough to give the father access to his newborn, much sooner than in a strange patrilocal environment where she is de facto under the authority of her mother-in-law. In a hybrid system, in which, when children are born, matrilocality is followed by patrilocality (for example, because the bridegroom first has to pay bridewealth by working for his parents-in-law for a while), then previous care experience will make it easier for the man to continue even after the grandmother and other maternal relatives are no longer there.[123]

The current reconstruction of the social relationships that influence the distribution and organization of work in the period in which the world only knew hunter-gatherers (that is, 12,000 years ago and earlier) does not mean, of course, that all hunter-gatherers have responded to this ever since. Where, subsequently, they were able to accumulate wealth as a result of extremely favourable natural resources and partly through the exchange of goods and services with horticulturalists and agriculturalists, very different societies were created. For example, certain hunter-gatherers were able to become more or less sedentary for large parts of the year as a result of the abundance of fish (salmon and trout migrations provided a regular food source), and thus also to develop hierarchical societies. Think of the indigenous peoples of the north-west coast of America, the prosperous maritime economies of the Aleut of Alaska and the Calusa of Florida and, in comparable areas in Asia, the Siberian Yupik.

Some of these peoples and their prehistoric predecessors (we are talking here of centuries-long enduring habitation) lived from about 500 BCE in large semi-sedentary settlements with chiefs, commoners and slaves, albeit on a small scale, yet were entirely dependent on wild food. In their complex social and material culture with large cedar-plank houses, some chiefs practised polygyny. Occasionally, they could also afford a bartered slave for status or childcare. Only families that failed to repay feasting debts lost status.[124]

More importantly, we should not forget that labour relations may also be unequal within families, simply because of age differences or because of specific characters. As a Dogrib (caribou hunters and fishers in Canada) man told an anthropologist half a century ago: 'With your dad, you kill yourself doing all the work. Going with your [elder] brother is just like going with your dad. He won't work hard. He expects you to do most of the work. So, you don't take your own brother very often [as a work partner]. You take your brother-in-law most of the time.'[125]

Ж

For most of the hundreds of thousands of years that modern humans have existed, up to 12,000 years ago, they provided for their existence solely by hunting and gathering food. Even now, a handful of people, the descendants of these humans, still live this way. By combining the latest insights from archaeology, primatology, anthropology and palaeogenetics, we can form a certain idea about the origins of human work and labour relations.

In any case, from the beginning of modern humans, we can assume a gradual development of a knowledge-intensive mode of existence, characterized by a long youth during which people could learn a lot from their parents' and grandparents' generations. This process led to the acquisition of more varied and higher-quality food and the use of on-site and off-site fire and landscape management. Low interbirth intervals, in turn, made it possible for youngsters to grow up among a larger group of siblings and peers.

The emphasis in modern research is on the high degree of interdependence in work and the cooperation that resulted from it. Another key component of daily work, the care of vulnerable babies and children, was primarily down to mothers, but band members also took responsibility for an important part of it. Defining work broadly, as is advocated in this book (that is, inclusive of care for family members and children), adult men spent 8 and adult women 10 hours a day engaged in it. Although this involved a considerable time investment, it is probably fewer work hours than the way of life that developed later. Social hierarchies were poorly developed, and subordination, other than that of children in respect of the elderly, was rare, let alone slavery. Internal labour relations within the household and the clan, consisting of a number of households, were rather characterized by reciprocity and cooperation. Life was nevertheless harsh, and predators and diseases and even aggression took their toll, so we cannot speak of a golden age. But this long period of time, when all humans were hunter-gatherers, still occupies a unique place in the history of work. Many of these elements, characteristic of the work of hunter-gatherers, would change with the further development of agriculture in the subsequent periods, and especially after 5000 BCE; at the same time, we can assume that a number of basics, acquired over such a long period, also continued to play a role. In particular, the satisfaction, pride and pleasure found in working, and the propensity to work in a cooperative way and to strive for equality in remuneration for effort. This will be explored in subsequent chapters.

2

FARMING AND DIVISION OF LABOUR, 10000–5000 BCE

The work of hunter-gatherers largely consisted of an extensive search for means of subsistence. When food became scarce, this pursuit moved further afield. The starting point for this search was Africa but, progressively, *Homo sapiens* spread throughout the Old World, south of the Great Northern Ice Sheet. At the same time, people were constantly having to adapt to different circumstances – climates, flora and fauna – and implement landscape management with the help of fire. Consequently, the daily diet varied enormously between Tasmania in the south-east and Ireland in the north-west, between South Africa in the south-west and Japan in the north-east; that is to say, in those parts of the world inhabited by humans around 20,000 years ago.

Around 12,000 years ago, or 10000 BCE, a gradual change in human food supply becomes visible, with humans effecting great changes in flora and fauna – far more than their hunter-gatherer forebears – and, consequently, in

A man, possibly representing a priest or God, feeding a flock of sheep on an Uruk-period marble cylinder seal, accompanied by its impression in clay.

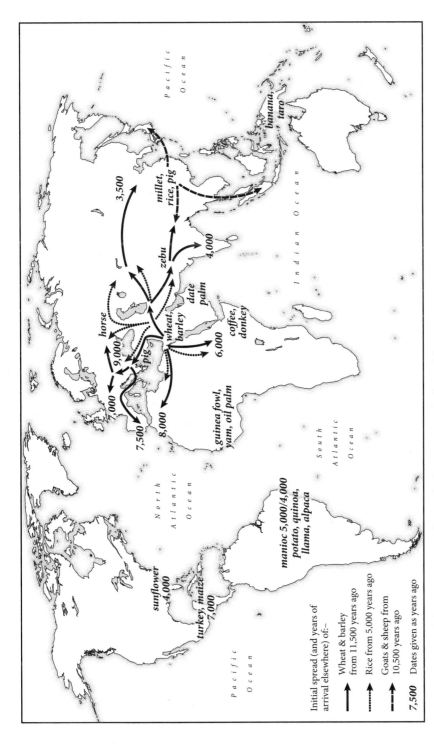

Map 2. Origins of domestication and spread of some grains and goat/sheep.

the utilization of available energy.[1] The qualitative transition in question is that of human consumption and the switch from wild plants to cultivated plants and from wild animals to domestic animals (cattle) and their products, resulting in a sharp decrease in the consumption of wild animals (except for fish).

Our unit of analysis becomes smaller in this chapter. From the labour relations within the band of hunter-gatherers we now switch to those within the peasant household, producing for its own consumption. These relations continue to be reciprocal, although gendered task divisions become more prominent. The next question, then, is how labour relations developed between these peasant households, united in 'tribes' of hundreds or thousands of households. Those between peasant households and emerging specialists like blacksmiths, potters and weavers may be envisaged – parallel to the Indian *jajmani* system (p. 143) – as the reciprocal local exchange of products and services outside of markets. With the relations between more and less successful farming households we encounter two models: the African (or Bantu) model, where inequality was insignificant for thousands of years, probably because of low population densities and ample opportunities for mobility; and the 'aggrandizer model', evidence of which is found in parts of Eurasia, mainly in the form of clear status differentials in burial practices.

A brief overview of what the specialists have to say about the 'Neolithic Revolution' (pp. 48–56) is followed by a much-needed concretization of what agricultural work entails (pp. 56–61). On that basis, we can reflect on the division of labour between men and women with respect to food production (pp. 61–5) and the link between the Neolithic Revolution and the unequal remuneration for efforts between households (pp. 65–72) that possibly emerged during it. This division of labour occurs within the wider context of the tribe and relationships between food-producing and other households, and also tentatively between leaders and their households, on the one hand, and their co-tribespeople or compatriots expected to pay on the other.

The Neolithic Revolution

The circumstances in which farmers and livestock breeders lived for thousands of years alongside hunter-gatherers and only later became dominant is a question that has occupied generations of archaeologists and is still not fully resolved.[2] Two assertions stand out, however: climate change and overhunting.

The climate change that occurred some 12,000 years ago caused a clear, albeit gradual, rise in global temperature.[3] These temperature increases initially facilitated population growth and further migration across the globe, quickly followed by an intensification of human work. The climate shifted from cold and dry to warm and wet, creating an environment in which plants and animals could thrive and, in turn, greater prosperity for our hunting and gathering forebears. Population growth due to the vast increase in plant foods on the steppes of south-eastern Europe and Siberia resulted in more contact and thus uniformity of products, for example, the similarly shaped microliths of the Early Natufian communities in the Middle East (12,300–10,800 years ago).

Prior to this climate warming, however, as we have seen, there was also a radical change in hunting methods.[4] As evidenced by the famous cave paintings of animals in various poses, prehistoric hunters had a strong preference for the meat of large-hoofed mammals. This preference remained unchanged during major climatic fluctuations until, from 30,000 years ago, the share of these meat supplies in the human diet declined dramatically, as demonstrated for several locations in western Eurasia. Given that the climate then stayed relatively stable and that there are no indications of culturally determined changes in taste, the most likely explanation for this appears to be overhunting of the largest animal species. As we saw in the previous chapter, this was superseded by individual hunters scouring for small animals and the increasing importance of the proceeds of gathering for the food supply. As will become clear, these shifts in the diet stimulated the domestication of plants and animals.

What we refer to as the 'Neolithic Revolution' is a fundamental change in our means of subsistence from extensive food-extracting ('living off the land') to intensive food-producing economies, in which humans took responsibility for the reproduction of their food through the domestication of plants and animals. While neither a revolution in the classical sense (a radical change in a *short* time) nor an invention, and certainly not the disappearance of hunting-gathering as a source of income, in the long run, the implications of this change for human history and certainly for the history of work are profound. Hence, in the absence of better knowledge, my use of the familiar metaphor, the Neolithic Revolution.

For several reasons, it is not easy to summarize this process, so essential to the history of work, briefly. Not least because it is unbelievably complex. That said, it is certainly not due to a lack of good, modern research; on the contrary. Indeed, it is no exaggeration to state that no subject dealt with in this book has been so rigorously overhauled in recent decades as the Neolithic Revolution. And it continues to be the case – it is not easy for a general historian to keep up.

The study of the origins of agriculture is no longer predominantly limited to the Near East, and prehistoric science is now actively practised all over the world. Moreover, it has rapidly become interdisciplinary, as illustrated by a symposium held in Mexico in March 2009, where participants included archaeologists, archaeobotanists, archaeozoologists, geneticists and physical anthropologists.[5] While the attendant specialists provided greater insight into the domestication of crops and animals, they were unable to agree on the reasons why hunter-gatherers swapped their stable mode of existence for the many insecurities of farming life. On the one hand, the simultaneity of many of the new 'inventions' in the cultivation of wheat, rice, sheep and cows in earth's far-flung places requires the search for a common cause. On the other hand, several specialists remain sceptical or find this premature and prefer to look for causes that apply to a more limited area.

In the search for causes, climate improvement (followed by population growth) and overhunting are primary factors, but the consequent human behaviours are also determinant. The periodic surpluses that were made possible by agriculture had to be divided, just like the proceeds of hunter-gathering. Since there are no indications of private ownership of land or herds in the first millennia of the Neolithic Revolution or in Africa until much later, the question arises about how these surpluses were distributed, and about how farmers dealt with windfalls. As we will see, for thousands of years, in Africa, when the group managed to, say, kill a large animal, the spoils were shared by way of redistribution. In Eurasia, however, a new phenomenon materialized, that of aggrandizers, who acquired a disproportionate share of the harvest for themselves and for their households.

While the reasons why hunter-gatherers became farmers may still be the subject of debate, the most important consequences are now established. This change in the means of subsistence initially represented great success for the human species: according to some authors, the global population increased tenfold from 8 million at the start of the Neolithic to 85 million in 5000 BCE.[6] At the same time, a gradual process of sedentarization and hence the accumulation of goods occurs, firstly of food and subsequently also of household effects and even valuables. It started with the semi-permanent establishment of hunter-gatherers in places that were so rich in natural nourishment that they no longer had to constantly hunt for their food. But this only became possible for larger parts of humanity with the development of agriculture.

This, too, was a lengthy process. In many parts of the world, farmers who employed the slash-and-burn method remained highly mobile. Every year, or every few years, an area of forest was burned down and crops were sown in the fertile ash. These farmers were thus continuously changing land. The specialization of certain farmers as pastoralists also involved a high degree of mobility. Finally, permanently established farmers could decide to move for all kinds of reasons – as evidenced by the immigration from the Old to the New World following Columbus's discovery of that continent.[7] These caveats aside, it remains the case that, since the Neolithic, humanity has become considerably more place-bound, which has had an enormous impact on the organization of work. It was a long-term process not least because it was by no means straightforward. Sometimes, farmers would even become hunters again.[8] That often happened when hunters had something to offer a neighbouring farmer. These hunters began to specialize, so that they could exchange their products with farmers such as the Athabaskans, who became bison hunters 1,250 years ago, and, later, the 'trappers' around the Arctic Circle.[9]

The Neolithic Revolution occurred in different locations in the world, independently of each other. It always went hand in hand with trial and error and it always took a very long time. Prior to the emergence in the Near East of agricultural economies based on domestic crops and livestock, there had been roughly 4,000 years of stable and sustainable subsistence economies founded on a combination of free-roaming, managed and fully domesticated resources.[10] In fact, three processes had to be completed before we can really talk about the predominance of the farming and/or herding activities of a particular community determining diet (up to this point associated with the products of hunting and gathering).[11]

First was plant and animal *management* – that is, manipulation of and some degree of control over wild species of plants or animals but without cultivation or morphological changes. This involves the systematic collection and consumption of the largest, tastiest seeds and fruits from wild plants and, subsequently, facilitating (unconsciously) their reproduction through defecation and by spitting out these superior seeds in close proximity to one's dwellings.

The next step was *cultivation*, or the intentional preparation of the soil for planting (initially) wild and (later) domesticated plants. This began with the conscious and literal weeding out of competitors in the vicinity of the increasing number of better yielding plants – also called 'plant nurturing' in 'wild gardens' – extensively applied in the Amazon region where cultivated plants such as cassava, cacao, coca and pineapple occurred.[12] Both of these steps promoted the growth of the most beneficial mutants of these plants.

Only then did the step of actual *domestication*, involving morphological or genetic changes in plant and animal species, take place. It is much easier to domesticate plants than animals. Plants rather quickly exhibit distinct morphological changes as a consequence of cultivating the best varieties, by selecting and sowing or planting seeds and rhizomes.

There are three distinct pathways in the animal domestication process.[13] Firstly, that of 'commensals', such as dogs, cats, guinea pigs, fowl and probably also pigs, adapted to a human niche. Then came the taming of goats, sheep and cattle. While commensals initiated the human–animal relationship by feeding on refuse around human habitats, these animals were initially focal prey hunted by humans for their meat. Subsequently, they were domesticated for a more stable and permanent supply. The third track is the 'directed pathway', whereby free-roaming animals (donkeys, horses, camels) are domesticated in order to obtain specific resources or 'secondary products',[14] for instance milk and derived products, wool, traction, and riding and pack transportation. The domestication process continues to this day: 'Humans and their domesticates exist in the symbiotic relationship of mutualism, as each species benefits from the other, in terms of its reproductive success. . . . It continues with each generation, as humans, plants and animals interact and certain phenotypic forms and behaviors are selected for.'[15]

Farming was only able to develop on the basis of all these steps, encompassing all the activities to obtain food by means of cultivating plants and the controlled herding of animals. Today, we know of at least twelve different places in the world where agriculture developed independently.[16]

It is simply not feasible to deal with all these fascinating innovations, even briefly. The first cases in the Middle East do, however, deserve a short discussion, partly because we now know that, throughout the Fertile Crescent, the management, cultivation and later domestication of plants and animals more or less went hand in hand.[17] Plant management had already started there ten thousand years before domestication. The actual domestication of cereals (einkorn and rye, followed by barley, emmer and oats) and thereafter pulses (lentils, chickpeas and faba beans) and figs, dates from at least 11,500 years ago. In some places, almonds and pistachios were also added early on.

At roughly the same time, we see the domestication of caprines (sheep and goats), cattle and pigs a little further north in the Fertile Crescent. In this case, it was preceded by centuries of management strategies by hunters, who mainly selected young, male animals as prey, thereby promoting the preservation of female breeding stock. Meanwhile, it is estimated that the transition from hunting to herding goats on the upper reaches of the Euphrates, in present-day Turkey, occurred already 10,500 years ago. In the first instance, wild goats were caught alive and fed in captivity. In a subsequent phase, more tame specimens were selected with a view to, ultimately, breeding domestic animals. Later, the same method was applied to sheep and then to cattle in the Zagros mountains on the border of Iran and Iraq. Pigs also belong on this list, although the starting point for their domestication (as in the case of dogs) should perhaps be seen more as the systematic feeding (and, ultimately, outmanoeuvring) of commensals scavenging for food around human habitations. In the case of pigs, the first form of management would have consisted of chasing young males. But this method is not appropriate to domesticate all animals. Captives such as cheetahs, falcons and elephants cannot be domesticated through selection and breeding over time; rather, wild specimens must each be tamed and trained individually to perform the desired tasks.[18]

Although these steps were taken sooner or later for all the different crops and domestic animals, in all parts of the world, Eurasia arguably still has an advantage over the Americas, tropical Africa and Oceania.[19] This has everything to do with its location parallel to the equator. This location along longitudes, not latitudes, means that the climate-dependent technique of domesticating animals and plants could spread rapidly over enormous distances. This, in turn, increased the chances of cultural cross-fertilization and of new inventions.

We can consistently distinguish three phases.[20] First, a crop or an animal is successfully domesticated in a particular area, in a process that takes thousands rather than hundreds of years. In the second phase, this invention is successfully imitated elsewhere within the same climate belt and, ultimately, a new species can be domesticated in this new location. The third phase now requires less time because the principle of domestication is already known.

The first phase of the independent domestication of crops and animals took place in western Eurasia and it commenced in the Fertile Crescent, where the Natufians were the first hunter-gatherers in what today is Israel, Lebanon and Syria. They lived in fixed settlements where they actively managed local wild plants for many generations, finally resulting in full-fledged agriculture.[21] Something similar occurred later in the east, in the river valleys of China, and, later still, elsewhere in the world, in New Guinea, the Americas and Africa. For example, in the Andes and Amazonia humans first managed manioc (5000 to 4000 BCE), and later potato, sweet potato, oca, quinoa, lima bean, common bean, peanut, and cotton barbadense as a fibre crop, and guinea pigs, llamas and alpacas became domesticated animals. The inhabitants of the Amazonian savanna subsequently developed a sophisticated system of ponds, canals, mounds and causeways to profit from the annual river inundations, thus maximizing fishing yields.[22]

The order in which new crops were developed and where exactly this happened is not particularly important per se. It is not a competition. Much more significant is the fact that the domestication of plants and animals occurred roughly at the same time and that people domesticated the same plants and animals independently of each other. The American archaeologist Diane Gifford-Gonzalez, an expert in zooarchaeology, commented on this with respect to Africa:

[The] choice of animals and plants is strongly driven by considerations of efficiency ... not the abstract efficiency of deterministic processual modeling, but the household manager's day-to-day assessment of marginal gains in time or nutrients that a new species, breed or strain offers. Quotidian agricultural and pastoral workload falls most heavily on reproductive-age women who also, in nearly all known cases, manage food resources at the household level, even among strongly patriarchal cultures.[23]

The second phase, the spread of domestic crops and animals from the Fertile Crescent across the rest of the world, was not simple one-way traffic from a unique centre, because elsewhere, such as in Africa, China and India, new crops were also being developed and new species of animals were being tamed and bred.[24] From the Fertile Crescent, grain cultivation spread in three different directions: from 9,000 years ago, simultaneously to Africa, via Iran to South Asia and via Anatolia to Europe.[25] The first farmers to head east reached the Indus Valley, where they mixed with the hunter-gatherers and introduced the winter rainfall crops wheat and barley and adapted them to the different climatic circumstances of the sub-continent, with its monsoon summer rainfall. At the same time, millet was being grown in northern China and rice near the Yangtze River. Both are monsoon summer rainfall crops, and their culture developed independently. From China, farmers spread these new crops in the direction of South East and South Asia around 5,000 years ago, and much later to Korea and Japan. Indian agriculture thus became a fortunate admixture of crops from two different and faraway sources.

A few centuries later, the urban Harappa culture, symbolized by the zebu, blossomed in the Indus Valley. These hump-backed cattle, domesticated locally, later spread to western parts of Asia and Africa. This is an example of the third domestication phase, which includes local domestications following the arrival of founder crops from elsewhere.[26] But the developments in the Fertile Crescent did not stop. Later, olives, almonds, grapes and date palms were introduced, and these products subsequently spread to neighbouring regions.

Today, we see these distribution patterns everywhere and, of course, they continue, albeit in a systematic and industrial way. The spread of, for example, the sweet potato from South America across the world in three waves is fascinating.[27] It initially spread from Peru-Ecuador, in a westerly direction, to Polynesia, between 1000 and 1100 CE, and from there to Hawaii in the north and New Zealand in the south. Thereafter, around 1500, the Spanish exported it from the Caribbean via the Atlantic and the Indian Ocean to South Asia, from where the new fruit eventually ended up in New Guinea. Finally, a generation later, it moved from Mexico, across the Pacific Ocean, to the Philippines and then on to China, Japan and, for the second time, to New Guinea.

Similar patterns of domestication and assimilation of plants and animals adapted elsewhere took place in all parts of the world.[28] Unfortunately, this concise history permits only a few examples. In the more spectacular cases it produced a single agricultural system with a dominant language family, such as the Indo-European language family in the west of Eurasia, the Niger-Congo language family in sub-Saharan Africa, and the Austronesian in the

Pacific. In lowland South America, this is not the case, nor is there strong and large-scale socio-political formation, hence the diversity of crop systems that has prevailed in Amazonia for the last 5,000 years.[29]

The function of this rather long list of 'agricultural inventions' for this book is manifold. Firstly, it follows that the Neolithic Revolution is a global phenomenon that took place everywhere, from 12,000 years ago onwards, except for far beyond the northernmost and the southernmost latitudes. Furthermore, it is an infinite process, as it were, and, after a false start, it was also an irreversible one. We still have many peasant families, farmer workers and plantation slaves to meet in this book, but for now it is important to understand how dynamic their role has been and how their work has changed over time.[30] Whether we take population size, the share of agriculturalists, cropland and pasture per capita, or pasture as a percentage of global land area, all these indicators demonstrate how agricultural productivity has increased over time. They also show how the landscape has been increasingly determined by agriculture, despite the percentage decrease in the population employed in this way in recent centuries. In short, although farmers play a leading role in this chapter but receive less attention later in this book, their work is not only indispensable for feeding the world's population, but their work is also incredibly dynamic.

Finally, the Neolithic Revolution led to great differences everywhere in the organization of human labour, although, as we have seen above, it did not extirpate hunter-gatherers initially. But before examining these social implications, we must look more closely at the most important type of work in human history – the work of farmers and livestock breeders.

Farmers at work

What do farmers do exactly? Let us begin this exercise in imagination with arable farming and, as in the previous chapter, with hunters and food gatherers, analogy will be employed where archaeology falls short. The last chapter relied heavily on more recent ethnological descriptions but, fortunately, regarding agriculture, we now also have access to descriptions from thousands of years ago. I will employ both here to conjure up an image of the earliest farmers.

Arable farming has a time horizon of at least one year. Of course, investments in buildings, equipment, wells, land improvement and irrigation also require a longer time perspective, but crops are alternated depending on the annual recurring seasons. Peak weeks, when there simply aren't enough hours in the day, are punctuated with months when farmers can only wait to see what their crops are going to do. Schematically, the following successive activities appertain to every crop: working the soil by digging it, but mostly by ploughing or harrowing, followed by or in combination with fertilizing; the sowing, weeding and irrigating of growing plants, followed by harvesting and for many crops threshing; and finally, the necessary processing for food preparation, such as the milling of flour.[31]

For slightly larger areas, the farmer swapped a spade for the ard (a simple scratch plough) and later for the deeper pulling plough, usually pulled by animals (initially cattle and much later horses, donkeys or camels). People also strained in front of the plough, as was the case in certain parts of China until the beginning of the last century.[32] Thanks to draught animals, arable farming and animal husbandry came together nicely from around 5000 BCE.[33] One medieval writer had an eye for the necessary skills in this regard: 'The skill of the drivers lies in knowing how to drive a team of oxen level, without beating, goading or ill-treating them. They should not be mournful men or wrathful, but cheerful, singing and joyous, so that by their tunes and songs the oxen may in some measure be heartened.'[34] Fertilizing with, among other things, mud and night soil (human manure) ensured that arable farming and cattle raising naturally functioned together. Before the invention of the cart, it was not possible to transport a lot of manure over longer distances.[35] There was usually a somewhat quieter period after the sowing or planting season, but since the crops needed water and it frequently rained too much or too little, water management was a key concern, especially when irrigating crops such as rice. Unfortunately, at the same time as the desired crops appeared, so did the weeds, making weeding an inevitable task. Crops, such as flax, that were sown using the broadcast method also needed to be thinned out.

Just how labour-intensive irrigation can be is clear from the description below of farming in the Azamgarh district (north of Varanasi, India) by the British colonial civil servant J.R. Reid in 1881.[36] At that time, mainly cereals, and in particular barley, were grown there. Where the fields could not be irrigated directly from nearby rivers and streams, water was collected in tanks and from there was raised into the fields, or from one channel into another at a higher level, by bailing.

In bailing, round shallow baskets made of wickerwork or of bamboo-matting, and called *dauris*, are used. Attached to the baskets are four strings, one of which is held in either hand by two labourers who stand opposite to each other on either side of the station [a small water reservoir] in little niches called *chaunrhá* or *paunrhás*. The basket is swung between the men, being carried above the water in the back stroke, and into it in the forward stroke. In finishing the latter, the labourers bring the basket up with a jerk, which throws the water that the basket carries with it on to the top of the lift (called *títhá* or *chaunrhá*). Fully two gallons of water are thrown up with one basket at each stroke, and from twenty to twenty-five strokes are made in the minute, according to the height to which the water has to be jerked. The height of the lifts varies from two to five feet, and the number of lifts is proportioned to the elevation above the stream or lake at which the fields to be irrigated lie.[37]

But that is only the start, because the water must now reach the plants:

There are two special methods of spreading tank or well water over dry fields. In one of these, known as *kiári*, the field is divided by little mounds, made with a kind of rake called *pharuhí*, into small rectangular plots (*kiárís*), and the water is allowed to flow of itself into these plots and fill them one after another. Poppy and all garden crops are watered in this way, and in the watering of sugarcane and indigo it is often adopted. The other method is by *háthá*. A convenient number of furrows or temporary water-ducts having been made across the field, a number of little round hollows or reservoirs are made at intervals along them. The water, having been turned into the ducts and reservoirs, is thrown from the latter over the parts of the field that are within reach by the distributor with a long wooden shovel or *háthá*. Less water is consumed in this method than in plot irrigation, and the distribution with the shovel is more equal than it would be, were the diminished quantity of water allowed to find its own way over the ground. . . . Barley, peas and other field crops, except rice, are irrigated with the shovel. In watering rice crops the tank water is simply bailed over the high mounds that surround the rice fields.[38]

These are long descriptions, but I include them deliberately. They demonstrate how much work something as simple as a good water supply can involve; and, equally, that each activity has its own techniques, equipment and specialized vocabulary. And this concerns just one of the multiple sub-operations involved in growing wheat or other crops. You don't need to have had an extensive education for this, but nor can it be called simple.

The subsequent processing, reaping and gleaning naturally appeal most to the imagination, because they encompass the reward for all that toil. A passage from one of the oldest poems in the world is appropriate here. Homer's *Iliad* (*c.* 750 BCE) reveals the apparent workings of a large grain farm:

> Another field rose high with waving grain;
> With bended sickles stand the reaper train:
> Here stretch'd in ranks the levell'd swarths are found,
> Sheaves heap'd on sheaves here thicken up the ground.
> With sweeping stroke the mowers strow the lands;
> The gatherers follow, and collect in bands;
> And last the children, in whose arms are borne
> (Too short to gripe them) the brown sheaves of corn.
> The rustic monarch of the field descries,
> With silent glee, the heaps around him rise.
> A ready banquet on the turf is laid,
> Beneath an ample oak's expanded shade.
> The victim ox the sturdy youth prepare;
> The reaper's due repast, the women's care.[39]

This verse mentions the sickle, but grains and grasses can also be cut with a scythe.[40] For other activities too, there are many different approaches and many different tools, depending on the crops, the soil, climatological circumstances and, of course, the time.[41] For example, threshing can be done by slashing with a flail, or with an animal-driven roller or board on a threshing floor.

The time horizon of the cattle breeder also covers a year, from the mating of the female animals to the moment when the young males, no longer of use, are ready for slaughter. At the same time, a cattle farmer must look ahead a number of years, or even beyond his own lifespan, on the one hand producing animals over several years that provide milk, wool or pulling power before subsequently being slaughtered – so after their peak reproduction years – on the other hand, fostering gainful characteristics over generations of breeding.[42] Daily care, of course, includes either feeding and watering or pasturing and possibly milking (including processing milk into butter and cheese). There is also periodic medical care and hygiene, including brushing and hoof care. In terms of breeding, mating is supervised once a year and, in areas with a temperate climate and therefore food shortages during the winter, the end of the year means, in principle, the slaughter of all male animals that are not necessary for breeding or otherwise (as a draught or riding animal).

There are perhaps bigger mutual differences in the work of livestock farmers than in the activities of arable farmers due to the generally lower mobility of the latter. The Russian anthropologist and historian Anatoly Mikhailovich Khazanov subdivides pastoral work into what he calls 'traditional societies'.[43] He assumes a general balance between agriculture and pastoralism within the food-producing economy of traditional societies, which, in turn, relates to the degree to which a community is sedentary. He thus distinguishes five types of pastoralism, depending on the importance of pastoralism for the community and, at the same time, according to the mobility involved. In terms of the type of work, it is directly related to how much the herdsmen must walk.

Firstly, there is sedentary animal husbandry in the form of household-stable animal husbandry. Depending on the climate, for one part of the year the livestock graze in pastures adjacent to the household's dwellings or the settlement and they usually return daily. For another part of the year they are kept in stables and enclosures and fed with stockpiled fodder.

Secondly, Khazanov distinguishes sedentary household husbandry, or stock breeding, with free grazing and without stables or stockpiled fodder. This form of animal husbandry is probably the oldest form of pastoralism and demands a lot of work from herdsmen.[44]

Thirdly, there are communities involved in herdsman husbandry or distant-pastures husbandry. This demands even more work from herdsmen. These communities fall into two interdependent sections. While the majority is engaged in sedentary agriculture, a minority of specialized herdsmen takes care of the livestock in pastures, sometimes quite far from the settlement. For part of the year, however, the animals are kept in enclosures, pens and stalls and fed with fodder. A special and well-known form is transhumance or 'yaylag' pastoralism. This enables people occupied with agriculture to use other areas, such as mountain pastures, as seasonal pastures when they are at their most productive. When the livestock return from the mountains they stay in lower zones near to the herders' villages.

Fourthly, semi-nomadic pastoralism may develop from the above-mentioned situation when agriculture (or hunting or fishing) is only secondary and supplementary, and pastoralism occupies most of the time of community members.

Finally, there is nomadism proper, whereby the whole community roams around and thus the term 'herder' acquires an entirely different social meaning, since it now means living close to the household or clan, who also roam with him. This specialism is the newest development and came into being later than the period covered by this chapter (the same might also be true for semi-nomadic pastoralism, see Chapter 3).

Returning to arable farming in general, the oldest farming communities remained highly vulnerable, especially to contagious diseases associated with farming. Agriculture also created a new sense of time, because people were no longer following their food – instead, the work now came to them, as it were, in seasonal peaks. And it went away again too. Put simply, farmers in the Northern Hemisphere worked ridiculously long days in the summer and had a lot of time off in the winter. This created an annual rhythm, dictated by the seasonal nature of staple foods. In medieval Europe, this meant that harvest holidays, followed by a series of festivals between Christmas and Mardi Gras and from Easter to Pentecost, occupied the low points in agricultural work. Midseason holidays like Midsummer, or, in England, Wakes week in August, corresponded with lulls in farm work or with annual fairs for hiring work folk.[45] These traditions are, of course, much older than Christianity.

Division of labour between men and women

The Neolithic Revolution was radical, but it took a very long time. In Mesopotamia, it took as long as 5,000 years before the overproduction was so large that the first cities could emerge; that is to say, before there were significant concentrations of people who did not grow their own food. During this long period between the first agriculture and the first cities, members of farming families, together with their neighbours, continued to hunt for a long time. Both modes of existence occurred in parallel and complemented each other. Nevertheless, specialization in work was gradually taking place, initially between men and women.

From the outset, there were differences between many activities of men and women, but, as we have seen, the differences for hunter-gatherers were still minimal. With the advent of agriculture, however, they became visibly bigger and the foundations were laid for the gender differences currently so central to societal debate.

One of the consequences of a better food supply, in particular the larger supply of grain, was the introduction of 'baby food' (for example, porridge), which meant that weaning could happen much earlier. After all, the availability of rich, soft carbohydrate weaning foods among agriculturalists resulted in shorter periods of lactation.[46] This led to another sharp reduction in the birth interval. Better-nourished mothers had more babies.[47] In hunter-gatherer communities, women can only take care of one child at a time, because they always have to carry the child with them during the search for food – despite the care of 'alloparents'. Only when the child can walk independently is there room for a younger brother or sister. In practice, this means that the interval between hunter-gatherer children is around four years. Among farmers, who live near their fields and orchards, the birth interval is reduced to, on average, two years.[48] Moreover, the menarche among women hunter-gatherers occurs later (about age sixteen) and their menarche–first-birth interval averages about three years. For present-day Euro-Americans, this interval is, on average, ten years and often exceeds twenty. Hunter-gatherers have a higher number of births, about six (as opposed to two now), and they nurse longer, typically about three years (as opposed to three months now), and more intensively. Finally, their menopause is usually earlier, in their mid-to-late forties (as opposed to early fifties now) – hence the lower risk factors related to women's cancers.[49] The Neolithic Revolution therefore meant an increase in women's work insofar as it concerns pregnancy, giving birth and raising children.

Infant mortality, however, remained enormous (up to 50 per cent). One reason for this is that early weaning replaces hygienic, easily digestible and nutritious mother's milk with 'an alternative that may be none of these'.[50] Early weaning, then, has both positive and negative consequences for mother and baby. Nevertheless, in net terms, more children remained alive and the population was still able to grow.[51] That said, life expectancy was short – indeed, half of ours. Variations in latitude and season aside, hunter-gatherers had a healthy diet with much less total fat, less saturated fat and less salt than, certainly, modern Americans. They took a lot of exercise and suffered far less from killer diseases and disorders like obesity, diabetes, hypertension, coronary heart disease and cancers, yet they still died early. This was the result of risks at work from dangerous and poisonous animals, but especially the inability to prevent or treat infectious diseases, specifically contamination from living in close quarters with domesticated animals. In contrast to the increase in reliable food production since the Neolithic Revolution,[52] there were many new risks, like an increased intake of salt and fat (from dairy foods, thanks to domesticated herds), alcohol and tobacco consumption and changing reproductive features.[53]

The necessarily greater stability of farmers, and certainly of arable farmers, meant they started investing in improvements to farmlands, building durable homes, and the possibility of stockpiling emerged. Many authors assume that this heralded the idea of ownership, including the idea that women represented a value and even that they could be owned by their husband. Consequently, sexual norms became stricter and virginity before marriage highly valued.[54] As we will see, there is evidence for this relation between the Neolithic Revolution and growing social inequality. We must exercise caution, however, as Africa demonstrates that there is no inescapable causal link between the two.

In most cases, while certainly not impossible, it is difficult to prove these theories about agriculture necessarily enhancing social inequality in this period. This shift has only been demonstrated convincingly for the so-called Yamnaya culture of predominantly male-oriented Indo-European pastoralists that spread over Europe and northern India 5,000 years ago (pp. 84–5, 89). In simple terms, this redirection, postulated for many parts of the world, from matrilinear to patrilinear lineage systems and from matrilocality to patrilocality means that, on her marriage, a woman went to live with her husband and therefore with her in-laws.[55] Alloparenting, which became even more important due to early weaning, was now de facto the task of the grandmother on the father's side.[56] More successful farmers (the 'aggrandizers', see pp. 69–72) expressed what they believed to be a bride's value by offering a bride price to her father, who was about to lose her labour.[57] In more extreme cases, this could even lead to polygyny. After all, if you can 'buy' one wife, why not buy more?[58]

Hrdy summarizes these processes succinctly as a 'great leap sideways'.[59] There are various reasons for this. Not only did more frequent pregnancies now place a much greater burden on a woman; a woman became more subordinate to the man within marriage, and the family of the man and therefore the mother-in-law increasingly determined the life of a married woman. Within the farm, this demanded more time than was previously the case with hunting and gathering, and it likely led to the development of more pronounced male and female tasks. Moreover, hunting became the exclusive domain of men, and greater demands were now made on child labour.

One of the consequences of this sideways leap pertains to the transfer of knowledge about crops. This proceeds differently in patrilinear and matrilinear societies, as has been demonstrated for many societies. Manioc cultivation in modern-day Gabon provides a good example – manioc being a staple food, originally brought by the Portuguese from Brazil. As is usually the case in Africa, the women are responsible for the food supply, and knowledge of food crops is passed from woman to woman, but in two different ways.[60] In the matrilinear communities south of the Ogooué River, a mother gives her daughter a few manioc cuttings when she moves to her groom's village. When the bride subsequently spots an interesting variety in a neighbour's garden she asks for a few cuttings to experiment with. Consequently, there is a much greater variety of species in the south than in the north. In Fang-speaking patrilinear societies to the north, a new bride arrives empty-handed and she receives her first manioc cuttings from her mother-in-law. She is thus initiated into her new clan, whose land she will work and to whom her children will belong. Here in the north, too, experiments are conducted with new cuttings from neighbours, but the choice is, of course, much smaller. As a result, the genetic diversity of this crop is also demonstrably lower there.

There are several reasons to assume that women in farming households now occupied a different position. But it is more difficult to ascertain what this meant in terms of concrete tasks. Were they, as valued 'property', watched more closely, and was their work restricted to the farm and its immediate environment? Collective hunting was, in any case, a thing of the past, and the significance of the band had also declined. Households became units in their own right. But, again, this was a very slow development, with many regional variations, and it must be located in the subsequent period rather than the earlier one. Farming communities do not necessarily consist of separate farms; they can now also live together in large houses. The anthropologist Claude Lévi-Strauss was fascinated by what he called 'house societies' and, indeed, many Neolithic 'great houses', which could accommodate an entire community, have been excavated.[61]

Of course, women were responsible for more than their pregnancies and their children on the farm. The earliest 'solid' evidence of this dates back to the beginning of grain growing in south-west Asia. Based on bone fragments, it has been observed that among the earliest rye growers in Syria, around 10000 BCE, women were responsible for milling grain. In this early phase, the still hard seeds required intensive rubbing or grinding to make flour and, in turn, porridge, which is easier to consume and possibly also to facilitate the weaning of babies. The women in particular show traces of this heavy work in the bones of their back, toes and knees. On this basis, we can assume 'a clear gender division of labour by the Neolithic . . . at least, while women processed food and attended their ever-increasing broods of children. For women, the Neolithic revolution meant a steady increase in labour, in both the work and the child-bearing senses'.[62]

That farming was primarily women's work is substantiated by similar research in North America. The starting point is the observation that highly mobile humans develop a long ridge down the length of the femur.[63] Conversely, this ridge disappears once we become sedentary under the influence of the agricultural revolution. Interestingly, this process does not always occur simultaneously among men and among women. And that is precisely the case among the people of the Cochise culture in what is now south-eastern Arizona. They switched to farming 3,500 years ago, but apparently farming was typically women's work, because only the men kept their pronounced ridges. This suggests that these men continued to hunt, perhaps for a thousand years or more. By the time the Spanish arrived, it was still the American Indian women doing the farming work (with the exception of the Pueblos). This implies a long – 3,000 years – sustained division of labour in that part of America between men who hunted and women who farmed.

In all cases, farm work meant an increased effort from every member of the household.[64] Time-budget studies show that peasant farmers and herders may have spent more, rather than fewer, hours per day at work than hunter-gatherers did. This is one of the reasons why, despite living alongside farmers, not all hunter-gatherers simply switched to farming. Finally, more work also meant a greater call on children, once they were old enough to help.

Division of labour between households and the seeds of inequality

It is important to emphasize that throughout the period covered by this chapter, we are, in principle, only talking about rural areas, because there were no really large agglomerations anywhere in the world. Jericho had 500 inhabitants in 9600 BCE and may have reached 70 houses with a thousand residents a few centuries later. Three thousand years later, 'Ain Gazal had three to four times as many inhabitants for a while. In sum, the cities in the Fertile Crescent at this time had a few hundred residents rather than a thousand or more. The oldest Chinese cities, which emerged much later, were certainly no bigger. In short, the largest agglomerations in the world at that time (including Jericho) were places that today we would call villages.[65]

If the Neolithic Revolution had such an impact on the division of labour between men and women, what impact did it have on social relationships beyond the household?[66] Bands – that is, units in which members of different households worked collectively at chasing their food – were being eroded, but what were they replaced with? While agricultural working units were certainly smaller than bands of hunter-gatherers, we may surmise that these peasant households did not operate totally autonomously. Two social developments with major implications for the history of work deserve our attention here: labour specialization between households and social relations between households that influence the rewards for labour.

Division of labour between households

Where farmers were so successful that they produced more food than they needed themselves, and where their numbers grew so much that concentrations of population became possible, certain people within their community could, in principle, be freed up for other work. That means specialization in the sense that 'fewer people make a class of objects than use it'.[67] In this early period, we are talking about pottery making, housebuilding and associated technology and textile skills. As we have seen for before the Neolithic Revolution, all of these techniques are found in various locations around the world but were not yet widely disseminated. The oldest fibres found date to 36,000 years ago, the oldest pots to 22,000 years ago and house floor plans or traces of housing are even older. Of course, there are also the stones and wooden implements (large-scale metalworking dates from a little later).[68] The question here, however, is whether these specialisms were already so developed that they were people's sole occupation or whether they were ancillary activities of farmers or possibly hunter-gatherers. In other words, were farmers and hunter-gatherers the only specialists (with typically male or female tasks) at this time, or were there already more?

In general, archaeological data suggests that, apart from potters and weavers, there were no other clear professional specializations in the first millennia of the Neolithic Revolution, although by the end of it some exceptions to this rule have been found in China. The reason for this general rule is simple: there was not enough demand for it. This is partly due to low agricultural productivity and partly to do with the climate zones in which agriculture developed. As will be elaborated in the next chapter, it was only from the seventh millennium that agriculture spread slowly from West Asia and Thessaly in a northerly direction to heavily forested regions, such as Europe. The necessary grubbing of forests led to such a demand for stone axes that specialized mining and production centres developed in the following millennia.[69] There were certainly also forests in the Fertile Crescent, but the areas where the earliest farming developed were nevertheless described as park and steppe landscapes.[70]

The Israeli archaeologist Gideon Shelach-Lavi notes that, remarkably, the construction of houses and settlements among the oldest farming populations in north-east China appear to have been carefully preplanned: 'houses and domestic structures are coordinated with each other; there also seems to be a clear separation between private and public spaces, production sites, ritual areas (including cemeteries), and so on'.[71] It seems to me, however, that this is not the earliest indication of a project developer and of contracting companies with carpenters, but rather a joint venture of farmers living collectively. Towards the end of our period, there is evidence of complex wooden structures of pile dwellings with mortise and tenon joints in the lower Yangtze River region. Perhaps we can rightly call their creator a carpenter.[72]

The long history of pottery making among hunter-gatherers in China led a little later to what we might call the first real potters. This is evident from the appearance of more sophisticated pottery, such as legged vessels, but especially of coloured decorations in the fifth millennium BCE. These were achieved by oxidizing iron minerals, requiring a high degree of control over the atmosphere inside the kiln. The subsequent standardization of pottery also points to the functioning of professional potters.[73] A product of another branch of the ceramic industry, the oldest bricks – not yet baked but unmoulded, unbaked mud bricks – had already been used for the first time a few millennia earlier in Baluchistan; nevertheless, the nature of the simple technique must be seen as an ancillary activity of the resident grain farmers.[74]

The further development of spinning, carding, twining, knitting, mending, weaving and other textile techniques was, above all, a domestic affair in which households primarily provided for themselves. Originally, clothing would have consisted of processed animal skins, as depicted in Palaeolithic rock drawings. In addition, the technique of braiding flax and hemp stems (then still wild plants) developed, as well as that for making rope, used for, among other things, fishing nets.[75] Neither technique yielded any fabrics, but they were steps in the right direction, whereby spinning and weaving developed separately and in combination with each other.

With the Neolithic and the emergence of regular agriculture, wool became much more available, and more regularly, than the felted wool collected from hunting and foraged from nature after moulting. In addition, industrial crops such as flax and hemp were grown. The decisive steps to spinning and weaving were probably first taken in the Near East. It has been documented for the Jordan Valley, with the oldest cotton fabric recorded, while the earliest woollen fibres are found in Central Anatolia, spinning stones in Kurdistan, linen yarns in Egypt and raffia weaving and bark cloth in Africa. All these finds and their dating continue to be modified almost daily due to new excavations, but apparently the Fertile Crescent was at the forefront of more than just agriculture. The next big leap was the invention of the hand spinning wheel in India in the first centuries of our era. In sum, such a low degree of specialization meant there was little room for large-scale exchange between households of farmers and specialized craftsmen. The trade flows during this period were still very thin and mainly concerned valuables such as semi-precious stones.

Still, there remains a possibility of professional specialization among farmers (and within this group possibly for arable farmers and livestock farmers) and hunters, who exchanged products with each other.[76] This may have happened in the broader context of other exchanges, such as that of marriage partners. Modern palaeogenetic research offers ever more examples of this, but such a scenario has also been reconstructed based on other data, such as from linguistics.[77] In Kenya, for example, in the first millennium CE, arable Luyia women went as wives to pastoral (proto-) Kalenjin. Christopher Ehret, an American scholar of early African history, deduces this from the fact that 'in contrast to the wide range of Kalenjin loanwords in Luyia, the Luyia words adopted into the proto-Kalenjin language, with one exception, relate to the activity that is and was anciently women's work in the Luyia societies. This set of loanwords consists principally of cultivation and cooking terms'.[78]

The exchange between farmers and hunters was not always easy to achieve, one of the reasons being that hunter-gatherers were often very wary.

Where they fear the disadvantages of trade for their egalitarian existence, such as the last representatives of this way of life in South America, there is the alternative of the widely reported practice of 'silent trade', in which hostile parties exchange products without meeting face to face. For example, the elusive Mlabri of northern Thailand at the beginning of the twentieth century left beeswax and honey on paths and received cloth, metal and salt in return. Some direct trade with neighbouring Hmong started only in the 1930s.[79]

The most extreme option is no trade at all. Amazonian foraging groups, like the Huaorani in eastern Ecuador, put more value on transferability than on use value in a deliberate attempt to distinguish themselves from settled horticultural neighbours and to refuse trade. The Huaorani and similar peoples refuse not only trade but also generosity, which is donor-initiated, hence potentially coercive: 'Sharing transactions, with their emphasis on entitlement (the donor's obligation to share, and the recipient's right to receive), form the basis of personal autonomy and egalitarianism.' This case provides a warning to interpretations that explain hunter-gatherers' societies exclusively in terms of want, thus robbing them of agency and history.[80]

Social relations between households: The seeds of inequality

The nature of hunter-gatherer societies is the starting point for the development of social relations. This is generally characterized as 'egalitarian', as we have seen in the previous chapter. There is a view that the term egalitarianism is used too widely: that it is 'best applied to simple hunter/gatherers or immediate-return societies, where there is no significant private ownership, no economically based competition, few wealth differences, and usually few prestige items'. The term 'transegalitarian' is used to describe the transitional form of more unequal societies, in the sense that: 'Where significant ownership of resources, economically based competition, and wealth differences occur but are not institutionalized as class distinctions, we refer to such societies as "transegalitarian" societies.' Even more unequal societies have been called 'chiefdom organizations'.[81] For the time being, however, we should not regard the concept of *ownership* as the ownership of the means of production (land, cattle), but as control over harvest surpluses. Signs of unevenly distributed property only come later.[82] The question now, then, is how to characterize the gradual transition between hunting-gathering and agriculture along these lines.

Let us again start from the important observation that the Neolithic Revolution created possibilities for saving food, much more than was the case among most hunter-gatherers. That also meant the possibility of enriching individuals and households to which they belonged and, consequently, of social differences. Not unimportant in this context is the fact that the strong numerical expansion of the now sedentary cohabiting group of housemates was made possible by the sharp increase in the labour productivity of agriculture. Hunter-gatherers lived together in groups of a few dozen people, in which household, extended family and band more or less coincide, but agricultural settlements in the Neolithic were already reaching hundreds to thousands of people.[83]

Higher production created opportunities not only for population growth, but, under specific circumstances, also for enrichment – in particular for the most successful and skilled farming households – as well as the desire and even necessity for it. After all, farming humans are, in a way, more vulnerable than food gatherers, as we have seen already. If the harvest fails or a herd is ravaged by an infectious disease then there is a danger of famine, not to mention the farming human's own greatly increased susceptibility to diseases.

The increased food production due to the Neolithic Revolution came at a price, however, not just economically but also in social terms. Saving for a rainy day became second nature to us, and if that means that someone else has to work harder for it, so be it. Perhaps this is the real beginning of human competition (often summarized simply as 'survival of the fittest'). Or it is the start of what De Waal calls the 'comeback': 'Social hierarchies may have been out of fashion when our ancestors lived in small-scale societies, but they surely made a comeback with agricultural settlement and the acculturation of wealth. But the tendency to subvert these vertical arrangements never left us. We're born revolutionaries.'[84]

Robert Kelly summarizes the differences between hunter-gatherers and farmers as follows:

Evolutionary ecology predicts that territoriality will result when resources are sufficiently dense and predictable to make the costs of defense worthwhile, and when population is high enough that, for someone outside looking in, the cost of trying to acquire a denied resource is worth the potential benefit. But the land that foragers need to survive is often so large, and population density so low, that physical defense of a perimeter is impossible, yet the cost of allowing unregulated visitors in can be too high.[85]

With the Neolithic Revolution and – despite all the risks of crop failures, livestock diseases, and so on – the greater chances of food surpluses, social inequality became feasible. The way in which that happened, however, reveals infinite variations, as a comparison of different criteria in early agricultural societies in diverse parts of the world makes clear.[86]

Tropical Africa offers the most impressive case; in particular, the expansion of Bantu-speaking agriculturalists over Central, Eastern and Southern Africa between 3500 BCE and 500 CE, but without the emergence of inequality. Throughout these millennia, these societies maintained a matrilineal (sometimes also matrilocal) and politically decentralized way of life, inclined to redistribution of resources, rather than to individual accumulation. Shifts to patrilineal and patriclan societies with greater inequality occurred rapidly in sub-Saharan Africa, albeit unevenly, from the late first millennium CE. This contribution of Africa to world history dismisses the still popular idea that humans took a wrong turn when we gave up hunting-gathering. Agriculture and egalitarianism are compatible.[87]

Where inequality developed, for example in the Fertile Crescent, it did so very slowly. Among the Natufians in the Levant (12500–9700/9500 BCE), a more favourable climate led to prosperity, characterized by the burial of the dead decorated with marine shells and bone and animal teeth pendants indicating differences in status, as well as through labour-intensive works such as the building of larger houses and the manufacture of mortars in addition to the older grinding slabs. These could have played a role in public feasting, but the evidence for large-scale food storage is currently lacking.

After a colder period came the millennium of the domestication of plants and animals (9600 until 8500 BCE). Settlements could encompass hundreds of people, ten times more than Natufian hamlets, helped by the fact that cereals are among the most suitable weaning foods. Food storage can now be demonstrated, as well as the exchange of exotic materials, but not yet the relationship with social hierarchy. Although there are clear signs of sharply declining mobility and possibly the emergence of permanent ownership, we must not forget that these villages had a lifespan of only a few hundred years.

Specific indications of inequality only become convincing in the last two millennia of the early Neolithic period (up to 6300 BCE). This is demonstrated in excavations from ceremonial centres such as in Göbekli Tepe in Turkey. An organized labour force was involved in the construction of this 'shrine'. The burials (accompanied by, among other things, exotic materials) reveal extreme status differences, and also distinguish poor and rich houses, the latter in the vicinity of cult places. Plastered skulls of adults and children belonging to a clear sub-group might point to a social elite. Despite all this, Price and Bar-Yosef remain cautious: 'In spite of the variety of evidence of the Near East, a fully convincing argument for social inequality in the Neolithic remains is hard to convey. One of the major difficulties in identifying emergent social differentiation likely lies in the simple fact that it is emergent and difficult to recognize.'[88] Strong evidence from sub-Saharan Africa, as we have seen, underscores their warning.

Feelings about what is socially just, and therefore also about what is a fair reward for work, are deeply anchored and therefore do not change effortlessly. So, we must seriously ask ourselves how people from more egalitarian societies, as described in the previous chapter, could resign themselves to strongly increased inequality; or, in the words of the American anthropologist and archaeologist Mark Aldenderfer: 'So, just how do some individuals get others to relinquish the fruits of their labour?'[89] According to him, we cannot ignore religion.

Of course, we can argue that 'aggrandizers', the men who managed to gain more of the wealth surplus, created social obligations of debt – frequently by offering feasts – which the many others unable to repay in kind had to provide in labour, but: 'How is it that individuals and groups come to accept that their debt is a "natural" condition?' In this case, religion can be seen as a powerful 'enabler' for cultural change, both for the aggrandizers who try to achieve this and for those threatened by change. If we assume that, in this period of thousands of years, social differentiation was repeatedly given a chance in Eurasia (but not in Africa), albeit without achieving a breakthrough, how, then, did it become acceptable? How could people accept that the work of one person was rewarded less than that of another, that one might even be able to force the other to do certain work? This requires a new system of norms and values, deviating from the egalitarian principles that had prevailed thus far.

Given that it is difficult to answer this question on the basis of archaeological remains from the time of the Neolithic Revolution, Aldenderfer has resorted to ethnographic material that describes comparable processes during the last centuries in the Americas and on New Guinea, borrowing the example of the Enga peoples in highland New Guinea and the religious changes that aggrandizers in the east of that region effected with the spread of the sweet potato and of pig farming. The extant Kepele cult, originally a simple boy's initiation ceremony, was expanded with a mythical, but direct, representation of wealth. In Aldenderfer's words:

> Importantly, much of this wealth was reinvested, in a sense, through the sponsoring of feasts, dances, and other performances. While the cult may not have extended hierarchy in the sense of big men to take on new social roles, it served as a justification for their continued violation of the egalitarian ethos. Ultimately, this allowed them to extend their efforts to participate in regional trade networks and to finance other major ceremonial events related to warfare and war reparations, among other things.[90]

But it wasn't only big men who attempted to move religion in a direction that was more in line with the new social relationships. Others with the same means could try the opposite. The Ain cult that emerged in the same area overtly challenged new big man-sponsored cult practices. For example, 'one of the cult prophets exhorted its followers to "continue killing pigs for the sun and eating meat until all are consumed; the sky people will replace them". Instead of alliances, hard work, and exploitation, wealth would be created simply by belief.'[91]

※

In this chapter, we have seen the first big change in the history of work. By gradually switching from hunting and food gathering to farming and animal husbandry, not only did food, health and population size change, but humans also became sedentary, the division of labour between men and women became sharper and the first cautious professional specialization occurred, as well as, in some parts of Eurasia, the seeds for social inequality. These may already have been sown within farming households due to the increasing division of tasks between men and women but were also evident between households in several places. This happened towards the end of this period as a result of unfair remuneration for work performed by the many for the

73

THE STORY OF WORK

few. Whereas before the advent of agriculture and animal husbandry remuneration was directly connected to the efforts made, from now on efforts and reward could diverge (although it took quite some time). So-called aggrandizers tried to take a large share of the surpluses that now existed, although they had to try to cover up this violation of one of the most fundamental social norms with generosity. In the words of the sixteenth-century judge and founder of modern political philosophy in France, Étienne de la Boétie:[92] 'theatres, games, plays, spectacles, marvellous beasts, medals, tableaux, and other such drugs were for the people of antiquity the allurements of serfdom, the price of their freedom, the tools of tyranny'.

Nevertheless, it seems fair to say that for thousands of years after the introduction of agriculture social equality persisted, certainly in Africa. Two other themes that we have developed for hunter-gatherers, based on, in particular, anthropological analogies, are less clearly documented for this period: in addition to the sorrows, the pleasures that accompany agricultural work as such, and the prevalence of working in the fields and with tamed animals. However, I am inclined to think that the numerous innovations not only in agriculture but also in the earliest crafts make this more than likely.

Does the story end now that we have become acquainted with the work of both hunter-gatherers and farmers, and of the few specialists outside agriculture (the carpenter, the potter and perhaps the priest)? According to the British archaeologist Steven Mithen: 'by 5000 BCE there was very little left for later history to do; all the groundwork for the modern world had been completed. History had simply to unfold until it reached the present day'.[93] The groundwork perhaps, but it is precisely in that unfolding that we find the fascinating history of work, as De la Boétie suggests and as Karl Marx (*Critique of Hegel's Philosophy of Right*), Antonio Gramsci or Aldous Huxley (*Brave New World*) have not neglected to convey over and over again. Humanity appears to be able to organize the work at hand in infinite variations.

3

EMERGING LABOUR RELATIONS, 5000–500 BCE

As shown in the previous chapter, the agricultural revolution created the basic conditions for potential overproduction of food and thus for comprehensive division of labour and, sometimes, for unequal labour relations. In reality, in comparison to hunter-gatherers, little had changed other than that work units had become smaller and gendered divisions of tasks more pronounced. Opportunities for structural societal change remained limited before further improvements in agricultural productivity disrupted this status quo.

Until now, the world had been one large natural landscape in which hunter-gatherers tried to sustain a living. Settlements arose – first in the Fertile Crescent and northern China and, tentatively, in north India and Central and South America – 'islands' where farmers attempted to conquer nature. At best, these farming settlements may be called villages. There were no towns to be seen at this stage, and any division of labour was rudimentary.

Prisoners escorted by a soldier on a victory stele of Sargon of Akkad. The hairstyle of the prisoners is characteristic of Sumerians.

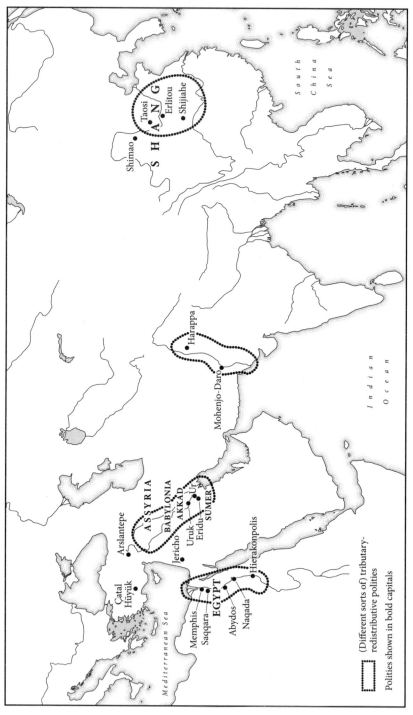

Map 3. Oldest cities (population centres) and polities.

Agriculture – increasingly diversified and increasingly intensive – extended over most of the inhabited earth's surface. Incidentally, there was more than just farming going on in this infinite countryside; mining emerged, and with it the processing of valuable rocks and metals.

But it was not until the rise of cities and, subsequently, of states that we see an explosion of labour specializations. This happened between 5000 and 500 BCE, first in the Fertile Crescent and Egypt, and later in the Indus, Yellow River and Yangtze valleys.

Various types of labour division became steadily more important. Firstly, a more pronounced division of labour emerged between men and women, related to an increased dependence on animal farming. Archaeological evidence suggests for the first time in human history a clear task division between male herders and female processors of animal products.[1] Secondly, there was a division of labour between the – relatively dwindling – groups of hunter-gatherers (of which fishers formed probably the most important sub-group) and farmers. In addition, there was a division within agriculture between arable farmers and livestock farmers. Finally, there was a division between urban and rural dwellers. In this way, 'complex societies'[2] emerged, comprising primarily arable farmers with livestock and, alternatively, livestock farmers, initially still without cities. In some places, large population concentrations did then emerge that merit the 'city' moniker. This happened first in Mesopotamia about 5,000 years before our era, and later in China and India. (In Egypt, as we will see, cities were much less important.) Trade between the city and the countryside meant that the artisan could obtain food and the farmer his tools. In addition, we see the rise of powerful livestock-breeder cultures that also specialized in the metal industry. Finally, even the minority of hunter-gatherers were incorporated into this pattern and, in general, they were no longer autarchic.[3] Whether voluntarily or involuntarily, the emergence of cities in parts of Eurasia and, from 3000 BCE, states, expanded this trend.

Even more radical than the implications for work specialization were those for labour relations, which changed profoundly in the three millennia between around 5000 and 2000 BCE. Firstly, let us take the hunters and food gatherers with their egalitarian practices and rules of reciprocity. They still inhabited most of the earth's surface, but their share of the global population was already in sharp decline. Then, there were the arable farmers. In the previous chapter, we saw how most of them maintained their reciprocal principles, but also how the 'aggrandizers' mechanism gave rise to the first

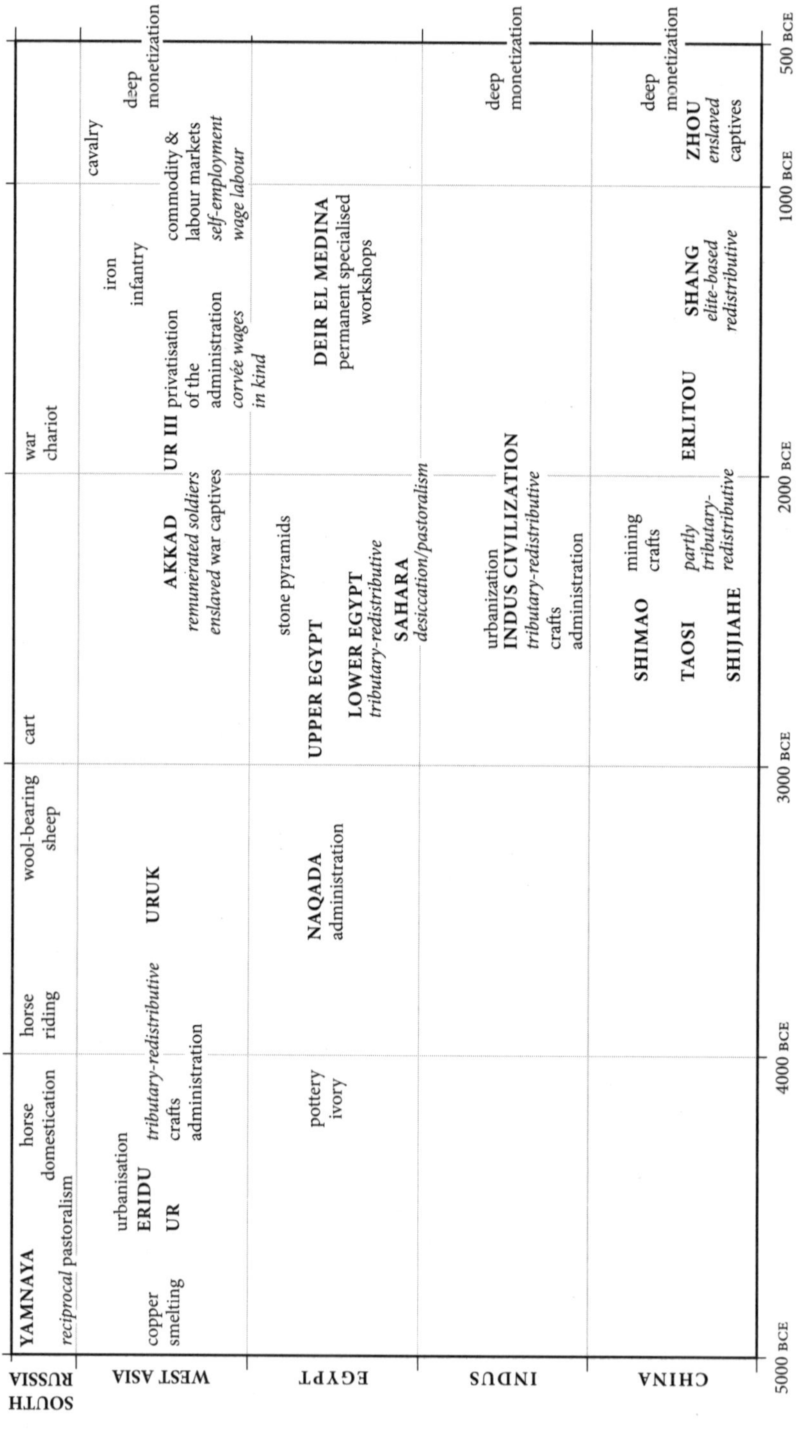

Technology/development markers (across the timeline, top band):
copper smelting · horse domestication · horse riding · wool-bearing sheep · cart · war chariot · iron · infantry · cavalry · deep monetization

SOUTH RUSSIA
YAMNAYA
reciprocal pastoralism

WEST ASIA
urbanisation
ERIDU — *tributary-redistributive* crafts administration
UR
URUK administration
AKKAD — *remunerated* soldiers *enslaved* war captives
UR III privatisation of the administration *corvée* wages *in kind*
commodity & labour markets *self-employment* *wage labour*
deep monetization

EGYPT
pottery ivory
NAQADA administration
stone pyramids
UPPER EGYPT
LOWER EGYPT *tributary-redistributive*
SAHARA *desiccation/pastoralism*
DEIR EL MEDINA permanent specialised workshops

INDUS
urbanization
INDUS CIVILIZATION *tributary-redistributive* crafts administration

CHINA
SHIMAO mining crafts
TAOSI *partly tributary-redistributive*
SHIJIAHE *tributary-redistributive*
ERLITOU
SHANG *elite-based redistributive*
ZHOU *enslaved* captives
deep monetization

Timeline (left to right): 5000 BCE · 4000 BCE · 3000 BCE · 2000 BCE · 1000 BCE · 500 BCE

Figure 3. The evolution of different labour relations 5000–500 BCE.

social disparities in what, until then, had fundamentally been reciprocal relationships. In Eurasia, some households managed to claim a larger share of the surpluses than others, with differences in wealth as a consequence. The crux was not so much in the unequal division of means of production as it was in the proceeds of work.

There are no good indications to suggest that private ownership was in vogue prior to 5000 BCE. That phenomenon also and especially occurred in, for example, livestock-breeding societies in the Eurasian Steppe, where disparities in wealth are evident from the graves of prosperous people. Here, the art of taming horses, horse-riding and, finally, the chariot were invented, and metalworking had a degree of sophistication. The increasingly inequitable labour relations in the 'countryside' and, in particular, the skewed growth of reciprocity in pastoral societies are dealt with in this chapter (pp. 80–90).

New labour relations primarily developed in the large population concentrations in the cities. Redistribution (let's call it reciprocity in disguise, and on a much larger scale) – that is, the division of labour and remuneration via centrally managed redistribution – was an innovation of Mesopotamian cities and, although less pronounced or less clear, of the first cities elsewhere in the world (pp. 91–5). It should be noted that the emphasis was sometimes much more on the tributary than on the redistributive side.

Finally, from around 3000 BCE, the first polities that warrant the name 'state' were created (pp. 96–112). In the first instance, they remained wedded to tributary-redistributive principles; indeed, in Egypt that continued to be the case for thousands of years. Other options were added, however. Firstly, these new polities grew to such a size that, during their mutual wars, male prisoners of war were no longer killed en masse; rather, they (and probably their wives and children) were made slaves – in principle belonging to and thus working for the polity. These states, embroiled in their defensive and offensive wars, also began to exempt and maintain subjects, in particular soldiers, for specific tasks. It is likely that the first wage labour was created in this way – albeit without a labour market. Parallel to this, we now see the first evidence of the private ownership of the means of production, specifically of land and cattle, but in the cities, too, of artisanal tools. This is how self-employed households that traded their products on the market came into being. And it was this that first made wage labour in the service of the self-employed possible on a larger scale – that is to say, the phenomenon of people without the means of production (especially land) working for someone who does, but for a reward: wage labour through the market. The question then is, how was the nature and level of this reward determined?

The labour relations in these old Eurasian states, represented here schematically but, in practice, in numerous hybrid versions, united elements of all the labour relations that we know today. Egalitarian relations according to the redistribution model now coexisted with slavery, wage labour, employment (of slaves and of freedmen) and self-employment.[4] Moreover, this mix could vary greatly per state. There was much less variation in tributary-redistributive Egypt, for example, than there was in Mesopotamia. The consequences for gender differences also varied considerably according to place and time. From the first urbanized and state societies, these combinations of labour relations spread throughout virtually the entire Old World. The differentiation of labour relations in sub-Saharan Africa and the New World took place significantly later and are dealt with in Chapters 2 (pp. 71–2) and 4 (pp. 160–72).

From this moment, human history can be understood as a competition between diverse constellations of labour relations, each with their own mix of cooperation and oppression. This determines the division of human history of the last 7,000 years into 4 sub-periods, of which that from around 5000 to 500 BCE is discussed in this third chapter.

Working in 'complex' agrarian societies: Increased inequality

Agriculturalists

Like the first roughly 5,000 years of the Neolithic Revolution (discussed in the previous chapter), initially, the development of arable farming was very slow; it was more extensive than intensive and also mixed with foraging for a long time. In these first millennia, the emphasis was mainly on what is called 'primary farming' – growing crops and raising livestock exclusively for food. From this, 'secondary products' now emerged, such as flax, milk and dairy products, as well as wool.[5]

Between 9000 and 3000 BCE, agricultural technology spread from the rainy areas in the Fertile Crescent (irrigation came much later) in an easterly, north-westerly, and southerly direction. Wheat, barley, sheep and cattle were found as far as north-west India and Europe and, after 5000 BCE, sheep, cattle and goats appeared in North and East Africa – but no further, because, ultimately, this 'Fertile Crescent food production complex' encountered monsoon climates in the south and Arctic climates in the north that were hostile to key winter crops like wheat and barley.[6]

Interesting for the development of professional specialization is the use of boats for transferring crops and livestock (pigs, cattle, sheep, goats), but also dogs and cats (for catching mice in granaries) to Cyprus as early as 8400 BCE.[7] Transport by ship also explains the spread of agricultural technology along the Italian and Spanish coasts.[8] Spectacular next steps included the colonization of the South Pacific, probably by farmers from Taiwan (from the Dapenkeng culture) between 3000 and 1000 BCE. They went first to the (already long-inhabited) Philippines and Indonesia, and from there they headed in both a south-westerly and south-easterly direction. Along with their cattle, they travelled first from the Philippines to Borneo, then to East Africa, eventually reaching uninhabited Madagascar at the start of our current era.[9] Another group departed via Indonesia and New Guinea, where the Lapita culture developed from 1300 BCE, for the Bismarck Archipelago and the Solomon Islands. But they did not stop at these previously uninhabited islands of Near Oceania, the one visible from the next. Indeed, manoeuvres to the still uninhabited Remote Oceania happened in several migration waves. A great leap of 800 kilometres, from Vanuatu to Fiji, took place between 1050 and 950 BCE; a century later, it was the turn of Samoa and Tonga. A discovery interval of some two thousand years then ensued, during which the simpler sailing canoe with outrigger was perfected and turned into the large ocean-going double-hulled sailing canoe. This eventually led to the colonization of New Zealand, Hawaii and Easter Island around 1200 CE. Long before, in the first half of the third millennium BCE, there was already an intensive merchant shipping trade (particularly of cedarwood from Lebanon) between Byblos and Egypt.[10] Thus, we can add the seafarer to our still concise list of early professions that includes hunter-gatherer-fisher, arable farmer and livestock breeder (and all combinations thereof).

As we have seen, farmers from the second key Neolithic centre, China's Yellow and Yangtze basins, who were familiar with cultivating short-grained rice and common millet, but also foxtail, soybean, chicken, cattle and the silk-worm, spread in a westerly, southerly and easterly direction – a process that, incidentally, took thousands of years. Comparable early distribution patterns are known for other areas where agriculture developed independently, albeit over shorter distances and with less spectacular consequences.[11]

Agriculture therefore spread beyond the first centres over greater areas, but the surpluses were still relatively small and, crucially, they were fickle. Meanwhile, social relations between workers remained fairly stable. Differences between farmers were still small, and the limited number of elite families with modest prosperity tried to bridge the differences that existed by holding festive meals and gift giving.

We can distinguish two opposing tendencies in these early agrarian communities.[12] On the one hand, emigration to new areas can be explained by the movement of younger offspring or farmers who missed out on inheriting significant entitlements to land, and of people in impoverished circumstances – possibly a reaction to apparent previous social oppression. On the other hand, archaeologists have noted, with some surprise, that it is precisely in newly claimed land, for example in Central Anatolia in 7400–6000 BCE, that so few status differences were visible.

But what exactly did these 'entitlements' entail? Almost certainly not property rights in our sense of the word; there are no indications of this (see also below for the Indus civilization). Rather, I tend to think in terms of claimed rights on parts of the communal harvest, or the right to determine ways of working at one's own discretion. In addition, it is conceivable that younger brothers no longer danced to the tune of older ones. But there are more signs of persistent egalitarian tendencies among early farmers at this time, such as communal grain storage.[13] Many farming communities also maintained the worship of female goddesses. If we can infer the relatively high status of women from this (which is far from certain), that could also indicate that men's and women's work were not yet valued so differently.

This probably very gradual transition, over thousands of years, from egalitarian to transegalitarian agrarian societies, via the phenomenon of 'aggrandizers' and subsequently into chiefdoms, is marked by innovations that point to greater prosperity. The earliest example is probably the quest for precious stones and, specifically, the further specialization of the (polished) stone tool maker. This was now probably more than just ancillary work.[14] A second example is the finding and processing of pure copper by Balkan farmers.

For a long time, the application of copper was aesthetic rather than economic. In comparison with other, already known materials, it was colourful, shiny, hard and durable and thus ideal as a sign of distinction.[15] Hammering out pieces had long been the only process for making jewellery, first known from Anatolia around 8000 BCE. Smelting from rock containing copper sulphide and copper oxide was invented 3,000 years later in both Iran and Serbia. This required a temperature of more than 1080 degrees Celsius, which can only be achieved with charcoal instead of wood as fuel and with the help of bellows. The ends of the bellows had to be made from ceramic material (clay tubes or *tuyeres* for bellow attachments), as did the crucible used to collect the molten metal.

The same principle was soon applied to silver and gold (copper has a smelting temperature of 1083, gold of 1064, and silver of 962 degrees Celsius). But not to iron. It took another 3,000 years or more before iron was commonly used among the elites of the Hittite Empire (1400–1200 BCE). The secret was not so much in the smelting temperature: the smelting of iron does not require higher temperatures than those needed to smelt copper, but very low partial pressures of oxygen are required to reduce iron from its oxide.[16] A little later than the sailor – and perhaps the shipwright – the (copper) smith now adds weight to our collection of professions, albeit with a much more prominent place in society. Indeed, various farming cultures put the smith on a pedestal. For example, smiths were sometimes buried together with their tools, castes of smiths were created (that is to say, they married within their profession) and not only material but also symbolic value was attached to their craft. The smith occupied a prominent place in the worlds of the gods; think of Hephaistos for the Greeks and Vulcanus for the Romans. African ethnographic literature is full of stories about smiths, and the art of smelting iron was associated with gestation and birth:

> The furnace was a woman, the iron bloom growing in the furnace was the fetus, and its male attendants were simultaneously husbands and midwives. In some instances, this equivalence was explicit, with furnaces modelled as women's bodies or bellows as male genitalia. More commonly, it was implied by the behaviour of the iron workers, who were often prohibited from sexual intercourse for the duration of the smelt and were frequently isolated in smelting camps to ensure compliance.[17]

The gradual differentiation of agrarian societies as a result of distinctions in entitlements, resulting in jealousies, and the availability of weapons, generally used to kill animals, may well have been the catalyst for the spread of violence on a scale that today we would call war. Shortly before the advent of agriculture, there were already petroglyphs of violent scenes made, such as of men shooting each other with bows and arrows, leaving dead and wounded.[18] How to interpret this in terms of social inequality, the division of labour and differentiation in labour relations at this time is far from clear. We must wait until around 3000 BCE to get some solid ground under our feet in this regard. This is when we see systematic inequality between workers gain momentum with the development of a specific version of livestock breeding, pastoral nomadism. What kind of work did that entail?

Specialized pastoralists

Livestock has a longer lifespan than most crops (with the exception of most trees) and is easier to transport and distribute, which is why livestock breeding contributes to the development of social inequality more than arable farming, certainly in the form of pastoral nomadism with large herds. This first developed in the south Russian steppes, in the so-called Yamnaya culture. In the region of the Dnieper and the Volga rivers, after 5000 BCE, hunter-gatherers succeeded in taming horses, there the most desirable source of meat in the winter – thousands of years after their southern neighbours managed the same with goats, sheep, cattle and pigs.

The great advantage of horses in these cold regions is that they are able to clear snow from the grass with the help of their large hooves. In this way, they can survive in the harshest of circumstances where other domesticated animals would have long since died.[19] In addition to meat and milk, horses and other livestock (which they did have to care for in winter), these people also lived from abundant stocks of fish that were easy to catch, especially in the Dnieper Rapids, as well as from wild plants, in particular goosefoot (*chenopodium*). They therefore had a rich and varied diet, even before they started growing grain on a small scale.[20] They were not only reasonably self-sufficient, but, after a time, they also had export products for trade with the south: first horses, other livestock and cattle products, and later also metals.

Once tamed, some 500 to 1,000 years later, horses were also fitted with a bit so that they could be ridden. Mounted shepherds could greatly increase their productivity. 'A person on foot can herd about two hundred sheep with a good herding dog. On horseback, with the same dog, that single person can herd about five hundred', said David W. Anthony, whose life's work is dedicated to the history of these nomads.[21] The use of four-wheeled carts around 3000 BCE (originally developed from sledges and sleds, probably in Anatolia), on which they could load and keep all possessions, made them even more mobile and their method of transhumance livestock breeding even more successful. This meant that they could keep large herds not only of horses but also of sheep and, especially, cattle. That was a crucial step, because the advantage of cows is that they provide twice as much milk as mares and five times as much as goats.[22] The advantage of keeping sheep increased enormously with the breeding of variants (for the first time in the Near East in 3400 BCE) that, in addition to meat and milk, also supply wool.

A geographical coincidence ensured that these nomads secured a second source of wealth: the presence of large reserves of copper ore in Kargaly and other places in the southern Urals, to the east of the Pontic-Caspian steppe.[23] They processed the copper ore with the help of techniques that had already been developed in the Balkans and Iran. In Sintasha, to the north of the Aral Sea, bronze was made by mixing copper with tin from the much more southerly Bactria. In Sintasha, around 2000 BCE, a final invention by the horse breeders on the steppes served to increase this trade with the south: horse-drawn war chariots with spoked wheels. Their speed and manoeuvrability meant that they were a popular alternative to the thousand-year-old solid-wheeled battle cart or battlewagon. The invention of the cattle-drawn cart also made muck-spreading possible, something that Anthony tells us facilitated farming by single families, rather than by communities with more cooperative communal labour. Single farms thus became viable, supporting larger communities.

From the last millennium BCE, horses became indispensable for warfare, and the cavalry was created. Pastoral nomads in Eurasia increasingly focused on the supply of draught and riding animals (sometimes sent complete with drivers or riders) to warring states (see below, pp. 97–9).[24] This was not confined to the steppes. As we have seen, sedentary agriculture, disposing of definite surpluses of vegetable food, and the skills to domesticate animals successfully could also lead, under specific circumstances, to the predominance of pastoralism over other forms of agriculture, in particular after migrations into arid zones. Initial household animal husbandry with free-range grazing could transform into herdsman husbandry, which, in turn, could develop into semi-nomadic pastoralism and, ultimately, into pastoral nomadism. This outcome was reached in five different regions, in chronological order: in the Eurasian Steppe, semi-deserts and deserts; in the Near East (Mesopotamia, Arabia,

Syria and Palestine); in the Middle East (Asia Minor, Iran, Afghanistan); in Africa; and, much later, in northern Eurasia.[25]

From the first and earliest case – pastoral nomadism in the steppes, semi-deserts and deserts of Eurasia – only a minority became specialized mounted nomads in the European and Kazakh steppes in the first millennium BCE. It goes without saying that there were many variations of this nomadic lifestyle in this huge temperate zone territory. The majority of them nevertheless shared some features: they herded mainly sheep and horses in a fixed seasonal pattern by trekking from north in winter to south in summer and back again. Sheep and horses were crucial, as they are also able to pasture in snow, as were their products, milk and meat and, to a lesser degree, blood – a diet to be supplemented with vegetable food that was exchanged or purchased. Goats were also herded, but were less important, and later, in the south, the Turks kept Bactrian camels and sometimes dromedaries (Arabian camels). The mountain sheep- and yak-breeding nomads of the Pamirs and of Tibet may be considered another sub-type of the Eurasian group.

As in the Eurasian Steppe, pastoral nomads in the Near East only very gradually developed their specialism. Herdsman husbandry and semi-nomadic pastoralism existed in the third and second millennium BCE. Sheep- and goat-herders, using donkeys for transport, lived in the outlying districts of agricultural areas and were engaged in agriculture as well. As a consequence of the desiccation of the 'Saharo-Arabian belt' that began about 2500 BCE, some pastoralists became nomads, which was also made possible with the domestication of the camel in roughly 1500 BCE. The animal (including 'milch camels') was mentioned as being among the stock of the biblical patriarchs Abraham, Isaac and Jacob. These animals became as indispensable for the Near Eastern nomads as the horse for those of the Eurasian Steppe.[26]

In contrast to the Eurasian Steppe, where sheep and horses were herded together, here we see separate pasturing of, on the one hand, sheep and goats, herds that had to be watered every 3 to 4 days and so could not move more than 15–20 kilometres from a watering place, and on the other, camels – recall the aphorism by a Polish poet that 'a camel can work a week without drinking, while a man can drink for a week without working'.[27] This separate herding entailed intergroup and intertribal specialization. Milk dominated the diet of Near Eastern nomads, supplemented with meat, and sometimes blood, and with substantial amounts of vegetable food – not only dates but also cereals acquired from farmers who allowed them onto their stubble fields in return for the manure left by their herds.

Pastoralism reached Egypt and that way also North and East Africa from the Levant between 5000 and 4000 BCE.[28] In the Sahara, the development of pastoral nomadism was a direct consequence of its increased desiccation between 2500 and 2000 BCE.[29] This forced its existing pastoralists and possibly already existing semi-nomads with donkeys to adapt to the new circumstances. Only the advent of the riding horse via Egypt and, in particular, the camel from the Arabian Peninsula made real nomadism possible between West Africa and the Horn. Between the pastoral nomadism of the Eurasian Steppe and that of the Arabian desert an intermediary type may be found in the Middle East in Asia Minor, Iran and Afghanistan.[30] This type, documented no later than the third millennium BCE, was based on the semi-nomadic pastoralism of the yaylag (transhumance; yaylag or yaylaq means summer quarter), with small stock kept in the mountainous parts of Iran and the Armenian plateau, supplemented by agriculture.

However, real nomads in these countries emerged from the Eurasian Steppe, mainly in the Middle Ages (we are making a leap in time here). They can be divided into two types: sheep and horse herding in the steppes of, especially, Iran, and the herding of small stock in the mountains, as practised by the Lurs, Bakhtiari, Quashghai and Kurds. A smaller immigration took place from the Arabian Peninsula, but because their dromedaries could not bear the cold of the Anatolian plateau, these Bedouins confined themselves to the provinces of Fars and Khuzestan in south-western Iran, where they combined pastoralism with the cultivation of date palms. Some even went as far as Makran and Baluchistan.

Agriculturalists and pastoralists compared

The idea of private property originated within pastoralism much more than within arable farming, in contrast to (sometimes rather romantic) notions of common ownership among itinerant tribes. The animals, at least, are owned by individuals or households, while the pastureland and watering holes are considered communal property of the large community that these families belong to. Upon closer consideration, this is also logical. Successful (nomadic) pastoralism depends on the quality of the shepherd's care for his herd, of which he or she knows every single animal. In sum, we can say that 'as a whole the wastage of manpower is less in extensive pastoralism than it is in agriculture'.[31]

In the majority of nomadic societies, nuclear families and separate households, sometimes comprising two generations, predominate. Among the nomads of the Eurasian Steppe, but also elsewhere in Asia and Africa, the patrilocal stem family is widespread. In this case, one of the married sons, usually the youngest, lives with his parents, and he inherits their stock and property after buying out his elder brothers.[32] Labour requirements in these relatively small households are seasonally determined, which implies that they are dependent on cooperative labour and other forms of mutual aid within the community. It follows that dependent labour, let alone wage labour, was difficult to develop in this type of economy.[33]

Cooperation and confrontation

The independence of pastoral society and the positive contribution to state formation has long been anathema in history – unjustly. Traditionally, the economy of livestock breeders from the Eurasian Steppe was exclusively seen as parasitic in relation to neighbouring arable societies, from China in the east, via India in the south, to Europe in the west. By contrast, Anatoly Khazanov has shown that, in addition to incidental and spectacular pillaging, a quotidian complementarity between the two modes of existence was, in fact, the rule. Arable farmers needed the products of livestock breeders and vice versa. We encounter this complementarity already in ancient Mesopotamia. It was mostly peaceful, but sometimes disastrous; the latter, of course, made much more of an impression.[34] In the words of the first-century Chinese historian Ban Gu, the rule of the steppe was to plunder the sown: 'The people of the Yi and Di are greedy and seek profit . . . Their food and drinks are not the same [as ours]. . . . They follow their herds across the grasslands and hunt for their living.'[35]

The earliest agrarian societies exhibiting significant inequality and violence are the so-called warrior societies of the European Bronze and Iron Age.[36] They originated between roughly 3000 and 2000 BCE with the spread of speakers of the oldest form of the Indo-European languages of the Yamnaya culture across the Pontic-Caspian steppe in two directions:[37]

westwards to Europe and southwards to India. Initially, they occupied the empty spaces between the already long-settled agriculturalists by converting forests into grasslands. These early Indo-European-language-speaking herdsmen, living closely together with their cattle and thus more resistant to related contagious diseases, may also have caused pneumonic plague among the agriculturalists.[38] For both reasons, initially there was little mixing with existing populations, but eventually these pastoralists replaced major parts of the original populations. And this happened in a very special way. According to the geneticist David Reich, the Yamnaya culture 'was unprecedentedly sex-biased and stratified. [It] left behind great mounds, about 80 percent of which had male skeletons at the center, often with evidence of violent injuries and buried amidst fearsome metal daggers and axes'. Its spread into Europe and South Asia replaced earlier agricultural societies 'with little evidence of violence, and in which females played a central role' by 'a male-centered society, evident not only in the archaeology but also in the male-centered Greek, Norse, and Hindu mythologies of the Indo-European cultures'. On the basis of the latest results of human genetics, Reich concludes: 'This Yamnaya expansion also cannot have been entirely friendly. . . . [The] preponderance of male ancestry coming from the steppe implies that male descendants from the Yamnaya with political or social power were more successful at competing for local mates than men from the local groups.'[39] It does not take much imagination to see what that has meant in practice.

The American geographer and historian Jared Diamond provides us with a much-needed concrete example of large-scale organized group aggression (call it war, if you wish) that only became possible from the moment when agriculture group size had become large enough for it to sustain for an extended period of time:

In a band, where everyone is closely related to everyone else, people related simultaneously to both quarreling parties, step in to mediate quarrels. In a tribe, where many people are still close relatives, and everyone at least knows everybody else by name, mutual relatives and mutual friends mediate the quarrel. But once the threshold of 'several hundred' below which everyone can know everyone else, has been crossed, increasing number of dyads become pairs of unrelated strangers. When strangers fight . . . many onlookers will be friends or relatives of only one combatant and will side with that person, escalating the two-person fight into a general brawl. Hence a large society that continues to leave conflict resolution to all of its members is guaranteed to blow up. That factor alone would explain why societies of thousands can only exist if they develop central authority to monopolize force and resolve conflict.[40]

Even more general is the sharp observation from Diamond's compatriot, the archaeologist Lawrence Keeley: 'One feature that makes war so terrible is not the human vice of violent aggression but the human virtue of courage. There would be no war if humans were cowards. They would be afraid to resort to violence because it might be returned and if attacked would run or acquiesce. Instead . . . humans fight back.'[41]

Agriculture per se may have created conditions for more group violence, but, as may now be clear, it requires much more than this. The immigration of pastoral herdsmen with a strongly patriarchal culture in a sparsely populated area inhabited by agriculturalists only accounts for one or two generations. The systematic killing or subjugation of vanquished men becomes an option. The enslaving of conquered populations is another. Nomads tend to refer to what we would describe as vassal-tributary relations as 'slavery'. In particular, 'real' slavery (meaning slavery according to the definition accepted by most historians today) could arise in nomadic communities in those situations where they subjugated farmers or sometimes also other nomads who kept different animals. The most extreme case is probably that of the stratification of the Tuareg in the Sahara – although later than the period dealt with here. The masters were the noble tribes of camel herders, also involved in the caravan trade and the slave trade; below them, vassal tribes of small stock herders; lower still, a semi-serf agricultural population; and, at the bottom of the pile, slaves used as herdsmen.[42]

In all these cases, the question for the millennia and centuries that we are discussing here is not whether systematic violence was involved in mass immigrations of pastoral herdsmen – that was unequivocal – but whether the labour relations of the vast majority of the population of, so far, reasonably independent farming households – whether or not they were specialists in arable farming or livestock breeding – had already changed substantially by then. There are insufficient indications for this, even though the number of aggrandizers almost certainly increased with the expansion of pastoral herdsmen societies.[43] There are indications, however, of the first urban societies and the states that followed.

Working in the earliest cities: Labour specialization and redistribution

The emergence of cities and urban societies was first possible when productivity had risen to such a level that enough people no longer had to depend on their own food production for their existence and therefore were able to leave their land. In this way, habitation concentrations – that is, cities – of artisans, priests and other non-farmers developed. At the same time, we now make the leap from a handful of different full-time professions to dozens if not a hundred or more.

We begin this story with the Fertile Crescent, that part of the world where the Neolithic Revolution had been a complete success – in contrast to an equally old agrarian region such as New Guinea or eastern North America – largely due to the balance of plant and animal nutrition. In the words of Jared Diamond:

> Thanks to this availability of suitable wild mammals and plants, early peoples of the Fertile Crescent could quickly assemble a potent and balanced biological package for intensive food production. That package comprised: three cereals, as the main carbohydrate sources; four pulses, with 20–25 percent protein, and four domestic animals, as the main protein sources, supplemented by the generous protein content of wheat; and flax as a source of fiber and oil (termed linseed oil: flax seeds are about 40 per cent oil). Eventually, thousands of years after the beginnings of animal domestication and food production, the animals also began to be used for milk, wool, plowing and transport. Thus, the crops and animals of the Fertile Crescent's first farmers came to meet humanity's basic economic needs: carbohydrate, protein, fat, clothing, traction, and transport.[44]

The oldest cities in the world were built in Mesopotamia: the cities of Eridu and Ur in the fifth millennium BCE and Uruk in the fourth, all three in the south of present-day Iraq. Here, we no longer find population concentrations of several hundred or perhaps even a thousand or two thousand people (as earlier in Jericho and Çatal Hüyük), but of many more. In the fourth millennium BCE, Uruk was greater in area than classical Athens and half as big as Imperial Rome.[45] Everywhere else in the world, cities emerged much later.

The division of labour in these earliest cities must have already been advanced.[46] We can deduce this not only from the high status of the material culture, but also from the stories originating from Eridu tribes – although they were only written down much later.[47] It is striking that various groups of professions worshipped the supreme god Enki as their patron saint, including leather workers, washermen, reed workers, barbers, weavers, builders, metalsmiths, potters, irrigation technicians, gardeners and goat-herds, as well as physicians, diviners, lamentation priests, musicians and scribes. This latter group already had its own vocational training by the beginning of the third millennium.

But there was more to it than group identity and possibly also professional pride; these early city dwellers also believed that people had to work hard and that this had been humanity's destiny since Creation. One of Eridu's stories, for example, is that the first generation of gods had each been assigned a specific task in order to keep the land well-tended and irrigated. Some had to carry the baskets with earth, while the 'great gods' acted as supervisors. When the gods of work start to complain, Enki, with the help of a number of goddesses, eventually creates man from clay and assigns hard work to human-kind. The gods celebrate the completion of man's creation with a banquet.

So, now we're talking about supervisors and hard work. Nevertheless, it seems that in these first urban societies, the toilers' lot was eased by an admin-istrative centre that handled the public exchange and redistribution of goods and took care of the workers. In Uruk, for example, the 'exchange in pre-state societies [was] heavily ritualized and conducted in the public eye to witness and approve the transaction. Even if the complexity of the Uruk economy demanded greater administrative supervision, as the sealings prove, this would not remove the need for public accountability'.[48] The invention, already in the fifth millennium, of the seal, usually in the form of a cylinder seal with a reverse intaglio impression, certainly points to an administrative need to facilitate the bulk storage and transport of goods. Their integrity was guaran-teed by sealed wrappings, and the seals were also very useful for collective storage facilities. This is the oldest tributary-redistributive society that we know. Every producer surrenders his surplus and this is then redistributed by the temple among non-farming fellow citizens.[49]

Important support for this interpretation of labour relations in the first cities comes from Denise Schmandt-Besserat's meticulous study of 8,162 baked clay 'tokens', 'counters', or 'counting devices', a few centimetres in diameter, which appear all over the Fertile Crescent.[50] The first pre-urban phase of this method of counting and registration is represented by sixteen different plain tokens, the most common of which were the cone, the sphere and the disc, for counting grain (they could denote a small basket, large basket, anything up to a whole granary), the cylinder for counting animals and the tetrahedron for labour. They came in small and large sizes. A small tetrahedron could represent one man's or one day's work and a big one a gang's or a week's work.[51] Thus, before the emergence of cities, Mesopotamian agrarian society was already so large-scale that tools for counting labour and the products of labour were considered necessary.

In the city-states from 4400 BCE onwards, a large number of more complex variants developed from these basic forms – mostly geometric, but sometimes also naturalistic forms with a variety of linear and punched markings. This meant more specific sizes could be indicated, such as grain content or land size, and animals could be distinguished, for example, fat-tailed sheep, ewes or lambs, but also manufactured goods, such as textiles, garments, vessels and tools; processed foods, such as oil, bread, cakes and trussed ducks; and luxury goods, such as perfume, metal and jewellery.

It is striking that most tokens are found in or in the vicinity of the public offices, warehouses and workshops of the central temple. We can deduce from this, and the fact that they were later strung together or kept in clay envelopes, with the number and type of tokens recorded in it, that they were used to keep track of everyone's contributions to the temple (for example, grain deposits in central silos) and that they formed the basis of the redistribution system. Arrears could also be recorded on the envelopes and the tablets that replaced the envelopes and their contents from 3500 BCE. In the aforementioned city of Ur, this administrative tributary-redistribution system was managed by the supreme god's priest-king, the moon god Nanna. At a certain point, the system took on the character of a tax or corvée, rather than the redistribution of collective production. Voluntarism also gave way to coercion, including public punishments for citizens who opposed this.[52]

Around 3000 BCE, violence and destruction brings an end to this first urban civilization. Gilgamesh is said to have built Uruk's city walls. In the new historical period, there are strong indications that society is organized much more hierarchically, that lords and workers emerge along with freedmen and slaves. This is dramatically articulated in the 'Lamentation over the Destruction of Ur'. Even the pleasure of work comes to an end:

That the hoe not attack the fertile fields, that the seed not be planted in
the ground.
That the sound of the song of the one tending the oxen not resound on
the plain . . .
That the song of the churning not resound in the cattle pen.[53]

For most other early urban cultures, there is an absence of detailed studies
like those available for Mesopotamia and we know too little about the labour
relations that may have prevailed there. Nevertheless, there are a number of
indications of the fact that the redistributive system that was made credible
for a number of cities in the Fertile Crescent also occurred elsewhere, such
as in Arslantepe in Central Anatolia.[54] It could also have existed a few centuries later in the city-states of the Indus civilization (2600–1900 BCE), whose
important centres were Harappa and Mohenjo-Daro in present-day
Pakistan. Although earlier ideas about the strictly egalitarian Indus society
have since been modified, the insignificance of war and, especially, the way
in which grain was harvested, threshed and stored, point in that direction.[55]
Agricultural technology was already highly developed; indeed, these people
were using ploughs with draught teams and carts. Notably, the harvested
grain was not threshed by farming households themselves. This is interpreted as possibly indicative of a communal or even centralized organization of production.

After 3000 BCE, the clustering and growth of sites also took place in
China, along the Yangtze and Yellow rivers and further north in Inner
Mongolia. The oldest Chinese city-states in the period between around 3000
and 1600 BCE were comprised of a central city, generally with a few thousand residents, and its immediate environs.[56] It was not only farmers who
lived in this area, there were also centres of craft production, such as the
stone quarries at Taosi and Erlitou.[57] In the quarries themselves, farming
households had a sideline producing flint shards as semi-manufactured
products. In specialized rural settlements, these shards were processed into
stone spades and other end products. That also happened in the city, and
from there they were even exported to other polities. How these semi-
finished and finished products were exchanged between the different places
is not known, but here, too, we already see an early form of non-agricultural
specialization.

Several urban settlements were as big as 250–400 hectares, and many were heavily walled. Most impressive of all is Shimao (2800–2300 BCE, in Shaanxi province, central China), surrounded by a stone wall that encompassed three enclosures. Such constructions presuppose a substantial accumulation of labour resources. Another such urban centre was Taosi (in Shanxi province, northern China). Measuring 280 hectares, it may have had several thousand inhabitants. The construction of just its main enclosure walls of pounded earth would have required 39,673 person-months (or a full year's employment for 3,306 men). At its peak, Erlitou, with 300 hectares (1900/1850–1550 BCE), had an estimated 18,000 to 30,000 inhabitants. These well-developed towns with highly specialized craft production demonstrate a great variation in degrees of hierarchy and, consequently, in the ways in which labour may have been organized and remunerated. On one end of the spectrum, there are towns with a high disparity between poor and rich graves, strong defence works and supplies of weaponry; and on the other, much more egalitarian societies.[58]

Taosi was an example of the former type. Its elite graves were more than ten times larger than the graves of commoners, and gender differences were also more pronounced, as men's graves were, on average, larger and richer than those of women. Human skeletons indicate greater differences between the elite and commoners in terms of the foodstuffs they consumed. At the same time, large storage cellars indicate the redistributive character of this society.[59] The military nature of this city-state is obvious, not only from its heavy defence works, but also from the sacrifice of humans, with the assumption that these are prisoners of war and not members of the lower strata of its own society.

In contrast, Shijiahe, in the mid-Yangtze region (2600–1900 BCE) had substantial walls, but rather as a protection against floods. It provided its inhabitants with drainage and sewerage by means of ceramic pipes, differences between graves were much smaller and the thousands of figurines and small ritual cups found are 'suggestive of inclusive rituals, in which the site's larger population and perhaps the rural communities that surrounded it as well, all participated'. Some form of redistribution system would have existed in all these versions, but in a much more inequitable form in the north than in the south. It would take until around 1600 BCE before we can speak of real (medium-scale) states in China, the best-known being that of the Shang (1600–1050 BCE; see pp. 111–12 below).

Working in states: The multiplicity of labour relations

State formation

As far as we currently know, the first states originate from around 3000 BCE. In contrast to agrarian societies, and even cities, states can determine labour relations and especially labour conditions for many more people, and, moreover, they can do this more drastically and more intensively.[60] States can develop out of cities or associations of cities, as happened in Mesopotamia in the third millennium and China in the second millennium, but they can also develop without these intermediate steps, such as in Egypt around 3000 BCE.[61] And successful city-states can also disappear again without the formation of a state, as was the case in the Indus civilization (2600–1900 BCE). These diverse ways in which they can arise largely determine the development of diverse new labour relations within them.

This section deals in particular with the extent to which the earliest states adopted the agrarian model of 'complex societies', with increasing inequalities, or that of the earliest cities, which were more redistributive in nature. It seems that the second prevailed initially, certainly in Mesopotamia, where a great continuity in cultures is visible (and the distinction between city unions and states is not always easy to make), but many elements of complex societies also crept in as a result of conflict – in particular unfree labour. In this mix, we now also find the first traces of wage labour, self-employment and labour markets (but still without money as a means of exchange: the influence of this on labour relations is the theme of pp. 118–27.

The Fertile Crescent

What changed in the labour relations of Mesopotamia when city-states and city unions gradually or abruptly turned into states? Was the original redistributive system around the central temples maintained on an even larger scale, or was there a significant shift with the transition from city to state? Given that the labour system, organized by and around temples, also persisted for a long time in the earlier states, two changes must be underlined here. Firstly, from the late third millennium, the effect of state formation on warfare and on large-scale enslaving of prisoners of war; and secondly, from the first millennium, the emergence of markets that, together with state bodies, determined the circulation of goods between households. This became the basis for self-employment and wage labour (in addition to the long-standing professional soldiers in state service).

One of the main characteristics of the economy of the Uruk culture, which from 3800 to 3200 encompassed many cities (and which therefore can be understood as a late city union, rather than as an early state), stretching over parts of Syria, Turkey, Iran and Iraq, was distribution and exchange. Because of the larger scale, more bureaucracy was necessary and everything was accompanied with more ritual, but the transition to bigger administrative units rather than a single city did not change the system as such. For a long time, the same is also true for the polities that followed from the third millennium.[62] This bureaucracy perhaps expanded most during the Third Dynasty of Ur (2112–2004 BCE), when redistribution between provinces was also organized. This is very similar to what we will see below for Pharaonic Egypt.[63]

Ultimately, the redistribution of products by the polity only survived on an incidental basis. Ashurnasirpal II of Assyria furnishes us with a later example. Having completed the palace of Calah, he invited 69,574 guests to a banquet that lasted 10 days. On the menu were, among other things, 1,000 fat oxen, 14,000 sheep, 1,000 lambs, hundreds of deer, 20,000 pigeons, 10,000 fish, 10,000 desert rats and 10,000 eggs. At first glance this seems to be the actions of another excessive aggrandizer, but, more significantly, it signalled the end of a tributary-redistributive state.[64]

Arguably, beyond Mesopotamia and more in the periphery of the Fertile Crescent, this redistributive character also applied to a number of states that from 1400 to 1200 qualified as members of the 'Great Powers Club' in the eastern Mediterranean basin and in the Near East. This includes well-known states such as Babylon (and over time Mitanni and Assyria), Hatti in Anatolia (the Hittites, succeeded by Arzawa with its capital Ephesus), Alashiya or Cyprus, Mycenae and the Minoan Empire on Crete.[65] It is important to emphasize a common feature of all these realms, namely, the central organization of workers for large-scale infrastructure (roads, ports and so on) and agriculture. Of course, these workers had to be fed and maintained by the state.

States, soldiers and slaves in Mesopotamia

State formation and the building of large armies usually go together. This has three implications for the history of work: the recruitment of soldiers' labour; the enslavement of growing numbers of prisoners of war; and some-times the forced removal of conquered peoples with the aim of coloniza-tion.[66] Around 2300 BCE, Sargon the Great, the ruler of 'all four corners of the world, of all lands under heaven from sunrise to sunset', established Akkad, the first large state in world history, with a territory reaching from the Persian Gulf far into Anatolia. We encounter both slavery and profes-sional soldiers in the surviving records of this kingdom.[67]

The 'invention of the military battle' and the phenomenon of the light infantry in the Fertile Crescent, after 1300 BCE, and its dispersal to other parts of the world, including Europe, meant further skilling and specializa-tions within this profession.[68] Essential for the success of states in this regard was the transport revolution. As we have seen, this was made possible by the taming of horses from 4000 BCE in the steppes north of the Black Sea and their deployment in wars, later with the help of horse-drawn battle chariots (1800 BCE). Manual military work is one of the earliest documented forms of free labour. Sargon wrote with regard to his military campaigns that '5,400 men eat before him daily'.[69] Moreover, senior officers were rewarded with the allocation of land.

At the end of a conflict there are prisoners of war. What is to be done with them? Should they be put to the sword or put to work? Most states chose the latter, an important, indeed, perhaps the most important, source of slavery. Slaves are originally hostages who are not killed, as is described explicitly much later in the Statute of Justinian, written 528–534 CE.[70] Thus considered, war – different from violence or aggression, which, as previously discussed, is much older – occupies a central place in the history of work.[71] Fighting 'real war' campaigns, defined as systematic and sustained violence aimed at defeating other people, required an army so large that it could only be success-fully maintained by a state. In turn, this state's income relies on farmers who can produce more than they need for themselves. At the same time – inter alia because of the absence of so many men departing for military campaigns – sufficient demand for labour exists in such complex societies so that war hostages can be profitably put to work, for example, in public works, instead of being killed off. The world record for the forced removal of prisoners of war for this period probably goes to the Assyrian Empire, which, from 900 to 600, deported no fewer than 4.5 million men, women and children. In the same period, all over the Middle East and the eastern Mediterranean, polities and especially their elites (and sometimes sub-elites) used slave labour.[72]

Despite the fact that an increase in prosperity, wars and social stratification go hand in hand and lead to slavery, we only find large concentrations of unfree men later. In Sumer, as early as the fourth millennium BCE, the concept of 'slave' was already equated with 'male person from a foreign country', indicating that captivity was the origin of slavery. The Hammurabi Code of around 1754 BCE shows that, additionally, purchase and debt can also lead to slavery.[73] Despite the occurrence of slavery – especially in the years following a war – free labour was probably still prevalent, and Mesopotamia was characterized by free farmers and free workers. In particular, the fact that numbers of slaves per owner or company were limited points in this direction: the highest documented number of slaves belonging to one owner, a banker, is 96.

Markets in Mesopotamia and the emergence of the self-employed, employers and workers

The fact that states began by employing soldiers and provisioning them with food, shelter and wherewithal, does not imply the existence of a labour market, however. For a real labour market to emerge, multiple employers are needed, who compete for wage workers and enter into employment contracts with them. To put it another way, in a labour market, wage workers can choose between different employers, and they can negotiate their wages – successfully or not.

These kinds of labour markets gradually emerged in Mesopotamia. The first traces are tentatively visible around 2000 BCE, but more convincingly after 1000 BCE, when, in addition to the state, now also cities, temples and, especially, the subcontractors hired by temples began to act as employers of labour in their own right. At the same time, commodity markets now regularly emerged.[74] We can find two types of buyers in such markets: firstly, independent producers who sell to and buy from each other, like the fisherman who buys grain from the farmer, the farmer who buys fabrics from the weaver and the weaver who buys fish from the fisherman, and so on. Secondly, professional soldiers or other hirelings who, when not in receipt of their maintenance in kind directly from the state, or without the time to produce their own food, used their wages to purchase grain, fabrics and fish at markets. Beyond the four labour relations already mentioned (reciprocal, tributary-redistributive, slave labour and the newly introduced wage labour), we thus encounter a fifth type: independent labour for the market (often called self-employment, including the family business arrangement in which women already played a role early on).[75] Finally, as already indicated, out of the contractors of temples and other organs of the polity also emerged the first employers of labour, thus bringing our count to a total of six labour relations. This is a crucial development in the history of work as no new basic categories have been invented by mankind since. From this point, the history of work may be conceived as an endless shift between these basic forms.

Various examples illustrate the expansion of the different kinds of labour relations that we know of in the states in the Fertile Crescent. The earliest polities for which sufficient relevant sources are available are the Kingdom of Ur under its Third Dynasty (Ur III, around 2112–2004 BCE) and some successor states, certainly the New Babylonian Empire (625–539 BCE) and the Persian Empire that assimilated it. Going beyond antiquated but persistent myths about an invariant 'Eastern despotism' or the 'Asiatic mode of production' in this part of the world, introduced by the classical Greek authors and their followers, a much more nuanced and interesting picture has emerged in recent decades.

The Ur III dynasty created a number of basic conditions for the emergence of markets, but probably not the markets themselves. Standard measures, replacing the earlier system of individual cities controlling their own system of weights and measures, was one of these conditions. The increased use of silver as the main unit of accounting and the circulation of this precious metal in the form of rods was part of this. That the appropriate amount of silver could be snipped off already comes close to a uniform payment system.[76] Given that Ur III bureaucrats worked within a strict central and hierarchical structure, the question is whether many transactions were actually settled in this way. Farmers had to hand over a large portion of their harvest – 43 to 48 per cent is calculated for the provinces of Umma and Lagash – and, in addition, willow and poplar, ceramic vessels, roof beams and leather sacks were collected as taxes. Herds of temple- and state-held sheep were also consigned to shepherds for care, subject to annual enumeration and inspection, and prescribed deliveries of wool, proportions of offspring, hides and dairy products. It is safe to assume that shepherds also kept their own sheep. As if that wasn't enough, corvée labour was imposed. These workers, organized in work gangs supervised by foremen, received allotments of barley, the quantity dependent on status, as well as annual allotments of low-grade wool or wool textiles.[77] There does not seem to be much room for monetary transactions in daily life here.

That became possible in the following centuries, between 2000 and 1600, when the 'privatization of the administration' rapidly took hold. Public servants became private businessmen, contracted for their services, but not owing political allegiance to any dynasty. They also began providing high-interest loans, up to 20 per cent interest on silver loans and 33 per cent rate on grain loans.[78] Evidence of the oldest salaries, expressed in quantities of grain or silver, or both, is found in texts from the eighteenth to the fifteenth century BCE, before disappearing from view again for a long time. The best known are the wage regulations in the Hammurabi Code. A conversion of the quantities of silver (0.23–0.28 g) recorded in the Code yields a standard wage of 6.2–8 litres of grain per day, per worker.[79]

In the nineteenth century BCE, Ashur's private merchants also established a profitable long-distance trade. Transported on the back of donkeys, they brought tin and textiles fabricated by their spouses to Anatolia in exchange for copper, precious metals and stones. Their well-documented business leads the historian and Assyriologist Gwendolyn Leick to conclude 'that Ashur in the twentieth century BC was primarily a capitalist trading state whose wealth depended exclusively on mercantile enterprise'.[80] Interestingly, in a text from the second millennium, we encounter the following clearly self-employed lady. A doctor, looking for his host, receives the following directions:

> Enter by the Grand gate and leave a street, a boulevard, a square, Tillazida Street and the ways of Nusku and Ninimena to your left. You should ask Nin-lugal-absu, daughter of Ki-agga-Enbilulu, daughter-in-law of Nishu-an-Ea-takla, a gardening woman of the garden Henun-Enlil, sitting on the ground of Tillazida selling produce, and she will show you.[81]

Both examples illustrate the possibilities for independent entrepreneur-ship already during the second millennium. However, for the time being, they seem not to have set a trend for Mesopotamia or the Fertile Crescent as a whole. We must wait for the next millennium for that. It has been demonstrated that, in Babylon, at least from 600 BCE onwards, self-employed labour and wage labour were much more prevalent than slave labour, that reciprocal labour was relatively unimportant outside the home and that tributary labour was declining sharply.[82] What is also striking is that payment for wage labour was reckoned in and paid out in pieces of uncoined silver and that wages were by no means meagre. Even slaves sometimes received wages instead of maintenance, so that, even though, juridically speaking, they were unfree workers bound to their owners, they could nevertheless acquire property of their own.[83]

In some cases, the archaeological record is so detailed that we can become acquainted with individual wage workers. In the so-called Mardonios archive, for example, cuneiform tablets inform us that in the years 484–477 BCE, three brickmakers named Abu-usursu, Bel-ana-merehti and Bel-ittannu hired themselves out as a team. Every month, they would mould and fire 11,000 to 12,000 large bricks, for which they received the sum of 21 shekels in silver.[84] Many such work teams were required. The construction of the city walls and the palaces of Babylon alone employed thousands of them at the same time.

Finally, different types of labour relations can be united in a single individual. Such combinations have also been documented for these ancient societies. Around 500 BCE, a cuneiform text from Uruk offers a striking example of combined labour relations in a market economy.[85] A subcontractor or executive at the time complained that it was impossible to obtain manpower for work on land belonging to a temple, because everyone was busy harvesting their own date crops – in short, self-employed labour was being combined with seasonal wage labour. The temple in this example, incidentally, also had slaves in its service, though not very many, because they reportedly lacked motivation and escaped when they could.

Egypt

The annual flooding of the Nile resulted in a form of natural fertilization with sludge, creating exceptionally favourable conditions for agriculture in Egypt[86] – at least on the narrow kilometre-wide strip of land on both sides and in the expansive delta and some oases. An average of nine farming households could feed an extra household without having to eat less and therefore could devote themselves to other activities.[87] This huge food surplus became possible from the fifth millennium with the introduction, from the Fertile Crescent, of, first, livestock breeding in Upper Egypt, and then arable farming in the Delta. From the fourth millennium, both types of agriculture were combined from south to north.

Historians are divided about the social purpose of this abundant income.[88] On the one hand, there is the traditional view, already well-voiced in the Bible, of Egypt as the land of slavery. Most historians now reject this idea and rather assume central taxation by the pharaonic state, which dominated the economy. At the other, far end of the spectrum, we find a recent plea to ultimately see classical Egypt as a market society. From the point of view of the history of work – allowing for a very modest role for slavery – the balance of the argument is clearly in favour of the proposition that, until its conquest by Alexander the Great, classical Egypt was a tributary-redistributive state with great influence on the division of labour and its revenues, and that labour markets of any significance only arose after this event (see pp. 118–27).

The rise of that almighty state is rather anomalous. In contrast to Mesopotamia, there was no long preceding period of city-states along the Nile.[89] The Egyptian state finds its origin in the fourth millennium, in the pastoral economy of Upper Egypt, where specialized workshops for ceramic products could also be found.[90] After 3500 BCE, the so-called Naqadan culture, which strongly emphasized the importance of funerary rituals with substantial animal and sometimes also human sacrifices, expanded to the north. This happened not through military conquest but through peaceful migration. River shipping connected all these small Naqadan settlements to each other, resulting in a standardization of products, measurements and product administration, reminiscent of the Mesopotamian tokens.[91] Access to arable farming in the north led to a significant expansion of political leeway.

Around 3000 BCE, this arrangement takes the form of a centrally guided state, initially ruled from Upper Egypt with centres such as Hierakonpolis, Naqada and Abydos, and from around 2700 BCE from Lower Egypt with centres at Saqqara and Memphis. After several centuries, the increasing scope of funerary rites[92] reached its apogee with the building of the pyramids at Giza. While, until around 1500 BCE, the new state is nowhere near as big in area as the examples that we first saw in Mesopotamia, the fact that it is formed by the banks of one great river means it is internally very coherent. Of course, the controversy about the nature of this state is encouraged by the fact that it covers an extremely long period of almost 3,000 years. Within it, the Egyptian state organized the work of its subjects centrally, but, of course, there were numerous variations. Firstly, the central state power experienced many oscillations. Its organized power was much more vigorous during formidable dynasties such as those of the pyramid builders than in the many 'intermediate periods' distinguished by historians. Secondly, it could exercise its power directly or via numerous bureaucratic layers and, in this latter case, there was, of course, scope for manoeuvre for these bureaucrats. More striking than these intermediate periods of failing central power and of the appropriation of power by priests and officials, which sometimes endured for centuries at a time, is the fact that the central state always returned in similar forms, until Roman times, when it essentially became a royal estate under the emperor, outwith the senate's administration.[93]

Due to the simultaneity of the great cultures in Mesopotamia and Egypt, both have frequently been compared to each other and there are, indeed, many similarities in terms of the organization of work,[94] but there are also great differences. Especially at the end of the period under discussion, they become increasingly clear. The main difference is the much greater urbanization of Mesopotamia and, as we have seen, the emergence of markets and new labour relations, while Egypt repeatedly returned to the original tributary-redistributive model.

Fundamental to this was the idea of the supreme king-god, who adjudicated over all products and workers and who could use them as he saw fit. In this view, private property could not exist and no one could decide their own work at their own discretion – neither as an individual, nor as a household or local community. That meant that all work and all the products of that work (not just crops and livestock, but also fish, salt, reed mats, and so on) were taxed in kind. On the other hand, in a few cases, the production was organized directly in the construction of temples and pyramids, as well as the armies necessary for all this. The first signals the tributary nature of the labour relations of most inhabitants of pharaonic Egypt, the second the redistributive character for the benefit of the minority who worked directly in the service of the state.[95] Farmers who had to work as soldiers combined both characteristics. Their labour was corvée, but it was enabled through the redistribution of agricultural products, levied on their co-subjects whose exclusive task was to produce them. That was most evident in the military service,[96] but also in, among others, state waterworks and expeditions to find ores.

This centralistic approach required a vast bureaucratic organization, for the administration of both the *domains* and the *estates*. The empire was divided into provincial domains, from north to south, established by a particular king, above all to guarantee the maintenance of the royal mortuary cult. Estates were a more specific institution, either a particular locality or a foundation, supplying a particular commodity. According to this definition, temples could also be counted among them, but it means, in particular, quarries, mines, construction sites and the like.[97] The part of the production that was levied as a tax (especially grain, but also fish and other products) subsequently went to the court (broadly speaking counting 5,000 to 10,000 members[98]) and the estates, to enable producers to devote themselves to their specialist work.

Since the total social product was distributed in this way, there was little room for trade outside of exchange at village level. Consequently, even foreign trade was monopolized by the state or the court. Merchants trading at their own expense and risk were not involved. The state monopoly of foreign trade – the import by Egypt of exotic goods such as timber from Lebanon and copper from Cyprus, for example – ensured that the goods became available for distribution among the big temples.[99]

The domains were entrusted to a senior official or to a temple, which thereby obtained all available means of production. In practice, it meant that all its residents had to deliver products and services if the state requested it. To that end, counts of livestock and other products were held in the Old Kingdom (until 2200 BCE), while registration agencies for workers operated in the Middle Kingdom.[100]

The lowest level of production was, in the first instance, coordinated by the village chief, who thus gained a higher status than his fellow villagers. For farmers – the vast majority of the population – this meant that by the time the harvest had ripened (March–April), a fleet from the state, the temples or the lord of the land berthed and took part of this harvest for storage in central silos. Eventually, only a small part would come back in the form of seeds for the following season, which started after the flooding of the Nile, between October in the south and December in the north. What was not collected was used to sustain the farming household. Within these narrow boundaries, one might even have spoken of having one's own inheritable farm. Viewed schematically, we can assume that of the total production: 10 per cent was paid in central tax; 10 per cent was kept back to be used for sowing; 40 per cent went to intermediaries (bureaucrats or temples, also referred to as 'landlords'); and 40 per cent was left to compensate the toilers on the land.[101] That is roughly the same order of magnitude of the remittances paid by Mesopotamian farmers during the Ur III dynasty.

Only thanks to the large yields from this irrigation agriculture – at least if there was enough water coming from Ethiopia without it turning into devastating floods – could this generate a reasonable income for the actual farmers. The fact that the population grew considerably in the long run is proof of this, according to Douglas Brewer, author of several books on Ancient Egypt. However, his estimates suggest that the daily grain yield per inhabitant fell from 18.16 kg per inhabitant around 4000 BCE, via 6.74 kg around 3000 BCE, to 3.92 kg around 2500 BCE. Thereafter, the downward trend slowed to a mere 2.08 kg per inhabitant per day in the Roman period. According to Brewer, Egypt's predynastic potential grain production was as much as 45 times what current Food and Agriculture Organization (FAO) guidelines state are necessary for a healthy diet; and even during Egypt's most populous period it amounted to nearly 5 times the recommended daily intake. 'Even if only half the cultivable land was planted with grain . . . production still ranged from 2.2 to 2.5 times the recommended daily allow-ance.' He concludes that 'it is easy to understand why Egypt was considered the breadbasket of the ancient world'. More importantly, it shows how the country could free up so many people to build all the monuments, and why its fame endures.

Of course, farmers' actual reward was heavily dependent on the extent to which they had to hand over their harvest. That could certainly be more than the already high average of 50 per cent that we have assumed above. This is beautifully articulated in the following two passages, fictional comparisons between the fate of the writers, on the one hand, and ordinary Egyptian farmers, on the other, recorded around 1850 BCE:

> Let me also explain to you how it fares with the cultivator, that other tough occupation. During the inundation he is wet through, but he must attend to his equipment all the same. He passes the whole day making and repairing his farming tools, and the whole night twisting rope. Even his midday lunch hour he spends doing farming work. . . . Now the land, free from the floodwaters, lies before him, and he goes out to get his team of oxen. When he has been tracking the herdsman for many days, he gets his team. He then comes back with it and makes for it a clearing in the field. At dawn he goes out to look after the team and does not find it where he left it. He spends three days searching for the oxen and finds them stuck in the bog, dead; and there are no hides on them either: the

jackals have chewed them up! He spends much time cultivating grain, but the snake follows him and eats up the seed as soon as it is cast upon the ground. And that happens to him with three sowings of the borrowed seeds.

Let me remind you of the plight of the peasant when the officers come to estimate the harvest tax, and snakes have carried off half of the grain and the hippopotamus has eaten up the rest. The voracious sparrows bring disaster upon the peasant. The remnants of grain left on the threshing floor are all gone; thieves have taken them away. What he owes for the oxen hired he cannot pay, and as for the oxen, they are dead from excessive plowing and threshing. And just now the scribe lands at the riverbank to estimate the harvest tax with a suite of attendants carrying sticks and Nubians with rods of palm. They say: 'Show us the grain!' But there is none, and the peasant is mercilessly beaten. He is then tied up and cast head foremost into a pool, where he gets thoroughly soaked. His wife is bound in his presence; his children are in shackles.[102]

Of course, this is a pastiche. So many simultaneous accidents would not have befallen one farmer in one season. It does, however, articulate that a tributary-redistributive system without markets is certainly not always heaven on earth. If we want to seriously consider the grain levies forced on Egyptian farmers by the pharaohs, then we must ask ourselves whether they got anything in return. The answer is probably in the affirmative, and not only in the sense that redistribution was properly done. There was a belief in a common, higher aim – an essential sense that everyone belonged to a large cosmic whole, in which, according to the state ethics (called *Maat*), social justice was an important norm, as expressed in a text from 2300 BCE. A high servant of the pharaoh summed up his life thus: '[H]aving spoken *maat* and done *maat* ... having rescued the weak from the hand of one stronger than he when I could; having given the hungry bread, the naked clothing and a landing to the boatless; having buried the one without a son; having made a boat for one without a boat.' This is an ideal, but it is not simply a construct of the ruling class to control the masses, because the same voice also says to his master: 'I am one who did what all people praise' and 'I did what the great desire and the small praise'.[103] The extent to which this ideal was respected by all subjects is not certain. In any case, the pharaohs did consider it necessary to promote the people's solidarity with the state, demonstrated most clearly in the construction of a series of small step pyramids at regular distances along the whole of the Nile. These miniature versions of the grand royal pyramids were intended to remind Egyptian subjects of the grand design for which they were toiling.[104]

Although the well-known depictions of agricultural work in ancient Egypt almost exclusively portray men, the size of the farms (around 3 hectares) nevertheless indicates that the labour of the whole household, of men, women and children, was required. Traditionally, pictures of ploughing and harvesting grain with sickles only show men, and likewise those of pottery making, stone carving, metalworking, construction and tanning; by contrast, we only ever see women gleaning, harvesting flax, weaving and doing household chores. Winnowing was done by men and women together. Shifts also occurred – for example, when the vertical loom was introduced in the New Kingdom (*c.* 1550–1070 BCE), men took over weaving from women.[105]

In addition to the large masses of farmers with their contributions through domains, there were also flagship estates, construction sites for temples, palaces and, in particular, pyramids, immense burial monuments surpassing all others in the world. We are already aware of large burial mounds and other organized construction projects based on corvée in various prehistoric and historic cultures, but the pyramids beat everything. Based on the amount of materials processed, we can roughly calculate how much labour their construction must have cost.[106] Large numbers apply here, and of particular interest to a history of work are the large numbers of workers whose labour had to be coordinated. We can distinguish a core workforce of 5,000 builders and, at the height of such projects, we must add a few tens of thousands more, up to 40,000 seasonal workers to quarry, ship, haul and build. These projects took place in the months when the Nile flooded, which meant that the construction materials could be rafted over the river and, at the same time, there was little work to do on the land. Initially, these funerary monuments were built from mud brick (a local adaption of an Uruk design),[107] but the step pyramid of King Djoser was built around 2650 BCE entirely from 600,000 limestone blocks (partly hewn nearby, and partly imported from the town of Tura) and 120 tons of granite, transported by ships all the way from Aswan. This hard stone could only be extracted with the help of copper chisels. For this pyramid alone this meant 70 tons of copper for hand tools. Here, we can certainly talk of serial production, something that eventually also applied to monumental sculptures. But this was just child's play in comparison with the 3 great pyramids that were commenced by his successors and that required no less than 20 million tons of stone.

We are, incidentally, well-informed about the work that took place on one of these estates, the grave builders' village Deir el-Medina, which, from 1525 to 1070 BCE, operated at the Ramesseum at Medinat Habu.[108] At its peak, 120 families lived here, tightly packed together, all of them specialists. Officials scratched notes about anything and everything on fragments that, fortunately, have survived in huge numbers. This gives us an unexpected view of countless details of their daily lives. We must not forget, however, that we are talking here about a very exceptional situation and about a small group of highly valued specialists within a short period of time.

At first sight, they are ordinary professionals. That is true when we look at their work, but is not the case when we examine their labour relations. Their entire life was one long hereditary corvée for the king. Neither they, nor their children, could really do anything else. On the other hand, the state provided for their basic needs, at least as long as there was enough work. If that disappeared, then they were sent outside of the village for much lower-paying jobs as part of the service staff. They were allowed to decide among themselves who met this fate, just as they arranged their entire internal organization themselves. It is striking that this was done using maritime terms. They divided themselves into port and starboard sides.

Within this strict framework, these 'state workers' exhausted all the possibilities of the system, in particular by making extra money and thus creating a sort of mini market. For example, some took on assignments from private individuals to make ancestral statues. In addition, their wives wove linen to order. They also allowed themselves liberties with respect to their water carriers, provided by the state. Many among this group of labourers worked themselves into an insurmountable state of debt, renting donkeys from craftsmen and others, which their subsistence wages of one-and-a-half sacks of grain a month could not pay for[109] – a clear case of the exploitation of one group of workers by another.

This already illustrates that we are not talking about one grey mass of unflagging workers. There was a clear differentiation in the wages according to types of work. The basic income of a simple craftsman amounted to 5 kg of wheat and 1.9 kg of barley per day, disbursed in units of five-and-a-half sacks per month. A foreman received seven-and-a-half sacks of wheat, a guard four-and-a-half, a boy two, and an unknown number of servant girls received three sacks between them.[110]

All being well, they could achieve a reasonable level of prosperity. The funeral of an ordinary worker, for example, cost the equivalent of 30 months' wages, which he had to save for during his working life. Where this redistribution system hit a snag, workers could try to improve their living conditions through collective action. For example, we know the first attested strike in world history was by the workmen of Deir el-Medina. When the administrators of this large temple repeatedly failed to distribute the usual quantities of grain to workers, the very principle of redistribution was violated. On the tenth day of the second month of the twenty-ninth year of Ramses III's reign, villagers refused to work any longer for the temple. They presented their case for this radical action: 'It was due to the hunger and thirst that we have come here. There were no clothes, no oil, no fish, and also no vegetables.' They marched in closed formation to the death temples where they held a sit-in. After a number of days, they got their way, but it soon went wrong again. Only resumption of the usual rations could bring an end to the action. There are many known examples of these kinds of strikes, until the dissolution of the village under Ramses XI (1103–1070/69). Although rightly called the first known strike in world history, this first collective action by working people was not about resistance by generally reasonably remunerated wage workers against entrepreneurs; rather, it was about their opposition to failing bureaucrats. Complementary to this is the self-consciousness of the craftsmen: see the following words of one of them just before 2000 BCE:

I know the secret of the hieroglyphs, the composition of ceremonial . . . I am a craftsman who excels in his art and is at the forefront of knowledge. I know how to estimate the proportions of figures and how they should sink and rise when they are sculpted in relief. I know the pose of the male figure and the appearance of the female, the poses of birds and cattle, the submission of an isolated prisoner when one eye sees the other, the gesture of a hunter as he harpoons a hippopotamus, the gait of a runner.[111]

There was no place in this society for large-scale slave labour. There wasn't even a word or a legal category for 'slave'.[112] There was only a more general term, under which all possible forms of dependent work were summarized. These kinds of dependent workers could possess ordinary property, however. Of course, prisoners of war were regularly taken, but they were, as it were, slotted into the existing system. Groups of prisoners of war were collectively housed on domains to deliver their share of corvée. This certainly also included domestic work in the households of senior officials. Furthermore, Egyptians convicted of evading corvée had to perform compulsory labour, and there was also debt bondage, just as in Mesopotamia. There is, however, no evidence for plantations or complete workshops run by slaves, and certainly not for slave markets.[113]

The ultimate proof of a lack of dynamics in the system of tributary-redistributive labour relations in Egypt is provided by the confrontation with the Greek world where, from around 500 BCE, fractional coins were introduced everywhere, as we will see in the next chapter. Although contacts between Egypt and its northern neighbours were intensive and silver had been imported from the Aegean Sea for centuries, this innovation, which spread rapidly throughout the Mediterranean world and the Levant, was initially ignored in Egypt. The *deben* copper weight unit (of 91 grams of copper) was still used as a standard value (or accounting unit), but that was not an existing item and therefore not a means of exchange. What were a means of exchange were cast gold rings, but by nature only the super-elite made use of them, primarily as a store of value.[114]

This only changed a few centuries later, with the conquest of the country by Alexander the Great, and even then still very hesitantly, as we shall see. For thousands of years, Egypt was a powerful state with a high material culture, an early developed writing system and a large degree of division of labour. But it was also a country without significant markets or cities and, consequently, without a demand for means of exchange in the form of money. And without demand, there was no supply.

China

In China, the first single polity that dominated the central and lower parts of the Yellow River basin was created in the Shang period (1600–1050 BCE). In this state, around 1200, Chinese script also developed as a resource for consulting oracles and for registering the results of these predictions.[115] Here, artisans, such as the many specialists in bronze casting, were sponsored and controlled by the state. As there was no formal system for levying taxes, this policy can best be characterized as an 'elite-based redistributive system'. Farmers were organized in work groups, called *zhongren*, which were managed by state officials and supplied with tools produced by the royal workshops. Besides collecting grain in the granaries, acquiring and redistributing salt and exacting corvée for public works, the Shang king led royal hunting expeditions that yielded considerable quantities of meat. The king and his large entourage were sustained during these expeditions by provisions from the local population.[116]

This hunt may also have served as a means of military training, because war was essential to the functioning of the Shang state, if only to provide for large numbers of enemies from the north-west, to be sacrificed in public. Its scale 'positions the Shang as one of the most excessive human-sacrificing polities in world history'.[117] The ceremonial killing of large numbers of people was to demonstrate and reaffirm the power of a king whose position was not institutionalized. When this institutionalization took place during the subsequent Zhou period, the frequency and scale of human sacrifice rapidly declined. We have already seen a similar pattern of bloody state formation in the earliest pharaonic dynasties of Egypt.

In this respect, the transition from the Shang to the Zhou period (1050–221 BCE) meant a great change for prisoners of war, but given that the wars did not stop, the question is, what happened to them? The answer is that they were put to public work en masse. We could, therefore, call them convicts, but since this term is generally used for domestic convicts, the term 'state slaves' is perhaps more appropriate. This probably happened on a modest scale during the Western Zhou (c. 1046–771 BCE), but subsequently expanded enormously – as is well documented for this period – during the Eastern Zhou (770–221). During the Western Zhou, cities were relatively small, mainly centres of aristocratic activity and numbering from several hundred to several thousand families. The largest during the Eastern Zhou, by contrast, counted tens of thousands of families. In any case, the elite had private land ownership under the Zhou. This is apparent from the designated burial grounds that each patrilineal kin now had, but little internal stratification was visible within these lineage cemeteries during the Western Zhou.[118]

We can only guess at the working relationship between farmers and the elite, but the contradictions during the Western Zhou must have been much smaller than those during the subsequent Eastern Zhou and much more pronounced than in the last part of this period, that of the Warring States (453–221 BCE). The major changes in this period, in which Confucius and Mencius emerge, are discussed in the next chapter.

Ӿ

In the millennia between 5000 and 500 BCE, not only did occupational specialization significantly advance, but, in particular, all the different types of labour relations that we know to this day emerged. Within farming societies, the possibilities for labour specialization were still limited. In Chapter 2, we saw, in addition to the original hunter-gatherers, the rise of farmers, while, in this period, alongside independent arable farmers, independent livestock breeders also emerged, as did specialists in metalworking and perhaps also sailors. With the advent of cities, the handful of professions quickly expanded to dozens and perhaps to more than a hundred individual professions. The normative split between typical men's and typical women's activities increased further, also in agriculture, as is visible in Ancient Egypt.

Where farming produced sufficient surpluses, cities could arise. There, the original form of reciprocity was followed up in a system of central tributary redistribution via temples or other central bodies. Strong ideologies defending the sacral position of those at the top of the social pyramid further cemented cooperation by the masses. We saw that most clearly in the Fertile Crescent, but also in the Indus, Yellow River and Yangtze valleys. That changed with the arrival of central states. This system retained its most pronounced tributary-redistributive features in Egypt. In other central states that emerged from the third millennium – directly from city unions in Mesopotamia and China – this redistributive system continued to exist, but it was attacked from all sides. That is to say that the skimming of the surplus became increasingly important and redistribution less and less important, certainly in material terms.

In addition, the employment of slaves arose everywhere, especially in the form of prisoners of war, whose lives were now generally spared. Initially, during the expansion phase of states, enslavement could temporarily take on large forms, but nowhere in this period did it control overall labour relations. And finally, the market was emerging, slowly but surely. That went with trial and error and certainly not in a straight line. Although still a subject of fierce debate among historians, it has now become clear that everywhere where the central authority was losing its grip on power, the opportunity arose for state officials not only to enrich themselves excessively, but especially to appropriate surpluses for themselves by taking control of production. These newly born entrepreneurs could thus outsource work to self-employed people or have it done directly by slaves or freedmen.

Tributary redistribution first occurred in Mesopotamia and, subsequently, in Egypt. Alternatives popped up regularly in both areas but were also reversed again. In Egypt, it remained successful until Greek and Roman rule, but it ended much earlier in Mesopotamia, roughly 3,000 years ago. From around 600 BCE, an irreversible process of marketing goods, services and work took place there. This was facilitated by money, in the form of silver bullion, which had been used for certain transactions for some time. Although copper was present in the Nile Delta, it was only used in limited situations as money of account, and never as a means of exchange. But we must also look beyond Mesopotamia for this important development. At roughly the same time, irreversible marketization was also taking place in China.

The debates about the pace and deepening of the marketing process, and thus about the occurrence of wage labour and about the wage rates of workers, are still ongoing for all three of these areas. The invention and large-scale introduction of currency and, in particular, of small coins – the process of deep monetization – was decisive in this regard. That is the theme of Chapter 4. It is not that the market economy as a universal principle breaks through then, but that it facilitates wage labour, especially, as an indispensable type of labour relations until this day.

In addition to the anthropological analogies that we previously had to rely on in order to know what people at work thought of their activities and their remuneration, evidence of their experiences and feelings emerged. Think of the Egyptian scribes, reflecting upon their own work and that of farmers. Alongside apparent satisfaction about working for a common goal, in turn making clear social distinctions in the form of tributary-redistributive societies acceptable, we also find complaints about unjust treatment, as well as pride in skills. What the enslaved thought remains a mystery, but, judging from what we will hear in the next chapter, we should not assume it was sheer resignation. It is even more difficult to know what men and women thought about gendered divisions of labour within the household – a theme for which the first written evidence only becomes available much later.

4
WORKING FOR THE MARKET, 500 BCE–1500 CE

Labour relations as we know them today developed a few thousand years ago in the first cities and states in Mesopotamia. In addition to the original reciprocity within gangs of hunter-gatherers (Chapter 1) and the independent work of farming households, probably according to the same pattern (Chapters 2 and 3), we witness a rise in tributary redistribution in the oldest cities there (pp. 91–5), and, in the ensuing states, first slavery and gradually also small self-employed producers for the market. Then, from around 1000 BCE the first employers and employees emerged (pp. 96–112). Egypt, however, remained largely committed to tributary redistribution (combined with the enslavement of conquered enemies) until the Hellenistic era, and we can safely assume the same applies later to nascent states in the valleys of the Indus, the Yellow River and the Yangtze, as well as (but without slavery) to most sub-Saharan African agricultural societies.

Sixteenth-century women and men sorting through silver ore at a workshop near the mine in Central Europe.

115

In the two millennia between 500 BCE and 1500 CE, the impetus for market economies, to which we were introduced in the previous chapter, now reached large parts of the population. To this end, new and handy means of payment were introduced in the form of coins with the value of a daily and hourly wage. This most remarkable innovation of small currencies greatly facilitated and promoted wage labour on a large scale (pp. 118–27).

In this chapter, we first follow the development of the earliest deeply monetized societies – the Mediterranean, north India and China – and their labour markets in different parts of Eurasia, with an emphasis on fluctuations between free and unfree labour (pp. 127–48). We then discuss alternatives to these societies: Firstly, the disappearance of the previously highly successful deep monetization in Europe and north India between around 400 and 1100 CE (pp. 148–60). Secondly, market-free, tributary societies such as those we have previously encountered in the Fertile Crescent and Egypt and that now arise independently in the Americas (pp. 160–72). And thirdly, there were, of course, still small-scale societies of hunter-gatherers, albeit increasingly marginal, with or without nascent agriculture, but still without significant state formation. This latter alternative has already been discussed extensively and will therefore not receive separate attention here.

Deeply monetized labour markets could thrive in sustainable, successful (urbanized) states. Interestingly, though, they could also disappear again. This reiterates the fact that it is not always easy to draw long lines of development in the history of work. Even more interesting is the return of monetized labour relations in the cities of India and Europe after 1000 CE (pp. 172–91). From that moment, work and labour relations in all the large cultural and economic centres across Eurasia became increasingly alike, as will become apparent in Chapter 5.

The emergence of deeply monetized labour markets does not mean that wage labour automatically prevailed. Indeed, sometimes it was quite the opposite. In the Greek world in particular the emergence of wage labour paid in small currency and mass unfree labour in the form of slavery appears to have been compatible and, as we shall see, there are also known examples of this elsewhere. Nor does it mean that (despite receiving less attention here) barely urbanized agricultural societies were now devoid of dynamics. Two brief excursions in this introduction must suffice to immediately dispel this misunderstanding.

The great voyages of discovery, which had stagnated thousands of years earlier (see p. 81), were now embarked upon again by farmers who sailed to the last uninhabited islands of the Pacific. Hawaii was finally reached in 800 CE and New Zealand between 1250 and 1300. Some even 'commuted' between Polynesia and South America, centuries before the 'great' European voyages of discovery. This is demonstrated by the spread of the sweet potato and possibly also of the bottle gourd from America to Hawaii, Easter Island and New Zealand. (The debate about possible Polynesian contributions to American cultures is ongoing.[1]) This required crossing thousands of kilometres of water and therefore sophisticated watercraft (outrigger sailing canoes) and exceptional navigational abilities. From the very first discoveries, regular contacts now became possible between these widely divergent islands. As with the emergence of cities elsewhere in the world, this implies a far-reaching division of labour and also a strict hierarchy onboard large ships.[2]

Nomadism also expanded further in various parts of the world. In East Africa, pastoral nomadism surfaces around 1000 CE, in particular the herding of cattle, in this case the long-horned, hump-backed sanga, bred in the uplands of Ethiopia. Riding animals were non-existent, so herders had to walk together with their animals – consequently covering rather short distances. Milk became a staple in their diet, followed by vegetable food (for women more than men; notably, vegetable food was not part of the Maasai diet), meat and blood.

Reindeer herding in the northern Eurasian tundra[3] only became widespread when the Samoyeds (who perhaps had once been red deer herders), under pressure from Turkic-speaking peoples, were forced to move northwards into the taiga. This started around 1000 CE and continued to increase until the beginning of the twentieth century. They would spend four to five months in winter pastures and two months in summer pastures, which meant that the distance of a few hundred kilometres in between had to be bridged in the other five to six months. During this trek, the herds (which varied from a few dozen to a few hundred) were moved every day, but otherwise migrations took place between once and three times a month. The work of reindeer herders' households thus involved moving camp, walking or riding, and meeting the needs of the animals in their care. Their main product, which also dominated their diet, was reindeer meat, supplemented with some plants, game and especially fish, as well as products exchanged with sedentary populations.

While work outside the largest states showed many variations, our attention must now turn to examining more closely the new versions of deeply monetized work in the different states of Eurasia, if only because the modern reader regards it as the most normal thing in the world to receive a wage in the form of an exact sum. We must also explore situations when this might not happen; or when it might not happen according to the agreements made. In this chapter, then, an initial picture of the behaviour of, in particular, self-employed workers and wage labourers emerges, with particular attention for scenarios in which their interests are seriously threatened.

Monetization and the remuneration of labour in Eurasia

The spread of wage labour is not impossible without, but is definitely greatly facilitated by, the invention of coins. Remarkably, in the centuries around 500 BCE, coins – currency in the form of standardized pieces of metal with a value signified by signs (text, figures, images) and guaranteed by the government – appear in three places around the world at roughly the same time (in China, in north India and in Asia Minor), although they were almost certainly 'invented' independently of each other.[4] Apparently identical conditions were met in these places: a sufficiently broad social demand for a manageable, standard means of daily exchange.

What is essential to our history of work is when these means of exchange also represent small values. For the payment of labour that means a value of a daily wage or less. The reason for this is simple: wage workers generally have little or no assets and therefore have limited credit. In practice, a worker can usually go a week (but no longer) without paying for groceries. For example, when he is paid his weekly wage in the form of coins with the value of a day's work, he can pay his various creditors at the end of the week without major problems. The same applies to self-employed producers such as peasants and artisans. Especially this last group cannot live without advances that equate to regular wage payments. Subsequently, we see the emergence of 'change', which greatly facilitates cash payments. In addition to coins with the value of a daily wage, any fully fledged, 'deeply' monetized cash economy must also circulate smaller fractions with the value of an hourly wage or less. These conditions were apparently met in the three afore-mentioned areas in the east, south and west of Eurasia in the centuries from 500 BCE.

This innovation is much more than a simple transition from wage payment in kind to payment in currency. Here, coins not only met a need, but, once in circulation, they, in turn, promoted the expansion of wage labour.

Economies with well-developed currency circulation can legitimately be referred to as a 'market economy'. Wage workers trust that they can do something useful with this money; employers trust that they can use it to attract the right workforce. The market economy is crucial for wage workers and self-employed workers precisely because of the greater freedom that, in principle, it affords them to use the rewards they receive as they see fit.

Comparing this major societal transformation in Greece and India, the English classicist Richard Seaford observes a growing awareness of individuality. In the new society:

> the well-being of the individual depends considerably on commerce, and especially with a *monetised* society, in which the possession of money frees the individual *in principle* (albeit not necessarily in practice) from the need for all socially defined relationships (reciprocity, kinship, ritual, etc.), and in which therefore the individual may seem to depend entirely on his own actions and beliefs, to be an entirely self-sufficient *self* (as opposed to others) and *subject* (as opposed to objects).[5]

West Asia and the Mediterranean

On one level, it is no surprise that coins were invented. After all, the necessary individual ingredients had long been present: the counting, measuring and registering of exchange, including work; payment in kind; and – more importantly – the giro system that resulted from urban development in Mesopotamia. The extraction, processing and purification of precious and base metals dates from even earlier, as does the manufacturing of 'plastic art', that is, carved or moulded objects, especially in the form of cylinder seals with negative images, and the use of 'tokens' (see pp. 92–3). An important step combining some of these elements was the creation of the Mesopotamian system of weights and measures as a condition for an accounting unit that was more detailed, more universal and more abstract than the hitherto gross value units of cows and slaves. This led, in the first instance, to the use of bars, often silver bars, according to the shekel weight system. The use of these silver bars for wage payment, however, was limited: they could be used to pay, at most, a 'gang', but not an individual worker, certainly not per day or per week.[6] The same is true for the first coins, which often still had a very high value, the equivalent of a month's rather than a week's work.

It did not take long, however, for the lower values to become established in most regions. The need for simple means of exchange for wage payments was important, if not decisive. The prevailing alternative explanation for the introduction of coins – the need for means of payment for long-distance trade – is not very likely.[7] Not only did trade exist for thousands of years before the use of coins, but it was by no means always necessary to use coins for long-distance trade, except for clearing (the sudden and imperative settlement of debts). But it is the fact that, from the outset, coins existed almost everywhere in different and especially *smaller denominations* that signals use by ordinary men and women, rather than large-scale trade between rich people. This, of course, also occurred, but, generally, the highest denominations (gold and gross silver) were used for this.

The production of small denominations first occurred in the Mediterranean in the fifth century BCE. Soon after 600 BCE, the first coins were made from electrum (a natural mix of 70 per cent gold and 30 per cent silver) in the kingdom of Lydia in Asia Minor. The lowest denomination (0.15 grams), one-thirty-second part of the largest one, was valued at no less than one-third of a sheep, which suggests that usage of these coins was still limited. In subsequent decades, Greek cities in Asia Minor and across the sea emulated these new means of exchange. In contrast to Persia, where gold darics and silver sigloi of one-twentieth of a daric (more than a soldier's monthly wage) were rarely subdivided, Greek cities produced many denominations from around 500 BCE.[8] Most small silver denominations weighed between one gram and one-quarter of a gram, the smallest only one-twentieth of a gram. This small silver could be used on a daily basis. A day's work (as well as the remuneration for a visit to a prostitute) was reckoned at 3 obols (1 obol = 1/6 drachm = 0.72 grams of silver). The smallest commonly available silver pieces of one-third of an obol therefore equalled roughly 1 hour's work.[9] A few decades later, the Greek cities of southern Italy and Sicily introduced fiduciary bronzes, equivalent in value to the smallest silver fractions but larger in size, so much easier to handle without worrying about losing them. Thus, they significantly facilitated wage payments and especially purchases of food provisions at the market by wage labourers and other low-income workers. However, it was not only small producers like peasants and free labourers who might be paid in cash. Slave owners could hire out their slaves to craftsmen and industrialists or allow them to work for wages on condition that they periodically return a certain sum to their masters (see pp. 138–9).[10]

The state, and in particular the city-state of Athens, was a major payer of money wages, especially through the army and navy.[11] In his last and longest work, the *Laws*, Plato succinctly characterized the situation in the first half of the fourth century: 'Money being necessary in the community for the daily buying and selling of the work of the craftsmen and the payment of wages, coin must be supplied.'[12] Like in Mesopotamia, wage labour was heavily stimulated in the Greek city-states by the great need for military labour, especially in the form of rowers and other crew members for warships.[13] From 480 BCE, Athens took on a leading role in the war against the Persians. As standard, a trireme had 200 men on board, 170 oarsmen from the *thetic* (working) class, each pulling 1 oar (the 62 on the upper level were the most important, followed by 54 each at the middle and lower levels), 6 petty officers, including the piper, 10 deck hands, 10 hoplite soldiers, and 6 archers. On a collision course, they could reach a speed of more than 13 kilometres an hour. This peak speed, whereby each rower developed 1/14 effective horsepower, was unsustainable, of course. Half an hour was already a lot. The triremes did not hold common soldiers, who travelled on troop carriers. Oarsmen were usually hired from the open market – except in case of emergency, as in 428 BCE when 42,000 oarsmen were simultaneously deployed against the Persians, which forced the Athenians to conscript citizens and even *metics* (*metoikoi* in Greek, or resident foreigners) and slaves.

The payment consisted of an advance of one month's pay at the rate of one drachma per man, per day; but during operations, half of the pay was withheld until disembarkation in order to avoid desertions. Leaving aside the risks of this type of work, the pay rate as such was not bad, considering that a minimal food ration cost two obols, or one-third of the daily wage sum. The system worked rather well in the fifth century, but in the fourth the Athenian state lacked funds and left it to the officers to find additional means to pay the men. Plundering friend and foe and exactions from allies became increasingly common. This may not have been very civilized, but we must bear in mind that the crew needed 300 kilos of food and 450 litres of water per day. The logistics of supplying armies on campaign has always been a nightmare, but at sea it is particularly difficult.

Indeed, it would be over very quickly if there were not enough food or water for days. The catastrophes of starvation and desertion were ever imminent for these fleets, ultimately ending in mutinies. Bonuses and advance payments were certainly not a luxury, especially not for the helmsmen and the upper-level oarsmen. A commander summarized the dilemma well in the fourth century BCE: 'For the more ambitious I had been to man my ship with good rowers, by so much was the desertion from me greater than from the other trierarchs. . . . [my oarsmen], trusting in their skill as able rowers, went off wherever they were likely to be re-employed at the highest wages.'[14]

The Greek coin system, with many and, especially, small denominations in different metals, subsequently conquered the western part of Eurasia via the Roman, Byzantine and Arabic empires. In order to better understand the social conditions for the demand for coins, we can learn a lot from a country where this invention was anything but easy. That was Egypt, as already mentioned briefly in Chapter 3 (p. 111).[15] Indeed, despite Egypt's strong links with the Greek world, and therefore also familiarity with the phenomenon of cash payments (in particular for payment of foreign mercenaries and in international trade), the use of money did not penetrate the Nile Delta – in contrast to the rest of the Mediterranean – until very late, and only then very hesitantly. The use of coins was only introduced after Alexander the Great conquered the country in 332 BCE, and initially in a very limited way. How exactly did that happen?

For a long time, coins were not used in what was by far the most important sector: agriculture, with its grain deliveries to the state. Other areas of the economy were monetized successfully only in the third century, in particular those in which Greek immigrants (5–10 per cent of the total population: soldiers and especially city dwellers of, for example, the brand-new Alexandria) were active, as well as in the oil, beer and some textile manufacturing industries, formerly in the hands of the temples, which became state monopolies. In addition to gross silver coins, fiduciary bronze coins also came into circulation in the 260s BCE.[16] This enabled the government to introduce a monetary poll tax, payable in bronze, on all male and female inhabitants. It also stipulated that all cash payments related to the monopolized oil production had to be paid in bronze, as did wage payments for work on infrastructure and on land reclamation in the Fayum Oasis, a desert basin immediately to the west of the Nile, south of Cairo. Initially, the smallest bronze coins (1 *chalkous*) equalled a quarter of a daily wage, or a loaf of bread; the largest (24 *chalkoi*, or 3 obols) half of the salt tax for females and a third that for males.[17] Thus, the simultaneous introduction of a poll tax and a series of five different denominations of bronze coins promoted the introduction of a wage economy where none had previously existed.

Corvée labour, to which the entire population was bound, provides the link between the originally cashless peasant existence of most of the Egyptian population and the cash economy of the cities and towns. Now, under the Ptolemies, this was transformed into compulsory work for a small wage, supplemented by seasonal wage work on estates.[18] Thanks to the large numbers of excavated documents and an excellent study by the German ancient historian Sitta von Reden, we now know that every form of wage labour, self-employment and everything in between occurred in post-Alexander Egypt. The same is true of payment methods. Depending on the circumstances, however, two forms (which, incidentally, can also be combined) dominated: subcontracting and direct employment – labour relations that have parallels in Egyptian tenancy contracts, also from before the Greek period. In addition, the tenant could simply work for his own account and at his own risk and pay a farm rent, or receive seeds and advances for seasonal labour from the landlord, which, of course, could be repaid later.

Subcontracting by an *ergolabos* who sub-employed workers to do the work proper (*locatio-conductio operarum*, in Roman law) mainly occurred in the maintenance of the irrigation system, stone cutting, brick making, construction work, carpentry, pottery, painting, transport and unskilled agricultural work. This could be advantageous for the state or large landowners because the disadvantage of the pre-payment of raw materials, tools and remuneration of labourers was balanced by shifting the recruitment and supervision costs of the workers. This was not without risk, of course, so the failure to finish the contract or to return any tools was made punishable with imprisonment.

Direct employment of wage labourers meant that the employer bore the costs of supervision himself, but could therefore monitor costs (subcontractors were only too happy to come up with extra work) and working methods and manage materials more precisely: 'So, direct-labour contracts prevail in the domestic context and in the care of domestic animals (horses, birds and dogs), as well as in all non-productive businesses, such as scribal and managerial jobs in a private and public context ... *ergolabiai* were preferred in any kind of productive activity, especially if this involved large groups (or "gangs") of workers.'[19]

Of course, hybrid forms also occur, and the same applies to the ways in which wages were paid: in money (*opsônion*), in food (*sitometria*, as in the pre-Greek period) or, most of the time, in both. The real level of the reward is conditional, of course, not least because monetary wages varied according to the work completed, but also because the quality of the grain used for *sitometria* was based on the status of the recipient. Daily rations were handed out in the form of bread, monthly ones in the form of flour. Traditional beer was no longer included and, like oil and linen clothing, often had to be bought at the market. The monthly *sitometria* 'was roughly sufficient for the upkeep of two people' and, given that, in the third century BCE, 'married couples and small families were by far the most typical household', it appears to have been a basic family income. Wages were usually paid as a combination of this food allowance and cash money, but real earnings were generally stable, given that the price of grain in this period barely fluctuated. Perhaps that is why we rarely hear about strikes, certainly not in connection with wage levels.[20]

The market continued to expand in late-Ptolemaic and Roman Egypt, also in villages.[21] In the Roman era, private land ownership increased to perhaps half of all tilled ground in the Fayum Oasis and three quarters in the Nile Valley. These landowners cultivated part of the land themselves and leased out other parts. The latter also happened with public land. In all cases, farmers had to hand over part of their harvest to the state, as was usual in Pharaonic times. That could be done directly on the village threshing floor, but the farmer could also deliver it to the public granary. In addition, tenants, insofar as they cultivated grain, paid their rent in kind to the landlord; for other crops, in particular fodder, which was much in demand in Egypt, they paid rent in money. As we have seen, they also needed money to pay the poll tax, for which all men aged 14 to 62 were liable. Smallholders therefore had to sell a share of their harvest on the market to get the necessary cash, or they also had to spend part of their time in paid employment on larger farms. Moreover, they could become heavily dependent on landlords by taking loans from them. The same could happen with wage workers. Of course, where large landowners exploited their lands themselves, such as one Appianus in Fayum in the third century CE, many workers were necessary[22] – many, but with a great variety in skills and levels of remuneration. So, slave labour did not play a significant role in this, but rather that of resident permanent workers (largely paid in kind), permanent but non-resident workers and casual labourers who were only paid in money, both by the hour and in piecework. The latter could easily make up more than half of the total workforce during harvest time.[23]

We do not know much more about the introduction of a money economy in the rest of the Mediterranean region than we do about those in Ptolemaic and Roman Egypt, but it is certain that, simultaneous to the use of cash, labour relations changed considerably there too. Later, we will discuss the relationship between free and unfree labour in these market economies. First, however, we must turn our gaze to the East, towards north India and towards China. Did the introduction of (small) money there have similar implications to those in the West?

India

As much as we know about the introduction of a money economy in the Mediterranean and, in particular, in Egypt, we know very little about the same phenomenon in India. But this does not make it any less important. The first occurrence and distribution of coins has now been dated a bit more clearly, but we are left largely guessing about its relationship to work. Although there were certainly contacts between West and South Asia around 500 BCE (for example, Indian mercenaries served in the Persian armies),[24] it is nevertheless likely that the invention of coins in north India occurred largely or even entirely independently. In particular, the totally different form that they took there – punch-marked or cast and often rectangular instead of mostly round, die-struck coins – points in that direction.

In the wake of a period of rapid urbanization and the extension of private property in the course of the fifth century BCE, north-west India (including what today is Pakistan) made the move from large silver coins to lower values.[25] From then on, 'bent bar'-type coins of a lower grade and minted fractions thereof also circulated.[26] These fractions are particularly important here: in addition to the standard of a siglos of 5.5 grams, there were not only double sigloi, but also half, quarters and even smaller fractions put into circulation, pieces of up to a twentieth and a fortieth of a siglos (0.13 grams): in total, no less than eight different denominations. At roughly the same time, minted coins appeared in other parts of north India too, sometime large ones, sometimes also smaller ones, but in the absence of systematic excavations and the registration of finds and a lack of written sources, there is little more to be said about this. What is significant, however, was the introduction everywhere of copper coins alongside the extant silver ones, evidently with the same practical advantages noted in the aforementioned Mediterranean case. So, what were they used for?

Some rare texts from the early years of the Maurya Empire (c. 321–185 BCE), especially the *Arthashastra*, provide economic information. The earliest known version of this important text is from the third century CE, but it is not clear what has been added to the original and precisely when in the five centuries since it was written. The text distinguishes between slaves, bonded labourers, unpaid labourers who worked in lieu of paying a tax or fine, casual labourers working for wages, piece-rate workers, individuals working for a regular wage and the self-employed. Paying out these wages and spending them in the market apparently posed no serious problems. Besides the silver *karshapana* of 3.5 grams and three fractions (the smallest, of 1/8 *pana*, weighed 0.44 grams), there were also four copper fractions ranging from 1/16 down to 1/128 *pana*. As the *Arthashastra* suggests that the lowest paid state servants received a cash wage of 5 *pana* per month, the hourly wage must have been about 5/200 = 1/40 *pana*; consequently, the smallest copper fraction equalled one-third of an hour's work. The highest paid bureaucrats received 800 times more and the famous prostitute Ambapali charged 50 *karshapana* a night.[27]

After the collapse of the Maurya Empire, a period of political fragmentation followed in the Gangetic plain, but with a 'concomitant spurt in urbanization with an increase in localized money economy'.[28] Comparable movements in the south of the sub-continent and on Sri Lanka, in which merchant guilds and Buddhist monasteries played a leading role, were only visible centuries later (see pp. 159–60).[29]

China

Fortunately, our knowledge of the introduction of coins in China and their usage is much better documented; indeed, rather excitingly, more sources become available every day. At the same time, this makes everything that follows provisional.[30] Cowrie shells and their bone and later bronze imitations (including 'ant-nose' coins), miniaturized spade blades (farming hoes) and bronze knives were used as burial gifts long before they functioned as units of account, let alone as means of exchange.

However, the flat, round cast bronze objects with a square hole, originally weighing 8 grams and bearing the characters *banliang* ('half-*liang*'), certainly may be considered as coins. It has recently been convincingly demonstrated that they were introduced by the western state of Qin around 350 BCE.[31] In the following century, in the north-east, competing systems of three-denominational spade money (the smallest was of the same weight as the *banliang*) and one-denominational knife money gave way to the *banliang*. This had already happened before the unification of China by the Qin, finally achieved in 221 BCE. Only in the south did cowries, imported from the Indian Ocean to Yunnan (probably from the twelfth century), subsequently sustain their monetary function for the next 500 years.[32]

Labour markets, currencies and society, 500 BCE–400 CE: China, Ancient Greece and Rome, India

With a little licence, we could say that, thanks to deep monetization, the labour market reached maturity in the main cultural centres of Eurasia between roughly 500 and 300 BCE. In a manner of speaking, it was only a matter of spreading the good news over the rest of the Old World, and then, of course, waiting for Columbus, before the remainder of humanity would also benefit from these institutional innovations. But the history of work is not that simple. The problem with such automacy is twofold. Firstly, deeply monetized societies can place large groups of workers outside the labour market (but not outside the market economy), especially those forced to work without being offered a notable monetary reward; and secondly, societies of this kind can also demonetize again.

History provides us with examples of both phenomena. The mix of free and unfree labour in deeply monetized societies will be dealt with in the following two sections, on the basis of three cases: the degree to which the state claimed labour for China; the issue of slavery among Greeks and Romans; and the emergence of the caste society in India. Chapter 4 (pp. 156–60) then follows the phenomenon of dramatic demonetization in the west and south of Eurasia between around 400 and 1100 CE – this is in sharp contrast to the greater continuity and prosperity witnessed in the Middle East and China.

State and market in China

In comparison to other parts of Eurasia, China is unique in maintaining a virtually mono-denominational system of very low value coins (equal to an hourly wage),[33] deliberately fiduciary in character, albeit with ups and downs over two millennia. Their production and circulation was on an almost industrial scale.[34]

What kind of society needed such means of exchange for daily use? The answer can only be that there are a number of different possibilities, ranging

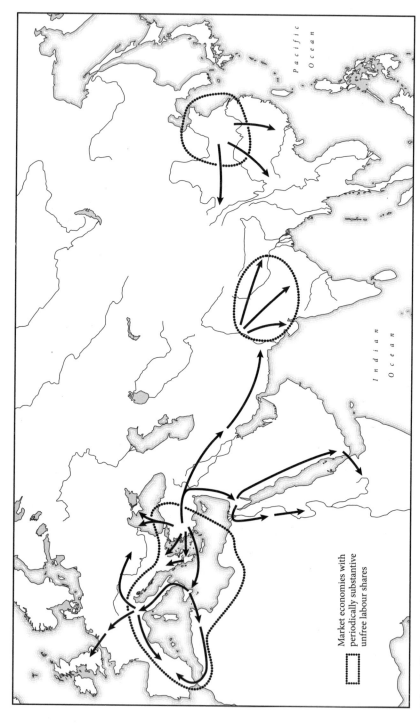

Map 4. Deep monetization, 500 BCE–400 CE.

from oppressive state interference in labour to a benevolent government. The Qin state is well-known for the immense 'Terracotta Army' that accompanied the First Emperor of China at his funeral in 210 BCE, as well as for the Great Wall. It is not by chance that it is characterized as one big 'command economy' and as one of the most successful war machines in ancient history. Little wonder, then, that Chairman Mao identified himself with the First Emperor.[35]

But that is only one part of the story.[36] By 350 BCE, the Qin was economically very successful, although not yet overstretching the capacities of its population as it would do at the moment of its sudden demise one-and-a-half centuries later. Unfortunately, the situation of the working population at the beginning of Qin is much less clear than in its final years, when the Great Wall, roads, canals, palaces and the Terracotta Army were being constructed simultaneously. We may therefore suppose that, only from this time, the economy was highly centralized.

Around 350 BCE, Duke Xiao, who ruled the Qin during the Warring States period (from 361 to 338 BCE), assisted by the statesman and thinker Shang Yang, introduced many institutional innovations in addition to the *banliang*, including a new fiscal system, weights and measures, conscription for the army and public works. Waged work became important, but less as part of a market economy (there was no land market) than as part of state-induced payments for conscripts for the army and public works.[37] The military was organized in a meritocratic way, inducing more social mobility than in the previous centuries. The government even defined one of its main tasks as being to 'love the people below'.[38] All economic activities, from agriculture and iron tool fabrication to public works, were either in state hands or closely supervised by the state. In the end, no less than 15–30 per cent of the male productive population was conscripted or directly involved in public works. As we have seen, they were paid in cash, but the archaeologist Gideon Shelach-Lavi, who made these estimates, makes the following comments:

This is a very high proportion of the workforce to have been taken out of the production of food and basic resources under great pressure. The indirect burden of the projects must also have been quite severe. Regardless of whether the people working on them were convicts or conscripts, or even if they were artisans that received payment for the work they did, the need to equip, feed, clothe and house them, even at a minimal level, must have been very expensive. We do not even have to estimate that taxes reached rates of up to 60 per cent in order to see that the burden on the peasants may well have been extremely heavy.[39]

Besides, those unwilling to obey the rules were punished with forced labour, a number of them even made state slaves in perpetuity.[40]

While initially this system appeared to be functioning well and guaranteed work and income for a sizeable part of the population, it ended in a nightmare in the hubristic final years of the Qin Dynasty.[41] The Han successors (206 BCE–222 CE) apparently sought to maintain many of the good aspects of the system, while avoiding the worst aberrations, in part by sacrificing efficiency.[42] There was still mass conscription for public work, but it was now restricted to thirty days during the period that peasants were free from the most urgent and time-consuming tasks on their farms. The Han also issued a new type of cash coins, the *wuzhu* (5 zhu, a weight term), successors and essentially similar to the *banliang*, but bearing a different text and weighing only around 3 grams. Salaries of 200 coins per month seem to have been the norm at this point, which, as was the case with the *banliang*, suggests a value of 1 hour's work.[43] The *wuzhu* production was enormous: 230 million pieces cast every year, or 4 per capita, which means a circulation of hundreds of *wuzhu* per capita around the beginning of the current era.[44] This is the best indicator of how widespread the monetary economy had become, in particular for the remuneration of work. What proportion may be considered self-employed work is hard to say, although given that the majority of the population were peasants, it is safe to say that it would have been significant. However, in the government sector, and now also in the private sector, there must also have been a considerable amount of wage work. Meanwhile, slavery was insignificant, though not convict labour.[45]

We find a strong opinion about the relationship between the state and the market with regard to labour from the famous historian Sima Qian (*c.* 145–86 BCE), who, based on the vicissitudes of China in the previous centuries, came to the following conclusion:

> Society obviously must have farmers before it can eat; foresters before it can extract timber resources; artisans before it can have manufactured goods; and merchants before they can be distributed.

But once these exist, what need is there for government directives, mobilizations of labor, or periodic assemblies? Each man has only to be left to utilize his own abilities and exert his strength to obtain what he wishes. Thus, when a commodity is cheap, it invites a rise in price; when it is very expensive, it invites a reduction. When each person works away at his own occupation and delights in his own business then, like water flowing downward, goods will naturally flow forth ceaselessly day and night without having been summoned, and the people will produce commodities without having been asked. Does this not tally with reason? Is it not a natural result?[46]

Another Chinese literate preferred to point to reality, rather than theory, and expressed compassion for his toiling compatriots. Po Chü-I (806 CE) voiced his doubts about fair compensation in the poem 'Watching the Reapers':

Tillers of the earth have few idle months;
In the fifth month their toil is double-fold.
A south wind visits the fields at night;
Suddenly the ridges are covered with yellow corn.
Wives and daughters shoulder baskets of rice,
Youths and boys carry flasks of wine,
In a long train, to feed the workers in the field—
The strong reapers toiling on the southern hill,
Whose feet are burned by the hot earth they tread,
Whose backs are scorched by the flames of the shining sky
Tired they toil, caring nothing for the heat,
Grudging the shortness of the long summer day.
A poor woman with a young child at her side
Follows behind, to glean the unwanted grain.
In her right hand she holds the fallen ears,
On her left arm a broken basket hangs.
Listening to what they said as they worked together
I heard something that made me very sad:
They lost in grain-tax the whole of their own crop;
What they glean here is all they will have to eat.
And to-day—in virtue of what desert
Have I never once tended field or tree?

My government-pay is three hundred 'stones';
At the year's end I have still grain in hand.
Thinking of this, secretly I grew ashamed
And all day the thought lingered in my head.[47]

A triumph of the (labour) market over the state, as advocated by Sima Qian, never fully and definitively occurred in China. An in-depth study of artisans in Han China by Professor of Early Chinese History Anthony Barbieri-Low reveals how important the work of conscripted artisans, convicted-criminal artisans and government slave artisans – alongside that of free workers – was in the centuries around the beginning of our era. This was no coincidence. In his words:

> [H]igh-level officials in charge of public works projects in early China used a cost-benefit analysis when determining the number, season, work duration, and assigned tasks for these different labor pools.... The cost of each labor group would be weighted and combined to arrive at a grand total of person-days needed for the project. The standard quotas for each group were strictly codified in writing: a certain amount of work expected in spring as opposed to winter; one woman can embroider as much as one man; a free artisan can accomplish as much as four convict artisans on skilled tasks.... As an imperial bureaucratic state, the early Chinese empire was ruled, not by autocrats waving royal scepters or by scholars brandishing moral texts, but by brush-pushing functionaries wielding information. Their databases consisted mostly of names attached to numbers: household registers, size and quality of land holdings, number of adult males liable for service, number of homeless migrants, etc. From this mountain of information, mind-boggling in its size and complexity for a precomputer age, grew the power to control the known world.[48]

The Han were the true successors to the Qin in this bureaucratic sense. Later dynasties were sometimes just as powerful, but often also much weaker. They were all variations on the theme of labour mobilization via direct recruitment by the state and, moreover, via the market.

The implications of all this are great and fit into one of the most important debates in social history that is directly related to the history of work: about the nature of classical antiquity, between the followers of

Michael Ivanovitch Rostovtzeff on one side and Karl Polanyi and Moses I. Finley on the other, a debate that has recently opened for classical China too.[49] The so-called Modernists 'argued that ancient economic life was very much like a budding version of our own, ruled by market-driven prices, high levels of monetization, productive cities and far-flung trade – all the hallmarks of incipient capitalism'. Against these Modernists, the Primitivists, who had the upper hand for several decades from the 1960s, contended that 'agriculture, and not commerce, was the dominant form of economic activity in Greece and Rome . . . that private trade was carried out only on a minimal scale, and usually only in luxuries . . . that Roman towns and cities . . . [were] parasitic centers of consumption and redistribution and not . . . productive industrial centers . . . [that] individuals were most concerned with gaining status, and [that] loans and investment were not made for economic purposes.'[50]

Meanwhile, the Modernist camp prevails once again, although it now seems that there is a synthesis that provides inspiration for new research. In the next section, we will encounter the fresh approach of Catharina Lis and Hugo Soly, who have written extensively on work and workers in pre-industrial Europe, but here we can summarize using the words of Barbieri-Low, who places himself 'squarely in the camp of the Modernists' in his study of artisans in Han China:

Many scholars now recognize that all economies since the rise of state-level societies display some level of commercialization, craft specialization, and market integration, alongside varying amounts of reciprocity, redistributive allocations, and state control. At different times, and under different historical circumstances, these variables might be located at different positions on a scale, though in no sense is the history of past economies a determined, unilinear trajectory.[51]

Barbieri-Low has incontrovertibly substantiated this position for China; below, I will show that this approach is fruitful for classical antiquity too. We will examine the extent to which it also applies to the third great classical monetary economy, India, and what the situation was regarding non-monetized economies following the emergence of state-level societies in pre-Columbian South and Central America and possibly in sub-Saharan Africa.

Monetization, free and unfree labour among Greeks and Romans

In the Greek world, independent, self-sufficient farmers dominated until around 500 BCE. Those lacking sufficient land sent expeditions to found 'colonies' elsewhere. Thus, Greek culture spread from the Aegean coasts to those of the Black Sea and the Mediterranean, with a heavy concentration in south Italy and Sicily. These Greeks were thus not only farmers but at the same time also sailors and soldiers.

The relationship between free and unfree labour has not been elaborated better for any civilization than it has for classical antiquity, that is for the countries around the Mediterranean and for the millennium from 500 BCE to 500 CE. For a long time, historians had established two characteristics in this regard: that the Greeks and Romans despised physical labour, and, consequently, that their economy leaned heavily on slave labour. Although it is not difficult to find examples and citations for both propositions among the great classical writers, the characterization of society as a whole being based on this must now be seriously questioned.[52]

Let us start with classical notions about work.[53] From a societal perspective, not only the traditional warrior was held in high regard, as in Homer's *Iliad* and *Odyssey*, but also his alter ego, the farmer. (After all, fighting wasn't a full-time occupation.) This ideal was intoned beautifully in *The Works and the Days* by the ancient Greek poet Hesiod. Productive labour was a core value in Greek thinking, with the legendary work of Hercules perhaps the most demonstrative expression of this. Greek expansion and colonization soon went from an extensive to an intensive phase, in which the Greek city-state, the *polis*, was central. The city-state was increasingly populated by people other than farmers, especially self-employed artisans and wage labourers (for the slaves who were also there, see below).

With the rise of this non-agrarian workforce, the problem then emerged of how to adapt existing political relations, with the bravest warriors at the top of society, to the new reality. This led to another invention, that of the famous Greek democracy (with the caveat that by no means all Greek city-states were democratic). Initially, this meant that political power no longer belonged only to the bully boys, but to all adult male household heads with their own farming business. After all, they were uniquely prepared to personally defend their farms and fields full of crops. Later, other male citizens followed, in their most radical form in Periclean Athens. With the citizenship law of 451/450 BCE, reiterated in 403/402, they even received an allowance to compensate for loss of income when attending political meetings and fulfilling political appointments. Thus, in this phase wage workers could also participate in democracy. According to conservative estimates, these wage workers and their housemates may have made up a third of the population around 400 BCE.[54]

But this shift caused some consternation among a number of controversial supporters of the old elite. Their most talented spokespersons said that only men who were not dependent on labour for their income were truly free to serve the common good. Wage workers were excluded. In that context, they reacted harshly to anyone who earned an income with their hands, and wage workers were, as it were, swept onto a pile along with slaves. The writers of the great tragedies, Sophocles and Euripides, the famous philosophers Plato and Aristotle and, in their wake, Xenophon, the Stoics and also the fathers of the Christian church and the scholastics, all defended the system of slavery, sometimes using racist arguments (Hellenes versus Barbarians), sometimes with arguments blaming the slave himself for his fate (lack of courage to die when imprisoned). The Cynics took an intermediate position, keeping open the possibility that an externally bound individual could still be free within. In any case, this starting point opens the door to a de facto recognition of the human nature of a slave, and therefore of his rights as a human. Only a handful of Sophists assumed a natural, inherent freedom, bestowed on every person by the gods. Indeed, the only people to reject slavery at this time came from within this philosophical school.

Because of the influence (which should not be underestimated) of authors such as Plato and Aristotle on classical thinking in later centuries – first in the Hellenistic and the Roman Empire and later in the Renaissance and in Western thinking generally (including the classically educated Karl Marx) – the widespread opinion has taken hold that the Greeks (and their students the Romans) were disdainful of wage labour. However, it is to the great merit of the aforementioned Lis and Soly that they have demonstrated that this view must be placed in a very specific context and certainly has no general validity.

On the contrary, entirely in line with Hesiod's glorification of farming, the talent and the dedication of the artisan and everyone who worked in the Greek world was appreciated and, indeed, praised – not only by big names such as the playwrights Aristophanes, Aeschylus and Euripides and philosophers such as Thales of Miletus, Protagoras, Democritus (remembered for his atomic theory of the universe) and the school of Sophists, but also by craftsmen themselves. This is most clearly reflected in the names that some put on their products.[55] Painters signed famous Athenian vases, sculptors their statues and some medallists signed coins, but less talented people were not left behind either. Professional pride must have been widespread, also among women. We know of examples of gravestones featuring professions such as priestess, midwife, nurse and even wool worker, jobs that were generally kept strictly within a household.

But was there really so much free labour in classical antiquity? Was slavery not dominant, as so many textbooks would have us believe? Slightly before and then contemporaneously with slavery, free labour became important in the classical period, dominated by several thousand Greek city-states around the Mediterranean and the Black Sea. An analysis of occupational titles in classical Athens suggests that 10,000 free citizens could be found in the non-agricultural sector, which contained as many unfree labourers; 170 different occupations are mentioned in the sources for this sector alone. Such extensive horizontal specialization of labour made it inevitable that the individual would need to acquire goods and services outside his immediate circle of friends, neighbours and family, and these craftsmen and merchants were the main users of coins and small change.[56] To what extent these people can be called wage labourers depends on how precisely their workshops were organized. Were they all independent small craftsmen who owned their own workshop, or did some of them work for others in exchange for wages – either as journeymen or as subcontractors?

Before the introduction of coins in the Greek *polis*, apart from a handful of skilled craftsmen, free labour existed only in the form of the *thetes*, who received regular sustenance from his employer in exchange for any work that was needed from time to time.[57] Unlike slaves, *thetes* could leave their employers, but most of the time that was not a real option. The introduction of money changed that, not because a new labour relationship had become possible, 'but because what could have been clumsy and rare became simplified and common'. *Thetes* ceased to exist as a category of workers and were replaced by others, called *penetes*, *latreis*, or *misthotoi*. They were often but not necessarily hired by the day,[58] worked individually or in gangs, and their wages were stipulated either by the day, by the *prytany* (one tenth of a year) or by the job.

Although wages in classical Greece were definitely an urban rather than a rural phenomenon, the cash nexus had a deeper impact on the countryside than might be expected at first glance.[59] The Greek peasantry operated on the basis of the contributions of all household members. Slaves were certainly not absent, as we will see, but their significance was limited in the countryside, and although many a peasant family sought to own a slave, it was difficult for most to buy one because, generally, slaves were not that cheap (roughly a craftsman's annual earnings). Peasants rather looked for alternative strategies to mitigate the risks of disappointing harvests, for example, by doing paid work for local patrons in times of emergency, who, in turn, were expected to assist their clients by offering seasonal wage labour. A more general strategy for younger family members, and particularly boys and men, was to perform wage labour elsewhere, especially rowing, mercenary service and also shepherding.

The crucial role that rowing in the state navy played in the introduction of the monetary economy has already been elaborated upon above with respect to Athens. Not only the labour markets for rowers but also those for mercenaries were thriving, and for the willing they offered work, wages and food. And it wasn't just in Athens. It has been estimated that, in any given year, between half and three-quarters of a million rowers were needed by states and private individuals throughout the Greek world. Furthermore, the demand for mercenaries, which dates back to the seventh century BCE, increased strongly in the bellicose fourth century and grew steadily thereafter. The nature of this demand for rowers and mercenaries has been described as 'a rather large and amorphous labor market constantly fluctuating in size and varying from place to place; yet, in aggregate, it produced a rather constant demand'.[60]

It was not just in the Greek world that free wage labour (both part- and full-time) was much more common than frequently thought; it was also the case in the Roman Empire. The best known, of course, are the endless numbers of Roman legionaries who were paid as professional soldiers for their services, partly in the form of board and lodging, partly in cash. During the Republic, soldiering earned about one silver denarius coin per three days; after Caesar's victorious return from Gaul, he raised the pay of a soldier to about one denarius every two days.[61]

But wage labourers and self-employed smallholders frequently occurred outside the army too, particularly in agriculture. At the same time, in the classical Mediterranean and Middle East, we also find slave labour in the countryside, but there are huge regional and temporal variations.[62] On the one hand, we have states like currency-void Sparta, where all work for the elite, concentrated in the town, was performed by slaves (*helots*). Something similar happened on Crete and in some other regions. On the other hand, there were many polities where unfree labour represented a small minority of the rural workforce. In general, the more successful a polity was economically, the greater the chance that it depended not only on free but also on unfree labour. At the top stood Attica and its main city Athens. Not only the 1,200 Athenian elite households depended for an important part of their income on slave labour in their sweatshops in town, in their silver mine concessions and on their farms, but also many other free citizens. Craftsmen and medium farmers could own a slave or two. In the fourth century BCE as much as one-third of the total population of Attica may have consisted of slaves. Not only Attica had a major slave population, but also Corinth and Aegina. This list is certainly not exhaustive. To the outer limits of the 'Greek' world, for example, in present-day Yemen and Ethiopia, thriving economies depended on the import of slaves.[63]

The supply of captives depended on a well-established maritime network of slave traders and their suppliers – especially pirates and warlords in Thrace (the eastern Balkans) and Phrygia in Anatolia, and in the western Mediterranean a similar network existed in the Punic world of Carthage. In sum, in the Greek world, consisting of over 1,000 *poleis*, comparative costs and output for the elites (and sub-elites) of slaves, tenants and wage labourers determined the proportion between these main categories of people providing agricultural work.

In the heyday of the Roman slave system in the second and first centuries BCE, the total slave population in Italy reached 2 or 3 million in a total population of 6 to 7.5 million (similar to the 32 per cent in the antebellum south of the US).[64] Slavery could not exist without free wage labour by smallholders at times when demand for labour peaked, especially during the harvest. Moreover, free labour dominated the urban scene, and many of these labourers were freedmen – former slaves. The famous *frumentatio* (the subsidized food price system for citizens of Rome) certainly made the employed unskilled labourer's daily wage of three-quarters of a denarius far from insignificant.[65] Perhaps work incentives even diminished after this special system was extended from grain to essentials such as free oil at the turn of the second century, or free wine in the early 270s CE. But the city of Rome was not the empire.

Free labour was not only complementary to slave labour, it was also a necessary incentive if slavery was to be maintained. As Xenophon aptly remarked: 'slaves, more than free men, need hope'.[66] This meant the hope of release, *manumissio*. This could be a generous act by their master, for example as a reward for loyal service, or, for a female slave, when a master officially wanted to marry her. But in addition to good behaviour, a slave was sometimes in a position to buy his freedom with saved money. In this regard, the Romans had the system of *peculium* and *praepositio*.[67] Like among Greek and earlier forerunners, this meant that slaves – especially the professionals among them, and certainly those with managerial skills – received permission to work for others and even to keep part of their earnings themselves. In this way, they could save for their release, and thus slaves could also participate in the money economy.

From the third century CE onwards, deep monetization suggests the increase of free wage labour. The production of medium and small denominations was restricted to debased *antoniniani*, and later to even smaller and uniform copper coins. In that respect, the western parts of the late Roman Empire came to resemble China, with its one denomination copper currency. In the east of the empire, the growing demand for small change, and thus the occurrence of free labour, is suggested by the replacement of local mint houses with new and extensive imperial minting houses after 270 CE. That was the time when urban decline in Thrace, Macedonia and Gaul coincided with urban prosperity and a thriving construction industry in Asia Minor and North Africa. It is also in these towns that we find guild-like collegia of artisans.[68]

But no matter which way we look at it, slavery, although not dominant, was and remained – albeit to varying degrees – an essential component of classical society. Where did it come from and how did it develop? In the period described by Homer and Hesiod, slavery only occurred on a small scale.[69] The palace of Odysseus, with its fifty palace slaves, is a good example of the slave-keeping elite. The sixth and fifth centuries BCE, however, saw the large colonization movement that distributed boatloads of Greeks from the Black Sea in the north-east to Marseille and Spain in the south-west, with Sicily and south Italy the core area for new colonists. Carthaginians did the same, and eventually the Romans followed in their footsteps.[70] The nature of colonization, together with the fact that, according to historian Tracey Rihll, 'much free land was available overseas, usually after the natives were captured, killed or expelled', led to slavery on a grand scale.

Rihll's theory that this colonization movement is related to the rise of the money economy and the emergence of democracy is interesting but speculative. After all, the availability of unfree labour also led to a coarsening of morals among free Greeks. This *hybris* (premeditated humiliation with violence) had to be restrained, otherwise the Greek city-states were threatened with falling apart. After experiments with a *tyrannos*, many Greek *poleis* came up with a form of democracy of free men as the best protection against mutual arbitrariness. Again in the words of Rihll: 'Ancient Greece was the first genuine slave society, and also the first political society. This was not coincidental. But slaves did not simply allow the classical Greeks the leisure time to participate in politics; rather, and more significantly, the growth of slavery in the archaic period prompted the Greeks to invent politics.'[71]

The importance of slavery fluctuated significantly in Athens, with slave numbers decreasing from 25,000 in the second half of the fifth century to an insignificant number after the Peloponnesian War ending in 404 BCE. Slave numbers grew again to more than 30,000 in the mid-fourth century, after which they declined to 20,000 at the time of Alexander the Great. One of the reasons for such great oscillations, apart from the political ups and downs in Athens, was the rule that children of free fathers and slave mothers took the status of the father.[72] Slave numbers increased sharply in the Hellenistic era due to the mass numbers of prisoners of war created first by Alexander and his successors, and later resulting from the Carthaginians' and Romans' conquest of Italy and mutual wars (in which ultimately the Carthaginians came off worst). The falling price of slaves in these centuries is illustrative.[73] In addition to this large supply, there was also a considerable demand for labour. Thus, Roman (smallholder) farmers and artisans were called on to serve in the army, for example in the Punic wars. This created a great need for substitute labour. We see the pinnacle of slavery in agriculture in the last two centuries before our era, as a direct consequence of the expansion of the Roman Empire, but above all in the crafts – because workshops were easier to supervise and more profitable – mining and shipbuilding as well as domestic slavery (here and elsewhere, having a slave was also a status symbol). They were also used as camp followers in the army, but as soon as slaves were needed to actively fight, they had to be made free.[74]

As we have seen, in the period 100 BCE to 50 CE, 30 to 40 per cent of the population of Italy were slaves, but for the whole empire it would not have been more than about a sixth, divided equally between men and women. To maintain these gigantic numbers, 500,000 new slaves were needed annu-ally.[75] A little less than half were available through natural reproduction, the rest came through enslavement. It is striking that by far the majority of this last group came from within the empire, with abandoned newborns providing an important supply. No wonder, then, that in this period of rapid acceleration, and especially of first-generation slaves who had known freedom, large slave revolts erupted, beginning with that between 198 and 184 BCE. The first (135–132 BCE), second (104–101 BCE) and third (73–71 BCE) servile wars in central and south Italy radiating out to Greece and Asia Minor are well known. The last, and the most famous, was that of Spartacus.[76]

Spartacus served as a cavalryman with the Thracian auxiliaries of the Romans. However, when they were deployed against the Maidi, Spartacus's own folk, he deserted. He was quickly captured and sold as a slave, aged about 25 years old. Subsequently, unlike most slaves, who were put to work in agriculture, he ended up, via Rome, in the privately owned gladiator arena of Capua. There he was forced to entertain the public in mano-a-mano fights that ended only after one had perished. By the spring of 73 BCE, he had had enough. Together with seventy fellow slaves, Spartacus escaped and headed towards Vesuvius, where he was soon joined by other slaves – in particular from Gaul, Germania and Thrace, who were more than happy to abandon their forced labour in the *villae* specializing in vines, olives and cereal crops – as well as by a number of free day labourers. Spartacus quickly emerged as a true general with trained and well-armed troops, at their peak 40,000 strong. For two years he managed to deceive and even defeat various Roman legions, until he was killed in battle in late March–early April 71 BCE. Remnants of his army continued to skirmish for more than ten years. The punishment for prisoners was horrible: 6,000 Spartacists were crucified along the 200-kilometre-long Via Appia from Capua to Rome.

Like a second Hannibal, Spartacus's aim was to bring the Roman Republic to its knees. Although his troops largely consisted of runaway rural slaves (who never linked up with those from the city), his objective was not to abolish slavery, let alone to overthrow class society, as many from the nine-teenth century onwards have suggested.[77] He did, however, clearly envisage a more egalitarian society of olden times. The spoils of war were distributed equally under Spartacus's supporters, and gold and silver traders did not enter his camp.[78] Perhaps important in this context is that he was accompa-nied from Thrace by his wife, a Dionysian priestess. This could have a deeper significance, given that there may already have been a link 'between rebel slave culture and Dionysian religiosity':

> a core of emotions and desires crystallizing around an ambiguous but potent message of liberation and subversion, capable of spreading from the lowest and most marginalized strands of society to the slave world itself. ... Spartacus' priestess companion would in this case have reaffirmed such a tie, and should have done so in a particularly suggestive way, given that, like Spartacus, she came from Thrace, where Dionysius was, in a sense, the 'national' god.[79]

With the Pax Romana, of course, an important source of slaves recruited for the empire dried up, although enslaved foundlings in particular remained a crucial alternative source. We therefore see a transition in agriculture to tenancy and sharecropping. According to some, the slave population at the beginning of our era still comprised 15 to 20 per cent of the total population of the Roman Empire. Others, such as the American Professor of Classics Kyle Harper, place this slightly lower, at 10 to 15 per cent and, for the fourth century, no more than 10 per cent.[80] According to Harper, this slave population would have remained at the same level for centuries through natural growth, and not because of waging war, as is often claimed.[81] A third of slaves were employed on specialized farms that produced for the market, as opposed to two-thirds in the households of the rich and, especially, the super-rich. In both cases, sexual service was part of their work, especially for young slaves.[82] Harper's main conclusion, however, is that the Romans were forced to maintain slavery despite the high costs because of the scarcity and therefore the expensiveness of wage labour. Where there were enough wage workers, such as in the densely populated Roman Egypt, and, as a consequence, their pay was low, there was significantly less slavery.[83]

The impression exists that slavery was less common in the late Roman Empire, and that, where it did exist, it was a more benign version. That said, we must still talk of a slave society, according to Andreau and Descat[84] – certainly when, from the fourth century, the numbers increased again due to warfare and the activities of slave raiders. This was despite a significant decrease in the use of children, traditionally ascribed to the influence of advancing Christendom.[85] This new religious movement never got around to abolishing it, however.

Hereditary professions in a market economy: India

As we have seen, India is one of the three earliest monetized economies in the world. However, like China and the Greco-Roman world, it also has its own characteristics, which are important enough for us to reflect on in a global overview of the organization of work. At the same time, South Asia is that part of the world where the most pronounced and ritually elaborated system of hereditary profession has arisen: the caste system, whose key characteristic for us is the heredity of professions within the male line in a strongly hierarchical society. How is that possible and, above all, when did it develop? Before, during or only a while after the rapid spread of deep monetization in India? The latter is most in line with expectations, but are there sufficient indications of that?

After all, one could argue that a complete caste society, certainly at village level, needs no market at all, let alone a means of exchange such as coins. Everyone in a village knows what his or her task is because it is passed on from parents to children. The only thing that still requires organization is the share of the harvest for that part of the population that does not grow its own food. For this, the solution of the *jajmani* system exists.[86] In this system, artisans in a village are supposed to deliver their goods and services, if required, to farmers, for which they receive a predetermined share of the total village yield after the harvest. In short, everyone's rights and obligations are fixed from birth, and markets and means of exchange are, arguably, superfluous. Thus, the classical Indian village is one big credit community based on reputation and enforceable social roles. This is in contrast to dealing with strangers, who always prefer a cash payment for goods and services over any other form of credit. This phenomenon is exemplified by Jewish merchants in medieval Cairo.[87] Mutual credit prevailed, and money was discharged only in exceptional cases (death, inheritance, and the like), while a mix of credit and cash payment was used by non-Jewish locals. Cash was only demanded from far-off trading partners, such as those in India.

The answer to these questions depends in the first instance on the precise dating of, on the one hand, the caste system (and consequently the *jajmani* system), and on the other, monetization and demonetization in India. As will be explained in more detail in Chapter 4 (pp. 159–60), deep monetization came to an end in South Asia from around 400 CE. The big question that arises here, then, is: did castes emerge before 400 CE, in a period of market expansion, or only afterwards, in a period of market contraction?[88]

Even earlier is unlikely. After all, as we have seen previously (pp. 55, 94), there are no indications of the origins of the caste system in the Harappa civilization, or of its destruction by 'Aryans' from the Yamnaya civilization. These nomadic cattle breeders who spoke an Indo-European language and entered northern India between 2000 BCE and the beginning of our era have long been seen as the inventors of the caste system, given that the *Vedas*, the oldest scriptures in Hinduism, are written in Old Indic, the language of these immigrants. Such an 'invention' is quite possible, but the more interesting question is what the exact age of the normative passages concerning the caste system in these writings is. Moreover, which parts of the population are they related to? Like all holy books, the *Vedas* were not created at one particular moment. These books are compiled from passages, the first of which, from 1500 BCE, came from the east of what today is Afghanistan, and later ones were conceived in the Delhi region around 600 BCE.[89]

Here, then, we are dealing with semi-nomadic immigrants, with cattle farming as the main source of income (although they were not unfamiliar with arable farming), who slowly but surely trekked from the north-west to the east of the north Indian plains, conquering many previously cultivated agricultural areas along the way. The vanquished, mostly farmers but also some hunter-gatherers, called *dasas, dasyus* and *shudras* in the *Vedas*, were assigned the status of slaves – as happened after wars everywhere else in Eurasia at that time. These slaves were regularly offered to priests. As a result of a series of wars of conquest, a society emerged in north-west India around 500 BCE consisting of four social layers: warriors (*kshatriya*); priests (*brahmana*); common people, including farmers and traders (*vaishya*); and the conquered, who, of course, had to perform forced labour (*shudra*). Most of the latter were women who carried out domestic services. So far, this was nothing special, and perhaps not even different from what was happening in western Eurasia with the immigration of the same Yamnaya, and certainly no caste system. Then, the term *varna* (later equated to caste) just meant colour – and in particular referring to skin colour, because the fair-skinned Aryans distinguished themselves from the indigenous people, who had a dark complexion.

Elements of what later became a 'caste society', such as it being taboo for higher castes to eat with, accept water from or touch the lowest caste, the prohibition of marrying outside your own (sub-) caste, and the inheritance of professions, only crystallized much later, and very slowly. We can follow this process to control upward social mobility using two scriptures. The first is the ideal-typical state theory *Arthashastra*, which we encountered earlier, composed by Kautilya in the period of King Ashoka (268–231 BCE). The second is the *Manusmriti* (*c.* 150 CE, often called the 'lawbook of Manu').[90]

The *Arthashastra* contains a simple classification of all inhabitants, starting with the Aryans. They are divided into four *varnas*: Brahmins, or priests; Kshatriyas, or warriors; Vaishyas, which now stands for traders; and Shudras, which now stands for the large mass of agriculturalists (often also colonists, assisted by the state), artisans and craftsmen. The members of each *varna* should marry within this group, but Kautilya is realistic enough to also list all the possibilities that could happen as a consequence of violating that decree. We can therefore assume that this was not a rarity. Further divisions, as found in the later *jati*, or sub-castes, are missing from this text. The most important non-Aryans, forced to live outside the perimeters of cities or villages, became outcasts due to heinous transgressions of the code of conduct, and the same happened to different kinds of people with whom the Aryans came into contact in their expansion to the east and the south (most frequently mentioned are the Chandalas). As far as was permitted, they were often deployed as guards and soldiers. Finally, there were the foreigners.

As we saw earlier, this classification is not the only one, because the extremely economically interested Kautilya also distinguishes between: slaves; bonded labourers; unpaid labourers who worked in lieu of paying a tax or fine; casual labourers working for wages; piece-rate workers; individuals working for a regular wage; and the self-employed (including Shudra colonists, assisted by the state); as well as 120 separate professions.[91]

Several centuries later, the Manu law book goes much further in distinguishing between the different population groups (it distinguishes no fewer than sixty-one castes) in its emphasis on endogamy and, based on this, in its differentiated choice and enforcement of punishments – inevitably, the lower that someone was in the hierarchy, the stricter the penalty.[92] A good example of this attempt to institutionalize social inequality is the provision that rice, pulses, salt, butter and ghee should be available for everyone, but a menial should receive only one-sixth of a gentleman's allowance of rice and only half his measure of ghee. Some differentiation on grounds of quality was also made: labourers, who needed plenty of nutrition, got the husks of rice and slaves the broken bits.[93] We are reminded here too of Varahamihira's ideal that 'a brahmana should have a house with five rooms, a kshatriya four, a vaishya three and a shudra two ... in each case the length and breadth of the main room should vary in order of superiority'.[94]

Such a serious violation of the natural ideal of equality, something we originally encountered with hunter-gatherers, required an ideology that could explain the sharp social differences, once the conquerors' logic had worn off, of course. In the *Upanishads*, the later commentaries on the *Vedas*, this takes the form of a belief that the soul passes from one life to another life: 'Souls were thought of as being born to happiness or sorrow according to their conduct in the previous life. From this evolved the theory of karma (action), which preached that the deeds of one life affected the next.'[95] This can be seen as an attempt to explain human suffering, without victims or perpetrators being able to or needing to change anything about the situation. By contrast, later, Vaishnavism taught that members of all four *varnas*, so even Shudras, could obtain final liberation in a next life through personal devotion to god. The Indian historian D.N. Jha points out that this devotion gained popularity among Vaishyas and Shudras and concludes: 'Evidently such a belief did not permit the masses to blame their miseries on human agency, and laid stress on the necessity of adhering to the duties traditionally prescribed for the varnas to which they belonged.'[96]

The caste society, however, was by no means an unstoppable force without opposition.[97] On the contrary, it encountered great hostility, and the *Arthashastra* and the *Manusmriti* can certainly be seen as attempts by the Brahmins to settle this ideological struggle to their advantage, rather than as reflections of the general social conditions of their time. The influence of these ideas must therefore have remained rather limited in India until the Gupta era, geographically at least, because they spread very slowly over the sub-continent, first in the north from west to east, and only then from north to south. Even more important is the emergence of counter-movements from the sixth century BCE, in particular Jainism and Buddhism.[98] Although neither argued in principle against the caste system, they provoked discussion about the existing ideas of the social order under the absolute leadership of the Brahmin caste, in particular by emphasizing compassion for the less fortunate, greater accessibility for women and members of lower castes to the movement and the belief that untouchables could also reach *nirvana* (this has undeniably influenced Vaishnavism). It is also striking that we only encounter the proper names of artisans, including leather workers, in the

Buddhist texts – inconceivable in the Brahminical worldview. Leather processing was, after all, regarded as one of the most contemptible professions. It is worth noting that Jainism was tailored more to the urban population and Buddhism to the needs of rural people.

Both movements had a large following for centuries: not least because the rulers of the Maurya dynasty (*c.* 321–185 BCE), who expanded Maghada into the first empire of India (from Kandahar in the west to Bengal in the east and Mysore in the south), turned first to Jainism (King Chandragupta), and then again to Buddhism (King Ashoka). Almost without exception, all the major successor states of the Mauryas, and thus also the successful economies in the centuries around the beginning of our era, were syncretistic. Think of the Indo-Greeks and the Indo-Parthians (with King Gondophares' sympathies with Christendom: it is suggested that he was actually Caspar, one of the three kings of the east), the Satavahanas (*c.* 50 BCE–150 CE) and the Kushanas (127–320 CE). As we have seen, a flourishing foreign land and sea trade, especially with the Mediterranean and the Persian Gulf, went hand in hand with urbanization, trade and artisan guilds (especially among the Shudras) and certainly also deep monetization.[99]

This dynamic gradually came to an end from the third century CE, especially in the north, during the deeply Hindu Gupta Empire, which flourished briefly between around 320 and 450 CE. Very striking at that time was the sudden end to the production of copper coins. For a while, it would have been possible to survive with all the old coins that had been produced in abundance in the previous centuries.[100] In contrast to the halt in production of small money, silver and gold continued as currency for a while. Certainly, the monetization of golden Gupta coins is known, but we must not be blinded by these artistic and high-quality gold coins. In seeking an answer to our question about when the caste system finally broke through with full force, it certainly appears that the Gupta Empire is the most eligible period, not least because it was followed by more than half a millennium of demonetization. The background to this demonetization (which, after the Guptas, applied equally to the production of silver and gold coins) is the decline in foreign trade, urbanization and of the economy in general, but for us, the most important implication, I would suggest, is the deployment of non-monetized labour relations in the caste system.[101]

In Indian history, the social changes of these centuries are analogous to something similar in Europe that is called 'feudalization'.[102] There has been much opposition to this term, but it seems certain that estates in the hands of priests, monks or warriors with bonded serfs working the land were becoming the dominant organizational principle. For example, the spiritual work to which Buddhist monks devoted themselves meant that others had to provide for their four necessities: clothing, food, bedding and medicine. Large central states disappeared, certainly in north and central India.[103] Professional differentiation fell sharply.[104] The ruralizing of trades and consolidation of guilds created new castes. This will also have meant the breakthrough of the *jajmani* system, in which the skills of hereditary artisans were employed by farmers in their village in exchange for a share of their collective harvest. The economic independence of women was also affected, according to D.N. Jha:

> The law givers . . . laid down inheritance rules which deprived women of their right to property and lowered the age of marriage, which took away their freedom to choose their husbands. As an unmarried girl a woman had to depend on her father, as a wife on her husband and as a widow on her son. She was, according to Manu, a seductress.[105]

Resistance to the phenomenon of independent Buddhist (mendicant) nuns may also have played a role in this, whereas in Brahmanic Hinduism the dutiful wife is the only model for women's virtuous and religious devotion.[106]

This radical social change also meant a repression of other religious views by the Brahmins, facilitated by a dilution of original Buddhism. This was accompanied by great struggle from around 300 CE, described in the *Puranas* as an age of social crisis, referred to as *Kaliyuga*. This meant 'a sharp antagonism between the higher and lower varnas resulting in the refusal of the shudras to perform production functions and of the vaishas to pay taxes'.[107]

The disappearance and re-emergence of markets: Europe and India, 400–1000 CE

The phenomenon of free labour – small, independent production for the market, as well as wage labour – as it had developed over many centuries in important parts of Eurasia from 500 BCE onwards was far from stable. And the relationship between free and unfree labour was equally precarious. We have already seen several examples of this, such as the fluctuating share of slave labour in the Roman Empire during its long existence, the different degrees of the state's reliance on its subjects' labour in classical China and the intricate prehistory of the Indian caste system. The period from roughly 400/500 to 1000/1100, however, offers the clearest examples of this instability, especially in the west and the south of these land masses. At the heart of this – the Byzantine, the Sassanian and the Arabic Empires (in shorthand, the Middle East) – the interplay of free and unfree labour of the Greeks and Romans continued for a long time.

Such dramatic changes and contradictions were less common in China, so will be touched on only briefly in this section. This is not to say that the Chinese history between the Han and the Ming periods is not interesting, including for the labour historian, but that the degree of deep monetization fluctuated there less and for shorter periods. The cash-coin system was never completely interrupted and, above all, coins from previous periods remained legal tender without major fluctuations in value. Periods with increased (Song) and decreased (Ming) coin production can be distinguished, which are also related to changes in labour relations.[108] In those centuries with a smaller coin production and weak central states, China consisted almost exclusively of small farms that paid tax – calculated in cash but paid in cloth or grain.

In the late Tang period, from the end of the eighth century, and under the Song an entirely different sort of state existed. The Song dynasty, in particular, was an exception to the Confucian tradition of a benevolent state that placed as little burden as possible on its farmers.[109] Basically, to buy off or combat the pressure from nomads at the northern border, an active state emerged that promoted economic development to raise the necessary revenue through tax in the form of cash. Deliberating on the notion that, during the Song period, China was a whisper away from its own industrial revolution, Professor of Economic History Kent Deng considers that: 'Counterfactually, if the stand-off between the nomads and the Song had continued for another 200 to 300 years, China might indeed have become a capitalist economy.' Trade and industry grew briskly and so did the cities. In just 8 years, from 1165 to 1173, the population of the capital city Hangzhou more than doubled from 550,000 to 1,240,000, making it the second city with more than a million residents, after Kaifeng half a century earlier. The total population in south China grew from 16.8 million in 1159 to 28.3 million in 1223.[110] It is safe to assume that the large urban population in particular consisted not only of self-employed people but also of large numbers of wage labourers.

We concentrate further in this section on the contrasting developments in Western Europe and India, on the one hand, and those in the Middle East, on the other.[111] Our index fossil is once again the distribution of small coins – that is, deep monetization as an indicator for free labour. This remained at the same level in the Middle East, but did, however, decline sharply on both its flanks, and we must therefore ask ourselves what this says about the organization of labour there, in contrast to the comparably much greater continuity of the market economies at the centre of the Middle East, as well as in China.

Roman labour relations continued and modified by Byzantines, Sassanians and Arabs

The Byzantine Empire was a continuation of the Roman Empire not only in name but also de facto.[112] In turn, it had a major influence on its new neighbours and competitors, the Islamic empires in the south and the Slavic empires in the north. Of course, not everything remained the same during the thousand years of its existence.

Let us start with continuity: In addition to free labour, slave labour continued to exist. As we saw in the last centuries of the Roman Empire, slavery did not come to an end with Christendom. The new religion did, however, plead for the proper treatment of slaves, and it rejected the enslavement of fellow believers – equals within the *societas christiana*. With a little licence, one could argue that the central identity of a citizen in classical antiquity was now giving way to that of fellow believers. This applied to both the Byzantine Empire and the Islamic states emerging from the seventh century – and that had particular implications for the existence of slavery.

This was primarily because the public law of the Byzantine Empire outstripped private law. Byzantine jurists in the eleventh century stated it simply: 'Compared to the emperor's power, the authority of the pater familias is nothing',[113] with all the implications of this for his power over slaves. This was also because the emperor was the head of a religious community with specific requirements regarding familial relationships and sexuality. In Christianity, the ideal of the inseparable, monogamous marriage was hard to reconcile with the free sexual relations between masters and slaves, and the marriage between a free man and a slave was equally at odds with the equality of all believers before God. A church marriage could only be concluded between free people. If a master wanted to marry a slave, then he had to let her go or buy her freedom. Their children were thus automatically free.[114] In this same context, Jews and Muslims were prohibited from owning Christian female slaves.

Yet, there were plenty of slaves in the Byzantine Empire, whether in rich households, in urban trades or in agriculture, although there are no numerical estimates such as those available for classical antiquity. The main source of new slaves was, of course, prisoners captured in the wars that the empire was constantly embroiled in, especially when these were non-(orthodox) Christians, such as the pagans of the Balkans, Muslims, Zoroastrians from the Sassanian Empire and, if it worked out that way, Latin Christians. Also notable was the common custom of selling oneself and one's children into slavery. Furthermore, slavery also existed as a form of punishment.[115]

Slavery and the slave trade in the Islamic states have many similar traits, but there are also some notable differences. Views on marriage differed greatly from those of Christians, and attachments of all kinds between masters and slaves were very common.[116] On the other hand, the children of a master and a slave girl were free and, subsequently, the mother could no longer be sold. The same was true in ancient Hebraic and in late Babylonian law, in contrast to Roman law.[117] Neither Christians, nor Jews, nor Muslims were allowed to enslave their fellow believers (of course, things were different for prisoners of war), but Muslims were also forbidden from selling themselves as slaves. Slaves in the Islamic world therefore had to be obtained through war or through the slave trade. Since the Byzantine Empire tried as much as possible to monopolize sources in the north, in particular the Balkans, the Islamic empires largely had to rely on other sources, in addition to slaves who were the spoils of war. In the ninth and tenth centuries, Jewish Radhaniyya traders played an important role in the supply from Western Europe to the Middle East.[118] Another difference between the Islamic empires and their competitors was the deployment of slaves as soldiers, which happened for the first time in the first half of the ninth century in the Abbasid Caliphate, and later systematically in Mamluk Egypt.[119]

Just as in the Roman Empire, there was also a large, if not greater, presence of free labour in Byzantium and, related to this, an abundant production (especially in the sixth and seventh, and again from the ninth to the thirteenth centuries) of copper money, in this case of *follis*, the equivalent of an hourly wage. Ten copper *follis* a day seems to have been the nominal wage for ordinary people, whereas qualified workers such as professional soldiers and craftsmen could earn anything from three to ten times more. Wage workers were mainly found in cities, where, incidentally, most slaves were found too.[120]

Initially, the Byzantine Empire's main competitor was the Sassanian Empire. How labour relations were organized there is unclear, but one difference between it and its Byzantine and Arabic opponents is immediately apparent: instead of forcing prisoners of war into slave labour, they used them as colonizers. Of course, they were bound to the land that had been assigned to them, far away from the border, but otherwise they were free.[121] There was also an important professional army that was paid in the copiously minted large flat silver *drahms*, but there was almost no question of deep monetization with the help of small silver coins or copper coins. Outside of the army, wage labour would probably not have been that important.[122]

Ultimately, the big winners in the battle between Byzantines and Sassanians were the Arabs. Initially, they continued the Byzantine system of mixed labour relations: a lot of slave labour, especially in the cities, but also a lot of free wage labour. As we have seen previously for the Greek and Roman world, we must also seriously wonder how important slavery was for Islam and whether we can really speak of a slave society there.[123] Although there was a long history of slavery in the newly conquered regions, last, under the Romans and Byzantines, and with the wars of conquest, new slaves became available, and eventually this type of labour relations became of minor importance. The Zanj rebellions and collective exodus of slaves of East African origin in southern Iraq, employed to clear salt off estate fields (869–883), appear to have played a role in this.[124]

From now on, slaves, and in particular female slaves, mainly appeared as servants in the private households of the well-to-do. How varied their background, status and professional specialization could be is illustrated by the following lively description from Samarra, the capital of the Abbasid Caliphate in the 860s. Following the assassination of the tenth caliph, Mutawakkil, in 861, his slaves were dispersed. One of them, Mahbuba ('the beloved one'), was a gifted singer-song writer who accompanied herself on the *'ud*, and the favourite of the deceased caliph. She ended up in the household of another slave, the Turkish military commander Bugha the Elder (hereafter called Wasif, meaning 'male slave'). The poet 'Ali ibn al-Jahm al-Sami recalls the following episode between the two:

> On one occasion I visited [Bugha] for a round of drink and good company. [At one point], he ordered the curtain [concealing the performers] wrenched aside and summoned the singers. They sauntered forward in all manner of jewels and finery; Mahbuba, without a trace of either jewels or finery, emerged dressed simply in white. She then sat, her head lowered, entirely withdrawn. Wasif invited her to sing, but she begged off. He said, 'But I implore you', and ordered that an 'ud be placed against her chest. Seeing that she had no option but to respond, she processed the 'ud to her chest and, accompanying herself on it, improvised lines of song:

> What Life can bring me pleasure / if I no longer find Ja'far there?
> A monarch, I saw him / bloodied and soiled with dust
> All who came unhinged [with grief] / or fell ill have long since recovered
> Except Mahbuba who / were she to see death on offer
> Would snatch all / that her hand could hold and thus be entombed.

> He continued: Wasif grew furious with her [as a result] and ordered her locked up. She was imprisoned and it was the last that anything was heard of her.[125]

The numerical decline (but certainly not the demise) of slaves in the Middle East after the ninth century does not necessarily mean a mitigation of the working conditions of slaves. There was, however, a whole spectrum of possibilities. On the one hand, there were skilled slaves who were allowed to keep the money that they earned outside the house, such as the slave girl that sang at weddings and births in tenth-century Kairouan. On the other hand, the master had the right to sexual intercourse with his slave, whether she liked it or not – even to such extremes as when he preferred to do that in front of others.[126]

Free labour nevertheless dominated agriculture and industry. Importantly, the Arabic tribesmen who made rapid military conquests possible were not rewarded with land, but were settled in newly established garrison towns like Basra (200,000 residents) and Kufa (140,000), and later in the new capital of Wasit, succeeded by Baghdad (500,000 residents around 800 CE).

Effectively obliged to abandon their pastoral way of life, they now obtained their income from regularly paid salaries (the lowest rate was 200 dirham per annum) and pensions. A little later, this pattern was repeated in Fustat (Old Cairo) and Alexandria in Egypt, Merv in Turkmenistan, and in the rest of the empire. Only in Al-Andalus (Spain) were there no military towns, but newcomers seem to have become property owners.[127]

In addition, there were industrial cities, such as Raqqa in Syria under Harun al Rashid. It has been shown that these too were cash-based.[128] The countless urban glass works, soap works, potters' kilns and looms will therefore also have been populated by free labourers. In the core areas, the latifundia disappeared at a rapid pace and were replaced by tenant farmers with farm labourers. Many small farming towns flourished, and cultivation was intensified with the help of irrigation channels all pointing in the same direction. The legal system also offered ample room for free labour.[129]

Periods of economic boom and decline alternated. In the following two-and-a-half centuries, small money disappeared, the cities emptied, industries vanished and nomadic troops living off the land were employed. For a century, the only places to escape this decay were at the periphery, in Fatimid Egypt, in Central Asia and in the east of Iran. The second Arabic growth period dates from roughly 1200.

Before we conclude the discussion of the boom in the Middle East and contrast it with the disappearance of the state and market in Western Europe and north India in the early Middle Ages, there is still one question that we must consider – the role of women, and in particular of the working woman, in Islam, such a relevant issue in the current social debate and one that is always traced back to the teachings of the Prophet. Did this role change with the arrival of Islam? And, if so, in what respects?

In a number of respects, the role of the working woman in Islam seems to be a continuation of the practice in the Byzantine Empire and, even more so, of classical antiquity. Here again, then, we see a great degree of continuity[130]: rather than a novelty, a consolidation of the classical tradition. Purely in this regard, there is no difference between women's labour and that of slaves. Let us begin with *the* symbol of the oppression of women in the current social debate about Islam: the veil. We find an equal emphasis on this symbol of chastity in the official ideology of classical Rome. It is said that Sulpicius Gallus, a consul in 166 BCE, divorced his wife when, one day, she left the house unveiled. He declared: 'By law, only my eyes should see you ... That you should be seen by other eyes … links you to suspicion and guilt.' But what does this view mean, in both classical antiquity and the Islamic world, for the daily work of women? That all married women had to stay inside and make themselves useful there?[131]

Not necessarily. Indeed, Islam brought renewal in the form of women's rights to property.[132] From this, it also followed that women could earn money independently and to which their husband was not automatically entitled. A specific consequence of women's property rights related to their own bodies, as is apparent from the following views on breastfeeding at that time:

> The fact that many jurists accepted breastfeeding as a remunerative activity and allowed that mothers could not be compelled to suckle their children, even with the prospect of a fatal outcome, means that a woman's milk was not ipso facto the husband's property in the eyes of the law but was seen as a commodity. This would seem to be a direct outcome of the legal stand that the wife's body and its reproductive qualities were her property. The recognition for this can be seen also in the legal articulation of wet nursing, for which service there was a hiring contract, practically the only hiring contract for females provided for in the notarial formularies. With this contract nursing mothers had the right to hire themselves out for the job and to keep their wages from their husbands in accordance with the separation of property within marriages. The husband's signature on the contract was necessary because he had to agree to give up his right to sexual intercourse with his wife during the period she was hired to breastfeed.[133]

The solution to the dilemma that women on the one hand – according to the accepted norms of classical antiquity – had to be at home as much as possible and, on the other hand, had the right to possessions and thus their acquisition through work, was simple: women worked at home as much as possible, including as wage workers. They are therefore found en masse in urban cottage industries, predominantly in spinning but also in weaving and embroidery. Jewish women in cities such as Cairo also followed this trend, and earned their money in the textile industry. In addition to these indoor activities, the sources also refer to occupations that must necessarily be carried out elsewhere. Much smaller numbers were involved, however. We have seen already the professional wet nurse, but we also come across occupations such as pedlar, medical doctor, midwife, occultist, astrologer, fortune-teller, organizer of marriage festivities, washer of the dead and professional mourner.[134]

Western Europe and north India
without markets, 500–1000

Simultaneously with the emergence of the Byzantine and Sassanian empires, labour relations in early medieval Western Europe and in India changed profoundly – but in a radically different direction. The population of Europe declined sharply, probably even by half, to 20 million, and remained at that level for half a millennium. Cities virtually disappeared after the end of the Roman Empire, accompanied by the outbreak of infectious diseases, but also the thinning out of the rural population.[135]

No wonder that the circulation of coins had also virtually halted, at least in comparison to the levels of classical antiquity.[136] This had grave consequences: 'The end of Roman rule meant the end of small change, an apparent trivial fact, but one with an important sequel. Wage labor cannot exist on a regular basis without a reliable and abundant coinage.' And that state of affairs was to last for more than half a millennium, because even the revival of coinage with the advent of the Carolingian pennies was relatively unimportant: 'The high exchange value of the pennies and their generally excellently preserved state argue against the idea that coins circulated rapidly through this society or that they served the needs of a wage economy . . . Regular wage labor in the Carolingian state was unknown . . . and no one lived by wages.'[137] Theoretically, the stoppage of coin production in Western Europe did not preclude the circulation of coins produced in the preceding ages, although, in practice, this did not happen very much.[138]

Now that wage labour and production for the market had dwindled as a serious income source in the first half of the Western European Middle Ages, the question arises about which system would now prevail: unfree labour, more self-subsistence or a mix of the two? A return to the pre-Roman Iron Age – in other words, a return to self-subsistence agriculture – was most probable.[139] In addition to the 1 to 2 per cent of the population in a few dozen cities of 10,000-plus inhabitants and another 5 per cent in places of between 500 and 10,000 inhabitants, the great majority of the population of Western Europe consisted of peasants who provided their own food and other basics such as flax and wool, leather, wood, clay and other construction materials. Cattle also served as draught animals.

However, a return to mainly subsistence agriculture in an endless country-side does not mean that peasants could keep all they produced. The ratios of ownership for farmland in Western Europe are unknown for the period of 500–1000. Since, at the end of this period, however, the distribution is estimated as one-third ecclesiastical property, one-third public property plus aristocracy, and so one-third free farmland, it may also have been the case in previous centuries, although there was much less nobility at that time.[140] Let us assume that roughly two-thirds of all cultivated land, and of course the best parts, were in the hands of spiritual and secular lords, then more than half of the population must have danced to their tune to a greater or lesser extent. Their status was referred to as *servus*, which did not necessarily mean 'slave', as in antiquity, but rather 'serf': that is to say, a land-bound peasant who was obliged to give up part of his production and time to the spiritual or secular lord. This could be as much as a third of the workforce of his household.[141] The rest he could consume, together with his housemates. From the duty to live and work on the estate, a hereditary right to the manor developed from the Carolingian era.

The hub of manorialism was in northern France and in the Rhineland, while in other parts of Western Europe it developed much less or not at all (such as in the northern Netherlands, northern Germany and Scandinavia). There, the free farmer was the rule. The larger farmers with plough and span (the *laboratores*) could, in turn, employ one or two serfs; the smaller ones were, of course, dependent on the labour of all members of their own house-hold. Because there was almost no investment in agriculture in these centuries, and this was therefore extremely labour-intensive, many people were needed to exempt a small number of people from the production of their own food. The property of the Chapter of Saint Symphorian in Autun, France, for example, included about a hundred farms, hardly sufficient for the sustenance of fifteen canons and a few servants.[142]

In the absence of cities and markets there was virtually no market economy – in comparison to the Roman era and the high Middle Ages – and so no labour specialization either. Practically everyone toiled on the land. Apart from the odd small town, labour specialization was primarily found in the monasteries that were founded with the permeation of Christianity from the end of the Roman Empire. In these centuries, we are talking about a few thousand.[143] These monasteries accommodated not only monks (or nuns) who divided their time between praying for 8 hours, working for 8 hours and sleeping for 8 hours, but also lay brothers. In addition to being self-sufficient, the abbeys also received proceeds from subordinate manors (owning roughly between a tenth and a third of the arable land in Europe), so that they were in a position to release a number of monks for activities outside of agriculture. Their size varied greatly, and while traditionally an abbot and twelve monks were sufficient to form a foundation, some were much larger.

Apart from the construction, maintenance and decoration of the monastery, the most specialized task of their residents was the copying and illuminating of books (book printing was only invented in the West at the end of the Middle Ages). The Benedictine monk Alcuinus wrote: 'It is a perfect task to copy Holy Books, and a copyist will never miss his reward. It is better to copy manuscripts than to look after vines. The last serves the stomach, the first serves the soul.'[144] Every monk was supposed to be able to read, and for the daily prayers and liturgy alone there were dozens of parchment manuscripts in the monastery. The parish clergy, whom they also supplied, had to make do with one or just a few. These figures are not very impressive and reveal the practical limitations of the spread of literacy. That does not mean that the monks were lazy; remember that the complete writing down of a book by a single monk took several years. In contrast to what one might think, it was not light work, as a Spanish monk sighed at the eighth hour of 27 July 970 after three solid months of continuous copying, 'bowed down and racked in every limb by the copying'.[145]

In spite of the fact that all Germanic peoples, who had assumed power after the Romans, were slaveholders, slavery was in considerable decline due to the deterioration of the economy.[146] Perhaps that is why, in 782, Charlemagne executed no less than 4,500 Saxons in Verden. They had been handed over to him by other Saxons, but, apparently, he had no use for them.[147] Crucial for the expansion of slave-taking operations was a sufficient demand – not the supply or the (lack of) moral virtues of suppliers. That is why between around 800 and 1000 the medieval slave trade in Europe was at its peak, when massive demand for slaves from the Muslim world met the Viking raiding network in north-western and eastern Europe. In southern Europe the Muslim–Christian clashes added to this, as did, finally, the Christian crusades against the 'heathens' in the Baltic. The equating, in practice, of the words *servus* and *sclavus* (Latin) or *saqaliba* (Arabic) makes it clear that the main recruitment area was shifting to the parts of Europe where Slavonic languages were spoken.

Economic changes played a much more important role in this decline in slavery than ideological ones such as the rise of Christianity. Certainly, manumission was a pious act for a Christian, but definitely not an obligation for a lord, let alone the right of a slave. There was, however, a growing agitation against the sale of Christian slaves. In the words of William of Malmesbury (c. 1095–c. 1143):

> They would buy up men from all over England and sell them off to Ireland in hope of a profit, and put up for sale maidservants after toying with them in bed and making them pregnant. You would have groaned to see the files of the wretches roped together, young persons of both sexes, whose youth and respectable appearance would have aroused the pity of barbarians, put up for sale every day. An accursed deed, and a crying shame, that men devoid of emotions that even beasts feel should condemn to slavery their own relations and even their flesh and blood![148]

The Church, however, never abolished slavery. Church slaves remained very normal for a long time, and, until late on, the German clergy turned a blind eye to the sale of heathen slaves to Muslims.[149]

Although the history of early medieval South Asia has attracted much less academic attention than that of Western Europe, everything suggests that the developments of labour relations there, in the same centuries, was broadly similar. That is to say, the diminishing of cities and markets, the sharp decline in the degree of monetization and, consequently, ruralization and the sharp increase in self-sufficiency for the majority of the rural population.

We saw previously that, already with the mighty Gupta dynasty, the production and, with some delay, also the circulation of copper money and of coinage in general had already disappeared from north India in the fourth century, only to return again in the thirteenth century with the expansion of the Islamic sultanates. South India and Ceylon, which at the beginning of the era produced hardly any coins – but did use Roman coins (especially silver denarii) – had already experienced a renewed deep monetization one to two centuries earlier, with the Cholas in the tenth century.[150]

In the meantime, 'feudalization' perhaps fulfilled a similar role for the organization of labour in the earlier-founded Buddhist and later Hindu and Jain monasteries, in particular in the Deccan sultanates (think of the Ellora, one of the largest rock-cut, monastery-temple cave complexes in the world) and Bihar, as it had for Western Europe.[151] They received a lot of land and, consequently, some of them became centres of learning, such as the monastery complex of Nalanda. The university founded there in the fifth century attracted scholars and students from far and wide. According to travel reports of Chinese Buddhist pilgrims from the seventh century, this institution is said to have accommodated 1,000 teachers, 10,000 students and no less than 9 million books. Even without taking these numbers literally, it is clear that the exemption of intellectual workers, as well as sculptors, painters and other construction workers, would have required a multitude of serf farmers paying remittances. Due to the extremely weak state formation, especially in the north, the payment of remittances to secular lords would probably have been less important here than in Western Europe.[152] What remained, above all, were countless small village communities, in which, as we have seen, the caste system could develop and embed.

Not surprisingly, considering the great cultural-religious influence of India on South East Asia, the same kind of labour relations appear to have prevailed there at this time: a non-monetized society of farming villages specialized in rice cultivation, also partly producing for temples and the elites associated with them.[153] The difference with India is that in South East Asia there was no preceding monetary period. The caste system there also played a different and much smaller role, at least later on. This was likely due to the prevalence of Buddhism, which spread from its Indian cradle in a northerly, easterly and south-easterly direction, only to eventually succumb to Hinduism in India itself.

In the most successful polities, such as the Khmer state of Angkor, in particular, an extensive system of corvée was of course necessary to achieve all the mighty building and construction works. This also involved slavery, as well as markets, but on the basis of barter and means of exchange such as cloth. This is most reminiscent of the pre-Columbian polities in America, especially those of the Aztecs in Mexico (see below). In South East Asia, however, there was a positive choice not to opt for a labour market with monetary remuneration. After all, in contrast to the Americas, the use of money was well known here, both from India and from China – only it was generally decided not to make use of this until much later.

Alternative state formation without labour markets: The Americas

The great cultures of the Americas prior to the arrival of the Spanish remain something of a mystery to the labour historian. They were as capable as their predecessors – the Greek world, Rome, India and China – of creating impressive and beautiful buildings, but they did not have any metal currencies. How, then, was the necessary work organized? Did workers receive payment in kind? Was the work done by unpaid slaves? Or, was all this implemented using corvée labour, imposed on otherwise self-sufficient farmers, whether or not via the kinds of tributary-redistributive methods seen in Mesopotamia and Egypt? And what about other forms of work, such as the recruitment and reward of soldiers and, most importantly of all, tilling the land?

In a recent global survey examining Eurasia and the pre-Columbian Americas, the Austrian historian Walter Scheidel states: 'Wherever governments want work to be performed for the state, they have a choice between contracting for the completion of such tasks and resorting to compulsion to get them done. While the former strategy is usually sustained by taxation of private assets and output, the latter often entails the imposition of labor services as a specific form of tax.' According to Scheidel, enforcement of labour obligations was the rule and the state's reliance on market institutions to undertake building projects among Greeks and Romans was the big exception.[154] Nevertheless, we have seen that in the period that this chapter covers there are many hybrid forms between Scheidel's two extremes, and that compulsion only partially addresses the issue. But let us take a closer look at the ins and outs of the matter in the best-known pre-Columbian societies in the Americas and the extent to which the solutions adopted there exhibit similarities with the other parts of the world that we have already encountered. This will also afford us insight into the place that work had in the Americas after 1500.

Bypassing countless smaller civilizations, although interesting in themselves (we will return to them at the end of this section),[155] here we will focus on the largest: the Inca, the Maya and the Aztecs. If my interpretation is correct, and wage labour was stimulated by the ample availability of means of exchange, then one could assume that in these materially well-developed societies without metal currencies, work was organized and remunerated differently.

As we have seen, this idea was strongly developed by the Hungarian anthropologist Karl Polanyi, who has had an extraordinary influence on the study of anthropology (via, for example, Marshall D. Sahlins) and archaeology and classical antiquity (via, in particular, Moses Finley).[156] He posited not only that reciprocity was much more important in world history before the Industrial Revolution in England than market exchange, but also that numerous civilizations existed according to the principle of redistribution. All production and therefore all labour was thus for the temple. The elite, responsible for the services there, then redistributed it among the population. These were, by definition, hierarchical societies, but a shared cosmological belief and a division experienced as fair promoted a general sense of prosperity and well-being. We have already seen examples of this in Chapter 3, in, among others, old Mesopotamia and Egypt.

Critics of a rather easy application of this model have rightly pointed out that there must have been firm indications of, in particular, the existence of large depots of redistributable food supplies. They are not convinced by the combination of beautiful temples and the lack of metal currencies, and they encourage archaeologists to look much more actively for marketplaces. They also warn against making too stark a contrast between the marketless Inca and the market-loving Aztecs, and all the others in between, as we will see at the end of this section.[157] We thus have advance warning about the following examination of pre-Columbian civilizations.

Small-scale agricultural communities become complex tributary-redistributive societies

The best-known tributary society of the Americas is the Inca Empire in the Andes (1431–1532/3). Like the Maya and Aztec empires in Mexico, the Inca could also build on a long tradition of predecessors, like the Chimu Empire (850–1450) in Peru. If my impression is correct, most other well-developed polities in the Americas can also be characterized as 'tributary', but that has yet to be investigated thoroughly. The study of these highly developed polities in Central and South America, before the 'Columbian encounter' or 'Columbian exchange', as the post-1492 events are currently described, is extremely important. After all, 'they represent the result of a natural experiment in independent parallel socio-economic evolution: in the absence of information transfers for up to 13,000 years, any institutional similarities that arose in the Old and New Worlds must be viewed as genuine analogues, as similar solutions to comparable challenges'.[158]

Archaeologists have tried to reconstruct the emergence of complex societies since the second millennium BCE by working back from the combined archaeological information and historical evidence (from Spanish descriptions as well as American Indian hieroglyphics) available for the Aztecs, Inca and, to a certain extent, the Maya and other American societies around 1500. A summary of some of their most recent results permits us to say more about the emergence and development of tributary-redistributive labour relations in the Americas at large.

The earliest American tributary-redistributive societies

Supposing that most developed (at least as measured in material achievements) societies in the Americas in the late Middle Ages, in particular the Inca, the Maya and Aztec polities, may be characterized by tributary-redistributive labour relations, questions arise, firstly, about the origin of this particular way of organizing work and labour relations and, secondly, about the degree of redistribution and the availability of a widely shared cosmological set of beliefs and values that justifies or at least irons out the inequalities inside such societies. In order to answer this question, we can skip over the first hunter-gatherer societies that abounded in this part of the world, and which even now still exist in small pockets of the Amazonian lowlands, and start with the earliest agricultural societies. After all, these were able to produce a surplus that opened the way to major shifts in labour relations. To what extent may we discern continuities and discontinuities between these societies and those of the Inca in the Andes and the Maya and Aztecs in Central America?

Agriculture as the main form of subsistence, and connected with this sedentarism, developed fully in Mesoamerica about 2000–1400 BCE. Apart from hunting, which had not been given up totally, early agriculture consisted mainly of slash-and-burn practices, sometimes supplemented with the cultivation of terraces. Important crops in Central America were squash and maize, and the main domesticated animals were the dog and the turkey, and in the Andes the llama and alpaca. Only then could villages develop, and the subsequent transition into towns took place regionally at different times.[159]

In Mesoamerica, the Olmecs of Mexico's Gulf Coast region may have been among the first to develop urban centres of more than a few thousand inhabitants (San Lorenzo had an estimated 10,000 to 15,000 inhabitants around 1100–950 BCE), followed by the Mazatán region in Chiapas. This implies an already large-scale division of labour, but the main question is whether this also implied a hierarchical society to such an extent that it changed the original mutual and reciprocal labour relations, as surmised for hunter-gatherers worldwide and also the earliest agriculturalists. This process has been studied in depth for the region of Oaxaca.[160]

According to the archaeologist Arthur Joyce's analysis of Oaxaca in southern Mexico (south of the Olmec and west of the Mazatán region), hereditary and therefore persistent inequality did not occur there before 700 BCE, when the Zapotec centre of Monte Albán started to grow.[161] He sees the preceding period as more characteristic of the 'transegalitarian societies' model – rising inequality without institutionalized hereditary status distinctions. This inequality generally manifested in the form of priests and nobles who played a crucial role in what Joyce calls the 'sacred covenant', which he considers to be the essence of social relations. These 'religious practitioners' were responsible for carrying out rituals in order to contact the deities and to petition them for fertility and prosperity. In Central and South America, this also entailed autosacrifice and the sacrifice of others, primarily captives taken in warfare. In Oaxaca, agriculture was introduced between 7000 and 4000 BCE, but was only organized in sedentary villages between 1900 and 1400 BCE. During the 'transegalitarian' period, the scale of agricultural and even craft production did not exceed the household, and trade took place between households without the involvement of communal or regional authorities. This period ended with the emergence of Monte Albán around 700 BCE and consequently endured in that part of Mexico for roughly one millennium.

Initially, status distinctions were still relatively modest in this new urban period, but gradually nobles acquired the right 'to mobilize goods and labor as tribute or sacrifices that enacted the sacred covenant and contributed to their ability to petition the gods on behalf of their followers'.[162] Originally, this should not be conceived of as centralization from above, but as a bottom-up process:

Social identities were increasingly differentiated by affiliations linked to crafting, long-distance contacts, wealth and status. People were also forging community identities inscribed in public buildings and communal cemeteries. The evidence suggests that practices of affiliation such as large-scale construction projects and communal rituals were corporate endeavors and not under the direction of a centralised authority.[163]

Interregional (rather than intraregional) warfare played an important role, and the 'innovation of human sacrifice', initially by nobles and later by priests, determined the fate of many a prisoner of war. The increasing power of nobles created tensions with the prevailing communal principles, and emigration followed. Those who stayed at Monte Albán were part of a society that can be characterized as one of 'tributary labour relations' and that may have lasted for 2,000 years. In the words of Joyce:

> Practices of affiliation that tied members of rural communities to Monte Albán included providing tribute (probably in the form of crop surpluses) as well as participation as warriors and laborers for the construction of monumental buildings. It is also possible that commoners worked the land of nobles as a form of tribute in the way they did at the time of the Spanish Conquest, although this is difficult to demonstrate archeologically. In return, people received the benefits of participation in ceremonies on the Main Plaza. People acquired social valuables such as decorated pottery and greenstone from the increasingly powerful leaders of the urban center. Nobles may have adjudicated disputes among their subjects.[164]

Interestingly, this coincides with a change in preparing maize from gruel or roasted cobs into tortillas, facilitated by the introduction of *comales*, or ceramic griddles. Both the causes and the consequences of this innovation are labour-related. In contrast to gruel or roasted cobs, tortillas can be easily transported, and they stay fresh for several weeks if toasted. They were therefore well suited to the increasing travel by residents of villages and small towns surrounding Monte Albán who came there to perform tributary labour, military work or to participate in rituals. The consequence of this much more labour-intensive food may have been increased work, especially for women. Moreover, increased labour demands may explain population growth, especially in the form of bigger family sizes.

Tensions between traditional leadership and the nobility may have led to a major political upheaval at Monte Albán, which brought a rather abrupt end to this once prosperous city. Although archaeologists have made great progress in the study of other early American societies, for more detailed research into work and labour relations we are particularly dependent on information about the three most recent, and therefore best-documented, big polities: the Inca Empire in the Andes and the Maya and later Aztec empires in Central America.

The Inca in the Andes[165]

The Inca Empire's achievements were astonishing. By the time of its surrender to the Spaniards in 1532, it stretched from northern Chile and Argentina to the south of Colombia and counted between 10 and 12 million inhabitants, whose labour had built 40,000 kilometres of roads in the mountains, linking 2,000 state installations. In addition, they undertook 'massive land modification programs, most notably by terracing mountain hillsides and harnessing the water flowing off the highest glaciers of the Western Hemisphere. And they could field armies in excess of 100,000 effectives, apparently without exhausting the land'.[166]

This nascent empire had started life in the mid-fourteenth century as a regional state focused on Cuzco, and its major expansion started as late as the early fifteenth century. The material remains thus testify to an incredible achievement in a very short time. How can this be explained? Mainly by combining all sorts of elements that we have already encountered in different cultures, the most important of which was forcing-cum-persuading major parts of its population to perform work for the state. And for those who did so, this was combined with an important redistribution of resources. Most significantly, the Inca did not use markets, and certainly not currencies.[167]

Before I provide a brief description of the way much labour was extracted, it is important to understand that this state did not control all labour efforts. During its turbulent expansion in northerly and southerly directions, the Inca had to deal with many different societies and their equally varied policies after conquest. A substantial part of the population (2 million males aged 25–50 and the members of their households – big families being an asset) had to perform labour duties, and about 3 to 5 million had been resettled. This labour consisted primarily of agricultural work, secondly of herding camelids (llamas, alpacas, guanaco and vicuña), used as pack animals as well as for their meat and wool, and thirdly of textile production. Some subjugated populations were assigned special duties, such as military service.[168] In return for the labour and expertise rendered, the government disbursed goods and facilities for maintenance.

Arable land was divided into three parts: for the state; for religious institutions; and for the peasants themselves. In the clear words of Father Bernabé Cobo, this worked as follows:

When the fields of Religion were finished, the fields of the Inca were immediately sown, and, in their cultivation and harvest, the same order was followed. All members of the people who were present came in a group, and with them the lords up to the most important caciques and governors, dressed in their best and singing appropriate songs. When they cultivated the fields of Religion, their songs were in praise of their gods, and, when they cultivated the king's fields, in his praise. The third part of the land according to the division above was in the manner of commons, it being understood that the land was the property of the Inca, and the community had only the usufruct of it. It cannot be determined whether this share was equal to the others or greater, although it is true that each province and town was given sufficient lands to support its population. Every year the caciques distributed these lands among their subjects, but proportionate to the number of children and relatives that each man had; as the family grew or decreased, its share was enlarged or restricted. No one was granted more than just enough to support himself, be he noble or plebeian, even though a great deal of land was left over to lie fallow and uncultivated. . . . When it was time to sow or cultivate the fields, all other tasks stopped, so that all taxpayers together, without anyone absent, took part, and, if it was necessary to perform some job in an emergency, like a war or some urgent matter, the other Indians of the community themselves worked the fields of the absent men without requesting or receiving any compensation beyond their food, and, this done, each one worked his own fields. This assistance which the community rendered to its absent members caused each man to return home willingly when he had finished his job; for it happened that when the Indian returned to his house after a long absence he might find that a harvest that he had neither sown nor reaped would be gathered into his house.[169]

From this description, it follows that reciprocal household labour was combined with hierarchical-redistributive work for temple and state. The mobilization of this labour was facilitated by the social basics of at least the core lands of Inca society, including the rights to farmland and water. Similar social, resource-holding units were found elsewhere, such as the *ayllu* kin group in Peru and northern Bolivia. *Ayllus*, whose populations could reach several thousand, granted households access to resources through usufruct. These resources were worked collectively, although elite members of the group had access to more diverse productive spaces. Labour was inherent to the continued existence of such communities and could not be bought or sold. While the clearly innovative Inca transformed their economic activities, they did so in a context where land, property and their yields were unassailable, no markets existed and labour was a social relationship.

Added to the existing, pre-Inca Andean societies' norms of reciprocity and redistribution was a similar state system, requiring rotating corvée (*mit'a*, conventionally spelled *mita*, meaning taking turns), which necessitated the construction of enormous state warehouses across the country in order to feed all those forced to work or to render military service. Apart from some 65 days that peasants could devote to self-subsistence farming, the remaining working time for anybody from the ages of 15 to 50 had to be available to the state, which not only organized all activities in detail, but also took responsibility for feeding and entertaining those working for the polity.[170]

In the last days of its rule, the system shifted from corvée to the creation of several specialized labour statuses, such as the 3 to 5 million resettled colonists, individuals (*yanakuna*) assigned permanent duties, including farming and household duties for the elite, as well as the assignment of adolescent girls (*aqllakuna*), separated from their families and *ayllu* and assigned to live in segregated and strictly supervised buildings where they wove cloth and brewed maize beer until they were married off to men being honoured by the state.[171]

Compulsion as such, however important in such a highly militarized society, does not explain sufficiently the success of the Inca model. Its efficiency contributed to the well-being not only of elites but also of the population at large, which had better access to foods and textiles, resulting in a better standard of living. Moreover, the general distribution of state ceramics, highly decorated in imperial styles, and bronze ornaments allowed 'an extension of the state ideology into ceremonial feasting and dress'.[172] The motivation for those performing all these efforts for the Inca therefore may also be explained by the attraction of the overarching ideology of the sun cult and its ceremony and public feasting, including human sacrifice of children and ritual warfare.[173] This ritual attraction was not infinite, however, as witnessed by the sudden disappearance of the sun cult and worship already by the early colonial years.[174]

The Maya in southern Mexico, Guatemala and Belize

Although the classic Maya states[175] no longer existed when the Spaniards arrived, a number of small successor states did function until well into the seventeenth century. Consequently, in addition to Maya hieroglyphic texts and archaeological excavations and surveys, colonial descriptions are also available for the analysis of Maya labour relations.[176] The classic Maya civilization of the Itzá state witnessed the shift from 'household economics' to a highly hierarchical polity in which all labour beyond that required for simple survival was organized for the construction and maintenance of drainage channels, enabling agricultural intensification, cities and temples.[177]

What did these developments mean for labour relations? The classical Maya seem to fit well into a state model, combining great ritual centres with agrarian-based, 'low-density urbanism' – together with roughly contemporaneous but even bigger South and South East Asian polities in Sri Lanka and Cambodia with large Buddhist complexes.[178] High harvest yields were made possible by impressive, centrally organized waterworks like tanks, river dams and canals, but most of all by smallholders. They must have provided the food and the workforce necessary to construct and maintain both these infrastructural conditions and the religious centres themselves.[179]

Ultimately, Chichén Itzá's classical and 'highly autocratic system of royal kings and dynasties' was not sustainable 'in the face of widespread overpopulation and exhaustion of resources'. And neither was that of the league of Mayapán, for that matter. What came instead were much smaller polities, less dependent on agriculture and more reliant on maritime resources. Mirroring what had gone before, they were highly urban in nature, with population concentrations of between 5,000 and 10,000 people.[180] These late-Maya polities did not, therefore, return to the more simple reciprocal systems of the early Maya societies before 800. Instead, 'while elite Classic populations were to a large extent integrated through the costly maintenance of an elite minority, Postclassic populations were most probably integrated through a rising standard of living locked into large-scale population participation in a commerce which emphasised economic efficiency and mass consumption'.[181]

The emergence of a market economy: The Aztecs of central Mexico

Together with the Inca, the last of the great pre-Columbian states was the Aztec Empire. It began in the thirteenth century in central Mexico with the arrival of Nahuatl-speaking migrants, originally nomadic hunters, from the north. In the next two centuries, as a result of frequent warfare and expansion, the Aztec Empire and its capital Tenochtitlan emerged.[182]

With the arrival of Hernando Cortés in 1519, the Aztec Empire was the second largest in the Americas, behind the Inca Empire. In just two centuries, the population of the Valley of Mexico exploded from 175,000 to 920,000, resulting in a population density of 220 per square kilometre, which was very high for a pre-industrial society. The total population of highland central Mexico was estimated at 3 to 4 million people. These extreme growth and density figures raise questions regarding the development of the means of existence as well as labour relations. Fourteenth- and fifteenth-century civilizations were dependent on one or more forms of intensive agriculture. In the Aztec case, this involved techniques such as terracing, irrigation, raised fields and house-lot gardens. Such intensive methods were found in earlier Mesoamerican civilizations, but the level of intensification in Aztec agriculture was new, transforming the natural environment into a cultivated landscape.[183] The majority of farmers could work without state interference, although the authorities were clearly involved in the building and maintenance of irrigation canals and the initial cultivation of raised fields in swamps. But most of the agricultural production of staple foods like maize and beans was 'almost certainly organized and operated entirely at the scale of the individual farm household'.[184] This is an essential difference with the Inca, who were heavily engaged in constructing a centralized infrastructure.[185]

Obviously, Aztec farming households were not producing food, cotton, maguey (a kind of agave for textiles, spun and woven by the women),[186] pottery, stone tools (especially those made from obsidian), paper or rope purely for their own subsistence.[187] Many of these goods were destined for taxation in kind (in addition to taxation in the form of corvée) and for the market – a market that can only be explained by an already sizeable urban population of roughly 30 per cent of all inhabitants of the valley of Mexico (or 10 per cent of highland Mexico).[188]

Markets – already existing before the advent of the Aztecs[189] – were indispensable for the exchange of all these goods, and there were many outside the capital. Within the capital, they were held daily, in the other cities and towns every five days, and less frequently in smaller places. The sellers were both the artisans who produced the goods and professional merchants. Diverging from the practice in Eurasia, where different forms of metal currencies were common, here cacao beans served as the smallest 'coins', lengths of cotton called *quachtli* used as capes were mid-value items, and T-shaped imitation bronze axes and other valuables (such as gold dust contained in goose quills or small fragments of tin) served as the most precious means of exchange. One cacao bean might buy you a tomato, a freshly picked prickly pear cactus, a *tamale* or a bundle of chopped firewood. A common-grade *quachtli* was valued at 65, 80 and 100 cacao beans, whereas 20 *quachtli* could support a commoner for a year in Tenochtitlan. Along these lines, 1 cacao bean might equate to the value of 1 hour's work.[190]

This entire currency complex – as a repository of value (but with a limited life span as far as the cacao beans are concerned)[191] and medium of exchange, although not universally exchangeable for all goods and services – bears the mark of a monetary system in development. As the archaeologist Michael E. Smith concludes:

> Clearly the Aztec economy was highly commercialized and dynamic, but it was not a capitalist economy. There was no wage labor, land was not a commodity to be bought and sold (except under limited circumstances), and opportunities for investment were limited to *pochteca* (merchants) expeditions. Marketplace trade gave the Aztec commoners and merchants a chance to advance themselves, but only up to a point. Aztec markets and the overall economy were embedded in a rigid system of social classes, and no amount of economic success would enable one to cross class barriers.[192]

How should we describe the labour relations of those independent producers who had to pay taxes and to perform services for the nobles?[193] Smith is rather emphatic about this: 'These great inequities might suggest that Aztec commoners were oppressed serfs leading bleak lives of servitude. This was not the case, however. ... Such duties [of commoners] vis-à-vis lords (5% of the population) typically rotated among the lord's subjects, with each family contributing several weeks of work each year.' In addition to this taxation, commoners occasionally had to perform corvée, such as the construction of a temple or canal system and, of course, military service, given that there were no mercenaries. Significantly, most of the Aztecs' battles took place during the dry season when there was little agricultural work to be done. The Aztec armies were huge. Spanish estimates vary between 40,000 and 100,000. The entire educational system was geared to training able-bodied men for military service. These were therefore not professional armies, and commoners would certainly have been conscripts or draftees.[194]

This discussion regarding the nature of the labour relations of peasants who had to perform labour and services for the nobility is reminiscent of social historian Gijs Kessler's critique of the one-sidedness of emphasizing the 'unfree' nature of Russian peasantry, without recognizing that, in fact, only a relatively small part of their time was spent on obligatory work for the nobility.[195] Other than these independent producers, there are no wage labourers among the Aztecs.[196] The group that comes closest to wage labourers are servants in noble households, but as no evidence of wage payments exists, this conclusion remains far-fetched.[197] By contrast, the situation regarding slaves is well documented. For example, the markets in the towns of Azcapotzalco and Itzocan were known as slave markets. People could become slaves through debt or punishment, but not by birth; slavery was not hereditary. Most slaves worked in the palaces of lords, women especially as spinners and weavers of *quachtli*. This may sound rather benign, but slaves could also be killed in order to accompany a chief into the afterlife.[198] Indeed, prisoners of war seem to have had the grimmest honour of exclusively being sacrificed to the gods, instead of being put to work as chattel slaves as was the habit in contemporaneous Eurasia and Africa.[199]

The emphasis on the empires of the Inca, Maya and Aztecs should not, however, lead us to think that all agricultural societies of pre-Columbian America were 'autocratic'. The anthropologist Richard Blanton suggests that there were a number of smaller agricultural communities that operated as 'collective societies'. This distinction may be a little bit too absolute, but it is important to understand that Mesoamerican societies like Tres Zapotes (400 BCE–300 CE), Zapotec (Monte Albán, 500 BCE–800 CE), Tlaxcala (1200–1520s) and possibly even Teotihuacán (100–550 CE) were much more dependent on peasant households that were reasonably taxed than on heavy forms of corvée.[200]

Stepping back and taking a look at the whole world around 1000 CE, we find an enormous variety of societies, from simple to complex, and within them a variety of labour relations. As we have seen, that certainly also applies to Eurasia, but that was about to change.

The return of the labour market in Europe and India, 1000–1500

The large differences in labour relations that had arisen between the different parts of Eurasia in the period 500–1000 were rectified in the subsequent centuries. Europe and India recovered and, around 1500, at the start of definitive globalization through the great voyages of discovery, the economies of Europe, the Middle East, South Asia and China resembled each other as much as or even more than they had done one to two thousand years earlier.

They had in common a high agricultural productivity that could feed a large urban population that specialized in other activities and deep monetization that facilitated wage labour and small-scale independent production on a large scale, as well as the increased significance of slavery. In addition, the specialization of free, urban small producers and wage labourers was accompanied by significant quality improvement, and also by the organization of professional groups.

In this section, the 'catching-up' of Europe and South Asia and, more particularly, India, will receive greater attention than the world of Islam and China, where the market economy had continued for 1,500 years, albeit with fluctuations.[201] Furthermore, there will be a significant weight placed on the late Middle Ages in Western Europe, if only because that was where the foundation was laid for European expansion in the early modern period, which forms the theme of pp. 244–75. More importantly for this part of the world, the reactions of the workers themselves have already been properly mapped out, something we caught glimpses of at the start of this chapter from the working Greeks, Romans and their contemporaries. For the first time, however, we can now study the quite systematic strategies and tactics of self-employed and wage labourers. Thus, in addition to structures such as labour relations and labour markets, the agency of thinking and acting working people becomes very visible.

The agricultural economy is at the root of the convergence of labour relations in the core areas of Eurasia. For this reason, we will briefly describe its development since the year 1000 for Europe and India, respectively, and finally for Eurasia as a whole.

Improving agricultural yields and urbanization in Europe

The catching-up of Europe and India in relation to the Middle East and China began with an improvement in food supplies, initially as a result of larger agricultural yields.[202] One of the first improvements we find, starting around 900 CE, is the transition from the two-field to the much more intensive three-field system. The three-field crop rotation system allowed for production on the same piece of arable land over a period of a year, with spring crops, such as barley, oats and leguminous crops (sown in spring, and harvested in summer or autumn), followed by a fallow period, then, in the next year, a third period of winter grain, mainly bread-grains like wheat or rye (sown in autumn or early winter and harvested in early summer), and then a fourth period of fallow, after which the same sequence started anew. Under the previous two-field crop rotation system, spring grains were planted in the first year, while the second year was fallow, followed by winter grains in the third year, and so on. In both systems, fallow periods were necessary for the recovery of the soil, but, under the three-field crop rotation system, the addition of leguminous crops among the spring crops had the same function due to their capacity to fix nitrogen from the air and thus fertilize the soil. Moreover, cattle could be penned on fallow fields, also enriching the ground with manure.

This shift to the new three-field rotation system substantially increased productivity per hectare (of course, provided that sufficient human and animal power was available). The increased production of oats and barley enabled farmers to feed horses properly, and to use them as draught animals for larger ploughs instead of oxen. This switch to horses was only possible with the introduction of harnessing, and in particular the shoulder collar, for horses, as well as shoeing (also used for oxen).

This also spared human labour. The rapid decline of slavery and the inadequate development of a human workforce under the conditions of serfdom would have been a catalyst for the invention and application of these kinds of labour-saving tools. In 1935, founding member of the Annales School of French social history Marc Bloch posited the following 'working hypothesis' in this regard: '[these] developments took place for the very good reason that they originated in the same need. Was the decline of slavery then a result of this? By no means: it was much more probably a cause, leading to a technical revolution, which was destined in its turn – we need hardly say – to have powerful repercussions on the structure of society'.[203]

Although it is difficult to disentangle cause and consequence in this shift of crop rotation systems, the final results become clear after a few centuries, as the average yield ratios (the ratio between grain seeded and harvested) rose substantially. France and England took the lead, certainly after 1250, with production gains of 60 to 70 per cent, later followed by the Low Countries. In addition to intensification, the available agricultural surface was also expanded significantly, mostly in Central and Eastern Europe in the form of colonization by land-starved peasants from northern Germany and the Netherlands, with their proficiency in diking and draining. Half a million colonists may have been engaged in these colonization projects by around 1300.[204] Lübeck became a point of departure for this movement, in the same way that Seville would for the colonization of America. In addition to these favourable developments, much more silver became available across Eurasia due to the Mongolian expansion at its centre. Consequently, silver became the common unit of account in China, India and Europe. Rightly, it is called the 'first silver century' by the Japanese economic historian Akinobu Kuroda.[205]

Even more important than the implications for agricultural work, the rise in food production in Western Europe for the first time since the Roman Empire enabled an increasing part of the population to engage in other activities and to concentrate in towns. But grain was not enough. More and highly nutritious food became available as a result of another development: the growing supply of sea fish from the North Sea and the North Atlantic, important not only for its nutritional value but also for the diversification of the diet.[206] In rural areas of north-west Europe, farms were usually not very big, but there was a marked difference between farmers and cottars. Farmers were tenants with holdings between 6 and 12 hectares, obliged to perform labour dues for their landlords. Small cottars worked less than 4 hectares; that was the minimum necessary to support a family of 4 in thirteenth-century England, and these households depended on extra work like harvesting and threshing for larger farms. In France, there was a similar relationship between *laboureurs* (farmers) and *manouvriers* (cottars).[207]

European city dwellers (defined as inhabitants of places with more than 10,000 residents) could therefore increase from 1 to 2 per cent in the early Middle Ages to *c.* 5 per cent in the high Middle Ages and 6 to 7 per cent in the late Middle Ages. If we also include the cities and towns of 500 residents or more, then we come to 6, 8–15, and 20–25 per cent, respectively. In most urbanized areas, such as in Flanders, that could rise to as much as a third.[208] As we will now see, this was accompanied by significant labour specialization, followed later by the expansion of industry in the countryside, so-called proto-industrialization.

Return of the market and urbanization in South Asia

Although the population development of South Asia at this time and, to a certain extent, even after 1800, remains terra incognita, there are enough indications for the 'catching-up' of this sub-continent in the period 1100–1500.[209] The background to this success is still ill-understood, but certainly also in India the positive effects of the 'first silver century' were felt after 1300. Certainly, cities encompassing up to 15 per cent of the population were a new phenomenon, as was the renewed monetization.[210] In the north, two successful states led to a revival of a typical urban and strongly mone-tized economy: the Sultanate of Delhi (1193–1526) and that of Bengal (1205–1576), whereas the smaller Jaunpur Sultanate, located between them, was also important in the fifteenth century.

It is not very clear what the establishing of a Muslim state such as the Sultanate of Delhi meant for existing labour relations. Previously, we saw how Islam certainly brought with it new ideas about work, especially for women, surprisingly, but also how much these were built on existing socio-economic structures. In this regard, then, it would not have been very different. So, how to distinguish the old from the new? What was new was the opportunity to completely or partially escape the strict caste constraints by converting to Islam. In that respect, individual conversion was perhaps more effective than collective conversion, because, in cases where entire groups of urban professionals switched to the new religion, they did not automatically reject previous group norms. The caste system, therefore, did not automatically disappear with Islamization.[211]

In any case, employment also increased outside of the cities, and not only in terms of agriculture and horticulture around the cities, but also as a result of the construction of canals around Delhi. For the poorer rural population, there was also an opportunity in the dry season, when there was not much farming to do, to supplement earnings as a mercenary, and thus also to adopt a new identity. In particular, peasants from Jaunpur specialized in this secondary work. The Muslim Barha Sayyids in Uttar Pradesh, for example, had a saying: 'Last year I was a Jolaha; now I am a Shekh; next year, if prices rise, I shall become a Saiyad.'[212] For this clan, the military profession was clearly seen as a way to rise socially. Soldiering was indeed one of the most important forms of wage work, and not only in Jaunpur. The Delhi sultan Alauddin Muhammad Khalji (1296–1316) was said to have spent 10 million tankas in cash every year on his 20,000 Turkish Mamluks, and a further 210 million tankas on his 900,000 cavalry men – certainly exaggerated figures for the cavalry, but, nevertheless, it emphasizes their societal importance. In addition, there was also wage labour for women; indeed, under the

176

aforementioned sultan, even the wives of large farmers 'had to take service in Muslims' houses' due to the heavy tax burden.[213]

The capital of medieval Bengal, Lakhnauti, also grew quickly.[214] In 1300, it had a marketplace that was a mile long, and by 1500 it had 40,000 inhabitants, including many foreign merchants from as far away as Afghanistan, Iran and China. According to a Portuguese visitor, its built surface measured 12 by 16 kilometres and 'the streets and lanes are paved with brick like the Lisbon New Street'. Its crafts and trades were concentrated in specific streets, like those for armourers, saddlers, silk and cotton producers. Besides Lakhnauti, Bengal counted five more important towns inland, all centres of industry, and extensive international commerce, which also involved the maintenance of a navy. In the countryside, rice was reaped three times a year, occasioning one sultan to use the epithet 'Mulk-i-Chaulistan' (the land of the rice bowl) for Kamrup, the location of one of his minting houses and a famous centre of wet rice culture.[215] Full of admiration, the famous Moroccan scholar and explorer Ibn Battuta wrote about fourteenth-century monetized Bengal agriculture:

> Nowhere in the universe have I seen a country where the commodities sell cheaper than here. . . . I have seen rice selling at the markets of this place at the rate of 25 rati of Delhi for a silver dinar. . . . I have seen milch cows in Bengal selling for 3 silver dinars. . . . The pigeons cost one dirham for 15 . . . a piece of fine cotton of excellent quality, and measuring thirty cubits, was sold in my presence for 2 dinars.[216]

Apart from an apparent labour specialization, exactly what labour relations dominated in Bengal is not very clear. We do know, however, that the economy was deeply monetized (cowries being the preferred subsidiary to the mainly silver coins) and that tax revenue was collected in cash. This points to the existence of a substantial number of peasants, craftsmen and possibly wage earners.

During this period, powerful polities – in this case the Hindu states of Chola and Vijayanagar – also emerged in the south of the sub-continent with equally well-developed monetary economies. The Chola Empire, which for some time also included Ceylon and undertook military expeditions to the Maldives, Bengal and the Indonesian archipelago, flourished from the tenth to the thirteenth century. From the fourteenth century, Vijayanagar became its successor, to a certain extent. Both empires illustrate that the re-entry of deep monetization and wage labour in South Asia were not necessarily foreign elements imposed on India from the outside, as the developments in the north might wrongly suggest.

In many respects, the Chola Empire, with its capital Tanjavur, was extraordinarily successful, much more so than any earlier south Indian state, with many more international contacts, rice cultivation with the help of irrigation and massive construction of temples.[217] The necessary labour for this was supplied by farmers and artisans, but also by agricultural workers – men and women. The gigantic production of copper coins by the Cholas both in India and Ceylon is a strong indication of the dominance of self-employment and free labour. Corvée was clearly of secondary importance, but slavery did occur, especially in domestic services. The cause was debt: people sold themselves to a temple as a last resort during famines, for example.

Here, the professional specialization necessary for this economic boom went hand in hand with a strengthening of the caste system, making social stratification increasingly complicated. A specific form of this was the emerging subdivision among craftsmen and agricultural labourers of so-called Right- and Left-Hand groups. The former considered themselves superior to the latter, leading to caste rivalries. In any case, we are dealing here with a society that was constantly on the move and that enabled social and geographic mobility, as evidenced by numerous religious sects and movements.

The later Vijayanagara Empire, with its eponymous capital, exhibits a number of similarities with the Chola Empire, economically, socially and ideologically.[218] Firstly, there was spectacular urbanization, with the capital growing to minimally 200,000 and maximally 500,000 residents in a short space of time. Other cities were smaller but still counted 10–15,000 inhabitants. Furthermore, we are almost certainly talking about a market economy, and, although firm figures are lacking, the circulation of small copper coins was probably not less than that under the Cholas, and in this case, too, we can speak of deep monetization. Taxes and tariffs also had to be paid in cash, and farmers focused on cash crops for urban markets.

Just as under the Cholas, village communities of self-employed farmers worked reasonably independently, kept their own accounts and collectively took care of paying taxes that were collected by tax-farmers. These were collected in kind for wet crops and in cash for dry crops, adding a level of enforced market participation to the process. Non-governmental shares were also allocated to village servants, including blacksmiths, carpenters, leather workers, water carriers, and money lenders, among others, in return for their goods and services during the year.'[219] Peasant and farmer production therefore went hand in hand with the reciprocal *jajmani* or *baluta* systems.

Artisanal products, like potter's wheels and metal tools and vessels, were probably made in family-run workshops and were traded nationally and internationally. The building of countless irrigation channels, water basins and aqueducts of course required many hands. Around 1520, the Portuguese Domingo Paes reported that: 'in the tank I saw so many people at work that there must have been fifteen to twenty thousand men, looking like ants, so that you could not see the ground on which they walked so many there were'. It suggests, in this case, recruitment via a corvée system: 'this tank the king portioned out amongst his captains, each of whom had the duty, of seeing that the people placed under him did their work'.[220] In the absence of further reports about an expanded corvée system, this could have been a one-off alternative for the use of wage workers. The organized protest in 1428–29 of agriculturalists and artisans against the heavy tax burden perhaps provides an indirect indication of the employment of paid construction workers instead of the imposition of corvée. In any case, the impressive standing army, consisting of Muslim and, later, Portuguese gunners, and foot soldiers recruited from forest-dwelling, non-peasant communities, was paid in cash.

Overview of Eurasia around 1500

Around 1500, Europe and India were back in the game, and there seems to have been a greater balance than before, over several centuries, between a number of major polities in Eurasia with similar economic and cultural achievements. From west to east, this relates to: Western Europe, despite it being politically fragmented; West Asia, increasingly united in the Ottoman and Safavid empires; South Asia, with its large sultanates and, somewhat later, with the Mughal and Vijayanagar empires; Ming China; and, later, Tokugawa Japan. This is well illustrated by a comparison of the distribution of the large cities in Eurasia between around 1100 and 1500 – despite all the problems that these kinds of quantifications bring with them. The figures in the literature for the Middle East vary widely, but there is no doubt that the largest cities in the world could be found there. Between 12.5 and 15 per cent of the population of the Mughal Empire may have lived in cities.[221]

I want to emphasise the 'greater balance' between the major Eurasian polities at this time, and certainly compared with the situation earlier, when the

Arab world and the Song civilizations were leading, and later, when Western Europe emerged at the helm. But we are fumbling in the dark when it comes to, in particular, the absolute standard in terms of wage levels, average income and other basic economic indicators, and also about the way in which these achievements were reached.[222] Hence, some have wondered whether it is possible to find underlying causes for the weaknesses and strengths of different medieval Eurasian societies (the so-called Great Divergence, see also pp. 245–8). In other words, the key question now is whether there were already profound differences below the surface in these politically and culturally equivalent centres of civilization in Eurasia, around 1500 and later, that would ultimately lead to the Great Divergence in subsequent centuries.

The full breadth of the debate cannot be traced here, but we will zoom in on the possible role of work and labour relations in the comparison. Many leading economic historians believe that we must look at institutions regulating market exchange, including forms of organization of work such as guilds, the remuneration of work and especially skilled labour, and citizens' access to the legal system.[223] Some aspects of this have already been dealt with in the previous comparison between the 'chasers' Europe and South Asia, but after a brief elaboration on the nature of work itself, we will discuss this in more detail.

Specialization and quality improvement of labour in the late Middle Ages

We have already discussed agriculture, so our attention now turns to other sectors. By far the most important industry in the cities was textile processing, and, in Western Europe in particular, the wool industry, such as that in the Italian and Flemish cities, but also in England, France and Spain.[224] In the thirteenth century, this was concentrated in small workshops of craftsmen practising their vocation, and a few journeymen and apprentices. They worked in a 'putting-out system', which meant that the looms were theirs but that they received the raw materials from an entrepreneur and processed them for a piece wage. It was also the entrepreneur who sold the ready products in the market. Urban industry was generally dominated by the textile industry elsewhere at this time, albeit for the manufacture of cotton and silk rather than wool.

Following the Black Death in Europe in the mid-fourteenth century, urban artisans focused more on luxury production, while the mass production of textiles shifted to the countryside. Merchant entrepreneurs found this cheaper because the cost of living was lower there, certainly where these rural weavers also worked a piece of land. This meant that the industrial wages were often lower there than in the city. Moreover, these cottage weavers generally did not organize themselves in guilds. Entrepreneurs did organize themselves, such as in the Grosse Ravensburger Handelsgesellschaft, established in 1380, which rapidly organized linen and fustian production in a number of Swiss cantons.

Concentration also took place in the cities as the main master artisans started delegating work to smaller ones, thereby violating the official egalitarian ideology of the craft guilds. The small masters thus became de facto wage workers.[225] In times of rising food prices, this could lead to rebellions of these small masters and journeymen, united in secret and illegal *compagnonnages*, such as in the years 1378–82 in parts of France, Flanders, England and Italy (the most famous being the revolt of the Ciompi – woolworkers and other commoners and small artisans in Florence – in 1378).

Specialization requires acquiring and transmitting professional competence.[226] This was rarely done via formal schooling (which only existed for theologians, lawyers and physicians), but rather by learning on the job. In small companies, apprentices copied the work of masters and their assistants, but more people were needed for larger projects. For the building of churches, temples, mosques and other tall constructions it was necessary to coordinate between the many specialists on large building sites so that all the individual elements worked together.

Of course, this also applied in the thousands of years before, you could say from the building of the Tower of Babel, but for the Middle Ages we have sufficient data for a comparative Eurasian overview.[227] Professor of Economic and Social History Maarten Prak compared the way in which, among others, Gothic cathedrals, Byzantine churches, mosques from Turkey to Delhi, temples in India and Cambodia and pagodas in Song China were constructed in practice. What knowledge was necessary for this and how was it transmitted? That was indeed a problem, because the hundreds of workers and builders on one site simultaneously were not only numerous, they were generally also illiterate and, due to the nature of their profession, some of them were also itinerant specialists who came from all over. This required collaboration and communication between local and peripatetic craftsmen.

The outcome of this comparison reveals surprising similarities between the different parts of Eurasia. According to the aforementioned Prak and his colleague Davids, *modular knowledge* could and, in fact, did substitute for *theoretical knowledge*. Coherent sets of proportional dimensions facilitated transmission between builders, and templates used, for example, by stone cutters, were derived from this. This modular knowledge was at the same time collective, acquired – and sometimes combined – throughout Eurasia via different social institutions: the family; the building lodge; the guild; and in all religious contexts, or, in the case of China, the state.

In the construction of cathedrals, as with the production of other goods, there was a need for three types of occupations, 'some requiring brain work, some trained skill of different kinds, some mere physical labour'. According to the British architectural historian John Harvey, from whom I derive this distinction, the middle category is distinctive from the other two, consisting of those who:

> have generalised aptitude and can switch from one job to another with little difficulty ... the man whose particular form of skill is the outcome of vocational training is, contrariwise, bound to that one method of earning his livelihood ... this underlies the frequency of demarcation disputes ... every craft composed of those with like skills forms a defensive – and sometimes an offensive – alliance against any who may threaten their livelihood. Similarly, if the methods of their craft are not very simple, they will include processes that can be safeguarded by secrecy.

And this key component is, in turn, connected to the cherishing of rituals 'believed to promote good fortune, to ensure fertility, to confer power'. It is not for nothing that craft is related to the German word *Kraft*, meaning power. Harvey connects the following observation to this:

> The association of craftsmen in the ritual of tribe or nation is of general occurrence and is in no way affected by the objective truth or otherwise of the underlying theory. Thus it is an irrelevance whether we accept that material crafts develop out of transcendent ritual, or adopt the materialistic hypothesis that the ritual grew out of antecedent material needs. In the latter case it is simply the effectiveness of craft skill that constitutes its power; in the former, the power is non-material, but breathes life into material operations.[228]

This is the context in which medieval knowledge was passed on within building specialities. Formal, multi-annual (in medieval England, for seven consecutive years) apprenticeship was one way to gradually master a craft. By 1300, the enrolment of apprentices was obligatory in London. The essence of apprenticeship was 'personal contact over a long time with opportunity of repetitive imitation of each process, and the learning by rote of recipes or other craft secrets'.[229] From the late Middle Ages, there was sometimes also an obligation to do an internship with masters in other cities, the so-called tramp (see pp. 234–5).

Where did all these craftsmen work? Mostly at home. As we have seen, businesses, at least in late medieval Europe, were small, both in the country-side and in the city. Yet there were also workplaces where larger groups of labourers worked together, which resulted in a specific dynamic developing there. This relates primarily to sailors and soldiers, but especially to the necessary infrastructural facilities that the army and fleet required (gun foundries, wharves, rope walks, and so on).[230] In fact, these were the only large businesses at this time. After the Ottoman Empire, the Venice arsenal was Europe's largest single industrial enterprise, with 2,000–3,000 workers.[231] Finally, of course, many labourers worked together on a more incidental basis, on large construction and infrastructure projects. When it comes to the construction of cathedrals and castles in Europe, we must think of groups of hundreds of people who worked simultaneously. For the construc-tion of Windsor Castle, for example, as many as 500 men were all working at the same time on-site for weeks at a time, and in one week there were 720. Because these kinds of projects took years and sometimes centuries, and occasionally were never finished at all due to lack of money, there were, in practice, fewer people actually working most of the time.[232]

Thus far, we have detected few fundamental differences across Eurasia in the technical organization of a number of activities, but that is not to say that every-thing was similar. In the last part of this chapter, we must zoom in on the strate-gies and tactics that workers used to defend their interests. As already stated, we must pay particular attention to the relevant institutions. These are, once again, firstly, the household (both its structure and marriage patterns) and, in a wider circle around them, all kinds of so-called market institutions. Economic histo-rians assume a strong relation between the quality of economic institutions and the average level of income. This certainly also includes the operation of market institutions that influence the remuneration of both self-employed and wage workers. In this vision, successful institutions – assumed to 'protect the powerless against the powerful' – include legal systems, and the importance they attach to the written word, as well as organizations solving the collective action problems of citizens.[233]

As shown on a few occasions earlier in this book, working people can defend their interests individually and collectively by resisting a deterioration of existing conditions, by trying to maintain the status quo and by striving for improvement. Let us see, then, how this applies to the period in question, for which much more data is available than for previous periods, and to what extent we can agree with the assumption 'that Western Europe, from as early as the late medieval period, had a relatively well-developed set of institutions. By contrast, South and South East Asian institutions were much less geared towards well-functioning markets'. For China, this relates to the first commercial revolution in Chinese history, during the Song, and to the second during the late Ming, and for Japan it relates to Tokugawa Japan.[234] I will return to the latter two cases in the next chapter, but the comparison of Western Europe with, in particular, South Asia and Song China certainly warrants attention here.

Individual protection of interests and the household

Existing standards of marriage and family formation have a profound impact on working life, especially for women.[235] The later they marry, the more work experience they can gain before they embark on the giving birth to and raising of children that will keep them largely occupied for years. If there is a big age difference with their spouse, they will be less able to act independently within the marriage. If they move in with their in-laws following the wedding, then that will limit their freedom of movement even further. When all this comes together, as has been documented in India, for recent centuries at least, then this could result in a significant difference with those parts of the world where other norms are upheld.

For Western Europe, the pope emphasized as early as the eleventh and twelfth centuries that a marriage ultimately depended on the mutual consent of the partners and not on that of parents or third parties. Forcing your children into marriage was even seen as sinful. This was the basis on which, in particular in north-west Europe, in the century of labour shortages that followed the Black Death in 1348, a globally atypical marriage (that in the meantime has become so familiar to many a modern reader) could develop. We begin with wage labourers. Because of the shortage of labour, they were able to set conditions, and their pay rose considerably, both nominally and in real terms. It is noteworthy that women in the English countryside benefited from this more than men. While previously their wages had been half those of men, the difference now all but disappeared. Young men and women could thus save for a wedding and independently search for a suitable mate. Marriages in north-west Europe were therefore not concluded until, on average, the age of 20. A widow often remarried. Indeed, the Wife of Bath in Geoffrey Chaucer's *The Canterbury Tales* married five times. Because not everyone was successful in this regard, there were also many unmarried people, as evidenced by the growth of beguinages. The nuclear family thus beat the multi-generational household as the nexus of labour income. This was advantageous for the independence of women, but there were also disadvantages. Members of a nuclear family were, of course, also vulnerable when one or two of the breadwinners were removed, especially later in life. Public and corporative forms of care for the poor endeavoured to fill this gap.

In this regard, there were significant differences within Europe between north and south, but those with Asia were even bigger. Economic and social historians Van Zanden, De Moor and Carmichael contrast the (West) European marriage pattern with that of Asia, and in particular that of China.[236] The dominant Confucian idea – still practised very liberally under the Song, but much more strictly from the Ming onwards – placed a strong emphasis on the value of the patriarchal peasant family. Marriages were arranged by parents at a very young age, and many girls were already handed over to their future parents-in-law as children. There, they provided labour in the farming household before and certainly after their marriage. In fact, they could never leave, because, once they had become a widow, they were not allowed to remarry. After all, this would mean an important source of labour leaving the patrilocal family. Everything was focused on the continuation of the male line, symbolized by the exclusive task of the pater familias to worship the ancestors at the home altar. Symbolic of the impossibility of women working outside the house was the Han Chinese practice of binding the feet of girls, an originally urban and elite phenomenon that later (from the seventeenth to the eighteenth centuries) also penetrated the countryside. In the same vein is the low value placed on daughters, leading to infanticide and, on the other hand, to the adopting of sons if the family line could not be continued in any other way.

Occasionally, China and India are mentioned in the same breath in this debate. That is tempting, because a patrilocal marriage system, significant age differences between bride and bridegroom, prohibition of widows remarrying (and even self-immolation, *sati*, especially in the case of Brahmin widows) and the survival of fewer girls than boys have all been reported for India in recent centuries. Whether and to what extent these characteristics already played a role there in the Middle Ages, and, in particular, whether they were limited to the elite or were more universally applicable, remains an open question. The aforementioned developments in the Chola and Vijayanagar empires suggest, in any case, something different: a strong social dynamic, such as greatly increased urbanization, wage work and independent managing of villages with extensive administrations.

In any case, an improvement of the position of the Indian woman on various points became possible for converts to Islam and, after the arrival of the Portuguese, to Christianity, and a little later to Sikhism. Although the marriage age of girls only increased by a few years and the age difference with their spouse decreased to the same extent, the new religions did permit the remarriage of widows. In addition, as we saw previously, the Islamic right of the woman to independently own property had important consequences for her right to work, at least insofar as was possible beyond the view of others – that is, indoors.

Individual protection of interests and the market

Once on the market, it is important to get good and well-paid work, or, in the case of artisans, commissions. For both the craftsman and the wage worker, the better practised, the better paid the work. This is the so-called skill premium, generally expressed as the difference between the wages of a skilled craftsman and those of an unskilled labourer. Getting well-paid work was particularly important in late medieval north-west Europe, where between a quarter and a half of households were entirely or partly dependent on wage work. In addition: 'In terms of life cycle, the breadth of the labour market may even have been larger than that. During their teens and (early) twenties, much more than half the population was engaged in wage labour (or as servants, apprentices, etc.) and wage employment was a normal part of the life cycle for almost everybody living in the countryside and the cities of England and the Low Countries.'[237] This dependence meant a sharp and increasing emphasis on training on the job and learning in general. Literacy and numeracy also increased significantly. In the Netherlands, it was up to half of all adult men and a third of women. Another division was that between the city and the countryside. It has been estimated that perhaps a quarter of the urban population was literate, compared to only a twentieth in the countryside. In the south of Europe and in other parts of Eurasia there was much less dependence on literacy. This had serious consequences for the nature, quality and mobility of workers.[238]

Seamen also voted with their feet and, from the thirteenth century, they increasingly shifted from being self-employed (until then, they had been profit-sailors, the partners of the captain and possibly also of merchants) to more general wage workers. In the event of an unwinnable labour dispute, they resorted to desertion. In the Mediterranean, this meant that:

> owner-captains' efforts to guarantee sailors' wages in the hundred years between about 1250 and 1350 closely coincided with the final breakdown of traditional, personal bonds between capital and labour in mediaeval shipping. ... Desertion from merchant ships, though it had not been unknown before the mid-thirteenth century, first became a significant problem at ports like Venice, Genoa, and Pisa during the hundred years between 1250 and 1350. Paleologo Zaccaria ... operated a small fleet of trading-galleys between Genoa and Byzantium during the early years of the fourteenth century. One of [his] routine activities ... was the sale of the legal rights to collect indemnities from the sailors who had deserted from his ships [to] professional collecting agents. For Paleologo, who employed hundreds of sailors on many different ships, this business practice simply constituted the most efficient way of minimizing his losses. For his sailors, the act of desertion proved to be a calculated gamble in which they accepted advances on their wages and then tried to lose themselves in the increasingly anonymous ports of the later Middle Ages. Offering to guarantee their sailors' wages was clearly one of the important ways in which thirteenth- and fourteenth-century owner-captains could hope to reduce the incidence of desertion from their ships.[239]

The Black Death not only caused the emergence of a different marriage pattern in Western Europe, but also opened up new opportunities for workers to protect their interests. An abbot in Tournai (Belgium) commented:

Due to the high mortality of men and women in the course of the previous year 1349, there were so many deaths among the wine-growers, navvies, craftsmen of all professions and in all families, that there was a large shortage of them. That is why many of the surviving manual workers were enriched by the possessions of the dead, while the others wanted a high price for their work.[240]

The demands for higher wages that workers could make in the time of labour shortages as a consequence of the Black Death were so threatening that, for the first time in history, national labour laws were enacted in Europe.[241] They were aimed at restricting the mobility of urban and rural workers under the guise of combating begging. Provence in 1348 and England in 1349 (the *Ordnance of Labourers*) led the way, obliging all able-bodied men to work. This was followed in 1351 by the *Statutes of Labourers*. All able-bodied men and women under 60 and without means of support were obliged to accept employment at wage rates equal to the average between 1325 and 1331, and no landowner or contractor could pay higher wages than those customary or hire somebody who had broken his or her contract with a previous employer. It was also forbidden to give alms to sturdy but intransigent beggars who refused to labour.

Similar measures were taken in Spain: in Aragon in 1349, and in Castile in 1351 and 1381. In this latter year, anyone who managed to grab a wandering beggar was permitted to put him to work for a month without pay. In Portugal, a whole series of similar laws were enacted between 1349 and 1401, including the introduction of a passport to hinder migration and to control begging and, in 1357, a law binding workers to their traditional vocation. And this list can be expanded with measures in France, Germany and other countries, all with the same objective, but also all with little effect, as the rising wage trend in this period demonstrates. Perhaps, however, it would have risen more rapidly without these measures to massively repress free movement of labour. In short, all this legislation to discourage the mobility of wage workers and craftsmen had little effect in Western Europe anyway. The freedom that slowly emerged from the eleventh century with the rise of cities was not suddenly lost.[242]

Collective protection of interests

Collective actions in the late Middle Ages that dealt directly with the issues of work and income took the form of peasants' revolts in the countryside and, in the cities, more incidentally in the form of hunger riots. In addition, there were crafts- and service guilds far and wide, which now, for the first time in history, have been extensively documented. Peasant revolts were, incidentally, different from peasant wars.[243] The latter, in the Netherlands, northern Germany and Switzerland in the thirteenth and fourteenth centuries, were successful resistance movements of large farmers against the expansion of feudal lords and of the state and could last for years. Peasant revolts, by contrast, ended less well. They were brief but fierce outbursts as a consequence of price slumps and thus income decreases for farmers and must, therefore, be situated after the Black Death, with the consequent sharp decline in the population. Perhaps the most famous is the Jacquerie to the north of Paris (1358), with at least 20,000 victims of the vengeful nobility. Another example is the rebellion of Wat Tyler in Essex and Kent against the poll tax (1381), but these revolts also occurred in Denmark, on Majorca and, later, in Germany. During Wat Tyler's revolt, labour was also expressed as a central theme by one of the leaders, the priest John Ball. His sermon containing the following phrase is famous: 'In the beginning all men were created equal: servitude of man was introduced by the unjust dealings of the wicked and was contrary to God's will. Whanne Adam dalfe and Eve span Who was thane a gentil man?'[244] The city of London also joined the uprising. We also see this element of rudimentary evangelism in the same period among the English Lollards and the Hussites of the Czech lands.

Without doubt the most important form of organization of working people in pre-industrial cities, and sometimes also in rural areas, are the guilds.[245] They occurred in many parts of the world, even in antiquity, but then disappeared again along with the cities. The medieval and early modern guilds exhibited the following features: they were more or less independent self-governing organizations of people with the same or similar occupations, aimed at furthering their common interests in almost any respect (economic, political, social, cultural or religious).[246] Four factors are important for the emergence and blossoming of guilds: urbanization, political economy, human capital and social relations.

The first, urbanization, is obvious, as concentrations of similar professions and occupations are likely to occur in towns and cities rather than in the countryside. Nevertheless, as we will see in Chapter 5, guilds could become such an appealing organizational model that they might sometimes be copied in proto-industrial regions in rural Europe in the early modern period. However, supra-local and non-urban guild-like organizations were not completely absent in the Middle Ages. For England, we know of, among others, the Tinmen of the Stannaries in Devon and Cornwall, with privileges going back as far as 1198, the Free Miners of the Forest of Dean and, above all, the Free Masons. The latter, in turn, inspired the masons' lodge of Strasbourg Cathedral, who had their privileges of 'freed masonry according to the English fashion' confirmed by the German emperor. In the German Empire, the miners also had similar forms of organization from the thirteenth century.[247]

But urbanization as such is not enough, as the political economy of a state must allow for such institutions. That was not the case under the Seljuks in Anatolia (where the older Byzantine guilds were discontinued), the Mongols in Persia and Iraq, the Mamluks in Egypt, the Mughals in India, or in pre-Ming China. New possibilities for guilds and guild-like institutions emerged, however, after the advent of the Ottomans in the Middle East, the Ming in China and the Tokugawa regime in Japan.

Human capital is also a prerequisite, as is demonstrated by the order in which occupational groups organize. First, the merchants, in Europe from the tenth century onwards, followed by the craftsmen from the thirteenth century and, finally, but to a much lesser extent, the journeymen (literally day wagers). The more literate a society, the better the chance that occupational groups are able to organize – see, for example, northern Italy and the Low Countries. As to the strategies and tactics of the merchant and craftsmen guilds, as a rule, they cooperated with the town government, which was also the authority to address any complaints to about competing guilds. That was different for the journeymen. Largely unorganized before the seventeenth century, but working in guild-based industries, they profited from the protection of their masters, but not always – and when interests clashed, they could demonstrate their power, very conscious of their freedom.[248]

Lastly, the strength of family ties matters, because, in order to prevail, guilds must take up functions that religious, caste or kinship associations are not able to do. Societies with weaker kinship ties, such as Europe since the late Middle Ages, therefore offer more opportunities for guilds than India, for example, with its strong caste networks. In north and north-east India, the economic boom of the late Middle Ages led to far-reaching forms of labour specialization in which new names for occupational groups emerged. The new specialism of spinning and weaving cotton was done by a group of people called Jolaha, the preparation of sugar by the *jati*, or caste, of the Modaka and that of jaggery by the *jati* of the Siuli. The extent to which and when precisely these professional groups came together, either as a sort of guild or as castes, as is undeniably the case in later centuries, is still difficult to establish.[249] China, where the earliest guilds were based not just on occupation but on place of origin, offers a clear illustration of the common quasi-family mechanisms. Equally, merchants from the same area and active in a distant city organized themselves, not coincidentally, as a quasi-family. Guild members, without exception male, treated their live-in journeymen and apprentices as members of the household, having absolute authority over them as they did over their own children. According also to this 'family model', it was difficult for women to work as craftspeople serving masters in foreign households; thus women too worked mostly inside their own home under the jurisdiction of the male head of the household, and, if he happened to be a member of a craft guild, they could work indirectly under guild regulations and even under their protection. But the almost complete exclusion of women from formal individual guilds worldwide meant that though widows might become heads of the household, they had to apply for special permission from the guild to retain their husband's journeymen or apprentices, and did not become a member themselves.

※

Deep monetization of already existing market economies has proved to be crucial for the development of free labour, both of self-employed and wage workers – all working for the market. This is demonstrated by the history of the Mediterranean, north India and China after 500 BCE and by all the societies that followed this path. Yet, as we have seen, these monetized market economies were anything but stable, certainly for the first 1,500 years. Moreover, there are many variants, both due to the many combinations with unfree labour as well as variants in the degree of state intervention in marriage and family systems. We observe other dynamics in the non-monetized parts of the world, namely, the blossoming of tributary-redistributive societies in South and Central America.[250]

With the proliferation of writing, we gain more insight into labour conditions and into the individual and collective strategies of working people and, in particular, wage workers. Despite elite counter-views, testimonies of pleasure in skills and a pride in work among common people from many societies have been preserved. Think of Mahbuba dressed in white, or the observations of Sima Qian or Po Chü-I. This includes the value of working together. Now, the thoughts and actions of the enslaved also reach our ears, most outspokenly in the form of slave revolts, notably that of Spartacus and the Zanj Revolt. Protests against unfair remuneration of the self-employed and wage labourers and their ensuing collective action and organization also testify to the universal ideal of egalitarianism in market societies – again, irrespective of elite views to the contrary – as do protests against enslavement.

These themes have only been touched on here but will be discussed more extensively for the following period, the centuries between 1500 and 1800. The question as to what extent the differences in the position of women at the base (the household) between Western Europe and other parts of Eurasia were already fundamental at this time remains insufficiently answered, certainly in the absence of good data for South Asia.

5
GLOBALIZATION OF LABOUR RELATIONS, 1500–1800

Despite a convergence of labour relations within Eurasia in the centuries prior to 1500, there were significant differences globally in the ways in which people organized their work around this time, and these differences would only increase in subsequent centuries. While humanity had now colonized the whole world – with New Zealand the last to be settled, around 1200 – the interconnectedness of the different continents remained limited. Before Columbus, the Americas were completely aloof from the rest of the world and the connections between north and south were also weak. Admittedly, the Indian Ocean, the China Sea and the European seas were busy with shipping, but they were much more reliant on land connections for mutual contact. The Italian Marco Polo and the Moroccan Battuta, who made long journeys through Asia, are the most striking examples. Only the sea voyages of Columbus from Europe to America, of Vasco da Gama to India,

Industriousness: a woman spinning while caring for swine and donkeys (1636).

193

and those of their emulators made cheaper and therefore more frequent exchange of people, goods and services possible on a global scale.[1] In terms of goods, think of the spread of many American crops, such as corn, tobacco, potatoes and tomatoes in Africa and Eurasia. This exchange was facilitated by the abundant availability of silver as a means of exchange. After the first silver century of Eurasia between around 1300 and 1400, we now witness a second, truly global, silver century. From a common unit of account across Eurasia, from 1600 silver coins now circulated intercontinentally.[2] Sometimes, in the beginning, this globalization went well, but it frequently went wrong, especially in the Americas and in North and Central Asia, where the discoverers treated the newly conquered areas as though they were 'uninhabited'.

Here, the central question is how labour relations and remuneration of work developed in the different parts of the world, no longer only autonomously but now also mainly in conjunction and often in confrontation with each other. Until the 'Great Discoveries' of the rest of the world by Europeans, the Americas, but also tropical Africa, Oceania and Eurasia, were largely independent and more introverted units. It was to be expected that, as a result of the new global contacts, further convergence of labour relations would take place in the following centuries. This is only partly true, however, especially in respect of Africa and the Americas. Three hundred years later, around 1800, Europe already dominated large parts of the world. Instead of imposing Western labour relations there – mostly free labour for the market – Europeans promoted and often introduced all kinds of unfree labour.

This process of convergence and divergence proceeded all in different ways and at a different pace, everywhere. The contact between Europe and Asia differed for centuries from that between Europe, America and Africa. While prosperous and powerful states in Asia allowed in European traders, they long determined the rules of the game themselves. It was only after around 1750, when Europeans began to play a key role in a few parts of Asia, that this also had consequences for the local way of working and for labour relations. This happened even later in Oceania.

In short, we must guard against simply projecting more recent global inequalities in prosperity and political power back to the era of the 'Great Discoveries', as if the inherently superior West just 'walked over' the rest of the world. In fact, it went rather differently. Remarkably, until the end of the eighteenth century, labour relations in parts of Eurasia, Western Europe, India, China and Japan developed in a similar way, namely by increasing the

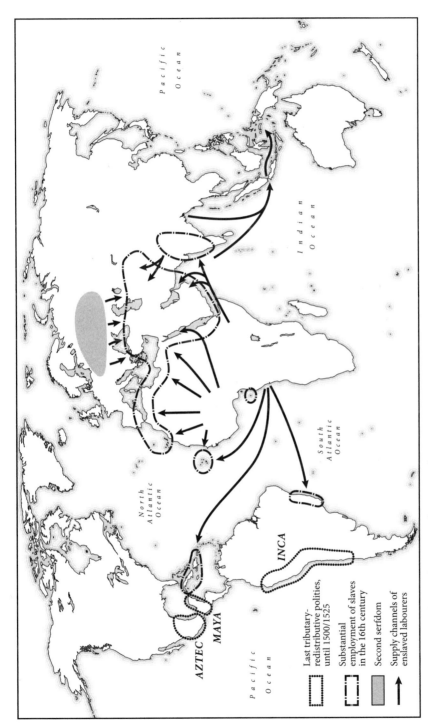

Map 5. Important labour relations in the sixteenth century.

input of labour on the market – that of men and, now, women and even children – called the 'industrious revolution'.[3]

However, this increased labour intensity in vast areas of Eurasia, in what was home to perhaps the largest part of the global population at that time, cannot hide the fact that Western Europe was stealing a march in other areas, to the extent that, from around 1800, it would dominate the whole world. This happened in a number of steps. Firstly, the discovery of the Americas swiftly culminated in conquest, and the existing tributary labour relations of the Aztecs and the Inca were upended, with great benefits for the Spanish and Portuguese and later the Dutch, French, English and other invaders. Secondly, captives sold to Europeans in the ports of West Africa were put to work as slaves on plantations in the Americas. Moreover, European demand stimulated African supply more and more. This had serious consequences not only for Africa, and, of course, for the slaves themselves, but also for the profitability of the plantations and for the availability of affordable American products on the global market. Enslaved labour also increased in South and especially South East Asia. Thirdly, the quality of workers, particularly in Western European cities, gradually increased in tandem with education and literacy. Together, these three developments provide an explanation for how, in a brief period from around 1750, Western Europe could eventually also impose its conditions on Asia, causing stagnation and even decline, or exacerbating existing problems: the so-called Great Divergence.

This chapter begins by discussing the dynamic changes within Eurasia, noting the key similarities between east and west. As we shall see, the common foundation (see Chapter 4) was the way in which labour relations between households were primarily organized via the market. From Ireland to Japan and from the Philippines to Portugal, the products of labour, insofar as they were not consumed within the household, were offered for sale and traded on the market. Small, independent farmers and artisans dominated. In addition, a significant number offered their labour and services for a wage. As had been the case in the previous period (so already for 2,000 years), this happened individually – in particular, soldiers, sailors, servants and farmhands offered their services – and collectively, via cooperative subcontracting, historical examples of which we will see below in relation to copper mining and processing and the minting of coins in Japan and China. In addition to free wage labour, in the sense of the individual freedom to conclude work contracts (including the necessary restrictions that these could entail), unfree labour in the form of slavery and serfdom also occurred in Eurasia. This was significant, but much less intense than elsewhere.

Work within these market societies intensified greatly in the period 1500–1800 – hence economic historians refer to this process as 'the labour-intensive path'. In agriculture, but also in the concomitant cottage industries, productivity per household sharply increased, because much more time could be spent on production for the market, not only by men but now especially by women and even children. As we will see, this change began in specific regions of Japan, China, India and Western Europe and subsequently spread throughout this large continent, as far as Russia – in addition to and as a feature of serfdom. Urbanization and the associated professional specialization usually increased in these frontrunning regions too.

Of course, regional diversity also occurred within this common trend of growing labour intensity. Within Europe, for example, a separation between west and east arose with the advent of 'second serfdom' in Eastern Europe. In addition, there was a 'Little Divergence' within Western Europe, whereby, first, the Netherlands surpassed northern Italy, subsequently the Dutch Republic overtook the southern Netherlands, and finally England overtook the Dutch Republic again.[4] In the most advanced areas, work became increasingly capital-intensive, resulting in a qualitative shift in England in the second half of the eighteenth century: the capital-intensive Industrial Revolution. Because this was still barely visible before 1800, it is a theme that will be addressed in Chapter 6.

After a detailed description of the spectacular labour intensification (in addition to the expansion of wage labour) in Eurasia (pp. 197–224), which, for many people, meant a longer life (in comparison with previous centuries, but, still very modest when measured against our own era), there then follows a discussion of the just as spectacular, but in this case negative, changes elsewhere. Firstly, the impact of globalization is treated in relation to the Great Divergence and discussions of slavery (pp. 244–79); then the labour-extensive path is followed with an examination of serfdom in Eastern Europe and Russia (pp. 279–89). This culminates in the situation around 1800, the starting point for the two final chapters, which cover the last two centuries.

The labour-intensive path in early modern Asia

We start our investigation of the labour-intensive path, that is to say the more efficient use of time by different members of the household, in the big centres of culture in Asia: Japan, China and India. As indicated, the expansion of free wage labour and associated labour relations will not be forgotten in this regard.

The Japanese historian Kaoru Sugihara – following Akira Hayami – advocates this scenario of a 'labour-intensive path'.[5] He states that we should not only look to the successful combination of capital and labour for an explanation of economic growth in market economies, but that we should also seriously consider a second possibility. That is the development of the quality of the worker and the degree to which this quality can be deployed – in principle, irrespective of the amount of capital invested.[6] The deployment of human labour in agricultural societies – that is, in the vast majority of the world in 1500 and long afterwards – is extremely seasonally sensitive. It is either running or standing still: running during harvest time and, to a lesser degree, during ploughing, sowing and especially weeding, and standing still in the intermediate periods. This pattern is not the same for men as it is for women. In some societies, men's work is limited primarily to a few tough weeks of harvesting or ploughing; in others, men mow, while the women bind the grain or turn the grass; in others still, dairy processing is typical women's work. Regardless, for both men and women (and, within this, age groups can also be distinguished) in a typical agrarian society, there is a lot of spare time. In principle, this can be spent productively by re-organizing existing cultivation or by commencing other activities at home or elsewhere. In particular, in the period 1500–1800, many places in Eurasia (with its forerunners and outliers) successfully experimented with filling this time within agriculture itself, in cottage and manufacturing industries, in services and so on.[7] In all cases, it is first and foremost about extra sources of income for the household without the withdrawal of labour from one sector to another.

Peasant households, farmers owning or leasing a small acreage, had the most labour power and the greatest need for extra income. It was decided within this unit which members would carry out which activities, and where, exactly, because the search for more work was not limited to the immediate environment. Thus, these are also the centuries in which seasonal work and other forms of temporary migration developed widely.

Japan

Tokugawa Japan provides a good example of changing agricultural production methods that led to a greater commitment to work. The country had shielded itself from the rest of the world by strictly regulating international movement of people and goods (from 1639, Chinese and Dutch ships were permitted almost exclusively, and only in limited numbers) and, because almost all available parcels had been exploited, land was much scarcer,

> and there was little room left for pasture. Plough and transport animals were used, but land was seldom available for the production of meat, dairy products or wool. Thus Japanese agriculture concentrated on the improvement of annual crop output per unit of land, with the use of human labour, manure, seeds and agricultural tools. Concern for fixed capital, in the form of cattle, fences and so on, or the sale of land played little part in the development of labour-intensive technology and labour-absorbing institutions.[8]

In the words of the American Japanologist Thomas C. Smith: 'Time was regarded as fleeting and precious, and great moral value attached to its productive use. Farmers made elaborate efforts to coordinate work and to stretch nature's constraints by the skilful use of early and late varieties, between row-planting, straw-covered planting beds, fast-acting fertilizers'.[9]

Besides the cultivation of staple foods, members of peasant households developed many other activities, as the following example of a village in a relatively commercialized district in south-western Japan around 1840 shows:

> Every able-bodied person works at salt making and other employment as far as farming permits. The average amount of arable land per farm family is only 2.1 tan of paddy and 0.6 tan of upland, and cultivation is relatively easy since the terrain is level. In time free from farming, men make rope and rush mats and other articles by hand; and women work in the salt fields from the third to the eighth month and during the rest of the year devote themselves exclusively to weaving cotton cloth, not even taking time to cut firewood and gather grass for compost [traditional female work].[10]

The importance of non-agricultural production in the countryside follows on from the assertion that it accounted for 40 to 50 per cent of regional production, although 'farmers' comprised around 90 per cent of the population of each domain.[11]

It is no coincidence that this labour-intensive path of economic development surged in Tokugawa Japan. After centuries of civil wars, two key political changes occurred with direct consequences for working Japan. Firstly, the Samurai were now concentrated in cities under direct supervision of the government. This initiated a period of centuries-long peace, but also of rapid urbanization. In 1600, only 3 per cent of the population lived in cities of more than 10,000 residents; 50 years later, this was already more than 13 per cent, and in 1700, 15 per cent. Some of these cities were very large: Edo (Tokyo), the seat of the government, had a million inhabitants; Osaka and Kyoto each had half a million; and several provincial cities recorded 100,000 residents. In order to achieve and maintain these numbers, and to compensate for urban mortality, continuous immigration from the countryside was required. That was difficult to maintain, not least because of the prosperity of the countryside at this time. Consequently, urbanization decreased again to 11 per cent in 1750, before climbing back up to 15 per cent in 1900.[12]

Secondly, taxation was based on the rice yield per village, thus the role of farming families became crucial.[13] This led to a special variant of the stem family, the so-called *Ie*, whose continuity was central. In large parts of the country, land ownership, status and also the name of such a family passed from the father to the eldest son, or, if that was not possible, to the son-in-law or an adopted son. Continuity of the *Ie* and of its name was paramount. The principle of the *Ie* was so central that businesses were also organized on this basis. This meant that the head of a family who required external labour would automatically be hiring a new 'family member', as it were. This was particularly the case when recruiting young people. Generally, they were aged between 11 and 14 years old and were hired for 5, 6 or more years of apprenticeship in return for room and board and a chance to learn a trade and, therefore, necessarily, also trade secrets. How, though, could you trust such a person and avoid buying a pig in a poke?

In fact, this problem was so big that the government got involved. At the start of the century, self-sale and pawn services were already banned, but, to eliminate rogue employment brokers (who conspired with the applicant to collect a nice advance and then would simply repeat the trick on another employer), in 1665–68 laws were introduced that required reliable guarantors for a bona fide labour contract. The written employment contracts were signed and sealed not only by the father of the candidate but also by guarantors who knew him or her. They guaranteed strict compliance, as is apparent

200

from the following example of a contract, concluded in 1776 with the large Maruo sake and soy sauce brewery in Tatsuno and signed by guarantor, parent and employee:

> Guarantee of Service. We aver that this Shige is sent to serve you for ten years from this year of the monkey to the coming year of the ram. She was born in Mino Otsu Gun Shihomata village as the daughter of Kisanji and we have known her family for generations so we stand as her guarantors. Her religious sect is traditionally Nishi Honganji [Pure Land Buddhism Jodo Shinsu]. We have her temple registration and she is not a member of the prohibited Christian sect. If she should become one, tell us immediately. She will not turn her back on government prohibitions. Furthermore, she is not a warrior, a masterless warrior or the daughter of one. If she could cause any trouble whatsoever, not to mention stealing money and running away or absconding, we will be sure that the shop master suffers from no difficulties at all. If at the end of the contract term you like her you may use this contract for however many years you like. This person is not to take time off or go to work for someone else during the contract period. If this should happen, she will accept whatever you feel is appropriate with not one word of complaint.[14]

This contract appears to be aimed only at protecting this large brewer, but, in fact, the employer was often left empty handed, when his employee did not do what he said. In such cases, the employer did not seek redress through the courts or via a guild, if there was one, but rather entered into a negotiation with the family and the guarantors. In most cases, the culprit – having offered apologies and compensation for any losses – was courteously taken on again, sometimes several times over. This was certainly the case when much of the apprenticeship had already been served and many production secrets were at stake. Equally, it was difficult for an *Ie*-based firm to fire a permanent employee, in much the same way as, say, parents would be reluctant to cast out an unruly child.

In addition to this permanent core of family members and workers with a long-term wage contract, there were also casual workers, often paid by the day. The largest companies could employ thousands of people, and these were, of course, not considered family members. Let us take the mining industry (gold, silver and copper) as an example, specifically the copper mines in the north of the country. In 1686, there were about 200,000 miners and 100,000 charcoal producers at 50 copper mines, 10,000 workers in refineries at Osaka and numerous seamen for the transportation of the copper to the smelters at Osaka and, from there, to Nagasaki, where, from around 1700, 90 per cent was exported: to China (60 per cent) and Batavia (30 per cent).[15] For a long time, Japan was the world's main copper producer. Aside from technological innovation in surveying, drainage, the manufacturing of strong iron digging tools and the refining technology, many labourers were needed, both men and women. The latter, the wives of those who worked in the mine, crushed and sorted the ore, together with their children. In 1837, they comprised 30 per cent of the workforce at the Besshi mine.

In the eighteenth century, problems with the water drainage in the mines led to compulsory reduction of production. The cause was a government-imposed wage cut, as a result of which drainage workers no longer came voluntarily to the mines. Instead, criminals and vagrants were rounded up; subsequently, peasants were drafted from the surrounding villages and, ultimately, inhabitants of big cities who had lost their family registration papers were mobilized. Rather than labour-saving technical innovation (possible due to knowledge of better pumping methods)[16] forms of forced labour were sought in this fully government-controlled sector. This included a compulsory truck system whereby the mine operators had a monopoly on the sale of rice to labourers, who generally lived and worked far from the inhabited world. They received this rice at preferential rates; in other words, the more workers there were, the more profit for the company shops. Consequently, there was no incentive to introduce labour-saving techniques. However, as a result of the abandonment of the free labour market, the remedy of labour-intensive production did not work either.

In sum, an important innovation in the nature and organization of labour occurred in the predominantly agrarian Tokugawa Japan. Firstly, work on the generally small farms became diversified, as a result of which there was not only a greater yield, but household members spent more hours working in the peak seasons, and specialist knowledge and certainly work discipline increased. Secondly, opportunities were also successfully sought to use the remaining time productively, for example producing, spinning and weaving silk and cotton. Any products of agriculture and cottage industry not directly consumed were sold on the market. This made it possible to purchase luxury products such as sugar again. As a result of these changes, planning, technical and general skills also developed within the household. In addition, wage labour in Japan expanded with the commodity chain from copper ore to cash coins (see pp. 205–10).

In agriculture itself, deep monetization was less dynamic. A village worked as a tax-paying unit and therefore was much more than just a collection of peasant households. According to Kuroda, '[i]t possessed common land for uses such as collecting fire wood ... Under these circumstances, various forms of labour exchange in proximate locations such as *yui* (labour exchange for agricultural work) dominated Japanese life. Under such a cohesive atmosphere, it is no exaggeration to say that day labour for a cash payment settled on the day would have seemed unsocial'. Instead, hiring day labourers was not a one-time but a continual transaction, and wage payments were deferred, sometimes by one month or even more.[17]

China

Tokugawa Japan followed the labour-intensive path within strict national markets because, for more than two centuries, its interaction with the global market was minimal, but labour intensification also occurred elsewhere in Asia – including in regions that were exposed to the forces of the international market, or where the stem family was less well developed, such as in the Yangtze Delta in China.[18] In the eighteenth century, about as many people lived there as in Japan, and, in many other respects, both parts of East Asia resembled each other, although there were also interesting differences.

Between 1400 and 1800, the population of the Jiangnan Plain in the eastern Yangtze Delta increased sharply, but the cultivated area hardly changed.[19] By far the most important source of livelihood was wet rice cultivation. This involved minimal animal energy, which was not essential for ploughing or for transport in the water-rich delta. Meat was supplied by pigs and poultry. The welfare level was high until late in the eighteenth century; indeed, as high as it was in England and more than double that of the rest of China. This success can be explained primarily by the gradual rise in rice yields as a result of dykes, canals, polders and windmill-driven square-pallet pumps from the Song to the mid-Qing.[20] Secondly, in the Ming-Qing era, a smart division of labour was introduced, whereby peasant men and women derived their income from a combination of farming, cottage industry and trade. In terms of cottage industry, the rapid rise of cotton growing and industry is particularly notable under the Ming, while the silkworm was cultivated by the wives of yet other peasants. The silk industry was, by contrast, concentrated in cities.

The labour-intensive path in China was also concentrated in farming households, but there were several key differences in comparison with Japan in this regard. For example, farms were divided up substantially, which meant that there were increasingly small plots for the yeomen (who accounted for half of the labour; the other half were free tenants) and a greater need for additional earnings. These Chinese farmers preferred to sell their products for cash in the marketplace, whereas their Japanese counterparts dealt with urban merchants who provided advances: freedom with risk versus dependence with more certainty. For agricultural labourers, this was mirrored by their gathering at central places, like bridges and marketplaces. There they hired themselves to the highest bidder against a daily wage in cash, paid immediately after the performance of the daily task.[21] The typical Chinese household deviated from that of the Japanese in other respects, too. Gender-selective infanticide led to a shortage of marriage partners for poor men. These were the sons of those who had inherited too little land to survive and who therefore became wage workers. Immigration into the countryside from outside the delta was negligible, because a deposit, usually the equivalent of three years' rent, was necessary to secure a tenancy. The large cities, such as Shanghai, were thus dependent on the immigration of surplus peasants from the delta.

In the surrounding countryside, smallholders were primarily engaged in rice growing, and their wives and any daughters (in addition to helping in the fields) were involved in the textile industry, especially cotton. They earned a little money from spinning but with weaving all the more, and, in the eighteenth century, the delta supplied the entire empire and even exported overseas. This dependence on exports would also prove to be a weakness, as competition from other parts of China began to increase at the end of the century.

There was renewed urban growth, not only due to the successful rice cultivation in the surrounding countryside, but also as a result of surplus peasant sons migrating to the cities.[22] Their first boom period dates from the Tang era and increased in the Song era. After a decline in the early Ming period, there followed a marked rise in the number of market towns again under the late Ming and the Qing. For a while, Nanjing was the new Ming capital. In both boom periods, not only were commerce and seafaring important but also religion. There were temples and monasteries in the cities, where the faithful of the countryside regularly went on pilgrimage. The lay Buddhist movement of the White Lotus was one of the best-known expressions of this, but there were also Daoist and other shrines that attracted pilgrims from far and wide. Although later strictly monitored by the court, here we are dealing with an important urban service to the countryside. At the same time, this strong bond between the city and the countryside reveals the purchasing power of peasants, the free time that they could afford and their opportunities for cultural education, including reading the pamphlets and books that were disseminated via the shrines.

Let us now turn from the industrious Yangtze Delta to the empire as a whole – and, in particular, to the development of skills in relation to the industrious revolution. This can be elaborated using some specific examples.[23] First, the circulation of useful knowledge, and second, as in the case of Japan, the commodity chain from copper to coin, a product that was so essential to this deeply monetized society.

With the opportunity to disseminate knowledge and literacy among the population, China was not in such a bad state. After all, book printing had already been invented there and in Korea in the eighth century.[24] This resulted in a more efficient method for reproducing manuscripts than simply copying them, which, in turn, allowed them to reach more people. In addition to copying texts, something that certainly did not die out quickly, more and more printed texts became available, especially in China where they were manufactured with the help of woodblocks (from which whole, ready-made pages were cut using a gouge). This differed from fifteenth-century Europe, which started to cast individual letters from lead. Chinese book production had already increased sharply under the Song, and it did so again in the period 1600–1800. Book scholars have tried to compare the number of titles and publications for different countries and continents, and it is not impossible that, at least until the eighteenth century, there were no major differences between Western Europe and East Asia in this regard.[25]

What seems more important to me is that a lot of printed matter was also able to reach the ordinary reader due to the fact that, from the seventeenth century, prices began to fall sharply. Hence, not only in Europe but also in China, book stalls, hawkers with books on their backs and, eventually, bookshops also appeared. In China, an estimated 30 to 45 per cent of men and 2 to 10 per cent of women were able to recognize some 1,000 different characters.[26] Some of them could also read more complicated texts and thus interpret them and show them to others.

As was the case everywhere, by far the most printed matter was of a religious and moral nature, but technical manuals also appeared, often illustrated and thus accessible to anyone with a technical mind. The Chinese government took the lead early on. Manuals for agricultural and textile technology were the most popular. One on rice farming and sericulture dates from the twelfth century; another from the thirteenth century also included cotton cultivation; and one from the early fourteenth century 'broke new ground by showing the details of the construction of tools, equipment and machinery used in farming and textile-making, and by integrating technical drawings and diagrams with texts [including] drawings of a winnowing-fan, a silk-reel, water powered bellows and irrigation equipment'.[27] In addition, manuals were published for construction, machine and equipment building, river control, salt making, paper making and printing, shipbuilding, and so on. Most importantly, such books were regularly reprinted.

The pinnacle of this kind of technological literature was the *Tiangong Kaiwu* ('The Exploitation of the Works of Nature') by Song Yingxing, published in 1637.[28] It was a summary of everything that had appeared in this field to that point, supplemented with observations by the author from his travels through the empire. Thanks to the fall in book prices, this tome became available to a broader section of the population, including traders and artisans. Its popularity is evident from the fact that it was reprinted within just a few decades. Curiously, however, in parallel to the *Tiangong Kaiwu* came a sudden end to China's technological lead. Large parts of the text were subsequently incorporated into a general encyclopaedia, but there was no longer any question of their own Chinese follow-up, other than perhaps in sub-fields. Furthermore, from the early seventeenth century, translations of European works appeared, with increasingly realistic technical illustrations. Consequently, it seems generally true that, for the seventeenth and eighteenth centuries, China was still at an advanced technical level, but that development in this regard had come to a halt. There are certainly exceptions to this rule, however, such as the publication in 1777 of an illustrated manual for printing with movable type (instead of block printing).[29]

The most impressive economic achievements come, as we have seen, from the expansion of agriculture, but also from mining and infrastructure, especially if we consider that the empire also expanded significantly as a result of various wars, reaching its current size around the mid-eighteenth century. The expansion of mining in the south has an extraordinary background. For centuries, China had sourced its copper, especially that for casting cash coins, from Japan, until that country decided to cut its exports in favour of its own coin production in the early eighteenth century.[30] China was thus forced to expand its copper mines in Yunnan and, indeed, it achieved this aspiration in a short space of time, despite major logistical difficulties. In the 1720s, Yunnan matched Japanese imports; in the 1740s, Yunnan was already five times more important, and in the 1760s its production was ten times more important than the imports from Japan.[31] Instead of importing ready-to-use copper bars via the relatively short crossing, by junk, from Nagasaki, the metal now had to come from thousands of kilometres away, from a southern border region that, at that time, was indirectly and, in reality, sometimes only nominally controlled by the emperor.[32]

Yunnan was rich in the minerals gold, copper, silver and tin, and was linked to both India and the rest of China by trade. In addition to these precious, non-ferrous metals, it also exported horses and salt, while cowries were imported from Bengal. The partial Islamization of the region will also have taken place via this route. China strengthened its hold on the area in 1682, mainly because of the great importance of the silver mines in Yunnan and, just across the border, in Burma and Annam. The total production of this region may even have equalled the amount of silver being imported from America.[33] Copper mining was also expanded, by as much as a factor of ten or more between 1716 and 1735. And that was by no means the end of the growth.[34] The main workforce, the capital and the technology were provided by Han Chinese from China proper, and most of the silver produced flowed back there. Local populations avoided the unhealthy and intensive labour in the mines, and there were even frequent rebellions of the various Miao people prior to their subjugation in 1727.[35]

From a technological and logistical point of view, the transport of, in particular, the copper from the mines to the metropolitan mints in Beijing was most impressive.[36] In the Qianlong period (1735–96), the bulk of Yunnan's copper output – between 2,000 and 4,000 tons per year – was transported first by porters, who carried it on their backs over land from the individual mines to several collection points, and, from there, to Szechuan and the harbour at Luzhou, situated on the Changjiang Yangtze River. Porters and pack animals had to cross the rugged terrain, including passes at altitudes exceeding 3,000 metres and notorious slopes of well over 1,000 metres. The government therefore tried, where possible, to replace land transport with that over water. This required removing as many as possible of the 132 rapids in the upstream rivers, such as the Jinsha. The engineering projects in this river between 1740 and 1748 amounted to 800,000 workdays, and still the end result was nothing to write home about.

Before being loaded into the river boats in Luzhou, the copper was officially weighed (and sometimes samples were even weighed twice to prevent obfuscation), packed into baskets or roped together in bundles, and then registered and numbered with the help of wooden tags that were tied to the bundles. For a convoy of 15–30 river boats transporting 600 tons (approximately 5 of these convoys took place annually), this strict and highly efficient process took 35 days, with accurate weighing requiring the most time. The journey then commenced by way of the Yangtze River, via Hankou to Yizheng and from there to the Grand Canal and on to the capital. Such a convoy required 750 crew, consisting of a core of helmsmen and boat masters, assisted by 30 oarsmen per boat on the stretch through the Three Gorges, who were exchanged roughly every 70 km. That amounts to labour productivity of 800 kg per person on board, all heavily supervised by magistrates and their staff, clerks, soldiers, runners and the like.[37]

Occasionally, sacrifices had to be performed, accompanied by feasts. At the beginning of the weighing at Luzhou, three pig heads and four smaller animals were sacrificed. At the intermediate stop in Chongqing, necessary for transloading, a great river sacrifice took place:

> All helmsmen, boat masters and skippers of the sampans and the transport brokers ... as well as the runners who accompany the convoy as guards of provide [sic] labour are invited to banquet seats [at tables upstairs in the temple building]. Altogether over 60 tables of wine seats. In addition, 8–9 tables of middle grade seats for one's own private servants, provide all with sea vegetables and surrounding small plates, and have them positioned to be able to watch the theatre inside the temple.[38]

After a journey of ideally eleven months from embarkation in Luzhou, the metal arrived in Beijing, where the copper was processed in two minting houses, that of the Ministry of Revenue and that of the Ministry of Works.[39] In the 1740s, their workforce of more than 3,000 men produced 0.7 to 1.5 million strings of copper cash per annum (a string containing 770 cash coins).

The technology necessary for supplying the biggest state on earth with small change required a combination of mass production and high technical specifications. While fundamentally fiduciary money, the public had to be prevented at all costs from distinguishing between different kinds of cash coins (as became customary, in fact, from the 1830s). This happened as follows:

> The coins were cast in large numbers in batches in two-piece moulds arranged vertically. Moulds were prepared from fine sand re-inforced with an organic binder and contained within a wooden box. A pattern of 50–100 'mother cash' (either individually made or identical copies of a single master cash) were pressed lightly into the surface and then a second mould box was placed face down on top. An impression was thus taken of both sides of the mother cash pattern. The mould boxes were then turned over and separated so that the mother cash remained on the lower mould surface. A fresh mould box was then laid on this and again the pair turned and separated. In this way a series of two-piece moulds were obtained. After clearing channels between the coin impressions and making a central runnel, the boxes were fixed together in pairs and, following a preliminary firing, metal was poured in. The result was a 'cash-tree' from which the coins were separated and subsequently cleaned up.[40]

Innovations in the period under scrutiny included the transition to brass, replacing the more expensive leaded bronze, the improved cleaning of the coins and the extension of the number of minting houses throughout the empire, involving many logistical problems in provisioning them with matrices and raw materials. Starting hesitantly in the early years of the century, all coins produced from 1527 onwards were made of brass by adding 12.5 per cent of metallic zinc to the copper. During this process, one-quarter of the zinc was lost through vaporization. This mass processing of zinc substantially predates its introduction in Europe. It is still debatable whether this zinc was initially imported from India or mined in China proper, which certainly was the case after 1620.

This complex manufacturing process was organized around furnaces.[41] In the 1730s, the fifty furnaces of the Ministry of Works and the twenty-five of the Ministry of Revenue – totalling seventy-five regular furnaces in the capital (apart from the assisting furnaces) – were in the hands of a dozen closely connected families. The furnace heads received money from the mints' superintendents, which they spent on food and other daily necessities for the craftsmen and workers and on money to be paid to them after each casting period. Then the bill was settled and, after the deduction of food and other expenses, the remaining wages were determined and then actually paid out monthly or after ten casting periods. The interests of the workers were protected through a series of in-built checks and balances: they themselves had to inquire about the market prices of rice, noodles and vegetables, and wages were paid out by the furnace heads to the individual workers, who were registered by name, age, appearance and native place, in public and under the supervision of the commissioner-in-chief of the mint. In order not to mix up recently produced copper cash coins and currency wages, these sums had to be paid out in silver.

The mother coins, prepared by the Board of Revenue, were made not only for the two minting houses in the capital, responsible for nearly half of the total coin production, but also for those spread over the empire. Because Yunnan was located so close to the copper mines, it had nine different mints in the eighteenth century, while most other provinces only had one. Twice a year, a new master cash was cut in Beijing for each province. After approval, it was cast in a few hundred mother cash copies by the Board of Revenue and sent to the respective minting houses. Each new master cash differed slightly from the preceding one, enabling the central authorities to check on the mint masters, who were deliberately kept in the dark about this minor change. This secured fabrication according to universal and uniform standards, but obviously this demanded a high degree of organization and control.

Concluding this overview of work processes in early modern China, questions are raised about how all those workers defended their interests. Did they do it individually or by organizing themselves? It follows from the above that households formed the organizational heart of early modern China. In contrast to Europe (see pp. 189–91, 232–5), craft guilds appear to play a minor role.[42] Common-origin organizations of migrants, while similar to guilds, were more characteristic.

In China, the patrilineal family dominated both rural cottage industry and urban crafts. The family represented the interests of its members, but members also had to defend their position within it. That was not always simple for the resident daughter-in-law. Skills, the basis of existence, were passed down the male line within the patrilineal family, but the daughter-in-law who married in from another village was frequently excluded from learning the most valued technical knowledge. An extreme variant of this is the habit of 'marriage resistance', meaning that parents were willing to let their daughters stay at home after marriage in order to keep these skills a family secret. From there, they worked as silk reelers in silk filatures, and sometimes they also lived with other women.[43]

Many villages and towns specialized in the making of specific products and, in such cases, it was the local group, rather than the individual family, that stood up for collective interests. The paper industry in Szechuan offers a good example of this kind of location-specific, group-wise production:

> the requisite skills do not fully exist until the moment when ... partners face and give a visual clue – a look or nod – to begin. In papermaking, such distributed skills are most evident in the production of large six- or eight *chi* paper (97 × 180 or 124 × 248 cm), molded by teams of two to four workers who synchronise their movements in a slow, rhythmic dance. Socially distributed skills also exist in the continuous operations around the vat, where teams of pulpers, vatmen and brushers work in close cooperation, and in seasonal steaming, where groups of labor-exchanging neighbors constitute a second site of skill reproduction.[44]

We have already seen how, elsewhere, this kind of collaboration mainly works according to the principles of cooperative subcontracting.

With respect to collective advocacy, artisans and traders from the same place or region worked closely together. In China, this was particularly the case with groups of specialists from the same place who temporarily practised their trade in cities and elsewhere, even abroad (for example, on Java). This kind of representation of interests is similar to that of Western European (and later Japanese) guilds, but one of the essential characteristics, legal recognition, was generally lacking from these so-called *hang* before the nineteenth century. Their main official task was therefore welfare of members and joint ritual functions.[45]

We see the same common-origin principles reflected among workers in the few large-scale industrial and mining units. For example, in the famous porcelain industry of greater Jingdezhen, with its hundreds of thousands of workers, eleven common-origin organizations were operating in the eighteenth century.[46] We see a comparable pattern among mineworkers in Yunnan.[47] The workers in the big minting houses in Beijing were strongly intermeshed, had their own apprenticeship system and apparently worked collectively and fairly independently per furnace. No wonder, then, that they were able to organize a number of major and partially successful strikes between the beginning of the eighteenth and the early nineteenth century. The most successful were those of 1741 and 1816.[48] Professor of Chinese History and Society Hans Ulrich Vogel gives us an idea of what happened in the wage conflict of September 1741:

> When Shuhede (the Senior Vice-minister of the Board of War) arrived on the scene with his troops he first had the mint surrounded. Then he went forward personally and attempted to persuade the workers and the craftsmen to despatch lucid representatives to come forward to talk with the officials. Shuhede reports that it first looked as if the workers and craftsmen who had hidden themselves on the earth mound would come down, but eventually they all began to shout and to throw bricks and tiles. In order to teach them a lesson, Shuhede told them that he would open fire on them if they continued to behave in this wicked and depraved way. Only after having fired several rounds of blanks did the workers and craftsmen desist from throwing bricks and tiles, though they continued to shout. Later on the soldiers of the Metropolitan Infantry Command marched forward to suppress the agitation.[49]

Negotiations ultimately brought about a compromise that saw wages increased, but not as much as the workers had originally wanted. More important than such collective actions born out of despair was the possibility for individual workers to have access to courts in cases of wage disputes. Professor of Chinese History Christine Moll-Murata concludes for eighteenth- and nineteenth-century Szechuan that 'to a certain extent, the "small people", who in their plaints and testimonies were required to refer to themselves vis-à-vis the authorities as "ants", harboured the hope that they would get their cash and acceptable working conditions by virtue of adjudication from the representatives of the state.'[50]

India

The combination of urbanization, increased agricultural production, labour intensification in rural households through a mix of peasant farming and cottage industry and, finally, the growth of wage labour that we have seen for early modern Japan and China also applies to India in those same centuries, but with two caveats. The first is that, as previously seen (pp. 143–8), Indian relations take a very specific form: the caste system. The second concerns the development of technical knowledge; that is to say, much less research has been done in this area for India than for the Far East, so what follows is still very preliminary.

In any case, what is certain is that the revival of urbanization and deep monetization that we observed in India from around 1100 gained new impetus in the sixteenth century.[51] Under the most successful Great Mughal Akbar and his initial successors – and probably also under his predecessors, the Suris – India experienced a boom period, politically, economically and culturally. The deep monetization indicates a strongly increased share of the wage-dependent population at that time, certainly in cities such as the government centres of Delhi and Lahore, but also the port city Surat. The earnings of wage workers also started increasing and, between around 1550 and 1650–80, their purchasing power was of the same order as that of their brothers and sisters in China and Western Europe.

The textile industry, in particular, experienced its heyday, and Indian silk and cotton dyed fabrics were world famous.[52] They were exported by sea and land to other parts of Asia, Europe and Africa. From the sixteenth to the eighteenth century, South Asia accounted for no less than a quarter of global textile production. Three production centres stand out: north-west India around Surat, Bengal in the north-east and Coromandel in the south-east.

There is insufficient data regarding the extent to which the consumption of the ordinary men and women who were responsible for this increased production also grew. Until the end of the seventeenth century, real wage growth in north India might point in that direction, but the subsequent decline suggests otherwise. The increased sugar production was, in any case, for domestic consumption. The same may also apply to some of the coffee, tea and opium. But increased income can also be converted into free time, and we do know a bit more about this.[53] In the eighteenth century, pilgrimages were very popular, drawing crowds of people to Hindu and Muslim shrines. The hajj of devout Muslims to Mecca is perhaps the best known of all. Around 1600, roughly 3 per cent of Indian Muslims made a pilgrimage to one of Islam's holiest cities once in their lives.

The question now is whether, as in the case of China and Japan, this gigantic industrial production of textiles and other Indian export goods from the countryside, such as pepper, opium, indigo, tea, coffee and saltpetre, was also established via a 'labour-intensive path' – or, more accurately, the extent to which the production of these goods provided the households of small farmers and peasants with more work and income. In a number of cases this is likely, but sometimes we just have no idea and sometimes we are pretty sure that this was not the case. The cultivation of sugar cane and cotton, but also in some regions that of indigo and poppies, could be perfectly combined with that of basic food grains, pulses and oilseed, because they required labour at different times of the year.[54] In addition, for women, there was spinning, which was not bound by caste restrictions and, in almost all households where it happened, led to a substantial increase in family income. The growing demand from the increased urban population, but especially from the international trade in these products, certainly stimulated the labour intensity of rural households.

Other export crops, however, were not produced by ordinary farmers, but instead by caste-tied specialists, including pepper in south-west India and cinnamon on Ceylon. This was also the case for the production of salt-petre, an essential raw material for making gunpowder in the course of the eighteenth century, and an increasingly important export product from north India.[55] Caste monopolies also played a prominent role in textile production, which, as a result, partly excluded peasants. In India, the activities of artisans and peasants had been so highly segregated for centuries, if not a thousand years, that it was almost impossible to unite them.[56] In 1625, a Dutch merchant concluded that:[57]

> In sum [the Indians] know to behave and occupy themselves with all things according to their caste or lineage, because everyone must do such business as his parents and ancestry has done, that is that a carpenter's son must become a carpenter and marry a carpenter's daughter, the same for a blacksmith, a tailor, a shoemaker, a weaver, and so forth, among whom each must marry and remain, if he wants to be esteemed, and when someone did not marry within his own lineage, he is despised and considered to be a disgrace.[58]

The weaving and the further processing of the highly successful Indian textile industry was thus also in the hands of specific castes that did this and nothing else. It was not an extra income for peasants. The booming textile industry in eighteenth-century Birbhum in Bengal illustrates this nicely.[59] The north-east of the district has been known for its high-quality silk since at least the seventeenth century, and cotton was added from about 1700. The fabrics were not woven by rice farmers (usually sharecroppers who were allowed to keep one-third of the harvest), but by the men of a particular Hindu caste (Tanti) and two particular groups of Muslims. This was done via a Kaufsystem, whereby they received an advance four times a year and were paid definitively once a year.

Part of the raw material was grown locally, by farmers, and, when demand peaked, it was also imported. Some of the final product was also exported, which meant that the busiest season for the weavers fell before the ships' departures, at the latest on 10 March, and therefore in the middle of harvest time. Both activities were therefore mutually exclusive not only due to social conventions but also economic ones. The weavers had to buy their daily food from the market rather than growing it themselves – with disastrous consequences in times of famine.[60]

Some of them procured yarn from housemates,[61] others from professional spinners. The latter were women, mostly widows, and worked irrespective of caste and creed. Spinning of the highest quality yarns could earn a spinner a maximum of Rs 1.75 per month, while a weaver could earn a maximum of double this, to which he could sometimes add the spinning wages of his female housemates. The strict separation between the professions – apart from the spinners – also meant that weavers' households sometimes migrated en masse, either to an area where their industry was expanding strongly, or from an area where it was declining sharply.[62]

Seen in this way, the Indian variant of labour-intensive industrialization therefore does not deviate considerably from that of Japan and the Yangtze Delta. Despite the caste system that makes India so special, the rapidly growing Indian textile industry in the seventeenth and eighteenth centuries did have a major impact. This resulted from the greatly increased employment opportunities for spinners beyond their own weavers' castes. In addition, the hidden unemployment of peasants reduced as a result of more intensive cultivation of the staple food rice, as well as of other crops, in particular cash crops – in addition to the already mentioned cotton, also sugar, silk and indigo.[63] The increased opportunities in spinning aside, India's caste restrictions contrast with Japan and China, with their combination of family income from smallholding and weaving as a cottage industry.

In particular, there were advantages for the non-weaver castes in the numerous activities that were necessary between the growing of cotton, on the one hand, and actually weaving and finishing the cloth, on the other hand. Farm work accounted for a quarter and spinning more than half of all the time necessary before the fabric could be sold. Warping and weaving accounted for roughly 10 per cent each. The historian Ian C. Wendt comes to a position for early modern south India that reveals how important the textile industry was for the shift in female household labour to production for the market.[64] Female labour in peasant households, which consisted of picking, cleaning and spinning cotton, contributed 41 per cent of the money income to peasant households owning 5 acres and as much as 52 per cent for those renting a similar plot. In weavers' families, warping and part-time spinning by women contributed 32 per cent of the monetary income of households owning 2 looms, 38 per cent of those with 1 loom, and 48 per cent in weavers' households without their own loom. But there was also a substantial number of women who were heads of households (mainly widows) earning the total money income. He concludes: 'Female labour contributed circa 5.5 pagodas or 20 rupees annually to many households, which accounted for between one third and one half of many households' total income. Women without male support, particularly widows, could earn a modest living wage for themselves and dependent children by spinning.'

The importance of women's contributions to the family's financial income is evident from all of this, and this also fits with the general theory of the labour-intensive path and the associated industrious revolution (see pp. 226–31 below). That the ambitions of economically active women could thus be stimulated is beautifully illustrated by a folktale from north India that was only published in the nineteenth century but is surely much older and fits nicely with the foregoing standpoint:

An ignorant milkmaid was going along with a pot of curds upon her head. As she trudged along the pleasant idea came into her noddle. 'I'll sell these curds; with the price I get for them I'll buy some mangos. I have at home already a few mangos, and altogether there will be more than three hundred. Some of them may perhaps go bad, but at any rate I'll have two hundred and fifty, and for them I'll get a fine price. Then I'll buy a green sari at the Diwali festival. Yes, yes, a green sari will become my style of face beautifully. And then! I'll take it, and put it on for the fair, and step

216

out proudly and show off the finery of my clothes and ornaments and the beauty of my face, bowing a hundred times at every step.' As she imagined all these fine things, the foolish milkmaid in her stateliness gave a lurch, and the curd-pail fell from her head and was smashed to atoms, and all the fine castle which she had built for herself was dissipated.[65]

The moral of this tale is unimportant for now; what is noteworthy is that the ambitions and desires of the 'ignorant' milkmaid are founded on industriousness and market orientation. This is an important recalibration of our ideas about the joint patrilocal family system that north India has in common with China and, according to the sociologist Monica Das Gupta:[66]

sons inherit equal shares of the property, although one son may have the use of additional land if the parents are living with him. Transfer of property and managerial authority takes place gradually, beginning with the sons working under the father's direction, and moving on to the sons taking over some of the managerial decisions as the father ages. Gradually the father becomes only a titular head. The sons move from cultivating their land jointly, to cultivating it separately, and later to formalizing the transfer and the division of the estate. This last step often takes place after the father's death.[67]

On the other hand, large farmers in particular tried to keep the farm intact as much as possible by limiting the number of heirs: a significant number of sons never married, and 'it was through a combination of female infanticide and non-marriage of men that households regulated their population growth'.[68]

It was not only in this regard that the position of women, and in particular of girls and young women, was very vulnerable. Das Gupta explains that the central bond in the Chinese and north Indian joint family is that between patrikin – between parents and children, and, in turn, between siblings. Indeed, the conjugal unit is seen as a potential threat to the bond and is actually discouraged from thriving 'by separating women from men all day in their place of work, and creating separate worlds for men and women to function in'. Thus, unlike in northern European families, the core unit is the household, not the couple:

Women marry into lineages other than their own, while men constitute the next generation of their own lineage. Thus it is the men who constitute the social order, and women are marginal to it. A woman is transferred to her husband's lineage upon marriage [at a very young age], and her own family gives up virtually all rights to her subsequent productivity. In her husband's home, her task is essentially biological: to bear children and to work. The social aspect of her persona is minimal, since it hardly matters which woman gave birth to a child: a child derives its social identity by dint of its position in its father's lineage. ... The powerlessness of women in the patrilinear joint family system of China and North India is at its peak during the early phases of a woman's marriage, which are the peak childbearing years. These are the years when a woman is subject to the stress of reproduction, and her children are very young and vulnerable.... Women themselves also suffer from greater reproductive stress because they are not in a position to take decisions about their own care if they are in their husband's home.

The consequence for the work of men in patrilinear joint families is that they 'remain members of the household and are ... underemployed in the family enterprise', or that they temporarily migrate and remit their earnings.[69] The question now arises as to whether this pessimistic picture also applies to those parts of the Indian population that took the 'labour-intensive path' from the seventeenth to the early nineteenth century and whether we should focus more on the mentality of the proud milkmaid. Unfortunately, a lack of research means that this question cannot yet be adequately answered, although it is not impossible that the gender norms as described by Das Gupta became petrified in the colonial era.[70]

Here, however, we must conclude with another way in which peasants could satisfy their great need for extra income without resorting to cottage industry (other than spinning), as was the case elsewhere in Eurasia.[71] That is to say, by pushing the boundaries of the system through seasonal and multi-annual temporal migration. This is different from the permanent migration of specific professions that, as we have seen, maintains internal cohesion, along with its associated norms and values. Seasonal and multi-annual temporal migration, whereby groups from different backgrounds come together to work, could, under specific conditions, lead to the disruption of existing ideas about the way in which work had to be done, in collaboration with whom and under which conditions. Think of Bengali sailors on Dutch East India Company (VOC) ships or of some professional soldiers.[72]

The gunpowder factory at Ichapur (north of Calcutta) in the late eighteenth century offers a good example.[73]

The manufacturing of gunpowder for the Bengal Presidency gained momentum as a result of the intensification of the English war effort from the 1780s, when a number of campaigns were fought against Tipu Sultan, also known as the Tiger of Mysore, and, later, simultaneous manoeuvres against the French (as far as Egypt!), the Dutch (on Java, Ceylon and in the Cape) and the Spanish (in the Philippines), in addition to all kinds of other enemies. The number of workers increased to some 2,500 in 1797, thus making it one of the largest industrial establishments in the world at that time. Apart from the director and his right-hand man, virtually all workers were Indians, including the supervisory staff. After the October rains, the men and women (one-quarter to one-third) arrived, most of them from the Burdwan-Birbhum-Midnapore area a few hundred kilometres to the west, as well as from Chittagong, even further away to the east across the Bay of Bengal. In May, most of them returned home to resume small-scale share cropping and cottage industry until the new season at Ichapur in the autumn.

At the government factory, leased to the Scotsman John Farquhar from 1787 to 1814, they performed their skilled tasks in shifts, 24 hours per day, 7 days per week, Hindus and Muslims, men and women from different parts of Bengal and Orissa, all intermingled in one big factory. Some of them had to overcome cultural objections, like the turners, who turned the composition of charcoal, saltpetre and sulphur into the necessary balanced mix for effective gunpowder. They were obliged to wear protective leather jackets, trousers, gloves and caps-cum-masks, anathema for Hindus. All ran the risk of becoming maimed or dying from the regular explosions of gunpowder. But risk also united them, because, by way of several collective actions, including strikes, they managed to obtain a formal pension scheme. From 1783, monthly pensions, equal to their final last salaries, became available for workers who had survived an explosion but were unable to resume work, as well as for the close relatives of victims who had not survived.

Originally, those entitled had to collect the money in person from the factory premises, a major impediment for those living hundreds of kilometres away. This was changed following the action of the Chittagong-based Khoosoomdi. One year after having received a message from the factory director that her young, unmarried son Chamaroo had been 'destroyed' by the explosion of Powder Mill No. 2 on 21 February 1797, she travelled all the way to the director's office at Ichapur in order to apply for a pension from him. She convinced Farquhar to change his policies on two important points: not only that, as a mother of an unmarried victim, she was entitled to the pension, but also that it had to be paid out in future at Chittagong. The director reported to his superiors that she and others had 'represented to me that the danger and expense of an annual journey from Chittagong to the Presidency [in this case Ichapur] for the pension has in a great degree frustrated the good intentions of Government, and that they humbly beg that the [Tax] Collector or some other officer at Chittagong may be authorized to pay them monthly at the spot'. Thus, it was decided, and so it continued in the decades to come.

As we have seen, while, compared to China and Japan, the Indian caste system is not necessarily detrimental to economic development and is also more flexible than it is assumed, it did, nevertheless, limit the opportunities for a labour-intensive path. It had other, possibly more positive implications, however. Although these three great civilizations each developed their own writing and counting systems early on, India still stands out in terms of its application of them, particularly in terms of passing on caste-bound professional knowledge from one generation to the next. Not only is formal training important in this regard, but also, in practice, transmitting 'tacit knowledge', undocumented professional competence and skill. The general level of education and the organization of vocational training is key to this.

India may have had an advantage in terms of vocational training, but probably none or much less in the case of general education. Craftsmanship was monopolized by the castes and, in principle, was fixed. From an early age, a boy would be able to copy and thus was slowly initiated into his father's skill. The question, of course, is the extent to which such a closed system was conducive to innovation. The low level of education, in any case, was not. In India – assuming that reliable information from a little later also applied to the sixteenth and seventeenth centuries[74] – the caste system limited education among Hindus: for sons of Brahmins who could afford it, it was the norm, just as it was the norm that they did not do manual work. Furthermore, the Banians, or merchants (increasingly committed to vegan and pacifist Jainism) had a well-developed commercial curriculum. But, like Brahmins and the writers' caste, they did not do manual work either. For Muslims, such restrictions did not apply formally, but, all in all, it is not surprising that the literacy and numeracy rates for India were among the lowest worldwide – noteworthy for such a developed country.

In any case, this hindered the dissemination of knowledge, certainly in combination with the limited production of books, which also limited the possibilities of a reading culture. In these centuries, India had only a few Western-style printers in Goa and Bombay, but Indian languages or Persian, the lingua franca of the Mughals and other ruling houses in India, were still copied by hand until the nineteenth century, which led to a very limited distribution. As for the use of the dominant Persian alphabet, the fact that, in 1727, Muslims in the Ottoman Empire were officially forbidden to print books will certainly have been of influence.[75]

From the labour-intensive to the capital-intensive path: Early modern Western Europe

The path of labour-intensive industrialization has been pursued successfully for centuries not only in Asia but also in Europe, shifting towards the end of this period, and particularly in England, to the capital-intensive phase that we call the Industrial Revolution. For that reason alone, but also because of trade contacts with the rest of the world, with all of the ensuing consequences, it is important to examine the history of work in this part of the world more closely. Let us start with the labour-intensive path in Western Europe, also in connection with the so-called industrious revolution. As in South and East Asia, there was also the scope in Western Europe to spend time more productively. Farm work was organized more efficiently, industrial activities tackled, and both were better coordinated. Finally, through different types of migrations, work in the city and sometimes distant lands were interrelated.

From a comparative perspective, there is little point in listing countries here (because, after all, at that time even the more substantial European countries were about the size of the biggest Chinese provinces). Instead, the labour-intensive path in Western Europe is addressed here mainly from different angles: specialization in increasingly efficient agriculture and associated migrant labour in the countryside; the so-called proto-industry, especially in the countryside, and the demand for products as a consequence of the industrious revolution; the urbanization in Western Europe, involving occupational specialization and organization, hubs of immigration and knowledge; multi-annual temporal mobility; and, finally, the implications of all this for the experience and worldview of working people.

221

Specialization in increasingly efficient agriculture

After the catastrophe of the Black Death, it took half a century for the population of Western Europe to return to its previous level. From then on, expansion of growing areas was only possible in a limited way. The population continued to grow, however, and even doubled between 1500 and 1800, primarily due to the intensification of agriculture. There was no longer much progress to be made in enhancing bread grain yields. Still, average yield ratios of the four principal grains (wheat, rye, barley and oats) in the British Isles and the Low Countries doubled in the early modern period, mainly due to heavy manuring, but they increased only half as much in the rest of Europe.[76] The real profit came from other crops instead. We therefore see the specialization of one region in livestock breeding for dairy production, another for meat production and yet another in horticulture or industrial crops.

Let us take one country as an example: the Dutch Republic, which imported most of its bread grain from Poland (via the Baltic), as well as from England, France and others.[77] As a result, there was room for livestock breeding in lower-lying areas, but also for flax (the raw material for linen), rapeseed (likewise for lamp and other oil), linseed (for oil paint), madder (red textile dye), hemp (for making wick, rope, tarpaulin and fishing nets, and its seed for soap), hops (for breweries) and tobacco in higher regions. The varieties were also greatly improved in livestock breeding. Compared to an ordinary milk yield of 800 litres elsewhere in Europe, that of Dutch Frisian cows was already 2,000 litres per year in the seventeenth century. At the same time, this meant 2.5 times as much work per animal for milking, churning and cheesemaking. Gardeners supplied vegetables, fruit and flowers (the famous tulips, originally from Turkey), first from open ground and later also from greenhouses. Tree nurseries exported all over Europe.

The results of all these innovations were so favourable that it paid to turn lands below sea level into polders, where the water had to be continuously pumped out with the help of windmills. Dykes and channels were also dug, both for drainage and to facilitate transport. The labour for specialized polder farms was partly supplied by the farmer and his household, with the dairy production of butter and cheese in the hands of the women: 'Rural households reorganized their activities; they shed from their work schedules a wide variety of tasks necessary to sustain the household in a regime of self-sufficiency and concentrated their efforts on the remaining tasks, the more strictly agricultural tasks. In a word they specialized. An indicator is the growth of the scale of production, and in areas predominantly engaged in livestock husbandry, the growth of herd size shows this development most clearly.[78] The average farm size also increased, especially following the disappearance of the smallest farms. Most important, however, was the specialization and intensification of farming households, be they owners or tenants.

On the heavy clay soils of Flanders-Zeeland-Holland and Friesland-Groningen, a number of permanent farmhands and girls were needed for ploughing, sowing and, above all, the time-consuming thinning, weeding and harvesting of all these crops. They were either resident and received a sum of money in addition to room and board, or they worked on demand as day labourers – and these day labourers also developed considerable agricultural skills. In Oakham (East Midlands) in 1610, the following distinction was made between two types of farm labourers: 'a "man servant, for husbandrie of the best sort, which can eire, sow, mow, thresh, make a ricke, thacke, and hedge the same; and can kill a hog, sheepe, and calfe" was to be paid Pounds 2 [per year], in contrast to "A meane servant, which can drive plow, pitch cart, and thresh, but cannot expertly sow and mow", who was to be paid only Pounds 1.'[79] Skills were increasingly important not only among full-time farm servants, but, as we will see below, this applied to migrant workers as well.

Migrant workers in the countryside

Due to the seasonal nature of this multitude of crops, including hay cultivation, in addition to all these local workers, labour from elsewhere was needed for specific months of the year.[80] This need was exacerbated by the disappearance of the smaller farms in the highly specialized agrarian regions. Where they still existed, in the less developed hinterlands and in the mountain regions of Western Europe, migrant workers were now attracted en masse by the arable farming regions. Sticking with the North Sea coasts, from Flanders in the south to Bremen in the north, around 1800, the flow of migrant workers swelled to as many as 30,000 people, who were hired in annually during the peak seasons, and then subsequently went home, only to return again the next year.

And the North Sea region was not even the greatest attraction in Western Europe: other major pull-areas were south-eastern England (East Anglia and Lincolnshire), the Paris Basin, Castile and its capital Madrid, the Mediterranean Coast between Catalonia and Provence, the Po Valley and Central Italy. In the three northern areas, 100,000 workers were involved annually, and in the four southern ones this was more than 200,000. That such work was carried out on a vast scale is clear from this description of the Campagna Romana in summertime: 'not seldom one meets six to eight hundred harvesters in the fields, forming a row that goes on for half an hour. From time to time a cry arises that passes down their ranks. Forty to fifty supervisors on horses ride along the row to urge the workers on and to see that they cut the stalks of grain as close to the ground as possible. Mules, laden with wine, bread and cheese, come and go with provisions. At night the workers sleep in the fields.'[81] Common to all these pull-areas is that, over the previous centuries, the farmers developed highly specialized monocultures, which only required a lot of work for part of the year; at the same time, there were hardly any peasants left locally to do that work. Fortunately, they were present in the surrounding regions – sometimes mountainous – where only small-scale farming was possible. Again, from the same report about Central Italy:

> It so happens that wealthy landowners or leaseholders from the Roman Campagna have agents in the département [Trasimeno] who take advantage of the miseries of winter by advancing a supply of grain to farmers in need. In repayment they merely require that their debtors come to the Roman Campagna for the harvest and in this way pay back part or all of their loan. These persons entrusted with the hiring of workers bear the title of 'caporale'. From the landowners, in addition to a double day wage, they receive a bonus of 25 French francs for each worker they take on. These workers in turn were given food and a sum of 4 French francs per work day, half of which they had to give back to pay off their debt to the landowner. Free of debt, a worker would ordinarily be able to take 25 to 30 French francs home with him.[82]

Despite the arduous work and the risk of malaria in the coastal plains, this additional wage was attractive enough for hundreds of thousands of Europeans, before and around 1800 (and millions a century later) to embark on a journey involving a week's walk there and back, year in, year out.

In contrast to farm servants, who received an individual hourly wage, migrant labourers generally worked collectively and for a piece wage, according to a system of cooperative subcontracting – for example, the migrant workers who took on the task of sowing, transplanting, weeding and harvesting the rice in the Po Valley. Rice was ready to be cut between late August and mid-October.

The harvest was accomplished in teams, each consisting of six men and six women. Not only did they cut the rice, they also threshed it and saw to it that the full sacks of rice were stored in the granary. Their pay was between one-fourteenth and one-thirteenth of the yield, which worked out at about 200 litres per person, or, transposed per day, 2.5 French francs. Thus, these types of groups organized the work entirely independently, so the employer only turned up at the start of the season to arrange the group contract and at the end of the season to pay the group's piece wages. This was a previously agreed sum of money based on their finished production of the right quality. The workers then divided the money among themselves at their own discretion.

Among the brickmakers of the small principality of Lippe-Detmold (Westphalia), who dominated the brick factories in large parts of Germany, the Netherlands and Scandinavia – apart from a small sum per worker for the job broker and after the deduction of the costs of communally purchased food – this happened as follows:[83] a few inexperienced youngsters who had to learn the trade were put on hourly wages, whereas experienced workers would receive a piece rate. The most experienced brickmakers (fireman, moulders and temperers) received the highest share, whereas the less experienced gang members (carters, upgangers and off-bearers) received half or three-quarters of the sum received by the most experienced gang leaders. Separately, the gang leader-cum-fireman received a fixed sum per worker for his supervisory work. Thus, all gang members had a direct interest in efficient cooperation for production. Seasonal brickmakers from Wallonia, south-west England and northern Italy used similar systems of cooperative subcontracting.

Complementary to cooperation in the workplace was cooperation between all household members. The following description, also from Westphalia, is by a civil servant in Diepholz in 1811, and demonstrates how peasant families combined agricultural work and linen production at home with seasonal migratory labour in Holland, where wages were twice as high, but so were the prices of daily necessities:

All people from my canton who go to Holland own only a small amount of land which doesn't yield enough to meet rents and duties. They must also choose this secondary work whose advantages, not to underestimate them, are more considerable than any other alternative. Nor is their absence a drawback in the least. Those who have travelled out are back by St. Jacob's [25th July, after which the grain harvest starts in Diepholz] and departure for Holland only takes place after the sowing season. This way workers miss only the hay-making which can be carried out by the female family members who remain at home. Because the Holland-goer takes pork provisions with him – from his own slaughtered pig – he realizes the maximum profit from his production and that is an advantage to the state that should be especially taken into account. Just so from a statistical point of view it is extremely important that practically every migrant to Holland carries along a piece of [his home-spun and woven] linen which on his own, without a middleman, he sells there for the highest possible price.[84]

Proto-industry

The textile industry grew significantly from the late Middle Ages, not only in rural Westphalia but also in many other areas in Western Europe. With a nod to the later Industrial Revolution, this was also called *proto-industry*. Until well into the eighteenth century, the most important raw materials were wool and linen and, to a lesser extent, silk and hemp (for fine and rough fabrics, respectively). It was not until the late eighteenth century that European production of all-cotton fabrics became important – until then, this was mainly concentrated in India, as we have seen. In these centuries, the vast majority of European production was consumed in the continent itself, with an important exception being raw linen for the clothes of slaves in the Americas. The combination of industrial (not only textiles, which are the focus here, but also metal and other sectors[85]) and agrarian activities within one household in Europe reveals an infinite variety, not only in the way in which this was organized, but also in the prosperity, or lack thereof, that it brought to the men, women and children involved. This mainly depended on different political-institutional arrangements and natural conditions.

It is not only the concept 'proto-industry' that refers to the later Industrial Revolution – so too was the connected key term *industrious revolution*, which occurred in early modern Europe. This concept represents the increased labour market participation of households and, subsequently, their increased consumption, and vice versa – both taking place within the framework of a new self-definition of the household, its members and their tasks. This industrious behaviour and mentality is at odds with the 'leisure preference' that has long been thought to characterize pre-modern men and women – that once they had earned enough they would stop and only begin working again when the need arose.[86] We have already encountered this industrious behaviour in Asia in the form of the labour-intensive path, and the following brief, chronological tour d'horizon will also clarify these processes for Europe based on the daily practices of the textile industry. The emphasis will be on the proto-industrial countryside and small towns.[87]

Northern Italy, which had been a frontrunner in the textile industry in the Middle Ages, lost its leading position in the sixteenth and early seventeenth centuries to the Netherlands, France and England. In particular, the textile industry stagnated in the large Italian cities. Recovery followed, after around 1650, now mainly in the small towns and in the countryside, where, in addition to wool, silk was now an important raw material, with women performing an increasing part of the production process. Moreover, domestic spinning and weaving of hemp was undertaken in rural households, mostly by women and children during the long winter months. Finally, after 1750, certain northern areas specialized in cotton and wool production.[88]

In the late Middle Ages, rural industry in the Low Countries was concentrated in Flanders, but with the rise of the Republic the centre of gravity shifted to the province of Holland, not least due to the mass emigration of Calvinist textile workers from the Spanish Netherlands, who, after 1580, wanted to escape the influence of the Catholic Counter-Reformation. In the north, this industry was initially located in the cities: Leiden was famous for its linen industry and what was soon to become its main industry, wool; Haarlem was known for its linen; and Amsterdam was a centre for finishing and international trade in textiles.[89] As in most European cities since the Middle Ages, weaving was a male profession, practised in guilds (or a comparable organization). Spinning, as well as hackling and carding – in short, all the preparatory activities – continued to be women's work, done mainly by female heads of households (generally widows) and unmarried adult women (whether or not living independently), in the first case often forming single-person households. In addition, many children – primarily outsourced orphan boys and girls – spun, carded and twined.

Men and women received piece wages, while almsmen (as well as almswomen and so-called charity children) received room and board and a small hourly wage. It was only when the textile industry declined in the eighteenth century that men supplanted half of all women involved in spinning wool. Something similar had happened previously in wool combing. It is tempting to assume that spinning women and weaving men automatically formed a couple and together were part of a (core) household. That certainly happened, but it seems that more spinners practised their profession independently, bought their own raw materials and even sold their own spun yarns. A number of them also took on independent staff, especially other people's children, including, as mentioned, orphans. A child could learn to spin within a month, but it took one to two years for a good quality yarn to pass through their hands at sufficient speed.

It is important to underline that, at least in Leiden, piecework rates for women did not differ from those for men, nor did labour productivity. And yet, as a rule, male spinners earned more than female spinsters. This was because the men mainly spun weft yarns, for which the rate was significantly higher than that for warp yarns, which were generally spun by women. We also find male spinners almost exclusively in the cloth industry and not in the less well-paid linen industry.[90] Boys and girls earned about the same piece wage for the same work, although this was a half to a third less than the adults. In practice, however, they frequently worked for an hourly wage. The income of married spinning women and their children was a necessary addition to that of an artisan, weaver or not. If there was no husband, as was often the case because women remained unmarried or lost their husbands early and did not remarry, then spinning yielded enough to lead a very simple life. This was provided, of course, that they remained healthy and could work six days a week – possibly supplemented with some poor relief at a later age. Those worst off, of course, were single women with children who were too small to work. In sum, people earned less from spinning than from weaving and, indeed, less than from working in construction.

Rural industry emerged, initially in addition to and later instead of the urban textile industry, both in the east and the south of the Republic. As a result of the lower wages in the countryside, in the course of the seventeenth century, merchants moved their orders for textiles from the cities to the countryside, both to North Brabant (wool) and to Twente (cotton). The division of labour there was roughly the same as in the cities, although here both men and women spun. The production and family relations were also very similar. In the eighteenth century, the wool weavers in Brabant switched from the usual Kaufsystem, whereby they independently bought yarn and sold textiles, to the putting-out system, whereby they received yarn from their client (a merchant, or *fabriqueur*), even if it was spun by their own wife and children who received their own wages from the same client!

In the booming rural linen industry in southern and central Flanders, the complementarity of industry and agriculture caused an explicit shortage of land for spinners and weavers looking to invest their extra earnings in a small patch, as demonstrated by the following observation in the year 1800:

> the village-dweller has the habit of constant work; and, since his primary
> desire is to work the land, he applies himself to do it with ardour, while at
> the same time devoting to the work of weaving or spinning of flax and
> wool all the moments which he cannot employ in cultivation. Many of
> the village-dwellers achieved some affluence from this advantageous
> regime, and desired to become farmers and not day-labourers. The land-
> holdings have been divided up astonishingly.[91]

It is unfeasible to treat the rural industry in all European countries, but we cannot, of course, ignore England. After all, this would later be the location of the Industrial Revolution (see pp. 293–304). In southern England, in the seventeenth century, servants' beds no longer consisted solely of straw and a blanket, but now had mattresses, pillows and sheets. At the end of that century, in Shropshire, the average number of pairs of sheets per bed had jumped from three to five, while labourers in Cambridgeshire had at least two pairs. Bed-curtains became more common, and among the prosperous even window curtains were spreading. Finally, the common man gradually had more woollen and linen clothes, as made clear from the fact that housewife's linen and local tailor's woollen work was now supplemented with ready-made clothes.[92]

The wool industry, the so-called new draperies, was concentrated in the Cotswolds (heavy white broadcloth), East Anglia (the lighter and less durable kerseys or worsteds made from combed wool) and the mid-Pennines in Lancashire and the West Riding of Yorkshire (both broadcloth and mixed linen-cotton fustians). Since the Middle Ages, the industry had shifted from predominantly towns to predominantly villages.[93] Like Western Europe in general, the increased share of wage workers in England was perhaps less notable than the increasing inclusion of women and children in the labour market and outside of the household.[94]

The increased consumption of wool and linen (cotton only became available to a wider public after 1750) meant a huge growth in employment not only for spinners and weavers but also for knitters of woollen clothing. Knitting for the market, originally a London speciality, emerged as a handicraft in the

Pennine Dales, shifting to the Trent Valley and, after 1750, to rural Leicester and Coventry. The linen industry was found on the Norfolk–Suffolk border.[95]

The organization of these kinds of industry, mostly (but not exclusively)[96] in the countryside and mainly in combination with small-scale agriculture, was extremely diverse, and many people combined several activities. Looking back on his life, Edward Barlow, born in 1642 in Lancashire, records of his youth: '[I] was forced to go to work with our neighbours sometimes when they had any need of me in harvest or making hay and suchlike work, and sometimes going to the coalpits, for we have many of them in our country and coals are very cheap. I used to go with our neighbours' horses and fetch horse-loads to burn.' Forced to leave school at the age of 12, he went to work in the local fustian trade, whitening cloth, 'A hard-working trade, for when we had done a day's work at the trade we had another to do about the cattle that we kept, looking after the horses and cows, dressing them and foddering them; and when we had no other work, as in the winter, for then they worked but little at the trade, then we must trash and hedge and ditch and do all other country work.' But all was not in vain. He writes about his savings, earned from fetching coal: 'Yet with that and suchlike work I made shift to buy me some clothes, and then I went to church on Sunday, which I could never do before for want of clothes to go handsome in. My father being poor and in debt could not provide us with clothes fitting to go to church in (so we could not go to church) unless we would go in rags, which was not seemly.' Moreover, for women, the new industrial tasks, 'were added on to rather than substituted for women's work in the home or in agrarian sidelines. Distaff spinning, hand knitting, lace making and straw plaiting remained common in parts of rural Britain well into the nineteenth century because they utilized the cheap labour of older women and children in particular, and they were popular because they could be done simultaneously with other tasks such as child care or walking to and from market or field work.' Ultimately, for all family members, 'the primacy given to manufacturing work meant less time to engage in food preparation, growing food and raising cows, poultry or pigs'.[97]

For northern Italy, the Netherlands and certainly also parts of England, we can observe a boom in rural industry in particular regions long before the Industrial Revolution. But there were also parts of the European countryside where these kinds of cottage industry did not take root. Why was this the case? Was there less seasonal unemployment there, or were people less industrious? Detailed consideration of rural Europe, region by region, constantly yields new combinations of livelihoods and new specializations. Some farms almost exclusively cultivated grain, some mainly industrial crops; sometimes large farms grew different but complementary crops which made it possible to have a large permanent staff, while others grew crops unilaterally but had peak times when labour was needed from elsewhere. Finally, there were peasants who had to supplement their income from agricultural activities by working as farmhands at large farms in the vicinity or as migrant workers far away, or with various kinds of cottage industry. In any case, the phenomenon of the simple, small, self-sufficient peasant farm without extra income had disappeared.

To illustrate, we can take the southern half of England, where the pattern is clear. Further to the west and in neighbouring Wales, farmers specialized in livestock breeding, with many opportunities for women in terms of caring for the cattle and in the processing of dairy products. In the east, the growing of grain dominated on large farms, where employment, more for men than for women, can be distinguished in the large numbers of married, independently living 'farm servants' and unmarried, live-in farmhands, typically called 'labourers' (and later 'boys').[98] Labourers, mostly boys from 14 and girls from 16 years old, were considered adults from their twenty-first birthday. The home counties in the far south-east had a very varied cultivation of not only grains but also fruit and industrial crops such as hops. The rural population there also found work in London and overseas.

Blossoming towns

The textile industry represented the largest economic sector in most European cities.[99] That had been the case already before 1500 and was still true for the early modern period. We have already seen how important this was and remained, not only in terms of employment but now also for the much broader development of labour. It could not operate, let alone grow, without a constant flow of labour migrants from the countryside. This concentration of energy and talent resulted in an intensive exchange of ideas in the areas of organization (in particular, the development of the guild system) and of knowledge, both technical and more general.[100] Two aspects of the early modern European city deserve our special attention: demographic development and professional specialization and organization.

Between 1500 and 1800, Europe gradually urbanized, while simultaneously the urbanized centre shifted from northern Italy, via the Netherlands, to

England. In 1500, the continent had only 17 cities with 40,000 or more inhabitants, more than half of which were in Italy. By 1800, this had risen to no fewer than 37 cities of more than 70,000 residents, with an accent on the British Isles, but now with a more balanced distribution over the continent than ever before – from Cadiz to Stockholm and from Glasgow to Palermo. The population increase of these cities was entirely due to immigration. Indeed, immigrants were indispensable for maintaining existing populations, simply because, in those centuries, more people died in the cities than were born there.[101]

The 'natural growth' of the early modern European city was thus negative. This was due to poor hygiene conditions and the increased risk of infectious diseases. City dwellers lived in close proximity to each other in houses without sewerage, with all the associated risks, especially when wastewater and drinking water became mixed. In the first half of the seventeenth century, cities lost, on average, 1 per cent of their population every year if this loss was not compensated for by immigration. The countryside was the biggest supplier, and, in total, some 20 million people traded the countryside for the city throughout Europe between 1500 and 1800.[102] In doing so, they also left farm work behind and entered the world of all kinds of artisanal crafts.

The specialization of crafts that had already begun in the Middle Ages now came to full fruition. Generally, we can state that the larger the city, the greater the diversity in industrial activities and services. This is nowhere better illustrated than in the case of the Dutch painters of the Golden Age.[103] They had no royal or spiritual patrons as the great Italian, Spanish and French masters did, and, on the whole, they produced not to order but rather stock for the market. To make a success of this – paintings, after all, were not food – they had to specialize radically. Their brethren in Flanders and Brabant were already ahead of them in this regard. One would specialize in flower or fruit still lifes, another in landscapes, city or seascapes or charming scenes in village inns. They could thus work quickly and try to earn a reasonable crust. From around 100 professional painters *c.* 1590, the figure grew to between 700 and 800 at the apogee of Dutch painting in the Golden Age around 1650.

These painters, the greatest of whom are still household names (Rembrandt, Vermeer, Hals, Steen), were considered by their contemporaries, and, indeed, regarded themselves, as craftsmen first and foremost. As such, they were also compulsory members of a craft guild. This form of organization originated in the Middle Ages (see pp. 189–91) but was certainly not yet on its last legs a few centuries later. On the contrary, in the medium- and large-sized cities of the Dutch Republic, the most economically advanced society of the seventeenth century, there were more guilds than ever, and also per capita.[104]

They naturally fulfilled their traditional functions by providing livelihood security to their members, who, thanks to a local government-approved monopoly, could try to sell their products for a reasonable price to a broad public. In Dutch cities, for example, unpretentious oil paintings were for sale for the price of an average day's wage. One of the guild's functions was promoting the transfer of necessary professional knowledge from master to pupil. Sometimes this was done explicitly, by instituting formal testing of professional knowledge by the board of the guild in the form of a 'master-proof', but more often than not it happened implicitly.[105]

Widespread skills among the working population were a sine qua non for economic development and for the success of the Industrial Revolution. A few clever inventor-types are not enough for that. After all, a great many artisans must be suitably motivated to come up with and develop labour-saving technologies, however small, as well as be willing to apply such improvements invented by others.[106] This requires formal training through apprenticeship, enabling the passing on of 'tacit knowledge' in practice – that is, undocumented professional competence and skills. The general level of education, the nature of education and the organization of vocational education are all crucial in this regard.[107]

If we consider that so many city dwellers were immigrants, it also means that the guilds operated as an integrating institution that also facilitated social mobility, especially where they maintained a number of rituals that everyone was obliged to participate in, firstly the burial of guild brethren and also (annual) meetings, whether or not followed by a feast. From this, an insurance system gradually developed in the Republic, which provided benefits not only in the event of death but also – albeit more limited – in case of illness or old age. In Amsterdam, these payments were not made on the basis of a pay-as-you-go system, but from the interest of invested capital, preferably long-term and fixed-income government bonds. Thus, a fully fledged mutual insurance organization for working people emerged in the eighteenth century.

The craft guilds' admission criteria were, of course, crucial, and here we see an interesting link between accessibility and urban growth – accessibility measured by the costs of acquiring civil rights and, moreover, of paying for guild membership, as well as other provisions regarding, for example, religion or family reputation. The rapidly growing cities in the west of the Netherlands appear to have had the most favourable conditions, while those of the slow-growing cities in the middle and the east were somewhat less generous and the stagnating cities in the west of Germany made it almost impossible for immigrants to become guild members. It is no coincidence that the latter was the most notorious area in terms of push factors for emigration to the Netherlands. On average, it took an artisan several months' wages to join a Dutch guild, while in West Germany it was more like several years, and candidates also had to practise the correct religion (in other words, that of the authorities) and, based on their pedigree, they had to prove that there were no 'dishonest' professions in their family, such as executioner or prostitute.

In all of this, however, we must not forget that a number of people were excluded from membership in any event, and that, in addition to the contrast between members and non-members, serious tensions could also arise internally.[108] Whether guilds were open to immigrants or not, women could almost never become full members (again, some Dutch guilds were an exception in this), even though they played a key role in the artisan businesses of their husbands, who were members.[109] Apprentices and servants were not full members or not members at all, a development that started as far back as the late Middle Ages. Itinerant traders were thwarted. In Western Europe – in contrast to the Ottoman Empire – Jews were almost always excluded, and Catholic cities barred Protestants and vice versa, with, once more, the cities in the west of the Republic as the major exception.

Serious tensions regularly arose within guilds between affluent members and their less successful 'brothers'. Contrary to the formal rules, great masters tried to act as subcontractors, creating de facto wage dependence for the minor ones. The 'brothers', who in theory had equal opportunities, had anything but, especially in the expanding industries. Resistance to this was sporadic and occurred primarily in sectors where assistants had to wait until kingdom come to become independent masters. The best organized were the journeymen hatters and journeymen cloth shearers.[110] Like the guilds of masters, they collected contributions from members, so-called boxes, on a regular basis, which were used not only for social assistance but also for strike funds. Their organizational ability was strengthened by the fact that, in large parts of Europe, journeymen were obliged to gain experience elsewhere, via the tramping system.[111] In Germany, they were called *Wanderfögel*, in France *compagnons*, and in the British Isles they were *travelling brothers*. As a result, they were definitely worldly-wise. They were also perfectly capable of organizing themselves. It is not surprising, then, that the hatters' assistants of the southern Netherlands did not think that their local strike funds were enough and organized a national network of interconnected common boxes that, in turn, were affiliated with similar organizations, in particular in France. These kinds of organizations and actions, which occurred all over Eurasia in different forms,[112] were actually the training ground for the unions of the future, as we will see (pp. 302–4, 381–8).

A large group of wage workers, generally referred to as 'servants', fell completely outside of the guilds and apprenticeship. Commonly, this implied living and working outwith the parental household for several years between the ages of, say, 15 and 25. Apprenticeships were mostly the domain of boys, servanthood mostly that of girls (but, especially in agriculture, also boys). Servants' labour contracts were organized in a completely unique way. Live-in servants were seen as part of the household and the patriarchal authority of the head of the household was law. This relationship was similar to that of the artisan's resident assistant or pupil. This ersatz parent–child relationship, with the parent enjoying almost absolute power, had already been disrupted in some medieval cities.

Let us take the Netherlands as an example.[113] Since the fourteenth century, in the IJssel towns, and since the fifteenth century in Holland, Flanders, Groningen and Friesland, the free labour-wage contract had become the rule. This implied the freedom to engage in wage work, and the possibility for both parties to resort to the courts for enforcement or dissolution of the contract. Civil not penal law ruled the labour market. In the Dutch Republic, no efforts were made to compel the poor to accept work offered (this only happened in the nineteenth century) or to officially set wage levels. Breach of contract by servants was seen as a serious offence and was met with the threat of confinement or forced labour; in reality, this never or rarely occurred. On the contrary, from the late seventeenth century, intermediate cessation of the contract gradually became easier and, in general, labour relations were characterized by increasingly impersonal human relations. No wonder that the seventeenth-century law professor Ulrik Huber considered corporal punishment of servants in the Dutch Republic 'intolerable and contrary to the dominant sense of justice'. Dutch servants were therefore able to earn a reasonable wage and even save. After all, unmarried live-in servants enjoyed room and board. This allowed them to qualify for the marriage market. It has been calculated that, at the top end, servants in the most well-off households in eighteenth-century Amsterdam could save a marriage budget that amounted to between one-third and half of the capital that her future husband – let us assume he is an unskilled man – could save in the same amount of time.[114] The big exceptions were sailors and soldiers. Until well into the twentieth century (and sometimes to this day), other rules applied to them because their captain or military commander acted in loco parentis. This included meting out corporal punishment.

Beyond the Netherlands, and especially in England and in the German states, domestic servants' rights in the direction of a completely free wage agreement developed much later.[115] Following the great shortage of labour since the Black Death, the Ordnance and Statute of Labourers (1349–51) and its ratification and elaboration in the Statute of Artificers (1562–63) curtailed the freedom of movement of English wage-dependent workers in every possible way.[116] The domestic servant law stipulated, among other things, that, in case of breach of contract, the employee fell under criminal law and, moreover, that the master was entitled to 'moderate chastisement'. Sir Thomas Smith summarized it as follows in his book on the Elizabethan polity:

[Servants are] for other matters [except as regards their service] in libertie as full men and women. [But according to their labour contract] If he be in covenaunt, he may not depart out of his service without his masters license, and he must give his master warning that he will depart one quarter of a yere before the terme of the yere expireth, or else he shalbe compelled to serve out another yere, or else he shalbe punished with stockes and whipping as an idle vagabond. . . . Thus necessitie and want of bondmen hath made men to use free men as bondmen to all servile services but yet more liberally and freely, and with a more equalitie and moderation, than in time of gentilitie slaves and bondemen were woont to be used.[117]

From the 1740s, these provisions were being undermined, leading to much more tramping and much more interlocal and interregional contacts. Criminal laws against 'combinations' now became dominant.[118] Nevertheless, the inequality between master (to whom civil law applied) and servant (to whom criminal law applied) was only officially abolished in England with the Employers and Workmen Act of 1875.[119]

Multi-annual temporal migrations

We have now addressed two major shifts that characterize the world of work in early modern Europe. Firstly, from agriculture to handicrafts and industry, partly coinciding with the migration from the countryside to the city. As we have seen, mobility is also a crucial force behind technical progress. Secondly, from household production to production for the market, epitomized by the industrious revolution and the deployment of women and children. A third must still be mentioned separately here. That is the shift to temporary migration. Not only seasonal migration, which we have already dealt with, but also multi-annual temporal migration. These are migrants whose aim is to work elsewhere only for a limited number of years, such as soldiers, sailors, tramping artisans and some domestics. We have just encountered the latter two categories; the first two now deserve special attention.

In these centuries, soldiers and sailors form a much more important category for Western Europe than for East Asia. Between the periods 1501–50 and 1751–1800, the number of soldiers in Europe quadrupled, while the population only doubled. In the same period, the number of sailors with high-seas experience doubled too (from 740,000 to 1.6 million).[120] As far as soldiers are concerned, the classic explanation for this gigantic increase is the variation in state sizes in Eurasia: extremely fragmented in the west versus large entities in the east. Simply put: the more states, the more borders, and the greater the chance of conflicts arising. The internecine warfare within Western Europe resulted in an above-average number of mercenaries moving around within Europe and later all over the world.[121] Later, in the Napoleonic era and especially during the two world wars, many more men would have to perform this kind of work, but this was only possible with general conscription. In the centuries prior to this, armies – which were increasingly becoming mass armies – were filled with professional soldiers.

As we have seen with seasonal workers, here, too, certain regions specialized in soldiering, and hence we encounter, in particular, Scottish soldiers, and an even greater numbers of professional soldiers from Switzerland and neighbouring south Germany, all over Europe. Although soldiers were all men, armies were also accompanied by a lot of women and children, the so-called camp followers. They took care of food and soldiers' other needs. Their numbers were considerable until around 1650, and there was one camp follower for every two soldiers. Later, these functions were increasingly carried out by professionalized support services and, by the eighteenth century, there was only one camp follower to every twenty soldiers, which still amounts to more than a million women for that century.

The soldier's work, of course, changed over these centuries, as the focus shifted to the improvement of firearms and the construction of elaborate fortifications, both leading to a greater distance between warring parties. The bigger armies became, the greater the chance of infectious diseases, especially in the barracks. Thus, the career of many a professional soldier ended not on the battlefield, nor in a much-hoped-for return home to make an attractive marriage with their saved-up salary, but in a foul bed in the midst of delirious and groaning fellow victims of dysentery, plague or cholera. The shift from hand-to-hand combat to manoeuvres culminated in the professionalization of the Napoleonic army. While the enemy used the usual 75 steps per minute, Napoleon managed to whip his men up to 120 or even 150 steps.[122]

Calculating the labour productivity of soldiers may be a tricky task; fortunately for sailors it is a bit simpler. Their greatly increased productivity from a best practice of 6 tons per sailor during the Great Discoveries to an average of 12 tons in the seventeenth century and up to 15–18 tons a century and a half later explains how it is possible that the European conquest of the world's oceans could take place with a relatively constant ratio of sailors in the population. While the Dutch were the first to take the lead in this regard, the English took over in the eighteenth century.[123]

Professional soldiers and sailors had a much more international labour market compared to other professional groups. That was perhaps most pronounced in the Dutch Republic, where half, or more than half, of all soldiers originated from abroad, as was the case for the sailors in the navy and manning the ships to Asia.[124] Their share was much smaller on short-haul routes and certainly in coastal navigation sea fishing. This is not surprising given that the ships were much smaller and that, with limited space on a fishing boat, preference was given to locals.

There are no indications of doubts about the loyalty and commitment of foreigners. Apparently, they were considered a fully fledged workforce and, consequently, they also received the same reward for the same work. Even the career opportunities of the many German sailors in the Dutch East India Company (VOC) were not significantly worse than those of the Dutch. The fact that they scored well in terms of literacy and numeracy may well have played a role in this. German VOC sailors fared much better not only than their compatriots who remained at home but even than their Dutch colleagues as well.

1. A group of people work together to hunt kangaroos in New South Wales, Australia, *c.* 1817. Most of the twenty or so figures are male, but some in the background could be women and children. The hunters use fire and smoke to direct the prey towards the archers.

2. The figures on this tile are enjoying a happy afterlife where they can catch fish and birds, and reap a bounteous harvest forever. This stamped brick was made to decorate a tomb in Chengdu, south-west China, in the later Han period (25–220).

3. An official supervises the collection of the state portion of the harvest in Luxor, Egypt, 1390–1380 BCE, while children are gleaning (two even fighting over the task) and men collect the ears of grain in baskets, thresh with the help of two pairs of oxen, and winnow with the help of fans. Two take a rest in the shadow of a tree.

4. Sailors can be seen aboard the ships at Ostia, the sea harbour of Rome, as port workers busily unload the vessel on the left-hand side. They may have been paid with a coin like this (a sestertius of Emperor Nero, 54–68), which was worth a few hours of work.

5. Agricultural labourers drive a pair of oxen as they plough the land in Cherchell, on the southern Mediterranean coast, 200–25. This is from a series depicting the four seasons, and the figure on the lower right is sowing grain in the freshly prepared soil.

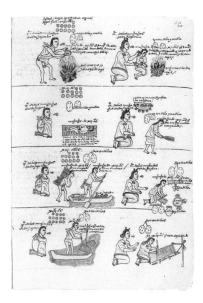

6. Workers are shown here completing each stage of the glass-making process in a shop in Bohemia, c. 1400; men mix quartz with ashes, transport raw materials to the oven, blow the glass and cool the oven.

7. Aged between 11 and 14, Aztec boys are shown here hard at work with their fathers (left column) and girls with their mothers (right column), Mexico, 1541. Not only their chores are shown, such as fishing, food preparation and weaving, but also the punishments inflicted by their parents for failing to do the tasks properly.

8. A group of four men and two women of the *dhobi* caste of professional Hindu clothes washers, cleaning garments for customers of higher castes ('gentile *mainatos* from Goa on the Kanara Coast who wash clothes for money'), *c.* 1540.

9. In this miniature from the *Surname-i Hümayun* (Imperial Festival Book, 1582) we see the cloth weavers with their banners and insignia in front of Sultan Murad III (left) and other spectators (right). This was part of the guild procession in the Hippodrome of Constantinople.

10. This Indonesian domestic slave has been taken by his master to Decima (Dejima, Nagasaki), the Dutch establishment in Japan, c. 1800.

11. Slaves sieving diamonds in running water are strictly supervised in case of theft, which would be punished with whipping. John Mawe (1764–1829) made the original sketch for this engraving in 1804–06 at Mandango on the Jequitinhonha River in Minas Gerais, Brazil.

12. Women are shown here nesting silkworms at Rikuchū in the countryside in north-eastern Japan, c. 1877. Once a year they place silkworms into special bamboo frames. Three to four worms will spin their cocoon in each pyramidal space, where they will be fed for twenty-eight days. After that, the women can begin spinning silk.

13. May Day 1897: five male workers, symbolizing the five continents, promote the eight-hour working day under the aegis of Freedom, with Equality and Fraternity. The American Federation of Labor had taken this initiative three years previously, and it had been adopted in 1889 by the socialist Second International.

14. Pay day: workers line up at the Braat machine-building plant at Ngagel, Surabaya (Java, Indonesia). This image is from a series of photographs taken for the twentieth anniversary of the factory in 1921, which specialized in building iron railway bridges and machinery for the sugar industry.

15. The man depicted here is the steelworker Lukashov, who worked himself up to the position of engineer in the 'Hammer and Sickle' factory in Moscow, 1932. 'Civilized life – productive work' was a message for the members of Komsomol, the communist youth organization, who had to set an example through their actions.

16. 'A glorious production model' worker proudly shows her Stakhanovite-like diploma and medal to her excited daughter and two sons; in the background is the factory where she works, China, 1954.

17. Assembly line workers pose for a promotional film at the Ford factory in Highland Park, Michigan, to mark the 10 millionth Model T in 1924. The first Model was made less than sixteen years previously.

18. A man reclines in his chair in the control room at the Point Tupper power plant in Nova Scotia, Canada, 2007. This photograph shows the advances of automation, and the minimum effort needed on the part of the worker.

However, such a truly international and free labour market was still exceptional in Europe at the time. Surrounding countries such as Denmark, the
German Hanseatic cities and the Austrian Netherlands, as well as France and
Spain and, above all, the major competitor England, recruited at most 10 per
cent foreign sailors and sometimes also resorted to the press, which involved
violently forcing residents to serve on the war fleet. In the European periphery
of the Baltic and the Mediterranean, both free and unfree sailors were recruited,
that is conscripts, convicts, prisoners of war and even slaves, both from within
its own population and from dependent states and slave-selling areas.

The low percentages of foreigners on English ships have an extraordinary background. England had a long tradition of warding off aliens, as
seen, for example, in the large-scale massacre of Jews in 1189–90, of Flemings
by Wat Tyler's men in the Peasants' Revolt of 1381, and the large-scale anti-
alien riots on Evil May Day in London in 1517. After the loss of Calais to
France in 1558, a law decreeing the expulsion of all Frenchmen was narrowly
defeated in Parliament by only a few votes. A proclamation in 1601 ordered
the expulsion of all black people.[125] Despite a brief period of greater open-
ness that saw the admission of Protestant refugees in the sixteenth century,
the country remained suspicious of foreigners, including the Scots, especially before the Union of 1707. This could also be seen in the restrictions on
the crews of the English merchant fleet. According to the Navigation Acts of
1651, three-quarters of sailors on English cargo ships had to be English, but,
in practice, this share appears to have been much higher. Not only did the
English government force English captains to reject foreigners (including
Scots before the Act of Union), but they apparently agreed wholeheartedly.

The Dutch merchant fleet was not only international, it was also intercontinental. Although the VOC, like all its European competitors, tried to
avoid allowing Asians to sail on the return trips to Europe, it certainly
recruited local personnel, both for its army and for its fleet, as well as for
other activities.[126] On the one hand, it simply could not do without it, on the
other hand, it was certainly not averse to it. The Dutch had learned this from
the Portuguese, who already in the sixteenth century were sailing with
mixed European-Asian crews, and they put this into practice much more
than the French and the English – parallel to the differences we already saw
in Europe.[127]

Even more striking – certainly compared to after 1800 – is that here, too,
sailors who did the same work also got paid the same. The only difference

between European and sometimes also Eurasian sailors, on the one hand, and Asian sailors, on the other hand, lay in the career opportunities that the VOC offered. Asians never made it further than the position of boatswain, the highest rank of non-commissioned officer. On the Dutch side, in addition to a racial-religious prejudice, language skills also played a role. Becoming an officer required passing the helmsman exams, and for that a good knowledge of the Dutch language was necessary. Given that Dutch functioned as the lingua franca in north-west European waters, this was not an insurmountable obstacle for Germans and Scandinavians, but it was for Asians.[128]

Seamen are an important category in the history of work for yet another reason. As a consequence of their inevitably close interrelationships on board, they also developed traditions of collective action early on, when they disagreed with their working conditions and circumstances.[129]

The experience and worldview of working people

With the major changes in labour relations in Western Europe in these centuries, ideas about work also changed, of course, both those of the elite about the labouring middle class and the labouring poor, and those of the working population about themselves. The shift from working for the household to working for the market that had already begun in the high Middle Ages was now given an extra dimension through labour specialization in the countryside (including proto-industrialization), but in particular as a result of the sharply increasing urbanization. This meant that work became decreasingly hidden within households and increasingly public. Consequently, many aspects of work were now arranged publicly and were articulated and discussed, potentially leading to social movements.

Let us begin with the flipside of all that hard work: anticipating free time. A fifteenth-century poem entitled 'Holidays', attributed to an English spinster, contains the following lines:

I've waited longing for today:
Spindle, bobbin, and spool, away!
In joy and bliss I'm off to play
Upon this high holiday.
Spindle, bobbin, and spool, away!
For joy that it's a holiday![130]

The Reformation also brought with it many attempts to restrict public free time, but these ideas had already been brewing. For example, in England, in 1495, efforts had already been made to instil work discipline by fixing a minimum workday.[131] During the transition of large parts of Europe from Catholicism to Protestantism, the number of official days off decreased dramatically. Until then, according to the word of the Bible, not only was the Lord's Day sacred, but there was also about the same number again of official church holidays. These were not holidays that already had to fall on a Sunday, such as Easter and Whitsun (Pentecost), but rather days like Christmas Day and 26 December (Boxing Day in the British Isles), Easter Monday and Whit Monday, All Saints' Day, All Souls' Day, Corpus Christi and so forth. In addition, there were the pilgrimages in Catholic countries, not affected by the Reformation.

In 1552, the English government tried to restrict public holidays to twenty-seven days per year. It may not have been an unmitigated success, because during the Puritan Revolution authorities attempted once more to eliminate traditional Catholic or Catholicized festivals and to impose a strict observance of sabbatical rest.[132] In the northern Netherlands, the Synod of Dordrecht in 1574 even stipulated that only Sundays should be celebrated as a holiday. Things were not as black and white as they appeared, but this did reinforce the long-standing trend to officially celebrate fewer Christian holidays. In sum, the maximum work year increased from 260–265 days around 1500 to over 300 after 1600, an increase of more than 15 per cent.[133] This meant that, for the Dutch, other than Sundays, there were only a meagre six public holidays left.

We have not, however, taken into account obligations of an entirely different nature in the above calculations of official days off, which meant that the working year was de facto shorter than one might think based on the above. Firstly, there was the not inconsiderable time involved in attending funerals. In contrast to baptisms and marriages, which could also be planned on a Sunday, many burials had to be held during the week because the dead body could only be kept briefly above ground. Given the high mortality, this obligation could be very time-consuming within the family circle and the neighbourhood, but the obligations extended even further, in particular to professional colleagues. The best-known case of this is probably the craft guilds in Europe and the Islamic world. Everywhere, we encounter the obligation – even on pain of a fine – to bury colleagues with the necessary decorum. For the larger professions in the bigger cities, this could involve many days a year.[134]

All this emphasis on time stems from the external monitoring of performance and therefore an intensification of effort. An important consequence of this was the search for stimulants – something to make the time pass more easily. The increased consumption of colonial products that could serve as such, like sugar, cocoa, tea and coffee, and not just among the elite but also among common folk who could now afford them, is an indication that the labour-intensive path and the industrious revolution had yielded increased earnings. At the same time, of course, such stimulants also make long and hard work possible and more bearable. In the army and the fleet, the provision of spirits had already become part of the standard repertoire since the early seventeenth century. The drinking of beer, much stronger than most modern beer, was standard for heavy agricultural work.[135] In addition to calories and a reduction in feelings of pain and fatigue, it also, of course, led to cheerfulness, and this should not be underestimated during hard work, and neither should singing while working. Think here, again, of the sailors with their shanties, but also of talking and especially singing during collective toil.[136]

Public statements about the value of working also increased sharply, if only as a result of the growth in literacy and the spread of the printing press. Occasionally, as in Spain, it took the form of admonitions – by both Enlightenment and Catholic reformers – of putting women in their 'proper' place, the household, where they had to fill their spare time with spinning. The vehemence of their arguments demonstrates precisely the widespread activity of women outside the household in labour and commodity markets.[137] Workers themselves could now express themselves to a large public, gather supporters and possibly also take collective action. We know about positive expressions of the pleasure of working from the circle of urban artisans. An anonymous French author around 1720 envisioned the following dialogue between a plane and its master:

> Little tool, pretty plane
> Your body is loyal and working
> Adorned with a quite beautiful head
> May you be preserved from tempestuous times
> Little tool, royal tool
> The work performs itself in front of you.

My master, please use me
You'll be happier than a king
You know that I'm unique
Among the tools in your workshop
The workbenches and the easels,
The rules, the mortise-gauges and the mallets
Appreciate my eminence,
Honour and revere me[138]

The great contradiction between the importance attached to work for the market and in the public space, on the one hand, and poor working conditions and rewards, on the other, now also leads to new visions and attempts to realize them. In the late Middle Ages, we have already seen the resistance of master craftsmen to powerful merchants (the Ciompi Revolt) and the peasant rebellions that followed the Black Death, led by the famous John Wyclif and Wat Tyler in England and John Huss in Bohemia. They sought their ideological justification in the original human state in the Earthly Paradise, according to the book of Genesis. From the sixteenth century, this was further engineered by 'utopians', who ultimately outlined a new world, without biblical references, in which working people were central. They are named with reference to Thomas More's *Utopia*, written in 1516, in which we find:

What kind of justice is it when a nobleman, a goldsmith, a moneylender, or someone else who makes his living by doing nothing or something completely useless to the commonwealth, gets to live a life of luxury and grandeur, while in the meantime a labourer, a carter or a carpenter or a farmer works so hard and so constantly that even beasts of burden would scarcely endure it? Although this work of theirs is so necessary that no commonwealth could survive for a year without it, they earn so meagre a living, and lead such miserable lives, that beasts would really seem to be better off.[139]

Although a pious man, More is not referring to the Bible here, but to more general principles such as the need for labour for society and, consequently, a fair distribution of the fruits of this labour among the small self-employed and wage workers. We see this also among many utopians who succeeded

243

THE STORY OF WORK

him. Just like *Utopia* (a non-existent country), the *City of the Sun* (1602) by the Italian Tommaso Campanella was not a real attempt to create a new society. Campanella did take up an old idea here, from the *Acts of the Apostles*, by propagating the community of goods (and, he adds, women) as a remedy against all social inequality. The Dutchman Pieter Cornelisz Plockhoy had similar ideas, but he had actually made a communal experiment along those lines in New Netherland in 1663–64.[140]

Much more important than pie-in-the-sky ideas and unsuccessful attempts to actually achieve ideals of equality, some of which, incidentally, did have a major influence on later developments, the early modern period saw massive collective actions, such as those of the Levellers and Diggers in England. These movements did not formulate new ideas about the place of work in society, but a related ideal that revolved around land for peasants, while their leader Gerrard Winstanley explicitly rejected wage labour.[141] Of course, this does not alter the fact that the increasing number of wage workers had a completely different view. An anonymous English ballad from the seventeenth century puts the following words in the mouth of an agricultural labourer:

I carefully carry home all that I earn.
Now daily experience by this do I learn;
That though it is possible we may live poor,
We still keep a ravenous wolf from the door.

I reap and I mow, and I harrow and sow,
Sometimes I to hedging and ditching do go;
No work comes amiss, for I thresh and I plow;
Thus I eat my bread by the sweat of my brow.

My wife she is willing to pull in the yoke,
We live like two lambs and we never provoke
Each other, but like to the laboring ant
We do our endeavor to keep us from want.[142]

Shifting global labour relations under European influence

The parallels between work intensification and economic growth in eastern, southern and western Eurasia in the early modern period (dealt with above, pp. 197–244) coincided with increasingly deep fractures between 'the West and the Rest'. These parallels and fractures are subsumed in the historical debates on what is called the 'Great Divergence' and the proliferation of enslavement and slave labour, not only in the Atlantic but also elsewhere. These two sides of the same globalization coin between 1500 and 1800 will be dealt with in this chapter (mostly on the links between Western Europe and the Americas, Africa and southern Asia), and in the next (on Central and Eastern Europe).

The Great Divergence, a brief discussion

For a long time, the world history of these centuries appeared simple to outline, at least from the long-dominant West European perspective. Despite a somewhat problematic Middle Ages, until recently, the West was still seen as superior. After all, it was the fortunate child of the marriage between classical antiquity and Christianity, raised in the Enlightenment and thus able to impose itself definitively on the rest of the world. That was perhaps unfortunate for the rest, but ultimately it was for their own good. The road to happiness lay in carefully copying Europe. This caricature has been tilting sharply for the last twenty years or so, not least because of the recent impressive and autonomous growth of the Chinese economy. The question of whether the West has in fact always been (and therefore will remain) superior is becoming more pressing. If the answer is no, when exactly did the economic performances of 'the West and the Rest' diverge and what were the causes of this? The consensus is now that these big differences between the west and the east of Eurasia are relatively recent. This historic debate about the European growth spurt and the lagging behind of Asia is conducted under the name of 'the Great Divergence'.[143]

This is more than the story of the literal survival of the fittest, although it may have looked like that in the Americas. But what was the situation in Asia? At what point did the 'colonies' of Portugal, the Netherlands, France and England cease to be nothing more than ennobled trading posts that were tolerated and used by Asian states? Was the 'isolationism' of states such as China and Japan with respect to European traders a sign of power rather than of weakness? In other words, to what extent is the European power expansion in Asia already a fact before 1750–1800, and to what extent can it subsequently be explained by the fundamental societal differences between the West and the rest?

In the context of this book, the question naturally arises about whether and how Western Europe built up an advantage over the rest of the world in this period with respect to the organization of work and labour relations.[144] Here, too, is a classic answer, albeit in two variants. Firstly, that Europe could enrich itself immeasurably by exploiting cheap and mostly unfree labour in the American colonies, which allows us to explain the Industrial Revolution and the development of power elsewhere in the world. The second variant is that Europe had developed superior economic institutions, including a free labour market and a successful apprenticeship system that optimized human capital and hence geographical and social mobility – institutions that first helped to unleash the 'Industrial Revolution' and to subjugate the whole world, and, subsequently, to educate the new subjects – from American Indians to sub-continent Indians and from Africans to Chinese – to the point where these beneficial institutions could be introduced everywhere.

Many sub-questions have been suggested: what do we currently know about the economic achievements of the different parts of Eurasia in the three centuries between 1500 and 1800? To what extent was the economy there specialized, including in relation to the degree of urbanization? To what extent could working people there develop, with increasing labour productivity as a consequence? How efficiently was the labour power of men, women and children deployed? What was the ratio of free and unfree labour? What opportunities did free workers have to take control of and improve their own destiny? And, finally, do the inevitability of the Industrial Revolution and the dominance of England, and, by extension, of Europe, over the rest of the world follow from such analysis?

So many questions, many of which were eloquently formulated already more than a century ago by the great sociologist-cum-historian Max Weber. So few satisfactory answers – still – mostly due to a lack of solid comparative studies of 'the West' and 'the Rest' (common expressions, themselves indicating implicitly the magnitude of this problem). Time and again this is deplored, but it does not prevent many a scholar from making far-flung statements about the comparatively great achievements of Britain or Western Europe.[145]

The Great Divergence debate has thus far taught us that the classical premise of Europe's intrinsic advantage from the Great Discoveries is no longer tenable, but also how difficult it is to make a meaningful comparison of the economic achievements of Western Europe, China, India and Japan.

According to some scholars, from 1650 to 1700 (that is, before the Industrial Revolution), the level of prosperity in the economic centres of Western Europe and China (the Dutch Republic/England and the lower Yangtze Delta, respectively) was still roughly the same, and this was set to continue for a while. Only in the course of the eighteenth century was output per agricultural worker in the Yangtze surpassed by that in England. More importantly, the income opportunities for farmers' wives and other family members to earn extra money from spinning and weaving cotton were eliminated by north Chinese and, later, in particular, European competition.[146] Others are less certain about the interpretation of the data and believe that the relative deterioration of the core regions in China as compared to the countries bordering the North Sea may have started at least a century earlier.[147] Regardless, everyone is in agreement that Song China was far more prosperous than Europe at this time, that subsequently Europe began to catch up, but also that, in terms of per capita income, the wealth differentials with China were not impressive until at least 1800.

Indian history has only received a fraction of the attention in the Great Divergence debate compared to Great Britain and China. The results for this part of the world are, therefore, even more uncertain. Only from the late seventeenth century did real wages in India start to lag behind those of Western Europe, differences that began to increase rapidly after 1800 because India stagnated while the situation in Europe improved rapidly.[148] There were also incidental disasters at an increasingly higher frequency. The first known and well-documented major famine in Bengal dates from 1769–70, with as many as 10 million victims. Previous years of scarcity were nothing in comparison. After this disaster, a new one followed in 1787–88, and there were many more to come.[149]

At least until around 1700 there seems to be no clearly demonstrable European superiority in terms of prosperity that can explain the rest of history, but were there perhaps fundamental differences in other areas? Many factors in the Great Divergence barely or simply do not relate to work and can therefore be set aside, but a few deserve further scrutiny. One example is the enhancement of the skills of the working population and the ability of the government to promote prosperity, themes that will be developed in the next chapter (pp. 296–8). Another related theme is the growth in income as a result of a greater input of work in Western Europe and, in particular, its effects – the greater consumption of luxury goods like sugar, coffee, tea and other exotic products, produced by unfree and thus utterly cheap labourers else-where in the world. This issue now deserves our close attention.

The expansion of unfree labour

We have concluded that, until the eighteenth century, the practice of labour as well as labour relations showed great similarities between the separate parts of Eurasia. It is true that more and more European ships were sailing to Asia and not the other way around, but the colonial impact of Europe on work in Asia as a whole was still extremely small at the time, except in a few spice regions. This was very different in the Americas and gradually also in the coastal regions of Africa. In the Americas, European labour relations based on the principles of the market economy clashed with fundamentally different tributary societies with hierarchical redistribution. There was no question of an equivalent exchange of experiences and ideas of the kinds that had long taken place in Asia, because the Europeans were quickly able to subdue the Americas militarily.

This in no way meant that the Europeans literally transposed their own forms of labour to the Americas. Even though they were the victors, they had to deal with and adjust to the practices of highly developed societies. Moreover, they introduced, very selectively, certain forms of work from the Old World (that is, unfree labour) and not, or only to a limited extent, others (free labour). This was partly due to the nature of the labour relations in the countries of the original colonizers, Portugal and Spain, where, around 1500, slavery was not unknown. In their wake, their competitors – the Dutch, English, French and Danes – also relied heavily on the use of unfree labour in the Caribbean and the supply of slaves there from Africa. All colonizers were, of course, stimulated by the increasing global demand for luxury products, which grew sharply in the context of the industrious revolution. Europe had an additional advantage in this regard because it could import products such as sugar, coffee and tea from all over the world, for cheaply extracted American silver.

Before zooming in on the Americas and Africa, let us first establish the state of the relationship between free and unfree labour, especially in south-west and southern Europe, from where European overseas colonizations orig-inated. Against the general late medieval tendency of labour for the market, with increasing emphasis on self-employment and wage labour, as we have seen, slave labour re-emerged there. This had definitely not disappeared in

Islamic regions, especially in the form of house slaves, who were always in demand among the elite. The well-to-do inhabitants of Catholic cities in the Mediterranean emulated this after the expansion of Genoa and Venice in the Black and Aegean seas in the fourteenth and fifteenth centuries. Especially in southern Russia they could tap into a flourishing slave trade. Fresh offerings were also secured in particular by the wars between Christians and Muslims, who both considered themselves entitled to sell prisoners of war of the other faith as slaves. Think of the Reconquista on the Christian side and the expansion of the Ottoman Empire on the other side.[150] In this context, for example, Pope Nicholas V in 1452 allowed the Portuguese king to sell all Muslims, heathens and other enemies of Christendom to the highest bidder. It is no surprise, then, that in 1488 Pope Innocent VIII gratefully accepted a Portuguese gift of 100 Moorish slaves and divided them up among his cardinals.

The use of slaves in the production of goods for the market was perhaps most common on plantations where cane sugar was grown. The expansion of this cultivation from the Middle East to the west therefore inevitably meant the expansion of slave labour.[151] Sugar cane was originally grown in India, Mesopotamia and the Levant. Under the aegis of Italian city-states such as Genoa and Venice, it was also established in Cyprus and on Crete by Crusaders and their descendants. From there, this lucrative cultivation expanded to Sicily, the Balearics, southern Spain and southern Portugal, eventually reaching the Americas in Brazil via the Canary Islands, Madeira, the Cabo Verde Islands and São Tomé.[152]

The demand for slaves, for a long time mainly from the east coast of the Adriatic, but especially from the Italian Black Sea colonies, was insatiable. Thus, even Christians sold Christians. Little wonder, then, that a significant drop in the price of female slaves followed the fall of Capua in the Kingdom of Naples in 1501. Africa, however, became the largest new supplier, partly because of the direct contact with sub-Saharan Africa, partly also because the supply from the Balkans and southern Russia had been cut off by the Ottomans.

The export of West African gold to the Roman mint houses from around 300 was a catalyst for the medieval expansion of Islam to the south of the Sahara that started, albeit hesitantly, in the ninth century. This intensification of trans-Saharan contacts gave rise to a northwards stream of slaves that flowed to the southern coasts of the Mediterranean, especially to Morocco. The Portuguese and Spanish, who conquered port cities in north-west Africa, learned about this source of slaves from the Moroccans. In addition to Berbers, whom the Arabic conquerors had traded in much earlier, they now also offered black slaves for sale. Egypt was another terminus for the slave trade. The rulers of that country, the Mamluks (who came to power in 1250), had great need for slaves, whom they also used as elite soldiers. They were supplied from the north by the Venetians, who bought their white commodities in south Russia, and from the south by nomads, who supplied black slaves from West Africa to Tunisia and Libya, from where they were sent on Genoese ships to Egypt.[153]

The demand for black slaves in the west of the Mediterranean and in the newly conquered Atlantic Islands increased rapidly when the Turks conquered Constantinople in 1453. This meant that after the Italians they now controlled the Bosphorus and, from that point, there was no longer a flow of Turkish-Mongol slaves from the Russian steppes, or of slaves from the Caucasus and the Balkans to the west. So, they were forced to look for another source. That was Africa, the west coast of which was now being discovered further and further southwards by the Portuguese. The Italians now even went to Valencia to buy their slaves. There, slavery was widespread in all kinds of industries, and the trade in prisoners of war (acquired in 'just wars'), prisoners of hijackers and pirates, and Mudéjars (local Muslims) sentenced to penal servitude, also flourished. By the end of the century, 40 per cent of the slave population of Valencia was black, and it is here that we must look for the roots of modern racism.[154] The earliest Portuguese and Spanish sources speak of Guinea as a place of origin, rapidly followed by Canary Islanders and Wolof, followed by Sérères (including Biafra), and after the Portuguese fort São Jorge da Mina (Elmina) was established in Ghana, also Ibo and Mandinka. It should be noted, however, that all this happened before America, which rapidly became the primary destination for African slaves, was even in European sight.

After the impermanent successes of Christians against Muslims in the twelfth and thirteenth centuries, embodied in the Crusader states and the Latin Empire of Constantinople, the fifteenth century witnessed a new and severe pressure from Muslim competitor states in the eastern Mediterranean. Consequently, Portugal and Spain tried to expand westwards and eventually to gain independent access to the East via new seaways. These attempts combined aspirations of military glory, economic profit and the expansion of the Christian faith. In competition with the highly successful Portuguese along the west coast of Africa, who acquired Madeira, the Azores and Cabo Verde, the Spanish conquered the Canaries, as well as a number of coastal places in Morocco. The Spanish behaviour in this archipelago in the decades preceding their discovery of the Bahamas is highly significant for what was to happen later in the Americas. Unlike Madeira, the Azores and Cabo Verde, which are believed to have been uninhabited, the Canaries were inhabited – not by Christians or Muslims, but by 'animist' people speaking a Berber language and commonly called 'Guanches'. Emulating the Portuguese sugar cane cultivation on Madeira, which had been introduced from the Algarve and, from 1452 onwards, was increasingly performed by slave labour, the Spaniards in the Canaries also imposed unfree labour on the Guanches. Moreover, they imported Muslim slaves from North Africa, but most of all black slaves from sub-Saharan Africa.

Against this background, we examine, firstly, labour relations in the Americas following the Spanish and Portuguese conquests, and, secondly, those in Africa, in a brief comparative framework of global slavery, in order to see how unique the Atlantic tragedy was.

Repartimiento and encomiendas in the Americas

When the first Europeans arrived in the Americas, they encountered a society in which labour was organized in ways that were entirely different from what they were used to. And the inhabitants of the Americas were no less surprised about the labour concepts of their new masters.[155] In places where hunter-gatherers dominated, such as Brazil, reciprocity was the rule, whereas in the great empires of the Andes and Mexico hierarchical societies were based on tribute with redistribution. Market economies such as those in Europe did not exist, and neither did the type of chattel slavery the Iberian peoples had become used to over the last centuries. Whereas the former subjects of the Inca and Aztec empires tried to maintain existing labour relations as far as possible, the newcomers tried to acquire the biggest possible share by adopting those elements that suited them and by introducing elements of market economy and chattel slavery where deemed necessary.

Not unimportantly, the conquerors were obsessed with purity, both of reli-gion and of race. Earlier forms of Iberian tolerance and mutual conversion between Christianity, Islam and Judaism, were now gradually being supplanted (not without tensions) by the regular expulsion of Muslim and Jewish minorities and a suspicion of converts. Mixed marriages in particular were mistrusted, and a keen sense of 'limpieza de sangre' (purity of blood) became dominant. For the Americas, this not only meant scrutiny of the religious background of new arrivals, but also strict rules regarding family formation. Catholic marriages – the only ones officially recognized in the Spanish and Portuguese conquests – were forbidden between free and unfree, but also between Europeans, Indians and Africans. In Spanish America, this rule was upheld officially until independence, and the Portuguese allowed marriages between Indians and white people only in 1755, but not between white and black people.[156] Nevertheless, a large population of mixed descent, called *castas*, grew quickly and was minutely distinguished in sub-categories. This strict categorization had various consequences for family life and, in turn, for the reciprocal division of tasks within the family. For most slaves, family life was out of the question; meanwhile, at the other end of the spectrum, *castas* with a reasonable source of income may not have had a family life dissimilar from Europeans or un-mixed Indians.

As a result of these two factors, the Americas saw the emergence of a unique composite of labour relations in the four centuries to come. For a brief period after 12 October 1492, when Columbus and his crew encountered inhabitants of the Bahamas for the first time, contacts were based on exchange of goods, and labour relations were not yet involved. However, the Spaniards and somewhat later the Portuguese did not arrive tabula rasa, as we have seen. To the contrary, they both had a clear idea of how to approach inhabitants of newly discovered lands as well as ample recent experience of dealing with those who had the audacity not to be compliant.

It comes as no surprise that against this background of labour relations in force in Spain and the colonization of the Canaries, the Spaniards had already imposed tribute on the indigenous communities in 1494.[157] This did not affect existing labour relations, as such, but two innovations introduced forms of unfree labour to the New World. First, the enslavement of prisoners of a 'just' (directed against infidels) war in the same year. And, most significantly, temporary (during a lifetime, not hereditary) distribution (*repartimiento*) of the Crown land to individual Spanish colonists from 1498 onwards, which was soon extended to include the indigenous who populated them and now had to render labour services. Although the Spanish Crown had explicitly forbidden the introduction of slavery in its new colonies across the Atlantic (apart from prisoners of war and criminals, see below), Columbus's decision to introduce corvée (*servicios personales*) by including the labour of the inhabitants in the *repartimiento*, could de facto lead to situations that came very close to it.

The difference between rendering services before and after the advent of the Spaniards was that, previously, the products of this servile labour went to the state, whereas afterwards they were sold immediately in the market and from the sales taxes were paid in coin to the Crown. This combination of land-cum-inhabitants distribution, introduced in 1503 in the Caribbean, is called *encomienda*, literally 'commission' (*encomendar* means to entrust). Officially, this measure was meant to fight 'laziness' and 'vagrancy', but it was also meant to protect the American Indians from outside violence, combined with instruction in the Catholic religion and the Spanish language.[158]

In former Aztec Mexico, Spanish conquistadores and soldiers partially replaced the traditional nobles as *encomenderos*, but otherwise the system basically followed the Aztec registration and bureaucratic systems.[159] Of course, how much work was demanded by the new lords from the nominally free peasants (under Spanish law they were neither slaves nor serfs) mattered a lot. There are reasons to suppose that the workload increased immensely, as the Nahua population of the Valley of Mexico was reduced by 88 per cent within 60 years, whereas the *altepetl* or city-state system, with taxes paid through the performance of work, had been maintained, and the white population had increased greatly. On the other hand, there are examples of more favourable developments, where self-employment for the market as it had existed under the Aztec rulers was continued or even extended, like the *repartimiento* production of cochineal by the indigenous people of Oaxaca in Mexico until its demise in the mid-nineteenth century. In Mexico, the *encomienda-repartimiento* blossomed between 1525 and 1575 but was finally abolished by the Crown and converted into a tax, to be paid partly in money and partly in crops. In more peripheral parts of Spanish America this conversion took place much later.

In Mexico, like elsewhere in Spanish America, in addition to the *encomienda-repartimiento*, there was another type of enforceable labour, the *repartimiento forzoso* or *cuatequitl*.[160] As the latter expression indicates, this originated from the Aztec era, when groups of peasants under their *caciques* could be summoned to perform public works. The Spaniards gratefully continued this system, inter alia for building their brand-new capital Mexico City, with public and ecclesiastical buildings and roads, and for part of their silver mining. Road building was crucial for the new masters. Previously, because Mexico had no pack animals, all transport had been done by *tamemes*, porters who carried baskets of 23 kilograms suspended from a tumpline across their forehead. Now, the freight became heavier and hours were extended. Although the authorities ordained in 1531 that they should work voluntarily for a daily wage of 100 cacao beans (1 real or 1/8 peso), the abuse did not end. One of the main problems with this corvée labour was its improper imposition in times of labour scarcity, when a *juez repartidor* could assign such labour for two weeks to haciendas for weeding and harvesting. Officially abolished in 1630, it continued in certain regions and sectors like mining until the end of the eighteenth century.

Of course, American Indians tried every possible way to evade this hated corvée when it was too hard, interfered with other necessary agricultural work or had to be done for abusive employers or through abusive intermediaries, even though it was stipulated that they should be paid for it beforehand 'in sounding silver on the table'.[161] Officials in the town of Palín in Guatemala vividly described how difficult it was to collect enough men for such a task:

> First it is necessary for the justices and the other leaders themselves to go from house to house citing individuals who are to work and to give them two or four reales of their advances, money that they receive with such repugnance that often all you can do is put the money in the house, for no one will take it. On the day indicated for the repartimiento the scene is sad. The officials with the policemen round up the men while their neighbours commiserate with them. The women, children and all of the neighbours hurl reproaches and curses on the operation, and finding no escape for their beloved husbands and sons, there are everywhere tears and hopeless cries. It seems more as if they were going to prison or the gallows.[162]

Variations of the *encomienda-repartimiento* existed for many parts of Spanish America, but perhaps those of the Andes are the best known. After the Spaniards had also conquered Peru, they repeated their bad habits from the north and adapted systems of compulsory labour already tested in Mexico. From the Inca they borrowed the *mita* system, which has become best known for the way it was used in Potosí (Bolivia) for the mining of its spectacular silver mountain, situated in a barren landscape at 4,000 metres. Discovered by the Spaniards in 1545, it became legendary worldwide, as far as India and China, where much of its produce ended up, converted into silver coins and ingots.[163]

Provisionally, the existing Inca recruitment system for public service (*mit'a* in Quechua means service)[164] was more or less continued. In 1572, Viceroy Francisco de Toledo introduced the Mexican method of the amalgamation refining process. This gave a boost to silver production and raised an immediate demand for a much larger workforce, which was not available locally. He therefore modified the *mita* for his own purposes and guaranteed a supply of sufficient labour to the Spanish mine owners on the condition that the Crown would receive one-fifth of the production and that the miners would be compensated for their compulsory work, which was time-limited. Some 14,000 adult males with their families, 40,000 persons in total, from 17 provinces in a radius of up to 300 kilometres, were drafted under the leadership of their own *caciques*. Around 1600, this impressive forced temporal mass labour migration from Lake Titicaca to Potosí 480 kilometres away looked as follows:

> I have twice seen them and can report that there must be 7,000 souls. Each Indian takes at least eight or ten llamas and a few alpacas to eat. On these they transport their food, maize and chuño [dried potatoes], sleeping rugs and straw pallets to protect them from the cold, which is severe, for they always sleep on the ground. All this cattle normally exceeds 30,000 head ... Only some two thousand people return: of the other five thousand some die and others stay at Potosí or the nearby valleys because they have no cattle for the return journey.[165]

The nature of the work was described vividly at about the same time by Father José de Acosta:

> They labor in these mines in perpetual darkness, not knowing day from night. And since the sun never penetrates to these places, they are not only always dark but very cold, and the air is very thick and alien to the nature of men; so that those who enter for the first time get as sick as at sea – which happened to me in one of these mines, where I felt a pain at the heart and a churning at the stomach. They always carry candles to light their way and they divide their labor in such a way, that some work by day and rest by night, and others work by night and rest by day. The ore

is generally hard as flint, and they break it up with iron bars. They carry the ore on their backs up ladders made of three cords of twisted rawhide joined by pieces of wood that serve as rungs, so that one man may climb up and another down at the same time. These ladders are twenty meters long, and at the top and bottom of each is a wooden platform where the men may rest, because there are so many ladders to climb. Each man usually carries on his back a load of twenty-five kilograms of silver ore tied in a cloth, knapsack fashion; thus they ascend, three at a time. The one who goes first carries a candle, tied to his thumb, ... thus, holding on with both hands, they climb that great distance, often more than 300 meters – a fearful thing, the mere thought of which inspires dread.[166]

In fact, the *mitayos* only complied with this harsh regime because they were able to earn more than the below-market rates received from the owners. After one week working as a mitayo, they would do the same work as free *mingas* for a higher salary.[167]

After the mid-seventeenth century, the *mita* was converted from a work to a monetary obligation. By paying this heavy tax (only abolished by Simón Bolívar in 1825), American Indians could avoid their obligation to trek to the mine, and many did. The Potosí mining labour force now became dominated by self-employed *kajchas*, who herded their own pack animals, as was practised in other silver mining areas in the Andes.[168]

The combination of thousands of labourers paid both low and high wages, their access to silver ore and the barren nature of the Andean landscape of Potosí triggered a vast market and service sector, dominated not by men, as was the case in the mines, but rather by women.[169] Fresh, raw and ready-made food was sold by Andean women, as were coca leaves essential for the miners, who chewed them to help the body function at high altitudes and to suppress their appetites. The same women brewed *chicha* (maize beer), which was likely to be sold by Spanish women as the authorities tried, in vain, to fight not only alcohol consumption but also its trade by American Indians and Africans.

Outside the great polities – those of the Aztecs, Maya and Inca – some of the other peoples of the Americas had also developed agriculture, but in a much more decentralized way. Redistribution of the fruits of their labour happened at a local level.[170] Here, the conquerors proceeded in a different way. The Catholic kings of Spain and Portugal delegated the tasks to integrate these kinds of matters to missionaries, predominantly Jesuits and Franciscans. Supported by the colonial state, missionaries established centres, learned the local language and tried to convert American Indians to Catholicism. But that was not all. They also imposed corvée for the church and the state against minimum wages in kind, paid out through the indigenous chiefs, and they facilitated a market economy, including taxation in kind.[171] In poorly endowed regions, village chiefs acquired key positions as intermediaries, and their power increased under the new rule. In more densely settled regions, like in the chiefdoms of the Mississippi Valley, economic patterns and the way colonizers adapted to them surpassed those of the old empires, and they gained much power over labour, although it was nowhere near as much as that in the strong states of Mexico and the Andes.[172]

The taming or disciplining of hunter-gatherers in order to change their reciprocal labour relations was another matter entirely.[173] Where the missionary approach across the Americas was well suited to getting a hold on decentralized agricultural communities, non-sedentary peoples were much harder to approach. This is not to say that their way of life stayed the same providing they kept out of the way. In the Gran Chaco, in modern northern Argentina, Paraguay and adjacent regions of Bolivia, lived the Guaycuruans, who only resolved to live in missions well into the eighteenth century, one-and-a-half centuries after their first contact with the Spaniards.

At the first meeting with the new colonizers, they added tamed horses and cattle to their usual prey, and soon discovered that it was highly profitable not to kill them immediately. Instead, they traded them to Spanish and *mestizo* fences, not averse to profiting from the misfortune of fellow Christians. Moreover, the Guaycuruans became able horsemen, which enabled them to hunt more wild game and tame cattle, and to take captives. In no time, they transformed from distant outsiders living their non-sedentary or semi-nomadic lives in the forest, marshes and savannas, into feared warriors who scorned the corn-growing sedentary Guaranis, who had transitioned to living in missions early on, and their Spanish allies.

After initial severe losses to epidemic diseases, like all American peoples after contact, Guaycuruan populations started to increase again in the seventeenth century, encouraged by the proceeds of trade in raided cattle, horses, mules and captives, as well as the produce of the forest: deer skins and honey. Their raiding parties swelled from a few dozen men afoot or in canoes to hundreds of horsemen who regularly attacked towns like Tucumán, Asunción and Santa Fe. At the same time, these successes induced their downfall – not only because the settlers improved their defences, but also and especially for ecological reasons, because the Guaycuruan started to deplete their own natural resources. Traditionally, native American hunters were governed by rules that limited a hunter's take to what was needed for survival, and game (unlike domestic animals), moreover, was believed to have a soul.

This sense had been lost, and their commercial harvesting of game forced most of them to become part of missions in the 1730s and 1740s.[174] For the women, used to collecting plants, the transition to a sedentary agricultural life was far less of a change than for the warrior-hunter men, who adapted to new ways of working very slowly. Guaycuruan men avoided working in the fields, and apart from hunting and the occasional raids on their neighbours, they preferred to become ranchers or craftsmen like blacksmiths, carpenters and builders of houses and carts.[175] All missions had a head start as a result of subsidies in the form of cattle and other animals, tools and clothing. In addition to having a priest to teach the new religion, hispanized *peones* were also hired as examples and tutors of the new ways of working. In the more successful missions, the Guaycuruan leaders resisted such paternalistic control and traded their community's produce with outsiders on their own terms.

The history of the confrontation between the indigenous peoples of Brazil and their colonizers is much more dramatic.[176] Certainly, there are various interesting examples of adaptation, but the overwhelming picture is one of annihilation. The colonizers needed land for sugar cane in the south and north, and in between, for cattle ranches producing hides for the European leather industry. They therefore needed indigenous labour, and they tried to acquire it by any means, which, as a rule, meant enforcement and enslavement. The skills of the *paulistas* (named after São Paulo), whites and *mamelucos* (of mixed descent) were notorious in this regard; they were even hired in central and northern Brazil to capture indigenous people. The town council of São Paulo in 1585 set the tone:

This land is in great danger of being depopulated because its [white] inhabitants do not have [Indian] slaves as they used to, by whom they always have been served. This is the result of many illnesses ... from which over two thousand head of slaves have died in this captaincy in the past six years. This land used to be ennobled by these slaves, and its settlers supported themselves honourably with them and made large incomes.[177]

A few decades later, the 'father of Brazilian history', Frei Vicente do Salvador, described how:

> with such deceptions and some gifts of clothing or tools to the chiefs, . . . they roused up entire villages. But once they arrived with them in sight of the sea they separated children from parents, brother from brother and sometimes even husband from wife . . . They used them on their estates and some sold them . . . Those who bought them would brand them on the face at their first [attempted] flight or fault: they claimed that they had cost money and were their slaves.[178]

This happened repeatedly in the subsequent centuries: seduction or capture, slaughter, forced labour and mass killing by contagious diseases caused the extinction of most of Brazil's native population – one way or another, and notwithstanding fierce armed resistance by many, or attempts to improve the situation by some missionaries and civil servants.

Forms of free wage and independent labour

What was the overall result of these initial phases of exploitation, enslavement and massive population losses? For some important parts of the Americas an answer is possible. From the late sixteenth century, about half of the rural population of New Spain (Mexico) consisted of peasants living under communal arrangements in their own villages and half of agricultural labourers working at the large *haciendas* owned by Spaniards and their offspring. By 1620, at least half of the agricultural land in the Valley of Mexico had been given to these colonists. In some parts of the colony, peasant families were also engaged in rural industries. The spinners and cloth weavers of Quito and its environs were even producing for export, which exempted them from the *mita*. Wages were low in comparison to those in the white settler colonies in north-eastern America, and the reasons for this are to be found in the old continent. There, the real wages in England were much higher than those on the Iberian Peninsula. Consequently, in order to improve themselves, Spanish and Portuguese commoners were much more easily satisfied in the southern parts of the New World, and this set the wage standard for *mestizos* and indigenous peoples.[179]

Two-thirds of the Mexican silver miners (in total 10,000 around 1600 and 50–60,000 around 1750) were wage labourers. They were paid partly in coin and partly in silver ore, according to piece rates (the *partido*). This may have to do with the general shortage of cash and especially small change in the countryside, but the labourers clearly did not deplore the *partido*. On the contrary, when the employers wished to abolish it, they met with fierce resistance from the miners. In 1766, they revolted in Real del Monte near Pachuca, and a long and successful strike ensued. In the end, the authorities stuck to the traditional remuneration arrangement, with its important piece wage component.[180] The similarities with the prevailing mode of remuneration in Potosí is obvious – this in contrast with the later explosion of gold mining in Colombia and Brazil, which was dominated by slave labour.[181]

Finally, most wage labourers and independent artisanal producers lived in cities, but there are two qualifications: the very uneven distribution of urban settlements throughout the continent, and the competition between free and unfree urban labour.[182] In what was to become Brazil, the Portuguese did not encounter big empires, and even agriculture was much less developed than it was further westwards. Many native Americans were hunter-gatherers or combined this type of work with slash-and-burn subsistence agriculture. Thus, the sedentary and agricultural Portuguese and, for a time, also the Dutch had to build their own type of society there from scratch, and, consequently, Portuguese America was hardly urbanized in comparison to Spanish America. Until the gold and diamond rush in Minas Gerais in the 1690s, the few Brazilian towns, like the capital Salvador de Bahía and São Paulo, were no match for big cities like Mexico City, Quito, Lima or Potosí. Here, free but poorly paid and poorly skilled artisans and domestic servants had to compete with slaves performing the same sort of work. The few urban industrial establishments, mainly textile and tobacco factories, were set up by the colonial state in the last decades of the eighteenth century. The Mexico City tobacco factory employed some 5,000 workers around 1800 and gained some notoriety following a strike by the women workers (over half of the establishment), who resisted the elimination of customary employee benefits and the raising of quotas. However, like in Europe and Asia, free wage labourers in the Americas generally worked in small work units.

Chattel slavery on American plantations

Slavery and other forms of unfree labour have been reviewed in passing in the preceding pages on Latin America. While it was certainly a widespread type of labour relation in the early modern Americas, it only became dominant in the Caribbean and Brazil. Although well acquainted with slavery at home, the Spaniards were not in favour of it in the New World, as we have seen. The only exceptions were prisoners taken in a 'just war' and criminals, although it should be noted that these were not few in number.[183] Indeed, between 1521 and 1524, at least 25,000 men and women were sold in New Spain, followed by many more tens of thousands in subsequent years. Most were employed in gold mining, where they received their basic food from *encomienda*-raised tax-in-kind. Because the contagious diseases that had decimated the original American population also hit slaves, their price shot up from 4–5 pesos (1527–28) via 50 (1536–38) to 200 pesos in 1550.

As a result, they had become as expensive as slaves from Africa. Consequently, these were now also imported into Mexico, having been introduced earlier to Hispaniola (this island was later divided into Haiti and the Dominican Republic), where, already in 1514, they outnumbered white people.[184] The importation of African slaves into Mexico was extended following the abolition of indigenous enslavement in 1548. Slaves in Mexico were employed in the silver mines (some 1,000 in 1600) and in the cloth factories.

Whereas African slaves in Mexico and most other parts of Spanish America were numerically insignificant, other areas were heavily dependent on them, in particular the Caribbean and its mainland coasts (under any master, be he Spanish, French, English, Dutch or Danish) and Brazil. In the Caribbean, they were mainly employed on plantations, in particular on sugar plantations. In Brazil – in addition to working on plantations – they also worked in the mines and, indeed, were found in almost any kind of job.[185]

Under the Treaty of Tordesillas (1494), which saw the pope divide the world between the Spaniards and the Portuguese, the latter were fortunate enough to receive the exclusive right to exploit both Africa and Brazil. This facilitated the combining of regions where they could buy and employ slaves. The Spaniards were therefore dependent on the Portuguese for the procurement of black slaves and, in 1518, they introduced a governmental licence (the *asiento de negros*) for those seeking to import slaves into their territories. Such *asientos* were exclusive contracts for individual merchants or mercantile companies to fetch a specific number of slaves (as a rule, 3,000 to 5,000 per licence) for a specific period. They were abolished only in 1834.

In Brazil, where the annihilation of the native population had been the most cruel, certain conditions ensured that the country was the largest slave country of the time: the earlier Portuguese experience with agro-industry on the Atlantic Islands; excellent conditions for sugar cane plantations; and their slave stations right across the sea on the coasts of Guinea and Angola.[186] In 1532, sugar cane was introduced to São Vicente (present-day São Paulo) and, in 1559, the king of Portugal allowed every plantation owner to import a maximum of 120 slaves from the Congo. In 1570, he officially prohibited the use of enslaved American indigenous, which opened the door to mass importation of slaves from Africa.

The acreage on plantations was divided into four, split between: sugar cane; crops like yucca or plantains to feed the workforce; forest land for firewood; and pastures for draught animals and beef cattle. Usually, sugar cane required replanting every year or two, but the environment in coastal north-eastern Brazil allowed for this period to be extended by as much as twenty years. Cutting the cane was the most important agricultural task during ten or eleven months of the year. This was done in teams, frequently consisting of a man and a woman, competing for the favour of the master and certain rewards. One team member cut the cane and the other cleaned, bundled and stacked the stems. The cane was transported to the mills on ox carts. Originally, the cane was crushed between horizontal mill stones; later, these machines were improved in Brazil by putting the rollers upright, moved around by oxen tied to a beam or, where possible, by a waterwheel. Windmills were only used on Barbados and some nearby islands to provide the necessary moving force.

The juice won from this process was boiled in large kettles. After 8 hours of field work, the slaves had to perform a mill shift. Another important task on any plantation was cutting and fetching the wood for the insatiable fires that were kept burning day and night. This was necessary because, if not processed quickly, the cut cane would ferment and lose sugar content. The sugar mill was only quiet at the beginning of the day, as workers waited for the new cane carts to arrive. After being boiled thrice, the cane juice or molasses was poured from the kettles into conical clay moulds, where it drained and crystallized. Finally, the sugar loaves were ground and put into boxes of 625–750 pounds (roughly 350 kg) each for export to Europe. Apart from these primary processes, each plantation needed carpenters, ironworkers, cooks, orchard keepers and laundry women. In total, even the smallest plantation needed fifty workers, but usually it was a few hundred.

In periods when the sugar price was high, the costs of purchasing a slave and his or her upkeep could be earned back within two years. In less profitable years this was four years, but, in any case, slave owners had no great incentive to treat their workforce carefully or to allow them to raise children; they simply bought new slaves. This situation prevailed until around 1800, when abolition, or at least its threat, drove prices up.[187]

The Dutch were the first northern Europeans to engage in the American sugar plantations.[188] When, following their revolt against the king of Spain (who also wore the Portuguese crown from 1580 to 1640) in 1595, the Dutch were no longer allowed to buy salt – necessary for preserving herring – on the Iberian Peninsula, they sailed to Venezuela. They became very well acquainted with the new continent by smuggling all sorts of contraband. After a twelve-year truce between the Dutch Republic and the Spanish Crown (1609–21), the Dutch West India Company was founded and subsequently conquered strategic parts of north-eastern Brazil and Portuguese Africa, which it managed to keep for decades. The Dutch emulated their predecessors in many ways, and thus got involved in both the slave trade and sugar plantations worked by African slaves. The Portuguese New Christians, who had found refuge in Holland and there reconverted to Judaism, played an important role in this. Some of these Dutch 'Portuguese Jews' maintained strong international trading networks and were now influential in the former Portuguese territories conquered by the Dutch, to which, by the way, we can add Curaçao and a few other Caribbean islands taken from Spain in 1634. After their expulsion from Brazil in 1654 (all the while maintaining posts in West Africa), the Dutch turned to the Caribbean (especially their slave entrepôt Curaçao, which supplied the Spanish) and Guyana (where they started slave plantations at Suriname, Demerara and Berbice).

They also taught their newly learned lessons to the French and the English, who also acquired trading posts in West Africa and started sugar and other plantations in the Caribbean.[189] None of these newcomers from the north entertained slaves at home, as was usual in the Mediterranean, but some, like the English, entertained peculiar labour relations, which mattered in the New World. Early on, the first English colonizers tried to rely on the labour of their own people, emigrated from home. The great majority of them arrived without their own means in the Caribbean (where the first permanent English settlement was at Saint Christopher in 1624, followed by

Barbados in 1627) or in North America (with the first settlements in Virginia in 1607). In any case, the harsh master-and-servant laws prevailed in the new colonics.[190] These included penal sanctions for breach of contract (as well as for 'fornication' and 'bastardy' for female servants in North America). Moreover, the settlers invariably arrived loaded with debts, usually incurred by paying their passage to the colony. These were passed on by the ship captains to their new employer and recorded in a written servitude contract. The main clause held that the thus indentured labourer was to redeem his indenture by unpaid labour for his master, who, in turn, agreed to provide board and lodging, including in case of illness.

Apart from such indebtedness, these wage labourers were tied for a long period to their masters. In 1642, Virginia stipulated for the first time statutory terms for servants migrating without indentures: four years for those over the age of 20, five years for those over 12, and seven for those under.[191] In the Caribbean, with its extremely high mortality among white people, this implied that there were very few really free labourers, notwithstanding the great number of arrivals from Europe. That was different in the parts of North America that had a moderate or cold climate, which enabled many an indentured labourer to serve his contract to the end and subsequently to choose freely an occupation and/or a master. Although penal sanctions for breach of contract were only abolished in the US in the early nineteenth century, white labourers and artisans did their utmost to emancipate themselves from the stigma of their status according to old English law by emphasizing their differences in comparison to black slaves. For example, to 'whip a Christian white servant naked' was officially prohibited in Virginia in 1705.[192]

On Barbados, after fifty cumbersome years of tobacco and cotton cultivation by English indentured servants with three- or five-year contracts, many eventually became small peasants.[193] Thereafter, agricultural labour began to be performed by (increasingly cheaper) slaves from Africa. In 1640, the average cost of a white indentured worker was about £12 sterling against £25 for a slave (though the costs of feeding, housing and clothing all had to be added to this, and, in addition, a white worker required payment in tobacco and land on expiration of the contract). As long as slaves were more expensive in comparison to indentured labourers, nothing changed on Barbados. But in 1670, the price of a slave fell to £15, and in 1683 to £12½. Moreover, slaves became permanent property and could be sold, and their upkeep was less expensive than that of indentured Europeans. Quickly, Barbados became dotted with sugar cane plantations worked by slaves and, at the same time, a concentration process took place at the cost of small properties.

The same happened on the largest English possession, Jamaica, and on the smaller Leeward Islands. Jamaica had been taken from Spain in 1655 and, initially, the English wanted to grow cacao beans there; but, like Barbados, Jamaica became an island with large sugar plantations and, by 1673, the enslaved plantation had already surpassed that of the free white population. Fifty years later, slave numbers had increased from fewer than 10,000 to over 80,000, while the number of white people stagnated. Jamaica's slave population further increased over the next 40 years, reaching 173,000 in 1760 – 10 times more than the white population and totalling nearly half of all slaves in the British West Indies. At that time, an average plantation in Jamaica held 204 slaves. Only the French island of Saint Domingue (later to become Haiti) had a larger slave population, with close to half a million slaves – about as many as Brazil. Cuba's slave population was still comparatively small (65,000 in 1780) but was increasing rapidly.[194] Second only to Brazil and the Caribbean in terms of slave numbers was the US at the end of the eighteenth century, where, after the 1680s, slaves had replaced indentured servants on the medium and large estates. In its modern territory, there were 700,000 slaves by 1790, 94 per cent of whom, located in Maryland and the states to the south, engaged mainly in the cultivation of export crops like tobacco, rice and, from 1790, also cotton.

Labour relations in the Americas had changed dramatically at the cost of the great suffering of its original inhabitants, of slaves brought there from Africa and of many others. The first post-Columbian century was the most brutal for the native Americans, although their ordeal did not end there. Nevertheless, by around 1600, work for the market by small peasant farmers and wage labourers had replaced earlier forms of labour relations. At the same time, slave transports from Africa increased, crossing the 2 million mark in the last quarter of the eighteenth century. The demand for slaves in the Americas may now be clear, but what about the supply side? What happened in Africa to make this possible?

Africa becomes the main source of slaves in the Atlantic

Africa's labour history cannot be written without slavery and slave transportations, both internally and to other continents. Nevertheless, it represents much more. In order to gain a complete picture of the labour history of Africa, we must start with some environmental basics. Sub-Saharan Africa was the opposite of the tropical and sub-tropical parts of South (and South East) Asia, where we have seen various forms of labour-intensive agriculture and industrialization, in virtually all respects. Population density in Africa was substantially lower than on other continents: about four people per square kilometre in 1750, or six times less than Western Europe (one of the implications being the persistence of egalitarian agriculture; see pp. 71–2). Intensive agriculture with the help of iron tools was not unknown, but it did not spread, because:

> not only was much land infertile, even the more fertile soils were usually thin and therefore easily degraded by ploughing or prolonged cultivation. . . . This was reinforced by endemic sleeping sickness preventing the use of large animals whether on farms or in transport . . . Thus human porterage was the only means of transport. Above all, access to land as a factor of agricultural production was effectively denied for several months of the year, in the sense that during the heart of the dry season there was nothing useful that could be done in farming.[195]

The transport problems were also a serious hindrance to trade, as human porterage made long-distance business much more costly than in other continents and thus restricted occupational specialization. It is not surprising that hunter-gathering sustained itself so much longer here than on other continents, although we should not imagine it as exclusively self-sufficient. For example, they provided important export products for the world market, such as ivory, wax for candles, and gum.[196]

These natural conditions led to three important consequences in sub-Saharan Africa. Firstly, agricultural work was even more seasonally divided than elsewhere in the world. In these centuries, it was all hands on deck outside of the dry season when there was a general lack of pack and draught animals. Incidentally, labour productivity rose in the long term as a result of 'the selective adoption of a long succession of imported crops or crop varieties of Asian or, after the inception of trans-Atlantic trade, New World origin, including plantains, maize, cassava and cocoa beans'.[197]

Secondly, a solution had to be found for the lack of work in the three dry months. Spinning and weaving, iron production and other crafts were on the programme for farming communities (I deliberately exclude the hunter-gatherers here). Zimbabwe experienced a peak in copper mining for the African market and gold mining for export across the Indian Ocean around 1400. Parts of West Africa also engaged in the risky mining of gold. Perhaps less than in agriculture, again, women's labour dominated here due to a strict division of exclusively male and female tasks. For example, in Benin, all weavers were women. Elsewhere in Africa, where weaving was an exclusively male task, a weaver could not function without eight to fifteen spinsters. By comparison, the number of men engaged in metal production was minimal. The felling of trees for fuel for the smelting of ores was typically men's work, especially that of hunter-gatherers.[198]

Thirdly, in the eighteenth and nineteenth centuries, it followed from this that African communities reacted to labour scarcity and labour abundance by valuing the acquisition of people, whether wives, children or captives. The oversupply of labour during a large part of the year, and especially that of men, tempted the elites to sell their surplus slaves to slavers from the north and east, but also, from the fifteenth century, to passing European ships. This was apparently so lucrative – as we shall see below – that slave trade went from being a sideline to the main business. Whereas until nearly 1700 European interest in African products had concerned mainly gold, it now shifted to captives. As a result, this self-propelling process accelerated now in a western direction, which lasted in total four centuries. There were three markets for enslaved Africans: America, which we have dealt with extensively; the Arab world (extending into India); and the internal African market. Everywhere, they were demanded for work, but the type of employment was different.[199]

Cross-Saharan transport of slaves did not start with the Islamization of Africa in the eighth century, but it certainly received an important boost in the ensuing centuries.[200] Whereas in classical antiquity the Sahara still formed a major barrier between the Mediterranean and tropical Africa and contacts were mainly restricted to the Nile and the Red Sea routes, the spread of Islam made a difference. North and south of the Sahara, Islamic states came into being, linked by religious and cultural ties that also enhanced trade, including slave trade, and traffic, including pilgrimage. Like Christians who justified the enslaving of captives in a 'just war', Islamic scholars such as Ahmad Baba al-Massufi from Timbuktu (1614) also found arguments in favour of slavery and slave trade:

The reason for slavery is non-belief [in Islam] and the Sudanese non-be-lievers are like other kafir whether they are Christians, Jews, Persians, Berbers, or any others who stick to non-belief and do not embrace Islam ... This means there is no difference between all the kafir in this respect. Whoever is captured in a condition of non-belief, it is legal to own him, whosoever he may be, but not if he was converted to Islam voluntarily.

According to the same logic, it was strictly forbidden for Muslims to sell enslaved people to non-Muslims.[201]

It is estimated that, over a thousand years, the numbers of slaves trans-ported overland from Africa to the north and north-east amounted to more than half the numbers shipped to the Americas in four centuries. This sounds impressive, but the intensity of the later transatlantic slave trade was five times that during antiquity.

Apart from the many other differences between these two destinations and the particular parts of Africa where the slaves originated, this difference in intensity is mainly the result of transport logistics. Most African slaves going north had to walk themselves through the desert to their new workplaces. Only slaves from Ethiopia (especially between the thirteenth and seventeenth centu-ries), Somalia and, later, coastal regions of East Africa were also transported by ships, to Arabia, Persia and India. Another important effect of the Islamization south of the Sahara was state formation in Western Africa. These new states (first Ghana, absorbed by Mali, which was then absorbed by the largest of all, the Songhai Empire) acquired prisoners of war from their 'heathen' or animist neighbours in the south. As a consequence, some of these took refuge in the tropical forests, while others converted to Islam in order to prevent further enslavement, which was, after all, forbidden among co-religionists.[202]

As we have seen, the closing off of the northern slave markets by the advancing Ottomans increased the demand for African slaves at the end of the Middle Ages, especially on the new Mediterranean sugar plantations spreading out into the Atlantic. When, gradually advancing southwards along the African coast, the Portuguese arrived in West Africa, they also met slave traders linked to supply chains in the interior. From then on, warring states could sell their supplies of captives both to the north and the south. And the south was going to take an ever-increasing share, because the Europeans with their big ships and demand for slaves in the Americas guar-anteed an insatiable hunger for slaves.

While the demand between the fourteenth and seventeenth centuries for African slaves from Ethiopia and Eastern Africa across the Red Sea and Indian Ocean may have been more or less stable, that on the other, western side of the continent rose after the Portuguese settled permanently at Elmina and São Tomé. Initially, the Europeans were mainly fascinated by something else, gold – traditionally monopolized by the Moroccans, who imported it from the gold fields near the Senegal, Gambia and Volta rivers all the way through the Sahara. West African exports of gold and slaves were balanced by imports of copper (in the form of rods and rings, also used as currencies), in particular, and, in addition, brightly coloured cloth and many other different goods, including cowries and beads for currency circulation.[203] With the development of the sugar plantations in the Atlantic and African islands (São Tomé and Principe) and, finally, in Brazil, the demand for gold, ivory and other African products was surpassed by that of 'black gold': slaves.

We have seen already how unfree American Indians were replaced by Africans in the course of the sixteenth century. The transatlantic slave trade increased dramatically after 1600, surpassing the trans-Saharan stream. Not only did the Portuguese step in, but also the Dutch, followed by the British and later also the French and other European nations. Over the centuries, 12.6 million slaves were transported from Africa to the Americas, half of those in the eighteenth century. The Portuguese, in the end overtaken by the Brazilians, took nearly half of the share, the British more than a quarter, the French more than 10 per cent and the Dutch 5 per cent.[204] In comparison to these main players, the share of the other nations was insignificant, although, at the end, after the British abolished the transatlantic slave trade in 1807, the most important slave states, Brazil and the US, became absolutely dominant.

In fact, the final part of the long, involuntary journey between the moment of capture and starting work as a slave went remarkably calmly. Indeed, fewer than 500 rebellions are known for the 36,000 documented transatlantic slave voyages.[205] Perhaps after several earlier escape attempts, many had simply given up in this final phase. Where that was not the case, it almost invariably ended badly for the slaves. In some cases, the attempt even ended in collective suicide. That was the case with the ship *Neptunus* from Zierikzee (in Zeeland, the province that accounted for 70 per cent of all Dutch slave ships), which in 1784–85 bought slaves in various ports between Sierra Leone and Ghana. The trade did not go very smoothly and therefore took too much time. Moreover, the sailors were unhappy, and slaves faced severe punishment at the slightest protest. When, on 17 October 1785, two hundred slaves had finally been brought on board by free Africans with their canoes, and the ship was prepared for the Atlantic crossing, the slaves successfully rebelled and took over the ship. The crew, together with the free Africans, grabbed a chance to flee. As a result, the slaves were lord and master, but also vulnerable to the hundreds of African salvage companies that gladly sold back rebel slaves to the Dutch. When the unholy alliance of an English slave ship and dozens of canoes belonging to free Africans threatened to overpower the rebels, the slaves put a fuse in the gunpowder and blew up the whole ship. Almost everyone was killed, and along with them their assailants, 400 men in total. In view of the number of victims, this was the most dramatic slave rebellion that ever occurred on board a European slave ship. Of significance for the history of work is the role not only of the crew of the *Neptunus* and the rebellious slaves, but of the free African recovery agents as well. This is how deeply the principle of unfree labour had penetrated Africa.

But the transatlantic slave trade was only part of a far greater drama. Apart from the Atlantic destinations, as we have seen, enslaved Africans were also exported to the Middle East and to the Indian Ocean. Of the over 20 million African captives between 1500 and 1900, roughly two-thirds left the continent to the west across the Atlantic and one-third departed to the north and east.[206] The total numbers of captives must have been substantially higher, however, as they had to walk great distances from the interior to the coast, many across the Sahara desert. The death toll before they arrived at the slave ships was enormous – according to some estimates, perhaps 4 million persons.[207] Finally, many were employed in Africa itself. Up to 1850, one-third of all surviving captives were retained in Africa, and after 1880 all of them. In sum, between 1500 and 1900, we are talking about the capture of easily 30 million sub-Saharan Africans (12.5 million across the Atlantic, 6 million to the north and east, maybe 4 million in casualties before transportation out of Africa and some 8 million inside Africa).

What was the impact on Africa? In one word: enormous. Not only for those 30 million enslaved, but also for those doing the dirty work of capturing, supervising and transporting them.[208] As might be expected, the effects of this were felt very unevenly geographically, and not only because coastal areas were more affected than the interior. The demographic impact may have been deepest in two regions: firstly, in Western Africa, where Arab traders exporting captives in northerly directions after 1600 were surpassed by Europeans heading west (it should be noted, however, that the former did not simply give up; indeed, over several centuries, millions headed in both directions simultaneously); and secondly, in 'West Central Africa', between Loango in the north and Benguela in the south, and comprising the key ports of embarkation: Luanda (2.8 million); Cabinda; and Malembo. In total, 5.7 million men, women and children were taken from an area not more than 900 kilometres wide as the crow flies. Together with the Congo River Basin, this coastal strip was most at risk.[209]

Millions of enslaved: impressive numbers, but composed of individual human beings. Only a few have been able to tell their stories of captivity in such a way that we can still hear them. One of these unique witnesses is Oluale Kossola, an Isha Yoruba from what today is Benin, who, aged 19, was captured by the king of Dahomey. He was subsequently sold to American slavers and forced into plantation work from 1860 to 1865, at the end of the Civil War. In 1927–28, he told his story to Zora Neale Hurston, a prominent member of the Harlem Renaissance Movement:

It bout daybreak when the folks dat sleep git wake wid the noise when the people of Dahomey breakee de Great Gate. I not woke yet. I still in bed. I hear de gate when dey break it. I hear de yell from the soldiers while dey choppee de gate. Derefore I jump out de bed and lookee. I see de great many soldiers wid French gun in de hand and de big knife. Dey got de women soldiers too and dey run wid de big knife and make noise. Dey ketch people and dey saw de neck lak dis wid de knife den dey twist de head so and it come off de neck. O Lor', Lor'!

I see de people gittee kill so fast! De old ones dey try run 'way from de house but dey dead by de door, and de women soldiers got dey head. Oh, Lor'!

Everybody dey run to de gates so dey kin hide deyself in de bush, you unnerstan me. Some never reachee de gate. De women soldier ketchee de young ones and tie dem by de wrist. No man kin be so strong lak de woman soldiers from de Dahomey. . . .

One gate lookee lak nobody dere so I make haste and runnee towards de bush. But de man of Dahomey dey dere too. Soon as I out de gate dey grabee me, and tie de wrist. I beg dem, please lemme go back to my mama, but dey don't pay whut I say no 'tenshun. Dey tie me wid de rest. . . .

When I see de king dead, I try to 'scape from de soldiers. I try to make it do de bush, but all soldiers overtake me befo' I git dere. O Lor', Lor'! When I think 'bout dat time I try not to cry no mo'. My eyes dey stop cryin' but de tears runnee down inside me all de time. When de men pull me wid dem I call my mama name. I doan know where dey is. I beg de men to let me go findee my folks. De soldiers say dey got no ears for cryin'. De king of Dahomey come to hunt slave to sell. So dey tie me in de line wid de rest.

De sun it jus' rising.

All day dey make us walk. De sun so hot! . . .

When we dere three weeks a white man come in de barracoon wid two men of de Dahomey. One man, he a chief of de Dahomey and de udder one his word-changer. Dey make everybody stand in a ring – 'bout ten folkses in each ring. De men by dey self, de women by dey self. Den de white man lookee and lookee. He lookee hard at de skin and de feet and the legs and in de mouth. Den he choose . . . he take one hunnard and thirty.[210]

If the preferences of the buyers had been decisive, only strong adult men would have been transported to the American plantations. However, the European ships were entirely dependent on what African traders wanted to offer and, as a consequence, women formed one-third of all their deportees. Over time, the proportion of males increased, possibly in relation to the strong upsurge of prices, which doubled between 1700 and 1750 and again between 1750 and 1800. By the early 1800s, they were five times higher in constant British pounds than around 1700.[211] Why African slave traders had so many women, as well as children, on offer both for European and for 'Arabian' buyers may have to do with the way Africans were forced into slavery: in war and also during raids, men may have resisted more success-fully, but may also have fought to their death. At the same time, African armies were accompanied by a train of women and children, which became easy prey for the slavers. Women were especially in demand for domestic service in the northern and eastern destinations, but also within Africa.

The consequences for the organization of work within sub-Saharan Africa were grave: the extraction of innumerable able-bodied workers from the labour force caused distorted sex ratios, but also the contamination of the slavery model, enhancing the share of unfree labour inside the continent and, finally, a specific diversification of certain occupations. This happened in several chronological steps.[212]

The first was Islamization, contemporaneous with the increasing demand for slaves in the countryside of the Abbasid Empire – in particular, in cash-crop production, salt production and land reclamation, but also as house-hold servants. In Iraq alone, 300,000 slaves were employed in the second half of the ninth century, many of them Africans, alongside Berbers, Turks and Slavs.[213] Secondly, with the Ottomans preserving Caucasian slaves for their own use, contemporaneous with the spread of sugar plantations in the Mediterranean, there was an increased demand for African slaves. Thirdly, the appearance of Europeans on the coasts of Africa was a catalyst for the development of American plantations. The years 1690–1740 were decisive, as prices surged and, simultaneously, the supply increased. Finally, with the demise of European demand in the nineteenth century, prices dropped, making possible an expansion of the Oriental trade as well as the growth of slavery in Africa itself. Indeed, around 1900, more slaves lived in Africa than ever before or after. The share of unfree labour inside the continent grew from 3 to 5 million in the second half of the eighteenth century to 10 million a century later, or from a maximum of 10 to 15 per cent of the total sub-Saharan population. Regionally, these percentages could be much higher. Estimates for the nineteenth-century Sokoto Caliphate in West Africa oscil-late between one-quarter and one-half.[214]

The extraction of countless able-bodied workers from the labour force was aggravated by desertion and by farmers (especially the animists and 'heathens' among them) who feared being enslaved fleeing to the forests and mountains, where they partially returned to a hunter-gatherer existence. The slavery model was certainly infectious, not only because taking war captives was profitable, but also because it stimulated kidnapping, judicial enslave-ment and impositions of taxation payments on slaves, all legitimized by concomitant African state institutions. Consequently, the labour force became predominantly female. Moreover, as many of these women were enslaved, polygyny became increasingly popular among African 'big men'; accordingly, married women's status declined from that enjoyed in monoga-mous marriages and existing kinship systems were corrupted. Women's work also included sexual services, as is clearly demonstrated by the prices at the Kano slave market in 1850. Males fetched 25,000–35,000 cowries (10–14 Maria Theresa thalers), while females were sold for 80,000–100,000 (32–40 thalers). More precisely, female children were priced at 30,000 cowries, young girls at 30,000–40,000, girls whose breasts had formed at 40,000–100,000, women with full breasts up to 80,000, but women whose breasts sagged less than 20,000 and old women 10,000 at most.[215]

The diversification of occupations took many forms.[216] Directly related to the institution of slavery was the proliferation and professionalization of warfare, including the usage of firearms. Between 1750 and 1807, the British alone sold at least 20 million guns to African merchants, as well as 22,000 metric tons of gunpowder and 91,000 kg of lead.[217] As all the captives had to be transported under surveillance, this also offered employment opportunities for caravan drivers. In West Africa in particular, many of these soldiers and supervisors were slaves themselves.[218]

As we have seen, gold was an important product, and the mining and transport of this precious good occupied many craftsmen. But hunter-gatherers were also necessary for African exports, as they hunted and butchered the elephants for their ivory tusks and collected beeswax and honey. Already the earliest available quantitative sources (Portuguese, from around 1500) demonstrate not only impressive amounts of gold being exported from Africa, but also ivory being exported to, especially, India. This suggests a sophisticated logistical operation involving mining, large-scale hunting, and overland transport to the coast and a concomitant workforce.[219] The same goes for other goods imported and exported, and for services like porterage, with men asked to carry loads of 25–40 kg over a distance of 25 kilometres a day, or canoeing on the rivers and between the coast and the big sailing ships waiting at the roadsteads. In the nineteenth century, commercial plantations for local and exportation crops (palm oil, peanuts, and so on) were founded, based on slave labour and often organized in gangs.[220]

Gendered divisions of labour are universal but possibly best visible in sub-Saharan Africa. Dating back to the different tasks among hunter-gatherers, as we have seen already in Chapter 1, they did not disappear with the advent of agriculture. It is not impossible that, in the African case, they were reinforced by the shifts in the working population as a consequence of massive enslavement of Africans over a very long period, in particular since 1600, as we have seen. In Africa, a coherent system of male and female roles has been registered by many anthropologists. A fine example that brings together many of the aspects of African labour discussed here is Jane Guyer's observation of traditional gender roles among the Beti in southern Cameroon in the 1970s:

Male activities were thought of in terms of warfare, hunting and tree-felling, however much or little time was spent in each. The male tools were iron and wood; the spear . . ., the hatchet . . . and the long planter . . . The male activities carried explicit military and phallic symbolism, including cutting down and building up, as with yam stakes and house poles. Men worked upright, climbed palm-trees to tap the wine or cut the fruit, prepared the tree-trunk barriers around the newly cut fields . . ., and the picket storehouses for yams. . . . The male milieu was the forest . . ., the source of the wood for tools and the most prestigious meat for the diet, the site of the hunt, the terrain to be conquered to open up a new field or prepare a new village site. The crops associated with male labor and male ownership were tree crops, crops of the forest fields, and crops which could be grown with the *nton*, the long-handled digging-stick. Women's milieu was, by contrast, the earth itself, the open clearings or the savanna . . . A woman worked in the fields, bending over the earth with her short-handled hoe . . . She cooked in earthenware pots, bending over the fire, fished by building earth dams across streams, bending into the water to trap the fish, and she 'cooked' babies in her womb. Bending over the earth to tend it, shape it, and coax it to produce was woman's attitude. Her crops were the savanna crops, planted with the woman's tool, the hoe.[221]

In sum, Africa became the main source of slaves in the Atlantic in this period. However, despite a lack of information on the early African economies and their organization of work, we should not make the mistake of primitivizing them, as was the dominant view in the nineteenth century, epitomized by Joseph Conrad's *Heart of Darkness* (1899).

Another reason not to do so is the resistance of captives and the enslaved against their oppressors. We have already encountered several examples of slave revolts. Although, as we have seen, resistance during their Atlantic voyage was much rarer, we cannot ignore the many testimonies of escape attempts at the point of destination, in the Americas, and also in Africa. As a result, a number of maroon states emerged. The most famous of all was Palmares in Pernambuco, Brazil, which endured for nearly a century. Another example is Berbice in 1763 (see p. 310). This permanent resistance to enslavement also explains the success of the further Islamization of West Africa around 1800.[222]

Overview: A global comparison of slavery, 1500–1800

How does the slavery that we have seen for Africa and the Americas in this period compare with the global picture? Sub-Saharan Africa adopted the market economy by shifting from predominantly small-scale and self-sufficient agriculture to mass-scale exportation of enslaved men and women and – in the slipstream – to the employment of those captured in Africa itself. In many parts of the Caribbean and in Brazil, slavery even became the dominant type of labour relations. This is not to say, however, that elsewhere in the world this phenomenon was insignificant.

In relation to African slaves, we have already seen that the Mediterranean, the Middle East and India also drew Africans for slave labour. But what about the importance of slavery in Eurasia as a whole?[223] Because of the immense impact of the slave trade between Africa and the Americas, two things are often neglected. Firstly, that in parallel to the dominant freedom of workers in the fully commodified labour markets of the far west, south and east of Eurasia, there was a significant number of unfree workers. In absolute numbers it was substantial, but as a proportion of densely populated Asia as a whole it was by no means as impressive as in other continents. In certain parts of Asia, however, it was significant, although never to the same degree as in the Americas. Secondly, that at the heart of that continent, slavery had prevailed in the steppes between China, India and Russia from very early on. We will discuss each of them separately, but for now it is important to know that, in absolute numbers, the slave trade in the Atlantic, in the Indian Ocean and in the steppes concerned similar numbers of people – in each case, between 1500 and 1800, over 10 million human beings.

Exemplary research into slavery in the regions dominated by the VOC has revealed, for example, that total numbers (including the Cape VOC) surpassed even those of the Dutch Atlantic slave trade – but also that in Malabar (south-western India), coastal Ceylon, north-western Java around Batavia and certain east Indonesian islands, slave labour was substantial compared to free wage labour and self-employment. The company as such was not the main employer, but rather some of its workforce, especially its middle- and high-ranking officers, facilitated, traded and exploited slave labour as a kind of side activity – mostly in the domestic sphere (not always easily separated from production for the market) and in leasing slaves to others. Occasionally, slaves were also employed in large-scale enterprises like the goldmines of Sumatra.

For the other European territories in Asia such research is sparse, but there is no doubt that the Portuguese, English and French were no different from the Dutch, let alone local rulers.[224] The reason is simple: upon their arrival, the Europeans adapted to the existing, thriving economies of Asia, including different forms of unfree labour. Deep societal cleavages like the caste system in, especially, southern India certainly enhanced the 'enslavability' of certain parts of the population, as evidenced by the heavy predominance of the lowest castes at the slave market of Dutch Cochin, and the different amounts of compensation according to caste in 1844.[225]

Ultimately, most of those who became slaves in the Indian Ocean World did so as a result of debt accumulated as a result of failing to pay fines, 'pawning' and not subsequently reclaiming children (especially girls) and kidnapping. This must be distinguished from debt bondage, entered into voluntarily as a credit-securing strategy. In fact, there were many more people 'enslaved' in debt bondage than there were actual slaves. However, when debt bondage became hereditary it was almost impossible to distinguish it from slavery. As well as debt, kidnapping and piracy (an alternative for war captives as common in Africa) ensured a constant flow of slaves in Asia. This is certainly the impression one gets from the slaving activities of polities like Sulu, Aceh, Bone, Bali and Lombok in Island Southeast Asia, still independent before 1850–70. Just like in Africa, the abolition of the maritime slave trade by the Europeans caused an increase in the local employment of slaves in certain regions, in total adding up to half a million by 1850.

Debt may have been the main reason working people were forced to give up their freedom in maritime South and South East Asia, alongside brutal kidnapping and being captured in war, but when we turn our eyes to the north, we see a situation much more similar to that in Africa and the Americas. For very good reasons, the immense steppes at the heart of the continent are often compared to an ocean, and the caravans crossing it along the famous silk route as ships plying the waves and connecting the empires of China, India, Persia, the Ottomans and Russia. As to their periphery, the steppes functioned as the origin of millions of slaves, but what was their destination? In some cases it was the competing empires, in others it was the steppes themselves. Sticking with the comparison, the steppes were not an empty space; indeed, its oases bear comparison with the Caribbean islands, where slavery became the dominant type of labour relations.

In order to understand this little-known centre of slave trade and slave employment, we must go back to ancient times, but in two periods in particular absolute numbers increased enormously.[226] The first was in the late Middle Ages, with the expansion of some Islamic states in an easterly direction towards India. The Turko-Afghan Ghaznavid Empire (ninth to twelfth centuries) centred in what today is Afghanistan, but stretching from Iran to the Indus Valley and from the Indian Ocean to the steppes, was famous for its military successes, but infamous for the numbers of captives it turned into slaves. According to a chronicle written after the conquest of the Indian city of Thanesar (north of Delhi) in 1014, 'the army of islam brought to Ghazna about 200,000 captives, and much wealth, so that the capital appeared like an Indian city, no soldier of the camp being without wealth, or without many slaves'.[227] Several decades later, 100,000 captives from Multan (now in Pakistan, west of Thanesar) entered the capital in the same way. The extension of the Delhi Sultanate in subsequent centuries followed the same pattern, with similar numbers of captives turned into slaves. The same is also true for the foundation of the Mughal Empire.

As elsewhere in Eurasia, differences of faith were crucial for the 'enslavability' of those captives who were not killed immediately during or after battle. As most of the empires and slavers involved (many of whom were Uzbeks) practised Sunni Islam, it meant that Hindus, Shi'ite Muslims, Buddhists, Orthodox Christians and Zoroastrians were most vulnerable as non-believers. In India, Muslim rulers confronted with an overwhelmingly Hindu population had to grant them protected (*dhimmi*) status, but that was not the case in the ever-contested border regions of the steppes.

After the logic of war follows the logic of trade. In the case of the millions of Indian and Iranian slaves being transported north, they were balanced by innumerable horses brought to the south, mainly employed by the cavalry. As we have already seen in the African case, horses cannot be well bred south of the steppes, and therefore were continuously in high demand. According to a Jesuit traveller in 1581, a contemporary saying among Punjabis engaged in this trade was 'Slaves from India, horses from Parthia'.[228]

Whereas in the empires bordering the steppes slaves were employed as domestics in affluent households, as soldiers and as specialized artisans (not strange given the caste-bound occupations in India), in the steppes they also performed a variety of less skilled and directly productive work. In sixteenth-century Central Asia, plantation-like farms belonging to big landowners in Uzbekistan were thriving by employing slaves for cultivation, the maintenance of irrigation canals and for tending their livestock. Artisans were highly sought after and could change hands from one conqueror to the other. After Tamerlane's sack of Delhi in 1398, thousands of skilled artisans were taken to Central Asia, where the masons among them built the Bibi Khanum mosque in his capital Samarqand.

The insatiable appetite for slaves in Central Asia and its borderlands may also be explained by the widespread custom of manumission of elderly slaves. Manumission after a number of years was certainly considered a religiously meritorious act. However, there may also be less altruistic motives behind the popularity of the manumission of slaves around the age of 50 in Central Asia. After all, it was at this age that the expense of clothing and feeding a slave began to outweigh the value of their work. As we have seen elsewhere, this fact of life is also reflected in the diminishing of price with age.[229]

In the eighteenth century, this type of slavery declined for both economic and political reasons. Economic because, instead of human beings, India now had textiles to offer in exchange for horses. The supply lines now shifted temporarily in the direction of Iran, where most slaves in the slave markets of Khiva and Bukhara hailed from in the eighteenth and nineteenth centuries. And political because the eternal struggle between steppe polities and their neighbours gradually came to a standstill because the great powers prevailed and met each other in Central Asia. There, they consolidated their borders. Of course, the Russians still made thousands and thousands of captives in the Caucasus, but the Great Game was over.

It has been estimated that, between the eleventh and nineteenth centuries, a minimum of between 6 and 6.5 million people were traded as slaves in Central Asia and Russia, 4 million of whom ended up in the Ottoman Empire and 400,000 in the Mediterranean via the Black Sea ports of Genoa and Venice.[230] To conclude this comparison, it may be clear by now that the exploitation and transportation of slaves in the Atlantic was not a unique phenomenon; indeed, it was matched in sheer numbers in various parts of Asia, especially in the steppes. What made slavery in Africa and the Caribbean so visible was the low population density in Africa and the intensity of the plantation economy in the Caribbean and coastal Brazil.

The labour-extensive path of Eastern Europe

We have now seen roughly two ways, worldwide, in which labour intensified after 1500 with a simultaneous and serious expansion of the market economy. Apart from all sorts of hybrid forms, as in South and South East Asia and the Mediterranean, we have seen market economies based, on the one hand, on the predominantly free labour of the self-employed and wage workers where this phenomenon already existed (such as in large parts of Eurasia), and, on the other hand, on the almost exclusively unfree labour of slaves in areas where there had previously been no market economies (in the Americas and in sub-Saharan Africa). Meanwhile, a large part of the earth's surface appears to have quietly escaped our attention: Europe to the east of the Elbe, and especially Russia, which expanded enormously in these centuries to Siberia and later also to Central Asia. There, a very special kind of market economy developed, in which mobility was severely restricted and – probably related to this – the labour intensity was very low. However, we should not simply dismiss these societies as primitive or contaminated by 'Eastern despotism', as has so often been the case. Russia, in particular, was extremely dynamic at this time, and although the labour relations were special, they can in no way be simply characterized as slavery. How should they then be characterized?[231]

In fact, slaves made up a surprisingly small part of Russia's population. Hereditary slaves accounted for only 10 per cent of the *kholopstvo*, and thus for 1 per cent of all inhabitants. In the majority of cases, *kholopstvo*, a category that was scrapped in 1725, can best be translated as 'servants', in the sense that they entered into a binding and fixed-term employment contract with an employer.[232] And although these employers had great power over them, including the right to impose penal sanctions, servants were not indebted to them. On the death of the master, the contract expired, and it was not hereditary. *Kholopy* were also allowed to marry. The fact that there were so few real slaves may be surprising, especially since the ongoing wars on the eastern and southern borders resulted in countless prisoners of war and millions of slaves over the centuries. Russia's opponents either sold their Russian prisoners of war as slaves or sold them back to the Russians for a ransom. Of course, the Russians and their Cossack allies also made prisoners of war. In contrast to their enemies, however, this did not lead to a large internal Russian slave market and slave labour. The Russians sold most of their captives to the Ottoman Empire. At the end of the eighteenth century, only Tatars and Circassians were kept to perform slave labour.[233]

Serfdom

While Russia was becoming an increasingly important conduit for valuable Asian products to Western Europe, Eastern Europe as a whole was also becoming the breadbasket of Western Europe in these centuries, as many farmers there specialized, leaving the growing of staple foods to others. Some other products, such as flax, hemp and tar, also made their way to the west, especially once Russia got its own ports on the Baltic (St Petersburg was established in 1703). Most notable with respect to the most important export product, grain, was the extremely low yield per surface area. The Russian 'yield ratios', the ratio between the amount of seed sown and the yield, were exceptionally low in comparison to the rest of Europe, and they remained so until well into the nineteenth century.[234] Although geographical location and climate certainly have something to do with this, the cause was primarily to do with the organization of work. In contrast to Western Europe, where the small- and medium-sized free farmers (owners or tenants) prevailed, Eastern Europe was dominated by large and very large farms in the hands of the nobility, the church and the state. They exploited their estates with the help of farmers, generally referred to in the literature as serfs.

These farmers were not free to leave the estate and thus were bound to the land and fully subjugated to the landlord, an arrangement introduced step by step from the late sixteenth century. In 1581, landowners successfully lobbied the crown to prohibit peasants' right of movement on St George's Day, the last of the holy days during which peasants had been able to leave their masters' lands and thus exert some degree of autonomy. More decrees followed in 1592–93, culminating in the Muscovite Law Code of 1649 (the *Ulozhenie*).[235] No less than 90 per cent of the Russian population was included under this.

It should be emphasized that, despite the implications of the term 'second serfdom' commonly used by historians, serfs are not the same as slaves, or even the same as the medieval serfs that we know from Western Europe in the Middle Ages. There are several reasons for this. Firstly, these farmers enjoyed some important rights, even though, in practice, they were systematically trodden on and curtailed, for example when they were sold separately from the land. In practice, they appeared to develop all kinds of initiatives to work outside their obligations with respect to the landlord by working for themselves, not only in farming but also in the cottage industry, and they were able to reap the benefits of this, partly or completely. Secondly, they had a considerable amount of time for other activities beyond those on the estate. From the eighteenth century, members of farming families began to work seasonally in the cities and participate in harvesting elsewhere – in return for a payment to their landlord and with his permission. And, thirdly, should the landlord provide too little space on or outside the estate, then fleeing to new areas of the ever-expanding empire was always an option – a widely used remedy, especially because runaway fugitives had de facto little to fear from the harsh punishments meted out against that offence. In sum, serfdom in early modern Russia seemed to be a combination of compulsory, inefficient labour for the estate and intensive labour for one's own household.[236]

Serfs either owed work (*barshchina*) or paid quitrent (*obrok*) to the owner of the land, and, of course, many combinations were possible. *Barshchina* entailed agricultural work, carting, and so on, for, in principle, half of the time. Often, when more men were available in a serf family, obligations were organized according to the 'brother for brother' principle, whereby one brother performed the seigneurial duties and the other was free to work the family allotment. In the nineteenth century, *barshchina* increasingly became defined as task work, leaving the peasant free to work his own family plot after the daily chores were done. Around 1800, the payment of *obrok* represented one-fifth of total income, whereas it rose to one-third around 1850. The net result for the peasant family was nevertheless positive, because income rose substantially in that half-century. *Barshchina* dominated in the fertile 'Black Earth' regions south of Moscow, and *obrok* in the less fertile parts to the north, especially in the so-called Central Industrial Region between Moscow and St Petersburg and the provinces east of that line. Over time, *obrok* became more popular than *barshchina*, so payment shifted from kind to money, plus 'soul tax' to the government.[237]

In 1678, more half of all serfs toiled on estates that were in the hands of the nobility, over 15 per cent on those owned by the church and the remainder on state property. The church estates were particularly vast: in 1762, Russian monasteries owned no less than two-thirds of Russian ploughed land and 70 per cent of landed ecclesiastical institutions. Each church estate owned more than 100 peasants, whereas only 13 per cent of the nobles exploited that many.[238] The large size of the Russian estates is most characteristic. In Russia, 4 out of 5 serfs lived on holdings of more than

200 persons – far bigger units than in the contemporaneous Americas, where self-management was the rule. Labour relations were thus far more impersonal, as the majority of serfs rarely saw their owners. The wealthier the Russian estate owner, the more absent he was. Instead, stewards (them-selves also serfs, sometimes replaced later by free Germans) were in charge, assisted by peasants per 100, 50 or 10 households, to 'require the lazy to work, not permit anyone to loaf, and punish those not wanting to labor', as one absentee landlord instructed his steward.[239]

There was a rigid gender-based division of work on the estates: 'men ploughed and sowed, carted, chopped wood, constructed buildings, cared for horses; women raked hay, reaped grain, milked cows, and cared for chickens, in addition to the indoor work of caring for children, cleaning house, cooking, spinning, weaving, and sewing.'[240]

The serf community and their household

Marriage was almost universal, especially in the fertile 'Black Earth' region south of Moscow.[241] Landowners advocated marriage – in church – of their serfs at a young age, in order to enable them to have as many children (and thus as large a workforce) as possible and to prevent non-marital sex. Co-residence and joint households were common, as they warranted econo-mies of scale, in particular where *barshchina* obligations could be shared. In the Central Industrial Region (Moscow province and to the north of it), households were much smaller and simpler. Besides these regional varia-tions, household size and composition also depended on landlord-specific policies and regulations regarding marriage. The lord could not only stimu-late marriage, but also impose fines and taxation on bachelors.

Russian peasants lived in communal villages under an elected *starosta* ('elder', but not necessarily the eldest, as many serfs did not want to spend time on this communal service), with a considerable amount of self-administra-tion.[242] The village (*obshchina* or *mir*) constituted the political representative of the serfs, receiving official government recognition and at least grudging seigneurial toleration, especially on *obrok* estates. All adult males were entitled to attend the regular meetings, at which heads of families could vote and records were kept by a peasant clerk. Certainly, these meetings, led by the *starosta*, were aimed at the interests of the estate, including *obrok* collection, regular reallocation of labour obligations and of allotments according to family size and composition, and selection of military conscripts. But they signified more than that, as becomes clear from the numerous petitions sent by the estate or village representatives to the owner and even to the tsar (although this was officially forbidden in 1767) to express dissatisfaction with their treatment.

Mistreatment as such was not the main catalyst for sending in petitions while seeking the redress of grievances, but rather anything that the serfs considered to be a breach of established norms, conceived of as their 'rights'.[243] The serfs shared an 'elemental suspicion of anything that upset established procedures' and cherished continuity in their relationship with the landlord. If petitions did not help, they resorted to a non-violent refusal to perform the required work. This *volvenie* (plural *volveniia*) could start with a petition and transform into a collective (village- or estate-wide) protest by way of a strike. If not resolved on the estate, these strikes led to an official governmental inquiry and often mediation. When that failed, soldiers could be sent in to pressure the serfs to give in, or even military courts to deal with the leaders. On a few occasions, protests turned into virtual uprisings of thousands of serfs. Although certainly not pure serf rebellions, two armed conflicts in the seventeenth century and two in the eighteenth century united so many of them that they cannot be isolated from serfdom as a system of labour relations. The 1774 rebellion included 3 million peasants. They had been addressed by the leader Emilian Pugachev as follows:

> By this decree ... we grant to all hitherto in serfdom and subjection to landlords the right to be faithful subjects of our crown, and we award them the old cross and prayer, heads and beards, liberty and freedom ... without demanding recruit levies, soul taxes or other monetary obligations, possession of the lands, the woods, the hay meadows, the fisheries, and the salt lakes, without payment or *obrok*, and we free all those formerly oppressed by the villainous nobles and bribe-takers and judges, all peasants and all the people oppressed by obligations and burdens ... those who hitherto were nobles, with their estates, those opponents of our power and disruptors of the empire and ruiners of the peasants, catch, kill, and hang them, and treat them just as they, having no Christianity, treated you, the peasants. With the annihilation of these enemies and miscreant-nobles, all may feel peace and a tranquil life, which will last through the ages.[244]

The most practised and most effective alternative to toiling for the landlord was not collective by way of petitions, *volveniia* or occasional rebellions, but private – that is to say, by organizing the efforts of all household members as much as possible independently of the landlord, either on the estate or outside.

Apart from the *barshchina* and *obrok* obligations, peasants were free to spend their working efforts as they liked. And they did. Late-eighteenth-century serfs and state peasants were selling more grain on the domestic grain market than large-scale landowners, and peasants had a virtual monopoly on the sale of specialized agricultural products such as hemp, flax and tobacco. They also performed skilled trades and specialized in weaving.[245] Most telling are the frequent complaints of landlords about the laziness of serfs in performing estate obligations in contrast to the zeal with which they worked their own plots – even to such an extent that one landowner directed that those serfs who, reportedly, refused to go to church in order to 'work secretly for themselves' should be fined and beaten, for 'nowhere on my estates do they work on Sundays'.[246] The landlords enjoined serfs to attend church and to observe Sunday and the many Church holidays, but having spent several days on *barshchina* obligations the serfs needed any spare time to tend their own crops.

Estates, organized according to *obrok* obligations, may have offered even more possibilities for independent work. Professor of Social Science History Tracy Dennison has demonstrated for the Voshchazhnikovo estate in the Central Industrial Region how most serfs engaged in crafts, trade, small-scale manufacturing and live-in services in cities, all permitted in exchange for tax payments to the lord – even to such an extent that for the eighteenth and nineteenth centuries in these and many similar cases we can speak of real labour, land, property, capital and retail markets.

At such *obrok* estates, all serfs were required to cultivate their share of the (by definition) communal land and to pay feudal dues (*obrok*), mainly in money, but also in kind. In kind meant deliveries of oats for the estate stables, wheat and rye for the lord's household, and some proportion of each for the estate granary, levied on the commune as lump sums, plus maintenance of village infrastructure, partially by labour paid from communal funds.[247]

In reality, several serfs who saw alternatives for better paid work on their own plot, in artisanal work or cottage industry hired fellow serfs to perform these tasks. The poorest households, especially, who were not capable of participating in the allotment of the land but were still obliged to perform their duties, were willing to act as wage labourers for their better-off co-villagers. This way there existed a true labour market inside the serfdom system.[248] Often simultaneously, some serfs worked as servants outside, carrying an internal passport, while employing co-serfs from inside or outside the village for wages, both as day labourers and as servants in husbandry. The commune, or *mir*, also hired wage labourers to perform routine tasks assigned as corvée labour, such as road or church building.

The social stratification that thus came into existence enabled the village elite to save money and even to 'buy' property. Officially, private property outside that owned by the lord was impossible, but, in reality, some lords – in return for substantial retributions – gradually recognized property rights of certain serfs and also facilitated the selling and buying of such 'property'. That way serfs could also set up workshops where they employed other serfs. Of course, the viability of such a quasi-formal system of enforceable property rights depended on individual landowners.[249]

Mobility

As long as obligations to the estate were fulfilled, out-migration was possible and, in principle, not opposed by the landlords, as, with their consent and the delivery of internal passports, they profited greatly from the earnings of the migrants. Even the 1649 *Ulozhenie* left this possibility open, and governmental decrees prescribed internal passports between 1719 and 1724. This type of temporal migration, with the landlord's consent, was called *otkhodnichestvo*.[250] As long as serfdom was the dominant labour relation in Russia, the urban labour market depended completely on these *otchodniki*. In 1840, half of Moscow's population consisted of these kinds of temporary migrants, who were serfs, most of them from estates with *obrok*, and in particular state peasants.

Distances of migration increased over time and, due to the rise in out-migration to cities, more immigration from the surrounding areas was necessary on *obrok* estates like Voshchazhnikovo. Several sub-groups can be distinguished among the *otchodniki*. First, those doing factory work, dominated by serfs and state peasants. Second, migrant craftsmen, traders and other kinds of entrepreneurs, many of them selling the products of cottage industry and other crafts at markets or by peddling.

The migratory factory workers were predominantly male, leaving women with household duties and peasant cottage industry a virtual women's monopoly. In order to avoid or to share the risks involved in this temporary migration, this trek was less an individual than a group undertaking, organized by *artel'* or *zemliachestvo*. *Arteli* (plural) were groups of peasants who jointly sought temporary or seasonal work. *Zemliachestva* (plural) were organized after arrival in cities or enterprises, usually more stationary and larger.

When difficult circumstances persisted and nothing helped, either collectively or individually, there always was the ultimate solution – leaving the estate without consent and escaping to a place out of reach of the landlord. The most eloquent proof of how many chose this option are the 3.7 million peasants who had emigrated to the newly conquered territories in Siberia, the Urals and the Volga by 1678. And this movement was to continue. Between 1727 and 1742, on average 20,000 serfs fled their homes.[251] Although the recapture of fugitive serfs was an important aim of the 1649 *Ulozhenie*, the tsar tolerated them in the southern border regions where they, together with Tatars and others, assimilated into semi-independent Cossack communities – of course, as long as they were prepared to cooperate in the defence and expansion of the empire.

They were certainly condoned in Siberia, because this part of the country was important as a source of furs for the surrounding empires.[252] Before its collapse in the fifteenth century, the Mongol Khanate of the Golden Horde and dependent states dominated this trade. The vacuum this left was filled by the Principality of Moscow and the lesser Muslim khanates of the Crimea, Astrakhan, Sibir and Kazan. The latter's conquest by Moscow in 1550, and the capture of Novgorod, were a boost for the fur trade. From its predecessors Novgorod, Kazan and Sibir, Moscow adopted the habit of levying a tribute, expressed in furs of different qualities, the so-called *iasak* (also called 'soft gold'). That is how an important section of hunter-gatherers became part of the global economy. Take the oath, administered in the early 1640s to the Bratsk people by Russian officials. They had to swear allegiance to the tsar: ' "on our faith, by the sun, by the earth, by fire, by the Russian sword and by guns." In the case of breach of oath "then, in accordance with my faith, the sun will not shine on me … I will not walk on the earth, I will not eat bread, the Russian sword will cut me down, the gun will kill me, and fire will destroy all our uluses [settlements] and our lands.'[253] But these trappers, cherished as long as they brought the soft gold, were not farmers, nor could they be easily turned into peasants. That is why the unofficial migration into Siberia, inconsistent with the 1649 *Ulozhenie* but consistent with imperial expansion, was so crucial. Many departed in groups, and in Siberia they formed communes, similar to those back home. Their status became that of state serfs, virtually the only category of serfs there. They had to pay *obrok* plus taxes in money and in kind (corvée), all organized in a military way. Only the church acquired the right to enserf its peasants, and no nobleman estates were allowed there. One exception was the peasants and soldiers who were prescribed to work at the rich Altai silver mines and some other mineral and metallurgical establishments in the Urals.[254]

Besides its original hunter-gatherers and escaped serfs, Siberia was populated by exiles – political, religious and criminal – and some categories of prisoners of war, especially Poles, Lithuanians and Swedes. At Poltava in 1709, 20,000 Swedish soldiers, non-combatants and women and children had been taken prisoner. By the creation of a juridical-penal mechanism that produced convicts, criminal exiles, rare before the 1649 *Ulozhenie*, helped the state to populate Siberia.[255] This was often accompanied by mutilation, as exemplified by a 1653 case: 'Those thieves and robbers who through their own fault would have been sentenced by previous ukases to death, will instead of the death penalty be knouted, have a finger cut from their left hands, and be sent to the borders with their wife and children, to Siberian and lower and border cities.'[256] Consequently, the execution of criminals became rare in Russia. After arrival in Siberia, their offspring became barely distinguishable from non-exiles. As has been noted, 'Deportation was the transmission belt linking the sovereign's punitive vengeance to the state's utilitarian exploitation'.[257]

In the south, the position of the fugitives changed after the Russians, under Catherine II, managed to conquer the vast open spaces by systematically subjugating the nomads from the Dniester to Dagestan, now proudly rebaptized Novorossiya. Instead of the 'right to refuge' in the so-called Don Cossack Host, to which the serfs fled, the serfs in the south now became free subjects of the empire. They originated not only from Russia, but also – as invited colonists – from Germany.[258]

Even one of the most awful aspects of the imperial labour system, military conscription, still contains some surprises.[259] After 1650, Russia switched from a mercenary army to conscription, definitively established by Peter the Great. Russia thus became the country with the highest percentage of conscripts (1–1.5 per cent) in Europe. What was horrifying was the obligation of landowners to supply men to the state, which took the unfortunate conscript away from his native land for ever. In 1793, the duration was reduced to twenty-five years, but that made very little real difference. On the other hand, these recruits were, crucially, also used for the expansion of the empire in an easterly and southerly direction. In order to permanently keep and defend the newly conquered territory, soldiers were established in these new areas as farmers, which gave them a relative degree of freedom again.

Russia thus entered the nineteenth century as a powerful and immense country with, at its centre, an overwhelming majority of serfs whose mobility was restricted by law and who were obliged to work for large landowners, as well as land-bound but otherwise independent peasant-soldiers in Siberia and Central Asia. Further to the west, as far as the Elbe, we also find a multitude of mobility-limiting measures that have so much in common with each other that they form a border between Western and Eastern Europe.[260]

※

Until 1500, the world had consisted of a number of large, separate islands, especially in the way in which people worked. Although hunter-gatherers still inhabited large parts of the earth's surface, they were marginalized to the (sub-)Arctic regions and to spots in the tropical rainforests of Africa and South America. Everywhere else, agriculture dominated. This was not only self-sufficient but also productive enough to generate surpluses. These were divided into two major models: in Eurasia, distribution via the market, and in the Americas and in parts of sub-Saharan Africa in polities, organized according to the redistributive model.

This disappeared rapidly there, not as before in Mesopotamia, for example, from inside out and gradually, but rather from outside in and in an extremely violent manner. Within the market model, free entrepreneurship of peasants and artisans with wage labour dominated, but, adjacent and simultaneous to this, confrontations between polities could lead to enslavement and, in turn, enslavement sometimes resulted in whole societies becoming highly dependent on slave labour.

With European maritime expansion, we reached a turning point, as all these separate islands came into permanent contact with each other. This led to the rapid demise of hunter-gatherers, the destruction of the last great redistributive societies, the retreat of reciprocity to the household and the expansion and intensification of the market economy. This expansion occurred in two ways: through the export of the market model and, simultaneously, through the expansion of unfree labour. Unfree labour became dominant in Russia as a result of the expansion of serfdom and in many other parts of the world through the sharp increase of chattel slavery. That was most intensive in the Caribbean and Brazil, increasingly so in Africa and possibly also in and around Central Asia. Although sheer numbers were equally impressive in the Indian Ocean, slavery there amounted to a much smaller proportion of the total population.

The extension and intensification of the market model affected all sectors. Peasants in Eurasia, by far the largest portion of the global population, intensified their work in all ways, both in actual agriculture and in cottage industry. Even the Russian serfs followed this pattern within the limits imposed by the system. This growing market orientation of the peasant household meant more work not only for men but also for women and children. The same happened in the rapidly growing towns and cities, and this also applies to sectors such as shipping and the military. The main motive behind this, partly under the influence of globalization, was more extensive consumption and new opportunities to consume above the absolute subsistence level. This is most evident in the increased sugar consumption, but also in the spread of stimulants such as tea, coffee, alcohol and opium, as well as textiles and, in Europe, cheap printing.

As a rule, workplaces were still small, whether we are talking about farms, those of craftsmen, or most American plantations. There were large work units, such as the armies, that had existed for thousands of years, and there were now many ocean-going ships, shipyards and arsenals, and other military workplaces. Russian serf estates and some Caribbean plantations were also large units. In terms of labour relations, slavery and serfdom, of course, meant subordination, with all the limitations this entailed for workers in terms of defending their own interests. Given that the memory of freedom never died, certainly not among the newly enslaved, the unfree constantly sought and found opportunities to defend their interests. Cooperation was a clear choice among free workers, especially in the cities, certainly where the polity permitted it. Artisans stood up for their interests in guilds and other types of fraternities (under which we may also list the Indian caste organizations of artisans). This is the picture that emerges of work and labour relations worldwide on the eve of what would later be called the Industrial Revolution: now totally globally connected but at the same time organized according to widely divergent principles.

At the start of the nineteenth century, power relations across the world were unrecognizable from those three centuries before. By 1800, the Great Divergence had taken place and the West was the winner of the power shifts that appear clearly from 1650–1700. With hindsight, this appears inevitable and thus pre-ordained. Moreover, until recently, this domination of the West over the Rest seemed immutable. This chapter has demonstrated that an attempt to analyse the history of work and labour relations impartially produces a much less linear result for the centuries between the 'Great Discoveries' and the 'Industrial Revolution'. Nevertheless, the cleavages were persistent and would deepen, as the story of work during the Industrial Revolution will tell in Chapter 6.

The increase in literacy, already visible in earlier periods, now yielded many testimonies of working people of all kinds, occasionally and indirectly even of the unfree. Think of Oluale Kossola, of Pugachev or of the fate of the rebellious slaves of the *Neptunus*. Such accounts confirm the impression, gained in previous chapters, that unfreedom was not at all self-evident or easily accepted as a fact of life. Nor was unjust treatment or unfair compensation of the self-employed or the waged workers. The testimonies of private household strategies to escape poverty or to improve one's work situation by migration, or of collective strategies, are numerous, attested, for example, by Khoosoomdi following the deadly accident of her son, or by Europe's craft guilds or the striking workers of Beijing's minting houses.

6
CONVERGING LABOUR RELATIONS, 1800 TO NOW

The final two centuries that are the subject of this and the next chapter will be more familiar to the modern reader than the preceding ones. Yet, it remains a challenge to characterize the last period of this book in a few words. What makes this era special? Perhaps most of all the fact that it is a period of global convergence of labour relations, albeit in fits and starts. Never before have so many people arranged their work in a similar way. Never before have they attempted to such a degree to improve their labour relations and labour circumstances collectively as well as individually. Central to this chapter are the different types of labour relations, culminating in the breakthrough of wage labour as the increasingly dominant framework. Parallel to this, the following chapter discusses the consequences of the shift in 'repertoires of action' in the representation of interests – primarily (but not exclusively) of wage earners whose share in society grew quickest. In particular, many new kinds of collective action emerged, with the state now playing an increasingly important role – despite ideologies that preached the opposite.

Diamond cutters, working by hand and at a mill (Amsterdam, 1875).

In order to better understand the shift in labour relations over the past two centuries, we cannot ignore the so-called Industrial Revolution. This gradually broke the dominance of agricultural work, which also led to completely new levels and patterns of consumption. The objective of work thus changed substantially: instead of it being a matter of pure necessity, for many more than had been the case in preceding centuries an improvement in the quality of life was now in sight.

In the last two centuries, labour relations – now primarily market oriented – shifted radically. The share of unfree labour fell sharply. The decline of unfree labour was heralded by the abolition of slavery, as a consequence of the Haitian Revolution (1791–1804), of the transatlantic slave trade by England in 1807, and of serfdom in Europe, the most famous example of which is the emancipation of the Russian serfs in 1861. These movements were provisionally consummated with the institution of the International Labour Organization in 1919 and the Universal Declaration of Human Rights in 1948. Success was not guaranteed, however. Time and again this tendency towards free labour was interrupted. Names such as Stalin, Hitler, Mao and Pol Pot speak volumes in this regard; and let us not forget the Kim dynasty in North Korea today. Like the share of unfree labour, that of self-employed labour also decreased, although much more slowly. This decrease was mainly due to the diminishing significance of the countless small farmers and artisans who, until then, had prevailed worldwide. The role played by domestic work declined as women increasingly began working for the market, within but now outside of the home, too. Of all three trends, free wage labour profited the most, not only in industry, but also in the service sector, both of which were primarily concentrated in cities. The increase in free labour also meant an increase in migration. The wage worker 'voted with his feet' and, where possible, sought better labour conditions, or, if unemployed, work elsewhere. This could be domestically, but also abroad. Sometimes, a temporary deterioration of working conditions was even accepted in this regard, as was the case with indentured labour.

The Industrial Revolution

The emergence and above all the spread of industrial society is perhaps the most obvious case of the global convergence of labour relations. After the introduction of agriculture, the Industrial Revolution is the most important change in the history of the working population – even though it is likely that no single country ever employed a majority of its workforce in industry.[1] Sticking with the terminology of the previous chapter: the transition from the labour-intensive to the capital-intensive path now became possible. This phenomenon was first visible in England in the course of the eighteenth century. I have deliberately chosen not to cover this episode in the previous chapter and instead tackle it here because, initially, it only affected a very small part of the population and its impact only gradually became clear in the course of the nineteenth century, even in the British Isles.

After a brief explanation of the nature of mechanization during the Industrial Revolution and its spread across England and, subsequently, the rest of the world, I would like to demonstrate in particular what it meant to work in industry that was increasingly concentrated in factories (its undeniable importance elsewhere, especially in transport and agriculture, will also be touched on). The crucial question was how to motivate people who were not used to being under the direct supervision of a boss to carry out productive labour under entirely new circumstances. This is the issue of work incentives.

Mechanization

So far, we have seen many examples of mechanization, that is to say people's use of tools so that their muscle and brainpower, and that of the animals working for them, could be utilized more efficiently; think of the spinning wheel and weaving loom, the potter's wheel and the cart. In addition to human, animal and plant-based energy sources, water power (via water and tide mills) and wind power (via sailing ships and windmills) had also been used by humans for centuries for production.

The Industrial Revolution is distinct due to its utilization of a new energy source – steam – which was no longer location-specific. A steam boiler that could drive a wheel with the help of a connecting rod could be located anywhere where there was sufficient fuel – mainly coal – available or where it could be supplied cheaply. The motive power of steam was already known to the Chinese, but as a curiosity, not for economic application.[2] The first industrial application occurred in coal mining, which was hampered by groundwater flooding the more deeply they wanted to dig. In 1712, Thomas Newcomen constructed a steam engine that could successfully power the pumps, allowing for the manual force used previously to be economized. Not only that, but the power of the pumps increased and, moreover, more coal became available to power yet more industrial steam engines. Canals were needed for the transport of coal, and a profusion was therefore excavated. A next big step was James Watt's steam engine, patented in 1769. This used five times less fuel than Newcomen's version, and Watt also designed a transmission mechanism enabling rotary motion. Thus, the steam powering of all kinds of machines became possible, including in the most crucial of all industries, textiles, which had seen the invention of many new machines. In the same year, Richard Arkwright had already made propulsion by water mills possible. Thus, between 1750 and 1800, the labour productivity of a cotton spinner increased 200-fold, an example that can be seen in many other cases in all branches of industry.

The next step was the steam propulsion of ships and trains, from roughly 1820. One simply cannot emphasize enough famous inventions and innovations in an overview like this, however brief. Let us never forget, though, that they were the result of long series of trial and error and that their introduction required much time, often more than half a century, while, at the same time, older technology was also significantly improved. Sailing ships, for example, were faster than ever at the moment when they were superseded by steamships in oceanic shipping.

Primarily American and German inventions followed in the late nineteenth and twentieth centuries. Electricity as a light source and as a source of communication (the telegraph, telephone, radio, television) found a special application in the electric motor. As a result, energy also became available for small-scale industrial production, as well as for household appliances. Not only did electricity replace steam, most visible in the case of electric trains, but also petrol. The petrol engine in cars (Carl Benz, 1885), followed by trucks, buses and coaches, ships and aeroplanes, has made every place in the world accessible, along with its products and people. In addition to the electric engine, the petrol and diesel engine have also found industrial applications. The use of nuclear fission (splitting the atom to produce energy) is currently the last breakthrough in a long line of inventions in the field of energy generation.

Hand in glove with inventions in energy generation are, of course, those in the field of chemistry and biotechnology. Just think of the paint and the pharmaceutical industries, of rubber, synthetic textiles and building materials, or fertilizers for agriculture. And let us not forget the application of all these innovations in healthcare. Finally, there is mechanical engineering, which automated human actions. The last big step in automation, of course, is the digital revolution of recent decades, with the latest application being nanotechnology and, so essential for industry, the possibilities of 3D printing, if only because of the changes this will bring about in the transport system.

It started in England and conquered the world

Why did the Industrial Revolution initially take place on one continent and why was one country, Great Britain, the first to make the transition from the labour-intensive to the capital-intensive path? Generations of historians have agonized over this, and the discussion remains unresolved. The fundamentally racist statements that assume a European, Anglo-Saxon or English genius that is superior to that of the rest of the inhabitants of this earth are utterly obsolete. Statements seeking explanations in the presence of raw materials, such as coals, are also too one-sided, as is the emphasis on the superior institutions that the country was assumed to have.

The understanding that the Industrial Revolution was actually comprised of countless small improvements and inventions in many areas and that these were based on diligent efforts to improve everyday artisanal practice through trial and error has led to a recent emphasis on the dissemination of useable knowledge. And this insight, in turn, points towards the single feature that has distinguished Western Europe from the rest of Eurasia, already from 1500 onwards: the availability of cheap printed matter that enabled technical improvements and knowledge to be widely disseminated, particularly among artisans.

Simultaneously, a number of maritime regions within Europe passed the industrialization baton from one to the other. For centuries, these were not big countries but successful smaller urban polities.[3] From northern Italy and, in particular, the city-state of Venice, the baton passed to the Low Countries, and especially the Dutch Republic (a federation of provinces and, most significantly, of city-states) and from there, at the end of the seventeenth century, to England, a centrally governed country with a partially elected parliament. These transitions meant the simultaneous success of ever larger states. England had the honour in this relay, as it were, of initiating the first industrial revolution at the end of the eighteenth century. Later, this role was taken over by the US and, to an extent, also Germany. And these forerunners inspired neighbouring states, such as France, Italy, the Low Countries and Switzerland, who initially enjoyed the advantage of imitating these pioneers. China and India are now in a similar position and are set to become the new technological leaders.

The successful new elements in the innovations taking place in England and the Scottish Lowlands – compared to their predecessors, in particular the Dutch Republic – were 'public science', and the participation in this was not only by the citizenry and artisans but also by 'improving' landlords. In concrete terms, this meant, among other things, the creation of literary and philosophical societies, as they were called then, which increasingly popularized the Newtonian way of thinking mechanically and scientifically, as well as their journals and public lectures (many given by itinerant lecturers) and the locales where inventions, in model form or not, could be admired. They bridged the gap between the propositional knowledge developed in academic science and the prescriptive knowledge of engineering.[4]

Indeed, the way in which knowledge and, specifically, useful knowledge was disseminated in a country has also proved crucial to the success of the aforementioned imitators. This also explains the great German accomplishments after 1850, in the so-called Second Industrial Revolution. A combination of good and compulsory (adult) education, *Gewerbeschulen* (industrial schools), whose graduates enjoyed reduced military service, and *Innungen* – a sort of guilds 2.0 – in collaboration with the state and employers ensured a flexible apprenticeship system that transmitted useful knowledge efficiently. At the same time, technical knowledge in England was increasingly becoming a closed shop, jealously guarded by the 'labour aristocracy' on the shop floor. The American economist Ralf Roland Meisenzahl notes rather sharply that: 'Older workers, who had little incentive to render their skills obsolete, were in charge of hiring and teaching apprentices, who then would be locked up in the old technologies themselves.'[5]

Intrinsically, there was probably no difference in the innate labour productivity of manual workers in the different parts of Eurasia, but there were variations in the conditions under which new technologies and production methods could be adopted.[6] These were the industrious revolution in the countryside and in the city, the free circulation of people and knowledge and the windfalls of the international maritime trade in specific parts of Europe, partly obtained with the help of unfree plantation labour. Nation states played a key role in all this by imposing protective tariffs on competitors.[7] As a result, the initially small differences between the extremes of Eurasia were soon magnified. They mutually reinforced each other, resulting in the Great Divergence, enabled by the Industrial Revolution and colonialism. Only decolonization and the end of the Cold War finally made it possible to narrow the chasm between the rich and poor in the world and thus the reward for labour. This is especially true for countries in East Asia, but, to date, much less so for those in in sub-Saharan Africa.

The discussion about when the breakthrough of the Industrial Revolution occurred in various countries – England around 1780–1800, Belgium around 1830, Germany around 1870, the US around 1900, and so on – often ignores the fact that, for a long time, only a small section of the population of these countries worked in industry and, within this group, only a small number worked in mechanized factories. Let us take England as an example. The Industrial Revolution was initially limited to the textile industry and, within this, the processing of cotton in particular. In parallel, the metal industry emerged and with it the expansion of the railway network, but it was not until the 1840s that industry achieved a broader base.

In the quarter-century between the Great Exhibition in 1851 and the 1870s, when England was dubbed the workshop of the world – subsequently superseded by the US and Germany – the country's industry reached a share of 40 per cent of the working population. It should be noted, however, that this was an all-time high and that it was also spread very unevenly throughout the country, with very little industry in the south, but, by contrast, a strong presence in the north and again in the Midlands and West Yorkshire. But there were also major differences within industrial businesses. Craftsmanship remained especially strong in London and other nurturing cities.[8] This pattern, in which only a minority of the working population were labouring in large factories and mines, was also found elsewhere, and these factories were also highly concentrated geographically. Think of the Ruhr region in Germany, Alsace-Lorraine in France, what is now known as the rust belt in the US, and the Urals and Donbass in Russia.

The organization of factory work

How should we imagine this factory work as it developed in the last two centuries? We saw in the previous chapter that, for centuries, in addition to the artisans in the cities, industry was primarily concentrated in the coun-tryside, in the so-called cottage industry. In both cases, work and living continued to coincide. Where water or wind power provided the propulsion, slightly larger work units were now possible. This was also true in industries that depended on heat, such as metal smelters, salt- and soapmaking plants, sugar refineries, textile bleacheries, dye and printing houses. In short, companies that had made large capital investments before the Industrial Revolution could now work profitably with only one or a few dozen workers. Those rare large industrial units that corralled hundreds or sometimes a thousand or more workers in one place were mainly state-owned companies such as army and navy workplaces, gun foundries, shipyards and the like, and then only a handful per country.

As was to be expected in a broadly supported industrialization process of trial and error, such as that in England, for a long time different organizational structures existed in parallel and were often also closely associated with each other. In any case, the classic contrast between traditional, idyllic craftwork and hellish factories is misleading.[9]

The different organizational structures do not neatly coincide with phases in technical development or with different branches of industry, or with regional differences. That is not to say that there is a total lack of logic, but the variations nevertheless are large. Firstly, you had artisans producing for end consumers, or, more often, for intermediaries. This second structure grew into the notorious sweating industry, in which subcontractors worked for other businesses in the sector for a piecework tariff but had the actual work done by people at home for a lower hourly rate, or sometimes also a piece rate – one of the worst forms of exploitation in industry, without a factory ever being involved.

Then, there were the many small workplaces that aimed, even before mechanization, for an optimal division of labour in terms of gender, age and skills, as was written in 1759 by the Welsh churchman, economist and political writer Dean Tucker:

The labour ... is very properly proportioned ... so that no time shall be wasted in passing the goods to be manufactured from Hand to Hand, and that no unnecessary Strength should be employed. For an instance of both Kinds, take one among a Thousand at *Birmingham*, viz. When a Man stamps upon a metal Button by means of an Engine, a Child stands by him to place the Button in readiness to receive the Stamp, and to remove it when received, and then to place another. By these Means the

Operator can stamp at least double the Number, which he could otherwise have done, had he been obliged to have stopped each Time to have shifted the Buttons: ... this single Circumstance saved alone 80 or even 100 per cent at the same Time that it trains up Children to an Habit of Industry, almost as soon as they can speak.[10]

In addition, mechanized workplaces emerged especially in the textile industry, albeit much later, ranging from a few workers to dozens or even hundreds of workers in one building, a factory centrally powered by water wheels and, later, steam boilers. The question then arose about how best to organize more workers than ever before in one place. A central chain of command was certainly a model, but, more frequently, factory buildings were de facto divided into smaller, more or less autonomous units, thus reducing an intermediate layer of managers.

Most common was the continuation of the old cottage industry model, transplanted, but fundamentally transformed, to the factory building.[11] Under this model, the owner or entrepreneur hired a number of spinners, weavers or other specialists on piece rates, allowing these men in turn to hire assistants or apprentices, whom they paid time wages. Mainly boys, girls and women, they could be relatives or neighbours, but in the fast-growing factory towns like Bolton in Lancashire they were not. This way, management problems were decentralized, but it needs no great fantasy to imagine how it enhanced the exploitation of many subaltern workers by an elite minority (just like the later notorious sweating industry, just mentioned and more extensively dealt with below, pp. 329–31). The more the 'master workers' chased their subalterns, the more money they earned, whereas their dependents didn't see a single penny more. One may wonder how such an unfair system could function for so long in, for example, cotton-spinning Lancashire. The secret lies, of course, in the hopes of the subaltern to one day reach the same position as the master spinner or weaver whom they allowed to exploit them for the time being – not unlike craft apprentices (p. 233), but with much less chance to reach their ultimate promotion.

A second, much more fair, model of avoiding heavy management involvement was the subdivision of the factory into several independent workplaces, where sub-tasks were performed in groups by reasonably autonomous workers ('internal contracting' or 'inside contracting').[12] In such a system, the boss didn't need to appoint underbosses, deputies and the like for the close and direct monitoring of workers to ensure sufficient production for an hourly wage. Instead, the emphasis was on controlling product parts and ensuring their smooth transition from one workplace to another. This traditional organizational structure involved the efficient collaboration of a number of 'cooperative subcontracting' units.

The shift between all these different organizational structures was very gradual and varied by sector, partly reflected in the average size of the company. For example, in 1815, cotton factories with fewer than 50 workers still dominated in Manchester, while, by 1841, factories of 100 to 250 were common, but in the same period, the number of factories with more than 500 workers hardly increased.[13]

Workers' actions and reactions

The fact that the productivity in the various economic sectors rose sharply and sometimes spectacularly does not mean that workers made visible advances in the short term. Although the standard of living debate has certainly not been resolved, a consensus is nevertheless beginning to emerge. The real income of English industrial workers – not just men but also huge numbers of women and children – barely increased before 1820 and grew only very slowly in the subsequent half-century. Moreover, this moderate profit was largely offset by worsening living conditions in the rapidly growing industrial cities. Indicators – such as life expectancy, infant mortality and height – that measured quality of life only show decisive improvements from the 1870s. In her recent summary of the debates of the last two centuries, British historian Emma Griffin said, 'modestly rising real wages appear a very small compensation for the high price extracted in terms of health, longevity and well-being'.[14] In any case, social inequality increased, and certainly that between factory owner and factory worker.[15]

No wonder, then, that the Industrial Revolution had a mixed reception among workers. And not only due to the often meagre reward for working hard and long hours: conditions were poor too. Just think of the noise from rattling machines that made it impossible to talk. In the textile industry, but also elsewhere, such as in the sawmills, sign language was necessary. This was in contrast to small workplaces or among larger troupes of workers who mollified work in the open air by singing shanties and other work songs.[16]

The gradual shift from small workplaces to larger factories and that between different organizational structures elicited three types of responses from workers: acceptance; adjustment; and resistance. The latter probably became the best-known, but, in fact, was rather exceptional (for more details on individual and collective response, see p. 375). The resistance to new organizational structures was not so much about the mechanization itself, but about the increased daily supervision and the replacement of collective piece wages with individual time wages; in a nutshell, it was about the loss of independence.[17]

Numerous incidences of machine breaking are known from the years 1760 to 1820, some of which were violent and even fatal, especially in cases where armed forces were deployed to protect the new machines, factories and their owners. Resistance was fiercer in some regions than others, with the south and especially the south-west of England standing out, but the regional spread of resistance and acceptance is not easily explained. What is clear is that resistance was more common in the countryside than in the big cities. In booming Birmingham, with its immigrants, for example, it was almost entirely lacking. The toughest resistance to new machines, in the form of Luddism, was found in rural Nottinghamshire, Derbyshire and Leicestershire in 1811–12. It was founded in 'the personal, kinship and other social connections within a workshop culture or small quasi-peasant community'. Highly disciplined 'guerrilla bands' were only able to carry out countless successful nighttime attacks on the new cloth-finishing machinery, stocking frames and power looms, as well as their owners, because everyone kept their mouths shut. Incidentally, Luddism is not an exclusively English phenomenon; it also is known from France, Germany, Switzerland, the Netherlands and Mexico, among others.[18]

Less heroic, but much more general and also successful for a long time, were attempts at adaptation, which highlight the creativity of workers. Adaptation or adjustment was mainly aimed at maintaining maximum freedom of action under the inevitably more intensive supervision of the worker, but in a such a way that the boss could live with it. A successful and widely used method was that of 'cooperative subcontracting' (as it was coined in the 1890s by the Fabian David Frederick Schloss) that we briefly encountered before.[19]

Cooperative (or collective) subcontractors usually combine more than one stage in the production process or undertake the process in its entirety and are remunerated as a group per item of finished product. In such a set-up, the organization of the labour process is left to the collective, and the employer's role is limited to the provision of raw materials and production establishments on the input side and quality control of the finished product on the output side. This is highly beneficial to the employer because any losses due to inefficient coordination and cooperation between workers are borne entirely by the collective in the form of a lower output and, hence, lower earnings. On the other hand, workers' own responsibility to effectively organize their collaboration in production provides them with significant autonomy and immunity from employers' oppressive oversight. In other words, mutual responsibility for the quality of the end-product and, thereby, levels of remuneration puts a premium on minimizing error rates among the different members of the collective and the effective application of available skills in the production process. The intra- and inter-generational transfer of occupational skills is accomplished through on-the-spot training, combined with differential redistribution of earnings according to skills.

Subcontracting units are often, but not necessarily, based on family groups. In both cases, the composition of the group is a major concern for all members as the weakest link ultimately determines the total result of the entire group.[20] Cooperative subcontracting has been extraordinarily wide-spread. Outside industry, we find it in seasonal agricultural gang work, within it in mining, house building and public construction, and in factories. Thomas Brassey, son of Great Britain's most famous builder of railways and thus probably the biggest private employer in the world, wrote in 1872:

> My father always preferred putting a price upon work, rather than paying by the day. . . . Piece work could not in all cases be adopted without some complications and difficulties; but my father always looked upon day work as a losing game; and all his work was done as far as possible by sub-contract, which is piece work on a somewhat larger scale. . . . Payment by piece is beneficial alike to the master and the man. The men earn higher wages, while the master has the satisfaction of obtaining an equiv-alent for the wages he has paid, and completing the contract which he has undertaken with far greater rapidity.[21]

This was not just a British oddity. A cross-cultural comparison between the organization of brick making in Western and Eastern Europe and India over the last few centuries reveals that these principles have been applied worldwide and apparently without much direct mutual influence, thus suggesting universal socio-psychological mechanisms in the organization of industrial waged work outside the household firm. We also find it in machine-building factories, in the printing industry and in many more industries. It is said to have been widespread around 1900 in the factories of all big European cities.[22]

Indeed, from about 1900, when it was probably at its peak, cooperative subcontracting was confronted with two declared enemies: on the one hand, the modern entrepreneurs and prophets of scientific management, and on the other, the modern trade union movement. We will discuss the trade union movement in the next chapter, but for now let us focus on the employers, and perhaps the most famous among them, the American Frederick W. Taylor, from whom the term 'Taylorism' derives. In 1911, he wrote:

> A careful analysis had demonstrated the fact that when workmen are herded together in gangs, each man in the gang becomes far less efficient than when his personal ambition is stimulated; that when men work in gangs, their individual efficiency falls almost invariably down to or below the level of the worst man in the gang; and that they are all pulled down instead of being elevated by being herded together.

What Taylor does not say is why workmen would behave like this, what has been called 'soldiering'. In fact, they knew very well that if productivity rose then the rates would be cut: 'A man producing too much on piece rate was seen as sacrificing his friends on the altar of his own greed; he was hogging higher pay, heedless of the rate cut it was sure to provoke. If on day rate, he was sucking up to the boss, likewise to his own gain and at the expense of his fellows.'[23]

As the comparative history of brick making discussed above shows, Taylor's statement is rather one-sided. However, it is important because, after about 1900, cooperative subcontracting had given way almost every-where, at least in the economically most advanced countries, to direct hiring based on individual contracts with time wages (with the possible exception of parts of the construction industry).

This new phase in industrial management of free wage labour will be elaborated below (pp. 388–97), but first we must track the emergence of free wage labour itself, also made possible by the demise of unfree labour.

The decline of unfree labour

In 1807, Great Britain passed legislation to abolish the slave trade, and the decision would never be repealed. Albeit slowly and certainly not in a straightforward and linear manner, over the last two centuries the slave trade, as well as enslavement and slave labour, has diminished or indeed vanished. The global demise of unfree labour is undeniable and, today, there is probably less unfree labour in the world than there ever has been since the introduction of slavery a few millennia earlier. How and why did the abolition of the slave trade and slavery occur? When and why were there hitches in this long-term development? And what is the current situation?

The abolition of the slave trade and slave labour: How and why?

The demise of unfree labour as a legally recognized, state-enforced system took place in two ways: from above and from below. From above, in the course of the last two centuries, states abolished the slave trade, followed by slave labour (while financially compensating the slave owners, not the liberated enslaved, who in a number of cases even had to pay part of the indemnification sum themselves)[24] and, finally, any penal sanctions in the enforcement of labour contracts. From below, as long as unfree labour existed, people tried to escape it individually by fleeing (think of the *marrons* in the Guyanas, or of Russian serfs absconding to the Cossack-dominated border regions of Russia)[25] or, where possible, by buying their freedom – and occasionally even by collective action in the form of revolts, as we have seen.

Given that the effect of abolition from above – partially pressured by collective action from below – has proved more effective overall, let us now examine the steps taken to achieve it.[26] Within the space of just a few years, three states decided to curb the age-old Atlantic slave trade from Africa: in 1803, Denmark outlawed the slave trade of its subjects; on 2 March 1807, the US president Thomas Jefferson prohibited the importation of slaves; and, on the 25th of the same month, Britain prohibited all its citizens from participating in the trade in and the transportation of African slaves. The British Slave Trade Act was by far the most influential, due to Britain's overwhelming maritime and colonial power, especially following the nation's victory over Napoleon in 1814–15. Moreover, the British were so serious about this issue that they tried to force other nations to enter into treaties to do the same. Such treaties included the right to search the holds of ships belonging to

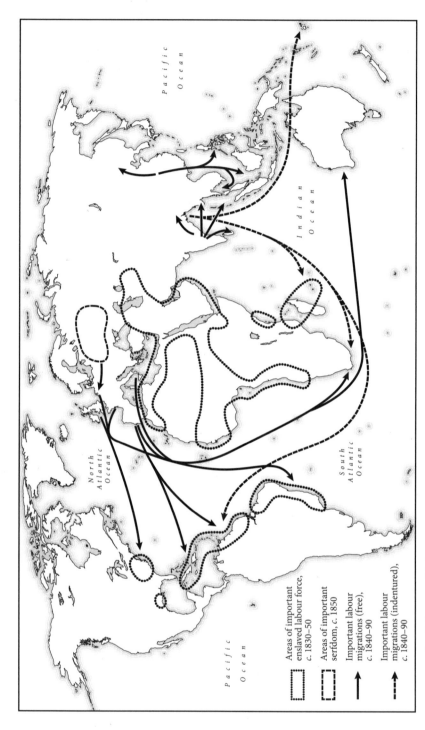

Map 6. Unfree labour and labour migrations in the nineteenth century.

treaty partners, the setting up of international courts to enforce these treaties and the liberation of enslaved men and women who were subsequently provided shelter in places such as Sierra Leone and, later, Liberia.

In fact, some Mediterranean states, infamous for the employment of slaves in the Middle Ages and the early modern period, never formally abolished slavery, although it rarely occurred there afterwards. In eighteenth-century Europe (and possibly for longer), Portugal was the only place where slavery played an important role.[27] In the period spanning c. 1600–1761, between one and two thousand slaves disembarked in the ports of Portugal annually. In the latter year, the entry of black slaves from America, Asia or Africa was forbidden; not for humanitarian reasons, but in order to prevent drainage of slaves from Portugal's highly profitable colony Brazil. Moreover, slaves who were already in Portugal were explicitly excluded from liberated status. In 1767, the decree was extended to mulatto slaves, and, in 1773, freedom was granted to children born of slaves in Portugal and to slaves with grandchildren in the country. All others remained slaves for life. No wonder that the demise of slave labour took so long in the Portuguese colonies.

At the eastern end of the Mediterranean, abolition was even slower.[28] Since the demise of agricultural slavery in the Ottoman Empire in the sixteenth century, the system had been largely restricted to elite households and male European slaves were replaced by female slaves, partially still from the Caucasus but mainly from Africa. In the nineteenth century, slaves may have comprised 5 per cent of the total population. From the middle of that century, slavery gradually became less important. After the Crimean War (1854–56), the Ottomans no longer enslaved prisoners of war or enemy subjects and, in 1857, the black slave trade was forbidden. Following Russia's defeat of the Circassians in the Caucasus – a traditional source of 'white slaves' for the Ottoman Empire – there was a steady exodus of Circassian slaves, along with their masters, into Turkey, reaching a peak in 1864–65. This implied a sudden but short-lived increase in slave labour there. Subsequently, the slave trade was increasingly frustrated, but as late as 1909, when the Young Turks officially abolished the white slave trade, they had to concede that slavery was recognized by the holy law of the Empire.

Moreover, the throttling of the transatlantic routes (with the most important exception being the Brazilian slave ships that, south of the English patrol ships, transited to Angola, Madagascar and Mozambique)[29] led to changes in the nature of slavery in the Americas and especially to an increase in slavery in Africa itself. Ultimately, the slave trade between Africa and the Americas was successfully frustrated: from 435,300 slaves traded across the Atlantic in the 1840s, the figure dropped to 179,100 in the decade thereafter and to 52,600 in the years 1861–67.

However, the abolitionist movement also prompted negative effects. As a result of the gradual frustration of the Atlantic slave trade by the British, those with vested interests in it, such as the Brazilians, were keen to circumvent these measures. And for a long time they were successful, because the procreation of existing slaves, together with the domestic slave trade, were not enough to meet the demand of the slave owners who did not want to shift to employing free labourers.

Slavery inside Africa increased, as exemplified by the Sokoto Caliphate in northern Nigeria, where it is estimated that, around 1900, between 1 and 2.5 million slaves were at work, predominantly in cash crop production but also as objects of conspicuous consumption for the elite. Despite British efforts to frustrate it, the export of enslaved Africans continued in the nineteenth century. Trafficking across the Atlantic now became rare, but numbers grew across the Sahara (where Darfur became a notorious slave-raiding state), the Red Sea and the Indian Ocean. It took until 1900 for this north- and east-bound trade to gradually stop. At the same time, the transoceanic slave trade had also been countered successfully elsewhere in the world.

Parallel to the fight against the slave trade ran that against slavery and slave labour itself, and this movement, too, was primarily based in England. In 1833, Parliament passed a bill to abolish slavery in all its colonies, except for those ruled by the East India Company. These would follow in 1843, and, somewhat later, those parts of India not directly under EIC rule, like Travancore, in 1855.[30] Other colonial powers would follow this example, including France in 1848, the Netherlands in 1863 and Spain with its important colony Cuba in 1886. But key independent states were rather late in forbidding slavery: indeed, it took a bloody civil war in America in 1865 (600,000 casualties in the name of a labour relations issue!), followed by a full century in which the southerners managed to frustrate the full enjoyment of civil rights by the formerly enslaved and their descendants. But in the aftermath trade unions also played a negative role, garnering criticism from prominent black leaders including W.E.B. Du Bois and Martin Luther King.[31] Brazil abolished slavery only in 1888. Among the last were Ethiopia in 1942 and Mauritania in 1981.[32]

The abolition of serfdom in Central and Eastern Europe also fits into this chronological pattern.[33] Although many countries emulated the abolishment of serfdom brought about by the French Revolution, like Prussia and Poland in 1807, the Baltic provinces of Russia in 1816–19, Wurttemberg in 1817 and Bavaria in the following year, other countries still had to wait for half a century or longer. In Austria, emancipation took place in 1848, in Hungary 1853 and in Russia 1861. Romania followed suit in 1864. Despite the Russian Emancipation Act freeing 11 million serfs in 1861 (nearly 50 per cent of peasants and 40 per cent of Russia's total male population), for decades many ex-serfs were still not free to move wherever they wanted. Indeed, large numbers of ex-serfs were bound by the *mir*, or communal peasant village, which was collectively responsible for paying generous compensation payments to their former masters.

All of these countries were struggling with the fact that they considered private property, including the ownership of slaves, sacrosanct. The solution was found in indemnification, paid for from the public purse, for former slave owners. In order to facilitate a smooth transition, former slave owners were also allowed a period of several years in which they could use their liberated slaves as 'apprentices'. In practice, this meant that, though freed, they had to work for their former masters for several more years in exchange for board, lodging, medical care and other maintenance. In fact, most freedmen decided not to stay after their apprenticeship and many plantation owners had to divide up their properties and rent them out to their former slaves-become-peasants or to deal with freedmen as sharecroppers. Freedmen also preferred labour contracts with anyone other than their former slave owners.[34]

An alternative was the employment of indentured labourers, that is, labourers bound by contract and under penal sanction to serve for a number of years on a single plantation. That is how tens of millions of 'coolies' from China, India, Java, Japan and some Pacific Islands (the 'Kanakas') ended up in places thousands of kilometres away from home like the US, the Guyanas, Mauritius, Ceylon, southern India and Assam, Malaya and Sumatra, and Australia. Like their predecessors from England and France (see pp. 264–5), they became indebted to their recruiters, who paid for their fare and passed them on to the plantation owners in order to work off their debts. It took them years to regain their freedom, after which they either returned home or settled as peasants in their new fatherlands. For nearly a century more, shades of unfreedom in the form of apprenticeship and indentureship followed the abolition of slavery, until Britain and other colonial powers finally got rid of indenture around the First World War. The American jurist Tobias Barrington Wolff characterizes this last form of legally unfree labour in his country as follows: 'The juridical category was different – the property right in a human being, now forbidden, was replaced with the generally accepted right of a creditor to enforce a debt – but the result was largely the same. The coercive power of the State was used to compel labor from poor (and usually black) workers, on threat of imprisonment.'[35] And this observation for the US reflected the situation in many other parts of the world where similar recruitment systems existed.

The protracted abolition of, first, the trade in enslaved labourers and, then, of enslaved labour itself was by no means self-evident or easy, as this brief overview suggests. The question arises, then: who were its main proponents and what was their motivation?[36] In fact, there were two, although not often working together or even in sympathy with each other. First, the enslaved in the Americas who tried to achieve their goal by revolts and revolutions and, second, citizenry – and especially workers – in Britain.

Marronage and slave revolts occurred regularly in the Caribbean and Brazil (see the Palmares revolt on p. 275). Most impressive was the revolt of the slaves along the Berbice River in Guyana that started on 27 February 1763 and lasted for more than a year. The suppression by the combined forces of European military, indigenous (American Indian) allies and black slaves who stayed true to their masters or, earlier on, gave up resistance was ultimately possible because of discord among the insurgents.[37] Such acts of evasion and resistance did not lead to the end of the institution until the Haitian Revolution. In 1791, the plantation colony Saint Domingue (the French part of the island of Hispaniola, now Haiti) was shocked by a slave uprising under the leadership of Toussaint Louverture. The freedom of all inhabitants, including the enslaved, was confirmed by the French Revolutionary Convention in 1794. But that did not guarantee its success. Opposition by slave owners of European and mixed European-African descent (the *gens de couleur*) and invasions by British and, later, Napoleonic forces (the emperor wanting to revert the decree of 1794) caused much bloodshed, and independence was only achieved in 1804. For the first time since the advent of transatlantic slavery, enslaved Africans and their descendants had freed themselves successfully in an entire country, although it came at a very high price.

Other abolitionists were predominantly, and rather remarkably, to be found in England, and their movement is an early example of a tenacious, broad-based popular movement that achieved its goal. Of course, its participants' motivations were diverse, and varied from Christian- or humanitarian-inspired Enlightenment thinking, departing from the same principle of the basic equality of all humans, to proponents of economic competition in absolutely 'free' markets. Among the latter, apart from free trade advocates, we should not forget the nascent working class and trade union movement in England. The British Society for the Abolition of the Slave Trade (1787–92) garnered widespread support, not only from academic and professional circles but also from clerks and artisans, who believed strongly in the ideal of the 'masterless man' and prepared to extend it to the colonies. Among the hundreds of thousands of petitioners from all over the country, 20,000 lived in industrial Manchester, which had 75,000 inhabitants.[38]

The movement was revived after the Napoleonic Wars, inspired by revolts in, among others, Demerara and Jamaica, and organized by the new Society for Mitigating and Gradually Abolishing the State of Slavery (1823) and the Anti-Slavery Society (1830), with 1,200 branch societies that advocated immediate liberation of slaves in the colonies. Now, colonial slavery was directly linked to the exploitation of wage labourers at home. An 1830 article by the anti-slavery agitator Richard Oastler, entitled 'Yorkshire Slavery', condemned the pitiless overworking of children and women by mill owners.[39] Even more pointed is the 1831 evocation of the contradiction between slave labour and wage labour by Mary Prince of Bermuda:

> I have been a slave myself—I know what slaves feel—I can tell by myself what other slaves feel, and by what they told me. That man that says that slaves be quite happy in slavery—and that they don't want to be free— that man is either ignorant or a lying person. I never heard a slave say so. . . . That's the reason they can't do without slaves, they say. What's the reason they can't do without slaves as well as in England? No slaves here— no whips—no punishments, except for wicked people. Let them work ever so hard in England, they are far better off than slaves. If they get a bad master, they give warning and go hire to another. They have their liberty. That is what *we* want. We don't mind hard work, if we had proper treatment, and proper wages like English servants, and proper time given in the week to keep us from breaking the Sabbath. But they won't give it.[40]

Fair and decent treatment at home and in the colonies appealed in particular to workers and to women. The Birmingham Ladies Negro's

Friend Society led the way in demanding immediate emancipation in 1831.[41]

After years of successful parliamentary reform and abolition, abolitionists, political reformers, Protestant revivalists and working-class movements in Britain went their own way again. The trade unions had to struggle for simple and basic legal rights, like the liberty to organize and to strike for the abolition of penal sanctions for breach of contract (see p. 404). The cause of abolition, inspired by Enlightenment ideas, now became more international, albeit not in the form of a mass movement. The Congress of Vienna in 1815 hastened the end of the slave trade, but without formulating sanctions of the kind that would appear in many subsequent international agreements. After the abolition of serfdom in Russia and of slavery in the US, the major slave countries left in the Western Hemisphere were Brazil and the Spanish colony of Cuba. Anti-slavery activists now turned to Africa.

With the European slavery legacy soon forgotten, this continent was now portrayed by missionary-discoverers like David Livingstone as the continent not so much of the Enslaved Victim as of the Enslaving Tyrant, with an accusing finger pointed towards both African rulers and Muslim slave merchants from the Middle East.[42] This provided the legitimation for the scramble for Africa and for the missionary zeal to convert the Africans to (various forms of) Christianity. The Paris, Berlin and Brussels conferences of 1867, 1884 and 1890 concentrated on the African traffic, leaving enough space for the old and new colonial powers to continue slavery and other forms of unfree labour for decades to come. This may be an important reason why European humanitarian movements paid much less attention to the continuation of different forms of unfree labour and unfree characteristics of indentured labour in Asia and the Pacific until the new world order after 1918.[43]

The League of Nations continued the practice of the preceding century, which had aimed at bilateral and increasingly multilateral agreements between states, thus trying to reach a global political consensus. In the nineteenth century, select passages from the Bible provided inspiration for the 'Powers of Christendom', and Christendom was considered equal to 'civilization'. Not everybody was convinced. In 1840, an English diplomat, commenting upon a move by the British ambassador in Istanbul to stop the slave trade in the entire Ottoman Empire, remarked that it met 'with extreme astonishment accompanied with a smile ... The Turks may believe us to be their superiors in the Sciences, in Arts, and in Arms, but they are far from thinking our wisdom or our morality greater than their own.'[44] Besides slavery, corvée now also became a target. Traditionally, it functioned as a form of indirect taxation in kind (through work) by governments, especially in less monetized societies like the colonies. Moreover, it also could be a form of unfree labour if the colonial state geared it to the compulsory cultivation of export products for which only a small remuneration was offered. The replacement of corvée in independent states with taxation in cash put a general end to it after the Second World War.[45]

Until rather recently, unfreedom within the household had gone unnoticed almost everywhere. Think of the mostly unmarried 'mixed couples' of male European colonialists and female colonized from Indonesia, Indochina and elsewhere. These women and their children were mostly cared for until the moment when the man decided to leave. Then, they had to return to their village. The following comparison, made in Haiphong (Vietnam) in 1910, is telling:

> In France, a peasant or worker who takes advantage of a neighbor woman makes reparations; and a man who by virtue of his position is able to abuse a younger or poorer woman contracts a debt that cannot be renounced. But without getting into any discussion of color or racial inferiority, social relations are not the same between the young Frenchman who lands on these shores and the native women who are more often than not offered to him.[46]

After the First World War, superiority in science, arms and economy enabled the North Atlantic to impose its ideas about free labour on other states. The members of the League of Nations (1919) committed themselves 'to secure and maintain fair and humane conditions of labor for men, women and children, both in their own countries and in all countries to which their commercial and industrial relations extend'. This refers, of course, to the colonies and 'mandate territories' that, at the time, remained omnipresent. There, the Western colonizers had to care for the 'preservation of the native populations and to supervise the improvement of the conditions of their moral and material well-being'. They also united in the 'endeavour to secure the complete suppression of slavery in all its forms and the slave trade by land and by sea'.[47] This became one of the tasks of the newly founded International Labour Organization (ILO). Because of the important influence of the international trade union movement, the link between the labour movement and the suppression of unfree labour was re-established. And it would be continued under the umbrella of the United Nations, the successor of the League of Nations, from 1945.

There has been an undeniable waning of unfree labour over the last two centuries. Yet, there are two reasons for a lack of triumphalism in this regard. First, in the same period, there were occasional but major setbacks, showing that, even in 'modern society', the re-enslavement of free people was not only feasible but could happen on a grand scale – consider Russia under Stalin, Germany and the territories it occupied under Hitler, China under Mao and a number of numerically smaller cases, such as Cambodia under Pol Pot and, to this day, North Korea.[48] Second, undocumented ('illegal') unfree labour has by no means been eradicated and continues to warrant our close attention.

Temporal returns to unfree labour: When and why?

The most frequent returns to unfree labour occur when prisoners of war are forced to perform labour during their captivity.[49] In particular, during the first and second world wars, for many years, Germany was trapped between different fronts – a working male population that was fighting and a shortage of labour. Whereas France heavily recruited colonial labourers and England depended increasingly on its female workforce, Germany tried to employ its POWs. In 1918, no fewer than 2 million prisoners were forced to work for the German Empire. Moreover, over half a million Polish workers, who had arrived as guest workers before the war, were considered per se sympathetic to the enemy and therefore forced to stay and work for the Empire as well.

The Second World War shows similar patterns, but on a much grander scale.[50] Already before the conflict, many foreigners (375,000 in 1938) worked voluntarily in Germany as a result of agreements between the German government and those of Italy, Yugoslavia, Hungary, Bulgaria and the Netherlands. After the conquest of Poland, a target was set to force 1 million Polish labourers, in particular Polish girls, to work in Germany. After the war began in the west, other nationalities were recruited, resulting in 2.1 million civilian labourers by the late summer of 1941. In addition, 1.2 million POWs, most of them French and Polish, worked in the Reich. By this time, the Nazis had apparently solved their serious labour shortages once and for all and believed they could afford to send Norwegian, Dutch and (most)

Belgian POWs back home – hence their lack of interest in taking prisoners during the subsequent attack on the Soviet Union. Of the 5.7 million POWs captured by the Germans, some 3.3 million died, most of them at the start of the war from starvation and disease.

It was not long before the Germans came to regret this brutal policy of neglect, once it became apparent, in early 1942, that the war would last much longer than anticipated and labour shortages once again became an issue. More and more inhabitants of territories under German control were forced to work for the Fatherland, and gradually even inmates of concentration camps were mobilized. In 1944, over 100,000 Hungarian Jews temporarily avoided the gas chambers when they were deployed in the war industry. In October 1944, Germany forcefully employed 8 million workers from 26 different foreign countries, including two million POWs. Together, they represented a third of the country's workforce. Clearly, civil prisoners had become much more important than defeated soldiers. Their fate, especially that of the Russians, Poles and others – mainly Jews and Gypsies – was harsh, and they were defined as *Untermenschen*, a label that meant they had little chance of survival.

Almost every war produces its own prisoners and, consequently, compulsory work is inevitable. These examples from Germany can easily be expanded with others from, for example, great warring states like Japan, or the US or China, countries marred by civil wars. The end of hostilities did not always mean an end to unfree labour by POWs and civilian prisoners, especially in the Soviet Union. The largest groups there comprised roughly 1 million Poles and, of course, defeated German soldiers, who only returned to Germany in the mid-1950s.[51]

Whereas many states returned temporarily to unfree labour in times of war, the cases of Stalinist Russia, Nazi Germany and China under Mao must be considered as structural. After the Russian Revolution and the Civil War, the Bolsheviks hoped to organize their alternative economy without markets. Instead, rational planning and scientific management with the party-state as the only employer, combined with well-motivated councils of workers, would, they believed, produce welfare for everyone.[52]

Stalin's impatience at how long it was taking Russia to achieve this utopia resulted in him imposing a number of measures to rob Soviet artisans, peasants and workers of any kind of freedom of choice. The October 1930 Decree on 'The immediate employment of the unemployed' stopped benefit payments without delay and applicants refusing work were struck from the rolls of the labour exchange. In 1938, the highly unpopular workbooks were introduced, giving the plant manager full power over the worker. A year later, social insurance rights were tied to the length of employment in one establishment. Finally, in June 1940, an act was promulgated for the 'prohibition of workers and employees from quitting their jobs of their own accord', and truancy was made a criminal offence.

All these measures were in force until the 1960s and, of course, they necessitated a vast enforcement apparatus. For this reason, the existing tsarist prisons for political dissidents were expanded into the infamous Gulag camps, made notorious by the writings of Aleksandr Solzhenitsyn. Besides political and other dissidents, these concentration camps and colonies for forced labour were mainly filled with citizens who could not be otherwise disciplined. It is estimated that between 1938 and 1950 some 7 million inmates or more were forced to work throughout the Soviet Union, especially in construction projects, mining and lumbering. This is over 20 per cent of the non-agricultural workforce of the country. On top of this, some ethnic groups were forcefully resettled where the regime needed them, and, as mentioned previously, millions of prisoners of war remained captive for many years in the Soviet Union following the Second World War.

After Hitler came to power in Germany and made the decision to go for territorial expansion and eventually to prepare for war, he trod the same path as Stalin.[53] First, prisons had to be adapted to house his political enemies, but quickly the labour force had to be geared towards the interests of the party-state, and finally forced labour in concentration camps formed the cornerstone of it all. For now, I will set aside the incontrovertible function of such camps for the annihilation of Jews and other *Untermenschen* and concentrate on their place in the history of unfree labour.

As Stalin was able to build upon the politics of his predecessors, so Hitler could use Weimar politics.[54] In a way, the Weimar Republic was ahead of the Soviets. The 1924 law on unemployment benefits strengthened the obligation for those on welfare to carry out compulsory labour, so-called 'welfare through work'. Since 1927, claimants of unemployment insurance could be assigned jobs by state agencies. This hit the young and the single in particular. The compulsory labour service (*Arbeitsdienstpflicht*) led to heated parliamentary debates in the early 1930s, which were, of course, silenced after the Nazis came to power. Indeed, the Nazis were quick to adopt this initiative and, in 1934, they numbered 10 per cent of the total German workforce.

Many more countries in Central and Eastern Europe, as well as Finland, Italy and France in the 1930s, followed the Weimar example of compulsory labour. The Civilian Conservation Corps, introduced in 1933 by Roosevelt in the framework of his New Deal, also shows a number of similarities (as well as differences, of course). Some countries included such provisions in their constitutions, including Spain in 1938 and France in 1946. Yet only the Soviet and German dictatorships developed a fully fledged system of unfree labour consisting of three elements: increasing restrictions on the movement of 'ordinary' workers; compulsory work for prisoners of war and inhabitants of occupied countries; and a combination of terror, extermination and enslavement of socially unwanted parts of the populations of both home and occupied countries.

These numbers subsequently dwindled as a result of full employment in Germany due to the preparations for war, but the unfree labour force grew again from 1938 to over 40 per cent by the time the Nazis were defeated in 1945. This was due, in particular, to the capture of foreign workers, who, as we have seen, were much more numerous than the still-impressive 2 million POWs. During the war, the SS was in charge of this huge enterprise. It not only employed its slaves directly but also hired them out to the state and private armament or militarily crucial industry enterprises – hence firms like I.G. Farben settling in Auschwitz, or Siemens in Ravensbrück.[55]

In the aftermath of the Second World War and following their own civil war, the Chinese Communist Party took power in 1949. The Party faced similar problems to those experienced by its Russian sister party thirty years before. In China, however, there was an even shorter 'honeymoon' period, of no more than five years, after which the state rapidly introduced a rigid policy of labour allocation, ending the mass migrations of the previous century that had been based on individual or household-level decisions. This policy had two faces: the immobilization of the bulk of the population at the place where they lived; and, simultaneously, the forced reallocation of workers.[56]

In 1955, the well-known *hukou* (household registration) system was implemented, a combination of the centuries-old Chinese family registers and – through Russian advisors – of the Soviet workbook system. This required all individuals to register in their place of residence, where they had to stay in their work unit (*danwei*), which entitled them to social and political rights, including benefits and education. A change of abode or workplace was forbidden without difficult-to-obtain migration certificates.

In order to prevent seasonal out-migration in the slack season, rural cadres had to keep farmers in the village by providing corvée labour to promote soil improvement, water conservancy and other public works. In 1960, the system was extended by demanding official travel certificates, compulsory for the purchase of train, bus and boat tickets.

On the other hand, the state had already been forcefully moving workers from the early years of the People's Republic. In the 1950s, millions of unemployed were evicted from the big cities – for example, 1.3 million people moved out of Beijing in the years 1950–57. From its inception, the People's Republic only took responsibility for the employment and welfare of its urban population. With famines the only exception, rural people – organized in self-reliant villages consisting of collective production teams – were responsible for feeding themselves. State grain rations were kept for the non-agrarian urban workers and for state employees. Rural people called these rations 'guaranteed harvest regardless of drought or flood'. In sum: 'By state reckoning, farmers produced grain for self-consumption and hence had little need for access to state grain supplies'.[57]

The Great Leap Forward and the Cultural Revolution may have stultified the immobilization policies of the 1950s, but the principle that migration to achieve individual betterment – by looking for another employer or employment – was selfish and therefore condemned remained firmly intact. This was juxtaposed with what was called the freedom of the masses, masterfully explained by the Minister of the Public Security Department in 1958:

> Naturally . . . there are some restrictions affecting the minority of people who think only of themselves and who blindly migrate without the slightest consideration for what is beneficial to both state and collective interests. For such people there is indeed a contradiction, but this type of contradiction definitely limits neither the citizen's freedom of residence nor movement. This is because the freedom regulated by the constitution is a guided freedom and is not anarchistic. It is a freedom for the broad masses, not an absolute freedom for a small number of 'individuals'. If one permits this small number of individuals absolute freedom, allowing them the freedom to migrate blindly without due consideration for the good of the state and the collective, this will naturally mean that the policy of arranging things according to an overall plan and implementing a plan for socialist reconstruction cannot be smoothly implemented.[58]

A second motive for denying freedom to its workers can be discerned in the 'Third Front Construction' episode when, because of the Sino-Soviet split in the late 1950s, China decided to disperse its key industries to remote mountainous areas in inner China. A third motive was the concentration and suppression of alleged and real enemies of the party and the system, which created the Chinese version of the Gulag.[59] There is a fourth, related type of forced migrations, which took place during Mao's Cultural Revolution. At this time, young people born and raised in cities had to be re-educated by working in the 'real' world of farming and manual labour: 'Up to the mountains and down to the countryside'. This involved no fewer than 17 million people in the decade between 1966 and 1976. A decade later, this piece of social engineering inspired Pol Pot in Cambodia, as it had inspired (and still does) the Kim dynasty in North Korea. Although the *hukou* had a much longer life, labour relations in China were definitively reformed from the 1980s onwards, when many of these types of unfreedom disappeared.[60]

Common to these cases are the ways in which all wage labourers are robbed of their freedom to change job, to organize themselves and to challenge employers and the state in order to defend or improve their position. They also share a state ideology that pledges to emancipate the 'true' workers and to enhance their condition. Alas, in all these cases, those who do not qualify are immediately defined as the enemy and suffer the consequences. What begins with austere measures for the unemployed who refuse to accept any job – a modern version of the medieval vagrancy laws – develops quickly, via workbooks, into complete immobility unless the state decides otherwise.

Ironically, all massive reversals of free labour in the twentieth century took place under the banner of a workers' paradise. Maybe that is also one of the reasons why these systems fail to survive for more than a few decades – North Korea being the ominous exception. It is noteworthy that, from the 1960s, the Soviet Union and the US competed in attempts to please the worker as a consumer and how, from the 1980s, the same has been true of China. In the Russian case, it ended in the demise of the communist system but without a properly working alternative. In the Chinese case, the system was modified but not disbanded while, to date, living standards have risen.

The actual situation: Continuities and change in unfree labour

Notwithstanding all reports about contemporary slavery, and however pitiful the fate of those affected, from a historical perspective unfree labour is a marginal phenomenon today. David Eltis, a Canadian expert in the history of transatlantic slavery, writes: 'I very much doubt if any of the slaves emerging from the hold of a slave ship after a two-month transatlantic voyage would sign on to the definitions of slave labor and trading implied by many modern discussions of the abuse of human labor.'[61] At the same time, we must ask ourselves how it is that, after two centuries of concerted efforts by states and international organizations to erase unfree labour, human trafficking still exists and that we know of so many cases of commercial forced sexual services and of debt bondage. Three key explanations offer themselves: the continuing legality of forced labour by prisoners and the unequal chances of getting imprisoned; the considerable time lag between formal abolition and the actual change of societal norms of slavery or other forms of widely recognized inequality like caste; and the easy abuse of 'illegal' workers, specifically 'undocumented' migrants, many of whom work as domestics.[62] These explanations – though certainly not all-encompassing – require further elaboration here.

As with military service, the imprisonment of criminals is not an infringement of the principle of free labour per se, but it can become so under specific circumstances. Any modern society includes a number of persons locked up for shorter or longer periods as a punishment for breaking the law. Arguably, prisons are necessary in any society that does not summarily kill all its criminally convicted. However, there is a big variety between countries in terms of numbers of prisoners in proportion to the entire population. Moreover, the more prisoners there are, the higher the likelihood that they will be put to work, even to the extent that a substantial part of the labour force comprises prisoners.

We have already seen examples of incidental surges of prisoners at work under dictatorships. To this we can add the pre-history of the Gulag in Russia. From the seventeenth century onwards, the tsars already sent their prisoners to Siberia. Before 1850, they counted thousands per annum, but by the end of the century this had already risen to over 10,000, not including wives and children. In 1885, 15 per cent were hard-labour convicts, 27 per cent forced colonists, 37 per cent 'communal exiles' (persons banished on account of their generally bad character by the village communities to which they belonged), 17 per cent were vagrants and 4 per cent were classified as political and religious exiles.[63]

Let us now briefly review some examples of above-average numbers or extremely harsh working conditions for prisoners in 'normal' or non-dictatorial countries. Before the American War of Independence, English prisons had disgorged some 50,000 of their inmates to the colonies, mainly to Maryland and Virginia. Scotland added thousands more. When this destination was barred after the Declaration of Independence, in addition to places like Penang Island, Australia became the main colony of debarkation for convicts. Between 1788 and 1868, some 160,000 were shipped in that direction. In its heyday, England annually evicted 2,000 of its citizens.[64]

France had an age-old tradition of sending prisoners to the galleys or subjecting them to hard labour in 'bagnes' (a kind of floating prison) in naval arsenals, before it started to send them overseas.[65] After the repression of the June 1848 uprising, Louis Napoleon sent more than 6,000 prisoners to Algeria, whence most returned. This was child's play compared to what happened some years later, when penal colonies were founded in French Guyana. Until 1938, about 52,000 prisoners and 15,600 banished individuals made the journey across the Atlantic. This destination, whose most famous prisoner was probably Alfred Dreyfus, was only abandoned in 1945. France opened a second destination, in addition to Guyana, in the Pacific, modelled on the Australian example. Between 1864 and 1896, New Caledonia received 20,000 prisoners, many of whom were *Communards*, plus 10,000 banished persons. This picture of some 100,000 forced evictions from France would not be complete without taking into account the thousands sent to the North African infantry battalions between 1889 and 1939 – and in a wider sense, the deportations within and between French colonies, such as French Indochina.

All these examples of imprisonment-cum-work may belong to the past, but some countries are notorious for the number of inhabitants they detain in prison, with the US prime among them. The particular significance of imprisonment in the US until today and, in particular, the predominance of ethnic minorities detained, may be explained to a great extent as a long-term legacy of erstwhile slavery. After Abolition in 1863, African Americans ran a tremendous risk of being incarcerated. White convicts nearly vanished from the prisons in the southern states, which not only extended their capacity dramatically but were now 90–95 per cent occupied by African Americans.[66] They had to work hard and were employed on public works and leased out to industries and mines, such as the iron and coal mines of Alabama and Tennessee during the 1870s to 1890s or the turpentine industry of southern Georgia and northern Florida. No wonder that during the 1880s average death rates in southern prisons were almost three times as high as in the north. State convict systems had ended by the 1920s, but the parallel system of debt peonage, again predominantly of African Americans, has an even longer life in the American South.[67]

South Asia offers another notorious example of the tenacious survival of unfree labour. Although the British had abolished the slave trade and slavery in their colony in the mid-nineteenth century, various estimates indicate that, still today, many millions and perhaps even more than 10 million Indians have to work for their employers-cum-creditors without any rights.[68] Like in the Americas (as explained by Tobias Barrington Wolff, p. 310), this is not just a question of people unable to repay their debts; rather – and more fundamentally – it is an issue of employers-cum-creditors belonging to a higher caste than their workers-cum-debtors. Moreover, the forebears on both sides of this economic divide also maintained such unequal relationships. Although at that time sanctioned by generally accepted custom, this is no longer the case before the law. Indeed, independent India has a long history of affirmative action for groups down the caste ladder, albeit with limited success.[69]

The practice may have diminished over time but it nevertheless remains vigorous. The fact that unfree labour remains embedded in traditional norms and customs may also explain why numerous initiatives by politicians and social activists like B.R. Ambedkar have still not succeeded in abolishing the phenomenon in India. It should also not be forgotten that, apart from the employers who profit from unfree labour and an upper class that feels little compunction to counteract the problem, unfree workers themselves can play a negative role in maintaining this state of unfreedom. In a study of servants-cum-debt peons (*halis*) in Gujarat, the Dutch sociologist Jan Breman observed a preference for short-term gain, in this case receiving credit, over long-term liberty:

> It is therefore more than doubtful that the *hali* strove to end his attachment. His being coerced to work is usually inferred from the condition that the servant was not allowed to leave his master as long as he was indebted to him. But the debt was rather fictitious in character and, if only for this reason, the term of debt slavery applied to this form of servitude is not very felicitous. Not only was repayment merely theoretical on

account of the *hali*'s minimal remuneration, but it was not envisaged by either of the parties. . . . [The master] tried to keep his debt within reasonable limits, as he well knew he could not recall it. The *hali*, on the other hand, did his best to maximalize it, and tried to get something out of his master as often as he could.[70]

The tenacity of unfree labour relations is not only restricted to regions where slavery once prevailed or where workers are subordinated on the basis of caste systems, like in Mauritania.[71] Even where there is no caste system or legacy of slavery, outsiders and children without adequate protection from family members remain vulnerable – even in Europe and North America, currently the continents with the best labour laws. Think of the 'undocumented' and the thousands of victims among them who attempt to gain entry to the promised lands of the United States of America and the European Union. But also think of children such as orphans and those 'fallen girls' that relatives, poor boards or the parish clergy want to get rid of. In recent years, there has been much commotion regarding cases of forced labour among these kinds of children in Roman Catholic convents, run by nuns in the Netherlands and elsewhere. In Ireland, between 1765 and 1996, over 30,000 girls were put to work, especially in laundries.[72]

The relative decline of self-employment

Two centuries ago, the majority of the working population lived off self-employed work for the market. This applied to all parts of the world, with the possible exception of the Pacific Islands and sub-Saharan Africa, where these kinds of markets remained underdeveloped. In addition, slavery and other forms of unfree labour and wage labour were important. Currently, roles have reversed and wage labour dominates, while unfree labour is much less important (which is not to belittle the fate of its victims) and the relative importance of self-employment has declined sharply, in particular due to the diminished role of smallholder farmers in global food production.

For both advocates of the free market and their opponents, this relative decline of smallholders, artisans, shopkeepers, peddlers and the like seems to have been self-evident and inescapable given the accelerating pace of the mechanization of work. The free market advocates ventured their capital on large-scale agriculture and industry, but then so did the communists. For example, in early 1957, Mao believed that the fate of the eternal Chinese farmer was sealed. Although at that moment China counted only 12 million industrial workers out of a population of 600 million, the Great Helmsman gambled all his cards on this minority:

> The number is so small, but only they have a future. . . . The peasants in the future will become mechanized and will be transformed into agricultural workers. . . . Right now there is the system of ownership by peasant-cooperatives. In the future, in a few decades, they will be changed to be like factories; they will become agricultural factories. In this factory, you plant maize, millet, rice, sweet potatoes, peanuts and soybeans. As for the bourgeoisie . . . they too will become workers. The several hundred million peasants and handicraft workers have now already become collective farmers; in the future they will become state farmers, agricultural workers using machinery.[73]

Not only did the Great Leader's prediction end in disaster, with the Chinese smallholder remaining alive and kicking for decades; globally, too, the self-employed worker is a much more resilient phenomenon than many had believed. The decline in their relative share is undeniable, but it has been slow and happened in fits and starts. In Western Europe, but possibly more generally, there is an important age aspect to the switch between wage dependency and self-employment:

> Up to the end of the nineteenth century, wage labor did not structure the whole life course of the majority of the population. Rather, it remained connected with early stages of the life cycle. Beginning at about 30, most people tried to establish themselves as independent farmers, craftsmen or tradesmen. . . . At age 40–49, self-employed or employers equalled the laborers; after age 50 they outnumbered them considerably.[74]

Peasants and smallholders

We have previously encountered the possibility for smallholders to intensify their agricultural activities on their own farm and to supplement these with cottage industry and wage work for others. This type of household economy – one that is sufficient for most or at least a substantial part of its own nutrition but which also produces for the market – is well documented for thousands of years of Chinese history, for early modern Japan, for the rice farmers with their irrigated plateaus in South East Asia, for the *chinampa* agriculture of Mexico and for the Low Countries, but is also a much more general phenomenon.[75] The large-scale mechanization of agriculture in the US from the mid-nineteenth century and later in other prosperous countries makes it easy to forget that tough but successful smallholders around the world still hold onto their existence.

Emphatically, this is a relative and not an absolute decline, because there have never been as many small farming households as there are at this time, comprising 2.5 billion persons. No less than 85 per cent of the 570 million agricultural farms worldwide cultivate less than 2 hectares and thus are readily defined as small peasants. Nevertheless, they still provide for the majority of the world's food supply.[76]

After all, small farmers in densely populated areas did not have and still do not have the choice to expand their farm, unless they supplemented their income by work in the city or emigrated to regions where land was still abundantly available. Their first option is therefore intensification; that is to say:

> producing relatively high annual or multicrop yields from permanent fields that are seldom or never rested, with fertility restored and sustained by practices such as thorough tillage, crop diversification and rotation, animal husbandry, fertilization, irrigation, drainage, and terracing. I am not talking here about amber waves of grain but about gardens and orchards, about rice paddies, dairy farms, and *chinampas* .... for all of them land is objectively a scarce good, agrarian production per unit area is relatively high and sustainable, fields are permanent, work takes skill and relatively long periods of time, decisions must be made frequently, and the farm family has some continuing rights to the land and its fruits.[77]

This focus on one's own farm in no way precludes active participation in commons, however.

A good example of such a society, where 'skill replaces scale', is the Swiss alpine village of Törbel in Valais Canton in the post-war decades.[78] The smallholders there focus on dairy farming for the market. In the long winters, the cattle must be fed on hay harvested from natural meadows during the summer. In addition, they maintain fields sown with winter rye and garden areas on slopes protected with occasional stone terrace walls. The steepest and smallest plots are tilled for potatoes or broad beans. 'To combat erosion in these canted fields, the Swiss fill baskets with dirt from the bottom of the slope and laboriously carry it up the top every spring. Tiny vegetable gardens planted with turnips and cabbages are made of well-hoed, raked earth in raised beds. The most extensive terracing is on stony slopes near the river, where vineyards are tended with hand tools.'[79] The maintenance of the fertility of the meadows requires great care in order to yield two crops of hay as well as to ensure enough for grazing. Irrigation makes it possible to situate these meadows as high as 2,000 metres. This irrigation system is collectively maintained in such a way that 'das heilige Wasser' (the holy water) is shared equally over the meadows of all participants in the commons.

A comparable organization of the activities of family members and the coexistence of individual and common property rights frequently occurs elsewhere. Take the Kofyar of the Jos Plateau in central Nigeria, who found an ingenious method for cultivating sweet potatoes, yam tubers, millet and sorghum on their small plots of land. To this end, they continuously make and repair ridges and basins to trap water, mounds for the sweet potatoes and conical heaps for the yams.

> Perhaps the most unique element in Kofyar agriculture is their means of restoring and in part creating fertile soil, which involves the transferring of organic material from the wild, the fields and the household to domestic animals, and the collecting of composted manure that can maintain the fertility and soil structure of permanently cultivated plots. During the nine-month growing season, the Kofyar confine their goats to a circular, stone-walled corral about 3.5 or 4.5 m in diameter, standing at the entrance to the homestead cluster of round, thatched huts. The goats are individually tethered and fed with grass cut in the fallowed fields around the village, or, in the latter part of the dry season when the bush has been burned, from the leaves of tree branches cut for the purpose. . . . A daily chore, often for women or children, is fetching the goat fodder and hauling their drinking water from the stream. The animals are fed more than they eat, and a layer of compost or mulch one to two meters deep accumulates over the course of the year, while dung

and urine also build up in the stable hut where the goats are kept at night. Just before the coming of the rains in March, this manure is dug out, loaded into baskets, and dumped into piles on the nearby homestead fields, which resident family members also use for elimination. In addition, during cultivation, weeds are turned under, and millet stalks are systematically buried under ridges. Every traditional homestead has a miniature hut near its entrance where ash from cooking fires is stored. Both fuel wood from the bush and sorghum stalks contribute to the ash, which is applied by the handful to peanut plants.[80]

Like their Swiss counterparts, Kofyar smallholders basically act as private households that mobilize all possible labour power of its members, men and women.[81] At the same time, they sometimes hire additional labour, but much more importantly they regularly engage in communal work with others. When unable to do all the work required for the millet, sorghum or yam cultivation they stage a 'beer work party'. In slack periods, women brew enough millet beer to compensate for the work of forty to eighty neighbours. Sometimes accompanied by a drummer, they collectively perform the job to be done, after which they are served the beer. Next time, it is another household that may count on the same help from their neighbours.[82] Between the more formal *mar muos* (farming for beer) and the small-scale household labour, most households also belong to *wuk* exchange labour groups of between five and twenty members. The members take turns working on each other's fields and are repaid with reciprocal labour.

Finally, let us not forget how important self-identity is for the self-employed producer. His or her control of the work process prevents, or at least diminishes, feelings of alienation. This is exemplified by the persistence of the small French winegrowers proud to be, or at least feeling that they are, 'their own boss'.[83] The success of the smallholders' households is also due to the ease with which the family's agricultural activities can be combined with household chores as well as frequent off-farm labour to supplement their income, when time allows for part-time employment as craftsmen, traders, artisans and wage labourers.

Despite this persistence of smallholding well into the twentieth century and recent stimuli such as small-scale mechanization and small-scale ecological farming, the global agricultural economy has been dominated for some time by economies of scale.[84] The division of commons in Europe, followed by mechanization and, finally, the state-supported Green Revolution have all played a role in this. Big farmers have long provided employment for temporary and permanent wage workers, but recently the full-time farm labourer in particular has largely disappeared. But that does not apply to peasants, however sharply their share in the total working population decreases.

Craft, retail and services

Just as it is not true that, in the modern world, the disappearance of peasants is inevitable, it is also not the case for craftsmen and other small entrepreneurs in industry, trade and services. Certainly, the emergence of large companies in recent centuries is evident, but, just like agricultural smallholders, the craftsman is a resilient phenomenon.

During the Industrial Revolution in Great Britain, the United States and elsewhere, there was the fear that the artisan himself would disappear and with him his skills. Such concern did not extend to small farmers, but the artisan was directly associated with not only the icons of Western civilization, such as medieval cathedrals, but also the Taj Mahal and other highlights of Islamic and Hindu architecture. Hence, at world exhibitions, the 'old' crafts of past centuries, or from distant lands, were invariably juxtaposed with modern mass industry. This is the basis of the Victoria and Albert Museum in London,[85] but also of the Henry Chapman Mercer museum in Doylestown, Pennsylvania.[86] Not only the competition of the machines but also the decline of the craft guilds in the nineteenth century in most European and neighbouring countries where they occurred, in which expertise was passed on from master to apprentice, was considered culpable (see p. 233).

Even without formal guilds, however, the apprenticeship system was sustained for a long time, in a number of cases to this day, especially in Germany.[87] That certainly applies to the liberal professions, partly in combination with mandatory university diplomas. These constitute closed professional orders everywhere, with strict admission requirements respected by national governments. The quality-of-service argument is the reason why the curbing of market principles is tolerated. Thus, the free establishment of shoemakers, carpenters or shopkeepers is the most normal thing all over the world, but the free establishment of, for example, doctors, dentists and other (para) medical professions, or notaries, is anathema almost everywhere. Migrants in particular suffer the most in this regard. Informally closed markets also exist, such as those of self-employed taxi drivers in many world cities.

This monopolizing of local and national markets of course promotes the continuity of independent professions. In quite another way, diesel and electric engines and, more recently, the computer have also made this possible. Mechanization and automatization were no longer dependent on large investments. Especially in metropolises, with their high demand, this led to extreme specialization. At the same time, however, it also risked the impoverishment of broad professional knowledge. Consider a report from 1861, prepared by Parisian workers for the London exhibition:

> the shawl designer divides up the work between eight different workers: the worker who composes the first design, the one who does the raw drawings, the one who then enlarges them on card, the one who picks out the main lines of the design, the one who checkers the outlines, the one who draws in the details, the one who transfers these details to the card and the one who fills them in. The apprentice becomes highly skilled, but is familiar only with one eighth of his trade.[88]

This division of work took place in the individual workshop as well as between workshops set up by workers throughout the neighbourhood. Thus far, nothing seems to have changed since the rise of the urban craftsman from the Middle Ages. There, too, we saw the specialization and impairment of his independence as a result of subcontracting. But this immobility is a façade, because, as we have seen, after 1850, in large sectors and especially in the big North Atlantic metropolises, artisans lost their independence, in extreme cases to the sweating industry. Their numbers continued to rise, but in the clothing and footwear industry in particular they became completely dependent on middlemen, who supplied them with semi-finished products, and sometimes also their tools and disbursements, for work according to precise specifications. This process is perhaps most accurately described by Charles Booth and his colleagues in his seventeen-volume *Life and Labour of the People in London*, compiled between 1886 and 1897.

According to Booth, self-employment, with or without a small number of subcontractors or wage labourers, was ascendant:

These small units of industry may sometimes be the survival of an old state of things, but by no means always. More often they are the form which the most pushing industries adopt in the struggle for existence. London is no doubt the stronghold of small industries, but London is the greatest of modern cities, and what is true of London is, I believe, not less true of all great cities – of New York and Melbourne, as well as of Paris and Berlin.[89]

Ernest Harry Aves, one of his collaborators, was of the opinion that a general theory explaining the preference for large or small production units, direct employment or subcontracting, time rates or piece rates was impossible, but he made many useful observations, two of which I will quote at length. The first concerns the shifts between wage labour and self-employment:

When only a very little capital is required in order to commence business 'on one's own account', the conditions are apt to be altogether too favourable to the multiplication of the small man. The cabinet-maker, for instance, can start operations, albeit inadequately and insecurely, with only £2 or £3 in hand. . . . Other determining circumstances are found in the nature of the market. If, in a trade in which little capital is required, the market be large, the demand fairly constant, and the buyers easily accessible, and if the practice of the market be to buy, either on order, or from chance producers offering for cash, then in that market will the small producer find his opportunity. By far the most important of such markets are wholesale, that is, when the small maker produces 'for the trade', and not for sale direct to the consumer. But it may be noted that the knowledge possessed by the small maker 'to the trade' that enables him to get a footing, not infrequently involves the somewhat unscrupulous use of information obtained as a wage earner. Thus we are told that in the wire-workers' trade the garret-masters frequently approach customers of the firm they had previously worked for, and offer goods at a considerably lower price. In this way either the order is obtained, or, after the customer has informed the firm of the lower price at which he can secure what he wants, the firm in its turn tells the workmen of the new competition, and prices and wages tend downwards all round. This operation is said to be one of the chief causes of the continued reduction of the prices of 'repeated' orders. Then if the small man does not succeed on his own account, he, to quote from our notes of evidence of a wire-worker (wage-earner), 'again seeks employment, cursing the bad pay and every bad condition for which he and his class are chiefly responsible'.[90]

Aves also had a keen eye for the labour relation between the small self-employed master and his handful of employees:

> *Ceteris paribus*, the small employer tends to impose harder conditions upon his workers, even though they be more irregularly enforced, than does the large employer. And some of the reasons for this are not far to seek. One of the most important is found in the fact that the small master often works himself at his own trade, and, working for his own hand, is apt to measure against his own eagerness the response of others whose interest in the total output cannot be so great as his own. He often maintains a very friendly relationship with the few workers around him, but his capital is small, his business interest is concentrated, and his employees consequently become, in a more intensified form than in the case of a large employer with a wider field of operations to divert attention, the human instruments of production out of whose energy his profits most directly and most obviously come. And the strength of his interest in their labour is reflected in the force and the strenuousness of his control.[91]

According to Aves, cut-throat industrial competition between small masters and the concomitant sweating system 'has been accentuated in a marked degree by the response that the producer has felt himself obliged to make to the popular demand for cheapness – that Janus-faced economic idol; making on the one side for comfort in life, but on the other constituting a shrine before which, though most worship blindly, many human lives have been and are sacrificed'.[92]

Finally, in output terms, big enterprise and wage labour took over in the twentieth century, sometimes under compulsion, as in Russia and China, as we have seen, but in most other parts of the world as a result of the scaling up of, especially, industry and transport, at the same time leaving a sufficient gap in certain sectors for all kinds of sweating and non-sweating practices. These challenges for the self-employed also have political implications, perhaps best exemplified by the Russian Revolution and its inability to deal with this part of the working population. But Western social democracy has also yet to formulate a consistent vision on earning one's living as a small independent producer. In France, for example, the blatant fiscal discrimination of small business as compared to wage earners provided a great boost to the conservative and anti-Semitic Poujadist movement in the mid-1950s.[93]

The return of self-employment and its impact

The demise of independent production was undisputed, at least until a few decades ago. However, with the economic crises of the 1970s, long-held views and practices of planned economies of scale were in question. Not only were many laid-off workers forced to earn a crust as small entrepreneurs, but a neoliberal ideology was rapidly emerging that put the ideal of free enterprise paramount with many consequences for laws and regulations with regard to the organization of labour (see pp. 420–1). Just as the petrol and electric engine had stimulated small industrial businesses in the early twentieth century, so did the computer a hundred years later, albeit mainly in the service sector. In part, this swapped one form of self-employment with another whereby the small retail business was replaced by internet shopping. The development of 3D printing seems to herald yet another phase.

The reduction in the share of domestic work

The position of the working woman in this period was fundamentally changed by a number of developments in medical science. Until the mid-nineteenth century, aside from some privileged areas in the North Atlantic, and much later in the rest of the world, women had many children, most of whom died in infancy. In wretched circumstances, they afforded their babies less care, certainly when this care came at the cost of the other (still) living siblings.[94] Thus, households were small, but women spent much of their life pregnant. In addition to the usual care for the surviving children, food preparation and other domestic chores, the married woman devoted herself primarily to productive work in and around the house. For the most part, this consisted of activities on the farm with the aim of producing food for the household. Step by step, this changed.

Already from around 1500, women were increasingly working directly for the market in the context of the industrious revolution, in particular in Eurasia, as we have seen. Spinning, for the moment, was the most important task added to women's work. This was certainly a widely accepted ideal, but, in the course of those centuries, women also became active outside the house-hold, as excellently illustrated for eighteenth-century Spain.[95] Child-rearing was not just a task for the parents but happened in the community, according to what is called the 'village model', whereby older children took care of younger children, and children were under less direct supervision anyway.

For centuries, this demographic 'model' was little tinkered with, notwith-standing the growing 'industriousness' of working women. Only the marriage age of women, the age difference between marriage partners and the degree of care for individual children could be influenced. The later a woman married, the longer she could gain independent work experience outside the house beforehand. The smaller the age gap with her husband, the greater the chance that a married woman could determine the nature and intensity of her work.[96]

A second step could be taken in the nineteenth century following discov-eries in the field of medical science, such as preventative vaccination and better hygiene. This led to greater numbers of children surviving and, there-fore, an increase in domestic tasks. It has been calculated that 'a baby adds about ten days' worth of tasks to the household per month'.[97] This great demographic transition occurred first in the cities, where there were the worst hygiene abuses and therefore the biggest gains to be made. Since this was linked to economic prosperity, community education got off the ground everywhere at the same time. The consequences for mothers were, on the one hand, that others looked after their children for part of the day, but, on the other hand, that children started working much later and therefore care for them increased.

Another hundred years later, effective birth control made its appearance in the form of the pill, approved by the American Food and Drug Administration (FDA) in 1960. Within a decade, what has been called the most effective invention of the twentieth century spread throughout the world, and some governments even turned it into active propaganda to stop the explosive population growth as a consequence of the demographic tran-sition. This had a dual effect on the work of women. Firstly, they were preg-nant less often, but, on the other hand, care for the few but therefore emotionally and materially expensive children increased sharply, especially when their education became the gateway to social success.

Against the background of these three transitions, we must locate the great shift from married women outside the household to productive labour for the market. In addition, unpaid domestic and educational labour has generally remained an important task for married women and mothers to this day.

From the Industrial Revolution to the demographic transition

As we have seen, the fact that women in or at home could combine productive agrarian or industrial labour with domestic tasks was one of the secrets of the industrious revolution. With the shift of industrial work away from farm and craft to centrally powered factories, this bond was slowly but surely broken. This happened first in England, then in Western Europe and North America, and later elsewhere, particularly in the textile industry, where there were already more working in the home industrial phase than men.[98] Given that the textile industry was much more important than other icons of the Industrial Revolution, such as metalworking factories, we can safely say that, in the first century of the Industrial Revolution, women and children were especially found in textile factories. Incidentally, it was not simply a matter of continuing traditions in a new location – the factory. Generally, women in agriculture and industry earned only half to two-thirds of what men received, but in the expanding industries their average daily wages could be higher.

How were married women in particular to combine both of their main tasks under these new circumstances, and how did the men and society in general respond? A greater number of offspring meant that, in the initial phase of the Industrial Revolution, more children were deployed as soon as they could be used productively, now also in factories with a lot of unskilled work. This eased the work of mothers and, at the same time, meant more income for the household. But women also found more work in domestic service, which, as a consequence, became feminized. There was increasing demand for this as a result of the growth of the middle class, who had more money to spend. This happened not only in Europe but also elsewhere. Around 1900, 15 to 20 per cent of the population of metropolitan India consisted of servants, a sector that was becoming increasingly feminized. The consequence was a devaluation of the status and the remuneration of this occupation. This menialization was certainly also provoked by a strong nexus between low caste and service.[99]

As we will see in Chapter 7, the Industrial Revolution and the tendency of entrepreneurs to continually cut costs, not only by increasing productivity by means of mechanization but also through employing women and children, led to counter-reactions. Firstly, from self-employed artisans who could no longer compete and who tried to stop mechanization, and, subsequently, through their organization in unions, which tried to increase their incomes through the forming of monopolies and the elimination of unfair competition from unskilled people, especially women and children. The bourgeoisie also protested against abuses of child labour, night work and the neglect of the household by women factory workers. Thus, the ideal came into being of the family man, who should be able to earn a decent family income, while his wife devoted herself to the household and the children.

From the demographic transition to the pill:
The heyday of the male breadwinner

For the time being, this led to the overburdening of both women and men. Some fragments from the childhood memories of Mrs Layton, born in Bethnal Green, in London, in 1855, speak volumes here:

> I was my mother's seventh child, and seven more were born after me – fourteen in all – which made my mother a perfect slave. Generally speaking, she was either expecting a baby to be born or had one at the breast.... My father, a well-educated man, was employed in a government situation, working from 10 a.m. to 4 p.m.... My father's position compelled him to keep up an appearance which an ordinary workman, earning the same wages, would not have had to do. He always went to business in nice black clothes and a silk hat.... In his spare time he learnt the trade of a tailor and was able to augment his small salary by doing work for people who knew him and by growing nearly all the vegetables the family consumed. He was a churchman who never missed the Sunday morning service, and he always relieved my mother by taking several of the children with him. In politics he was a Conservative, but was always tolerant. A good husband and a good father up to a point, he left the responsibility of the whole family to my mother. She it was who had to start us all out in life. As our family increased and my father's wages remained stationary, it was neces-sary for my mother to earn money to help to keep us in food and clothing. The clergyman's wife was very fond of her, and always had her to nurse her

when there was a baby born or illness of any kind. My eldest sister had to stay at home whenever there was a new baby at the parsonage, and we took it in turns to take my mother's baby there to feed at the breast three or four times a day, for it generally happened that my mother had a baby dependent on her for the breast when our clergyman's wife had her babies. When my mother was away, my father gave out each morning before he went to his work the portion of food for each of us for the day.[100]

Large families meant not only an increase in household duties, but with the increased prosperity – however modest – housing became better and all kinds of household chores were added, especially in those households that could not, or could only rarely, afford to employ a servant or workman. Resident and nearby relatives had to offer a solution here, where possible, something that was also promoted in the twentieth century as people gradually were able to grow old healthily. Thus emerged the phenomenon of indispensable grandmothers, who held everything together, most acutely, for example, in the Soviet Union, after the first and second world wars.

Of course, households had to be able to afford the luxury of the middle-class ideal of the male breadwinner with his stay-at-home wife. The epitome of this ideal is expressed, for example, by this engineer in the Dutch textile town of Tilburg in the 1880s:

Factory girls cannot become decent housewives, and when the male labourer is lucky enough to marry a decent girl who served in a proper household for five or six years, and therefore knows how to manage a household, in that case this man is very fortunate. However, when the labourer marries a factory girl who knows nothing about housekeeping and will find his house in chaos after coming home, he will go to the pub and destroy himself. The woman plays a large part, and this pleads against women working in factories.[101]

In Western Europe, the chances of working-class families achieving this ideal increased from the late nineteenth century, when, first and foremost, real wages for trained workers increased.[102] It was only then that a better paid, unionized worker could proudly declare that his wife did not have to work and, instead, could ensure a well-kept home and 'washed and brushed' children, whom she would encourage to go to school so that later they could do better than their parents. Thus, the breadwinner–homemaker ideology took hold and women's work disappeared from public life. Of course, this does not alter the fact that productive women's labour was still needed in poorer working-class families, where the expansion of sweating industries and also the demand for women servants offered opportunities. The same was true for poorer farmers and agricultural workers.

Sometimes, the rise of the male breadwinner was interrupted and the trend was even temporarily reversed, such as in the exceptional labour shortages during both world wars and their aftermath. Since all able-bodied men were called to arms in countries with general military conscription, a major problem arose in terms of keeping the economy going – not only in the war industry behind the front, where there was an insatiable appetite for bombs, grenades, uniforms and suchlike, but also on farms, in factories and in offices. In countries such as Germany, as we saw in the First World War, prisoners of war were deployed en masse and forced labourers were also used in the Second World War; in France, it was workers from the colonies, but in England and the US it was mainly women. The English unions spoke of 'craft dilution' and wished to cooperate only on condition that the women would disappear back into the kitchen after the war.

Nonetheless, this mass participation of women in the labour market, however exceptional and temporary, had a long-term effect – not only in terms of the introduction of women's suffrage after the 'Great War', but also through the even more massive participation of women in the Second World War. Famously, government propaganda in the Second World War, in the form of popular songs and posters, aimed at recruiting women to ship-building and other heavy industry, personified by, for example, Ronnie the Bren Gun Girl in Canada and Rosie the Riveter in the US.[103] Even Nazi Germany, which, like many other corporatist countries, had exalted the curbing of women's wage labour as one of the pillars of its ideology (in Germany elaborated by 'marriage loans' for women agreeing to leave the labour force) had to back down on this point in the last years of the war.[104]

The most extreme lack of men occurred in Russia, where the First World War was followed by an equally long period of civil war. Subsequently, the need for women in the labour market continued as Bolshevik state ideology required the deployment of all productive citizens and collectivized family responsibilities.[105] There was not, then, a partial retreat of housewives such as that in the rest of Europe and in North America. Moreover, the post-war communist states of Central and Eastern Europe practised female labour mobilization. In the German Democratic Republic, for example, the female participation rate grew from 64 to 80 per cent between 1960 and 1971, whereas in the German Federal Republic it dropped from 40.9 to 37.6 per cent over the same decade.[106]

No wonder that the Soviet Union was also at the forefront in the field of birth control, though its takeup varied. From 1920 to 1935, induced abortion was legal, and then again from 1955 to 1968 – after a hiatus due to the massive losses in population as a result of collectivization, famines and the 'Great Patriotic War'. The fact that many women resorted to abortion was, of course, also fostered by the want of practically everything that mother and baby needed. The same pattern existed in Eastern Europe in the Russian sphere of influence between 1945 and the fall of the Berlin Wall.

In 1979, China attempted to limit its population with the one-child policy as one of the main instruments of social engineering. This measure, implemented by means of a contraceptive intrauterine device, surgically inserted after having a first child, and sterilization after having a second child, also significantly increased the productive engagement of women.

The last half-century: Dual income couples, single mothers and single women

From 1960, the contraceptive pill quickly became the most popular and the most effective method of birth control in Western Europe and North America. Despite resistance from, among others, the Roman Catholic Church, birth rates fell sharply, which greatly stimulated the entry of women into the labour market, and women's independence generally, leading Harvard Professor of Economics Claudia Goldin to speak of the 'quiet revolution' of the 1960s and 1970s, with expanded horizons for women being a potent reason for the disappearance of early marriages and altered identities, including the retention of their surname upon marriage. Women now more accurately anticipated a career in relation to their formal education.[107] A side effect, which, in turn, led to the need for women to seek an independent income, was the increase in divorce and what is known as serial polyandry.

In terms of the domestic duties of mothers, the emphasis now shifted from household chores to the raising of the admittedly much reduced numbers of children, for whom an ever better education was strived for.[108]

This was also possible as a result of the diffusion of basic facilities such as running water, electricity and the flush toilet and, subsequently, of the 'engines of liberation', such as the electric washing machine, the vacuum cleaner, the refrigerator, the dishwasher and the microwave.[109]

Despite this great concern for upbringing, the (especially middle-class) social norm of domesticity and of the stay-at-home wife could now be definitively broken. We have found earlier motivations to do this here and there.[110] In the US and some Western European countries, from the late nineteenth century to the early 1920s, in addition to factory girls, a group of independent female workers in professions like teaching and clerical work emerged. Most of them, however, left the workforce on marriage due to the considerable social stigma regarding the work of married wives outside the home. Between the 1930s and 1950s, however, constraints on married women's work eased, and not only because of the previously mentioned effects of the wars. Marriage bars for teachers and clerical work – regulations that forced single women to leave employment upon marriage and barred the hiring of married women – until then very common, were now lifted. Part-time work now became possible in certain occupations, too. Between the 1950s and the 1970s, older groups of married women entered the labour market as mothers resumed the jobs they had quit in order to take care of their babies and younger children.

From the 1970s, in the affluent West – affected for the first time since the Second World War by economic crises – the dual income couple with few children has now become the norm.[111] Given the increased number of divorces (see above), however, between 10 and 25 per cent of households worldwide are headed by women. Fathers are out of sight here, and this share is increasing. In Botswana, Swaziland, Barbados and Grenada, 40 per cent of families with children live without a father. Incidentally, given that the contribution of fathers to household income and to the functioning of the family is certainly not always assured, it is possible that children in families with only a mother are better fed than those in two-parent families, as has been shown in, for example, Guatemala, Kenya and Malawi.[112] One of the solutions for women without a steady husband is serial polyandry, as seen in Africa and the Caribbean, as well as among the urban poor in Europe and North America.[113]

Nowhere has the transition of women from the domestic economy to the labour market been so great as in China in recent decades. The migration to major cities also included tens of millions of girls. In the diary and correspondence of one of them, Chunming, born in Hunan in 1974, who, at the age of 18, left for Guangdong against her parents' wishes, we read of both the old and new world in China. Firstly, the new, from her diary entry of 29 March 1994:

> We were paid today. I got 365 yuan. After repaying a fifty-yuan debt, I still have three hundred yuan. I want to buy a watch, clothes, and personal items. How will I have any left over? . . . Summer is here and I don't have any clothes . . . and I must buy a watch. Without a watch, I cannot make better use of my time. As for sending money home, that is even less possible. Next month after we are paid, I will register at the Short-hand Secretarial Correspondence University. I must get a college diploma. I certainly did not come to Guangdong just to earn this two or three hundred yuan a month. This is merely a temporary stopping place. This is definitely not the place I will stay forever. No one will understand me, and I don't need others to understand me. I can only walk my own road and let other people talk![114]

At the same time as she is thinking of a career beyond the plastic moulding department where she works, she is linking up with the old world and writing to her illiterate mother:

> Mother, I have knit you a sweater . . . If I weren't knitting you a sweater, I could have used this day to read so many books. But Mother, sometimes I think: I would rather be Mother's obedient daughter, a filial daughter, and even throw away those books I want so much to read. Mother, I have knit my love for you in this sweater.

These big steps in the shift of the labour of married women are only partly true for women who remained unmarried and childless, partly because they frequently lived in relatives' households and were assigned duties there. Nor did these steps mean that women and men now took care of the housekeeping equally. Income and career chances are currently still better for men than those for women, largely due to the fact that women still more often combine the care of children and the home with their professional lives – although grandparents (increasingly healthy at a higher age) and professional crèches and childcare facilities have eased a woman's tasks substantially. These pay and career differences to the detriment of women are more pronounced in some countries because women have part-time jobs, while in others pregnancy and maternity leave have negative effects on women's careers, including where they are facilitated by the state.[115] Furthermore, recently, we have also seen a sometimes curious reversal of this global trend. In India, women are now dropping out of the workforce as the social standing of families rises, because that means that they are able to stay at home, even with adequate school certificates – a cultural and now increasingly also a political ideal of the Hindutva movement.[116]

The increase in free wage labour

In previous periods, wage workers were still a minority. They were primarily young men and women who hired themselves out during the first part of their work cycle. Think of domestic servants (both women and men, mostly live-in), of journeymen, whether or not living with their masters, of sailors operating in much larger units, and, especially, of soldiers. In addition, there were, of course, civil servants charged with administrative duties on a more permanent basis, but especially also the wage workers in large state-owned companies such as powder factories, arsenals and the mint.

Increase in numbers of wage workers and hours worked

All these categories increased absolutely but also relatively in the nineteenth century. There were more servants and journeymen due to the growing prosperity and thus greater purchasing power of the bourgeoisie, especially in Western Europe. There were more seamen as a result of the increased transport, especially of steamships. But, above all, there were more wage workers employed directly or indirectly by the national state. Think also of the slowly expanding civil service, professional soldiers (also necessary in an army of conscripts) and of the railways and the postal service, increasingly monopolized by states.

The greatest increase in wage labour, however, initially occurred in industry, which recruited its workers from among men who had previously been journeymen, but mainly from among former self-employed small-holders and craftsmen (and, to a lesser degree, from among ex-slaves/serfs), and, eventually, also from among women who exchanged a part of their domestic work for wage work, as we will see (pp. 341–60). Incidentally, the transition from self-employment to wage labour often went very smoothly. Many of them had already been prepared as sharecroppers or via the putting-out system, whereby they wove or spun at home in the service of the same entrepreneur who took care of raw materials, machines and distribution and paid weekly advances on piece wages.

In some cases, the transition to wage labour also meant a shift from collective to individual labour relations. When the Anglo-Persian (later, Anglo-Iranian) Oil Company made preparations for drilling for oil in 1905, it initially recruited from among the Bakhtiari pastoral tribes in south-west Iran.[117] The company agreed a sum of £2,000 per annum with the principal spokesmen of the tribe in return for the supply of 80 guards to protect the drilling sites. Although the guards were supposed to receive 100 tomans (£35¼) per year plus fodder for their horses, apparently the Bakhtiari chiefs had pocketed the oil company's money and the poor guards were left to meet their needs by 'other means'. They only started receiving their wages directly from the head guards in 1909. On top of this institutional obstacle, a real market had to be established outside the old tribal agreements. In the words of the oil company: 'The wages, of themselves, could do little . . . to keep the men in service unless opportunities were provided of purchasing with the wages those commodities and comforts not obtainable in nomadic life. It was not enough to give money; ways of spending the money also had to be provided.' This transition to wage labour has accelerated in the past two centuries, parallel to the transition from agriculture and craft (both of which had many self-employed workers) to industry. In 1950, two-thirds of the world's population were still engaged in agriculture (mainly smallholders) compared to one-third today.[118] Secondly, in addition to jobs in industry, more and more jobs were added to the 'tertiary' sector in trade, transport and services.

Increasing numbers of people started working directly for an employer, whether or not via a manager – and for a long time, for many hours of their lives. As we have seen, the numbers of hours that people were working had been growing since the Reformation in Europe in the sixteenth century, and especially in the Netherlands. In the eighteenth century, a second, more serious and much broader attack on free time took place.[119] In 1754, the Austrian Empress Maria Theresa abolished – with permission from the pope – as many as twenty-four Catholic holidays, despite fierce opposition. Mounted police had to be sent to force Viennese shopkeepers to open their businesses at 11 a.m. on 23 April that year, St George's Day.

In England, without specific legislation, the working year was also extended substantially. Around 1830, earning a living in Britain required, on average, more than 300 eleven-hour days, or 3,300 hours net per year, leaving only Sundays plus seven days at Christmas, Easter and Whitsun for recovery. This number had grown substantially from 2,300 in London and 2,800 in northern England in 1760, via 3,300 in London and 3,000 hours in the north in 1800. This strongly shrinking difference between the capital and the north is explained by the vanishing in London of 'St Monday' – the habit of taking the first day of the week off, especially by men, to recover from the weekend – somewhere between 1750 and 1800. This custom was already insignificant in the north by 1760, where, between 1800 and 1830, we observe the demise of a large number of religious and political festivals. This must have already happened previously in London. In the same half-century, on average, people also started work earlier in the morning, making the working day half an hour longer. Around 1800, people worked, on average, from seven to seven, minus breaks of between one and one-and-a-half hours.

Remarkably, this extension of working hours had already occurred before 1800; that is, long before the advent of mechanized factories, which only took place in England on a large scale from the 1860s. At the same time, it implies that those whose income shifted to factory work were subject to the will of the employer for the majority of their waking life. All this applied *a fortiori* to the rapidly growing number of servants, especially those who lived in with sir or madam.

As we will see in Chapter 7, factory hours diminished from the mid-nineteenth century, initially only very slowly, and subsequently, from the First World War, stepwise and more quickly. Around 1920, earning a living in Britain demanded an average of 2,400 hours, compared to the 1,700 hours required around 2000.

Finally, wage dependency also meant increasingly visible unemployment, because the worker no longer regarded himself, or was regarded by others, as a self-employed person who was simply looking for a new assignment. This earlier version of unemployment was never registered, except sometimes in the context of craft guilds. Rather, now, these were dependents who lost their income as a consequence of decisions by the employer – leaving it to the government to come up with a solution (see pp. 394–5).

The implications of scaling

The massive transition to wage labour meant not only going to work for someone else in their workplace, factory or office, and not at home, for many hours a week, but also doing so together with dozens, hundreds and sometimes even thousands (and in China up to tens of thousands) of others that – certainly after 1900 – one had not chosen to work with oneself, and in other spaces and under other conditions than one was used to at home. We immediately think of relentlessly rotating iron machines in which one could easily lose one's fingers, hand or more, and of dark and stuffy premises. Many of these poor conditions, however, were just as prevalent and perhaps even worse in the cottage industry.

Furthermore, the increase in scale also meant a growth in the potential for industrial accidents, especially in the chemical industry. For example, where traditionally the danger came from explosions in gunpowder factories, whereby sometimes dozens of workers were killed or mutilated, there have been many industrial disasters in recent history, the worst of which may have been in Bhopal.[120] The Union Carbide pesticide plant in this Indian city leaked more than 40 tons of methyl isocyanate gas on 2 December 1984, killing an estimated 10,000 people in the first few days and causing 15,000 to 20,000 premature deaths in the following two decades.

This transition to wage labour in central workplaces was primarily made possible by the availability of central motive power for industrial and transport companies. This led to large companies at transport hubs and to a rapid urbanization that allowed urban workers fewer and fewer opportunities to combine their work with farming. In the history of mechanization, much attention has been paid to famous inventors, such as Watt, Edison and Marconi, but it is all too easy to forget how the state often led the way in innovation, in particular through the army, the navy and the big ministries, and sometimes state-owned companies such as the mint, naval yards or powder factories.

Not only the tools and their motive power but also the worker himself became the object of serious study, especially in the US.[121] One of the first to undertake such a study was the Englishman Charles Babbage (the 'father' of the computer), but the most famous was undoubtedly the next generation's Frederick Winslow Taylor, an American who systematically studied the time required for industrial activities, culminating in 'scientific management', ergonomics and 'human factors' techniques, and with respect to the economy, 'labour economics', 'labour (industrial) relations' or 'manpower economics'. Kindred spirits, as well as Taylor, apparently devoid of any modesty, called such an approach 'The One Best Way'.[122] But not everyone was so sure about it. The Danish-born and highly experienced toolmaker Nels Peter Alifas, the American Federation of Labor's representative for machinists employed in government arsenals and navy yards, explained directly to Taylor why motivated and responsible workers opposed his time study:

> [One means] by which an employee has been able to keep his head above water and prevent being oppressed by the employer has been that the employer didn't know just exactly what the employee could do. The only way that the workman has been able to retain time enough in which to do the work with the speed with which he thinks he ought to do it, has been to keep the employer somewhat in ignorance of exactly the time needed. The people of the United States have a right to say we want to work only so fast. We don't want to work as fast as we are able to. We want to work as fast as we think it's comfortable for us to work. We haven't come into existence for the purpose of seeing how great a task we can perform through a lifetime. We are trying to regulate our work so as to make it an auxiliary to our lives. Most people walk to work in the morning, if it isn't too far. If somebody should discover that they could run to work in one third of the time, they might have no objection to have that fact ascertained, but if the man who ascertained it had the power to make them run, they might object to having him find it out.[123]

Frank Bunker Gilbreth and his wife Lillian Moller Gilbreth positioned themselves alongside and, in part, opposite Taylor with their motion studies. In his *Motion Study* from 1911, Frank Gilbreth made a detailed analysis of the movements of bricklayers and of the collaboration between bricklayers and hodmen. In particular, the height of the scaffolding with respect to the wall under construction (to be precise, 'twenty-four inches above where the bricklayer stands') and of the platform on top of it, where the bricks and cement stand ('three feet above where the bricklayer stands; that is about one foot higher than the top of the wall where the brick is to be laid'), ensure that the bricklayer can work upright and this, in turn, leads to much greater labour productivity. Gilbreth even boasts that 'the workman's output can always be doubled and oftentimes more than tripled by scientific motion study'.[124] This increase would lead to both a reduction in costs for the employer and a wage increase for the bricklayer employed on piecework.

In contrast to Taylor, the Gilbreths realized that this outcome was not guaranteed for everyone and that the unions feared that extremely high outputs per man may, as they call it, 'work all of their members out of a job'. Although the unions were well aware that increased productivity generally led to a reduction in general living costs, and they were certainly not against that, they did not want their local organization to pay the consequences. Monitoring of the correct piece wage rates and of access to specialisms seemed, to them, a safer strategy.[125] No wonder that Lillian Moller Gilbreth, mother of thirteen children, also applied scientific management to home-making. Her famous *Kitchen Practical*, a design for a modern kitchen with electrical and gas appliances, was based on the methods of scientific management in order 'to free up their time for paid work, to integrate male family members into the performance of domestic tasks, and to demonstrate that home life and work life were analogous spheres, both requiring management skills and human practices'.[126]

Scientific management was indeed applied by its protagonists and further developed in practice by entrepreneurs such as Henry Ford. The Americans conveyed their ideas worldwide and they were eagerly received almost everywhere, especially later by belligerent states.[127] In some countries, national schools of scientific management emerged, with socialists playing an active role, such as in France. The most famous is the popularity of these kinds of ideas in the Soviet Union. Lenin, Trotsky and Stalin were proponents of it. Indeed, in a speech published in the daily *Pravda* in 1918, Lenin characterized Taylorism as a system that blended: 'the refined cruelty of bourgeois exploitation with a number of most valuable scientific attainments. ... We must introduce in Russia the study and the teaching of the Taylor system and its systematic trial and adaptation.'[128] This popularity also applies to other dictatorships, incidentally, such as Italy under Mussolini, and Germany under Hitler, the dictator who singled out Henry Ford for praise.

The rise of labour sciences, occupational physicians, company doctors and departments for personnel issues and human resource management fits within this same framework.[129] From the employer's perspective, this concerns efforts not only to make workers work as efficiently as possible, individually and collectively, but also to select the best possible workers and, once found, to bind them to the company. To this end, internal career paths

opened up in large companies. Here, as in the case of efficiency, the government once again set the example with the ranking system in the army and
the promotion of good soldiers to non-commissioned officers. Modern
employers are doing well in this respect given the average employee tenure
in many Western countries of roughly ten years. This means that, on average,
employees only change employer a few times in their working life. Such
commitment to the company varies per country, however. It is strongest in
Japan, followed by France and the Netherlands, but much lower in the US,
Canada and Australia (with an average employee tenure of around seven
years). In the US, it was a long time before the traditional hiring and firing
by the foreman was replaced. Under the influence of scientific management,
welfare initiatives and vocational schooling, personnel (later renamed
'Human Relations' or HR) departments became the rule in big industry in
two waves, in the two world wars – partially to take the wind out of the sails
of the trade unions, partially to accommodate them.[130]

Consequences for the autonomy of the wage worker

The most drastic change for industry workers was that increasing numbers
of them could no longer work at home and therefore completely at their own
discretion, but instead had to carry out the orders of others every day in
factories and offices. They could not even determine their own time any
more, because of the imposition, standardization and initial extension of
working hours.[131] This transition was more gradual in some countries than in
others. In Britain, time discipline was imposed on factory workers by locking
out those who did not show up punctually. A female winder in Preston,
Lancashire, reported to her union in 1915: 'On Monday morning when
I went to work I had just got my foot on the threshold of the door when
the door was slammed to and my foot was caught between the door and the
door jamb. I pushed the door open with my hand and as I entered the
manager was standing there who said to me: "Outside – you are not coming
through". Bolting out latecomers must not be interpreted merely as a display
of authority, because the same or an even better effect could have been
achieved by imposing severe fines for tardiness. Instead, it seems to have
been the logical consequence of British factory owners' and workers' mutual
perception of their relationship: 'Shutting workers out did not lay claim to
the labor power lodged in the person of the offenders but treated them as

though they were contractors [as in the traditional putting-out system] who had not taken due care to meet delivery deadlines and therefore deserved suspension of the contract. The struggle was over the acquisition of the product.'[132]

In nineteenth-century Germany, by contrast, many textile factories did not yet have fixed start and finish hours. Unpunctuality was rather treated as a denial of labour power, which could be counterbalanced by fines. Already in 1812, workers in the wool industry in Düren on the lower Rhine had to register by way of minute-by-minute check-in clocks. And textile mills in Germany extended this use of punch-in clocks at the turn of the century. On the other hand, as soon as a worker made his or her labour power available to the employer, he was accordingly 'at work' at all times on site. Workers claimed that this included, for example, when making coffee, changing their clothing, waiting for materials and receiving their pay (in 1906, mill workers in Mönchengladbach even requested that their pay be brought to them at their machines). Such claims became accepted and offered a first step toward demands for payment for vacation time in Germany.[133]

No matter which system was implemented, clocks became important everywhere that work was centralized. There are sporadic examples of this already before the advent of factories, such as in Leiden, where in 1516 a clock tower was built to keep fullers' servants in check, or the VOC shipyard in Amsterdam, which had a work clock hanging above the central entrance gate for the 1,100 workers.[134] Classic English factories also all had large and clearly visible clocks, and the idea was also exported to the colonies. In 1850, a clock tower was built at the workshops in Roorkee (north India), erected especially for the building of the Ganges Canal, which occasioned Director Proby T. Cautley to give the following appraisal: 'this item being indispensable for securing regularity of attendance. A flag staff on the top of this tower, regulates by the rise and fall of its appended flag, the periods for collecting and dismissing the parties [of ground workers] on the grounds between Roorkee and Mahewar.'[135] Even greater control was achieved in the same classic English factories, as they were often built as a fortress, with a central gate with porters controlling every entry and exit, and all spaces were only accessible via a central courtyard. This also made it easy to control all internal movements. A visitor to a rotunda-like coarse cloth factory at Knightsbridge in 1843 observed: 'On the summit of the building, at a considerable elevation, is a small square room, provided with windows on all four sides. From this an extensive view may be obtained in every direction.' An increase in the size of machines after 1850, as well as the introduction of steel girders and new techniques for supporting weight in the 1890s, permitted the creation of large factory halls which facilitated supervision.[136]

The new dependence on factory workers was most clearly expressed by the fines they risked for poor-quality work, unnecessary chatting and much more. Fines could be deducted from wages for all kinds of behaviours not tolerated by the employer. In view of the completely different ways in which workers in England and Germany defined themselves, they also responded completely differently to this. British weavers categorically rejected these kinds of measures, because, in their eyes, they had a contractual relationship with their bosses, who therefore could only have something to say about the quality of the end product. They thus considered it an inappropriate form of exploitation. In the words of a female Yorkshire weaver in 1890: 'The masters smoke a tremendous lot of four-penny cigars, and the two piece wages [fines] last week were for cigars.' Their German colleagues, by contrast, did not reject the principle, but constantly negotiated its fairness and level.[137]

In the course of this process, the dominant pay system shifted from piece wages (collective or otherwise) to individual hourly wages, and from group to individual contract – all this under the influence of the central workplace and direct supervision. The better the employer could monitor the individual employee, the more certain the employer could be about the fairness of the wages paid – at least in his eyes. All this, of course, necessitated a thick intermediate layer of supervisory and administrative staff. Despite the examples cited, this was a particularly American innovation.

How do you motivate a worker who has lost his autonomy?

Naturally, the loss of independence for the person working in a factory has radical consequences for his or her motivation. Dancing to someone else's tune in exchange for an income is one thing, but doing your best, or your extra-best, is something else entirely. No wonder that, after their liberation, most slaves became peasants or self-employed artisans rather than wage workers, as we have already seen (p. 309). They had heard enough commands.

In order to better understand the transition from self-employment to wage labour and the associated shift in motivation, we must first consider the question of what, given the need to earn a living, motivates a self-employed person to do his best. It is pleasure in the work and professional pride. And competition also plays a role in the latter, especially among young people. Consequently, the question arises: to what extent does this also apply to wage labourers?

According to the Tillys, an employer, as we have seen in earlier periods, has three types of incentive at his disposal: compensation ('the offer of contingent rewards'); commitment ('the invocation of solidarity'); and coercion ('threats to inflict harm').[138] Of course, these analytical distinctions in no way preclude strong mutual relationships. On the contrary, the Tillys say that these 'threats of harm often concern possible withdrawals of contingent rewards, whereas long-term threats and rewards shade over into invocations of solidarity. Behind "Do a fair day's work and you'll get a fair day's pay" or "Doing good work will bring honor to your family's name" lurk implicit threats: "If you don't do a fair day's work, you'll be fired" or "If you do poor work, your parents will know about it".[139] A slave owner or a superintendent in a concentration camp is more likely to reach for the means of coercion, but with the help of the whip alone, he does not get much done. That is why he will also try to get more and better work done by providing slightly better food and by granting all kinds of small privileges. Perhaps, sometimes, it will even be a pat on the back or a compliment. An employer with free wage workers, on the other hand, will try to foster motivation through wages, but he will also use many other ways to try to encourage commitment and, ultimately, he also has forms of coercion available to him, albeit within the law, if only the right to fire someone.

We find a specific mixture of all three types of incentives in the Kimberley diamond fields in South Africa. The De Beers Consolidated mining company first gained experience with a closed station for the hundreds of convict labourers it hired from government. This experience was, in the eyes of the management, positive in almost every aspect: convict labourers were more disciplined than free wage labourers, they cost less, were cheap to maintain by economies of scale and could be prevented much more easily from stealing diamonds than their non-convict counterparts. By 1889, urged to keep miners together for capital-intensive underground production, De Beers had decided to accommodate all its 10,000 free (that is, non-convict) African miners in closed compounds. The general manager, Gardner Williams (immigrated from the US), explained the advantages of this to his shareholders: 'Our natives are better housed and better fed than uncompounded natives and are better paid than miners in any of the European countries. Those unfit for work, either through sickness or on account of injuries received in the mine are taken free of cost in the Company's hospital which adjoins the compound. There are fewer accidents under the present system than there were [earlier on] in the open workings.'[140] Let us take a closer look at these three forms of labour motivation with respect to wage labourers.

Compensation

One of the main implications of paying an hourly wage is the need for much more monitoring of individual performance. How else can the performance of the individual worker be determined? As previously seen, the large employer's answer came in the form of supervision of time work, rather than promoting labour productivity through piece wages. In its turn, scientific management emerged from this increased supervision. Remarkably, there are enormous differences in the need for control across industrialized countries, which cannot be easily explained. In 1980, the number of clerical, service and production workers per manager (that is, administrative and managerial workers) varied from between five and ten in the US, the UK, Canada and Australia, between twelve and nineteen in Scandinavia (except Sweden), Austria, Belgium, France and Japan, and between as much as twenty-two and twenty-eight in some other European countries. These variations in 'span of control' cannot be related directly to variations in piece and time work, as can be demonstrated by the cases of neighbouring Norway and Sweden, where close to 60 per cent of all hours worked in industry were on piece rates. However, the national span of control in Norway was 11.4 production workers per manager compared with more than double (25) in Sweden.[141]

The obvious question is why piece rates, if they require lower supervision costs, have not become more dominant than time wages. Union resistance is one reason (see below, 7b), but another, perhaps even more important, factor is the fear among workers of rate cutting. Workers have two strong weapons against this threat but tend to favour a submaximal productivity level: deliberate go-slows, and a desire to ensure the 'avoidance of the sanctions suffered by the rate buster, who will at best be ostracized, thus acquiring a reputation with management for being hard to get along with, and will at worst be physically attacked by his workmates'.[142]

In this discussion about compensation and the advantages and disadvantages of time and piece wages, we can usually assume that, as a rule, workers are paid in cash. And, in general, this is true, certainly in industry, but to induce workers to perform even better, extras were sometimes provided, primarily in the form of stimulants. In the Northern Hemisphere in the nineteenth century that was often spirits, such as gin or vodka. In the twentieth century, synthetic products also became available. An extreme example is the provision of these products to soldiers. The German Army made massive use of the drug Pervitin (methamphetamine, comparable in effect with crystal meth) during its invasion of the Netherlands, Belgium and France in May 1940 and later during the war against Russia. In this Blitzkrieg, tank crews and infantrymen could remain awake and deployable for 48 hours.[143] Although not in the same degree as in wars (think of the Americans in Vietnam), strong drink and drugs are still very much sought after in arduous professions, such as among truckers or sex workers.

Compensation according to individual performance may have a positive effect on labour productivity, but like the Russian commitment schemes that we will encounter below, competition could get completely out of hand, as was the case at the infamous Texas-based energy company Enron. Inspired by the economist Milton Friedman and by the biologist Richard Dawkins and his *The Selfish Gene*, the company's CEO, Jeff Skilling, later imprisoned, instigated cut-throat competition within his company. The Dutch primatologist and ethologist Frans de Waal believes this is an example of the misinterpretation of evolutionary biology:

> Skilling set up a peer review committee known as 'Rank & Yank'. It ranked employees on a 1–5 scale of representing the best (1) or worst (5), and gave the boot to everyone ranked 5. Up to 20 percent of the employees were axed every year, but not without having been humiliated on a website featuring their portraits. They first were sent to 'Siberia' – meaning that they had two weeks to find another position within the company. If they didn't, they were shown the door. The thinking behind Skilling's committee was that the human species has only two fundamental drives: greed and fear. This obviously turned into a self-fulfilling prophecy. People were perfectly willing to slit others' throats to survive within Enron's environment, resulting in a corporate atmosphere marked by appalling dishonesty within and ruthless exploitation outside the company. It eventually led to Enron's implosion in 2001.[144]

Commitment

Commitment can be achieved and encouraged in many ways, and this does not even have to be done by the employer. Intrinsic pleasure in work and its enhancement is easily achieved by, for example, singing during work performed collectively. In an analogy of military music and music during sport, Gilbreth notes that: 'The singing of gangs at certain kinds of work, the rhythmic orders that a leader of a gang shouts to his men, and the grunting in unison of the hand drillers, show the unifying as well as the motion-stimulating effect of music and rhythm.'[145] He also gives examples of playing the phonograph, playing music and reading out loud as highly effective for the 'silent trades', and cites an example of a German who reads out loud to Mexican tobacco packers.

Extrinsic motivation enhancement without direct compensation is epitomized by the army, which provides a workplace where occasional pats on the back take the permanent form of epaulettes and medals. But medals also occurred away from the battlefields and the barracks. It is probably no coincidence that in nineteenth-century Russia, where serfs were already difficult to motivate, medals were also pinned outside of the army. This tsarist tradition was expanded under the communists, who, partly for idealistic and partly for purely economic reasons, were constrained in terms of applying unlimited individual compensation.[146] Incidentally, communist leaders were also inspired, if they were not having their hands forced by what was going on abroad. We have already seen Lenin's positive opinion of Taylorism, but now there was also admiration, which soon turned into fear for Italian (*Dopolavoro*) and German (*Kraft durch Freude*) mass organizations.

Under the rubric of socialist competition during the first Five Year Plans, labour productivity was stimulated by individual piecework and by bonuses and privileges like housing, 'deficit goods', educational institutes and sanatoria. So far, so good, but besides these material rewards, commitment was honoured by way of special flower-laden tables in factory canteens, and the most outstanding achievements were rewarded with medals like the Sovnarkom (Council of People's Commissars) state prizes, the Order of the Red Banner of Labour, and – the highest of all – the Order of Lenin. By publishing their names in the national daily *Pravda*, the recipients of these medals became an example for others.

Challenged to mark International Youth Day on 1 September 1935, Aleksei G. Stakhanov and two assistants attempted an over-fulfilment of norms in the Central Irmino mine in the Donbass coal region. Starting at 10 p.m. on 31 August, Stakhanov managed to cut 102 tons of coal with his jackhammer during his 6-hour shift, or 14 times his shift norm. This was a well-orchestrated event, which included the presence at the coal face of the editor of the mine's newspaper. Stakhanov earned 200 roubles, instead of his normal wage of 23–30 roubles, for his efforts, but that was only a minor detail, as became clear very soon. Immediately after this achievement, at 6 a.m., an extraordinary meeting of the local party committee was convened, which called it a world record for productivity. Lewis H. Siegelbaum summarizes this remarkable session in his book on Stakhanovism:

> Stakhanov's name was to be prominently displayed at the mine's honor board; he was to be given a bonus equal to one month's wage; an apartment among those reserved for technical personnel was to be made available to him and his family, and it was to be equipped with a telephone and 'all necessary and comfortable furniture'; the miners' union was to provide Stakhanov and his wife with passes to the cinema and live performances to the local workers' club, and places at a resort. A special meeting for hewers, with obligatory attendance by sectional party, union, and managerial leaders, was to be addressed by Stakhanov, and sectional competitions for the best emulator were to follow. Finally, 'all those who try to slander Stakhanov and his record' were warned that 'they will be considered by the party committee as the most vile enemies of the people.'[147]

Much more than the individual achievement of Stakhanov, this famous case reveals how commitment was orchestrated from above, with the clear purpose to stimulate emulation. And this was exactly what happened, nationwide after *Pravda* – instigated by the People's Commissar for Heavy Industry Ordzhonikidze – started to report about this record and, within a fortnight, coined the term 'Stakhanovite movement', and 'recordmania' swept the country, peaking in November 1935. Stakhanovite brigades sprang up, assembled among workers who had already distinguished themselves, and closely resembled the shock brigades of the late 1920s, followed by the All-Union Conference of Stakhanovites and Stakhanovite schools (on-the-job training courses by leading Stakhanovites). This movement appealed especially to young males, whereas women were less likely to become Stakhanovites than men:

Let's say that I have a mother and a wife. My mother is old and cannot work in the kolkhoz, but she can work around the house and take care of the children. Now, in this case, I and my wife can both work quite easily, put in all the work-days we are supposed to, and thereby become Stakhanovites. But you on the other hand are married, your wife had several children and there is no grandmother in the house to take care of them. Then, your wife cannot work very much … But my wife, who has an older woman in the house, can be a Stakhanovite and get a little suckling pig.[148]

But those who did, like Pasha Angelina, the first female tractor brigade leader, attained rock star status. Her commitment, not only to shock work, is illustrated by the following *chastúshka* (a humorous folk song with high beat frequency) that she recited:

Oh, thank you dear Lenin.
Oh, thank you dear Stalin,
Oh, thank you and thank you again
For Soviet power.
Knit for me, dear mama
A dress of fine red calico.
With a Stakhanovite I will go strolling,
With a backward one I don't want to go.

No wonder that she complained to the Tenth Komsomol Congress that she often was surrounded by a hundred people shaking her hand and pulling at her jacket.[149]

The great risk of this recordmania was, of course, rate busting: over-achievement in a piece rate system leading to the raising of output norms by the managers. This was most feared by experienced workers, who liked to work cooperatively at a pace that could be maintained also in the long term, with earnings divided among the *artel'*-minded group. But apart from rising tensions between over-zealous persons and the rest, managers were also at risk, because the continuous breaking of records seemingly proved that the previous norms they had set had been too low. Many were accused of sabotage and consequently dismissed, or worse, imprisoned and even executed. It was not long before both 'backward' workers and staff became the victims of indiscriminate and serious persecution. The chaos of this episode has been compared to the revolutionary Persimfans Orchestra, which, in 1917–18, tried to perform without a conductor.[150]

But this kind of competition promotion is certainly not limited to communist systems. Gilbreth also recommended competition to promote labour productivity in the US, so-called athletic contests between teams of bricklayers. He suggested promoting extra interest in these contests by assigning gangs of men of different nationalities to the different scaffolding beds. If this was not feasible, then tall men might be put on one bed and short men on the other, or the single men were pitted against the married men, or eastern 'pick-and-dip' men against western 'string-mortar' men.[151] He thus placed great emphasis on the social cohesion of the members of a team. This he called the commonality of 'creed', by which he meant religion, nationality, and so on. In short, everything that might act as a bond of sympathy between workers, or between workmen and their foreman, superintendents or employer: 'it is a recognized fact that instructions of the foreman or the employer will be more apt to be carried out where there is a bond of sympathy between the employees, the foreman, and the employers'. He goes even further to illustrate this: 'The motions of a bricklayer working upon the wall of a church differing from his own religion are often vastly different from those that he is careful to make when the congregation to occupy it coincides with his belief.' The extreme and excessive attempts to increase commitment that we have seen here in relation to Russia should not make us forget that a pat on the back and encouraging words are much more common, if not universal. These were converted into internal promotion in slightly bigger companies with an 'internal labour market', which were ubiquitous from the late nineteenth century. Instead of recruiting workers from the external labour market, employers prefer to fill internal vacant jobs by offering them to their own workers whom they deem to be promising.[152] In reality, in big companies, this even leads to the planning of a completely internal career, from recruitment to retirement, with one and the same company.

Coercion

Of the three methods for promoting labour productivity and quality, coercion is perhaps the least important among free wage workers, but it is certainly not insignificant. The possibilities for this depend – as with unfree labour – on legal regulations and their enforceability. We can distinguish three forms among free wage labourers: the almost complete authority of the employer with resident staff; the employment contract whose compliance is enforceable through criminal law; and the contract requiring mediation through the civil court. The first two have lost much if not all ground in the last two centuries. Below is a brief overview of the development of these three forms, insofar as they have not been discussed previously.

The view that a live-in employee should obey the employer as a child would obey a father stems from the time when all labour was organized within the household and not via the market. Households could thus exchange children to gain experience elsewhere, but the authority of the head of the household where the child was staying was never in question. In the last two centuries, we mainly encountered this among live-in apprentices, whereby parents or guardians concluded a contract with provisions about pay and a learning trajectory with a boss, over the head of a child. But also among servants, where this learning aspect was much less pronounced, this principle had long been advanced. Think of the late abolition of corporal punishment for servants in Germany.[153]

A variant of this is the labour relation between soldiers and their superiors in the army or between seamen and their (sub-) officers (note the terminology!) onboard ships. We find the last vestiges of this in the form of disciplinary punishments by ships' officers on board ships and in the form of martial law, including in peacetime.[154] As we have seen, in Europe and Europe-dependent areas, the view that a labour contract should be enforceable by the mediation of criminal law dates from the years of labour shortages as a consequence of the Black Death, after the fourteenth century. This did not end in most countries until the nineteenth century (see p. 404).

The alternative view – that a labour contract is encompassed by general contract theory and that any breaches should be resolved as much as possible by good consultation and, when this is not successful, in the civil courts – dates from at least Roman times, but only became valid for larger parts of continental Europe with the French Revolution, and from the end of the nineteenth century the Anglo-Saxon criminal approach was also discarded elsewhere. As always, the ultimate dominance of the civil law approach to employment contracts, and with it the limitation of the element of coercion within the repertoire of work incentives, was a matter of trial and error. In the interbellum, in particular, all kinds of governments once again tried to limit the freedom of labour, as we have seen. Via workbooks, forced employment of the unemployed, extension, denial of social security and, ultimately, forced employment, the governments of Russia and Germany, in particular, forced their citizens and those of the countries that they occupied or controlled into line. For Russia, see, for example, the 1938–39 legislation that recriminalized infractions previously under the purview of the comrades' courts.[155]

Mobility

As the history of work incentives already shows, the freedom of the wage worker is best and ultimately expressed in his ability to switch bosses. This freedom can, but does not have to, involve moving home or migration – moving across administrative boundaries. Where factories and other big employers were increasingly concentrated in large places, the growing opportunity arose to switch employers within the same place of residence or, with improved transport possibilities, to commute.

For tens of millions in the nineteenth and twentieth centuries, however, a shift in labour relations primarily meant a shift to free wage labour (for the mobility of unfree workers, see pp. 309–10) as well as geographic mobility, and the same was true for wage labourers who changed jobs. The wage worker voted with his feet by looking for better employment conditions or, in cases of unemployment, work elsewhere. Whether mobility and migration meets with success is, of course, an entirely different question. Even a temporary deterioration of employment conditions could prove acceptable in this regard, as was the case with indentured labourers. But, for all kinds of reasons, not everyone leaves as a result of mass dismissal and consequently massive unemployment, which is how 'rust belts' can arise.

Mobility levels, already substantial in different parts of Eurasia in the early modern period, as we have seen in Chapter 5, doubled in the second half of the nineteenth century and even tripled by comparison in the first half of the twentieth century, only to drop substantially later.[156] This may not come as a surprise if we think of the well-known mass migrations from Europe to the Americas, especially from the 1840s, once steamships diminished transportation costs and risks. However, equally important were the not-so-well-known migration flows of 'coolies' from South Asia and the colonization of Manchuria. In East Asia, mass migrations became possible after the opening-up of China, Japan and Korea. To these three waves of permanent mass migration and many more minor ones we must still add the temporal (at least for the survivors) multi-annual mass migrations of soldiers, mostly drafted since the French Revolution. Even more important than this long-distance mass mobility were the effects of urbanization, which caused major shifts from self-employment in agriculture to wage labour in industry and services. It gained momentum in Western Europe from as early as 1800, and in the US somewhat later. Both experienced urbanization levels (that is, the proportion of inhabitants of cities over 10,000 inhabitants) of 30 per cent, in contrast to 13 per cent for the world as a whole in 1890. Together, they explain the all-time high in mobility in the first half of the twentieth century. In both parts of the rich world, we see temporal returns to isolation, first after the First World War and, finally, at the beginning of our own century. An intermediate form of temporal migration is the temporal allowance of pure labour migrants from whom all rights of the native populations are withheld. This occurs everywhere, but notorious in this respect are the Gulf States.[157]

High mobility gained pace in other parts of the world later than in Europe and North America, and, finally, in China from the 1970s onwards. After several state experiments with immobilization and the simultaneous allocation of labourers to specific projects (as already discussed), labour migration to the east coast has been massive in recent decades, although, much like in the Gulf States, without offering essential social rights to these migrants. The Chinese American journalist Leslie T. Chang has written a masterly portrayal of the many 'factory girls' among them, exemplified by Lu Qingmin, or Min, originally from rural Henan province, who migrated 1,000 km south in 2003, at the age of 16, to a factory in Guangdong province:

> In the village where Lu Qingmin was born, almost everyone shared her family name. Ninety households lived there, planting rice, rape, and cotton on small plots of land. Min's family farmed half an acre and ate most of what they grew. Her future appeared set when she was still a child, and it centered on a tenet of rural life: A family must have a son. Min's mother had four girls before finally giving birth to a boy; in those years of the government policy limiting families to one child, enforcement was lax in much of the countryside. But five children would bring heavy financial burdens as the economy opened up in the 1980s and the cost of living rose. As the second-oldest child, Min would bear many of those burdens. ... In the late 1990s, both of Min's parents went out to

work to earn money for their children's schooling. Her father worked in a shoe factory on the coast, but poor health drove him back. Later her mother went out for a year. Min boarded at a middle school in a nearby town but returned home every weekend to cook and wash clothes for her father and the younger children. Almost all the young people in her village had gone out. When Min was still in middle school, her older sister, Guimin, went to work in a factory in Dongguan. . . . Guimin came home for the 2003 lunar new year holiday and took Min away with her when she left. Min had one more semester of school, but she wanted to save the tuition and get a jump on the job hunt. She was thrilled to be leaving home; she had never ridden on a train or seen a factory.[158]

※

This first chapter about the last two centuries is entitled 'Converging labour relations' because free wage labour has been gaining pace worldwide at the cost of all other types of labour relations, whether unfree labour (which tenaciously held on until 1900 and sometimes subsequently flares up again to this day), independent production or work within the household. At the same time, and mainly in the last century, the non-working part of the population, whether babies or children still at school and pensioners, also gained weight in society, as we will see in Chapter 7.

This important shift in labour relations received a significant boost as a result of what is called the Industrial Revolution or Revolutions. Consequently, an increasing number of workers were no longer able to perform tasks according to their own plan in a closed peasant or artisanal household, but instead worked in larger units with others and under the direct supervision of another worker, or a boss or his staff. The motivation to work, to work hard and to work according to a plan has therefore shifted to the employer or his ever-growing number of assistants and managers.

These persons, most of whom are also wage labourers but with a different status, are confronted with the problem of which mix of work incentives to apply in a given situation in order to make workers perform optimally. Compensation by means of wages seemed to be preferable and therefore gained weight, but both commitment and coercion remained in the mix. The fact that this mix was necessary – rather than simply sheer coercion, as commands most of the attention in classical labour history – testifies to the role and influence of workers, now cooperating as labourers in much larger numbers than was the case previously in their households. Testimonies of working women, men and even children now become abundant, and these receive more detailed attention in the next chapter. They represent self-conscious persons, proud of their work but also deeply convinced that they deserve better. Think of the former slave Mary Prince, or of Mrs Layton, Chunming, Lu Qingmin, or the exalted Pasha Angelina. Add to this compassionate observers such as Booth, Aves and Alifas, or empathetic scholars like Netting. And let us not forget those on the other side, like Brassey, Taylor or Gilbreth, interestingly accompanied by Lenin and Mao.

The behaviour and feelings of working people described in this chapter provide the framework for the next one, which, chronologically, runs parallel. In it, we will follow in particular the wage labourer in his efforts to defend his position vis-à-vis powerful employers. This does not happen in a vacuum but in the framework of states, which assume different tasks in regulating the labour market, from extreme abstention to extreme centralist organization, leaving the welfare state after the Second World War somewhere in between these extremes.

7

THE CHANGING SIGNIFICANCE OF WORK, 1800 TO NOW

The crucial changes to labour relations in the last two centuries, described in the previous chapter, had a number of implications. These are related to the massive shift of work from within households to outside and, consequently, the increased need to publicly regulate work and labour relations. The three most important implications of this are: the changed meaning of work and free time in people's lives (pp. 363–75); an entirely different self-organization of, in particular, the increasingly dominant group of wage workers (pp. 375–97); and the continuous amendment of labour legislation and regulations (pp. 398–421). These three implications are the focus of this chapter.

Due to the global shifts in labour relations from unfree to free labour and from self-employment to wage labour, the significance of work changed and there was increased space for other activities in people's lives. A contributing factor in this regard was the gradual shift in the last century from heavy

Azerbaijani cotton worker and politician Basti Bagirova at the cotton harvest in 1950, the fifteenth anniversary of the Stakhanovite movement.

manual work to lighter mechanized work and to intellectual work. The income from self-employment and wage labour increased slowly but surely and with it grew free time and the opportunity to consume. Life became more than just a vale of tears; that is to say, improvement came within reach of more than just the happy few. It became worthwhile to invest in training and education, and thus the lives of children became more important. Children went to school more and therefore went to work later.[1] More and more people reached a stage in life where they could not or even did not have to work. All this led to leisure becoming more important, initially in rich countries and more recently in many other parts of the world.

These changes and shifts did not happen automatically. Various groups of working people and, in particular, wage workers, have made a major contribution to this, individually and through self-organization. Initially building on the self-organization experiences of self-employed craftsmen and their helpers and the experience of 'spontaneous' collective movements, including strikes by all kinds of workers, the workers' movement developed and, in particular, the trade unions. A key stimulus for this was the international and soon-to-be global exchange of ideas and experiences.

Collective actions and organization were not limited to the employer–employee relationship. After all, under the influence of these major shifts, labour laws and regulations had to be constantly adapted. From rules within the household regarding parents, children and slaves, they became increasingly public and shifted from being local to national and, ultimately, international. The employment contract and remuneration, job placement, workers' right to association and to meet, and legislation in the area of working conditions and social security increasingly determine the lives of working people.

The growing national legislation with respect to work and, simultaneously, the steady democratization have enhanced the role of the state in determining the rules around the labour market and labour relations. From this, welfare states of various shades have emerged, but, as recent history is teaching us, not without serious challenges.

Work and leisure

The long-term tendential global shifts in the last two centuries, from unfree to free and from self-employed to waged labour, have had important implications for the appreciation of work in general and also for different types of work. In previous chapters, we have observed that the elite's demeaning and pejorative opinions on work mean we are quick to forget other, more positive voices, inter alia from urban craftsmen. This positive appreciation of work now becomes much more dominant. Among the physiocrats, agriculture and agricultural work were most highly appreciated. Similarly, the Scottish economist and philosopher Adam Smith still believed that 'the labour of farmers and country labourers is certainly more productive than that of merchants, artificers and manufacturers', although in the next sentence he appears to refute this prevailing physiocratic idea: 'The superior produce of the one class, however, does not render the other class barren or unproductive.'[2] In the nineteenth century, the emancipation of industrial versus agricultural labour was quickly achieved, though moral objections to mechanization, deskilling and urbanization were long-lived and, in a way, still survive today.

From the time of Adam Smith and, somewhat later, the political economist David Ricardo, labour has pre-eminently been considered the source of productivity, and – especially since Karl Marx – as the sole source of value. Communist, socialist, Christian, National-Socialist and fascist propaganda all exalted labour. Moreover, and more generally, in recent centuries and across the political spectrum, labour has come to be accepted as the foundation of society – if not out of conviction then as a necessary result of the fact that universal suffrage has made the working class, conceived of as both important producers and consumers, an important political force for the first time in history.

The combination of continuing occupational specialization and improving labour productivity has had many effects. To start with, there has been an explosion of the world's population, from 1 billion in 1800, 2 billion in 1925, 4 billion in 1975 and 6 billion in 2000 to a predicted 8 billion around 2025. Next, there has been a much slower but, nevertheless, undeniable rise in living standards of the majority, in particular in the twentieth century. This implies higher life expectancies, often lower working hours and the prospect of improving one's social position by social and/or geographical mobility, thus stimulating investments in childhood education.[3]

Consequently, work occupies a diminishing proportion of our life: in comparison to our parents and grandparents, most people nowadays start their working life later and work fewer days and hours during their working life, and an increasing number of us can expect to live a number of years as a pensioner. We must therefore consider more closely the development of working time and free time and the balance between the two over the last two centuries among different types of workers in different parts of the world.

Starting work later

We have previously seen the general rule that children were involved in household activities as soon as possible – little by little and learning by example. That was the rule for by far the largest part of the population and it involved no formal education. Twenty years ago, the anthropologist Barbara Polak described this process for Bamana children in Mali:

> [At harvest] three-year-old Daole begins to pluck beans from the tendrils. After he has filled the lid with a handful of beans, his interest fades. [He] carelessly leaves the lid with the beans lying on the ground and goes looking for some other occupation. Five-year old Sumala looks out for a corner not yet harvested and picks as many beans as will fill his calabash. [He] keeps doing this for more than a half hour. Eleven-year-old Fase has been busy harvesting beans since morning. He works as fast as his father and grown-up brother and only takes a rest when they [do]. Fase is fully competent with regard to harvesting beans. He even takes on the role of supervising his younger brothers and checks their performance from time to time.[4]

Similar scenes can still be found among the poor and the modestly self-employed in countries without efficiently controlled compulsory education, although increasingly rare in the past century and a half. How did this change take place?[5]

We must start at the point when children's work moved outside of the home. Initially, this happened mainly in a family context: the head of the household went to work in a factory or a mine and took with him as many members of the household, including children, as necessary. Consequently, child labour not only came indirectly under the supervision of third parties, but it also became much more visible, especially for critics of the new factory industry. This was further reinforced when employment contracts became individual and children ended up working directly under factory bosses.

As a result, legislation to limit child labour was enacted and, simultaneously, a movement to promote compulsory education emerged. This started with the English Factory Act of 1802, which set a maximum of 12 hours a day for pauper apprentices in textile mills, and which was followed by the more effective and far-reaching 1833 Factory Act. Generally, the effect of this kind of restrictive legislation was minimal, not least because it could be systematically evaded by employers and parents due to a serious lack of inspectors and the ridiculously mild penalties.

Mandatory and free full-time school attendance of the kind seen in mid-nineteenth-century Prussia was certainly much more effective, although only the rise of real adult wages at the end of the century became decisive, because it allowed parents to abstain from using their children to supplement their income.[6] By 1900, most of Western Europe required compulsory school attendance until the age of 12 or 14. This did not prevent child labour in family enterprises, like a peasant farm or a shop, however. Many children still worked before and after school and during school holidays, which were sometimes arranged to facilitate obligations such as the potato harvest in autumn.

On the other hand, based on pure necessity or a weighing-up of interests that many readers may find difficult to comprehend, parents continued to push or even exceed the limits of the legislation. The collaboration of parents with recruiters of child soldiers or in child prostitution is an extreme example of this. Of course, most vulnerable were those children outside the protection of a family, many of whom experienced extremely high mortality rates. Those who lost their mothers – and many women did die in childbirth – ran the risk of ending up in an orphanage and being put to work. Take the example of the demand of cheap, and therefore often, child labour in the white settler colonies. Indeed, London's street children had already been sent to Virginia while it was still a British colony. Later, homesteaders without children in the 'pioneer era' in the American West also had a great need for labour. By 1929, about 200,000 children from orphanages and foundling homes in cities on the east coast had been carried in 'orphan trains' to families in the West and Midwest.[7] But the most extreme type of exploitation of children (mainly) without parents takes the form of child soldiers in a number of countries, especially in Africa and Asia.[8]

Nevertheless, statistics on literacy and school attendance teach us a clear lesson, even if we allow for the possibility of combining working for wages and attending school full time.[9] In the heyday of the British textile industry, for instance, half-time work in the morning and half-time school in the afternoon was common practice. Whereas previously only elite families, sometimes grouped into castes as in the case of the Indian Brahmins and

Kayastha (scribes), had the means and the ambition to postpone work for their children by sending them to school, work specialization and rising standards of living extended this practice to wider sections of the population. In 1800, slightly more than one-tenth of the world population over the age of 15 had attained at least basic education, but by 1900 this had become one-third, by 1950 one-half, and today it is over 80 per cent. This attainment is spread very unevenly over the globe, however, with sub-Saharan Africa and, to a lesser extent, South and South East Asia lagging far behind the rest.[10] The geographical and temporal variations are also broadly explained by something as simple as dependency ratios: 'child labour is surely normal in an economy containing a high proportion of children'.[11]

Concomitantly, we can be sure that the age at which people started to work has risen substantially. In the mid-nineteenth century, worldwide, on average, children went to school for one year, in 1910 for two, in 1950 for more than three, and today it is an average of eight years, with the aforementioned regions still lagging behind.[12] This suggests that, globally, we now start working at around the age of 15, rather than at the age of 7 or earlier.

Working hours and days

As we have seen, where workers can determine their own working time, the boundaries between household labour (with peaks and lulls in agriculture), the care for household members and self-employed work for the market can be quite fluid. Nevertheless, all agricultural societies already had formalized periods of public rest, either in the form of fixed days per week (think of the Jewish, Christian and Muslim traditions of a mandatory weekly day of rest), or in the form of regular festivals (as in the Hindu tradition, including the Kumbh Mela). The two could be combined by celebrating fixed saints' days. On a personal level, people could take days, months or even years off for pilgrimages, as we have seen in the case of the hajj.

These customs and conventions were not immutable, even if they were grounded in religious convictions. We have already seen that, as part of the Reformation in Europe, public free days for religious reasons had been restricted, thus substantially increasing the annual number of working days. The history of working time over the last two centuries has been even more dynamic. The advance of wage labour gave employers a chance to extend working times to unprecedented levels until the counterforce of the organized labour movement brought them down stepwise to all-time lows in the last quarter of the twentieth century, at which point they seemed to stabilize or even increase slightly again. Soon, the same organizations advanced the idea of an annual holiday for wage labourers. The increase in general incomes in the West, especially after the Second World War, made this idea feasible and also attractive for the self-employed and for society in general. Later, it would be emulated elsewhere in the world.

The growth in the number of workdays that commenced during the Reformation continued in England during the Industrial Revolution. The trend towards extending the working year is reflected in, for example, the number of days on which the Bank of England remained closed. In 1761, this was still forty-seven. It had reduced to forty-four days in 1808, forty in 1825, and then it rapidly decreased to eighteen in 1830. By 1834, it was a mere four, namely, Good Friday, Christmas Day, 1 May and 1 November. In addition, Boxing Day (26 December) was not usually worked in England. It took until 1871 for Boxing Day, Easter Monday and the first Monday in August to be added by law. Such a law was particularly revolutionary for England, with its state church, because these days were no longer regarded as religious festivals, but as secular days of leisure, especially Boxing Day. In the cradle of the Industrial Revolution, then, the tide of the ever-increasing work year had turned, at least with respect to public holidays.[13]

Even more crucial, of course, is the length of the working day. Indeed, one of the best-known consequences of early industrialization was the extension of the working day for wage workers in factories, along with a wearying labour of women and children. Inevitably, workers responded with absenteeism, especially on St Monday, when the intoxication of the free Sunday would be slept off. Bosses even tolerated this from good workers.

More structural than St Monday were the legal measures introduced to restrict maximum working hours.[14] Step by step, the infamous 12-hour work-days and the even longer work periods of nineteenth-century factory opera-tives were limited and reduced, first for women and children, and then for men. This happened initially in some white settler colonies like Australia and New Zealand, and later in the North Atlantic, revolutionary Russia and other countries. Preceding the legislation histories of separate countries, this impor-tant first stage was completed with the establishment of the 8-hour working day. In many countries, this occurred during the turbulent end to the First World War. A few years later, a 48-hour (rather than a 45-hour) workweek prevailed in the most important branches of industry in Western Europe.[15]

The labour movement, which for decades had championed the 8-hour workday, vaunted its achievement, in particular during its May Day celebrations. France's socialist prime minister Léon Blum, who dared to introduce a 40-hour workweek in 1936, remarked emotionally that, on the rare occasions when he left the ministry for a long walk through the banlieues of Paris, he saw roads teeming with bicycles, tandems and motorcycles ridden by colourfully dressed working-class couples, who seemed to radiate a natural and simple coquetry about their free time. It was not just that they no longer sat in a pub, or had more time for their family, but, said Blum, 'they had gained a perspective on the future, they had gained hope'.[16]

Ultimately, the radical reduction of the length of the workweek in France in 1936 was not sustainable, but this ideal soon became reality elsewhere. Already in 1940 in the US, and following post-war reconstruction, many European countries adopted a five-day workweek by adding a free Saturday, totalling a maximum of 40 hours. In 2000, France reduced the maximum to 35 hours. In fact, these figures should be seen as thresholds above which overtime (for blue-collar workers) and rest days (for white-collar workers) kick in.

Another reduction of working hours took place with the introduction of paid holidays. The cumulative effect of these three measures – reduction of working hours per day, per week and per year – was most clearly visible in the last decades of the twentieth century. In one of the world's most prosperous countries, Germany, the annual working year has decreased from 3,000 to 3,500 hours in 1870 to 1,500 in 2005.[17]

We should not, however, simply calculate the average number of hours. As we have seen, agricultural work is characterized by sharp peaks and troughs, with harvest peaks seeing workers toiling from the crack of dawn until they could no longer see their hand in front of their face. This was offset by long idle periods, especially in the winter in northerly areas. The occurrence of night work – known to place an extra burden on the human organism – has also increased significantly. Originally, the lack of adequate and cheap lighting meant that night work was exceptional. Bakers were a well-known exception. With the spread of artificial light, however, night work and 24/7 shift work increased sharply, sometimes in the face of long-established taboos.[18] Combating night work was initially also an aspect of social legislation, but it has long been quiet on this front.

Economic growth was the decisive change that led to short-time working in the North Atlantic from the 1950s/1960s. The worker could now buy more with less work. To maintain that purchasing power, the same worker and his or her partner have had to work more hours since roughly the 1980s. Until the 1970s, the number of hours worked per job averaged between 1,900 and 2,000 per year. Subsequently, we see a divergence, and today it is 1,400 to 1,500 in France and Germany, 1,700 in the UK and 1,800 in the US. The gain in Western Europe is the upshot of shorter workweeks and longer vacations.[19] In Japan, the number of hours worked is much higher due to extreme forms of overtime, with all the associated negative health consequences.[20] Whereas for many working people in the North Atlantic work had long been an (admittedly necessary) exception and leisure time had become the rule and the purpose of life, the pendulum now appeared to swing to the other side again.

At the same time, as labour came to be considered as the main if not sole source of wealth, a new distinction emerged. Because of the growing role of education, the esteem for white-collar work grew at the expense of blue-collar work, increasingly considered to be purely manual and therefore menial. Yet, this development was far more striking in Europe and Asia than in the US or other white-settler colonies, with their traditional labour shortages.[21]

We must not lose sight of the fact that this reduction in working time has always concerned wage workers, in particular those working in middle-sized and large companies. Key sectors fell outside of this, namely, the rapidly growing army of servants, who had to be available day and night and satisfy themselves with a few hours off on Sundays. The working hours of the self-employed and the semi-self-employed in the sweating industry echoed this reduction, albeit from a distance.

This initial, and ultimate, trend towards fewer working hours is also visible beyond the richest part of the world, albeit to a lesser extent and with significant delay. The growing chasm between rich and poor countries that, until recently, seemed irreconcilable sometimes makes us forget that there has been a certain shift from work to leisure time in poor countries too. An example of this is the growing popularity of pilgrimages such as the hajj.

After a decline in the nineteenth century, the pilgrimage of Muslims to the holy places of Mecca and Medina regained significance, following the emergence of regular and cheaper steamship connections. Numbers of pilgrims increased after the Second World War, from more than 100,000 in 1950, through around a million in 1974, to 3 million in 1985. Given that the total population of the Muslim *ummah* at the time amounted to 750 million people, and supposing they reached an average age of 50, as many as 20 per cent of them would experience pilgrimage once in their life.[22] In reality, the figure is probably lower, because some of them travelled to these holy sites more than once. Still, the time that Muslims spent on pilgrimages must not be underestimated, firstly because there were many more holy places that attracted pilgrims, and secondly because of the time that such a journey took up.

While before the war, the annual hajj drew approximately 300,000 pilgrims, in 1937 250,000 Muslims visited a shrine in Senegal, several hundred thousands went to a site in the Nile Delta and nearly 100,000 travelled to one in Algeria. It is easy to go on like this, for example by listing the six most important shrines for Shia Muslims outside of Mecca, four of which are in present-day Iraq, but it is much harder to compile historical statistics in this regard.[23]

These pilgrimages took a long time. Indian pilgrims who chose the sea route departed in March and returned in September. Those who had not spent too long travelling within India from their residence to the seaport were away from home for half a year. It was only the introduction of steamships that reduced the total time of the pilgrimage to a few months, and at the end of the twentieth century, the plane cut this to a few weeks. Prior to this, the journey overland from Damascus took a total of three months, and from Cairo it was five.[24]

I have spent some time reflecting here on the significance of the pilgrimage in the life of a devout Muslim. Although the hajj could certainly be combined with economic activities, it is still largely a pastime that must be distinguished from work in the strict sense, but which also cannot be characterized as leisure time. It falls clearly within the obligations that, as noted in the Introduction, Nels Anderson described as 'roles in which status must be earned, and the effort may be highly satisfying. The effort may be equally as satisfying as leisure activity'. The same is true for pilgrimages in other religions. The implications of this for the problem that we are dealing with here – that is, the time when people are not available for work in the strict sense of the word – nevertheless seem limited. The time spent on the hajj is, on average, likely to amount to no more than a few workdays a year for the total world Muslim population.[25] In general, we arrive at an average 'loss' of, at most, one day per year for the one-off great pilgrimages, a few days for the lesser ones that are undertaken several times in a person's life or even annually, and perhaps a week for funerals.

Finally, let us not forget that working hours within the household – in the form both of unpaid work in family enterprises and of classic care and daily housekeeping – were rarely if ever affected by the regulation of working hours outside.[26]

Retirees

Until rather recently, increased life expectancy automatically meant that, on average, people could work more years. Especially in the last century, however, this increase has become so impressive that, for many, a life after finishing a working career has become possible. We can be sure that this applies to a majority of the population wherever average life expectancy passes 70 years of age. As with education, this has happened at different moments in different parts of the world – in Western Europe and its offshoots already in the 1950s, in East Asia in the 1980s, in Latin America and the Caribbean in the 1990s and in most of the rest of the world after 2000, with only sub-Saharan Africa lagging far behind.[27]

At the end of the nineteenth century, men over 65 were still gainfully employed in the most prosperous countries, but 50 years later this had become a minority, and later in that century the age brackets of 60–64 and even 55–60 were to follow this trend.[28] This became possible with the introduction of nationwide pension schemes. They were based on centuries of experience with the mutual pension schemes of small occupational groups – as a rule, of craftsmen, sometimes including their spouses, as we have seen in Chapter 5 (p. 233). At the same time, the positive appreciation of retirement gained ground. Two cohorts of Parisian workers on the point of retirement in 1972 and 1984 demonstrate this shift in attitudes:

> The younger cohort had a more positive view of retirement, either as a mixture of rest, family life and chosen activities (often useful ones), or as a new stage in life with more social, intellectual and leisure activity. Retiring 'early', that is, around 60, gradually became, between the mid-1970s and the mid-1980s, not only socially acceptable, but the new social norm. . . . Retirement was seen as a positive stage of life by the majority of the mature active population.[29]

In recent decades, a counter-movement has started. In many countries, retirement ages are rising again due to the heavy costs of pension schemes. Apart from demographic reasons (a less favourable ratio between active and inactive individuals), this is also caused by the diminishing willingness of governments to contribute.[30] And for the growing number of self-employed without pension provisions, stopping work at an early age is neither an attractive nor a realistic prospect in the light of waning welfare state provisions for the elderly.

The balance between working and free time

The culmination of this was a divergence between the meaning of leisure time and work. Both became more important. On the one hand, free time is highly valued, because it allows you to enjoy (read: consume) your wages. On the other hand, it requires work, indeed hard work. Already in 1884, the Scottish entrepreneur (and later MP) Alexander Wylie pointed an accusing finger at his fellow captains of industry and at economists who, according to him, tried to justify lengthy workdays and unfair social inequality with spurious arguments. Wylie argued that, ultimately, poor workers are just as much the victims of the desire for luxury as their bosses are.[31] That is to say, they spend a disproportionate amount of their wages on alcohol, tobacco and the excessive consumption of sweets, rather than on healthy foods, educating their children or saving it up for less fortunate times via consumer co-operatives, mutual insurance and building societies.

A few years before, Paul Lafargue, the Creole son-in-law of Karl Marx, wrote his passionate and satirical *The Right to Be Lazy* (*Le droit à la paresse*). In this pamphlet, he did not so much defend laziness as the right to free time for workers, which, he believed, could easily be facilitated as a result of the successful mechanization of the previous century. As if intoning a prayer, he concluded his tirade against the exhaustion of the workers with the appeal: 'O Laziness, have pity on our long misery! / O Laziness, mother of the arts and noble virtues, be thou the balm of human anguish!'[32] Instead of consuming what the workers produced, the bourgeoisie should grant them higher wages, which would enable them to work far fewer hours. More optimistic than Wylie, Lafargue believed that the choice for workers would be obvious. Instead, the bourgeoisie – if stubborn – would perish because of their gluttony, their drinking and their greedy, decadent behaviour.

A futuristic echo of this appeal can be found in a statement by the Russian artist Kazimir Malevich, in his *Laziness as the Real Truth of Mankind* of 1921: 'Everything that was done in the past was only the work of man; in the present man is no longer alone, but with machinery. In the future only the machine, or something that is similar to it, will remain.'[33] Now, a century on and a plethora of such predictions later, we know that work has not stopped because machines have taken over. Ultimately, we still work because of our propensity to consume more and better (this also applies to healthcare, particularly expensive in the absence of proper public provisions). The Tillys pointed to this paradox by interviewing adults from forty countries in 1995. The respondents were asked to choose between two options: 'Work is the important thing – and the purpose of leisure time is to recharge people's batteries so they can do a better job', or 'Leisure time is the important thing – and the purpose of work is to make it possible to have the leisure time to enjoy life and pursue one's interests'. A wide variation appeared across countries. Roughly two-thirds in Brazil, the Philippines and Saudi Arabia rated work more important than leisure, whereas half or more in the Czech Republic, Denmark and Great Britain put leisure first.

Particularly striking, according to the Tillys, was the inverted relationship between attitudes and behaviour. 'In other words,' they conclude:

> the more people claim to value work for itself, the less they work; the more they work, the less importance they place on work. Why? One explanation is that as countries become wealthy, two things happen. On the one hand, standards of living rise and consumption is increasingly commoditized, requiring additional income-earning labor . . . to live at a generally accepted standard. On the other hand . . . People are more likely to be working for someone else and correspondingly less committed to work for its own sake. So as nations grow richer their people work more and like it less.[34]

This at least goes for paid work, which invariably maintains a high status. It also explains the motivation of many pensioners to carry on in one way or another. At the same time, it emphasizes – apart from lower incomes – the problems of those outside the workforce, in particular the jobless. In the 1960s, an unemployed English miner expressed his ambivalence to work and leisure perfectly: 'Frankly, I hate work. Of course, I could also say with equal truth that I love work. . . . Nor have I ever met anyone who liked work, or to be precise, liked what blokes such as me understand by the term . . . It would seem clear that it isn't really work that we are talking about, not the thing in itself, but its association.' What this association means is expressed by another unemployed man: 'You felt you were playing part in the community [when working]: it was all right for someone to go to work from nine till six and bring a certain amount home ... You weren't shoved on the scrap-heap, rendered useless ... Well, you might as well be dead.'[35]

Promotion of interests: Individually and collectively

Anyone who works is apprehensive about the deterioration of his or her working circumstances and of the remuneration for that work. At the very least, they will try to maintain the status quo and, if possible, improve it in relation to earlier conditions or compared to others. This promotion of interests occurs individually, but, outside the household and under certain circumstances, also collectively (see, for earlier periods, Chapters 4 and 5).[36] If we concentrate here on the wage worker, then the individual strategy will focus first on the employer and his representatives. For the self-employed, the same applies to their client(s). In both cases, it is ultimately about entering into and complying with the most favourable contractual obligations possible. As we have seen, the choice for education precedes this, as do other household strategies, including marriage arrangements.

The collective strategies of the self-employed, employees and employers – insofar as they are not related to each other – include, firstly, the formation of alliances with fellow sufferers and, secondly, the effective manipulation of public opinion. In the last two centuries, this has also meant a shift from local to national and even international and global. The options in both strategies then vary according to the economist Albert Hirschman's famous systematics between *loyalty* (actions aimed at maintaining the status quo), *voice* (striving for improvement) or *exit* (if nothing helps to openly or secretly evade or circumvent the situation).

This analytical distinction between individual and collective strategies and tactics does not preclude strong links between the two in the life of individuals, as well as at the national level. In immigration countries like, for example, the US, Canada and Australia, the initial predilection of newcomers for individual betterment resulted in a substantially longer working day and year than in their European countries of origin. There, working hours were diminished by the collective action of trade unions and political parties, and, in particular, also by the extension of holidays (see pp. 368–9).[37]

Individual strategies

In terms of individual strategies among artisans' apprentices, servants of small self-employed businesses and wage workers, we should think of strategies to forge a good relationship with the boss and with co-workers, of attempts to keep learning, and of migration. Let us imagine that very concretely. An English working-class boy, who entered the labour market at the age of 10, following the premature death of his father in 1900, had already worked it out, or at least his mother had: 'I went accompanied by Mother to a very well-known second-hand clothes shop in Salford, Herzog by name. I was fitted out with coat, trousers, shirt, stockings and shoes for the sum of four shillings and sixpence, which was a lot of money in those days. ... The following Monday morning my mother accompanied me "looking for work" and we were not long in finding it.'[38] In addition to making a good impression on the boss, the relationship with co-workers also counted. We have seen already how, for example, all the members of a gang of Lippe seasonal brickmakers had a direct interest in efficient cooperation in production (p. 225). This entailed not only working efficiently together but also social skills, as these workers shared food, free time, and also twin cribs during the season; in short, they shared everything, night and day. Every year, before the start of the season, gangs were recomposed anew on the basis of reputation. The best workers could make it to gang leader.[39]

As these two examples show, the way in which one joins a company is already determinative of subsequent mutual relationships. Most people with a job have never seen the inside of a labour exchange or commercial recruitment agency, while others have visited them many times; yet others used to consult adverts in newspapers, and nowadays their job search starts on social media.[40] There are, indeed, numerous ways to find employment, ranging from the very personal to the anonymous. Take Pol de Witte, the son of a Ghent cotton spinner: 'One night in December 1857, Pol's father came home, announcing that his young scavenger had left, and that he would take his son with him from then on. There were two advantages: the pay of 3 francs [to the scavenger] was saved and the boy would learn to work. Pol was nine years old at the time. After vehement protest by the mother and her son, Pol started working next morning.'[41] Personal mediation may be used to solicit a job or an apprenticeship, to enter school (aimed at a particular job or profession) or to switch roles between firms or within a (big) firm. In the latter case, this involves so-called internal labour markets that exist not only in big firms, such as railway companies, but also in large institutions like the army, the navy and the church.[42]

A less personal way of finding a position involves job intermediation by way of professional networks, like guilds, the *compagnonnage*, trade unions and employers' organizations. Essentially, commercial and public employment services or labour exchanges are anonymous. In nineteenth-century Europe, mediation by guilds diminished, only to be partially replaced by similar structures. In central and southern France, for example, some 200,000 *compagnons* embarked on a *tour de France*, travelling between affiliate guesthouses that provided mediation, as well as viaticum if necessary.[43] Similar structures existed in the German-speaking world and, in a way, still exist. In the twentieth century, public labour exchanges gained importance, mainly because of their role in the execution of unemployment provisions. In recent decades, commercial mediation has been ascendant again.[44]

Whereas decisions among co-operative workers about career opportunities were taken independently, workers engaged individually were much more dependent on their supervisors and bosses. In a metal-polishing factory in New Delhi at the beginning of this century, it was observed that among the necessary social skills to survive among mates and bosses was the ability to banter, often in a highly sexualized manner:

> There is ... the sheer delight in the play of touching, grabbing and displaying the male genitalia, as a way of embarrassing and entertaining each other. At the end of the shift, when several workers cram into a single-person latrine and adjoining small chamber to bathe, one must not only struggle to scrub oneself off of the caked dust and grime of the day with the abrasive detergent soap provided by the company, while taking care to avoid accidental fingers, elbows, or knees in the eyes within the congested space. One must also keep a check on one's underwear, which everyone wears inside the bath, lest it be pulled down to one's knees by someone or some persons working in concert, followed by uproarious laughter as the hapless fellow pathetically tries to pull it back up.[45]

Foremen in this factory also engaged in such horseplay, and suggestive remarks were made about homoerotic services rendered in order to advance one's interests.[46] This may be an extreme way of ingratiating oneself with supervisors and bosses, but the importance of maintaining good relations with superiors, either by working properly or by appearing to do so, is obvious. The Chinese factory girl Chunming, whom we met earlier, quickly understood how it worked, and improved her position, albeit at a price.[47] On 26 March 1996, she wrote in her diary: 'My promotion this time has let me see the hundred varieties of human experience. Some people cheer me, some envy me, some congratulate me, some wish me luck, some are jealous of me, and some cannot accept it . . . As to those who envy me . . . I will only treat them as an obstacle on the road to progress, kicking them aside and walking on. In the future there will be even more to envy!' The Chinese American journalist Leslie T. Chang comments: 'Chunming studied the higher-ups in her factory, as intent as a biologist with her specimens. She observed that when the head of the human resources department gave a speech, he was so nervous that his hands trembled. Around the new year, a manager on the factory floor ignored her until she boldly wished him a happy new year; he responded warmly and gave her ten yuan in a red envelope, a traditional gift.' Chunming reflects on this experience in her diary: 'From this incident, I understand: Some people who have always seemed unapproachable may not really be so. You just need to make yourself a little more approachable.' Chunming also defended and advanced her position by taking courses. In fact, no job promotion was possible without training. Becoming a good craftsman took many years of apprenticeship, as a rule as a resident. Factory workers managed with less, but those who wanted more took evening classes. Big firms, interested in a stable labour force and therefore in an effective internal labour market, may also offer such classes, or occasionally paid training. Large enterprises are well-known for this (one of the secrets that explains the phenomenon of Japan's 'salary men'), as are certain government jobs around the world, in particular in the armed forces.[48] The overall trend in job training over the last century has been for the extension of general and professional education for youngsters, and incidental but regular refreshment opportunities for most of the workforce.

The mirror image of individual promotion of workers' interests is the behaviour of employers. Just as workers choose their bosses, the same is true vice versa. A number of factory owners, particularly interested in a stable and reliable workforce, but at the same time with idealistic motives, did aim at maximizing profit, but believed that they could guarantee success by investing in the well-being of their workers in many ways. On the occasion of the delivery of his hundredth steam engine in 1873, the Dutch machine builder

Charles Theodoor Stork invited his 500 to 600 employees to the Bourse in Deventer. Seated at long tables, 'each with his plate, glass, and half bottle of wine in front of him', they listened to his views on labour relations, expressed in plain language in the local dialect:

> [Manufacturers] work with the pen and with the head, which is even more difficult than with the hands and they often have concerns that you don't know about this. . . . There are those who think that [manufacturer and workers] are hostile to each other, but they are quite wrong: if everything is as it should be, then we should treat each other as good friends. The workman must trust that the manufacturer ... thinks well of him, that he considers the good and considerate worker to be his neighbour, as a man created by God and not as a machine.[49]

Stork is also clear about why he differentiates between wages according to performance, and it is not because the government in The Hague has ordered him to do so:

> Everyone gets reward for his work, the industrious and careful and those who understand work well. That is a good law, a law that applies everywhere. That is a law that is not made in The Hague, where the gentlemen who make the country's laws meet, but one that says the industrious and the careful fare better than the lazy and those who do not want to fit in. That is the law of our Lord and that is why this law is good!

Each country has a number of such examples, albeit in varying degrees. Almost without exception, employers like Stork, running family enterprises rather than joint stock companies, might pay better wages and provide clean working places, as well as schools, housing and parks. These employers not only tried to avoid and prevent social conflict; they also carved out a role for themselves in the wider society – not only by hoping that colleagues would follow their example but even by setting a standard for government. As Dolf Kessler, the first director of the Dutch steel producer Koninklijke Hoogovens, put it: 'We must always be one step ahead of the social legislator'. The same applies, to a certain extent, for the Indian Tata Iron and Steel Company, who have been the owners of Hoogovens since 2007.[50]

Moreover, the attitude of factory owners and management is also prone to change.[51] From paternalistic types such as Stork, it shifted, in the sellers' market after the Second World War, to, in particular, highly trained engineers who were preoccupied with production capacity and thus a good relationship with workers and their organizations. And via the buyers' market in a period of overcapacity (1965–90), when the power in companies ended up in the hands of sales and marketing managers (inclined to leave the actual production to innumerable subcontractors), we have finally landed in a situation where business managers and financial gurus rely on control of the distribution channel through branding. The fact that the personal link between management and labour has weakened so severely is important for our subject. Add to this the explosion of the remuneration levels for business executives, made possible by diminishing fiscal progressivity in the absence of the countervailing power of organized labour,[52] and it becomes clear that the strategy of individual wage dependents must also change, both individually and collectively (see below).

If it is impossible for a worker to improve his situation or, worse, if he or she cannot prevent its deterioration, finding a new job offers new opportunities. This turnover of labour has aptly been called 'the individualistic strike'.[53] The chances of success, of course, depend on general trends in labour demand and on specific circumstances. Turnover rates are highest among low-trained temporary workers and general labour – a classic example was during the heyday of US immigration. Ultimately, the individual strategy of wage labourers often turns out to be purely defensive. A corollary for the self-employed is the serial start-up of new businesses, occasionally accompanied by insolvencies and bankruptcies.

From about 1840, geographical and, as a consequence, social mobility is most pronounced. Urbanization and international migrations are the clearest examples of this.[54] Urbanization increased rapidly in Western Europe after the Napoleonic wars, in Russia from a half-century later and in Asia in the twentieth century. International migration, which has long been of great significance, rose sharply when steam shipping greatly reduced the costs of passenger transport over water; the railways subsequently did the same for land transport. The most spectacular migration flows – all in the same order of magnitude of 40 to 50 million between 1840 and 1940 – promoted by these developments were those from Europe to North and South America, those of South Asian and other indentured labourers to sugar and other tropical plantations in America, Oceania and Asia, and those of south Chinese farmers and agricultural workers to the north-east.

This is not to mention the migrations of sailors and, especially, soldiers in the context of the numerous colonial and other wars, including the first and second world wars.

No matter how big and dramatic the step was from smallholder to factory worker, from the countryside to the city and from one continent to another, this kind of transition occurred gradually rather than suddenly (as in the case of the above-mentioned Bakhtiari pastoralists) by way of stepwise migration. A man goes to work somewhere else, for example, and once successfully established he brings over his sister, his friend, and so on. Or, a worker emigrates first from the countryside to a small town, and subsequently to a large city. This even goes for the Russian serfs and their descendants, for example.[55] Already in the course of the eighteenth century, some had the opportunity to work part of the year in urban industries, when they could be missed from compulsory service. Following the abolition of serfdom in 1861, they continued this custom to a much higher degree, and with the redistribution of land additional income from work in urban industry and migrant labour was essential in many regions of the Russian Empire.

The aggregate result of these numerous individual decisions to opt for loyalty, voice or exit have contributed substantially to the major shifts in labour relations over the last few centuries. The classical case involved people who decided to give up their small farm or craft enterprise to go to work in a factory, in their local or neighbouring town or overseas – mostly combining geographical with professional mobility. Due to the shift to increasingly important wage work in the last two centuries (mainly at the expense of small independent business; see pp. 323–32), repertoires of action, collective forms of action and, of course, also organization developed in this direction. This relates to the emergence of the collective voice of the self-employed in parallel to that of wage workers. In this regard, we can distinguish between incidental collective action and permanent organizations like mutual benefit societies and trade unions.

Incidental collective action

In the preceding periods, we have encountered a few major forms of collective action, including strikes of groups of wage workers without the existence of a permanent organization (erroneously called 'spontaneous' strikes; I prefer the term 'incidental') and rebellions and other forms of resistance by, especially, enslaved people, as well as by artisans, shopkeepers or petty

traders. These forms have not vanished, although some have lost importance. Let us first consider more closely the following forms of collective
action outside of permanent organizations: sabotage; collective exit; charivari; petitions; consumer boycotts; and, above all, the strike.[56] The choice for
a specific form from this repertoire of action (or, as is often the case, a
combination thereof) depended on, among other things, the attitude of the
authorities. And with illegal actions, such as the destruction of personal
property, or when strikes were declared illegal, secrecy was often paramount.[57] Pure wage workers were often more vulnerable than their self-
employed counterparts who, for example, still had an extra form of income
because they owned a piece of land.

Sabotage was already found in the early phase of the Industrial Revolution,
when machine breaking swept England and France (see p. 302). But like
the collective exit, it was much older than this (see, for example, p. 152 on
the Zanj rebellion in the ninth century).[58] Indeed, in the 1840s, a combination of the two (and other tactics) was used by seasonal brick moulders
employed on the Ganges Canal works, close to Roorkee in northern India,
to prevent piece wage reductions of 12.5 per cent.[59] The more than a thousand moulders, united in production gangs, probably based on regional and
caste bonds, initially tried collective exits. Clearly lacking an understanding
of the deep roots of the conflict, one of the English executive engineers
reported:

> their combined and frequent efforts to evade the doing of a fair day's work,
> or to extort from us a higher rate of pay [than the recently reduced one],
> caused much anxiety to all concerned in the manufacture of bricks. If an
> attempt was made to coerce a moulder, or even if fault was found with the
> quality or quantity of work performed by one or more of them, the whole
> would quit working collectively, taking their moulds in their hands, and
> walk to their huts, in spite of all remonstrance. I can well remember that
> they served us in this manner twice in one week at Roorkee.[60]

In the next phase of the conflict, the new machinery, which threatened the
monopoly of the moulders, was constantly being sabotaged and new attempts
were made to reverse the pay cuts. When all this turned out to be to no avail,
fires broke out among the thatched sheds of the public works department at
Roorkee. The engineers had no doubt that this was arson but were unable to

catch the perpetrators. One of them commented: 'I am inclined to think that the cause which has led to this wanton destruction of property has been discontent of the moulders at the rate of wages which they at present receive ... it is probable that the nearly general dissatisfaction found vent among the leaders of the malcontents by active participation in this outrage, which the remainder either approved or would take no active steps to prevent.'[61] Interestingly, the moulders ultimately prevailed. In the end, the engineers who had wanted to reduce total production costs by up to 25 per cent were able to achieve a reduction of 16 per cent in the short term, but at the expense of 'an infinite deal of trouble', as one of them concluded. More importantly, in the long run, wage rates were not reduced, the brick machines were no longer active and, once again, bricks were made by hand.

Public humiliation of those who break community rules, called charivari or the 'donkey ride', is best known as a punishment for men who break their promise to marry a girl after getting her pregnant, marrying couples with an extreme age difference or for wife beaters, but it also occurred in labour conflicts. Both unpopular bosses and, especially, strike breakers were sometimes called to order in this way. Dishonoured persons were placed on a pole or paraded or ridden around the streets in a wheelbarrow, serenaded by discordant 'rough music'.[62]

Petitioning can be seen as a safety valve for those lacking formal rights in politics, but whose concerns nevertheless may be considered, if only to prevent worse. They are integral instruments of government in any non-democratic society, but may also have a longer life. Moreover, contention over innumerable work issues have been formulated in this way (as discussed in Chapter 5).[63]

Consumer boycotts are generally a means to express dissatisfaction about prices or about political issues, such as the ban on imported Outspan oranges from South Africa during Apartheid.[64] The Outspan boycott was clearly linked to labour issues, as is the word 'boycott' itself. While the practice is much older, the word is derived from Captain Charles Cunningham Boycott from County Mayo, Ireland, who, in 1880, refused to receive rents fixed by his tenants and was subsequently confronted with their violent protests. An example of wage workers using this weapon comes from London's East End. In order to improve hours and working conditions, bakers went on strike in 1904. Those employers who agreed to their wishes received a union label to put on their products, while the others were boycotted. The women who did the shopping played a crucial role: 'A few days after the strike began, the smaller master bakers attached the union label to their product, as the Jewish women refused to buy any other. It was the custom of grocers to stock bread. Women would first buy their provisions, then ask for a loaf. The grocer was left with so much unsold bread that he immediately switched to a union-based supplier. It did not take long before the union's demands were agreed by every master.'[65]

This was a successful action by unorganized consumers supporting a strike organized by a union. However, in contrast to the conventional view, strikes in the past and possibly also in the present have frequently not been initiated by trade unions.[66] We have already seen a number of examples in this section (but see also, for example, the strikes in the Ichapur gunpowder factury, pp. 219–20). Instead of multiplying those examples here, we will briefly discuss a few key dilemmas facing workers on strike. By stopping (or also slowing down) work and, consequently, inflicting damage on employers, workers try to force them to give in to their demands. Excluding non-economic demands like the boycotting of foreign goods for political reasons or the political system of a country, strikers may leave the workplace, may close it off for suppliers or customers or may occupy it without working, as in the sit-down or sit-in. They may do so for a (pre-announced) brief period of time (lightning strike) or, at least as an objective, indefinitely. They may attempt to shut down one establishment or all establishments of a business or sector simultaneously, or instigate a consecutive series of brief work stoppages at many firms (rolling strikes). The outcome is, of course, determined by the enduring power of the workers, now without wages, and that of the employers, now without income from their sales. The great number of strikes in history demonstrates that this outcome is uncertain. Although employers as individuals are many times wealthier than their workers, the latter – by means of solidarity, including savings (by way of collections or in the form of a strike fund) – are certainly not defenceless, provided that they maintain unity. This is perhaps the most difficult aspect, in particular when the employer manages to engage strike breakers, actively supported by the police force that has to protect them when facing picket lines.

The emergence and subsequent growth of central workplaces made the organization and eventual success of a strike much more feasible. Andrew Ure, the Scottish physicist and author of *The Philosophy of Manufactures* (1835), remarked that British proto-industrial textile workers were 'scattered over a wide track of the country' and that, because they were also 'mutual competitors for work and wages', they rarely managed to 'conspire with one another, and never with effect against their employers'.[67] As we will see below, he was soon to be proven wrong. From the second half of the nineteenth century, not only the concentration of workers but also the growing interconnectedness of national economies enhanced the phenomenon of transnational waves of conflict.[68] Thus, the years following the first and the second world wars are conspicuous, but for different parts of the world other strike waves are also visible in between, for example, during decolonization. As we have seen, these waves have had major implications for the position of the workers.

The patterns are fuzzy for recent decades. Against pessimism about the effectiveness of the strike weapon in the rich 'core countries', we find rising collective actions in eastern and southern China from the late 1990s.[69] Remarkably, these strikes of mainly young migratory workers of recent peasant background are, by definition, not organized by trade unions. The unions play only a mediating role between the striking workers, on the one hand, and the government as the dominant actor and the employers, on the other.

To give an example, in the summer of 2005, 20,000 workers went on strike in 18 enterprises in the Dalian Development Area in China.[70] Consequently, each of these factories, all Japanese except for one Korean firm, raised their salaries and abolished a number of practices, including the issuing of short-term contracts and speeding up assembly lines. This successful result for the strikers is not self-evident, however, given the fact that, in 1982, the Chinese government revoked the freedom to strike, previously included in the constitutions of 1975 and 1978. On the other hand, in 1990, China's People's Congress approved the 144 Convention of the ILO calling for 'tripartite consultation'. In reality, this is very hard to practise in China, where the unions are entirely dependent on the government. Not surprisingly, the workers at Dalian averted the unions only a few hours before the beginning of the strike. In one company, 'a note was slipped under the door of the union office in the morning, which declared the intention of the strike action that took place four hours later.' In another company, union cadres 'visited dormitories to persuade workers to stay away from the strike, only to find that all of the dormitories were empty; it turned out that a mobile phone message about the visit of the union cadre had been disseminated among the workers and that they had been asked to "disappear"'.[71]

Permanent organization

Guilds and guild-like organizations vanished from most countries from 1800 onwards, but only gradually, and even now they are not totally absent (think of closed national organizations of highly skilled professionals like medical doctors).[72] Partially inspired by these old organizational forms (see pp. 232–5) and means of collective action, new types of organizations have emerged, in particular co-operatives, mutual benefit societies and trade unions. Their occurrence in specific countries at specific times greatly depends on the legal possibilities to start such organizations.

Mutual societies and co-operatives

Mutual aid is not a new, nineteenth-century phenomenon. In the preceding five centuries, craft guilds had already developed elaborate schemes of mutual help in order to cover the costs of a decent burial, sickness, old age or other mishaps of life. This tradition, which primarily concerned master craftsmen, was also emulated by journeymen's guilds or similar organizations, in particular in those trades where there was little chance of workers becoming masters themselves after a few years.

In addition to the most common form of mutual aid, disbursements to members in need by way of mutual insurance or benefits could also be rotated.[73] So-called *roscas* (rotating savings and credit funds) functioned as illustrated in the following example of a *cycle* or *sheet* among Indian migrants on Mauritius around 1960:

> A man or woman calls together a group of friends and neighbours. Suppose there are ten of them, and each puts in Rs. 10. They then draw lots and the winner takes the Rs. 100. (Sometimes the organizer automatically takes the first 'pool'.) The following month each again puts in Rs. 10, and another member takes the resulting Rs. 100; and so it continues for ten months until each member has had his Rs. 100.[74]

Another form of mutual aid is the distribution of benefits among a group as we saw in the case of 'beer work parties' (p. 327).

Most *roscas*, monetized or not, were based on trust and required minimal administration compared to mutual benefit societies or co-operatives. This, combined with neglect by trade unions, is also why these and similar organizations are popular among migrants. Mutual insurance requires a distant time horizon. Guilds with compulsory membership were well suited in this regard. Trade unions, too, although legally unable to compel workers to join, emulated this model with success – in the rich countries, until the welfare state took over most or all of these functions.[75] To a lesser degree, corporate funds, set up by management, and commercial or doctors funds could become competitors. Mutual organizations in particular offer a useful alternative for private loans, which often left poor people without collateral dependent on creditors and, in extreme cases, in lifelong bondage.

Already documented for the Roman Empire and for the medieval and early-modern guilds, mutual benefit societies spread quickly with the expansion of wage labour. Based on a membership of workers in a city in the same trade, they frequently combined several functions. Apart from providing mutual insurance, these societies also enhanced sociability and communal respect, in particular by staging public funerals of their members, all of whom were obliged to attend in smart attire. On an economic level, such societies also functioned as consumer co-operatives. The step to a more active defence of interests by way of petitioning and occasional strikes was imminent, and many developed into trade unions – or, they offered an alternative to unions, as the latter were often forbidden. It is noteworthy that mutual benefit societies have hardly ever been banned, if only because they alleviated poor relief. In England, for example, mutual benefit societies were generally called 'friendly societies' and were recognized as early as 1793. Trade unions, by contrast, were still facing many impediments as late as 1867.

Producer co-operatives are democratic, profit-sharing organizations that give members a say in the management.[76] They emerged, briefly, in the mid-nineteenth century among craftsmen and, in a much more restricted way and therefore much more successfully, among peasants and farmers. In order to fight or avert unemployment or to abolish middlemen, craftsmen could produce communally rather than on their own private account. This was facilitated by the communal purchase of raw materials, tools or machinery and by communal sales of their products. Successful sales often proved the most difficult aspect of such producer co-operatives. Notwithstanding strong work ethics and the elimination of excessive profits, this form of cooperation, attempted many times, has not been very successful overall.

What has been a success, at least for small farmers in Western Europe, has been the common purchase of means of production and the ability to access cheap credit loans via a co-operative bank. Best known is the bank founded by the nineteenth-century German social reformer Friedrich Wilhelm Raiffeisen, who propagated self-help. His ideas were emulated over most of continental Europe and even beyond. The initial project to pool members' savings in order to provide low-cost long-term loans then developed into the joint purchase of seed and fertilizers and of operating resources such as machinery to be used by co-op members, and the common storage and sale of harvest products at the most favourable moment and independent of merchants.

Trade unions

Whereas craft guilds defend the interests of those self-employed in a specific local trade and mutual benefit societies aim at reducing the personal risks of their members – not necessarily but often workers – trade unions typically unite workers who want to influence wage levels and working conditions. Despite these differences, the nascent trade unions worldwide in the eighteenth and nineteenth centuries borrowed many tactics, strategies and rituals from their predecessors, and the collective actions of all these entities ran parallel for a very long time. This is aptly called the 'artisanal phase' of the labour movement.[77] Prior to the twentieth century, trade unions were more numerous than the aforementioned older organizations in only a very few countries in Western Europe.[78]

The legal framework in which trade unions could function is discussed below (pp. 398–400). Here, it suffices to remember that they were permitted in most countries quite late in the nineteenth century. Indeed, before trade unions were empowered with full rights, there had been a greater chance that they would resort to illegal actions, including violence. Between the 1820s and the 1860s, the brickmakers' organizations in and around Manchester tried to establish a closed-shop system in order to prevent employers from selling bricks outside the area and, in particular, below conventional rates. Their aim was to compel factory owners to employ union members and give them a fair piece rate for moulding and, if need be, advances as well as employment to dig clay in winter when moulding was impossible. Any employer not prepared to obey union rules could expect strikes and, if that failed to have an effect, also violence. Needles or broken glass were hidden in the moulding clay, green bricks were destroyed, workshops were burnt down or factory horses' hamstrings cut with razor blades. As these words of the union man attest, sometimes matters took a turn for the worse: 'After a master had infringed upon the rules of the society, a deputation was appointed to wait upon him, and after having been waited upon, if he still acted contrary to our rules, or refused to comply with our requests, a general meeting was called. We there discussed the case, and we decided that the only course left open to us was what would be called by persons not belonging to the union an unlawful course.'[79] There are reports of subsequent personal assaults, attempted poisonings, nightly arson on adversaries' houses, shootings, and even the murder of a police constable in 1862, which was followed by the trial and execution of one of those found guilty.

The further development of already existing journeymen's organizations was one way to start a trade union, as it became clear to more and more journeymen that they would never attain the status of an independent master. That was certainly true for those that had already joined a factory. The fact that Lancashire mule spinners hired and trained their own assistants, as we have seen, meant that they controlled the supply of labour and could therefore unionize their trade effectively early on by making agreements with employers on detailed piece rate lists, short-hour working during trade slumps, seniority rules in case of lay-offs and, finally, conciliation arrangements.[80] But many early trade unions also united small independent craftsmen, such as the self-employed diamond workers that stood at the cradle of the socialist trade union movement in the Netherlands.[81]

Trade unions were able to expand following the repeal of restrictive legislation. Everywhere the foundation was a local or supralocal organization of workers in the same trade or branch. A first proliferation of trade unions and similar organizations took place in Western Europe in the decades before 1848. The revolutions that took place around that year – which were about much more than labour issues – mostly ended in disappointment and also in a lull in labour activity. Only after four decades did activities pick up again, now mainly under the banner of socialism.[82] Successful attempts were also made in Western Europe at this time to form national federations, first trade-wise and subsequently uniting as many wage workers as possible across all economic sectors.

This was also the period when ideologies matured with respect to the nature of the labour–employer relationship. Two basic positions emerged. The first was taken up by the (mainly Christian) trade unionists, who believe that cooperation is the best way forward and that open conflict is only neces-sary in exceptional circumstances.[83] The second position, meanwhile, was occupied by anarchists, syndicalists and socialists who regard employers and their workers as two distinctive 'classes' that, in principle, have antago-nistic interests, and they thus believe that class struggle is necessary. Revolutionary syndicalists even propagate 'class war' to be waged through ongoing guerrilla warfare, while socialists, by organizing not only trade unions but also political parties, essentially want to rely on the state to achieve their goals. The extension of voting rights to workers and small independent producers enhanced the chances of those labour movements that were willing to exploit the political opportunity. By participating in and winning elections, they expected that, once in power, they would be able to change, in a democratic way, the rules governing the labour market; hence they called themselves social democrats. The communists, who split from the socialists in the early twentieth century, aimed to take over government by force, as they did for shorter (133 days in Hungary in 1919) or longer periods (more than 70 years in Russia, and even more in China, given the communists remain in power today).

These different interpretations of the nature of the clash of interests between employers and workers resulted not only in different organizations but also in fierce competition among them. Whereas in the early phase of trade unionism it would have been highly unlikely that workers in the same trade would organize along different ideological lines, this became the rule later on, especially nationally and internationally. Conversely, national orga-nizations could force local ones to show their colours. Before the Second World War, anarchist and syndicalist trade unions played an important role, especially in southern Europe and Latin America. Ideological controversies and other rivalries contributed to a schism in trade unionism. In Mexico, a country with far-reaching labour rights since its 1910 revolution, workers' organizations sprang up, with textile workers already counting 425 local unions affiliated to 8 different national federations in 1940.[84]

As the Cold War evolved, the main competitors emerged as communist and socialist trade unions. Frequently, the latter's tactics imitated those of Catholic and Protestant trade unions in the few countries where these played a significant role. This became possible as the social democrats exchanged the dogma of class struggle for that of the 'social market economy' (in Germany called the Rhineland model) following the Second World

War.[85] Thus, trade unions like the American Federation of Labour (AFL) also became increasingly apolitical.

The development and dissemination of trade unionism across the globe occurred through imitation, as had previously been the case with guilds, mutual benefit societies and the like. Migrants and, especially, sailors played an important role in this regard. This is obvious in the case of white settler colonies, but it also happened in tropical colonies, not only as a result of workers imitating their counterparts elsewhere, but also top down. This could be in the form of the missionary zeal of communist, socialist, Christian, national, international and supranational organizations (like the socialist and communist internationals discussed below), but also of religiously inspired movements; think of the Catholic Church and the papal encyclical *Quadragesimo Anno* (1931) and its predecessor.

Trade unions utilize various strategies and apply many tactics to achieve their goals, but at the centre is the collective bargaining of wages and work conditions, aimed at collective labour agreements. This requires considerable diplomacy, but in the knowledge that they have recourse to the ultimate bargaining lever – the threat of strike. If applied, this threat is the ultimate test of the union's ability to impose its will on the employer or employers, but notably also to control its workers. When a union is able to force the employer to make union membership a condition of employment, we speak of a 'closed shop'.[86] In fact, this is the same procedure that was followed by the craft guilds. Indeed, the closed shop was particularly popular and successful among the skilled crafts in nineteenth-century Europe and, more recently, in England.

The unification of workers, of course, provoked the unification of their counterparts, employers. Conventionally competitors, under the pressure of collective action and a united workforce they now attempted collective bargaining as a strategy and, in addition, put pressure on local or national governments to choose a side. Broadly speaking, for a long time, politicians and employers belonged to the same social class, with the latter having a much bigger chance of enforcing their conditions than their workers. Among their strategies was the organization of factory- or firm-based trade unions, meant to compete with unions controlled by the workers independently.

These employer-organized unions are called yellow unions. Even more extreme was the imposition of yellow-dog contracts, particularly widespread in the US in the interwar years before new arrangements under the New Deal saw the blossoming of trade unions in subsequent decades. The polar opposite of closed shop arrangements, the yellow-dog contract is 'a promise, made by workers as a condition of employment, not to belong to a union during the period of employment, or not to engage in certain specified activities, such as collective bargaining or striking, without which the formal right to belong to a union is wholly valueless'.[87] In post-war Japan and Korea, too, fierce battles between trade unions and employers who established competing top-down unions are not uncommon. Several trade unionists in the Korean shipbuilding industry even committed suicide in a final attempt to save their independent unions and to win disputes. One of them, employed at the Hanjin Heavy Industries wharf at Busan, occupied his crane, No. 85, 35 metres above the ground, from 11 June until 17 October 2003. In his suicide note he wrote:

> Managers seem to want blood with their naked swords. Yes! I will offer myself up as a sacrifice if you want. But we badly need to get a result from this struggle. . . . Using claims for damages, provisional seizure, criminal charges, imprisonment, and dismissal, managers seek to change our union into a 'vegetable union', and workers into 'human vegetables'. If we could not transform this labor control policy through our present struggle, all of us would only fall over the cliff. So, whatever may happen, we must continue to struggle until we win. I am only thankful and at the same time sorry to comrades who have been with me and believed in me.[88]

Cooperation between local trade unions dealing with one or several local factory owners developed into national federations, whose main aim was collective bargaining on a national scale, at least where wage levels did not differ too much regionally.[89] This way, terms of work and pay for specific groups of workers were excluded from competition. The next step was 'social ownership' at the firm level: economic power sharing and employee involvement in business decision making and strategy setting, exemplary in Scandinavia and Germany during the flourishing of the welfare state.[90]

The outcome of all these negotiations over the last two centuries is a much better position for wage labourers in countries where unions have developed most and have met with success than in countries where they have not materialized for various reasons. The same can be said about different sectors within countries, the clearest example being India. There, trade unions and collective bargaining are restricted to the 'formal sector', covering only 7–8 per cent of all wage workers. Wages, and especially social security, are much higher in this sector than they are in the 'informal' or 'unorganized' sector.[91]

Not by chance, the global waves of strikes after the two world wars more or less coincided with the success of unionization and union density. This has never been higher than it was in the 1950s and 1960s, although this success would not last long. Without doubt, union membership and union density have been decreasing worldwide over the last half-century. There are many reasons for this. The main ones are (in different order for different parts of the world and for different economic sectors and branches of industry): changing political structures and globalization; professionalization of trade union functionaries leading to alienation from rank-and-file members; discontinuities of firms and, consequently, the loss of unionists' expertise and traditions; and the increasing heterogeneity and casualization of the workforce intrinsic to the shift from industry to services in the rich countries[92] (for more detail, see p. 423 below).

The unavoidable result of organizational success was the professionalization of full-time paid union leaders and their staff and, as a consequence, more anonymous internal relations. Collective bargaining in particular could result in internal conflict between functionaries and the rank and file. After all, negotiators on both the employers' and the unions' side must be firmly in control of their members to ensure that they adhere to the contract for the agreed period. Dissatisfaction with professional trade unionists may induce the rank and file to so-called 'wildcat strikes' in order to reach better terms of contract.[93]

One simple reason for the demise of trade unions in the rich countries is the closing-down of factories and mines and their subsequent shift to low-wage countries elsewhere. Between 1969 and 1976, 22.3 million jobs were lost in the US with the closure of some one hundred thousand manufacturing plants.[94] Bruce Springsteen sang about deep frustrations in the US, for example about the closing of a textile mill in *My Hometown* in 1984; similarly, Ewan MacColl lamented the coal miners' situation in England in *Miner's Wife* in 1960. These concerns remain crucial to North Atlantic politics today.

Of course, new jobs are constantly being created, but the point here is that the old plants were heavily unionized and that the generations-old experience of collective action was lost – lost in desperate defensive actions such as the year-long strike by Arthur Scargill's National Union of Miners against the closure of the English coal pits. And in other countries, the learning process taking place in new plants in terms of dealing with the power relations between wage workers and management had to be started almost from scratch. Moreover, the outsourcing of tasks to subcontractors diminishes the long careers of wage workers during which they can garner trade union experience.

Another reason for de-unionization is the growing heterogeneity of the workforce in these countries from the 1960s onwards.[95] In the US, for example, women, immigrants and African Americans in particular entered realms thus far dominated by autochthonous white males.[96] Their trade unions, always alert to preventing wage cuts, were traditionally suspicious of these groups, who, they believed, were supposed to be satisfied with inferior working conditions. This was exacerbated by the propensity of employers to use immigrants as strike breakers in the pre-war years. This inclination towards the exclusion of newcomers perceived as culturally alien also weakened the unions. The unions' upholding of seniority rules for lay-off benefits favoured their long-time members, but at the same time alienated youngsters and other outsiders.

This is not to say that the inclusion and active participation of migrants, ethnic minorities or women is easy for traditional trade unions. The Austrian social democrat Adolf Braun made the following observations in 1914:

While male workers start and finish working and take their breaks at set times, the hours of work of female workers are very frequently, one might even say as a rule, unlimited. When women come home from the plant with its set working hours, they find manyfold tasks awaiting them, often for people they must care for in addition to themselves, with respect to cleaning, clothing, cooking, and often not for themselves alone but for others as well, not only for their husbands and children but also for subtenants, lodgers and the like. ... Arriving home late, the road home from the meeting, across long distances at night, often through poorly lit areas, presents no problem for male workers but does for female ones. This is why often even female workers recruited as members of the industrial organizations have greater difficulty becoming fully involved than their male counterparts.[97]

Of course, in addition to these structural reasons, the political framework also matters. There are huge differences between countries when it comes to unionization, depending on the nature of the parties in power and their cooperation with employers' and workers' organizations. The presence of leftist politicians in government, union involvement in unemployment benefits and the size of the labour force in unionizable industries explains these variations. Around 1980, union density was highest in Sweden, Denmark and Finland (80 per cent or more). In Iceland, Belgium, Ireland, Norway, Austria and Australia it was between 50 and 79 per cent, and only 20–49 per cent in the UK, Canada, Italy, Switzerland, West Germany, the Netherlands and Japan, with the lowest rates, below 20 per cent, in the US and France.[98] Occasionally, more peculiar circumstances can explain national differences. In France, for example, membership fluctuates heavily as workers can easily drop out between strike waves and join again as conflict surges.

These figures also reveal how state policies directly influence the longevity of trade unions.[99] Where welfare states delegate crucial executive functions to trade unions (especially with respect to unemployment benefits), such as in Scandinavia, membership is automatically high. Where this is not the case, as in most other Western European countries, figures are much lower. In particular, the general binding agreement of collective labour agreements disincentivizes joining a union. This is the case in the Netherlands, for example, where free riders and loyal, subscription-paying members alike profit equally from attractive offers from trade unions. In recent decades, as we will see, the proliferation of subcontracting, temping agencies and payroll constructions have made the work of trade unions much more difficult than it was in the classical factories that dominated the landscape from, say, 1850 to 1980.

Where this is compounded by the state frustrating or suppressing trade unions, membership is even lower. Trade unions in the sense of independent organizations have been and are still forbidden in dictatorial regimes. Or they are entirely subsumed by the state, in a corporatist way (compulsory cooperation of employers and workers under the guidance of the state), as witnessed in Fascist Italy and National-Socialist Germany, or in a communist way as in Stalinist Russia. More recently, military regimes in Latin American, European and Arabic countries have abolished trade unions, put their leaders and active members in prison or set up rival organizations under strict state control. Under new centralist leadership, these mock-unions (also called 'yellow unions') certainly have a cultural role to play, but they cannot perform their essential independent function of co-determining labour relations.[100]

In addition to the many structural factors at play in other countries, the low figures for union membership in the US are a direct result of racial segregation and various waves of checking, counteracting and suppression.[101] Trade unionism started early in the US, boosted by experienced immigrants and, in the late nineteenth century, the successful Knights of Labor (founded in 1869, it propagated co-operatives among farmers, shopkeepers and labourers). Employers, often hand in glove with civil authorities, adopted serious counter-measures, including legal action, espionage, violence and terror. Perhaps the most infamous example is the 1892 strike at Carnegie's steel plant at Homestead, managed by Henry Clay Frick, who invoked the assistance of 300 armed security men of Pinkerton's National Detective Agency and, after their defeat, a further 8,000 men from the Pennsylvania militia. They were to stay for 95 days and, with the help of strike breakers, ensure Frick's victory. There are many more instances of worker militancy, in particular in the period from the First World War until the 1930s, when trade union rights were confirmed and extended by the Wagner Act (1935). Many of these achievements would be restricted by the Taft-Hartley Act of 1947, followed by McCarthyism. What had once been a powerful movement was thus reduced to mainly shop-floor action by skilled workers.

This is not the place to repeat the history of trade union internationalism, with the exception of one particular aspect: its influence on labour legislation and therefore labour conditions transnationally and even globally. Many attempts at such cooperation have been made, but the most successful is undoubtedly the International Labour Organization (ILO), founded in 1919.[102] It builds on long traditions of transnational and international cooperation between workers. It began with journeymen's organizations linking towns, like the French *compagnonnages* or German *Wanderburschen*. In the nineteenth century, other organizational forms emerged, again among migratory workers crossing borders, like sailors (for both, see pp. 237–40). Such cooperation aimed at preventing the importation of strike breakers from other countries (as successfully achieved between Spanish Galicia and northern Portugal between 1901 and 1904) and at reducing competition between workers in the same industries in different countries. This may be rather defensive, but these contacts also enabled them to learn from each other, at least where workers in different countries worked for the same multinationals. For example, in the 1990s, the International Metalworkers' Federation (IMF) maintained files on more than 500 of such companies.[103]

The various 'Internationals' may be famous, but their effectiveness varies immensely, from boosting the morale of participants to organized revolution.

Preceded by some earlier initiatives, like the London-based Democratic Friends of All Nations (1844–48/53), the First International (the International Working Men's Association, 1864–76) was still small. The Second International (1889–1916) had many more members in different parts of the world, and also lasted much longer. But it was also deeply divided on many issues: not only ideologically (socialists versus anarchists) but also on practical matters, as became clear when it discussed international labour migration during its 1904 and 1907 congresses. Notwithstanding the high ideal of international solidarity, the successful trade unions and labour parties in white settler colonies squarely opposed free immigration of 'non-whites'. More generally, racist attitudes vis-à-vis colonial populations were widespread in the labour movement until far into the twentieth century, even after the movement had advocated decolonization.[104] But solidarity between labour organizations in different European countries also appeared much more superficial in that fateful summer of 1914 than previously anticipated.

Trade unions and political parties worked together in these 'Internationals', but in 1903 a separate Secretariat of National Trade Union Confederations was established by mainly North Atlantic socialist trade unionists. In 1913, it was renamed the International Federation of Trade Unions (IFTU) and in 1949 it was succeeded by the International Confederation of Free Trade Unions (ICFTU). They were rivalled by similar syndicalist, Christian and communist federations of national trade unions.

All these international organizations, whether uniting trade unions from a particular sector or all types of member organizations sharing the same ideology, sought to influence public opinion, and a number also appealed directly to governments. The League of Nations (and later its successor, the United Nations), founded after the First World War, became the natural focus point of such attempts. The ILO came into being in 1919 as part of the Versailles Treaty, which declared that 'peace can be founded only on social justice'. Helpfully, key politicians had been convinced by the usefulness of the international trade union movement in their bid to sidestep 'the long shadow of Russia'.[105] In its turn, only a month after its foundation, the ILO used its Washington Convention to attempt to convince member states, by diplomatic means (unlike trade unions, the ILO cannot use strikes as a lever), to adopt legislation regarding labour standards, such as the maintenance of the 8-hour day and the 48-hour week for industry.[106] Its major achievements include measures against slave labour and the slave trade.

Work and the state

Influenced by major shifts in labour relations and in the strategies of those involved – both individually and collectively, both 'spontaneous' and via more permanent organizations – the character of society has changed radically in the past two centuries. More and more rules were needed as work shifted from primarily the household to the public sphere. And those laws and regulations relating to work had to be constantly adjusted.[107] National states became dominant at the expense of local authorities. And, ultimately, they also moved to international and supranational agreements (consider the abolitionist movements against the slave trade and slavery). Partly due to the emergence of national schools of law and partly due to democratization, large differences in laws and regulations arose in practice, as a result of which it is often difficult to see the wood for the trees.

Two traditions stand out among this enormous variety: the Anglo-Saxon one and the continental European one. A distinction is made in the Anglo-Saxon tradition between still-relevant labour regulations based on statute law dating back to 1349 in England, determined by the government and popular representation, and the much more important common law, determined by judges on the basis of jurisprudence, which goes back to the late sixteenth century.[108] On the European continent, following the French Revolution, national and systematically codified law replaced previous local regulations and its courts for those laws (enshrined in a constitution and, in addition, in separate codes, such as a civil code, a criminal code, a *code de commerce*, a *code de travail*, a *code de justice militaire*, and so on). English colonies initially followed the mother country on this point, but later, a number, such as the US and certainly Australia, increasingly combined this with the continental European model of codified law. How all of this is arranged of course matters greatly to self-employed litigants, wage labourers (individually and collectively), employers and their respective legal advisors (large unions, for example, have legal departments).

Nevertheless, during the last two centuries, we may discern a great wave in the North Atlantic and its offshoots, and in the last half-century also increasingly beyond – from regulation and corporation (households, estates, guilds and so on) in the ancien régime, to deregulation and decorporation in the first half of the nineteenth century, to reregulation and recorporation in the century thereafter and, finally, to another period of deregulation and decorporation since the end of the twentieth century.[109] Prepared by the banking crisis of 2008, the pendulum may now be swinging in the opposite direction, influenced by the coronavirus pandemic, although it is unclear for how long.

Incidentally, the development of decorporation warrants an observation with respect to households, where we do not find any recorporation from the late nineteenth century. As a nuclear work unit, the household eventually and definitively lost power. How did all this play out for labour within the household, for the self-employed and for wage labourers? This last group, increasingly more important than the first two, as argued in Chapter 6, will receive by far the most attention. Since we have already briefly discussed the legislation regarding unfree labour, we can bypass it here.

Labour relations that, initially, were primarily arranged within the household, that is to say the relationships between the head of the household, (usually) his partner and other adults and children – but also slaves, if present – now increasingly had to be cast in public laws and regulations. This is particularly evident in the discussions about child labour: can the state take over care duties and thereby the legal authority of the father (and, via him, of the mother) in the household? That was certainly not self-evident in the nineteenth century. In the course of a debate about protective legislation with respect to child labour in 1877–78, a Belgian MP resolutely opposed this with the following argumentation:

> a worker is also a father . . . There is no doubt that the state, in the public interest, can regulate certain professions, such as, for instance, the art of healing, or the art of producing medicines; the state can protect birds that eat insects to ensure that they are not killed, and domestic animals so that they are not mistreated. But there is one being which the state cannot touch without touching ourselves, and that is the being that is united with us through all the fibres of our souls, that is, our child.[110]

By the turn of the century, however, this debate was certainly in favour of protective legislation. But the curtailment of a husband's authority over his wife, her labour and her earnings would take almost another century.

Meanwhile, less controversial was the view that education could help an individual, as well as the national economy as a whole.[111] This is evident from the increased labour productivity due to the success of primary education in the US in the nineteenth century. Of course, we should not underestimate the effect of the immigration of a young and aspirational cohort from the Old Continent, but it took until around 1900 for the UK and, later, also France and Germany to level up. It took France and Germany until the 1960s to surpass the UK due to the devastation of two world wars. By the 1980s, they had caught up with labour productivity in the US, leaving the country of General Motors, Ford and Chrysler trailing.

The explanation for these developments is education. The US, which by around 1945 had been close to achieving universal secondary education and, subsequently, had made great progress in the extension of higher education, was outflanked by Japan's general education levels, due to the US's privatization of quality universities with consequently higher thresholds. In contrast to the moderate diversity in primary and secondary education in the US – and to a lesser degree also in the UK – there is a deep gulf between well-endowed private and less well-endowed public tertiary education since the 1980s and 1990s.

Due to Japan's national and widely available education system, with its emphasis on general skills, the country was able to develop an alternative to the American managerial model. Instead, Japanese firms could and were willing to rely on their shopfloor workers' capacities to detect and immediately correct problems on the production floor. Whereas, according to the Canadian economist William Lazonick, American managers tended to see the independent judgements of skilled shopfloor workers as a threat, their Japanese counterparts were only too glad to rely on them. This largely explains – together with extremely low immigration figures – the phenomenon of the Japanese 'salary man': regular workers with lifetime employment and totally devoted to their firm in successful export industries. Japanese labour law accommodated this model. We must add a caveat here, however. Like the exclusion of women and children from the success of the adult male English textile workers in the nineteenth century, Japanese women largely functioned as a 'secondary labour force'.[112]

Since governments had attained centuries of experience of regulating commercial practices, much less changed for the self-employed in these centuries. With the gradual abolition of guild monopolies in some countries and the sudden elimination of them in others, the equal freedom for all individuals to contract and compete in the marketplace appeared to have been achieved, but it has not been that simple. Think, for example, of the small farmers who often missed out in the distribution of the commons. But also with regard to, in particular, the leasing of land, the renting of business premises and the prevention of usury in moneylending, there was still much to be organized.[113]

We will not delve further into this here, but instead concentrate again on the category for which the most has changed: wage workers. Historically, we can distinguish three phases: to begin with, the breakdown of the corporative order in favour of the purest possible market operation around 1800, whereby the labour contract became sacred; then, during the nineteenth century, attempts by workers to make this functioning of the labour contract more equitable, to acquire the right to associate and meet and, ultimately, the right to strike (see p. 404); and, finally, the phase in which the state began to play an increasingly active role, alongside employers and employees, especially in the twentieth century in the form of the welfare state, including its partial degradation since the end of the same century.

Market instead of corporatism

The French Revolution, which had proclaimed the liberty and equality of each individual adult male citizen, sought to liberate that person from all impediments imposed by estates and corporations.[114] According to d'Allarde, the rapporteur for the deliberations leading to the abolishment of guilds in March 1791: 'The ability to work is one of the first rights of man. This right is his property and it is without doubt ... the first and most sacred property which cannot be invalidated by prescriptions.' When, however, immediately afterwards, printers, carpenters and farriers collectively resisted salary reductions by using their new political freedom of assembly and association, Le Chapelier (d'Allarde's fellow MP), while acknowledging the need for higher salaries to guarantee true freedom, radically advocated the prohibition of all coalitions, both of workers but also of employers: '[those] formed by workers to raise the price of their working day and the ones formed by entrepreneurs to decrease [such rates]'. He explains his paradoxical opinion as follows:

> While all citizens should certainly have the right to assemble, citizens practising certain professions should not be allowed to gather for their purported common interests. The state is no longer a corporation, only the private interest of each individual and the general interest remain. No longer may anybody campaign for intermediary causes or use the corporate spirit to alienate the citizens from the state ... We must restore the

principle of free agreements about each labourer's working day between individuals; each worker is then responsible for fulfilling his agreement with his employer.[115]

Although not based on the principles of the French Revolution, the Anglo-Saxon tradition in the nineteenth century also tried to reduce the employer–employee relationship to the bare principles of a contract related to the offer and payment of services for a limited period of time between two individuals; specifically, 'men of full age and competent understanding ... contracting ... freely and voluntarily', in the words of the British judge Sir George Jessel in 1875.[116] Three decades later, an American Supreme Court judge, Justice Peckham, formulated the same principles in a similar way in his verdict on the question of whether the state of New York had exceeded its constitutional powers by imposing a maximum number of working hours for bakers. According to him, state interference had to be strictly limited to 'safety, health, morals and general welfare of the public'. However:

> Clean and wholesome bread does not depend upon whether the baker works but ten hours a day or only sixty hours a week. ... In our judgement it is not possible in fact to discover the connection between the number of hours a baker may work in the bakery and the healthful quality of the bread made by the workman. ... There is no contention that bakers as a class are not equal in intelligence and capacity to men in other trades or manual occupations, or that they are not able to assert their rights and care for themselves without the protecting arm of the State, interfering with their independence of judgement and of action. They are in no sense wards of the State.[117]

Striving for fair market conditions

In reality, wage earners and employers were not equal at all, not least for strictly formal reasons – and least of all in the Anglo-Saxon tradition, for a very long time. In England, until 1867, workers (but not employers!) still had to face criminal punishment for breach of contract, which was a serious impediment to collective action by trade unions, as exemplified by the great strike of 1844 in the northern English coal fields:

The agents of Radcliffe Colliery [in Northumberland], by false pretenses brought thirty-two Cornish miners to supplant the old pitmen, and engaged them for twelve months at 4 sh. per day. . . . After the second fort-night the viewer offered these men 4 d. per tub, and they all, with the exception of four, absconded. . . . A reward of £50 was offered for the apprehension of the runaway Cornish men. The Newcastle police captured four of them, brought them to the Amble in gigs, together with a *posse* of police. The poor fellows were kept from the Monday night till . . . on the Tuesday night they [successfully] attempted to make their escape. . . . The others who absconded were arrested by the North Shields police force, and a steam-boat, carrying the police force and the special constables, was sent to bring them to Alnmouth, and thence to Alnwick, to answer for their conduct before the magistrates.[118]

Despite this impediment, textile unions in the industrial heart of Britain had managed to come up with peculiar arrangements with employers, as if combination laws were non-existent for them.

In contrast, the French *Code Civil* (Article 1781) did not include any penal sanction on the breach of contract, but, at the same time, the word of the employer should be accepted as the truth and the worker was not allowed to call witnesses in any court hearing.[119] In another respect, too, French (and in emulation many continental) workers enjoyed more freedom than their brethren across the Channel. There, debtors of small means were severely prosecuted, put in special debtors' prisons, or banished to North America or later to Australia (see p. 321).[120] In France and many continental countries, by contrast, debt was defined as a commercial problem, not as a criminal offence. The *livret ouvrier* (abbreviated to *livret*), an obligatory personal work pass, introduced in 1749 under the ancien régime, listed references from succes-sive employers. It was given a new function when reintroduced in 1803 (this law would be repealed in 1890). On the one hand, mayors now became responsible for delivering and registering the *livrets*, and workers found without this document were to be arrested and sentenced as vagrants. On the other, '[w]hereas the old common law would allow the employer to retain a worker who was in debt by exerting economic pressure [the *livrets* now] allowed debts to be circulated from employer to employer. . . . That meant that the new employer became responsible for reimbursing the previous employer by deduction from the worker's future wages up to a limit of one eighth.' And the system worked pretty well, as evidenced by the successful mediations of the industrial tribunals (*conseils de prud'hommes*).[121]

In spite of the success of arbitration and conciliation in France in the first half of the nineteenth century, the bare market system, even without the unfairness of the Anglo-Saxon penal sanction for breach of contract, proved to be untenable. According to the German dictionary, edited by the famous linguists Jacob and Wilhelm Grimm, *Gewerbefreiheit* (freedom of trade) must end where *Gewerbefrechheit* (impudence of trade) begins.[122] And it was exactly this sensitivity for *Gewerbefrechheit* that would grow after the mid-nineteenth century, when the hopes for arbitration and conciliation as a panacea were waning, in particular in Britain. Think of the role of artisans and workers in Chartism in Britain and in the 1848 revolutions in France and Germany. The focal point became the workers' right to form associations in order to improve their own bargaining power by collective industrial action, including the strike weapon.

From the second half of the nineteenth century, workers in more and more countries gradually gained the legal right to unite into trade unions. Previously, this had only been legally possible in a few countries, for example in the UK, albeit with severe restrictions on action.[123] Although the Combination Acts of 1799–1800 propagated mediation and arbitration and made industrial action an offence, workmen nevertheless were allowed to associate peacefully to improve wages and conditions of work. In 1825, these organizational restrictions were repealed, but until 1867 workers still faced criminal punishment for breach of contract, which was a serious impediment to collective action by trade unions. In France, the *compagnonnage* and, during the 1860s, many trade unions were tolerated, but the latter were only legalized in 1884.[124] Many other European countries emulated these principles. It took most of the nineteenth century to ensure the legal right everywhere to set up a trade union that was allowed to wage collective action, and to abolish frustrating legislation along English or French lines.

Trade union rights were not unanimously declared by all countries, as they eventually were in Britain, France and most other European nations. The US, for example, offers a very messy history of tensions between a constitutional right to organize and continuous hostile court rulings of the kind pronounced by Justice Peckham. Even the federal National Labor Relations Act (NLRA, also called the Wagner Act), based in the First and Thirteenth Amendments of the American Constitution and enacted by

President Roosevelt in 1935, has not put an end to this.[125] It will come as no surprise that the Europeans afforded their subjects in the colonies such rights much later than at home.[126] In many other countries of varying political shades, including communist countries, trade unions have been forbidden or totally subsumed in order to render them powerless.

Growing state concerns about the labour market

From the second half of the nineteenth century, the national state became an increasingly important player in this process of reregulation and recorporation. It also became an independent actor in terms of being a legislator and enforcer. In fact, it had long been so in its role as employer, especially of soldiers, sailors and civil servants, and the significance of this role increased with the nationalization of companies and especially with the abolition of private ownership of the means of production in communist countries. In the welfare states, the sharp increase in tax revenues was also partly used to facilitate numerous civil servants carrying out these new tasks.[127] This new role, essentially meant to counter assumed equality in the labour market, could have various and overlapping political backgrounds: from defensive conservatism (think of Bismarck in Germany, but also of papal initiatives) via social-democratic consensus, to radical attempts at making workers' rights dominant.

In terms of the forms and domains, we find state interference by way of the continuation and expansion of the conciliation or arbitration that we have seen before – voluntarily in the US and the UK and compulsorily in Canada, Australia and New Zealand, for example.[128] A second domain concerns the protection of those not considered capable of defending their own interests – first children and women, and only later all industrial workers – as seen in a plethora of factory acts and concomitant state-run inspectorates. In this field, we can speak of an international movement in which best practices (of course defined along political convictions) were tried out and emulated, famous examples being the Factory Act of Japan (1911) and the Labour Union Law of China (1924).[129] Crucial here is which workers are included and which are not, as exemplified by the Indian case, where the vast majority of wage earners, defined as belonging to the 'informal sector', are not protected at all by the state.

In addition, we also see in the twentieth century that the national state took over the traditional role of local authorities to directly promote the well-being of its inhabitants, and especially of the wage recipients within it, and increasingly to determine the lives of working people through national labour legislation. This went much further than income policy through differentiated taxation, combined with poor relief.

What were the attempted solutions in the welfare states? If only to offer an alternative for socialism, considered as extremely dangerous, all industrializing countries attempted some form of regulation of safety and working hours in the factories. Equally important was state interference in insurance matters. As we have seen, in case of conflicts, mediation, sometimes by special courts, was also offered. A next step was state interference in labour market intermediation, the setting of minimum wages and, finally, unemployment provisions, apart from poor relief.[130]

In the following, I focus in particular on some important forms of workers' insurance, and especially those against work accidents, sickness and unemployment before the First World War. The two main varieties of workers' insurance, emulated in one way or another worldwide, developed in Britain and Germany.[131]

Insurance schemes against accidents, sickness and unemployment: Two models

In Britain, for a long time, the state's basic response was the enhancement of 'self-help', especially in the form of mutual insurance against temporary incapacity to work due to sickness and accidents, organized by Friendly Societies, mostly established independently of the masters. The state attempted to improve the quality of the services of these societies by requiring their registration. In contrast, the Prussian states and, from 1871, the Reich also relied on self-help, but by turning it into a compulsory, contributory, state-controlled insurance. They did so because, while (much later than England) introducing *Gewerbefreiheit* (breaking guild monopolies and thus allowing free immigration into towns), they felt compelled to take over part of their social security provisions. Firstly, and more generally, the new 1842 Prussian poor legislation applied to all resident Prussian citizens employed on a regular basis, including servants, journeymen and craftsmen. Secondly, and more specifically, the Prussian *Gewerbeordnung* of 1845 authorized local authorities to reimpose the requirement to belong to local trade-specific journeymen funds. Additionally, when Prussia abolished its monopoly over mining between 1854 and 1865, it maintained compulsory membership of the *Knappschaften*, invalidity insurance financed by mine owners and workers alike, dating from the sixteenth century. Such legislation formed a precedent for further compulsory insurance under state direction. Leaving aside – however interesting – a comparison between British and German approaches to insurance against accidents and sickness,[132] we will concentrate here on insurance against unemployment.

Unemployment provisions and job mediation

Insurance against unemployment, at least for a limited period of time, is one of the oldest but also most difficult aspects of the provisions of guilds and mutual benefit societies.[133] It is difficult because in organizations with members from one and the same trade, all of them could be affected simultaneously, but in more mixed organizations, too, a downturn of the trade cycle would leave any system struggling with near-insurmountable difficulties. Hence such provisions, where they existed, always included many restrictions. Most of the time, provisions only took effect after a certain period and were only in place for a short time. The alternative was poor relief, but mostly in return for participation of the temporarily (and therefore 'respectable') unemployed in works that were considered to be useful, in particular public works. In the words of the British minister Joseph Chamberlain in 1886: 'By offering reasonable work at low wages we may secure the power of being very strict with the loafer and the confirmed pauper.'[134] On a local scale, the public works solution encountered many obstacles.

Once again, we detect important differences when comparing the national social policies of Germany and Britain in the late nineteenth century. In Germany, unemployment insurance existed in only a few towns, whereas in Britain the National Insurance Act of 1911 included compulsory insurance against unemployment. Once more, the question arises: why were there such big differences in two modern and successfully industrializing countries?

The British solution of 1911 entailed compulsory weekly payments by the regularly employed (workers 38 per cent, employers 38 per cent and government 24 per cent) in unemployment-prone sectors, mainly building and construction. Disbursements only kicked in after one week and for a maximum of fifteen weeks per year. Unemployment caused by a strike was excluded. On the other hand, the state subsidized voluntary unemployment insurance by trade unions. After the First World War, long-term mass employment resulted in this being extended to all sectors in 1921, and to the conversion of a flat-rate benefit into one including dependents' allowances.

In Germany, as in many continental European countries, the so-called Ghent system prevailed – that is to say, the provision of only local subsidies to local trade unions. Unions accepting such subsidies had to strictly separate their unemployment funds from their general means, which could be used to compensate members for loss of income during a strike. Here, the tradition of the local labour exchange was much older than in Britain. Between 1869 and 1900, they were free of government control, but subsequently they had to operate under a licence in order to foster transparency. As an increasing number of trade unions included unemployment benefits in their package, they also tried to occupy part of the job mediation market. In 1903, non-profit mediation accounted for 30 per cent of such mediations. Private employer-controlled job mediation, of course, offered plenty of opportunities for the blacklisting of labour activists and other critical workers.

By 1904–05, Germany counted 216 public labour exchanges against only 21 in England. Their success in Germany was partly due to the trade unions' adoption of unemployment insurance, from 1911 subsidized according to the Ghent system. It was executed by local governments who partially drew from charitable contributions, but increasingly from public means. This contribution increased benefits by 50 per cent for a defined maximum number of days. The establishment of labour exchanges, managed equally by members from employers' and workers' organizations, enabled the participants to judge whether unemployment was genuinely voluntary. The composition of the management in fact favoured more skilled labourers because their unions could run unemployment insurance funds much more successfully. For the same reason, this helped them to unite workers in a particular branch. Politically, the acceptance of the Ghent system in German towns signals a fundamental change in German welfare policy and the acceptance of trade unions 'as legitimate actors in the regulation of social problems'.[135]

Nevertheless, it concerned only a minority of the German towns and urban workforce because it presupposed the power of the socialists, the trade unions and their supporters to convince a town government that subsidizing workers' unemployment funds was a good idea. In Belgium, this was the case in Ghent, but in most German towns political majorities were not in favour of workers' organizations. Hence the British solution was more successful because 'organized labour was effectively integrated as part of the British political system'.[136] That was not the case in Germany, where a far smaller proportion of the labour force was unionized than in Britain.

The emergence of welfare states

All measures and legislation discussed so far may be seen, at best, as institutions to improve or even optimize the functioning of the market and, at worst, as stopgaps for an essentially unjust system. Those who adhered to the latter interpretation have tried to eliminate the market or most of it by getting rid of (big) employers. In communist states, however, sickness, old age and other lifecycle problems are present as well, and there, too, insurance has been accepted as the best solution, although not voluntarily or compulsorily paid for by the workers themselves but rather financed by general taxation.

Other states had been preparing in a practical way for the exigencies of the welfare state long before the concept even came into being. They did so by employing more and more wage workers directly. Before the introduction of military conscription, many states acquired the necessary managerial skills by maintaining professional armies. The execution of military conscription also asked for plenty of bureaucratic and managerial skills. The expanding tasks of the national state in the nineteenth and twentieth centuries – including staff for the colonies – also reflected this.

The social legislation reviewed above was the result not only of collective action but also of individual voting behaviour.[137] With the expansion of suffrage and voting rights to large parts of the population, not only was the state forced to intervene increasingly and more intricately in the work of its citizens-no-longer-subjects; states also cherished the pretension that it was best to provide good working conditions and a good income, and they promised their citizens the best of all worlds – the welfare state in all its variations. These promises were particularly strong during and after the world wars: in exchange for the untold sacrifices of its citizens for the nation, in turn, the state would ensure that the citizens' lot definitively improved. Thus, all the suffering would not have been for nothing.

These mutual expectations of the majority of working voters and the promises made to them by elected officials led to serious political tensions that dominated the last century, forcing employers into the role of lobbyists, if nothing else due to their smaller numbers – a role that they naturally played with verve. Already before the First World War, the powerful Central Association of German Industrialists (based on the iron and steel conglomerates) saw the approaching storm. Following the 1911 law on a separate white-collar insurance, Alexander Tille, a leading member of the association, commented:

> This is a legislative measure based neither on destitution nor on regard for the maintenance of the nation's strength. It is merely an aspect of so-called social policy, i.e. of consideration for the wishes of those voters to whom it is desired to show consideration. If it becomes a custom in Germany that, whenever any particular group of the population wishes to be maintained in greater comfort, the government makes a law to satisfy their wishes, it will not be long before we are in a socialist state.[138]

His prediction would prove true quicker than he had thought or feared, but he was too pessimistic about the resilience of his organization and that of other employer organizations in a parliamentary democracy, as history would demonstrate time and again.

In most countries, the welfare state has never been declared, nor has it been abolished as such. An exception, albeit not utilizing this precise term, is the seizure of power by authoritarian parties who promised utopia from the outset. The Russian Revolution and its imitators are the most famous examples, and also corporatist regimes, in particular in the interwar period, which rendered parliamentary democracy redundant in favour of the greater happiness and welfare for all – except for their scapegoats, of course.

Yet, it also did not emerge out of the blue. The emerging nationalism in the nineteenth century paid increasing attention to the population's workforce and wanted to deploy it for the fatherland. The concern for its enforcement ensued later. A fine example comes from Japan, where the *Factory Girls' Reader*, a simple textbook for young, female textile workers from 1911, wrote about the necessity of 'Working for the Sake of the Country':

> Everyone, if you all work to the utmost of your abilities from morning to night, there can be no loyalty to the country greater than this. If you do not work thus and stay idly at home, the country of Japan will become poorer and poorer. Therefore, work with all your might for the country's

sake, enabling Japan to become the greatest country in the world. Everyone of you, no matter what your age, you would not want to become a burden to your father and mother who have to toil unceasingly.... For your own sake, for your family's sake, for your country's sake, devote yourself heart and soul to your work.[139]

The First World War brought the first acceleration in the willingness of parliamentary democracy – not coincidentally only then having come to full maturity – to guarantee forms of income and other welfare. This was no longer intended as a remedy and, in extremis, to prevent serious social unrest, but as a universal right for all those committed to the salvation of the nation, de facto for all workers and in particular for wage workers and the self-employed. The concern for wage dependents was primarily expressed in the prevention of mass unemployment, if only because it was the biggest threat – in the short term, because of demonstrations or, in the worst case, the looting of shops, or in the long term, due to punishment in the elections and the change of political parties in power.

As we have seen, on the eve of the war, legislation was already being passed in the core industrial countries. However great the differences in implementation were between different countries, the general tendency was to regulate welfare not only locally but also nationally, and thus uniformly, and to combat not only the most extreme poverty but, increasingly via obligatory insurance, that of, especially, the wage dependent (something that subsequently became active labour market policy). The precondition for this was the discovery of the phenomenon of unemployment. That sounds strange now, but until the 1890s the word 'unemployment' was rarely used. Whereas the French census of 1891 offered no possibility to register someone as unemployed, that of 1896 did so for the first time. Now an explicit distinction was made between those voluntarily unemployed (persons aged 65 and over were regarded as no longer active and hence not among the unemployed) and the real jobless.[140]

This awareness among statisticians of unemployment as a structural phenomenon originated in the discovery of the regularity of trade cycles in the last decades of the nineteenth century. This discovery is reflected in the Minority Report of the British Royal Commission on the Poor Laws of 1919. Traditionally, its concern had been with casual unemployment, but now the proposal was to abandon the much-hated local relief programmes and, most significantly, the alternative: instead of the traditional remedies, the report proposed counter-cyclical variation in work contracted by the central government departments. The labourers engaged in such projects should be rewarded with normal wage standards. The report also raised the issue of funding these works by borrowing from underemployed capital during a depression, to be repaid during a boom.[141]

The First World War, which ended the long nineteenth century, with its endless series of official and less official reports on the poor and then on the unemployed, brought about a new period of intensified activity. Two causes of this major change during the war stand out clearly: firstly, massive state intervention in national economics, including the labour market (among other things, at the cost of employers' initiatives);[142] and secondly, claims by workers on social security in exchange for the sufferings of war, claims that had to be taken seriously as a result of widespread revolutionary threats.

As the Great War turned out to be more than a single campaign with a handful of major battles, governments increasingly had to mobilize their national resources, now including the labour market. Major parts of the labour force not only were channelled into military service, but simply never returned. Around 16 million combatants died or were lost in the war, and another 20 million were wounded. In order to meet increased production targets, more and more men and, in particular, women (see pp. 337–8) were drawn or even forced into the labour market, especially into the war industries.

In the revolutionary years that followed the Armistice, governments started to proclaim the right to paid work for their citizens – echoing an old claim by the French revolutionaries of 1848. As the first democratic constitution for Germany, the *Weimarer Verfassung* of August 1919, stated in Article 163: 'Every German will be offered the possibility to take care of himself by paid labour. As far as appropriate labour cannot be provided, his basic needs will be cared for.'[143] But it was not only in the defeated countries that workers claimed their rights. In Britain, in March 1919, Lloyd George's cabinet refused to return to the gold standard (abandoned in 1914) out of fear of the prospect of unemployment, especially among demobilized soldiers. For the first time in British history, unemployment took political priority over the opinion of the Bank of England and the Treasury. As we have seen, in many countries, compulsory state-induced unemployment insurance and state-organized labour exchange became intertwined. After a try-out of the combination in 1911, Britain was the first country to intro-duce a virtually universal compulsory unemployment scheme connected to the labour exchanges in 1921. Other countries, like Sweden, developed a dual system, in which the government dealt with unemployment insurance and employers and unions cooperated in labour mediation.

The Great Depression of the 1930s re-intensified the debate about ways to steer the labour market. While Germany adhered to the primacy of politics, Britain emphasized understanding the workings of the market. Guidance was offered by the now widely accepted conclusions of the 1909 Minority Report and by William Beveridge's new and influential book *Unemployment: A Problem of Industry* (1930). Beveridge, intellectually cooperating with Keynes, understood that unemployment is nothing more or less than an economic problem of matching supply and demand in the labour market.[144] As a result of these intellectual developments, the liberal government in the 1930s again abandoned gold, thus enabling exchange-rate policies that, in addition to protectionism, favoured competitiveness and thus employment opportunities. It also promoted labour exchanges, counter-cyclical works of 'national utility' and, above all, national insurance for those in cyclical trades – relieving unemployment, but not curing it.

Most central, eastern and southern European countries adopted different measures, much more heavily biased towards a primacy of politics over economics. Germany's answer was a total state monopoly of labour market regulation: not a universal right to labour but the universal duty to work became the point of departure, years before Hitler came to power. In fact, strong labour market politics or even dictatorial measures became widely accepted in view of the new situation. At the Geneva Conference of 1934, Harold Butler, the director of the ILO, saw no problem in saying that Italy, together with the US, the Soviet Union and Germany, was at the forefront of creating a new economy. He praised Italy's progress 'in the construction of the corporative system that breaks away with economic theories based on individualism'. This was all the more remarkable since, by that time, unemployment in Italian industry was two-and-a-half times higher than in 1929. Most of the policies of the Italian fascists were not new. Their semi-official international recognition, however, shows how deeply the Depression had influenced the ideological approach to labour policies worldwide.[145]

Not only in those countries that were already heavily centralized in the 1930s but also in others like Britain, the Second World War signalled a rapid expansion and intensification of government intervention in the economy, even more so than in the First World War. London now accepted a fiscal policy aimed not only at funding the war but also at fighting inflation (the great problem in the preceding war) by keeping personal budgets down. This revolutionary Keynesian integration of national budget and national accounts would endure in the post-war decades. From 1942, comprehensive manpower planning was organized by a Ministry of Labour and National Service. The Treasury lost its central role, as illustrated by the proliferation of economists in the government bureaucracy and a growing trust in rational intelligence as a way to resolve social problems, which was also seen during reconstruction after the war. Liberals like Beveridge and Keynes became more important than Conservatives and Labour. They wanted to reform the existing economic system without threatening private property.

The 1944 White Paper on Employment Policy distinguished between frictional, structural and general unemployment and pleaded for 'high and stable' employment. Beveridge's programmatic publication of that same year was entitled *Full Employment in a Free Society*. He advocated a strong role for government planning in the public sector, though private investment would continue. These ideas deeply influenced politics not only in Britain but across Europe. Because of the increased competition between the two great socio-political systems, Western European governments were now even more convinced than they had been after the First World War that they had to respond to workers' claims by introducing fundamental changes to social and economic policies.

Notably, as the Cold War gained momentum in the 1950s, while economic growth proved possible beyond imagination, the welfare state became the norm in Western Europe – to such an extent that nothing seemed more normal than this state of affairs. A combination of scholarly insight and political will seems to have resulted in a solution to 'make' society. The general optimism about what was seen as the result of Keynesian economic policy was expressed by Michael Stewart in his *Keynes and After*. In this widely read Penguin pocket reader, first published in 1969, reprinted several times and translated into many languages, this senior advisor to the Wilson Labour government was happy to announce:

Mass unemployment was brought to an end by the Second World War. It never returned. Despite dire predictions in 1945, Britain has now enjoyed full employment for more than thirty years. Such a tremendous transfor-mation might be expected to have many causes. But in fact the evidence points to one cause above all others: the publication in 1936 of a book called *The General Theory of Employment, Interest and Money* by John Maynard Keynes.[146]

The period is also characterized by an emphasis on international agreements. European governments considered them essential to the success of the welfare state. It was thought that only agreements of this kind could prevent a country from being drawn into a crisis by another one, with unforeseeable consequences. Britain was particularly active in pursuing such agreements in the late 1940s and early 1950s, especially through the Economic and Social Council of the UN (ECOSOC), but largely in vain because of American opposition. In the end, the GATT (General Agreement on Tariffs and Trade) was the only device left after the still-birth of the ITO (International Trade Organization) and the short-lived Bretton Woods Agreement. This was a far cry from the Keynesian ideals of the 1940s.

Before continuing the saga of the welfare state, after it was challenged deeply during the economic world crisis of the 1970s and after, let us briefly turn to the communist variant, and its competition with the democratic variant, as briefly described, both within Europe and in the rest of the world.[147]

The Soviet Union was the first country to take radical measures to ensure a just income for its working population.[148] By cutting out profit for employers and embracing the ideal of equality of the French Revolution, a workers' paradise would be created on Earth. The reality was different. The objective facts are that, until at least the 1950s, the USSR remained an agrarian society largely living under harsh climatic circumstances. That could, of course, be said about Canada as well, but what is different are the disasters on Russian soil caused by two world wars and a protracted civil war, together lasting some thirteen years, in the period 1914–45. The Soviet leadership was perfectly aware of this. It therefore preached that the masses should be patient and that, before entry into the heavens of real communism – the welfare state, communist-style – could be achieved, a transition period of 'socialism' was necessary.

Under transitional 'socialism', wage differentials were still deemed necessary as labour incentives to overcome economic problems of low productivity and low industrialization. This refers to what Marx wrote in 1875 in his *Critique of the Gotha Programme*. According to him, the first phase is one in which goods are still scarce and people need extra incentives to work for the final goal. That goal is communism when there is not only abundance but when also, ultimately, this abundance is distributed from each according to his ability, to each according to need. Lenin wrote in the margin of his own copy of the first printed edition (1890–91) of this book the biblical judgement 'he who does not work, neither shall he eat'. In total alignment, Stalin flatly called the egalitarianism of the trade unions, dating from before the revolution and still powerful in the early 1930s before the purges, 'petty-bourgeois'. As late as the 1960s and 1970s, Soviet academic economists were stating that 'excessive equality' would threaten the building of communism – the main objective of socialist society.[149]

These constraints between the ideal of communism and its welfare rights, as promulgated in several constitutions between 1918 and 1977,[150] and the realities of a revolutionary transformation of the country into a modern industrial state under extremely adverse circumstances, determined the peculiarities of the Soviet welfare state. In order to meet the needs of the people, the USSR distinguished between free-of-charge services, in particular education between the ages of 7 and 17–18 (plus partially kindergarten and free tuition and stipends for universities) as well as medical care, and the remaining goods and services at subsidized prices.

In order to enable people to buy their food, pay their rent and so on, the state, which in principle as owner of the means of production disposed of all goods and services produced, made transfer payments to particular groups. This included pensions and sickness benefits (but no unemployment benefits after 1930!), maternity benefits, child allowances and a few more – plus, of course, cash wages. In the 1950s and 1960s, the hope was expressed that even more goods would be transferred from the ability to pay for them to distribution 'according to need'. The Party Programme of 1961 – Khrushchev's vision of a welfare state – claims that this real communism would apply to things like bread, housing, urban transport and meals in factory canteens. But these claims have never been realized.[151]

Reality was harsh, however, and Stalin departed from the idea that the peasantry, now members of collective farms, would take care of themselves. For the rest of the population, mainly state employees under conditions of full employment, only disability pensions were needed for the victims of industrial accidents and, from 1941, of war accidents. All others in need were idlers, wilfully refusing work. It was only recognized in the 1960s that this could not be maintained, as substantial parts of the population officially lived in poverty. Out of a total population of 230 million in 1965, no fewer than some 50 million state employees and their dependents, plus 30 million kolkhoz members, lived below the poverty line.[152]

This points to a dramatic failure of the Soviet-style welfare state, even if real income per capita may have doubled between 1965 and 1990.[153] Fortunately, reality was not entirely bleak, due to the inventiveness of the Russian population. In infinitely creative ways, it circumvented the rules and improved living conditions at the household level with the live-in grand-mother as the indispensable centre.[154] This was thriving babushka-household-welfare as a compensation for a very bleak state welfare. As a result, popular scepticism about the state's pretensions became widespread following failures to deliver social policies in the 1970s and 1980s. Therefore, and apart from all sorts of unfreedom, perestroika, involving the introduction of markets in the place of central planning, came as no surprise.

The competition between communist and capitalist (including socialist) worldviews gained a boost after the Russian Revolution. Not only did both sides try to overthrow each other by economic and political means, but also the appeal of their material success, especially apparent from welfare provi-sions, played a role now. The virtues of 'really existing socialism' were propa-gated by communist parties worldwide under the strict control of the Communist International (Komintern) based in Moscow. Stalin declared to the world about the 1936 constitution: 'the working class of the USSR is completely new, liberated from exploitation, a working class the like of which the history of humanity has not known'.[155]

In the interwar period, this competition was especially visible in the colo-nies of the Western powers. There, the colonizers' welfare pretensions had only recently emerged and, in general, had not yet been very successful. So, the communist model could successfully boast of the availability in Russia of free education and medical care when even the most idealistic proponents of enlightened colonialism had to confess their impotence in these fields.

The extension of communism after the war, eastwards to China and westwards to Eastern and Central Europe and the Balkans, put the wind in the sails of the communist appeal, including in parts of the world where colonizers were reluctant to give up their power. Propaganda regarding different types of welfare played a central role in the Cold War.[156] Happy workers on Chinese and Russian posters may have played a role, supplanting hard facts about the proletariat's real income in material terms. More important, however, was the communist promise, just as before the war, of free education and free medical care (notwithstanding the poor performance of these, evidenced by very negative demographic developments) and the right to work, as well as the early closing of the gender gap in education and low social inequality. More than Angola, Mozambique or Vietnam, Castro's Cuba offers the perfect example of an application of this overseas.

But the Western idea of the welfare state also had a wider appeal. That is often forgotten in all the gloom about austerity measures in the West. In the democratization wave of the 1980s and 1990s, in which many military and other dictatorships died, the civic movement simultaneously promoted a better reward for work and more security of existence.[157] We see this in, for example, Argentina and Brazil, but also in South Korea and Taiwan in this period. In South Korea, four decades of authoritarian rule came to an end with a civic movement in which the general strike of 1996–97 played a decisive role. In their simultaneous demand for democracy and redistribution, social welfare workers and their trade unions and reformist elites worked together.[158]

In the backlash of neoliberal market reforms that quickly followed, in particular with the Asian Financial Crisis of 1997 and the global banking crisis of 2008, many of these achievements survived. Everything was nibbled away from the universal social insurance scheme that was introduced in South Korea from 1997, especially in the sphere of old-age pensions, but its national health care programme proudly remained in place. The welfare gains of the early 2000s in Brazil and especially Argentina have suffered most.

After the demise of the Soviet Union, only China is left as a powerful protagonist of communist welfare, in particular after it has been able to realize impressive economic growth figures and recently also to invest heavily in poor Asian and African countries. Maybe because the Western world no longer shows pride in its welfare achievements, China seems to have recently lost its inclination to do so too. Overseas investment and economic growth are the new slogans, leaving recipients and the rest of the world in the dark about other possible objectives. The spread of the communist welfare example definitively seems to have vanished from the scene, to be replaced by the New Silk Roads.[159]

The welfare state in trouble

Nowhere else has the welfare state been jeopardized more than in the country that started it all. In 1985, Margaret Thatcher's Conservative government published the White Paper 'Employment: The Challenge for the Nation', with its central message that the government has only to create a climate in which private enterprise can flourish. The main difference with the 1944 White Paper was the rejection of the government's responsibility for welfare; its only task was to 'set the framework for the nation's effort'.[160] It should concentrate its efforts not on the demand side, as in 1944, but rather on the supply side of labour, by training young people, by propagating better management and wage moderation and by starting an extensive programme of 'deregulation'.

The change in international perspective between the 1944 and the 1985 White Papers was striking. In 1985, there was no longer any talk of international cooperation, only of national policies: 'external events are treated as entirely exogenous, outside any control of government'. Arguably, this reflects the decline of Britain's international power over the previous forty years, but also the fact that 'its perceived scope for successful action [was] reduced almost to vanishing point'.

Although the trend towards the deregulation and reduced pretensions of the welfare state is evident in all countries in the North Atlantic, there are still substantial differences between the US, Britain and the Continent. In the US, the distinction between the privileged, white, male breadwinners and other wage earners was pronounced long before Reagan. In 1960, the American public intellectual Paul Goodman, in his peculiar and provocative style, had already contrasted the working poor in America ('Negroes, Puerto Ricans and Mexicans, migrant farm labor') that were 'outside society' with, on the one hand, the factory workers, and on the other:

> the vast herd of the old-fashioned, the eccentric, the criminal, the gifted, the serious, the men and women, the *rentiers*, the freelancers ... Its fragmented members hover about the organization in multifarious ways – running specialty shops, trying to teach or to give other professional services, robbing banks, landscape gardening, and so forth – but they find it hard to get along, for they do not know the approved techniques of promoting, getting foundation grants, protecting themselves by official unions, legally embezzling, and not blurting out the truth, or weeping or laughing out of turn.[161]

The much greater income inequality in the US compared to Western Europe, which goes hand in hand with rising labour productivity, can be explained by the drop of the federal minimum wage. Still the highest in the world in the 1950s/1960s, it has dropped by 30 per cent since the 1970s and 1980s.[162]

In the European countries, to a certain extent, the 'Rhine Economic Model'[163] is upheld against the neoliberal model of Reagan and Thatcher, with social justice versus efficiency; compromise, consensus and cooperation versus confrontation and competition; long-term stability versus dynamism and change focusing on short-term results; and finally, a concept of government as a difficult yet vital partner, with a mutual dependency between government and the economic actors, versus a modest government that should be kept at arm's length. It is remarkable that Germany, despite its major difficulties in uniting the two former parts of the country after 1989, has stuck to the principles of the Rhineland economy. And also outside Europe we cannot simply speak in an overly pessimistic tone of the demise of the welfare state; think again of the examples of South Korea and Taiwan. China, too, deserves special attention, and very recently even India.

This does not mean that nothing has changed on the European continent. The welfare state has clearly lost part of its pretensions, certainly after the deep financial crisis of 2008. The outcome is an increase in social inequality, as pointed out effectively by the French economist Thomas Piketty, who indicates the drop in the share of national income going to labour.[164] To be clear, this is primarily about the widening gap and less about the stagnation of incomes at the bottom, in particular of wages over the past four decades. Despite the widespread availability of mobile phones and other electronic devices, Piketty believes that the real available income per household of 'the bottom 50 per cent by income' barely grew, if at all, in these years, certainly in the US. And again: this is despite a sharp increase in labour productivity,[165] not only in continental Europe, but – as might be expected – certainly also in Britain and the US. This growth in inequality perhaps hides an even more important phenomenon: the stagnation in social mobility in the North Atlantic. Whereas in the first half of the twentieth century, workers there got used to improved standards of living generation after generation, this mobility has clearly slowed down. For many, like those in the American 'rust belts', it has simply vanished in recent decades. Many workers and small independent producers have simply lost hope of any improvement for themselves and for their offspring in the long run.

As already indicated several times, most countries, with the US and the UK taking the lead, adopted diametrically different socio-economic policies from 1980. In democratic countries there was also sufficient electoral support for this, in particular because wage workers turned their backs on social democratic parties (Labour in the UK, the Democrats in the US, and so on). According to Piketty, this collapse of the working-class vote for socialist, communist and social-democratic parties was directly linked to 'the reversal of the educational cleavage', coinciding with a significant expansion of educational opportunities and upward social mobility in the post-war decades: 'the less educationally advantaged classes came to believe that the parties of the left now favor the newly advantaged educated classes and their children over people of more modest backgrounds'. In France, for example, 'those [working-class] children and grandchildren who managed to make it to the university (and particularly those who earned the more advanced university degrees) are the ones who continued to vote for the parties of the left with the same frequency as the less educated voters of 1956'. And, as he shows, this does not only apply to France.[166]

The growth of income inequality within countries is now even becoming a global phenomenon. At the same time, the deep gap in economic performance between the different parts of the world is closing, in the first place due to the rapid rise of China, but now also due to India – with a completely different political system – having made gains.

We have already seen the expansion of wage labour between 1500 and 1800, mainly as an extra source of income for peasants outside the rare and generally still small towns. After 1800, it increasingly became the sole source of income – and is currently so for the majority of the global population. The advent of wage labour has had a number of implications for the way we look upon work and how we, as working humans, try to defend our interests, individually, collectively and in the political framework.

Initially, it brought about the phenomenon of the male breadwinner ideology, which has only recently been receding in order to include all workers. Alongside examples of apartheid and inside-outside thinking, we have also seen the advent worldwide of the norms of horizontal cooperation, job pride and fair labour relations. Think of the mainstream Tille or the more extreme positions of Lafargue and Malevich. And let us not forget all those examples of collective action that we have encountered in this chapter. Think, finally, of the principles on which the ILO and the United Nations are built, however problematic their execution.

The close connection between industrialization, efficiency and wage labour has also tilted the ratio between working time and leisure time. Whereas in earlier times, most waking hours had to be spent on work, in the last century leisure and schooling have taken that position. It should be noted that in the 'Global North' this movement halted a few decades ago, but not in the 'Global South', and especially not in China in recent decades. In particular, if we take the household as a unit of analysis, in the 'Global North' we observe another increase in the hours worked by husband and wife together. However, their compensation in real terms, per hour, appears to have been stagnating for a number of decades. Economic growth accompanied by an equal distribution of welfare, which was the norm in the 1950s and 1960s, is over.[167]

More hours per household spent on the job enables it to increase consumption, primarily in the rich North Atlantic and its offshoots, but at a price – and with the undoubtedly detrimental consequences for the environment, including climate change (a theme that is beyond the scope of this story). To exaggerate slightly, the more prosperous workers do not have enough time to spend their earnings. And notwithstanding the passing of the first, the second and the third industrial revolutions (an expression borrowed from Jeremy Rifkin), the availability of jobs has not diminished.

Wage workers defend their interests differently from their self-employed counterparts, who still today mainly rely on the strength of the household. Apart from private strategies, among which geographical and social mobility are especially important, wage workers have also further developed what is called their repertoire of collective action. Trade unionism immediately comes to mind, but historically we may discern many more types of collective action and of organizations. The balance between private and collective strategies is continuously moving. After periods of success for trade unionism following the First World War and especially the Second World War, this type of organization is now clearly in trouble.

The successes of classical collective action have brought about the welfare state in many different forms worldwide. Common is the increasing role of the state as an arbiter of the labour market and as a provisioner of welfare. This has become an integral part of the democratic process.

But to what extent, for how long, and what are its implications? That, as well as a general reflection on the nature of work from a long-term perspective, is the theme of the Outlook that concludes this book.

OUTLOOK

One of the questions that arises at the end of this deep history of work across time and space is whether it informs how work will be organized and undertaken henceforth. What does the historical record suggest about what needs to be done in order for us to better control our collective future? Certainly, general lines can be distinguished – in the last centuries, for example, as a result of watersheds like 'The Great Transformation' (the mechanization by steam power that led to the declining importance of agriculture in industrializing countries), 'The Second Great Transformation', in which, from around 1970, services took the lead over manufacturing while states simultaneously loosened their grip on the market and, finally, the robotic transformation that we find ourselves in now.[1] If we survey the entire history of work, however, there are reasons enough to be suspicious of simplistic fault lines, based, in particular, on the experience of rich countries over the past few centuries. Yet we can conclude with four crucial elements that have become clear over the book's trajectory.

Artist Frans Masereel's response to an industrialist's opinion that 'in order to continue to exist, the world must produce more and talk less' (1919).

423

My primary reservation about over-simplistic predictions is the fact that all the major developments described here invariably evoked unexpected reactions. Appearance does not preclude disappearance. You only have to think of how market economies functioned for a millennium in Western Europe and India between 500 BCE and 500 CE, only to suddenly disappear again for half a millennium or more. Another example is the rise, fall and rise again of unfree labour within market economies. Despite the abolition and serious prosecution of slavery in the nineteenth century, and despite the establishment of the fundamental rights of working people in the Treaty of Versailles, it was not all that long ago that major countries such as Russia, Germany, Japan and China partially retrogressed to unfree labour. The transition of the housewife into the labour market has also been interrupted several times, as have fluctuations in the extent to which the ideal of the welfare state is embraced. The stagnation of remuneration and job security in especially the rich countries in recent decades (summarized in concepts such as flexibilization and precarization) can also be counted as types of reactions.[2] Or, in that context, the recent massive Keynesian state aid to companies and working people following the outbreak of the coronavirus pandemic – something that prior to this seemed absolutely unthinkable.

Secondly – and previous examples already point in this direction – the nature and vehemence of these reactions are not easy to predict; at least, not as easy as, say, a strike resulting from a massive cut in wages. Take, for example, the contradiction between the emergence of the workers' movement, which peaked one hundred years ago, and the current lack of successful collective actions to improve working conditions. And all this is taking place while the wealth gap within countries, between the richest inhabitants and the rest of the population, has been widening and deepening for decades. This increase in social inequality without apprehending the expected 'classic' social counter-movement seems new, unless we are convinced of an exact and thus ineliminable parallel between the emotional compensation offered by the 'nativist' (often referred to as populist) exclusion movements of the interwar period and those of today.

Thirdly, under the influence of digitization, there has been an unprecedented global convergence of prosperity levels and consumption patterns between countries in the past decades and a similar confluence of rewards for work. Simply put: at last, the Chinese are better off, while Europeans and Americans (and in particular the white males among them) must accept a standstill or even a step back. This is a new detail in a truly globalized world for which there are no historical parallels. Moreover, we are also seeing the re-emergence of counter-movements, as 'offshoring' (moving production to low-wage countries) is once more provoking a turnabout due to robotization in the North Atlantic and due to rising labour costs, especially in China: so-called reshoring. China, in turn, is not sitting still and is now seriously pursuing factory automation. This is not surprising for a country that stands on the cusp of ageing, something that has already begun in Japan and South Korea.[3]

Fourthly, and certainly not unimportant, for most states, globalization means an erosion of democratic decision making at the national level. Capital is withdrawing itself from the rules of play agreed within nation states. But it is also taking labour with it with the rise of the informal economy, if we define this as 'socially legitimate [in contrast to the criminal economy] paid work that is not declared to, hidden from, or unregistered with, the authorities for tax, social security and/or labour law purposes when it should be declared'. Where capital cancels the national contract, labour reaps the bitter benefits. In the European Union, some 10 per cent of the total labour input in the private sector is in the informal sector, representing 14.3 per cent of total gross value added (GVA, varying from 25 per cent in Poland, Romania and Lithuania to 7 per cent in Germany). It is even more impressive beyond Europe, with some 60 per cent of non-agricultural workers – based on a survey of 36 developing countries – being primarily employed in the informal economy.[4]

Seen in this light, globalization means the termination of the national social contract in the North Atlantic, or the failure to pursue it where it has already been weak for a long time. Large companies choose countries with low production costs (including low wages) and low taxes and pay their top management and shareholders from the increased profits. Workers are deployed as flexibly as possible. One of the techniques implemented is the outsourcing of services, made possible by employment agencies. Think of the altered power balance between European trade unions and the big internationals (the American trade unions hardly play a role). Consequently, the mentality and political preference of many working people, who feel victims of this, are also changed. Among this group, there is a rising hope that protectionism and restriction of international labour migration is the best solution.

If simply tracing historical lines is not easy or perhaps not even feasible, then I propose an alternative strategy in order to gain some insight into where we now stand as working people. I will begin with a brief discussion

of a number of scenarios that have been gaining ground in the recent literature. Subsequently, and also finally, I would like to consider the results of this
exercise in light of the main constants that the history of human work seems
to yield. Because they too exist.

Currently, there are a number of future scenarios circulating, most of
which do not concern us here because they have nothing to do with, or are
only very indirectly related to, labour.[5] The following five, however, deserve
our attention:

Firstly, the current dominant system of market economies (referred to as
'capitalist') is unsustainable, whether or not it is located in a democratic
society.[6] The most well-founded analysis of this is by the Dutch historian
Bas van Bavel, who, based on historical arguments, expects the current
market economy to perish irrevocably due to its internal weakness. Others
think that the past century of growing free labour, which has been increasingly well rewarded, was an exceptional period, not only with regard to its
history but also with respect to the future.

Secondly, the market economy is in deep trouble, as evidenced by
increasing social inequality within the rich countries – which, of course, is
different from the inequality between countries, which is decreasing sharply.[7]
As detailed in Chapter 7, the remuneration for work in rich countries, and
especially the US, has dropped to such low levels that precarious working
people need public assistance – and so taxpayers subsidize employers who
underpay their employees.[8] Piketty in particular is struck by the absence of
collective action and socio-political engagement to halt the diminishing
wages for labour in democratic countries, in the first place by restoring
strongly progressive taxation. He and others (such as the British Professor of
Development Studies Guy Standing) warn of the opportunities this political
inertia from the left offers right-wing identitarian politicians and the (potential) victims it will create.[9]

So far, so pessimistic; but there are also optimists out there.

Thirdly, while recognizing the crisis of the current system, optimism
about the renewal power of 'capitalism', especially through state intervention, prevails. This is the mainstream position of both policymakers and
academics in democratic countries.[10] There is a growing awareness of how,
until now, it has flourished under state protection (also in the US), demon-
strating that the market and the state deliver the strongest possible combination. This is evidenced by government efforts to eliminate or at least

mitigate the mismatch between the demand of the labour market for computer-literate workers and the supply of predominantly low-educated and/or non-tech-savvy unemployed.

Fourthly, there are those diehard neoliberals who see fewer problems; indeed, they only see opportunities. Despite recent deep economic crises, such as that of 2008 and the outbreak of coronavirus in 2020, they believe in the disappearance of the wage worker and put their faith in the new human, an entrepreneur and professional with their own business, always in search of opportunities. This self-employed working hero of the future will, moreover, be extremely mobile and would go in search of new challenges all over the world.[11]

Fifthly, there are those – both optimists and pessimists – who share an expectation regarding the final acceleration of technology, the most important consequence of which for this book is robotization.[12] Accompanying this would be an unprecedented shift in the balance between work and free time. The optimists among them herald the leisure time that this would deliver; the pessimists fear mass unemployment and an even more drastic drop in purchasing power and thus in demand. In addition, robotization would bite its own tail and the greying workforce would give a helping hand in this regard. A third variant, which is not so easy to characterize as either optimistic or pessimistic, is entirely related to the large multinationals that are the driving force behind robotization. The majority of nation states appear to be against global monopolies but, with the exception of China, they are no match for behemoths such as Amazon, Apple, IBM and Microsoft. These tech companies seem increasingly able to determine the public's taste. The ultimate consequence of this is the reduction of the citizen, and therefore also of the working citizen, to a mere consumer of ready-made fare. The ultimate 'Bread and Circuses' society – Yuval Harari's 'Age of Shopping' or even Aldous Huxley's *Brave New World* (1932).[13]

Having surveyed the whole history of work, then, what can this survey tell us about what to expect of its future? While no single scenario can be clearly argued to hold (or not), we can react to a number of established, even celebrated, projections in relation to the future of work: the 'end of capitalism', increased inequality, the role of the 'free' market in distributing work and pay, and the consequences of robotization.

The inevitable end of 'capitalism'?

Bas van Bavel's interesting and excellently documented vision of the last thousand years convincingly shows that economic 'capitalist' frontrunners, the major market economies – from the Abbasid Caliphate of Baghdad to the United States of America – inevitably ran into trouble after a few centuries and, consequently, had to surrender the baton again. This *translatio imperii* is undeniably a recurring phenomenon in history. It is, however, not so much the loss of the top position that is remarkable, but perhaps more the fact that, in most cases, the 'losers' were not much worse off in the long run. The system was not *that* self-destructive. Compare, for example, the prosperity of the Dutch today, even though the country's Golden Age was already a long time ago. The same is true for northern Italy, the southern Netherlands, the Dutch Republic, the UK, and the US losing its competition with East Asia.[14] And why would that not continue with other shifts in dominance in the foreseeable future?

Van Bavel has, of course, thought of this. He does not deny that, in the past, it may have been possible for losers to recover, albeit on a more modest footing, but he believes that this is no longer possible in our heavily globalized world in which old-style empires are simply not viable. But is this convincing? Think, firstly, about China. Whatever the weaknesses of this centrally managed market economy, it is certainly not yet buckling under the weight of globalization and global capital owners. And what of the argument posited by some labour historians about the exceptional nature of free wage labour? The big question is whether the undeniable precarization of sections of the workforce in recent decades is sufficiently broad and deep to be simply extrapolated to the future.

Increasing social inequality?

And so we come to Piketty's irrefutable assertion of the growing income disparity especially in the rich countries since the 1970s and 1980s. Prior to this, the incomes of wage workers had increased; subsequently, they stagnated, while, at the same time, the top incomes skyrocketed.

But the story does not end here. Against this stagnation of labour income stands the long-term growth of other forms of income for the ordinary man and woman, as we have seen in Chapter 7 (pp. 409–21). The pronounced disparity in income inequality in the North Atlantic, ushered in by Reagan and Thatcher's long-prepared ideological victory march, should not close our eyes to the almost paradoxical growth of social security expenditure and transfer payments, through taxes in the form of housing benefits, tax credits, child benefit and national insurance benefits, as demonstrated for England by Peter Sloman, who calls this 'the paradox of rising welfare spending in an age of neoliberalism'.[15] This entails a substantial shift in the portion of income of working-age adults with children being paid not by employers but by or via the government; the latter being less in the form of cash benefits and increasingly in the form of social insurance, housing subsidies, good free or state education and the like. For Great Britain, around the beginning of the new millennium, this meant that 'the increase in household earnings inequality was largely unwound by the tax and benefit system'.[16] Not only was this a shift away from dependence on employers (and collective action) and towards government officials, but it also meant, in particular, the latter's direct involvement in household finances. This type of assistance is, after all, 'means-tested', and this type of testing (increasingly digital) can be far-reaching and undermine autonomy within domestic relations.

We find proponents not only, predictably, among the political left (think of the Programa Bolsa Família, introduced in 2003 by Brazil's President Lula) but also among ideologically right-wing economists and politicians, who are sometimes pro forms of redistribution via a (Universal) Basic Income. The most famous example is the intellectual champion of the free market, Milton Friedman, who had already started developing his proposal for a Negative Income Tax in the Second World War.[17] For him, the difference between both approaches lies in the level of contribution, and most of all in the implementation of government control. In both cases, however, we see an undeniable increase in the gap between work and pay and a shift of employers' responsibilities to government.

In the context of this history of work, it is perhaps no surprise that the widening wealth gap within countries appears to be a centuries-long legacy of institutionally and ideologically anchored unequal appreciation and reward for labour. This is apparently separate from the traditional self-congratulations of aggrandizers and their universal support for ideologies that demean wage labour. It also contradicts their currently widely propagated belief that high rewards stem from like efforts and innate talent.

Societies dominated in the past by slavery, explicit caste hierarchy or more modern forms of institutionalized inequality, such as racial segregation and apartheid, seem to be, as it were hereditarily, the most burdened (which is not to say that the rest of the world, including Europe, is without sin). Think of the recent extreme increase in inequality in India, despite serious attempts since independence in 1947 to promote social opportunities for disadvantaged caste members via the constitution (1950, drawn up by Ambedkar, himself born a Dalit), which, in turn, facilitated affirmative action by way of 'reserva-tions'[18] – and also despite efforts to build a welfare state *à la* Beveridge, which, unfortunately, ended in a deep gulf between a protected 'formal' and an unprotected 'informal' sector.[19] In the US, too, affirmative action, as pleaded for by James Baldwin, Martin Luther King and Malcolm X, is a long way from delivering the desired result, as the Black Lives Matter movement does not fail to emphasize. Think, too, of post-apartheid South Africa, but also of Brazil, another example where the legacy of slavery (abolished just 130 years ago) looms large. The strongest example, of course, is the stubborn prevalence of value systems favouring inequality – despite utterances to the contrary – in the oil-rich states of the Arab world.[20]

Thus far, an inner circle of (especially male) citizens has shared at least a minimal number of rights to work and fair compensation. But the difference between *us* (adult males) and *them* (the others) does not stop there, certainly not in a world with great geographical mobility. In every country there is also an outer circle of working people who only partially belong and who only enjoy some, or none, of the legal benefits of inner circle members. They are, primarily, legally employed foreign workers. They always have fewer rights, even within the European Union, and sometimes far less, as is the case in the Gulf States and Saudi Arabia.[21] Finally, there are the disenfranchised illegals, the *sans-papiers*. The most extreme version of the outer circle is a society exploiting a minority of *Untermenschen* without any form of remuneration. The Second World War has shown us many examples of this, and, unfortu-nately, we cannot say the possibility can be ruled out in the future.[22]

The logical follow-up question is why collective action in the face of the increasing welfare gap has become so rare, in comparison with the previous century. Arguably, there is not, in fact, a total absence (remember, for example, the fierce protests in South Korea). And we can also see the partial success of affirmative action, or at least the promise it holds, for instance in India in relation to the lower castes and, in general, for women.[23]

The lack of a strong, collective counter-movement can perhaps be explained by the fact that, precisely as a result of a century of collective action, on average, the underclass in the North Atlantic now enjoys a historically reasonable level of prosperity (again because of the aforementioned transfer payments). Yet pervasive inequality still prevails, and I would add that the lack of counter-movements today could precisely be a consequence of the psychological ramifications of that inequality on those worst off: that is, that energy has been diverted from the real problem – social inequality – to excluding others, as is evident in the prevalence of populist fears regarding immigrants and minorities (see p. 424).[24]

Will the market resolve distribution problems?

Not on its own, though this is the omnipresent neoliberal vision on the distribution of work and pay via the market (already a century old, but still going strong). It was not the case in the past, as England's heavily protectionist and mercantilist measures, at the expense of the Dutch Republic and, later, of the US, demonstrated during the long Industrial Revolution. History is in fact replete with examples of exactly this successful limiting of market forces, which yielded the greatest possible benefits for some states. This is the rule rather than the exception. The neoliberals who are optimistic about the blessings of the market and *only* the 'free' market distribution of work and pay have misread not only their history lessons but also the contemporary scenario in which the ideal of a world dominated by small entrepreneurs is highly unlikely.

Here, the recent coronavirus crisis speaks loud and clear. The biggest victims in rich countries are undoubtedly small business owners and freelancers – notwithstanding the gigantic sums that governments in rich countries have been forced to allocate to save them from certain destruction.[25] The prospects for unprotected migratory workers worldwide are equally bleak. This contrasts, in particular, with organized wage workers with a permanent contract, although their position will also be threatened in the long term in the event of a global economic crisis as a result of the pandemic.

Paradoxically, although competition at the lower end of the labour market is increasing, it is declining at the top. Outside of China and, in a certain sense, perhaps India, the food industry is globally dominated by Unilever, Bayer and Procter & Gamble, the energy sector by Philips, Siemens and General Electric and the aircraft industry by Boeing and Airbus.[26] This seems to contradict the greatly reduced workforce of these large companies. In 1974, the Dutch electronics giant Philips had almost half a million employees, compared to 37,000 now, and that was not because the company was in crisis, or because its products were not in demand – and also not because the company simply split into 10 units, each with 50,000 employees.

The explanation for this kind of development is deeply rooted in the proliferation of subcontracting. And where many wage workers are still physically working together, for example in the gigantic distribution centres located alongside motorways which are rapidly replacing shops in town centres, this is happening not only as a result of endless subcontracting but also as a result of payroll constructions. The American economist David Weil offers many examples of this, including the following:

> A member of a loading dock crew working in Southern California is paid by Premier Warehousing Ventures LLC (PWV) – a company providing temporary workers to other businesses – based on the total time it takes him and members of his crew to load a truck. PWV, in turn, is compensated for the number of trucks loaded by Schneider Logistics, a national logistics and trucking company that manages distribution centers for Walmart. Walmart sets the price, time requirements, and performance standards that are followed by Schneider. Schneider, in turn, structures its contracts with PWV and other labor brokers it uses to provide workers based on those prices and standards and its own profit objectives.[27]

Aside from the low hourly wage rate that all this leads to and, as a consequence, a lot of overtime, it also results in an extreme fragmentation of workers in the workplace. In the above example, they are still working in shifts, but, as a rule, this is not the case and we see working people employed by a temporary employment agency, paid via a payroll company, but obliged to adhere to the standards of a multinational that itself only supervises this whole process through a host of intermediaries. This is not only alienation but also isolation, about which more below.

Does robotization promise a new utopia?

As we have seen, automation is centuries old. The contemporary iterations of this, robotization and digitization, are omnipresent, but the implications for work are much harder to judge, however obvious they seem to be.[28] The dramatic reduction of working hours as a result of mechanization has already been promised for a century and a half. Think, for example, of the famous British philosopher Bertrand Russell, who, in 1918, stated in *Roads to Freedom* that 'with the help of science ... the whole community could be kept in comfort by means of four hours' work a day'. Or consider the over-confident title of the eloquent James Livingston's 2016 book: *No More Work: Why Full Employment is a Bad Idea.*[29]

A drastic reduction of working hours has undoubtedly occurred for many, certainly in the North Atlantic World that both Russell and Livingston are targeting, but, remarkably, it has been stuck, already for more than half a century, at around 40 hours per breadwinner and 60 to 80 hours per household. The fruits of automation are being converted into increasingly sophisticated low-priced consumer articles, but not into more free time. How is that possible? The explanation can be found in the proliferation of endless intermediate layers in the occupational structure. Direct producers are decreasing in number, but before goods reach the consumer, a much larger number of intermediaries has already interfered.

There are various reasons for this. The most important is perhaps the need of consumers, consumer organizations, national governments and international partnerships (such as the World Health Organization, but also trade treaty watchdogs) for control and security in an increasingly anonymous world with long and complicated production chains. In other words, striving for a level playing field on a global scale. There is no room to systematically elaborate this further here, but we should note the sobering observation of the Californian technology columnist Farhad Manjou. Himself the son of a pharmacist, he observes that 'most pharmacists are employed only because the law says that there has to be a pharmacist present to dispense drugs'.[30] Think also of the proliferation of the legal profession (especially private law experts in the Anglo-Saxon tradition),[31] or of specialists in detecting, fighting and preventing cyber-crime – the other side of the shining medallion of digitization. Without striving for completeness, think also of the flexibilization of work that requires much greater coordination, the fight against burn-out and other work stress complaints. The same applies to the demands of *éducation permanente* in the computer age. If everyone must constantly upskill in order to stay up to date, then many more 'upskillers' are necessary, including specialists in digital support.

Apparently, we need more inspectors, controllers and supervisors, more auditors of auditors of auditors and so on, *ad infinitum*, in the private and in the public sectors, both in the position of wage worker and in that of the hired-in freelancer. Either way, so far new jobs are being created faster than old jobs are disappearing. The ageing population in the North Atlantic, as well as in Japan, South Korea and soon in China, resulting in more paid care tasks is also mentioned frequently. This is all true, but this book suggests a more profound explanation for the unstoppable advance of this counter-intuitive phenomenon: our essential need to work.

Work: The long historical lines

Let us now take a step back and survey what our exploration of the entire history of human labour has revealed. I detect three crucial elements.

Work as meaning, especially social meaning

We relate to each other through work. This book shows, in every register, that although work is clearly driven by need (the naked *homo economicus*), mankind also works because it produces self-esteem and elicits esteem from others.[32] This is something that endless leisure simply cannot provide. No one has articulated this better than the German American philosopher Hannah Arendt: 'The blessing of labor is that effort and gratification follow each other as closely as producing and consuming the means of subsistence, so that happiness is a concomitant of the process itself, just as pleasure is a concomi-tant of a healthy body ... There is no lasting happiness outside the prescribed cycle of painful exhaustion and pleasurable regeneration.'[33] Her American student, Richard Sennett, creatively advanced this theory, but narrowed it down to 'pragmatism' by referring to William Morris and John Ruskin, meaning – rather remarkably for an academic – that you work with your hands: 'The craft of making physical things provides insight into the tech-niques of experience that can shape our dealings with others. Both the diffi-culties and the possibilities of making things well apply to making human relationships.'[34] Both observations fit nicely with the ideas of David Riesman, who wrote in *The Lonely Crowd: A Study of the Changing American Character* (1950): 'men need to feel adequate: to hold down a job, and then to be related to life through consumership is not enough. ... [The] burden put on leisure by the disintegration of work is too huge to be coped with: leisure itself cannot rescue work, but fails with it, and can only be meaningful for most men if work is meaningful.'[35] This desire for work as such, separate from the level of remuneration, perhaps also explains the amazing adaptability of younger generations to shifting contracts, as demonstrated for the US by the sociolo-gist Beth A. Rubin, who said that they will consider any job or assignment as long as they can work, and as long as they can participate.[36]

Cooperation as a basic need of men and women

Precisely because work is as much about self-esteem as it is about gaining respect from others, cooperation is essential – in a small community like a household, as well as in a workshop, an office or a factory. As we saw, the oldest, even prehuman, desire is to work together, to cooperate. To quote the primatologist Frans de Waal again: empathy 'builds on proximity, similarity, and familiarity, which is entirely logical given that it evolved to promote in-group cooperation'. This is in contrast to 'the trust-starved climate of modern business [which] spells trouble and has recently made many people deeply unhappy by wiping out their savings'.[37] One of the causes of this lack of trust are the long lines between management and the people who actually do the work, examples of which we have already seen. In this regard, whether that person is a wage worker or a lone freelancer no longer matters.

The large experimental medical and social science laboratory that we have all been living in since the outbreak of the coronavirus pandemic has meant that many more people, including those with better labour contracts, have experienced this deeply. Grateful for the opportunity that digital resources provide to work from home, and by turning households into workplaces again after more than a century (think of the abuses of the 'sweating industry'), we are now becoming 'zoombies', according to the organizational behaviourist Gianpiero Petriglieri: 'any professional used to working face to face is deprived of subtle cues that they have learnt to process implicitly. Their conscious mind has to strain for new cues to make up for those familiar ones'.[38] That is why video calling and meeting, forced upon us by our work (whether or not occasioned by a pandemic), are so tiring, and even exhausting. In the end, physical presence is essential for working together.

A fundamental need for fairness

Since the earliest times, we have known the tendency of some individuals to eat more of the social cake than their due, at least according to the egalitarian principles that we have all shared since the beginning of human history. We have also seen that these 'aggrandizers' cannot do this with impunity but must compensate the community, even if it is only symbolically. There is thus a socio-psychological limit to social inequality.[39] In a negative sense, this was reflected in the general moral outrage at the bonuses and other benefits of bankers during the banking crisis of 2008. A smaller but more recent example is the call in many countries to improve the pay of healthcare workers in response to the coronavirus pandemic. In other words, egalitarianism is very much in line with the recognition of individual differences, especially in terms of effort. Piketty articulates it as us needing 'a clear vision of human equality ... a vision that fully recognizes the many legitimate differences among individuals, especially with respect to knowledge and aspirations, and the importance of these differences in determining how social and economic resources are deployed ... the ideal socioeconomic organization must respect the diversity of aspirations, knowledge, talent and skills that constitutes the wealth of humankind'. The lack of this vision was one of the main factors in the failure of the Soviet Union.[40] People strive simultaneously for fairness and egalitarianism within their group (and this can also mean within their groups of men or women) and for the fulfilment of individual aspirations and hope.

We have encountered two socio-political solutions in this book that reconcile both of these things: redistributive theocracy and the income-levelling welfare state and its predecessors (namely, the notions of a 'just price', documented across Eurasia for over two millennia).[41] In the various theocracies that we have met, egalitarianism is regulated from above and must channel human aspirations and hope on condition of a strong, justifying ideology. In this way, a small elite is legitimized as ruler-priests of a widely shared cosmic global and societal vision. Think of classical Egypt and the pre-Columbian civilizations, but also of an 'ideal state' like the Soviet Union, or even of caste systems.[42] As long as they could ensure sufficient redistribution – whatever we think of it now – this can be sustained for centuries or even millennia.[43]

The welfare state is an explicitly egalitarian-inspired attempt to structure our society in such a way as to create the most favourable mix of livelihood security for many and a toleration of a limited number of aggrandizers.[44] History, and even our most recent history, teaches us that, thus far, this mix has a shelf life of only a number of decades, as it is also easily threatened.[45] Although cautious about feasibility, recent proposals for profound internationally coordinated fiscal reforms point in the same direction.

We must add a historical caveat here. This striving for fairness, as we have seen, almost inevitably leads to 'us and them' thinking: fairness for our kind of people, but when it comes to others we are quick to make an exception, not only in terms of access to work but also in terms of working conditions and remuneration. Here, others can range from slaves or lower castes to 'foreigners' of all shades. This applies both to formal inequality regimes, based on legally

436

regulated slavery and serfdom, as they existed until a century and a half ago (think of the US, Brazil and the Arab states, as well as Russia) and to apartheid and the exclusion of large sections of the working population (South Africa before Mandela, the Gulf States and Saudi Arabia), as well as to democracies.

Regarding the latter, in particular, as fairness for 'us' disappears, the tendency to exclude 'others' increases. What is called the 'social-nativist trap', a retreat into defending national, ethnic and religious identities with countless victims as a consequence, has been particularly apparent since 2000.[46] But, ultimately, so has the opposite: the more fairness in the reward for 'our' work, the greater the willingness to let others share in this in a democratic way. This underscores the importance of fairness all the more.

In addition to old propositions, new proposals for a more just and sustainable society have flourished in recent years, reinforced by an increased awareness of our global dependencies under the influence of the corona-virus pandemic. They emerge from the bottom up, in the form of platform co operatives and other 'commons'-like ways of organizing work, and, from above, in the form of cost calculations in which the social and environ-mental effects of production are passed on in full and also in the form of much more progressive taxation.

Any choice for the future organization of society is, of course, shaped by the experiences of millions of working women and men who have passed before us in the preceding pages. For by far the longest period of human history (98 per cent or more), they were organized in small bands of hunter-gatherers. From about 10,000 years ago, they increasingly developed into peasant households. Collaboration between these households resulted in labour specialization in cities, later city-states and, ultimately, in territorial states. Later still, they were based on theocratic tributary redistributions, soon to be replaced by markets from about 2,500 years ago. It should be reiterated here that markets for goods, as well as for labour and services, are not a recent phenomenon. Since 1500, they have become dominant, and for decades they have been the only way of struc-turing the economics (outside the household) we know today.[47]

In this phase of history, the idea is growing that we have a new opportu-nity to decide on a continental or even a global scale what our working lives will look like. Our long past as humankind suggests strongly that when making such choices, we must not lose sight of the three principles – meaning, cooperation, fairness – that can be derived from this story of work.

NOTES

A NOTE ON HISTORIES, METHODS AND THEORIES OF WORK

1. Cf. Lourens & Lucassen 1992.
2. Weber 1909, 55–73, 181–2. A powerful summary of the discussion is provided in Ehmer & Lis 2009, 9–10; Lis 2009, 57 and Lis & Soly 2012 (on this influential book, see the debate in *TSEG*, 11 (2014), 55–174; cf. for classical antiquity: Loomis 1998; Van der Spek 2004; Migeotte 2009, 2–3, 173–8; Von Reden 2010, 8–11; Feinman & Garraty 2010; W.V. Harris 2011, esp. ch. 12; Andreau & Descat 2011, 91–4; Temin 2012; J.M. Hall 2014; Zuiderhoek 2015; Erdkamp 2015; Launaro 2015; J. Lucassen 2014a, 2014b, 2018a and 2018b.
3. Van der Linden 1989, ch. 8.
4. For a marvellous intellectual pedigree of these development phases since Marx, see Van der Linden 1989, 235–60.
5. Chayanov 1966 (cf. Dennison 2011, 12–17); Polanyi 1944, esp. 43–4 (cf. Wagner-Hasel 2003, 148–9).
6. Concisely in Polanyi 1944, 43–4, partly as a critique of Adam Smith. For the debates among anthropologists and archaeologists: Maurer 2006; Feinman & Garraty 2010; Peebles 2010; Haselgrove & Krmnicek 2012.
7. J. Lucassen 2018a. See also W.V. Harris 2011, chs 1, 11 and 12; Lipartito 2016.
8. Van Bavel 2016, 272–3. His approach diverges from the European claim to uniqueness by, among others, the influential Wallerstein: see Feinman & Garraty 2010, 176; J. Lucassen 2018a.
9. Milanovic 2019, 2, 12; De Vito, Schiel & Van Rossum 2020, 6; on the history of market economies: Van der Spek, Van Leeuwen & Van Zanden 2015.
10. Respectively: Kocka 2018; Safley & Rosenband 2019; Harari 2014; Beckert 2015 ('war capitalism', 1600–1800/1850); Manning 2020; Lazonick 1990; Piketty 2019; Versieren & De Munck 2019. Of course, most authors are more subtle than suggested here. Cf. Kocka & Van der Linden 2016.
11. De Vries & Van der Woude 1997.
12. For an excellent critique see Chalcraft 2005. A related problem plays a part in the discussion about the extent to which China can or should be called 'capitalist'. See e.g. Rosefielde & Leightner 2018, esp. 22, 58; Piketty 2019, 606–36; Milanovic 2019, 87–91.
13. Admittedly, Harari 2014 and Manning 2020 do not seem to face this problem.
14. Quoted in D.M. Lewis 2018, 99.
15. Cf. Arendt 1958, 79.
16. A pedigree in J. Lucassen 2006b; Eggebrecht et al. 1980; Castel 1995.
17. Bücher 1919 (5th edn). On him, see Wagner-Hasel 2011; Spittler 2010; and the contributions to Backhaus 2000. Bücher's achievements, based on extensive reading of secondary literature on the history of work worldwide, available at the time, are all the more remarkable since most recent overviews restrict themselves to (Western) Europe.
18. Veblen 1914; Arendt 1958. See also Tilgher 1977 and Budd 2011.
19. For the development of labour history: Van der Linden & J. Lucassen 1999; Heerma van Voss & Van der Linden 2002; J. Lucassen 2006a and 2018a; Van der Linden 2008; Van der Linden & L. Lucassen 2012; De Vito 2013; Hofmeester & Van der Linden 2018; Bosma & Hofmeester 2018; Eckert & Van der Linden 2018; De Vito, Schiel & Van Rossum 2020. For my earlier, limited endeavours to write a more general history of work, see J. Lucassen 2000 (only Europe), and 2013.
20. By far the most impressive is Lis & Soly 2012 (from classical antiquity), which I lean on extensively. This is followed by Komlosy 2018 (from the 13th century); Simonton & Montenach 2019 (1 vol. on classical antiquity, 1 vol. on the Middle Ages, 4 vols for the later periods); and Cockshott 2019. Shryock & Smail 2011 provide arguments for starting early in history, as do Africanists Ehret 2016

and Suzman 2017 and 2020. For a global economic history: Roy & Riello 2019; for global history: Beckert & Sachsenmaier 2018.
21. Netting 1993, 1; Linares 1997. For a comparable method: M.E. Smith 2012a.
22. Cf. Safley 2019. Segalen 1983 and Thomas 2009 provide good examples.
23. There are a few important exceptions, however: see my concise discussions of the analytical value of the concepts 'capitalist' and 'modern' (above); the links between anthropology, archaeology and history (ch. 1); the implications of the Neolithic Revolution for inequality (ch. 2); the controversy between 'modernists' and 'primitivists' (ch. 4); the links between monetization and labour relations (ch. 4); the impact of the Industrial Revolution (ch. 6); and the extension of unfree labour in the last centuries to date (ch. 6).

INTRODUCTION

1. They limit themselves to the period of capitalism since the (late) Middle Ages (cf. Charles Tilly 1981, chs 7–9; Van der Linden 2009). Early examples of a thoughtful attempt to define work and labour: Jevons 1879, 181–227; Jevons 1905, 71–119.
2. Tilly & Tilly 1998, 22–3. Their definition fits well with that used by the ILO; cf. Van der Linden & Lucassen 1999, 8–9; for definition issues and for the difference between work and labour, see also Conze 1972; Sahlins 1972, 81; S.L. Kaplan & Koepp 1986; Pahl 1988; Applebaum 1992; Thomas 1999; Kocka & Offe 2000; McCreery 2000, 3–4; Ehmer, Grebing & Gutschner 2002; Weeks 2011; Budd 2011; Graeber 2019.
3. Cf. also Van der Linden 1997b, 519.
4. Tilly & Tilly 1998, 23–4; for a different take on 'usable', see Applebaum 1992; Budd 2011; cf. Ulin 2002.
5. Zürcher 2013.
6. One can search the extensive register of Tilly & Tilly 1998 in vain for concepts such as leisure, vacation/holidays, weekend or pension.
7. This global picture is based on so-called time-budget studies, which represent the amount of time individuals (animals or humans) allocate to mutually exclusive activities; Anderson 1961, 102–7.
8. Anderson 1961, 39.
9. Anderson 1961, 40.
10. Anderson 1961, 42–9; cf. Thomas 1999, 256–7.
11. For the fundamental concept 'labour relations' as used in this book: Hofmeester et al. 2015. This is much more encompassing than the mainly modern North American 'industrial relations' studies with their emphasis on (collective bargaining) relations between management and unionized workers, see Budd 2011, 1–2.
12. For income pooling according to a 'work cycle' see Lucassen 1987 and 2000. For inequality with the household: Bras 2014, also referred to as 'cooperative conflict' (Sen 1989). For slaves within the household: Culbertson 2011a; Tenney 2011; Muaze 2016. For separate budgets of husband and wife within the same household in Senegal: Moya 2017. For household ideologies in sinic countries: Rosefielde & Leightner 2018, ch. 9.
13. Also called 'coping strategies': Engelen 2002; Kok 2002.
14. Feinman & Garraty 2010.
15. Cf. Netting 1993, esp. 17ff (on Marx and Chayanov), 64 (on needless dichotomies).
16. This is the definition developed in the IISH-Collab on *Global Labour Relations 1500–2000*. See Hofmeester et al. 2015.
17. Tilly & Tilly 1998, 73–5, 87. See also pp. 350–8.
18. Lourens & Lucassen 1999; Kessler & Lucassen 2013; see also pp. 302–4.
19. Incidentally, this does not exclude cooperation between employer and employee, as explained in esp. pp. 389, 395.
20. Price & Feinman 2012; See also the triangle in K. Davids 2013a (not only state and market but also religion).
21. Manning 2013; Lucassen & Lucassen 2014.
22. De Zwart & Van Zanden 2018.

CHAPTER 1 HUMANS AT WORK, 700,000–12,000 YEARS AGO

1. Gilbreth 1911, 76. For another interesting parallel by Bücher, see Backhaus 2000, 165.
2. I use the expression *modern humans* (as in Reich 2018), where others speak of *Homo sapiens* or of 'anatomically modern humans (AMH)'. Cf. Shryock & Smail 2011, ch. 3; Hatfield 2013, 8–10. Other authors date the first modern humans to 300,000 or 200,000 years ago (cf. Manning 2020, ch. 2), but I do not think this difference has any bearing on the arguments developed here.

3. Hrdy 2009, 205–8.
4. De Waal 2005; Hrdy 2009; Hatfield & Pittman 2013 (including Hatfield 2013). Remarkably, Suzman 2020 does not adopt this line of thought. Diamond 1992: three million years ago, chimpanzees and bonobos went their separate ways (his kind of comparison tacitly implies the improbable assertion that the behaviour of non-human primates has not significantly evolved since then; for a critique see Roebroeks 2010).
5. Hrdy 2009, 116–18.
6. Hrdy 2009, 164–7. She notes that, in the majority of cases, exclusively male hunting is unsuccessful.
7. De Waal 1996; cf. Pagel 2012; Hatfield & Pittman 2013.
8. Milton 1992, 37; De Waal 1996.
9. R.B. Lee & Daly 2004; Suzman 2017 and 2020.
10. Hrdy 2009, 79; Lancy 2015, 123–5.
11. I thank Wil Roebroeks for these insights.
12. Pagel 2012, 6; cf. Hawke 2000; Coxworth et al. 2015.
13. Hrdy 2009, 85–95; cf. Kaare & Woodburn 2004; Aiello 2007, 20; Shryock, Trautmann & Gamble 2011, 39.
14. Morgan 2015; Pagel 2012, 278–80. On the thorny question of how and when language originated: Shryock & Smail 2011; Hatfield & Pittman 2013; Villa & Roebroeks 2014; Manning 2020.
15. Aiello 2007.
16. Aiello 2007, 23; also Mussi 2007 on the Neanderthals.
17. Kaplan et al. 2007; for the period of apprenticeship, see the paragraph 'Hunting and gathering food in practice' below.
18. Nunn 2018.
19. E.A. Smith et al. 2010.
20. Hrdy's hard-to-prove hypothesis that matrilocality is essential for the development of alloparenting (Hrdy 2009, 143–5, 151–2, 171–3, 180–194) is, in my opinion, superfluous here. Cf. Trautmann, Feeley-Harnik & Mitani 2011, 166, 172.
21. Historiographies of prehistory: Barnard 2004; Graeme Barker 2006, 4–17; on the development of the comparative method and the role of anthropology: Kelly 1995, 1–37, 43, 49, 345–8. Cf. Adovasio, Soffer & Page 2007. No matter how many mistakes are made, the comparative method is simply indispensable for a historical analysis such as this book.
22. De Waal 1996 and 2009. He positions himself in line with Pyotr Kropotkin (*Mutual Aid*, 1902: who 'had an inkling about it'; and *The Conquest of Bread*, 1906) and especially Robert Ludlow Trivers, the originator of the theory of reciprocal altruism, an approach related to that of John Rawls. For the opposing traditions of 'the war of all against all' (Hobbes; Huxley; Durkheim) versus Rousseau to Kropotkin: R.B. Lee & Daly 2004, 1; Kelly 1995, 1; Graeme Barker 2006, 44. Polanyi talks of 'reciprocity' with 'symmetry' (Polanyi 1944, chs 4–6; Polanyi, Arensberg & Pearson 1957; Dalton 1971).
23. Caveats are well-formulated in Ames 2010, who stresses that humans, also in small-scale societies, have a capacity for inequality and egalitarianism, while conceding that it is possible that they 'work better and are more likely to persist if prestige competition is repressed' (37).
24. De Waal 2009, 20–1; cf. Nystrom 2005.
25. Cf. Hatfield 2013, 13–14 (humans profit from a dual inheritance system: genetic and cultural) and Trautmann, Feeley-Harnik & Mitani 2011 (humans' evolutionary success is based on the characteristics – partly shared with different species of apes – of kinship recognition, incest avoidance, pair-bonding and overlapping generations).
26. De Waal 2005, ch. 6; De Waal 2009, ch. 7; cf. Mithen 2003, 506.
27. Pagel 2012.
28. See contributions in Roebroeks 2007 (especially Anwar et al. 2007, 235–40 and Leonard et al. 2007, 35); Roebroeks 2010; Erlandson 2010; Pawley 2010; Shryock & Smail 2011; Langergraber et al. 2012; Hatfield 2013; Villa & Roebroeks 2014; Reich 2018; note his warning on p. xxi: 'the field is moving too quickly. By the time this book reaches the readers, some advances that it describes will have been superseded or even contradicted'.
29. Pagel 2012, 33–5; Hatfield 2013.
30. M.P. Richards 2007, 231; cf. Binford 2007.
31. Earle, Gamble & Poinar 2011. Cf. Heckenberger & Neves 2009; Bar-Yosef & Wang 2012; Manning 2013 and 2020.
32. R.B. Lee & Daly 2004, 466–7; cf. Mithen 2003, 10. For population densities: Kelly 1995, 221–32; also Hrdy 2009, 26; De Waal 2009, 23; Klein Goldewijk 2011; Pagel 2012.
33. Reich 2018, see esp. his maps on 88, 156–7, 197, 202.
34. A.B. Smith 2004. Cf. Binford 2007, 196–204; Guthrie 2007, 160; Roebroeks 2010, 31–5. For the great similarities between Neanderthals and modern humans, see Villa & Roebroeks 2014.

35. For other capacities, see Joordens et al. 2014; more on early hominin tools in Suzman 2020, ch. 3.
36. Kelly 1995, ch. 3; Graeme Barker 2006, 60–2.
37. Schrire 2009; cf. Sahlins 1972, 8–9. This type of comparison is now part of the 'interdependent model' (Kelly 1995, 24–33), which recognizes different sorts of interdependence among hunter-gatherers and agricultural or horticultural neighbours.
38. R.B. Lee & Daly 2004, xiii, 1–3. I will, in general, use this reference for the *CEHG*, rather than refer to the dozens of *CEHG* authors by name, unless it concerns important and explicit ideas; cf. Sahlins 1972, 48.
39. R.B. Lee & Daly 2004, 3; Schrire 2009.
40. R.B. Lee & Daly 2004, 175–87, 215–19, 231ff.; Dewar & Richard 2012, 505; cf. Suzman 2017 and 2020.
41. Kelly 1995, 24–33; see Rival 2004a for a balanced overview; see also Schrire 2009.
42. R.B. Lee & Daly 2004, 3–4; cf. Graeme Barker 2006, 42–4.
43. Kelly 1995, 162–203, quotation at 185; cf. Suzman 2017, ch. 3.
44. Sterelny 2013, 315–18.
45. Liebenberg 2006. In the documentary 'The Great Dance', these hunting methods were filmed in 1998 and 2001; cf. Suzman 2017, 274 and ch. 12.
46. Kehoe 2004, 37–9; cf. Mithen 2003, 288–91; cf. Graeme Barker 2006, 66–9, 237–8.
47. Shnirelman 2004b, 149; for similar cases cf. also R.B. Lee & Daly 2004, 158–9.
48. About the difference between animal (stimulus enhancement) and human learning (social learning, leading to more sophistication and refinement over long periods of time): Pagel 2012, 38–45; cf. Hatfield 2013, 13–19.
49. Binford 2007, 198; cf. Lancy 2015.
50. MacDonald 2007a and 2007b.
51. Scherjon et al. 2015; Suzman 2017 and 2020.
52. Reich 2018, 26–7.
53. Much of the dating of what follows remains controversial. Stiner et al. 2011; Hatfield & Pittman 2013; Manning 2020; Suzman 2020; for China: Bar-Yosef & Wang 2012.
54. Roebroeks 2014; cf. Shryock & Smail 2011; Ehret 2016, 47; Pagel 2012, 59–68 (he attributes this jump to a growing population after 100,000 years of 'random drift' that caused small populations to lose information, slowing the pace of cultural evolution; for a critical note see Vaesen et al. 2016; Hatfield & Pittman 2013.
55. Mithen 2003, 31, 518 fn. 7; A.B. Smith 2004; Graeme Barker 2006, 31; Binford 2007, 197–9; Guthrie 2007; Zeder 2012, 172; K. Brown et al. 2012; Germonpré et al. 2014; Ehret 2016, ch. 2; Suzman 2017, ch. 8; Manning 2020.
56. Kelly 1995, 31–2, 117–20; cf. Graeme Barker 2006, 47–9.
57. Mithen 2003, 371–80.
58. Bar-Yosef & Wang 2012, 330.
59. R.B. Lee & Daly 2004, 327, 329; McConvell 2010, 169ff.; hafted tools are already known from the Neanderthals, see Roebroeks 2010, 31–5.
60. Rival 2004a, 80–1.
61. Shnirelman 2004b, 131. And those who, today, still cling to existence as hunter-gatherers have not stood still either. Think of fishing and the trappers in the northern polar regions who work commercially.
62. E.g. Gurven & Hill 2009.
63. Endicott 2004, 412; cf. Mithen 2003, 131–2; Kelly 1995, 297–301; MacDonald 2007b, 396.
64. Sterelny 2013, 319–23.
65. E.g. R.B. Lee & Daly 2004.
66. Toussaint 2004, 340; the use of fire and the preparation of food started 1.5 million years ago with *genus Homo* (Leonard et al. 2007, 37–8; cf. Roebroeks 2010, 34).
67. Tonkinson 2004, 344–5.
68. R.B. Lee & Daly 2004, 337, 350, 354.
69. R.B. Lee & Daly 2004, 205–9; cf. Suzman 2017 and 2020.
70. Ichikawa 2004; see Ehret 2016, 48 for the preference for 'Batwa' over 'Pygmy'.
71. Vidal 2004.
72. This task division is unknown in the northern polar regions: R.B. Lee & Daly 2004, 138–9.
73. Respectively, Griffin & Griffin 2004; Ehret 2016, 399; Haas et al. 2020.
74. Peterson 2002.
75. Roosevelt 2004, 88; Haas et al. 2020. For recent similarities in both men and women catching fish: R.B. Lee & Daly 2004, 299–301.
76. Villotte & Knüsel 2014.

77. Again, the dating is controversial: Hrdy 2009, 276; Shryock & Smail 2011, 73; Pagel 2012, 258–62; Manning 2020, 68. Whether clothing is the cause or the consequence of humans' light body hair remains unclear, because both are possible. Also, because smearing the body with fat, sleeping close to each other and burning fires are possible strategies against the cold, as shown for Yámana of Tierra del Fuego, Argentina.
78. Hansell 2008.
79. Scherjon et al. 2015.
80. Adovasio, Soffer & Page 2007, 177–91, 212–15; cf. Shryock & Smail 2011, 73.
81. Tonkinson 2004, 344–5.
82. Sahlins 1972, 10–12, 28–32.
83. Sahlins 1972, 19, 38–9; Roebroeks 2014.
84. Clottes 2002, 6; González-Sainz et al. 2013.
85. Powell, Shennan & Thomas 2009; Vaesen et al. 2016, however, warn against an all-too-easy use of the demographic argument.
86. Manning 2020, 125–7.
87. Feinman & Garraty 2010.
88. Tonkinson 2004, 344–5.
89. R.B. Lee & Daly 2004, 238.
90. Pandya 2004, 245.
91. R.B. Lee & Daly 2004, 206; Sahlins 1972 (on Sahlins: Kelly 1995; Suzman 2017 and 2020).
92. Hrdy 2009, 22–3, 26.
93. Kelly 1995, 14–23 (quoting Bruce Winterhalder).
94. Kelly 1995, 20, 346–7.
95. Sahlins 1972, 53; Lancy 2015.
96. Hrdy 2009, 299.
97. Hrdy 2009, 268–9, 298.
98. Eaton & Eaton 2004, 450.
99. R.B. Lee & Daly 2004, 95; Suzman 2017 and 2020 reports considerably fewer working hours for hunter-gatherers, partially because of his emphasis on men.
100. Lancy 2015, 30, 66–70.
101. R.B. Lee & Daly 2004, 196.
102. Arcand 2004, 98.
103. Eaton & Eaton 2004, 450, 452.
104. There is a good overview in Kelly 1995, 21; see also Sahlins 1972, 14–24; Eaton & Eaton 2004, 450; R.B. Lee & Daly 2004, 95, 196; Suzman 2017 and 2020.
105. Cf. Hrdy 2009, 143–52, 171–94.
106. There were limits to the caring tasks of hunter-gatherers; they simply could not permit themselves to maintain immobile dependents, hence the frequency of infanticide and senilicide: Sahlins 1972; Hrdy 2009.
107. Yetish et al. 2015. Moreover, among hunter-gatherers, the care of (even sleeping) babies continues through the night: Hrdy 2009, 145–7.
108. Sahlins 1972, 19, 23, 35–6.
109. Hrdy 2009, 91.
110. Nystrom 2005, 36; cf. Suzman 2020, 99.
111. I owe this interesting interpretation of social obligations/leisure to Wil Roebroeks.
112. Sahlins 1972, 64.
113. This idea is not new. Lewis Henry Morgan speculatively called the way of life of native Americans 'communism in living'. This inspired Marx in 1881 and especially Engels in 1884 to coin the term 'primitive communism': Graeme Barker 2006, 54–5; Kelly 1995, 29–33; cf. Flannery & Marcus 2012.
114. Rival 2004a, 81–2; Mithen 2003, 126.
115. Dunbar 2007, 97; Anwar et al. 2007, 246–9.
116. Dunbar 2007, 93, 96; cf. Manning 2020; Suzman 2020.
117. Kelly 1995, 209–13, where he explains that 'the magic numbers 500 and 25' show more variation than is thought; Mithen 2003, 129, 529, endnote 13.
118. Dunbar 2007, 98–9.
119. Dunbar 2007, 102.
120. Kelly 1995, 10–14, 270–92.
121. Hrdy 2009, 271–2, 286–8; Kelly 1995, 270–2 .
122. De Knijff 2010, 51–2. This matrilocality is not specific to all primates: Langergraber et al. 2012.
123. Hrdy 2009, 143–52, 171–94, for, among others, the contrast between fathers among hunter-gatherers and among farmers; for bridewealth, see Kelly 1995, 277–89.

124. R.B. Lee & Daly 2004, 5, 27, 32–4; Kelly 1995, 288–92, 302–8; Mithen 2003, 298.
125. Kelly 1995, 277, quoting June Helm.

CHAPTER 2 FARMING AND DIVISION OF LABOUR, 10000–5000 BCE

1. Hoffman 2009; Manning 2020; Suzman 2020.
2. Graeme Barker 2006; Whittle & Cummings 2007; Shryock & Smail 2011.
3. Mithen 2003; Graeme Barker 2006; Stiner et al. 2011; Manning 2020.
4. Stiner et al. 2011, 250–3; cf. Sterelny 2013, 317.
5. Price and Bar-Yosef 2011; Flannery & Marcus 2012; Ehret 2010 and 2016 for the role of linguistics.
6. R.B. Lee & Daly 2004, 466–7; Graeme Barker 2006, 398–401 is much more cautious.
7. Graeme Barker 2006, ch. 2.
8. Rival 2004a.
9. McConvell 2010, 178; R.B. Lee & Daly 2004, 39; A.B. Smith 2004, 388.
10. Zeder 2011; cf. Netting 1993, 28–9.
11. For the following: Graeme Barker 2006; Price & Bar-Yosef 2011; Zeder 2011 and 2012; Whitehouse & Kirleis 2014; Manning 2020; Suzman 2020; cf. Whittle & Cummings 2007; Gifford-Gonzales & Hanotte 2011.
12. Heckenberger & Neves 2009, 253 call this 'plant and animal management'; in earlier publications it is often called 'cultural control'.
13. Zeder 2012, 171–81; cf. Gifford-Gonzales & Hanotte 2011.
14. Graeme Barker 2006, 145.
15. Gifford-Gonzales & Hanotte 2011, 3.
16. Price & Bar-Yosef 2011; Zeder 2011 and 2012; H. Xiang et al. 2014; Whitehouse & Kirleis 2014; Shelach-Lavi 2015; Ehret 2016.
17. Zeder 2011.
18. Zeder 2012, 177–8; Diamond 1998, 159, 169.
19. Graeme Barker 2006, 404–5; cf. Anthony 2007, 462–3.
20. Diamond 1998, 97ff.; Ehret 2016 claims much earlier dates for Africa than most other authors.
21. According to Ehret 2016, 35–7, 51–2, they were of African stock.
22. Roosevelt 2004, 89–90; cf. Graeme Barker 2006, ch. 7; Mithen 2003, ch. 2; Prestes Carneiro et al. 2019.
23. Gifford-Gonzales 2013.
24. Reich 2018, 100, 150–1; Ehret 2016.
25. Reich 2018, 96: in Europe it led to the fusion of existing hunter-gatherers with blue eyes, dark skin and dark hair with immigrating farmers with light skin but dark hair and brown eyes. This resulted in northern Europeans with blue eyes, light skin and blond hair.
26. Mithen 2003, ch. 43; Gifford-Gonzales & Hanotte 2011; Gifford-Gonzales 2013.
27. Roullier et al. 2013.
28. On Africa: Gifford-Gonzales & Hanotte 2011; Gifford-Gonzales 2013; Ehret 2016; Fourshey, Gonzales & Saidi 2018.
29. Heckenberger & Neves 2009; cf. Anthony 2007; Manning 2020.
30. Klein Goldewijk 2011.
31. Amin 2005, 112–24, 290–319 (for India c.1870–1880); Hommel 1969, 41–81 (for China c.1900–1920).
32. Hommel 1969, 42–4.
33. Graeme Barker 2006, 356–7, 368.
34. Thomas 1999, 333 (from the *Fleta*, a treatise written in Latin on the common law of England, c.1290).
35. Anthony 2007, 72.
36. Amin 2005, 291–3, 297.
37. Amin 2005, 292.
38. Amin 2005, 297.
39. Thomas 1999, 335 (translation by Alexander Pope, 1715–1720).
40. J. Lucassen 1987, 52–8; Lambrecht 2019.
41. Khazanov 1994, 19.
42. Zeder 2012, 174.
43. Khazanov 1994, 19–25. He is not talking about modern dairy farming, where the income of fully sedentary farmers is entirely or largely dependent on livestock.
44. Khazanov 1994, 24; cf. Mithen 2003, 77–8; Diamond 1998, ch. 9.
45. Cross 2001.
46. Adovasio, Soffer & Page 2007, 269.

47. Lancy 2015.
48. Diamond 1998, 105, 98.
49. Eaton & Eaton 2004.
50. Lancy 2015, 101.
51. Lancy 2015, 109.
52. Note the caveat in Anthony 2007, 155: domesticated animals can only be raised by people morally and ethically committed to watching their families go hungry rather than letting them eat the breeding stock. Seed grain and breeding stock must be saved, not eaten, or there will be no crop and no calves next year.
53. Eaton & Eaton 2004, 450–1. Cf. Sahlins 1972; Roosevelt 2004, 88–9; Shryock & Smail 2011, 72, 74.
54. Lancy 2015, 31, 85–7, 304–25.
55. Hrdy 2009, 274–5; De Knijff 2010, 49–50; Gronenborn 2007, 80–4; Bentley 2007; cf. Kok 2010, 218–31ff. For the maintenance of matrilocality in the Neolithic Revolution in Thailand: Bentley 2007, 129, fn. 2.
56. Lancy 2015, 141–4.
57. Hayden & Villeneuve 2012, 100–3.
58. Sterelny 2013, 313–15; Henrich, Boyd & Richerson 2012; Lancy 2015, 85–7; cf. Ehret 2010, 138; De Knijff 2010, 49–50.
59. Hrdy 2009, with a nod to Jared Diamond's 'great leap forward' for the innovations 50,000 years ago.
60. Delêtre, McKey & Hodkinson 2011.
61. Bradley 2007; for China, see Shelach-Lavi 2015, 70–86, 97–8.
62. Matthews 2003, 78; cf. Peterson 2002; Graeme Barker 2006.
63. Adovasio, Soffer & Page 2007, 247–9, 268–9; cf. Peterson 2002.
64. Sahlins 1972, 41ff.; Diamond 1998, 10–106; Mithen 2003, 165–6, 495; Hrdy 2009, 299; Lancy 2015, 268–9; this is a major theme of Suzman 2020.
65. Mithen 2003, 58–9, 83–4; K.-C. Chang 1999, 46.
66. In what follows, I refer to households as a unit, fully aware that within this unit there are differences not only in the division of tasks (as we have just seen) but also in power (see, among others, Costin 2001, 275).
67. Costin 2001, 276. Like the dating of agricultural innovations, that of the earliest crafts is now also under discussion, see e.g. Ehret 2016 and Manning 2020.
68. See ch. 3.
69. Bellwood 2013, 148; for Africa: Ehret 2016, 60–1.
70. Graeme Barker 2006, ch. 4. No clear picture emerges for China on this point. *Idem*, ch. 6; Shelach-Lavi 2015, chs 3 and 4.
71. Shelach-Lavi 2015, 71.
72. Shelach-Lavi 2015, 108–9, 122.
73. Shelach-Lavi 2015, 87; for Europe: Graeme Barker 2006, 357–64; Gronenborn 2007, 77–84; for Africa: Ehret 2016, 57–9.
74. Graeme Barker 2006, 131–2, 159–60.
75. Costin 2001, 286; cf. McCorriston 1997; Ehret 2016; Manning 2020.
76. Hoffman 2009, 146 (he even talks of 'commercial hunting'); cf. Schrire 2009.
77. Bentley 2007.
78. Ehret 2010, 382–3.
79. R.B. Lee & Daly 2004, 276, 280.
80. Rival 2004a, 81–2.
81. Hayden & Villeneuve 2012, 95–6, 99; cf. Flannery & Marcus 2012; Manning 2020.
82. Borgerhoff Mulder 2009; E.A. Smith et al. 2010. Cattle, however, lend themselves more to appropriation than land: Shryock & Smail 2011, 257.
83. Kelly 1995, 221–32; cf. Ingold 2004, 400.
84. De Waal 2009, 161.
85. Kelly 1995, 203; Graeme Barker 2006, 56–7, 70.
86. Drennan, Peterson & Fox 2010; Feinman 2012.
87. Ehret 2016; Fourshey, Gonzales & Saidi 2018. This contradicts another Africanist, Suzman 2020.
88. Price & Bar-Yosef 2012, 161.
89. Aldenderfer 2012, 78; cf. Hayden & Villeneuve 2012.
90. Aldenderfer 2012, 86.
91. Aldenderfer 2012, 88; cf. Hayden & Villeneuve 2012, 132.
92. Shryock & Smail 2011, 64–5.
93. Mithen 2003, 506.

CHAPTER 3 EMERGING LABOUR RELATIONS, 5000–500 BCE

1. Peterson 2002, 125.
2. For this term: Matthews 2003, ch. 3; Wengrow 2006, 151–3: however, greater societal complexity can go hand in hand with material simplification.
3. Moreover, an evolution from farmers back to hunter-gatherers also occurred sometimes: Diamond 1998, 53–7, 63–5.
4. See the taxonomy of global labour relations as explained in the Introduction.
5. Wengrow 2006, 23–6.
6. Bellwood 2013, chs 6, 7, 9.
7. For the earlier history of maritime navigation related to the original expansion of modern humans, which entailed crossing straits of up to 200 kilometres: Manning 2020.
8. Bellwood 2013, 146–8.
9. Reich 2018, 199–204; cf. Ehret 2016; Manning 2020.
10. Wengrow 2006, 148–50; Gifford-Gonzales 2013.
11. Bellwood 2013, chs 6, 8, 9.
12. Bellwood 2013, 131, 147.
13. Bellwood 2013, 143, 150.
14. For Europe: De Grooth 2005; G. Cooney 2007, 558–61; cf. Bentley 2007, 125 ff.; Gronenborn 2007, 77–9.
15. Killick & Fenn 2012, 562; in Africa, the use of copper and iron took place in a more egalitarian setting (Ehret 2016).
16. Killick & Fenn 2012, 563; cf. Anthony 2007.
17. Killick & Fenn 2012, 567 (quotation); E.W. Herbert 1984 and 1993.
18. Nash 2005.
19. Anthony 2007, 200–24.
20. Anthony 2007, 127, 174–7, 321–7; for Egypt-Sudan cf. Wengrow 2006, 17–19, 25; Romer 2012, 8–10.
21. Anthony 2007, 222 (quotation). For the latest theory about the origin and distribution of Indo-European languages: Reich 2018; Manning 2020.
22. Regarding lactose tolerance: Khazanov 1994, 96; Pagel 2012, 263–4; De Knijff 2010.
23. The following after Anthony 2007, 67, 72, 277–9, 382–405, 425.
24. Khazanov 1994, xxxi–iii, 15ff., 122 ('The non-autarky, in many cases I would even say the anti-autarky of their economy').
25. For the following: Khazanov 1994, 44–59, 65–9, 89–122.
26. Khazanov 1994, 99; cf. Diamond 1998, 390–1; Mithen 2003, ch. 51.
27. Khazanov 1994, 55. The poet was Julian Tuwim (1894–1953).
28. Wengrow 2006, 59–71.
29. Khazanov 1994, 63–5, 106–11; Wengrow 2006; Ehret 2016.
30. Khazanov 1994, 59–63, 102–6; Atabaki 2013.
31. Khazanov 1994, 123, 152; Atabaki 2013, 165; cf. Wengrow 2006, 63–5 for a critique of the primitivization of pastoralism.
32. Khazanov 1994, 126–7; 143–4 (patrilineal descent also prevails among nomads, but may have been preceded by matrilineal descent, which still exists among the Tuareg).
33. Khazanov 1994, 130ff.
34. Anthony 2007, 321–2.
35. Shelach-Lavi 2015, 250.
36. I.J.N. Thorpe 2005; Parker Pearson 2005; cf. Pagel 2012, 88–98.
37. The following after Reich 2018, who has been inspired greatly by Marija Gimbutas.
38. Reich 2018, 98–114, 234–41.
39. Reich 2018, 237–41; cf. Seaford 2020.
40. Diamond 1998, 277, 286; cf. Hayden & Villeneuve 2012, 129; for competition between groups of hunter-gatherers forced to compete as a result of the changing climate and environment: Keeley 2014.
41. Keeley 2014, 30.
42. Khazanov 1994, 160–2, 181, 278–82.
43. Cf. Hårde 2005; cf. Fontijn 2005, 152; Kristiansen 2012; Hrdy 2009, 29–30, 169, 274; De Waal 2009, 22–4.
44. Diamond 1998, 141–2.
45. Leick 2002, xvii, 48; Matthews 2003, 109–10; Mithen 2003; K.-C. Chang 1999; R.P. Wright 2010; Beaujard 2019.
46. Leick 2002, 43–8, 77–8; Matthews 2003, 98–9; Wengrow 2006, 36–8, 76–83, 135–7; R.P. Wright 2010, 160–6, 183–7, 222–3.

47. Leick 2002, 22–3, 69.
48. Leick 2002, 52; cf. Van de Mieroop 2007, 55–9.
49. This concept gained prominence via Karl Polanyi (1886–1964): Polanyi 1944, chs 4–6; Polanyi, Arensberg & Pearson 1957; Dalton 1971. What Polanyi calls 'redistribution' with 'centricity' was called 'Leiturgie' by Max Weber: Weber 1909, 80–91, 181, and Weber 1976, 153, 211, 818.
50. Schmandt-Besserat 1992; cf. Van de Mieroop 2007, 28–35.
51. Schmandt-Besserat 1992, 150–3, 161–3, 189.
52. Schmandt-Besserat 1992, 179–83.
53. Leick 2002, 137.
54. Anthony 2007, 283–4; cf. Van de Mieroop 2007, 202–3, 220–2.
55. R.P. Wright 2010, 205–6; more hesitant: Kenoyer 2008; Wade 2017; cf. Seaford 2020, 18.
56. Shelach-Lavi 2015, esp. chs 7 and 8; cf. contributions in Underhill 2013. Traditional claims for an earlier state 'Xia' (e.g. K.-C. Chang 1999) cannot be archaeologically substantiated.
57. Liu, Zhai & Chen 2013.
58. Shelach-Lavi 2015, 131–2, 155–6, 188, 224; He 2013; Xu 2013.
59. Shelach-Lavi 2015, 156; He 2013, 266; Liu, Zhai & Chen 2013, 286. Note that not all regions mentioned shared the same language (Bellwood 2013).
60. Cf. the definition of empires by Sinopoli 2001, 441–4: 'large states with heterogeneous ethnic and cultural composition ... A primary goal and/or consequence of imperial incorporation is the extraction of wealth, in the form of subsistence and other resources (including *human labour*)'. My emphasis.
61. Wengrow 2006, chs 2–5; cf. Beaujard 2019.
62. Leick 2002, 52–3, 76–80, 158–60.
63. Van de Mieroop 2007, 78–84.
64. Van de Mieroop 2007, 233–6; Fernández-Armesto & Smail 2011, 144.
65. Kelder 2010; Fischer 2007 (though Garlan 1995, 3–35 emphasizes the slave character of this society); cf. Garcia-Ventura 2018; for similar polities much later in Africa, cf. Monroe 2013.
66. Leick 2002, 145.
67. Leick 2002, ch. 4; Van de Mieroop 2007, 64–73; Matthews 2003, chs 4–5 offer arguments about why, a thousand years earlier, Uruk might be a candidate for this honour; cf. Van der Spek 2008, 33–9. Van de Mieroop 2007, 45, 51 speaks of the Early Dynastic Period (2900–2350) of politically divided city-states.
68. Van de Mieroop 2007, 143–8, 182–3, 230–3; cf. Anthony 2007; Shelach-Lavi 2015, 257.
69. Leick 2002, 95; cf. Van de Mieroop 2007, 231.
70. Rotman 2009, 19, 26, 211 ('Servi autem ex eo appellati sunt, quod imperatores captivos vendere iubent ac per hoc servare nec occidere solent').
71. Parker Pearson & Thorpe 2005; T. Taylor 2005, 232 turns matters on their head by assuming that, in prehistory, forced labour existed 'in the same way as access to drinking and water is assumed'.
72. Van de Mieroop 2007, 233; cf. Gelb 1972; Culbertson 2011a and 2011b; Tenney 2011; Kleber 2018; D.M. Lewis 2018; Beaujard 2019.
73. Leick 2002, 187. According to Asher-Greve 1997, militarization could also have had a very different effect: an emphasis on the differences between men and women.
74. Jursa 2010; Van de Mieroop 2007; Matthews 2003, 182–8; Oka & Kusimba 2008. Trade is much older in origin, and archaeological findings suggest that it already occurred in the earliest stages of human prehistory when groups of hunters and food gatherers exchanged rare goods without much interaction and sometimes even without physical contact (for 'silent barter', see Wicks 1992, 12).
75. Barber 1994, ch. 7.
76. Leick 2002, 124–5. The earliest example of (forced?) silver payments that she gives occurred c.2250 (Ibid., 99). See also Heymans 2018.
77. Adams 2006, 158–67.
78. Van de Mieroop 2007, 93–4, 115.
79. Scheidel 2009, 438–40. Compared with Ancient Egypt, this is quite favourable.
80. Leick 2002, 203, 205; Matthews 2003, 120–2; Van de Mieroop 2007, 94–103.
81. Leick 2002, 164 (without a more precise date).
82. Dandamaev 2009; Jursa 2010; Van der Spek 1998 and 2008; cf. Pirngruber 2012, 20–6.
83. Dandamaev 2009; Jursa 2010; Van der Spek et al. 2018. For money without coins: Heymans 2018.
84. Jursa 2010, 261–3, 680. There is no mention of moulding and firing bricks in this source, but I infer as much from production figures for the manual shaping of bricks in later times (cf. Lourens & Lucassen 1999; Kessler & Lucassen 2013; W.P. Campbell 2003, 30–7).
85. Jursa 2010, 662–3.
86. The following primarily based on Romer 2012 and 2017, whose spelling of personal names I also generally follow; cf. Donadoni 1997; Wengrow 2006; Wilkinson 2010.

87. Romer 2012, 70; cf. Brewer 2007; K.M. Cooney 2007, 162.
88. Brewer 2007; Bleiberg 2007; Moreno García 2008; cf. K.M. Cooney 2007, who talks of a 'mixed economy'.
89. Wengrow 2006, esp. 33–40, 263–8.
90. Wengrow 2006, 158–64; Romer 2012, 64–71.
91. Romer 2012, 169; Bleiberg 2007, 182.
92. Romer 2012, ch. 6; on p. 114 he is critical of Wengrow 2006.
93. Moreno García 2008.
94. Kelder 2010; cf. Moreno García 2008; Hayden & Villeneuve 2012.
95. Fernández-Armesto & Smail 2011, 144; Romer 2017, 133–9.
96. al-Nubi 1997; Spalinger 2007; K.M. Cooney 2007, 164; Moreno García 2008, 119, fn. 59.
97. Kelder 2010, 117ff.
98. Romer 2012, xxxv; Romer 2017, 134.
99. Kelder 2010, 63–4, 82–3 (the exchange of precious goods by messengers could also include elite military forces and seaworthy sailors; cf. Leick 2002, 95, 99).
100. Moreno García 2008, 110, 144.
101. Brewer 2007, 145; cf. Katary 2007.
102. Caminos 1997, 16–17.
103. Ockinga 2007, 253–4.
104. Romer 2012, 325–7.
105. Moreno García 2008, 118; cf. Brewer 2007, 134; on women's labour: Feucht 1997; Stevens & Eccleston 2007.
106. Romer 2012, 276–85, 309–13, 319–20, 357, 363, 381; on harbour and maritime work: Romer 2017, 259–72, 478–80, 379–414.
107. Romer 2012, 192; Romer 2017, 135–6.
108. Exell & Naunton 2007, 94–7; K.M. Cooney 2007, 168–73.
109. K.M. Cooney 2007, 171.
110. K.M. Cooney 2007, 170; Valbelle 1997, 39–40 and 44; cf. this with the much smaller quantities that were left over for farmers.
111. Romer 2017, 497.
112. Loprieno 1997.
113. Moreno García 2008, 123–42. For debt bondage, see 118, 136; cf. Romer 2017, 492.
114. Von Reden 2007; Bleiberg 2007, 181–3; Moreno García 2008, 112–14, 146–9; Romer 2017, 136–7; Heymans 2018.
115. Shelach-Lavi 2015, 196–7, 217–20, 242–6; cf. Yuan 2013; Jing et al. 2013.
116. Shelach-Lavi 2015, 222–3.
117. Shelach-Lavi 2015, 255, cf. also 224–5. Note that the workforce of prisoners of war as slaves is apparently not considered; cf. Yuan 2013; Jing et al. 2013.
118. Shelach-Lavi 2015, 226, 269–305.

CHAPTER 4 WORKING FOR THE MARKET, 500 BCE–1500 CE

1. Kirch 2010; Pagel 2012, 36–7; Roullier et al. 2013; Reich 2018, 199–204.
2. This also meant the possibility of bartering over long distances and thus even the return to a sort of gatherer existence on certain islands, such as Yap, with its intriguing monetary system. See Gillilland 1975.
3. Khazanov 1994, 41–4, 111–15.
4. J. Lucassen 2007a (introduction), 2014b, 2018a; Mooring, Van Leeuwen & Van der Spek 2018; cf. Maurer 2006; Haselgrove & Krmnicek 2012; J.M Hall 2014, 275–81; Seaford 2020. Kuroda 2020 provides the best introduction to monetary history.
5. Seaford 2020 (quotation on 61; italics in original); cf. Kuroda 2020, 41, 145, 202–3.
6. Haselgrove & Krmnicek 2012; cf. Aubet 2001, 138–43; Leick 2002, 99, 125; Kuroda 2020. Heymans 2018 points to small fractions in hoards of 'hacksilber' but not to a relation with wage payments. Nevertheless, Jursa 2010 is convinced about this link.
7. P. Spufford 2008.
8. H.S. Kim 2001 and 2002.
9. Cohen 1992, xiv, 22 (fn. 92); Garlan 1995, 77; Schaps 2004, 156; J.M Hall 2014, 277 (smallest Athenian silver coin, C5th, weighing 0.044 grams or 1/16 obol, or 1/48 standard daily 'minimum wage'); D.M. Lewis 2018, 40, 43. Cf. Jursa 2010 for low-weight silver chips in Mesopotamia's long 6th century BCE.
10. J. Lucassen 2007a, Introduction (after Garlan 1995; Cohen 2002; Burke 1992).
11. Loomis 1998, 257; Trevett 2001, 25; Ashton 2001, 92–4.

12. J. Lucassen 2007a, Introduction, 23.
13. After Gabrielsen 1994, ch. 5.
14. Gabrielsen 1994, 124.
15. Von Reden 2007 and 2010. Slavery remained of secondary importance, also under the Ptolemies, certainly in the productive sector (131–6). For the Roman period: Howgego 1992; Van Heesch 2007; Verboven 2009.
16. Von Reden 2007, ch. 2, 303–4.
17. Von Reden 2007, 60–5 (the annual salt tax for men was 1.5 drachm [= 9 obols = 72 chalkoi] and for women 1 drachm).
18. Von Reden 2007, 81 (60 per cent of the population in a large stretch of Middle Egypt were cultivators; 40 per cent were part-time farmers).
19. Von Reden 2007, 148.
20. Von Reden 2007, 138 (quotations), 147–8. Faced with the dramatic fall in wages and income in the longer term (Scheidel 2010, 453; cf. Brewer 2007, 144) Von Reden 2010, ch. 6 emphasizes the price stability and a high degree of internal market integration in the 3rd century BCE in contrast to more intense fluctuations of prices in the 2nd (Ibid., 154).
21. Rowlandson 2001; Harper 2015; Erdkamp 2015.
22. Rathbone 1991; cf. Bagnall 1993.
23. Launaro 2015, 177.
24. Witzel 2006, 460–2.
25. Thapar 2002; Chakrabarti 2006 (at the same time there was also unfree labour).
26. Bopearachchi 2015, I, 82–92. Indian sigloi have a lower silver content than the Persian sigloi (which are a completely different type), cf. J. Lucassen 2007a, 28–9; Bhandare 2006; Shrimali 2019.
27. Kautilya 1992; cf. Chakrabarti 2006; Jha 2018.
28. Bhandare 2006, 97.
29. H.P. Ray 2006; Majumdar 2015; for trade in the Indian Ocean: Seland 2014; Mathew 2015; Boussac, Salles & Yon 2018.
30. See Wang 2004, 9–16; J. Lucassen 2007a, 29–32; Scheidel 2009, 137–43; Haselgrove & Krmnicek 2012, 239–40; Thierry 1997 and 2015; B. Yang 2019.
31. Thierry 2015.
32. The *monetary* function of cowries in China often causes misunderstanding, inducing authors to date the monetary usage of cowries far too early (e.g. Harari 2014, 197–8). Cowries found in early Shang graves, however, had no monetary functions, as suggested by Yuan 2013, 337. See Jing et al. 2013; Shelach-Lavi 2015; B. Yang 2019.
33. Pines et al. 2014, 320 (fn. 8 to ch. 6 by Robin D.S.Yates): prior to 221 BCE, 'if one was poor and could not pay the fine, one could pay it off by working for the government at six cash per day if you received food, or at eight if you did not'. By implication, a daily ration could be procured for one-quarter of the wage, which contradicts Scheidel's assertion (2009, p. 182) that the Qin conscripts did not receive cash wages.
34. Thierry 2015, 442.
35. Pines in Pines et al. 2014, 234.
36. Pines et al. 2014; cf. Falkenhausen 2006; Shelach-Lavi 2015, ch. 11.
37. Cf. Barbieri-Low 2007, 7–9.
38. Pines et al., 2014, 19–28; cf. Falkenhausen 2006, 417.
39. Shelach-Lavi in Pines et al. 2014, 131.
40. Pines et al. 2014, 27 (Introduction), 223 (chapter by Robin D.S. Yates), 310 fn. 18 (chapter by Gideon Shelach-Lavi); Barbieri-Low 2007, 10, 212ff.
41. For comparisons with the collapse of the Maya Empire: Shelach-Lavi 2015, 121, 132–3, 308.
42. Shelach-Lavi 2015, 137–8; M.E. Lewis 2015, 286–94.
43. Wang 2007, 67.
44. Scheidel 2009, 11, 199.
45. Scheidel 2009, 4, 19, 76; M.E. Lewis 2015, 286–94.
46. Barbieri-Low 2007, 43 (translation Burton Watson).
47. Thomas 2009, 533–4 (translation Arthur Waley 1919).
48. Barbieri-Low 2007, 254, 256.
49. Barbieri-Low 2007, 26–9; cf. Lis & Soly 2012; for artisans in later periods of Chinese history: see Moll-Murata 2018.
50. Barbieri-Low 2007, 27.
51. Barbieri-Low 2007, 18.
52. Banaji 2016, 14 prefers to characterize the (late) Roman economy as 'proto-modern', rather than 'pre-capitalist'. See my discussion of the terms 'modern' and 'capitalist' in the Introduction.

53. Lis & Soly 2012, in which existing theories (e.g. Arendt 1958, ch. 3) about the contempt that the Greeks supposedly had for work are turned upside down; Budd 2011; Hofmeester 2018; for China, see Barbieri-Low 2007, 36–66.
54. Lis & Soly 2012, 28.
55. Lis & Soly 2012, 48–51.
56. E.M. Harris 2002, 70–3; Vélissaroupolos-Karakostas 2002, 134–5; Kyrtatas 2002, 144–5; D.M. Lewis 2018.
57. Schaps 2004, 153–74 (quotation on p. 153); J.M. Hall 2014, 214–21, 262–8, who, remarkably, characterizes sharecroppers, wage labourers and debt bondsmen before 500 BCE as 'various classes of unfree status' (p. 219).
58. Cohen 1992, 61 (the preference for daily payments in Athens may have had to do with 'social values inhibit[ing] citizens from working on a continuing basis under another person's control'), 70–3.
59. Gallant 1991; D.M. Lewis 2018 (who sometimes disagrees strongly with colleagues, e.g. Garlan 1995; Andreau & Descat 2011); Zurbach 2014.
60. Gallant 1991, 134 (strictly speaking this quotation pertains to rowers, but it is fully consistent with what he says about mercenaries later on in the text).
61. Van Heesch 2007; Verboven 2009.
62. Mainly after D.M. Lewis 2018; cf. Garnsey 1998; Temin 2012; Erdkamp 2015; Launaro 2015.
63. Cf. Hrdy 2009, 275; Ehret 2010, 131–5; Rotman 2009, 57, 198.
64. Kolchin 1987, 53; cf. D.M. Lewis 2018, 281, fn. 45.
65. Cf. W.V. Harris 2011, 38.
66. Andreau & Descat 2011, 88.
67. Andreau & Descat 2011, 82–91, 107–8, 149–56.
68. Verboven 2011; Garnsey 1998, 77–87, 154–62, see esp. 86; Launaro 2015, 177; Erdkamp 2015, 31–2; Banaji 2016.
69. Rihll 1996; Andreau & Descat 2011; D.M. Lewis 2018.
70. For this date, see Van Dommelen 2012. The colonization had already begun in small numbers earlier, in the 10th century. Like most authors, Rihll 1996 puts the high point in the 8th–6th century.
71. Rihll 1996, 111; D.M. Lewis 2018.
72. Garlan 1995, 71–3; Rihll 1996; Schaps 2004; Jameson 2002, 171.
73. Garlan 1995, 40, 61.
74. Andreau & Descat 2011, 120–8.
75. Andreau & Descat 2011, 46–65. For the Roman slave trade, see also W.V. Harris 2011, ch. 3.
76. Schiavone 2013; cf. Andreau & Descat 2011, 141–9; W.V. Harris 2011, 286. For slave revolts in the Greek world, see D.M. Lewis 2018.
77. Schiavone 2013, 97–103; Gregory of Nyssa (4th century CE) was the classical author who went furthest in the direction of a plea for abolition, but even he did not call for actual abolition: Andreau & Descat 2011, 136, 169.
78. Schiavone 2013, 41–4, 59–61, 116–17.
79. Schiavone 2013, 27–8, 68–9 (quotation on p. 69), 74; Andreau & Descat 2011, 144.
80. Andreau & Descat 2011, 14, 41–52; Harper 2011, 38–60; see also W.V. Harris 2011, 61. For Athens c.400 BCE and 350–310, Garlan 1995, 61–6, 72–3 comes up with double this, which can be explained by the much shorter periods, in which there was massive supply due to wars. For free labour in Athens, see Migeotte 2009, 93.
81. Harper 2011, 67–91, this in contrast to W.V. Harris 2011, 62–75, 88–103.
82. Harper 2011, 59–60: 'The top 1.365 percent of Roman society thus owned the bottom 5 percent of Roman society.' For the main sexual function of slaves, see *Idem*, ch. 6.
83. Harper 2011, 150–1, 157–8, 162–79; cf. Rotman 2009, 114–16; J. Lucassen 2013, annex 1.
84. Andreau & Descat 2011, 158.
85. On the other hand, parents were allowed to rent out the labour of their children for 25 years: Andreau & Descat 2011, 162; cf. H. Barker 2019 for a critical view on the supposedly mitigating impact of Christianity, which she calls 'the narrative of Christian amelioration'.
86. Sharma 2014.
87. Stillman 1973.
88. I will not discuss other caste societies, as documented e.g. for Africa (Ehret 2016, 218–26) and the Pacific, esp. Hawaii (Flannery & Marcus 2012, 332–48); Barbieri-Low 2007, 56–63: 300 BCE–200 CE Chinese artisans were not caste-bound to their profession as they seemed to enjoy at least some possibility of upward social mobility.
89. Jha 2018, 2020. Unless otherwise stated, I follow his interpretation, which is heavily inspired by Damodar Dharmanand Kosambi and R.S. Sharma. Cf. Thapar 2002; H.P. Ray 2003; Boivin 2005; Chakravarti 2006; Parasher-Sen 2006; Witzel 2006; Stein 2010; Olivelle & Davis 2018. Seaford

2020, 213–16 dates the full blossoming of the caste system too early. For the latest dating of the immigration movements to India, see Reich 2018, ch. 6.

90. Klass 2020, 21–5.
91. Kautilya 1992, 33 53, 69, 88–9, 446–55; cf. Thapar 2002, 62–8, 122–5, 154.
92. Jha 2018; cf. Witzel 2006, 482–3; Olivelle & Davis 2018. The Manu law book was accepted much later, at the end of the eighteenth century, by the English as the Hindus' sacred laws – *shastras* – of choice.
93. Fernández-Armesto & Smail 2011, 145.
94. Jha 2018, 160.
95. Jha 2018, 59–60.
96. Jha 2018, 161–2.
97. See also Witzel 2006.
98. Cf. Thapar 2002, 164–73; H.P. Ray 2003, esp. 245ff.; Falk 2006; Parasher-Sen 2006, 441–4; Witzel 2006.
99. H.P. Ray 2003, 165–87; Kearny 2004, 31–55; Tomber 2008; on guilds: Subbarayalu 2015 (cf. Verboven 2011 for Rome).
100. Jain 1995, 136–8; S.R. Goyal 1995; Sharma 2014. See also Wicks 1992, ch. 3; Shankar Goyal 1998; Thapar 2002, 460–1. Shrimali 2002 convincingly refutes the main arguments of Deyell 1990 (which received much acclaim: Subrahmanyam 1994, 11–15); cf. Deyell 2017; Shrimali 2019.
101. So far, the oldest dates for strong group endogamy that geneticists have found are between 2,000 and 3,000 years ago for a Vysya group in Andhra Pradesh (Reich 2018, 144) and between 1,000 and 1,500 years ago for a Patel group in Gujarat (Pemberton et al. 2012); cf. Chaubey et al. 2006; Bittles 2005. This could be consistent with my dating of the simultaneous breakthrough of castes and demonetization, if we accept that endogamy has spread through society in a top-down manner.
102. For objections to this analogy, see Stein 2010, 106–8.
103. And with that, up to the 12th century, also political-economic texts such as the *Arthashastra*, see Pollock 2005, 63–4 (cf. Kautilya 1992, 823). For more continuity in the south: H.P. Ray 2006.
104. Jha 2018, 128, 159; H.P. Ray 2003, 224.
105. Jha 2018, 130–1 (quotation), 155; Stein 2010, 87–90; Falk 2006, 147–53; Jamison 2006; cf. Kautilya 1992, 69–70 for women's labour in his time: spinning and weaving for wages; prostitution (in state brothels); live-in servants; and slaves. Shrimali 2019, 186 cites the price of 50 *karshapana* for an outcaste or *shudra* woman maid servant at the beginning of our era.
106. Jamison 2006, 204–9.
107. Thapar 2002, 462–6; Jha 2018, 130, 153 (quotation), 161; Sharma 2014; Habib 2004.
108. J. Lucassen 2005, 430–2; M.E. Lewis 2015; Deng 2015; Guanglin 2015.
109. Deng 2015, 326 (quoting Eric Jones). He compares the Song in this respect with the late Qing. It is striking that exactly in both periods, and almost exclusively at that time, multiples of coins were made, thus leading twice to brief periods of a multi-denominational currency system in China.
110. Deng 2015, 326; cf. M.E. Lewis 2015, 302.
111. For demonetization in Ethiopia after *c.* 650 CE, see Ehret 2016, 201–7, 283.
112. Banaji 2016; Rio 2020.
113. Rotman 2009, 176, 179 (quotation).
114. Rotman 2009, 32, 41, 121; cf. Rio 2020, 136–41, 225–30; H. Barker 2019.
115. Rotman 2009, 173–6.
116. According to T. Taylor 2005, these slaves included a significant number of sex slaves, exploited during their transportation and following their onward sale. The words used by the Arab chroniclers (such as the important Ibn Fadlan, who travelled from Baghdad to Kazan on the Volga in the 920s) for slave-girl and slave-boy, *jariyeh* and *ghulam*, both had clear sexual connotations; cf. H. Barker 2019.
117. Rotman 2009, 159.
118. Rotman 2009, 57–81; cf. Ott 2015; T. Taylor 2005, 229–30.
119. Zürcher 2013; Chatterjee & Eaton 2006; H. Barker 2019.
120. J. Lucassen 2007a, 38–9, after Laiou 2002, in which C. Morrison 2002; C. Morrison & Cheynet 2002. Also Rotman 2009, 95–107, 198–200.
121. Rotman 2009, 33–4, 36, 44.
122. Heidemann 2010, 53–4.
123. Shatzmiller 1994, 38–40; Shatzmiller 2007, 150; cf. Heidemann 2015, parts discussed in more detail in Heidemann 1998, 2006, 2007, 2009a, 2009b, 2010, 2011.
124. Kennedy 2015, 401; Van Bavel 2016, 84–5.
125. Gordon 2011, 73–4; cf. Toledano 2011. NB. White is the colour of mourning.
126. Shatzmiller 2007, 98–9, 159–60.
127. Kennedy 2015, 391–7; cf. Hofmeester 2018.
128. Heidemann 2006.

129. Nasr 1985; Udovitch 1961; J. Lucassen 2013.
130. Cf. Kennedy 2015, 390ff.
131. Sebeta 1997, 535; for Greece: Barber 1994, 273–83; for (Jews in) the Islamic world: Hofmeester 2011, 146; H. Barker 2019.
132. Shatzmiller 1994 and 2007 (quotation on p. 101).
133. Shatzmiller 2007, 129.
134. Hofmeester 2011, 151.
135. Russell 1972; Verhulst 1999; Buringh 2011, 71–5, 78, 290. For the Roman Empire: Scheidel 2009, 11.
136. J. Lucassen 2007a, 40, heavily inspired by Bloch 1954, 11–33 and P. Spufford 1988.
137. Epstein 1991, 28–38.
138. Hodges & Cherry 1983, 141.
139. For a characteristic of this, see De Hingh 2000.
140. Buringh 2011, 432; Rio 2020.
141. Slicher van Bath 1963a; Rio 2020, 135 demonstrates that household slavery 'is more likely to have yielded hard-line practices of unfreedom'.
142. Slicher van Bath 1963a, 49; Slicher van Bath 1963b and 1963c.
143. Buringh 2011, 77–94.
144. Buringh 2011, 81.
145. Buringh 2011, 347.
146. See Wyatt 2011 and Rio 2020. They point out that, after antiquity, slavery (especially of women) did not disappear from Europe – and it was certainly not abolished – and neither did the enslavement of prisoners of war. See also pp. 157–9.
147. McKitterick 2008, 104; cf. Harper 2011, 497–509.
148. Rio 2020, 33.
149. Arnoux 2012; Toledano 2011; H. Barker 2019.
150. J. Lucassen 2014b; Deyell's (1990) suggestion that low-value coins filled the gap left by the disappearing silver coins in the era c. 500–1000 CE is unconvincing. See Shrimali 2002 and 2019. Although it is difficult to date the expansion of cowries as small change in Bengal, their presence has certainly been well documented there since the 14th century (B. Yang 2019) and in Orissa and Bihar until the 19th century.
151. Thapar 2002, 344–5; H.P. Ray 1986, 82–9; Fletcher 2012. For manuscript production in India, see Buringh 2011, 104–5, 150–1, 156–7.
152. Thapar 2002, chs 9–10.
153. Wicks 1992; Coe 2003; Lieberman 2003; Scheidel 2015a; see B. Yang 2019 for cowries as money from 1300.
154. Scheidel 2015a; Monson & Scheidel 2015; For a more nuanced approach: Barbieri-Low 2007, 254–6.
155. For a kaleidoscopic overview, see Mann 2006.
156. Cf. Feinman & Garraty 2010. See also Maurer 2006 (who characterizes Polanyi's work as 'a compendium of exotica coupled with a morality tale about the world that "we" have lost') and Peebles 2010.
157. Feinman & Garraty 2010, 175. For the Maya, see also Pines et al. 2014, among others, p. 308 (notes). See Diamond 1998, 53–63.
158. Scheidel 2015a, 2. For the history of work and labour relations, early information on Africa remains sparse compared to America, see Kusimba 2008; Monroe 2013; Ehret 2016.
159. M.E. Smith 2012b, 31; Joyce 2010, 51–3, 66–83; Kolata 2013, 123.
160. Lau 2013.
161. Joyce 2010.
162. Joyce 2010, 111.
163. Joyce 2010, 116, 142.
164. Joyce 2010, 147–8.
165. Mainly based on D'Altroy 2002 and 2015; Kolata 2013; cf. La Lone 1982 and 2000; Morris 2008. For earlier civilizations: Kolata 1993; Lau 2013.
166. D'Altroy 2015, 31; D'Altroy 2002, ch. 9.
167. Kolata 2013, 139–45.
168. D'Altroy 2002, ch. 9, esp. 207: 'the general principle was to be generous with those who capitulated'. For alternatives in several pre-Inca warring polities, see Lau 2013, ch. 4.
169. Quoted by Kolata 2013, 101–2.
170. D'Altroy 2002 and 2015; Kolata 1993, 205–42 argues that the Andean Tiwanaku civilization (c. 500–1000 CE) shared many characteristics with the Inca in terms of the social organization of agricultural production.
171. D'Altroy 2002, chs 8–9; D'Altroy 2015, 49, 54; Morris 2008, 310–2; Gil Montero 2011; Kolata 2013, 92–6, 110.

172. Earle & Smith 2012, 277–8.
173. Morris 2008, 309–10; D'Altroy 2002, ch. 7; Kolata 2013, ch. 5.
174. D'Altroy 2002, 176, cf. also 286.
175. Classical period 250–800/1000 CE, capital at Tikal; later capitals at Chichén Itzá c. 800/850–1100/1200 and Mayapán c. 1100/1200–1441.
176. Demarest 2004; M.E. Smith 2012a, 14–15; Canuto et al. 2018.
177. Andrews 1993, 54; Canuto et al. 2018. Demarest 2004 is very reluctant to draw such conclusions.
178. Fletcher 2012; Pyburn 2008 (heavily inspired by Netting 1993 and Stone, Netting & Stone 1990).
179. Andrews 1993, 49–52.
180. Andrews 1993, 48–9; Canuto et al. 2018 estimate the total population of the Central Maya Lowland around 700/800 CE at some 10 million, i.e. some 100 per km²; cf. Demarest 2004.
181. Andrews 1993, 59 (quoting W. L. Rathje).
182. M.E. Smith 2012b and 2015; for continuities with earlier periods see Hirth 2008.
183. See M.E. Smith 2012b, 69; see Earle & Smith 2012.
184. M.E. Smith 2012b, 77.
185. Earle & Smith 2012, 240–1, contrasting the *territorial* Inca state with *staple finance* strategies of state funding and little commercialization and the *hegemonic* Aztec state with *wealth finance* strategies and strong commercialization; cf. Kolata 2013 for a different use of *hegemony*.
186. Sinopoli 2001, 456; Joyce 2010, 50 remarks that this 'enhanced the demand for and value of female labour and put women at the forefront of resistance to requests for increased tribute'; Beckert 2015, 15.
187. M.E. Smith 2012b, 81.
188. M.E. Smith 2012b, 94–107 (all luxury craftsmen and a number of utilitarian craftsmen – some of them organized in a kind of guild – lived in the cities).
189. Earle & Smith 2012, 264.
190. M.E. Smith 2012b, 111, 116–19, 125, 170; Giraldez 2012, 152.
191. Giraldez 2012, 154.
192. M.E. Smith 2012b, 126.
193. M.E. Smith 2012b, 134 for quotations.
194. M.E. Smith 2012b, 52, 61, 130–4, 142–3, 154, 161–3, 321; M.E. Smith 2015, 73, 102–4.
195. Kessler 2012; see Chapter 5.
196. Giraldez, 2012, 154 and in personal communication, however, questions why, in 1518, porters and other native labourers would have asked for wages to be paid out by the Spaniards in cacao beans unless they had previous knowledge of this practice.
197. M.E. Smith 2012b, 134, 136, 145–6.
198. M.E. Smith 2012b, 112, 116, 125, 141–2, 161, 212, 214, 225; D'Altroy 2002, 172 (many more victims than during Inca human sacrifices, whose victims were mainly Inca youngsters); Berdan 2014,190–1.
199. M.E. Smith 2012b, 154, 161, 210, 222–5; cf. Joyce 2010, 50, 62.
200. Wade 2017.
201. Guanglin 2015.
202. Slicher van Bath 1963a, 1963b and 1963c; Arnoux 2012.
203. Bloch 1967, 176–82, quotation 182; Arnoux 2012. He also stresses the redistributive effects of the tithes, enabling not only an income for the clergy but also the survival of the village poor and disabled; Beck, Bernardi & Feller 2014.
204. Scammell 1981, 40–7.
205. Kuroda 2020, ch. 6.
206. Hoffmann 2001.
207. Lis & Soly 1979, 1–8, 14–16; cf. Arnoux 2012.
208. Buringh 2011, 74, 290–1, confirmed by increased book production, which, of course, now also occurred commercially, beyond the monasteries; *Idem* 348–58, 427–40.
209. Guha 2001; Lardinois 2002; Krishnan 2014.
210. Chandra 2014; Grewal 2014; Hussain 2003.
211. Moosvi 2011.
212. Kolff 1990, 10, 18–19 (quotation on p. 18), 58. A Jolaha, or weaver, was considered the lowest caste, while Shekh stood for scholarship and religious functions in the community. For unfree labour: Levi 2002; Hussain 2014, 114–16.
213. J. Lucassen 2014b, 30 (after Deyell 1990); cf. Kulke & Rothermund 1990, 168–81; Subrahmanyam 1994; Habib 1994 (quotation about women on p. 103); J.F. Richards 1994.
214. Hussain 2003, esp. ch. 8; cf. Wicks 1992, ch. 3; Beckert 2015 for cotton.
215. Hussain 2003, 260.
216. Wicks 1992, 104; B. Yang 2019 for cowrie currency.

217. K. Hall 1994; Thapar 2002, ch. 11, for wage work, esp. p. 378; Ramaswamy 2004, 2011,
218. Sinopoli & Morrison 1995; Sinopoli 2001; K.D. Morrison & Sinopoli 2006; cf. Appadurai 1974.
219. Sinopoli & Morrison 1995, 91.
220. Sinopoli & Morrison 1995; Kulke & Rothermund 1990, 193–6 agree with Burton Stein's critique of the characterization of Vijayanagar as an example of 'military feudalism'.
221. Chandra 2014; K. Davids & Lucassen 1995; Shatzmiller 1994, 55–68; Van Bavel 2016.
222. For attempts to measure and compare these levels, see De Matos & Lucassen 2019; De Zwart & Lucassen 2020.
223. Van Zanden 2008; Van der Spek, Van Leeuwen & Van Zanden 2015.
224. Lis & Soly 1979, ch. 2; Cohn 2007; Van Nederveen Meerkerk 2008; Riello & Roy 2009; Beckert 2015; Van Bavel 2016.
225. Lis & Soly 1994; Harvey 1975, 38–9.
226. Prak & Wallis 2020.
227. Prak 2013; cf. K. Davids 2013b; Harvey 1975; Erlande-Brandenburg 1995, 80–85; Ramaswamy 2004.
228. Harvey 1975, 8–18 (quotation on pp. 8 and 9); Victor 2019.
229. Harvey 1975, ch. 3 (quotation on p. 48); Victor 2019.
230. Zürcher 2013.
231. Scammell 1981, 132; Ágoston 2005; J. Lucassen 2012a and b.
232. Harvey 1975, 71; Erlande-Brandenburg 1995.
233. Van Zanden 2008, 337, 351.
234. Van Zanden 2008, 337, 349.
235. Van Zanden, De Moor & Carmichael 2019; however, Segalen 1983 suggests that Western Europe was less deviant from e.g. India.
236. Van Zanden, De Moor & Carmichael 2019, 24, 27, 39, 42, 46, 53, 56, 233–43.
237. Van Zanden 2008 (quotation on p. 348); Van Zanden, De Moor & Carmichael 2019.
238. Buringh 2011; for a later period, see M. Spufford 1995.
239. Jackson 1989, esp. 627–8; cf. K. Davids 1994.
240. Blockmans 1980, 845–6; cf. Beck, Bernardi & Feller 2014.
241. Lis & Soly 1979, 48–52; Harvey 1975, 39–40; Cohn 2007; Humphries & Weisdorf 2019. This is also one of the earliest examples for Europe that states and not cities (to whom the economic and labour policy had been left until then) became involved with this issue. Cf. Brady 1991, 137; Prak 2018.
242. Cohn 2007; Dumolyn 2017.
243. Slicher van Bath 1963a, 189–94; Lis & Soly 1979, 52 also mention the Languedoc, the Rhineland, Spain, Bohemia and Scandinavia.
244. Slicher van Bath 1963a, 192; cf. Arnoux 2012, chs 6–7.
245. See also 5b and also 6c and 7b; for Qin China: Pines et al. 2014; cf. for earlier periods: Verboven 2011; Subbarayalu 2015.
246. J. Lucassen, De Moor & Van Zanden 2008.
247. Harvey 1975, 24; Lis, Lucassen & Soly 1994.
248. Sonenscher 1989; Lis & Soly 1994; Knotter 2018, ch. 1.
249. Hussain 2003, 264–5; Mazumdar 1969.
250. We might add the matrilineal smaller polities in tropical Africa (increasingly patrilineal and unequal after 500/1000 CE, see also p. 71; the Sahel also changed under the influence of trans-Saharan contacts from c. 1000, see Ehret 2016 and Green 2019); and maybe at a local rural level the Indian *jajmani* system.

CHAPTER 5 GLOBALIZATION OF LABOUR RELATIONS, 1500–1800

1. Abu-Lughod 1989; Vogel 2013; Deng 2011; Van Dyke 2005; Kirch 2010; Roullier et al. 2013; De Zwart & Van Zanden 2018; Manning 2020.
2. Kuroda 2020.
3. De Vries 1994, 2008, 2013. For a recent, though not very impressive, critique: Safley 2019.
4. K. Davids & Lucassen 1995; Van Bavel 2016.
5. Sugihara 2013. In my opinion, De Vries 2013, 80 overstates the differences between Western Europe and Asia.
6. Sugihara 2013, 20–1.
7. Sugihara 2013, 59.
8. Sugihara 2013, 25. So, there was only space for reclamation, see L. Lucassen, Saito & Shimada 2014, 372–4: In 1600–1750 the total acreage of arable land increased by 40 per cent, most of it before 1690,

by converting riverbeds, bays, coastland and marshes into paddy fields, where the Champa variety of rice (imported from China, despite it being unpalatable for most Japanese) could withstand waterlogged conditions very well.

9. Sugihara 2013, 27, 202; Matsuura 2016.
10. Sugihara 2013, 26 (NB. 1 tan ~ ¼ acre); cf. Beckert 2015.
11. Nagata 2005, 6.
12. L. Lucassen, Saito & Shimada 2014, 385–7.
13. Nagata 2005. For the *Ie*: Fauve-Chamoux & Ochiai 1998.
14. Nagata 2005, 141.
15. Izawa 2013, 19; cf. also Shimada 2006, 45–56, 94–101, 143–9, Nagase-Reimer 2013 and various contributions to N. Kim & Nagase-Reimer 2013 and Nagase-Reimer 2016. NB. There appears to be a problem with these numbers of workers. Imai 2016, 12–14, writes that the Besshi mine in 1713 (which then accounted for ¼ of the national production) had no more than 2,825 workers (incl. 600 charcoal makers), although she adds (p. 13, fn. 2) that for two locations we do not know how many people worked there.
16. Mathias 2013, 303.
17. Kuroda 2020, 34.
18. Pomeranz 2013; cf. Kuroda 2020. Cf. Huang 1990.
19. Li Bozhong 2003, 142–7.
20. Li Bozhong 2003, 173.
21. Kuroda 2020, 32–4.
22. Von Glahn 2003; Li Bozhong 2003; Deng 2011 and 2015; Guanglin 2015.
23. Huang 1990, chs 3 and 8.
24. Moll-Murata 2018, chs 7–8; Moll-Murata 2008a, ch. 3.3; K. Davids 2013a, ch. 2; Van Zanden 2013.
25. Moll-Murata 2018, 250–3; K. Davids 2013a, 70–1; Van Zanden 2013 disagrees with this.
26. This is a much larger share of the population than the top of the intellectual pyramid, consisting of the literati, who were the product of a meritocratic exam system that was, in principle, open to everyone wanting to obtain a job and, with the help of diplomas, subsequently forge a career in the civil service (Moll-Murata 2018, 256–9).
27. K. Davids 2013a, 120; for nuances, see also K. Davids 2013b.
28. K. Davids, 2013a, 138–42.
29. Moll-Murata 2018, 222–4, 277–8.
30. Shiuh-Feng 2016.
31. This can be seen from a combination of tables in Shiuh-Feng 2016, 115–17 and Lin 2015, 163–4, 169–70.
32. Vogel 2013, ch. 3.
33. Y. Yang 2013.
34. Shiuh-Feng 2016, 89–94; cf. Kuroda 2020.
35. Cf. Giersch 2001 for a nuanced picture of the encounters between Han Chinese and others.
36. Dieball & Rosner 2013; Lan 2013; Shiuh-Feng 2016. A small part of this copper went to mint houses in Yunnan itself.
37. That is low when compared to sailing ships at sea, see J. Lucassen & Unger 2011.
38. N. Kim 2013, 182.
39. Wang et al. 2005 and Moll-Murata, Jianze & Vogel 2005, esp. Vogel 2005.
40. Wang et al. 2005, 5.
41. Vogel 2005; Burger 2005; Lin 2015; Jin & Vogel 2015.
42. Moll-Murata 2008b, 2013; Pomeranz 2013.
43. Pomeranz 2013, 118–19; Moll-Murata 2018, 271–2. According to Birge 2003, 240, the position of women deteriorated from the Yuan dynasty: 'From Ming times on, daughters rarely received land as part of their dowry . . . and widow chastity became the litmus test of family and community virtue'.
44. Pomeranz 2013, 119.
45. They therefore resemble most larger and large traders, who, often based on family connections, organized themselves in various cities outside of the guilds and maintained mutual contacts, see Gelderblom 2013.
46. Moll-Murata 2013, 257.
47. Y. Yang 2013, 99ff.
48. Vogel 2005.
49. Vogel 2005, 411.
50. Moll-Murata 2015, 276.
51. Vanina 2004; Moosvi 2011; Mukherjee 2013; Beckert 2015; For wages, De Zwart & Lucassen 2020; De Matos & Lucassen 2019.
52. Parthasarathi 2001 and 2011; Riello & Roy 2009; I. Ray 2011; also Sukumar Bhattacharya 1969, 172ff.

53. Mukherjee 2013, ch. 3; Pearson 1994, 51ff.; for China: K. Davids 2013a, 125ff.
54. R. Datta 2000; For the late 18th and 19th centuries: Van Schendel 1992, 3–8; Buchanan 1986a and 1986b; Amin 2005, 211–19, 289–346, 332–6.
55. On saltpetre, see Jacobs 2000, 96–100; Buchanan 1986a, 549–55; Colebrooke 1884, 110–15; Sukumar Bhattacharya 1969, 141–5; For indigo: Van Santen 2001; Van Schendel 2012.
56. Roy 2013, 113: Only impoverished farmers or land workers from far away were hired out as factory labourers. They probably had enough time spare. In any case, as late as the 1940s, the average working year for males in India was only 182 days; cf. Pomeranz 2000, 212–15, 146–8.
57. Caland 1929, 74. Cf. Van Santen 2001. Mobility across caste lines was nevertheless possible, as stressed by authors from Colebrooke 1884, 104–7 to Vanina 2004, ch. 4 (esp. 125) and Parthasarathi 2011, 59–60. My strong impression is that these are exceptions that will confirm the rule and the norm of occupational endogamy.
58. I am grateful to Ed van der Vlist for this translation from Old Dutch.
59. R.K. Gupta 1984, 150–60; Sukumar Bhattacharya 1969, 173–84. For the cotton workers of South India: Parthasarathi 2001 and 2011.
60. Cf. R. Datta 2000, 185–213 and 294–304.
61. For South India, Parthasarathi 2001, 13 suggests that it was still possible that cotton weavers with small families hired labourers ('coolies') to prepare the yarn bought at the market with part of their advance. Cf. Wendt 2009.
62. R.K. Gupta 1984, 212, fn. 50. Cf. Parthasarathi 2001, 11–14, 29–32, 119–20; Subramanian 2009; and Ramaswamy 2014.
63. R. Datta 2000; cf. Parthasarathi 2011; Beckert 2015.
64. Wendt 2009, 211 (quotation), 212. For an even stronger distribution of activities among castes in western India, see Subramanian 2009, 257–60.
65. Amin 2005, 360: Fable XI, first published in Hindi in 1873. Note the similarities with the seventeenth-century poem 'The wife of the Gujar or Cowherd' (Raghavan 2017, 98). A French version is at least as old as 1240 (Arnoux 2012, 286–7: he points to the Sanskrit Panchatantra as the probable original). For women see also Moosvi 2011.
66. Das Gupta 1998. Although her empirical evidence does not apply to the current period and variations in family structure existed within India (Parthasarathi 2011, 73–5), I still assume that I can use her observations here.
67. Das Gupta 1998, 446–7.
68. Das Gupta 1998, 451–3.
69. Das Gupta 1998, all quotations from 450–9.
70. Denault 2009.
71. Roy 2013.
72. Van Rossum 2014; for the groupwise closed migration of weavers, see Ramaswamy 2014.
73. J. Lucassen 2012a and 2012b; for firm and factory size, see Pollard 1965 and Huberman 1996.
74. Bellenoit 2017; cf. Sugihara 2013, 29–30: 'It is also possible that the East Asian core regions might have valued mass literacy more than the South Asian counterpart.' Cf. Studer 2015, 33.
75. Van Zanden 2013, 326–8, 339–40. NB. The peak of manuscript production in the Arabic world was in the period 800–1200, so also much earlier; see also Buringh 2011.
76. Slicher van Bath 1963b and 1963c; Muldrew 2011 for England.
77. Bieleman 1992; cf. De Vries 1974; J. Lucassen 1987.
78. De Vries 1974, 136–7.
79. Muldrew 2011, 19.
80. J. Lucassen 1987. For a recent overview of seasonal migrations since 1500: Lucassen & Lucassen 2014.
81. J. Lucassen 1987, 117 (original December–January 1812/1813); cf. Lambrecht 2019.
82. J. Lucassen 1987, 118.
83. Kessler & Lucassen 2013.
84. J. Lucassen 1987, 96.
85. Ebeling & Mager 1997.
86. De Vries 1994, 2008, 2013. For a good discussion of this concept: Muldrew 2011, 14–17.
87. Ogilvie & Cerman 1996; Ebeling & Mager 1997; Beckert 2015.
88. Fontana, Panciera & Riello 2010, 277–85; cf. Belfanti 1996.
89. Van Nederveen Meerkerk 2007; see also Van Nederveen Meerkerk 2006, 2008 and 2010.
90. Van Nederveen Meerkerk 2007, 289–90.
91. Vandenbroeke 1996, 104–5.
92. M. Spufford 1984, 110–34 and 2000; cf. Muldrew 2011, esp. ch. 4; Thomas 2009, ch. 4; Humphries & Weisdorf 2019 show the income effects for England.
93. Holderness 1976, 86–92; Hudson 1996.

94. Based on Lancy 2015, 17 (more childcare); De Moor & Van Zanden 2006, ch. 5. and Van Zanden, De Moor & Carmichael 2019; for household strategy within and outside of patriarchal households, see Cashmere 1996; Bourke 1994.
95. Holderness 1976, 86–92; Hudson 1996; M. Spufford 1984 and 2000.
96. Snell 1985, ch. 6; cf. Van Nederveen Meerkerk 2007; Lis & Soly 1997.
97. Quotations from Hudson 1996, 64 and 65. King 1997 (a study about the West Riding of Yorkshire) points out that the families were very close and continued to be during this process. Women married young, on average at the age of 22, while their husbands were at most one or two years older. Parents were therefore still alive in most cases and assisted when necessary (mothers weaned their children early, which indicates that productive work took priority). In sum, he outlines a close-knit proto-industrial village community.
98. Snell 1985 83–4; cf. Muldrew 2011, 18–28; J. Lucassen 1987, 264–7.
99. For guilds outside Europe see Prak 2018, ch. 11.
100. Prak 2018; Prak & Wallis 2020.
101. K. Davids & Lucassen 1995, Introduction; Lucassen & Lucassen 2010, 19–32; cf. De Vries 1984; Prak 2018.
102. Lucassen & Lucassen 2010, 32. Here, I ignore the push factors, such as the frequent misery of war that mainly occurred in the countryside.
103. Prak 2008; Bok 1994; De Vries & Van der Woude 1997, 342–3.
104. Reininghaus 2000; Van der Linden & Price 2000; Prak, Lis, Lucassen & Soly 2006; J. Lucassen, De Moor & Van Zanden 2008; Epstein & Prak 2008; Teulings 2019; Prak & Wallis 2020.
105. Epstein & Prak 2008; K. Davids 2013b.
106. Mokyr 2015.
107. Prak & Wallis 2020; cf. K. Davids 2013a, 138: 'After catching up with China in the circulation of technical information in script and print, Europe went through a set of further changes that were unmatched in the Ming or Qing Empires.'
108. Sheilagh Ogilvie (2007) has an especially keen eye for the negative sides of the guilds; cf. Sarasúa 1997. Most recently this has been critically discussed in Prak & Wallis 2020.
109. Schmidt 2009; Van Nederveen Meerkerk 2006 and 2010.
110. Knotter 2018, ch. 1.
111. Dobson 1980; Barret & Gurgand 1980; Truant 1994; Reith 2008.
112. De Moor, Lucassen & Van Zanden 2008; Prak 2018, ch. 11.
113. J. Lucassen 1995, 382–3; cf. Carlson 1994, 94–5.
114. Boter 2016.
115. Hay & Craven 2004; Pesante 2009; Deakin & Wilkinson 2005.
116. Steinfeld 1991; Humphries & Weisdorf 2019; for forms of unfreedom in Scotland: Whatley 1995a and 1995b.
117. Steinfeld 1991, 98; cf. Pesante 2009, G.R. Rubin 2000.
118. J. Lucassen 1995, 398.
119. Hay & Craven 2004, 116. For the inferior position of farm servants in Germany before 1918: Biernacki 1995, 309.
120. Lucassen & Lucassen 2010. Unfortunately, no estimates are available for South and South East Asia.
121. Lucassen & Lucassen 2014, Introduction, 44–5.
122. Furthermore, in order to encourage speed, supplies were abolished, see Rieksen 2020; Zürcher 2013.
123. J. Lucassen & Unger 2011.
124. Van Lottum, Lucassen & Heerma van Voss 2011; Van Rossum 2014.
125. Van Lottum, Lucassen & Heerma van Voss 2011, 332–3.
126. Van Rossum 2014, 79–80, 95–7.
127. Van Rossum 2014, 80–8.
128. Van Rossum 2014, 281–7.
129. Rediker 1987, 2014; Van Rossum 2014; Jaffer 2015.
130. Thomas 1999, 256–7 (translated from Middle English by Brian Stone).
131. Cross 2001, 502; Humphries & Weisdorf 2019; for attempts to control labour time already in the medieval textile industries, see Stabel 2014; for other sectors: Victor 2019, 134, 145; Versieren & De Munck 2019, 80–1.
132. Cross 2001, 502.
133. De Vries & Van der Woude 1997, 615–17; Noordegraaf 1985, 58–9.
134. Prak 2018; Teulings 2019.
135. Muldrew 2011; on stimulants in early modern Europe, see also Roessingh 1976, 73–98.
136. C.A. Davids 1980; Rieksen 2020.
137. Sarasúa 1997.

138. Barret & Gurgand 1980, 196; cf. Amelang 2009.
139. More 1995, 243.
140. Looijesteijn 2009 and 2011.
141. Thompson 1968, 24–6; Skipp 1978, 105–7; Thomas 1999, 535.
142. Thomas 1999, 145–6.
143. The impetus was given by Pomeranz 2000; Parthasarathi 2011; Vries 2013. For a discussion about that book, see *TSEG* 12 (2015); Studer 2015; more recently, see many authors (including Pomeranz himself) in Roy & Riello 2019.
144. Of course, these are not the only factors. Much of the debate concerns, e.g. the availability of coal. For a reasonably complete overview, see Goldstone 2015, 19 in his review of Vries 2013. One of the factors in his list is labour, described as 'abundance/scarcity, intensity/industriousness, wages, and quality or human capital'. For an interesting comparative discussion of the human capital factor, see Prak 2018.
145. Including otherwise excellent studies like Humphries & Weisdorf 2019, 2883; Prak & Wallis 2020, 309, 315. Prak 2018 is much more cautious.
146. Goldstone 2015; Beckert 2015.
147. O'Brien & Deng 2015.
148. De Zwart & Lucassen 2020.
149. R. Datta 2000, chs 5–6. Mukherjee 2013 provides a more favourable picture of the grain trade.
150. Verlinden 1991; Walvin 2006; H. Barker 2019; Rio 2020.
151. Phillips 1991; Hofmeester & Lucassen 2020.
152. Verlinden 1955, 1977, 1991; Phillips 1991; Walvin 2006; Eltis & Richardson 2010; Ehret 2016; Green 2019.
153. H. Barker 2019; cf. Verlinden 1991, 71; Scammell 1981, 106–8; Green 2019; see B. Yang 2019 for the simultaneous exports of Maldivian cowries via the Mediterranean to sub-Saharan Africa.
154. Blumenthal 2009; for black as a racial category see also H. Barker 2019.
155. Berthe 1991; McCreery 2000; cf. Semo 1993; M.E. Smith 2012a.
156. McCreery 2000, 94.
157. M.E. Smith 2012a; cf. Allen, Murphy & Schneider 2012.
158. McCreery 2000, 22–6; cf. Berthe 1991.
159. M.E. Smith 2012a, 291–2.
160. The term *repartimiento forzoso* is from Berthe 1991, 104.
161. McCreery 2000, 39.
162. McCreery 2000, 49.
163. Barragán Romano 2016, 2018; cf. Cole 1985; McCreery 2000, 31–3, 41–3; Mangan 2005; Gil Montero 2011.
164. Cole 1985, 1; according to Barragán Romano 2016 and 2018, *mita* in Quechua and Aymara means to work by turns.
165. Gil Montero 2011, 309.
166. Cole 1985, 24; cf. Mangan 2005, 26–7.
167. Barragán Romano 2018.
168. Here, I combine the arguments of Gil Montero 2011 and Barragán Romano 2018.
169. Mangan 2005.
170. E.g. among the Timucua in what is now northern Florida and southern Georgia, see Milanich 1996, 134–6, 173–6.
171. Milanich 1996, 190–5.
172. Milanich 1996, 137, 160–6; Hemming 1984.
173. Saeger 2000; cf. Hemming 1984, 538.
174. Saeger 2000, 138–40.
175. Saeger 2000, 65–76.
176. The following based on Hemming 1984; cf. Kars 2020 for the Guyanas.
177. Hemming 1984, 506.
178. Hemming 1984, 517.
179. Allen, Murphy & Schneider 2012, 887. To this were added the plagues of debt peonage (*peonaje*) and the truck system (the obligation to buy goods from the shop of the employer or one of his relatives), but especially after the colonial period, see McCreery 2000, 64–5; Semo 1993, 156–7.
180. McCreery 2000, 63, 65–7; Semo 1993, 88–9.
181. McCreery 2000, 56–60; Hemming 1984, 536–9.
182. McCreery 2000, ch. 3.
183. Berthe 1991; cf. H. Klein 1986.
184. McCreery 2000, 25–7.

185. Muaze 2016 for domestic slavery in Brazil. African slaves also became important in Peru as a consequence of the increased wealth after Potosí. They were shipped via Cartagena (now Colombia) and Portobelo (now Panama), transported across the Isthmus, and then shipped to Callao, the entry port of Lima, see H. Klein 1986, 28–35; cf. Green 2019.
186. Moya Pons 2007, 16, 22–5, 57–63, 71–2; McCreery 2000, 48–54; cf. Bosma 2019.
187. McCreery 2000, 53.
188. Moya Pons 2007, 39–47, 57–63; Emmer 2000; Ribeiro da Silva 2012; Meuwese 2012.
189. Moya Pons 2007, 50–74, 86–94.
190. Galenson 1981 and 1989.
191. Tomlins 2004, 120; Bailyn 1988.
192. Tomlins 2004, 122.
193. Moya Pons 2007, 68; cf. Galenson 1986.
194. Moya Pons 2007, 67; H. Klein 1999, 32–46; Galenson 1989.
195. Austin 2013, 203 (quotation); higher density estimates in Green 2019; Ehret 2016. For the use of metal tools in Africa, see also E.W. Herbert 1984, 1993; Schmidt 1997.
196. Thomaz 2014; Ehret 2016.
197. Austin 2013, 203.
198. E.W. Herbert 1984; Austin 2013; Thomaz 2014; Ehret 2016; Green 2019. For seasonality in Africa: Hurston 2018.
199. Manning 1990; H. Klein 1999; Lovejoy 2000, 2005 and 2011; Walvin 2006; Eltis & Richardson 2010; Toledano 2011; Green 2019.
200. For slavery in classical antiquity, when black Africans were not preferred over other slaves, see pp. 134–42. The demand for slaves, also from Africa, increased substantially during the Abbasid Caliphate in Iraq (Van Bavel 2016, 68–71; Gordon 2011).
201. Lovejoy 2011, 43.
202. Lovejoy 2005, 19–33; Green 2019.
203. E.W. Herbert 1984, 113–23; Hogendorn & Johnson 1986; Beckert 2015; Green 2019; B. Yang 2019; Kuroda 2020.
204. Eltis & Richardson 2010, 23. These figures are still changing a bit due to new research. See Candido 2013; Paesie 2010; Van Rossum & Fatah-Black 2012.
205. Paesie 2016; for Asia cf. Van Rossum 2015b, 19–20, 36.
206. Eltis & Richardson 2010, 5; Lovejoy 2005, 15; cf. Toledano 2011.
207. Manning 1990, 171.
208. Green 2019; cf. D.M. Lewis 2018, 271.
209. Eltis & Richardson 2010, 136–53; see also Candido 2013, also for Lusophone and Luso-African involvement in taking captives.
210. Hurston 2018. I used the excellent Dutch–English edition 2019, 94–8, 108.
211. Eltis & Richardson 2010, 159–66. For the prices, see H. Klein 1999, 110.
212. Manning 1990.
213. Van Bavel 2016, 68–70. Cf. Gordon 2011.
214. Manning 1990, 170–1; H. Klein 1999, 126–7.
215. Manning 1990, 97–8, 113–23, 130–3; Lovejoy 2005, 3, 81–152, 355–84.
216. Cf. Candido 2013, 171–5.
217. Lovejoy 2000, 109.
218. Lovejoy 2005, 17–19.
219. Thomaz 2014, 77–80, 84–7.
220. Lovejoy 2005, including a discussion of *murgu* (the payment made by slaves to their masters for the right to do wage work on their own account) and *wuri* (a proportional payment to their masters for the right to trade on the basis of one tenth of a day's earnings): see 206–26.
221. Quoted in E.W. Herbert 1993, 222–3.
222. Green 2019.
223. Vink 2003; Van Rossum 2014, 2015a, 2015b, 2021a, 2021b; Mbeki & Van Rossum 2016; Brandon, Frykman & Røge 2019; Van Rossum et al. 2020; Van Rossum & Tosun 2021.
224. Singha 1998, 154–8; Chatterjee 1999, esp. ch. 1; Chatterjee & Eaton 2006; Levi 2002, 278–9; G. Campbell 2011 and 2012; Clarence-Smith 2015; G. Campbell & Stanziani 2015; Van Rossum et al. 2020; Van Rossum 2021b.
225. Saradamoni 1973; Reid 1998, 129–36; Reid 1999, 181–216; Vink 2003, 149–51, 156–7.
226. Kolff 1990, 10–15; Levi 2002; Stanziani 2014; G. Campbell 2011, 54–61. Peaks occurred in 200 BCE–200 CE, 800–1300 and 1780–1910, and he estimates that, over 2,000 years, total numbers (including 1.5 million from Eastern Africa in the 19th century) far exceeded the 12 million involved in the transatlantic slave trade. We must add to this the probably even more important overland trade in 'Hindu India and the Confucian Far East'; see the 8–9 million slaves counted in India for 1841.

227. Levi 2002, 281.
228. Levi 2002, 280; Kolff 1990, 11.
229. Levi 2002, 287.
230. Stanziani 2014, 88; cf. Toledano 2011; H. Barker 2019.
231. Kolchin 1987; Dennison 2011; Stanziani 2014.
232. Stanziani 2014, 61–72.
233. Stanziani 2014, 85.
234. Slicher van Bath 1963a, 280–2, 330; Kolchin 1987, 152; Dennison 2011, 35–6. The same applied to crops such as peas, hemp and linseed.
235. Gentes 2008, 26.
236. Stanziani 2014, 55–6.
237. Kolchin 1987, 69, 151.
238. Kolchin 1987, 27, 39; Stanziani 2014, 120–1. NB. Clerical property was secularized in Russia in 1764 and in the Ukraine in 1785.
239. Kolchin 1987, 57, 62, 73 (quotation).
240. Kolchin 1987, 217.
241. Kolchin 1987, 73–5, 108, 212–17; Dennison 2011, 62–7, 87–92.
242. Kolchin 1987, 200–7; Dennison 2011, 93–131; Budd 2011, 22 for religious implications.
243. Kolchin 1987, esp. chs 5 and 6; Dennison 2011, 42–3.
244. Kolchin 1987, 249–50. The 'old cross' refers to the dissenting movement of Old Believers.
245. Kolchin 1987, 334–43.
246. Kolchin 1987, 74 (quotation), 108, 224.
247. Dennison 2011, 230.
248. Dennison 2011, 149–80.
249. Dennison 2011, 132–48; some better-off serfs could even buy serfs, of course – as with land and property – only with the permission of the lord. As a rule, this practice was aimed at finding a substitute military conscript for the army (Dennison 2011, 169–71).
250. Kolchin 1987, 335–40; Gorshkov 2000; Moon 2002; Dennison 2011, 166, 171–8.
251. Stanziani 2014, 56; Kolchin 1987, 28–30, 279. In Siberia, in 1678, there were no privately held serfs, and in 1719 only 3.4 per cent of its population were privately held, the others being state serfs, see Kivelson 2007.
252. Kivelson 2007; Boeck 2007; Znamenski 2007; Gentes 2008.
253. Kivelson 2007, 35.
254. Gentes 2008, 101–3; cf. Whatley 1995a and 1995b for the status of Scottish miners.
255. Gentes 2008, 48–57.
256. Gentes 2008, 50.
257. Gentes 2008, 57.
258. Boeck 2007; Kessler 2014; Sunderland 2014.
259. Zürcher 2013; Kolchin 1987, 282–3.
260. Dennison & Ogilvie 2007.

CHAPTER 6 CONVERGING LABOUR RELATIONS, 1800 TO NOW

1. No other topic has been debated more extensively in economic and social history, e.g. Pollard 1965; Lazonick 1990; Huberman 1996; Voth 2000; Rider & Thompson 2000; MacRaild & Martin 2000; Berg 2005; Allen 2009; Van Zanden 2009; Horn, Rosenband & Smith 2010; E. Griffin 2010; Stearns 2015; Greif, Kiesling & Nye 2015; Beckert 2015; Roy & Riello 2019.
2. Pomeranz 2000, 63–8; Deane 1969; Berg 2005; Broadberry, Fremdling & Solar 2010. The figure for spinning comes from Deane 1969, 87.
3. K. Davids & Lucassen 1995.
4. Mokyr 2002; K. Davids 2013a and 2013b; cf. Prak & Wallis 2020.
5. Meisenzahl 2015, 330.
6. Kessler & Lucassen 2013.
7. Magnusson 2009; Broadberry, Fremdling & Solar 2010; Beckert 2015; Wong 2016.
8. J. Lucassen 2021.
9. Berg 2005. Cf. Schloss 1898, 1902 (on Schloss: W. Brown & Trevor 2014); Pollard 1965; Jacoby 1985; Lazonick 1990; Huberman 1996.
10. Berg 2005, 204. NB. This text is not meant to be cynical.
11. Lazonick 1990; Huberman 1996.
12. Knotter 2018, 22–3; cf. Pollard 1965, 51ff; Jacoby 1985; Lazonick 1990; Huberman 1996.
13. Berg 2005, 198.
14. E. Griffin 2010, 160; Humphries & Weisdorf 2019.

15. Cf. Jones 2015, 404.
16. Meissner, Philpott & Philpott 1975. We can distinguish work where talking and singing was impossible (not only in heavy industry, but also where concentrated cerebral work was required) from that where it was possible and that where talking is necessary (think of hairdressing or retail work).
17. Berg 2005, 192, 253–4, 282–3; cf. Kessler & Lucassen 2013, 285–6.
18. Geary 1981; J. Lucassen 2006c; Horn 2010; Beckert 2015.
19. Here, I closely follow Kessler & Lucassen 2013, 262–3. Cf. Pollard 1965; Shlomowitz 1979; Lourens & Lucassen 1999; J. Lucassen 2013 and 2021; Berg 2005; for subcontracting under conditions of limited freedom: Whatley 1995a and 1995b.
20. Lourens & Lucassen 2015, 2017; cf. Versieren & De Munck 2019.
21. Lourens & Lucassen 2015 and 2017, 23 (quoting *On Work and Wages,* 3rd edn, 1872).
22. Kessler & Lucassen 2013; cf. Pollard 1965, Lazonick 1990.
23. F.W. Taylor 1911, 72; cf. Kuromiya 1991. Taylor had been a gang boss himself, see Kanigel 2005, 147, 162–7 (quotation on 163).
24. Piketty 2019, ch. 6.
25. Kolchin 1987, 7, 37, 245–6; cf. for Africa: Lovejoy 2005, 207–26.
26. Van der Linden 2011a; Brass & Van der Linden 1997; cf. Hurston 2018, and the various chapters in these two volumes.
27. Verlinden 1977, 1020–46. For Portugal: Boxer 1969, 265–6 and Godinho 1992, 19–20; for the Portuguese Empire in western Africa: Kloosterboer 1960, 67–78; Green 2019.
28. Toledano 2011; Erdem 1996; Hofmeester & Lucassen 2020; cf. Nieboer 1910, 136–7.
29. On pre-European and European slave transports from and to Madagascar: Dewar & Richard 2012, 506–7. On the effects on the Americas: Heuman & Burnard 2011, chs 6–8; on Africa: Pallaver 2014; Green 2019.
30. Saradamoni 1974; Baak 1997; Singh 2014.
31. Beckert 2015; Piketty 2019, chs 6 and 15; Greenhouse 2019.
32. On the Dutch East Indies, see Baay 2015; Van Rossum 2015a, 2015b; Van Rossum & Tosun 2021. For the long train: Kloosterboer 1960; for Ethiopia: Fernyhough 2010.
33. Blum 1978; Kolchin 1987, esp. Epilogue; Burds 1991; and especially Dennison 2011, 231–3.
34. Espada Lima 2009.
35. Quoted in Van der Linden 2011b, 29.
36. Blackburn 1988 and 2011.
37. Kars 2020; cf. Dewulf 2018; see also the Palmares revolt (p. 275). It is important to realize that protests of slaves are lacking in regions where slavery was intimately connected with caste hierarchy, as in Kerala: Saradamoni 1974.
38. Blackburn 1988, 144. Later in the century, the Cuban labour movement played a similar role, see Casanovas 1997.
39. Blackburn 1988, 440–1.
40. Blackburn 1988, 443.
41. Blackburn 1988, 444.
42. Eckert 2011, 351; Seibert 2011.
43. For the following: Zimmermann 2011.
44. Zimmermann 2011, 470; cf. Zilfi 2010, esp. 220–6 for opposition from the 'ulema'.
45. Van der Linden & Rodríguez García 2016. For Korea, see Miller 2007. For compulsory cultivation in the Dutch East Indies, see Breman 1989 and Van Rossum 2021a. Generally, military conscription as such is not considered an infringement of the principle of free labour, but it can become so under certain circumstances (especially if very lengthy, say over three years).
46. Piketty 2019, 290–1.
47. Zimmermann 2011, 481, 488; Bales 2005, 40–68 on international agreements against slavery.
48. Breuker & Van Gardingen 2018.
49. Bade 2000, 232–45, 287–92; Roth 1997; Westerhoff 2012.
50. U. Herbert 1990, ch. 4.
51. U. Herbert 1990; For Japan, see e.g. Palmer 2016; for the defeated Kuomintang soldiers in China: Cheng & Selden 1994, 648. According to Kay & Miles 1992, some post-war 'European Volunteer Workers' in Britain, e.g. those from the Baltic states, looked suspiciously like unfree labourers.
52. The following after Kössler 1997; Van der Linden 1997a; Piketty 2019, ch. 12.
53. Roth 1997.
54. Homburg 1987; Patel 2005.
55. Mason 1966; For similarities between Germany and Japan in WWII, see Boldorf & Okazaki 2015.
56. Cheng & Selden 1994; Shen 2014; J. Li 2016; Piketty 2019, ch. 12; cf. Netting 1993, 109ff., 232ff.
57. Cheng & Selden 1994, 660.
58. Cheng & Selden 1994. For the famine caused by the Great Leap Forward, see Dikötter 2010.

59. Frankopan 2019, 103–6.
60. On Korea: Breuker & Van Gardingen 2018.
61. Eltis 2011, 139; cf. Budd 2011, ch. 2; Van der Linden & Rodríguez García 2016; Kotiswaran 2017.
62. Kotiswaran 2017.
63. Kennan 1891, vol. I, 255; vol. II, 458.
64. Coldham 1992; Bailyn 1988; E. Richards 1996. For later vagrancy laws, see McCreery 1997.
65. Pierre 1991. Other colonial powers had similar penal colonies, like the Netherlands at Boven-Digoel (New Guinea) from 1926 to 1942.
66. Santiago-Valles 2016, 89–90; Piketty 2019, 581–2.
67. Pizzolato 2016. For the long-term negative effects of black slavery in the US: Angelo 1997; Krissman 1997; cf. Hurston 2018; and in Brazil (esp. debt bondage in Amazonas): Bales 1999 and 2005.
68. Molfenter 2016; Breman 1996; Olsen 1997; Baak 1997; Bales 1999; G. Campbell & Stanziani 2015.
69. Drèze & Sen 2013; Piketty 2019, 345–61.
70. Quotation in Van der Linden 2016, 321; Singh 2014.
71. For Ghana, see Akurang-Parry 2010; for NGOs continuing the tradition of the abolitionists, see Bales 2005.
72. Costello et al. 2015.
73. Cheng & Selden 1994, 652.
74. Ehmer 1996, 65.
75. Stone, Netting & Stone 1990; Netting 1993; Blum 1978; Vanhaute & Cottyn 2017.
76. Vanhaute & Cottyn 2017, 3; cf. Segalen 1983.
77. Netting 1993, 3.
78. Netting 1993, 34–41; cf. for France: Segalen 1983.
79. Netting 1993, 35.
80. Netting 1993, 31–2.
81. This may be less obvious than it seems, as cultural norms regularly prevent women from doing productive work, e.g. among the neighbouring Muslim Hausa (Stone, Netting & Stone 1990, 11).
82. Netting 1993, 73; Stone, Netting & Stone 1990.
83. Ulin 2002.
84. Netting (1993, 321) predicted: 'But densely settled areas of traditionally intensive production, like the great irrigated areas of Asia, will remain smallholder bastions, and zones of increasing population pressure in Africa and Latin America may move gradually in the same direction.'; cf. Vanhaute 2021.
85. Barringer 2005. See also Crossick 1997b, 1–15.
86. He was also the man behind Hommel 1969 (orig. 1937) and an inspiration for Henry Ford's Museum of American Innovation in Detroit, which, incidentally, also glorified the Industrial Revolution.
87. Cf. contributions to Crossick 1997a; Haupt 2002; De Moor, Lucassen & Van Zanden 2008.
88. Bourillon 1997, 229.
89. Booth 1904, 57–8.
90. Booth 1904, 113–14.
91. Booth 1904, 117–18.
92. Booth 1904, 119. For the sweating industry also Schloss 1898 (who was one of Booth's collaborators); cf. W. Brown & Trevor 2014.
93. Piketty 2019, 591–5, 771–2, 789.
94. Hagen & Barrett 2007, based on research among the Shuar in Ecuador.
95. Sarasúa 1997.
96. These are the main variables presented in De Moor & Van Zanden (2006) to explain the historical differences in 'girl power'. For other variables, see, among others, Brinton 2001.
97. Lancy 2015, 155; cf. Segalen 1983 for female farm work.
98. Berg 2005, ch. 7; E. Griffin 2010, ch. 5; for Japan, see Tsurumi 1990.
99. Berg 2005, 137; Sinha, Varma & Jha 2019; Sinha & Varma 2019.
100. Davies 1977, 1–8; cf. Segalen 1983 for France.
101. Boter 2017, 80–81.
102. E.g. MacRaild & Martin 2000, 26–7; Boter 2017; Van der Vleuten 2016.
103. De Moor & Van Zanden 2006, 45–7; Heald 2019.
104. Wulff 1987; Tonioli & Piva 1988.
105. Siegelbaum 1988, 217–223.
106. Daniel 1989, 42–4.
107. Lancy 2015; Segalen 1983, ch. 7 and Conclusion.
108. Boter 2017; cf. Brinton 2001; Van der Vleuten 2016.
109. Goldin 2006, 5; Heald 2019.
110. Goldin 2006, 3–8.

111. The oil states form an important exception, not because many of them are Islamic, but because of the large incomes of their citizens, see Ross 2008.
112. Hrdy 2009, 167. NB. This is not a new phenomenon: in England in 1574–1821, over a quarter of households were headed by a single person; widows accounted for 12.9 per cent of households (Berg 2005, 157). Cf. Hahn 2002.
113. Hrdy 2009, 171.
114. L.T. Chang 2009, 51–3. For a male counterpart, see Pun & Lu 2010. Also Chow & Xu 2001; S. Li & Sato 2006.
115. See the special edition of *The Economist*, 26 November 2011.
116. *The Economist*, 7 July 2018.
117. Atabaki 2013 (quotation on 168).
118. Vanhaute & Cottyn 2017, 3: 96 per cent of agriculturalists today are smallholders and 85 per cent of those in the Global South work less than 2 hectares.
119. Voth 2000.
120. J. Lucassen 2012b; Broughton 2005.
121. Jacoby 1985; Kanigel 2005; Wood & Wood 2003; Suzman 2020, ch. 13.
122. Wood & Wood 2003, 441, 629 (as expressed in 1910 by Louis Dembitz Brandeis and in 1911 by Edward Mott Woolley); cf. Lazonick 1990.
123. Kanigel 2005, 520–1.
124. Gilbreth 1911, quotations on resp. 83 and 92–3.
125. Gilbreth 1911, 62–3, 71–2.
126. Graham 1999; Englander 2003, 234–5; Heald 2019, ch. 9. For corporate welfare, in which employers saw themselves as 'corporate fathers', their welfare workers as 'corporate mothers', who took care of the employees as 'corporate children', see Mandell 2002.
127. Kanigel 2005, 486–550; Schneider 2003. For the influence of plantation slave management on these later developments, see Van der Linden 2010.
128. Kanigel 2005, 525; cf. Siegelbaum 1988, 1–2.
129. Gilbreth 1911; Jacoby 1985.
130. Kohli 2000, 378 (figures for 1980, 1985, 1990 and 1995); Lazonick 1990.
131. Zijdeman 2010; Netting 1993, esp. 76–7.
132. Biernacki 1995, 105–21, quotations at resp. 106 and 111 (cf. also 359: 'the assumption that they took charge of a loom to manage it for a profit, as if they were petty commodity producers'); Budd 2011, 50–2.
133. Biernacki 1995, 367, 375–6.
134. J. Lucassen 2006d.
135. J. Lucassen 2007b, 77–9.
136. Biernacki 1995, 134–40.
137. Biernacki 1995, 425–31 (quotation on 426).
138. Tilly & Tilly 1998, 74; Van der Linden & Lucassen 2001; Budd 2011; For England see Pollard 1965. For a popular management application focusing on commitment: Amabile & Kramer 2011; for historically determined, cultural differences: Alam 1985.
139. Tilly & Tilly 1998, 74.
140. Turrell 1987, 149–63, quotation on 158. For a different view on the wage levels, see 170–1.
141. J. Lucassen 2001, 13–14; Tilly & Tilly 1998, 205.
142. J. Lucassen 2001, 13–14; Van der Linden 2008, 180–1, 185–6; Meyer 2019.
143. Ohler 2015.
144. De Waal 2009, 38–9, 211.
145. Gilbreth 1911, 48–9; cf. McNeill 1995 about the effect of dance and exercise as emotional means of communication.
146. Siegelbaum 1988; Benvenuti 1989; cf. G.R. Barker 1955.
147. Siegelbaum 1988, 71–2.
148. Siegelbaum 1988, 172.
149. Siegelbaum 1988, 182, 230–1.
150. Benvenuti 1989, 46.
151. Gilbreth 1911, 15–16; for an explanation of these two bricklaying methods, see 78.
152. Tilly & Tilly 1998, 217–27.
153. Wierling 1987.
154. Zürcher 2013. Think also of the closed compounds in Kimberley (Turrell 1987) and of the dormitories in the silk industry in Japan (Tsurumi 1990).
155. Siegelbaum 1988, 204–5; Brass & Van der Linden 1997, 354.
156. Lucassen & Lucassen 2014, pp. 31ff., in which cross-cultural migration rates (CCMRs: 14–16) are used to compare the different parts of Eurasia. This study does not provide similar data for the other continents; Manning 2020.

157. Kotiswaran 2017; Röschenthaler & Jedlowski 2017.
158. L.T. Chang 2009. Quotations from 9–10.

CHAPTER 7 THE CHANGING SIGNIFICANCE OF WORK, 1800 TO NOW

1. Lancy 2015; Van der Vleuten 2016; Heywood 2018.
2. Adam Smith 1812, 535. Cf. the comment by the editor J.R. McCulloch on 803–4 (notes 218–19) and Schumpeter 1972, 629–31. More generally, see Lis & Soly 2012.
3. Van Zanden et al. 2014.
4. Cited in Lancy 2015, 269. I have shortened the text slightly, but not essentially.
5. Cunningham 1995; Cunningham and Viazzo 1996; Cunningham 2000; Rahikainen 2004; Goose and Honeyman 2012; Heywood 2018.
6. Van der Vleuten 2016; B. van Leeuwen & Van Leeuwen-Li 2014.
7. Lancy 2015, 282, 384–93.
8. Huynh, D'Costa & Lee-Koo 2015.
9. Goose & Honeyman 2012, 18.
10. B. van Leeuwen & Van Leeuwen-Li 2014; for the impact of different types of colonization, see B. Gupta 2018.
11. Goose & Honeyman 2012, 4–5.
12. B. van Leeuwen & Van Leeuwen-Li 2014; Drèze & Sen 2013.
13. Pimlott 1976, 81, 145–6; cf. Bailey 1978; Suzman 2020.
14. Cross 1988 and 1989; Hennock 2007; Huberman & Minns 2007.
15. Karsten 1990 also offers a good past history; Heerma van Voss 1994.
16. As quoted in the editorial introduction to Lafargue 1969, 78.
17. Huberman & Minns 2007; cf. Ehmer 2009a; McBee 2019.
18. In the 19th century, Zulus in South Africa feared being outside at dark (Atkins 1993, 91–2).
19. Piketty 2019, 515–16.
20. Yamauchi et al. 2017; Suzman 2020, ch. 14 (also for other countries).
21. J. Lucassen 2000, 8–9.
22. Pearson 1994, 51–58. Numbers have been fluctuating in recent decades due to logistical problems, and the previous impressive increase seems not to have continued.
23. Pearson 1994, 37–8.
24. Pearson 1994, 134–5, 149–50.
25. If we assume, firstly, that the effect of the increase in pilgrims and of the shortening of the duration cancel each other out and, subsequently, that, around 1600, the average working life of a pilgrim was 35 years, then that meant an absence for him (or her) of 5 months or 125 working days. This equates to an average of four working days per year. For the total Muslim population that meant less than one day per year.
26. Antonopoulos & Hirway 2010.
27. Zijdeman & Ribeiro da Silva 2014.
28. Ehmer 2009a and 2009b; Hennock 2007, chs 10–11 and 191–192: in the German case, the Law of 1889 combined provisions for old age and invalidity, and the sums spent on invalidity greatly surpassed those spent on pensioners over 75 in good health.
29. Ehmer 2009a, 132.
30. M.H.D. van Leeuwen 2016, 220–1; Hu & Manning 2010.
31. Wylie 1884, 53–4.
32. Lafargue 1969, 123, 136. In the same pamphlet, he also condemned migratory cooperative subcontracting because such workers, whether Auvergnians in France, Scots in England, Galicians in Spain, Pomeranians in Germany or Chinese in Asia – 'races for which work is an organic necessity' – were stupid toilers 'that love work for work's sake'; cf. Arendt 1958, 87–90.
33. Quoted from the Dutch translation in J. Lucassen 2013, 32.
34. Tilly & Tilly 1998, 114.
35. Burnett 1994, quotations on 189 and 295–6; cf. the more abstract S. Li & Sato 2006; Ehlert 2016.
36. Although this theme is elaborated here for wage workers *c.* 1850, it is much broader, see e.g. most recently, Brandon, Frykman & Røge 2019. Cf. also Lis, Lucassen & Soly 1994; A. Bhattacharya 2017.
37. Hirschman 1970; Huberman & Minns 2007; Jacoby 1985; Lazonick 1990, chs 4–6; Huberman 1996 (also on a local level).
38. Rose 2012, 301; for the following also T. Wright 1867.
39. Lourens & Lucassen 2015 and 2017. See De Waal 2009 on solidarity, but also Rosenblatt 2006; for fair and equal remuneration and competition among primates, see De Waal 2009, 185–6, 195–7, 229ff.

40. J. Lucassen 2000, 43–55. On careers, see Mitch, Brown & Van Leeuwen 2004; on intermediation, see Wadauer, Buchner & Mejstrik 2015.
41. Scholliers 1996, 110–15.
42. Tilly & Tilly 1998; Wadauer, Buchner & Mejstrik 2015.
43. Truant 1994; Haupt 2002.
44. For labour arrangements for Indian IT-specialists abroad, infamously known as 'body shopping': B. Xiang 2007.
45. Ramaswami 2007, quotation on 208.
46. For examples from the maritime sphere, see Van Rossum 2014. Think also of the (lack of) agency of women in the framework of the #MeToo debate.
47. L.T. Chang 2009, 58–9. Cf. Chow & Xu 2001; S. Li & Sato 2006.
48. Tilly & Tilly 1998, 216–27. Think also of the excessive overwork in Japan as discussed earlier (p. 370).
49. Löbker 2018, 70; cf. De Gier 2016.
50. Bouwens et al. 2018 (quotation on 48); cf. Hennock 2007, 339–40. For conflicting views on Tata's social policies since the 1870s, cf. the more traditional Laila 1981 with the more critical Mamkoottam 1982; S.B. Datta 1986; Bahl 1995.
51. With thanks to Dr Chris Teulings for his suggestion regarding the following passage. Cf. Milanovic 2019, 25; cf. Suzman 2020, 352–9.
52. Piketty 2019, 421–2, 533; Milanovic 2019.
53. Jacoby 1985, 32, 137.
54. For the following, see Lucassen & Lucassen 2014. Also J. Lucassen 2000, 26–40, 65–7; Manning 2013 and 2020.
55. Stanziani 2008 and 2009a; Dennison 2011. For freedmen in Brazil: Espada Lima 2009.
56. Of course, such forms may also be used by individuals (e.g. the abscondment of slaves), as well as by permanent organizations, in particular strikes, but also e.g. petitions. Atkins 1993 offers a nice combination of the different forms in nineteenth-century South Africa. Brandon, Frykman & Røge 2019 offers an excellent overview of all forms of action by free and unfree labourers and everybody in between.
57. Rediker 1987 and cf. the mariners pp. 238–40.
58. For violence and sabotage, see Van der Linden 2008, 174–5, 181–2; for collective exit, see 175–8. For collective exit in the form of the *uytgang*, see Dekker 1990, 387–91; for go-slow or ca'canny see pp. 351, 384.
59. J. Lucassen 2006c, 545–51.
60. J. Lucassen 2007b, 70.
61. J. Lucassen 2007b, 74.
62. Van der Linden 2008, 175, 197; Biernacki 1995, 438–41.
63. Van der Linden 2008, 175, 211, 253; Heerma van Voss 2002; cf. M.B. Smith 2012, 393–4, 397.
64. Van der Linden 2008, 211–15.
65. Van der Linden 2008, 215.
66. Van der Linden 2008, 179–207.
67. Quoted in Van der Linden 2008, 190.
68. Van der Linden 2008, 298–312.
69. Chen 2010; Pun & Lu 2010; K. Chang & Cooke 2015; cf. L.T. Chang 2009.
70. Although proper labour conflict statistics are unavailable for China, note the rise of labour disputes in arbitration from 135,000 in 2000 to 314,000 in 2005, involving 801,042 employees in 2003 (Pun & Lu 2010, 509).
71. Chen 2010, 114. Dormitories are necessary given the *hukou* system that severely hampers the settlement of rural migrants in cities, see Shen 2014.
72. For the survival of guilds or some of their functions in Germany (as compared to Great Britain, Northern Italy and France), see Biernacki 1995, ch. 6. Also Van der Linden 2008, 224.
73. Van der Linden 2008, 84–90; cf. Moya 2017.
74. Quoted in Van der Linden 2008, 85.
75. M.H.D. van Leeuwen 2016; Van der Linden 2008, 91–4, 109–31.
76. Van der Linden 2008, 151–69.
77. The expression was coined by Lenger 1991. For continuities with the pre-industrial period, see Epstein & Prak 2008, Introduction.
78. Boch 1989; J. Lucassen 2006b and 2006c; Christensen 2010; Knotter 2018 (esp. ch. 3); for the Islamic world, see also R. Klein 2000.
79. J. Lucassen 2006c, 528–33, quotation on 531.
80. Huberman 1996; Christensen 2010. This craft control model frustrated the adoption of the American managerial alternative in the UK (Lazonick 1990).

81. Van der Linden 2008, 220; Knotter 2018.
82. Biernacki 1995, ch. 9; Huberman 1996; cf. Van der Linden & Rojahn 1990.
83. Biernacki 1995, 423–5; Van der Linden 2008, 226–7; Heerma van Voss, Pasture & De Maeyer 2005; W. Thorpe 1989; Van der Linden & Thorpe 1990.
84. Christensen 2010, 765.
85. The German Social Democratic Party (SPD) accepted 'capitalism with a human face' at its congress at Bad Godesberg in 1959, see Reinhardt 2014.
86. Van der Linden 2008, 225, 232–3, 251; see also Biernacki 1995, 286–7 for closed shops for apprentices.
87. Van der Linden 2008, 227–32, 240; cf. Jacoby 1985; Lazonick 1990. Money may also be extorted from both employers and workers by third parties, so-called *racketeers* who try to interfere in the negotiating process. Such practices could also corrupt and compromise trade unions (Witwer 2009; Greenhouse 2019).
88. Shin 2017, 632. Damages: management threatened strikers that they would each have to pay for damages caused by what it called an illegal strike. More generally, see C.-S. Lee 2016 for the important role of trade unions more recently.
89. See Van der Linden 2008, 254–7 on the positive and negative implications; also Deakin & Wilkinson 2005.
90. Piketty 2019, chs 11 and 17.
91. Sabyasachi Bhattacharya & Lucassen 2005. For the shipbuilding industry, see Fahimuddin Pasha 2017; for brick making, see J. Lucassen 2006c; for trade unions in South Asia, see Candland 2001.
92. Cf. Benner 2002 and 2003.
93. Van der Linden 2008, 247–57; Greenhouse 2019.
94. Perchard 2019, 78.
95. Cf. August 2019; Tilly & Tilly 1998, ch. 9; Penninx & Roosblad 2000; Pizzolato 2004; Marino, Roosblad & Penninx 2017.
96. For example, on the US textile industry, see Blewitt 2010, 552, 555. In the American South, work, labour markets and trade unions were racially segregated (Van der Linden & Lucassen 1995; Greenhouse 2019). The active membership of African Americans, especially during the Second World War, and their experiences in Europe during and after the war, contributed to a slow change; see also Heald 2019 for trade unions feeling threatened by female labour force participation during the world wars.
97. Quoted in Van der Linden 2008, 245–6.
98. Tilly & Tilly 1998, 246–50; for the US: Jacoby 1985; Greenhouse 2019.
99. Knotter 2018; Greenhouse 2019.
100. For India, see also Tharoor 2018, 190–1 and Van der Linden 2008, 223.
101. Tilly & Tilly 1998, 249–53; cf. Jacoby 1985; Montgomery 1987 and 1993; Lazonick 1990;Van der Linden & Lucassen 1995; Blewitt 2010; Greenhouse 2019; Jaffe 2021 describes a number of new bottom-up initiatives for unionization in the US.
102. Van der Linden 2008, ch. 12; cf. Van Holthoon & Van der Linden 1988; Knotter 2018.
103. Van der Linden 2008, 264.
104. Weill 1987; cf. Van Holthoon & Van der Linden 1988; Van der Linden & Lucassen 1995.
105. Van der Linden 2008, 263.
106. Cross 1988 and 1989; Heerma van Voss 1988.
107. Steinmetz 2000; Van der Linden & Price 2000. Cf. Tomka 2004; Frank 2010; Fineman & Fineman 2018.
108. Deakin & Wilkinson 2005, xi–xxiii provide a thorough overview of regulations still valid in this respect for England and Wales (not including Scotland with its separate case law, see G.R. Rubin 2000, 292–3), listing 249 cases between 1598 and 2004, and 103 statutes, of which 21 for 1349–1597 and 82 for 1598–2002. Similar listings in Fineman & Fineman 2018, 392–8.
109. Piketty 2014 and 2019. Naturally, there is a lively debate about the numerical substantiation of his work. As far as I can see, however, this has no consequences for the way I draw from this milestone study. Additionally, Segal 2020 points to growing inequality from 'entitlements over labour' by top income groups that can afford to buy the labour of others for their personal consumption, especially domestic servants of all kinds – a return to the pre-war years, I would suggest.
110. Simitis 2000, 189.
111. The following is based on Piketty 2019, 528–47.
112. Lazonick 1990, 284ff.
113. For the English enclosures, see inter alia Snell 1985. For landlords and their tenants, for usury and credits, see Steinmetz 2000, chs 13–20.
114. Simitis 2000, 186–7; Hennock 2007; cf. Rimlinger 1971; Van der Linden 1996; M.H.D. van Leeuwen 2016.

115. Olszak 2000, 141–2.
116. Simitis 2000, 191.
117. Simitis 2000, 181–2. Cf. Zietlow 2018, 67–8.
118. Steinfeld 2001, 11–12; cf. Steinfeld 2009; Frank 2010.
119. Cottereau 2000, 208–12.
120. Johnson 2000; White 2016.
121. Lis & Soly 2012, 499, 504–6; Delsalle 1993; Steinfeld 2001, 243–6; Cottereau 2000, 208–12; also Horn 2010.
122. Simitis 2000, 186.
123. Thompson 1968; Pelling 1976; Dobson 1980, 121–2; Rule 1988; G.R. Rubin 2000; Hay 2004; Frank 2010.
124. Olszak 2000, 145.
125. Van Wezel Stone 2000; Zietlow 2018; Greenhouse 2019.
126. Steinfeld 2001, 246–9 for the colonies and 253–314 for the US.
127. Piketty 2019, 367–8.
128. Van der Linden & Price 2000.
129. Garon 2000; Shieh 2000.
130. For private and state poor relief, see Hennock 2007, chs 1–2; for minimum wages: Piketty 2019, 530–3.
131. Hennock 2007.
132. Kocka 1980, 1981; Bichler 1997; Veraghtert & Widdershoven 2002; Hennock 2007; M.H.D. van Leeuwen 2016.
133. Hennock 2007, chs 16–17.
134. Hennock 2007, 295. For the agricultural labourers, he advocated 'three acres [1.2 hectares] and a cow' in 1885.
135. Hennock 2007, 320 (therefore also labelled proto-corporatism).
136. Hennock 2007, 328. For later developments, see M.H.D. van Leeuwen 2016; Ehlert 2016. For China, see S. Li & Sato 2006.
137. Steinfeld 2009; Greenhouse 2019.
138. Hennock 2007, 287.
139. Tsurumi 1990, 94; this contributed to the later phenomenon of the 'salary man' (see above).
140. Eichengreen & Hatton 1988, 5; Burnett 1994.
141. Tomlinson 1987, 6; Sloman 2019.
142. Fitzgerald 1988.
143. Lins 1923, 825.
144. Renwick 2017; also Rimlinger 1971.
145. Tonioli & Piva 1988, 241.
146. Tomlinson 1987, 106; Sloman 2019 demonstrates that this was by no means a one-man-show.
147. I will refrain from describing the competition with the fascist, nationalist and other corporatist models, because this covers a much shorter period. In the key model countries, the corporatist experiment existed only for one or two decades. Only Franco in Spain and particularly Salazar's Estado Novo in Portugal lasted longer. This country is also important because of its colonial policies. Besides, Japan competed with the welfare pretensions in the European colonies, e.g. with the Dutch in Indonesia.
148. M.B. Smith 2012, 2015a & 2015b; McAuley 1991; also Rimlinger 1971; Madison 1968; Cook 1993; Tomka 2004; Piketty 2019, 578–606; Milanovic 2019.
149. McAuley 1991, 195. Cf. Article 12 of the 1936 Constitution: 'the man who will not work, shall not eat', which sounds like the apostle Paul in 2 Thessalonians 3 (Kloosterboer 1960, 174).
150. M.B. Smith 2012; Cook 1993.
151. McAuley 1991, 193, 204; M.B. Smith 2012, 395–7.
152. McAuley 1991, 197.
153. McAuley 1991, 203–4. According to his reconstruction of the 'real expenditure out of social consumption funds (SCF)'; Cook 1993. For other communist countries: Tomka 2004; Candland & Sil 2001.
154. Kessler 2008. Besides, until the late 1970s, only a quarter of persons of pensionable age received old age pensions, and the sums were extremely low. McAuley 1991, 205–6; cf. M.B. Smith 2012, 392, 397–8.
155. M.B. Smith 2012, 389.
156. M.B. Smith 2012, 394–7; Tomka 2004.
157. C.-S. Lee 2016. A more extensive comparison (but only for the period 1945–1980) can be found in Haggard & Kaufman 2008.
158. Song 2009. Cf. Van der Linden & Price 2000.

159. Chow & Xu 2001; S. Li & Sato 2006; Dillon 2015; Frankopan 2019.
160. Tomlinson 1987, 163–5 for this and following quotations; Piketty 2019; For Britain, Sloman 2019, for the Netherlands, Heijne & Noten 2020.
161. Goodman 1960, esp. 59–63. He distinguishes three statuses in American society: the Poor, the Organization and the Independents.
162. Piketty 2019, 531; Milanovic 2019.
163. Albert 1993. Cf. Candland & Sil 2001; Fellman et al. 2008; Piketty 2019.
164. Piketty 2014 and 2019; cf. Greer et al. 2017; Williams 2019; Sloman 2019.
165. The key figures in Piketty 2019, 21–3, 260–1, 419–23, 492–3, 525–7.
166. Piketty 2019, chs 14 and 15, quotations on 755. The 'classist cleavages' 1950–1980 have been exchanged for 'identitarian cleavages' 1990–2000 (958); Milanovic 2019, 56–66.
167. McBee 2019, 166–72 is also very clear about more and more work and thus the fact that there has been no increase in wealth since the 1970s.

OUTLOOK

1. The terminology is Polanyi's. This classification in Baldwin 2019.
2. J. Lucassen 2013, 25–31; Feinman 2012; Standing 2016; Piketty 2014 and 2019; Williams 2019; Sloman 2019; Heijne & Noten 2020; Manning 2020.
3. Ford 2017; Frankopan 2019.
4. Williams 2019, 111, 115. And the ILO appears to watch on helplessly.
5. In particular, scenarios of major military conflicts up to and including a third world war, but perhaps more importantly, of climate change (Manning 2020). People contribute to this not only as consumers but also as producers, which has consequences for the labour movement (Fitzpatrick 2017).
6. Van Bavel 2016; cf. Piketty 2019, 546–7. Van der Linden 2008 and Stanziani 2019 emphasize the exceptional nature of free wage labour in comparison with unfree labour relations in global history since 1500.
7. Piketty 2014 and 2019. For a similar argument, which emerged at roughly the same time, but which caused much less of a stir, see Luzkow 2015. See also Lawlor, Kersley & Steed 2009; Trappenburg, Scholten & Jansen 2014; Ford 2017; Jensen & Van Kersbergen 2017.
8. Piketty 2014 and 2019; Standing 2016. Add to this the phenomenon of food banks in rich countries, whose need has become more evident than ever during the coronavirus pandemic.
9. Although the analysis of Manning 2020 concurs with that of Piketty 2019 in many respects, Manning elaborates in more detail about the environmental challenges (Piketty 2019, 235, also 254–5). Cf. also the tenor of Drèze & Sen 2013.
10. Van der Spek, Van Leeuwen & Van Zanden 2015; Piketty 2019; Milanovich 2019 (although all are critical with respect to current developments).
11. For this position see inter alia Sloman 2019; Budd 2011, 38–9 for historical roots. An early example is Wells 1914, ch. 3 ('Off the Chain'), in which he praises all forms of global migratory labour as the pinnacle of the new, totally free working person and which could also contribute to world peace.
12. Baldwin 2019 (clearly more optimistic than Ford 2017 and certainly more positive than Harari 2014 in this regard); Cockshott 2019 (under the condition of automation within a socialist planned economy).
13. Harari 2014, 388–91, 436–7.
14. K. Davids & Lucassen 1995; cf. Lazonick 1990; Van der Spek, Van Leeuwen & Van Zanden 2015.
15. Sloman 2019, 17; for an average of tax receipts spending in Germany, France, the UK and Sweden, see Piketty 2019, 428, 458–60, 530, and for low incomes and transfers in the US, 526–30. For the Netherlands, see Heijne & Noten 2020.
16. Sloman 2019, 206–7.
17. Remember that producers have a structural need for consumers of goods and services, including medical services and many kinds of communication, as nicely exemplified by the reversal of accepted macro-economic wisdom in the Global North during the coronavirus pandemic by guaranteeing jobless incomes from tax money.
18. Piketty 2019, 929–53. Cf. Drèze and Sen 2013, and Tharoor 2018 for the ideological backgrounds of anti-egalitarian Hindu nationalism.
19. Ahuja 2019.
20. Piketty 2019; G. Campbell 2012; Green 2019; Greenhouse 2019. In the end, only solutions such as Manning 2020 proposes may offer solace.
21. Piketty 2019, 649–55. He demonstrates that the Middle East is 'the pinnacle of global inequality'.
22. In my estimation, it is possible, purely economically, to maintain for decades a minority of, say, 5 to 10 per cent of under-consuming *Untermenschen*, but not of a quarter or more of the population.

Here, I assume states – the majority – who produce for an important domestic market, like Nazi Germany. States with a dominant export sector can, of course, afford even more apartheid; think of Apartheid South Africa and the Gulf States, but also of the Antebellum South.

23. Piketty 2019, 352–7, 360–1. Do not forget here their individual strategies, such as e.g. migration.
24. Perhaps the redistributive theocracy is not as obsolete as we think, if we consider the neoliberal redistribution that seduces the impoverished white workers and independent producers in some countries to vote for anti-union and racist candidates and political parties.
25. Heijne & Noten 2020, 70.
26. Heijne & Noten 2020, 78.
27. Weil 2014, 2; cf. Guendelsberger 2019; Greenhouse 2019; Jaffe 2021; and the sweating phenomenon (see pp. 329–31).
28. Ford 2017; Baldwin 2019; Garcia-Murillo & MacInnes 2019; cf. Benner 2002 and 2003; Suzman 2020, ch. 15.
29. Quotation in Sloman 2019, 69; Brynjolfsson & McAfee 2014; Livingston 2016.
30. Ford 2017, 167.
31. Cf. Deakin & Wilkinson 2005.
32. I am aware that this goes against the idea of 'anti-work politics' (Weeks 2011).
33. Arendt 1958, 107–8 (perhaps superfluously, the final sentence should not be interpreted as Christian self-sacrifice, but as a direct physical satisfaction resulting from the performance of an accomplishment).
34. Sennett 2008, 8, 287, 289.
35. Quoted by McBee 2019, 157; cf. Clark et al. 2018 for the importance of relationships at work (and at school), of work that is more than a negation of joblessness and of parity through work; also Thomas 2009, esp. chs 3 and 4; Budd 2011, chs 6, 7 and 9.
36. B.A. Rubin 2012; cf. Harari 2014, 437–44. On the excesses in Japan and the recent 'workism' of millennials, see pp. 338–41, 370, 410. Suzman 2017 and 2020 considers this boundless desire to work (ultimately going back to the Neolithic Revolution), together with consumerism, to be the major problem of our era; cf. also Graeber 2019. Jaffe 2021 warns against the risk that the neoliberal system is the sole profiteer of our 'devotion to our jobs' as it 'keeps us exploited, exhausted and alone' as the subtitle of her book screams out loudly.
37. De Waal 2009, 221 (he refers to the financial crisis of 2008).
38. Petriglieri 2020, in which he refers to the ideas of the psychotherapist William F. Cornell.
39. See Manning 2020, 249–56. Trappenburg, Scholten & Jansen 2014, for example, have also observed a slow return of 'decent wages', which, in their opinion, is a form of 'remoralization' in the direction of the so-called Tinbergen Norm. This is traditionally (but without any clear evidence) attributed to the Dutch Nobel laureate for economics in 1967. This standard sets the ideal difference between a minimum and a maximum wage inside organizations or enterprises at 1:5, depending on education, effort, responsibility and drudgery.
40. Piketty 2019, 593–4.
41. Van der Spek, Van Leeuwen & Van Zanden 2015.
42. The current society, incidentally, has more caste characteristics than one might be inclined to think. In particular, the comparatively high pay of certain occupational groups, such as professionals (and senior managers), can be explained by this rather than by long and expensive education, as is usually the case. Just ask yourself why that education should necessarily be so expensive. The reason is hidden in the mechanism itself. See also Piketty 2019, 540–51.
43. I do not see something like this being repeated on a global scale in the near future, but with the most modern means of communication it cannot be entirely ruled out.
44. This can, of course, go very well with the application of other standards elsewhere, see L. Lucassen 2021.
45. Some only think of catastrophes, such as Scheidel 2017; for an implicit critique, see Piketty 2019, 959. For an extremely cynical variant, see Joseph Goebbels' comment on the allied bombing raids in 1944: 'The bomb terror spares the dwellings of neither rich nor poor; before the labor offices of total war, the last class barriers have had to come down.' (Mason 1966, 141).
46. Piketty 2019, 241–6, 645–59, 862–965. In a more general sense, he calls this the 'border question'.
47. Hence the provocative title by Milanovic 2019: *Capitalism, Alone: The Future of the System that Rules the World.*

BIBLIOGRAPHY

LIST OF ABBREVIATIONS USED

CUP   Cambridge University Press
EHR   *Economic History Review*
IRSH   *International Review of Social History*
JESHO   *Journal of the Economic and Social History of the Orient*
OUP   Oxford University Press
TSEG   *Tijdschrift voor Sociale en Economische Geschiedenis* [*The Low Countries Journal of Social and Economic History*]

Abu-Lughod, Janet. *Before European Hegemony: The World System* A.D. *1250–1350* (New York: OUP, 1989).
Adams, Robert McC. 'Shepherds at Umma in the Third Dynasty of Ur: Interlocutors with a World beyond the Scribal Field of Ordered Vision', *JESHO*, 49 (2006), pp. 133–69.
Adovasio, J.M., Olga Soffer & Jake Page. *The Invisible Sex: Uncovering the True Roles of Women in Prehistory* (New York: Smithsonian Books/Harper Collins, 2007).
Ágoston, Gábor. *Guns for the Sultan: Military Power and the Weapons Industry in the Ottoman Empire* (Cambridge: CUP, 2005).
Ahuja, Ravi. 'A Beveridge Plan for India? Social Insurance and the Making of the "Formal Sector"', *IRSH*, 64 (2019), pp. 207–48.
Aiello, Leslie C. 'Notes on the Implications of the Expensive Tissue Hypothesis for Human Biological and Social Evolution', in Wil Roebroeks (ed.), *Guts and Brains: An Integrative Approach to the Hominin Record* (Leiden: Leiden UP, 2007), pp. 17–28.
Aktor, Mikael. 'Social Classes: Varna', in Patrick Olivelle & Donald R. Davis (eds), *Hindu Law: A New History of Dharmashastra* (Oxford: OUP, 2018), pp. 60–77.
Akurang-Parry, Kwabena O. 'Transformations in the Feminization of Unfree Domestic Labor: A Study of Abaawa or Prepubescent Female Servitude in Modern Ghana', *International Labor and Working-Class History*, 78 (Fall 2010), pp. 28–47.
Alam, M. Shahid. 'Some Notes on Work Ethos and Economic Development', *World Development*, 13(2) (1985), pp. 251–4.
Albert, Michel. *Capitalism versus Capitalism* (London: Whurr, 1993).
Aldenderfer, Mark. 'Gimme That Old Time Religion: Rethinking the Role of Religion in the Emergence of Social Inequality', in T. Douglas Price & Gary M. Feinman (eds), *Pathways to Power: New Perspectives on the Emergence of Social Inequality* (New York: Springer, 2012), pp. 77–94.
Allen, Robert C. *The British Industrial Revolution in Global Perspective* (Cambridge: CUP, 2009).
Allen, Robert C., Tommy E. Murphy & Eric B. Schneider. 'The Colonial Origins of the Divergence in the Americas: A Labor Market Approach', *The Journal of Economic History*, 72 (2012), pp. 863–94.
Amabile, Teresa & Steven Kramer. *The Progress Principle: Using Small Wins to Ignite Joy, Engagement and Creativity at Work* (Boston: Harvard Business Review Press, 2011).
Amelang, James S. 'Lifting the Curse: Or Why Early Modern Worker Autobiographers Did Not Write about Work', in Joseph Ehmer & Catharina Lis (eds), *The Idea of Work in Europe from Antiquity to Modern Times* (Farnham: Ashgate, 2009), pp. 91–100.
Ames, Kenneth M. 'On the Evolution of the Human Capacity for Inequality and/or Egalitarianism', in Douglas T. Price & Brian Hayden (eds), *Pathways to Power: New Perspectives on the Emergence of Social Inequality* (New York: Springer, 2010), pp. 15–44.
Amin, Shahid (ed.). *A Concise Encyclopaedia of North Indian Peasant Life: Being a Compilation of the Writings of William Crooke, J.E. Reid, G.A. Grierson* (Delhi: Manohar, 2005).
Anderson, Nels. *Work and Leisure* (New York: The Free Press of Glencoe, 1961).

469

Andreau, Jean & Raymond Descat. *The Slave in Greece and Rome* (Madison, WI.: University of Wisconsin Press, 2011).

Andrews, Anthony P. 'Late Postclassic Lowland Maya Archaeology', *Journal of World Prehistory*, 7(1) (March 1993), pp. 35–69.

Angelo, Larian. 'Old Ways in the New South: The Implications of the Recreation of an Unfree Labor Force', in Tom Brass & Marcel van der Linden (eds), *Free and Unfree Labour: The Debate Continues* (Bern: Peter Lang, 1997), pp. 173–200.

Anthony, David W. *The Horse, the Wheel, and Language. How Bronze-Age Riders from the Eurasian Steppes Shaped the Modern World* (Princeton/Oxford: Princeton UP, 2007).

Antonopoulos, Rania & Indira Hirway (eds). *Unpaid Work and the Economy: Gender, Time Use and Poverty in Developing Countries* (Basingstoke: Palgrave Macmillan, 2010).

Anwar, Najma, Katharine MacDonald, Wil Roebroeks & Alexander Verpoorte. 'The Evolution of the Human Niche: Integrating Models with the Fossil Record', in Wil Roebroeks (ed.), *Guts and Brains: An Integrative Approach to the Hominin Record* (Leiden: Leiden UP, 2007), pp. 235–69.

Appadurai, Arjun. 'Right and Left Hand Castes in South India', *The Indian Economic and Social History Review*, 11(2/3) (1974), pp. 216–59.

Applebaum, Herbert. *The Concept of Work: Ancient, Medieval and Modern* (Albany, NY: SUNY Press, 1992).

Arcand, Bernard. 'The Cuiva', in Richard B. Lee & Richard Daly (eds), *The Cambridge Encyclopedia of Hunters and Gatherers* (Cambridge: CUP, 2004), pp. 97–100.

Arendt, Hannah. *The Human Condition* (Chicago/London: University of Chicago Press, 1958).

Arnoux, Mathieu. *Le temps des laboureurs: Travail, ordre social et croissance en Europe (XIe–XIVe siècle)* (Paris: Albin Michel, 2012).

Asher-Greve, Julia M. 'The Essential Body: Mesopotamian Conceptions of the Gendered Body', *Gender & History*, 9(3) (1997), pp. 432–61.

Ashton, R.H.J. 'The Coinage of Rhodes 408–c.190 BC', in Andrew Meadows & Kirsty Shipton (eds), *Money and its Uses in the Ancient Greek World* (Oxford: OUP, 2001), pp. 90–115.

Atabaki, Touraj. 'From 'Amaleh (Labor) to Kargar (Worker): Recruitment, Work Discipline and Making of the Working Class in the Persian/Iranian Oil Industry', *International Labor and Working Class History*, 84 (Fall 2013), pp. 159–75.

Atkins, Keletso E. *The Moon is Dead! Give us our Money! The Cultural Origins of an African Work Ethic, Natal, South Africa, 1843–1900* (Portsmouth, NH: Heinemann, 1993).

Aubet, Maria Eugenia. *The Phoenicians and the West* (Cambridge: CUP, 2001).

August, Andrew. 'Work and Society', in Daniel J. Walkowitz (ed.), *A Cultural History of Work in the Modern Age* (London: Bloomsbury, 2019), pp. 127–40.

Austin, Gareth. 'Labour Intensity and Manufacturing in West Africa', in Gareth Austin & Kaoru Sugihara (eds), *Labour-Intensive Industrialization in Global History* (London/New York: Routledge, 2013), pp. 201–30.

Baak, Paul E. 'Enslaved Ex-Slaves, Uncaptured Contract Coolies and Unfree Freedmen: "Free" and "Unfree" Labour in the Context of Plantation Development in Southwest India', in Tom Brass & Marcel van der Linden (eds), *Free and Unfree Labour: The Debate Continues* (Bern: Peter Lang, 1997), pp. 427–55.

Baay, Reggie. *Daar werd wat gruwelijks verricht: Slavernij in Indië* (Amsterdam: Atheneum, 2015).

Backhaus, Jürgen H. (ed.) *Karl Bücher: Theory – History – Anthropology – Non-Market Economies* (Marburg: Metropolis, 2000).

Bade, Klaus. *Europa in Bewegung: Migration vom späten 18. Jahrhundert bis zur Gegenwart* (Munich: Beck, 2000).

Bagnall, Roger S. 'Managing Estates in Roman Egypt: A Review Article', *Bulletin of the American Society of Papyrologists*, 30 (1993), pp. 127–35.

Bahl, Vinay. *The Making of the Indian Working Class: The Case of the Tata Iron and Steel Company, 1880–1946* (New Delhi: Sage, 1995).

Bailey, Peter. *Leisure and Class in Victorian England. Rational Recreation and the Contest for Control, 1830–1885* (London/New York: Routledge, 1978).

Bailyn, Bernard. *The Peopling of British North America: An Introduction* (New York: Vintage, 1988).

Baldwin, Richard. *The Globotics Upheaval: Globalization, Robotics, and the Future of Work* (Oxford: OUP, 2019).

Bales, Kevin. *Disposable People: New Slavery in the Global Economy* (Berkeley: University of California Press, 1999).

Bales, Kevin. *Understanding Global Slavery: A Reader* (Berkeley: University of California Press, 2005).

Banaji, Jairus. *Exploring the Economy of Late Antiquity* (Cambridge: CUP, 2016).

Barber, Elizabeth Wayland. *Women's Work: The First 20,000 Years. Women, Cloth, and Society in Early Times* (New York & London: W.W. Norton, 1994).

Barbieri-Low, Anthony J. *Artisans in Early Imperial China* (Seattle & London: University of Washington Press, 2007).

Barker, Geoffrey Russell. *Some Problems of Incentives and Labour Productivity in Soviet Industry: A Contribution to the Study of the Planning of Labour in the U.S.S.R.* (Oxford: Blackwell, 1955).

Barker, Graeme. *The Agricultural Revolution in Prehistory: Why did Foragers become Farmers?* (Cambridge: CUP, 2006).

Barker, Hannah. *That Most Precious Merchandise: The Mediterranean Trade in Black Slaves, 1260–1500* (Philadelphia: PENN, 2019).

Barnard, Alan. 'Images of Hunters and Gatherers in European Social Thought', in Richard B. Lee & Richard Daly (eds), *The Cambridge Encyclopedia of Hunters and Gatherers* (Cambridge: CUP, 2004), pp. 375–83.

Barragán Romano, Rossana. 'Dynamics of Continuity and Change: Shifts in Labour Relations in the Potosí Mines (1680–1812)', *IRSH*, 61 (2016), pp. 93–114.

Barragán Romano, Rossana. 'Extractive Economy and Institutions? Technology, Labour and Land in Potosí, the Sixteenth to the Eighteenth Century', in Karin Hofmeester & Pim de Zwart (eds), *Colonialism, Institutional Change, and Shifts in Global Labour Relations* (Amsterdam: AUP, 2018), pp. 207–37.

Barret, P. & J.-N. Gurgand. *Ils voyageaient la France: Vie et traditions des Compagnons du Tour de France au XIXe siècle* (Paris: Hachette, 1980).

Barringer, Tim. *Men at Work: Art and Labour in Victorian Britain* (New Haven/London: Yale UP, 2005).

Bar-Yosef, Ofer & Youping Wang. 'Palaeolithic Archaeology in China', *Annual Review of Anthropology*, 41 (2012), pp. 319–35.

Bavel, Bas van. *The Invisible Hand? How Market Economies Have Emerged and Declined since AD 500* (Oxford: OUP, 2016).

Beaujard, Philippe. *The Worlds of the Indian Ocean: A Global History, vol. I* (Cambridge: CUP, 2019).

Beck, Patrice, Philippe Bernardi & Lauren Feller (eds). *Rémunérer le travail au Moyen Âge: Pour une histoire sociale du salariat* (Paris: Picard, 2014).

Beckert, Sven. *Empire of Cotton: A Global History* (New York: Knopf, 2015).

Beckert, Sven & Dominic Sachsenmaier (eds). *Global History, Globally: Research and Practice around the World* (London: Bloomsbury, 2018).

Belfanti, Carlo Marco. 'The Proto-Industrial Heritage: Forms of Rural Proto-Industry in Northern Italy in the Eighteenth and Nineteenth Centuries', in Sheilagh C. Ogilvie & Markus Cerman (eds), *European Proto-Industrialization* (Cambridge: CUP, 1996), pp. 155–70.

Bellenoit, Hayden J. *The Formation of the Colonial State in India: Scribes, Paper and Taxes, 1760–1860* (London & New York: Routledge, 2017).

Bellwood, Peter. *First Migrants: Ancient Migration in Global Perspective* (Chichester: Wiley Blackwell, 2013).

Benner, Chris. *Work in the New Economy: Flexible Labor Markets in Sillicon Valley* (Malden, MA: Blackwell, 2002).

Benner, Chris. '"Computers in the Wild": Guilds and Next-Generation Unionism in the Information Revolution', *IRSH*, 48 (2003), Supplement, pp. 181–204.

Bentley, Alex. 'Mobility, Specialisation and Community Diversity in the Linearbandkeramik: Isotopic Evidence from the Skeletons', in Alisdair Whittle and Vicki Cummings (eds), *Going Over: The Mesolithic-Neolithic Transition in North-West Europe* (Oxford: OUP, 2007), pp. 117–40.

Benvenuti, Francesco. *Stakhanovism and Stalinism, 1934–8* (Birmingham: Centre for Russian and East European Studies, 1989).

Berdan, F.F. *Aztec Archaeology and Ethnohistory* (Cambridge: CUP, 2014).

Berg, Maxine. *The Age of Manufactures: Industry, Innovation and Work in Britain*, 2nd edn (Abingdon, Oxon: Routledge, 2005).

Berthe, Jean-Pierre. 'Les formes de travail dépendant en Nouvelle-Espagne XVIe–XVIIIe siècles', in Annalisa Guarducci (ed.), *Forme ed evoluzione del lavoro in Europa: XIII-XVIII secc.* (Prato: Instituto F. Datini, 1991), pp. 93–111.

Bhandare, Shailendra. 'Numismatics and History: The Maurya-Gupta Interlude in the Gangetic Plain', in Patrick Olivelle (ed.), *Between the Empires: Society in India 300 BCE to 400 CE* (Oxford: OUP, 2006), pp. 67–112.

Bhattacharya, Ananda (ed.). *Adivasi Resistance in Early Colonial India: Comprising the Chuar Rebellion of 1799 by J.C. Price and Relevant Midnapore District Collectorate Records from the Eighteenth Century* (New Delhi: Manohar, 2017).

Bhattacharya, Sabyasachi & Jan Lucassen (eds.). *Workers in the Informal Sector: Studies in Labour History 1800–2000* (New Delhi: Macmillan, 2005).

Bhattacharya, Sukumar. *The East India Company and the Economy of Bengal from 1704 to 1740* (Calcutta: Mukhopadhyay, 1969).

Bichler, Barbara. *Die Formierung der Angestelltenbewegung im Kaiserreich und die Entstehung des Angestelltenversicherungsgesetzes von 1911* (Bern: Peter Lang, 1997).

Bieleman, Jan. *Geschiedenis van de landbouw in Nederland 1500–1950* (Amsterdam: Boom Meppel, 1992).

Biernacki, Richard. *The Fabrication of Labor. Germany and Britain, 1640–1914* (Berkeley: University of California Press, 1995).

Binford, Lewis R. 'The Diet of Early Hominins: Some Things We Need to Know before "Reading" the Menu from the Archeological Record', in Wil Roebroeks (ed.), *Guts and Brains: An Integrative Approach to the Hominin Record* (Leiden: Leiden UP, 2007), pp. 185–222.

Birge, Bettine. 'Women and Confucianism from Song to Ming: The Institutionalization of Patrilineality', in Paul J. Smith & Richard von Glahn (eds), *The Song-Yuan-Ming Transition in Chinese History* (Cambridge, MA: Harvard UP, 2003), pp. 212–40.

Bittles, Alan H. 'Population Stratification and Genetic Association Studies in South Asia', *Journal of Molecular and Genetic Medicine*, 1(2) (December 2005), pp. 43–8.

Blackburn, Robin. *The Overthrow of Colonial Slavery 1776–1848* (London/New York: Verso, 1988).

Blackburn, Robin. 'Revolution and Emancipation: The Role of Abolitionism in Ending Slavery in the Americas', in Marcel van der Linden (ed.), *Humanitarian Intervention and Changing Labor Relations: The Long-Term Consequences of the Abolition of the Slave Trade* (Leiden/Boston: Brill, 2011), 155–92.

Bleiberg, Edward. 'State and Private Enterprise', in Toby Wilkinson (ed.), *The Egyptian World* (London/New York: Routledge, 2007), pp. 175–84.

Blewitt, Mary H. 'USA: Shifting Landscapes of Class, Culture, Gender, Race and Protest in the American Northeast and South', in Lex Heerma van Voss, Els Hiemstra-Kuperus & Elise van Nederveen Meerkerk (eds.), *The Ashgate Companion to the History of Textile Workers, 1650–2000* (Farnham: Ashgate, 2010), pp. 531–57.

Bloch, Marc. *Esquisse d'une Histoire Monétaire de l'Europe* (Paris: Armand Colin, 1954).

Bloch, Marc. *Land and Work in Mediaeval Europe: Selected Papers*. Trans. by J.E. Anderson (Berkeley/Los Angeles: University of California Press, 1967).

Blockmans, W.P. 'The Social and Economic Effects of the Plague in the Low Countries: 1349–1500', *Revue Belge de Philologie et d'Histoire*, 58(4) (1980), pp. 833–66.

Blum, Jerome. *The End of the Old Order in Rural Europe* (Princeton: Princeton UP, 1978).

Blumenthal, Debra. *Enemies and Familiars: Slavery and Mastery in Fifteenth-Century Valencia* (Ithaca/London: Cornell UP, 2009).

Boch, Rudolf. 'Zunfttradition und frühe Gewerkschaftsbewegung: Ein Beitrag zu einer beginnenden Diskussion mit besonderer Berücksichtigung des Handwerks im Verlagssystem', in Ulrich Wengenroth (ed.), *Prekäre Selbständigkeit: Zur Standortbestimmung von Handwerk, Hausindustrie und Kleingewerbe im Industrialisierungsprozess* (Stuttgart: Steiner, 1989), pp. 37–69.

Boeck, Brian J. 'Claiming Siberia: Colonial Possession and Property Holding in the Seventeenth and Early Eighteenth Centuries', in Nicholas B. Breyfogle, Abby Schrader & Willard Sunderland (eds), *Peopling the Russian Periphery: Borderland Colonization in Eurasian History* (London/New York: Routledge, 2007), pp. 41–60.

Boivin, Nicole. 'Orientalism, Ideology and Identity: Examining Caste in South-Asian Archaeology', *Journal of Social Archaeology*, 5(2) (2005), pp. 225–52.

Bok, Marten Jan. 'Vraag en aanbod op de Nederlandse kunstmarkt, 1580–1700', PhD thesis, Utrecht University, 1994.

Boldorf, Marcel & Fetsuji Okazaki (eds). *Economies under Occupation: The Hegemony of Nazi Germany and Imperial Japan in World War II* (London/New York: Taylor & Francis, 2015).

Booth, Charles, assisted by Ernest Aves. *Life and Labour of the People in London, Second Series: Industry, vol. 5: Comparisons, Survey and Conclusions* (London: Macmillan, 1904).

Bopearachchi, Osmund. *From Bactria to Taprobane: Selected Works*, 2 vols (New Delhi: Manohar, 2015).

Borgerhoff Mulder, Monique et al. 'Intergenerational Wealth Transmission and the Dynamics of Inequality in Small-Scale Societies', *Science*, 326(5953) (30 October 2009), pp. 682–8.

Bosma, Ulbe. *The Making of a Periphery: How Island Southeast Asia Became a Mass Exporter of Labor* (New York: Columbia UP, 2019).

Bosma, Ulbe & Karin Hofmeester (eds). *The Life Work of a Historian: Essays in Honor of Marcel van der Linden* (Leiden/Boston: Brill, 2018).

Boter, Corinne. 'Marriages are Made in Kitchens: The European Marriage Pattern and Life-Cycle Servanthood in Eighteenth-Century Amsterdam', *Feminist Economics*, 23 (2016), pp. 68–92.

Boter, Corinne. 'Dutch Divergence? Women's Work, Structural Change, and Household Living Standards in the Netherlands, 1830–1914', PhD thesis, Wageningen University, 2017.

Bourillon, Florence. 'Urban Renovation and Changes in Artisans' Activities: The Parisian Fabrique in the Arts et Métiers Quarter during the Second Empire', in Geoffrey Crossick (ed.), *The Artisan and the European Town, 1500–1900* (Aldershot: Scolar Press, 1997), pp. 218–38.

Bourke, Joanna. 'Avoiding Poverty: Strategies for Women in Rural Ireland, 1880–1914', in J. Henderson & R. Wall (eds), *Poor Women and Children in the European Past* (London/New York, 1994), pp. 292–311.

Boussac, M.-F., J.-F. Salles & J.-B. Yon (eds). *Re-Evaluating the Periplus of the Erythraean Sea* (New Delhi: Manohar, 2018).

Bouwens, A.M.C.M. et al. *Door staal gedreven: Van Hoogovens tot Tata Steel, 1918–2018* (Bussum: TOTH, 2018).

Boxer, Charles R. *The Portuguese Seaborne Empire, 1415–1825* (London: Penguin, 1969).

Bradley, Richard. 'Houses, Bodies and Tombs', in Alisdair Whittle & Vicki Cummings (eds), *Going Over: The Mesolithic-Neolithic Transition in North-West Europe* (Oxford: OUP, 2007), pp. 347–55.

Brady Jr., Thomas A. 'The Rise of Merchant Empires, 1400–1700: A European Counterpoint', in James D. Tracy (ed.), *The Political Economy of Merchant Empires* (Cambridge: CUP, 1991), pp. 117–60.

Brandon, Pepijn, Niklas Frykman & Pernille Røge (eds). *Free and Unfree Labor in Atlantic and Indian Ocean Port Cities (1700–1850)*, IRSH, 64, Special Issue 27 (2019).

Bras, Hilde. 'Inequalities in Food Security and Nutrition: A Life Course Perspective', Inaugural lecture, Wageningen University, 4 December 2014.

Brass, Tom & Marcel van der Linden (eds). *Free and Unfree Labour: The Debate Continues* (Bern: Peter Lang, 1997).

Breman, Jan. *Taming the Coolie Beast: Plantation Society and the Colonial Order in Southeast Asia* (New York: OUP, 1989).

Breman, Jan. *Footloose Labour: Working in India's Informal Economy* (Cambridge: CUP, 1996).

Breuker, Remco E. & Imke B.L.H. van Gardingen (eds). *People for Profit: North Korean Forced Labour on a Global Scale* (Leiden: Leiden Asia Centre, 2018).

Brewer, Douglas. 'Agriculture and Animal Husbandry', in Toby Wilkinson (ed.), *The Egyptian World* (London/New York: Routledge, 2007), pp. 131–45.

Brinton, Mary C. *Women's Working Lives in East Asia* (Stanford: Stanford UP, 2001).

Broadberry, Stephen, Rainer Fremdling & Peter Solar. 'Industry', in Stephen Broadberry & Kevin H. O'Rourke (eds), *The Cambridge Economic History of Modern Europe, Vol. I: 1700–1870* (Cambridge: CUP, 2010), pp. 164–86.

Broughton, Edward. 'The Bhopal Disaster and its Aftermath: A Review', *Environmental Health*, 4(1) (2005), pp. 1–6.

Brown, Kyle et al. 'An Early and Enduring Advanced Technology Originating 71,000 Years Ago in South Africa', *Nature*, 491 (22 November 2012), pp. 590–3.

Brown, William & Jonathan Trevor. 'Payment Systems and the Fall and Rise of Individualism', *Historical Studies in Industrial Relations*, 35 (2014), pp. 143–55.

Brynjolfsson, Erik & Andrew McAfee. *The Second Machine Age: Work, Progress and Prosperity in a Time of Brilliant Technologies* (New York: Norton, 2014).

Buchanan, Francis. *An Account of the District of Purnea in 1809–10* (New Delhi: Usha, 1986a).

Buchanan, Francis. *An Account of the District of Shahabad in 1812–13* (New Delhi: Usha, 1986b).

Bücher, Karl. *Arbeit und Rhythmus* (5th edn) (Leipzig: Reinecke, 1919).

Budd, John W. *The Thought of Work* (Ithaca/London: Cornell UP, 2011).

Burds, Geoffrey. 'The Social Control of Peasant Labor in Russia: The Response of Village Communities to Labor Migration in the Central Industrial Region, 1861–1905', in Esther Kingston-Mann & Timothy Mixter (eds), *Peasant Economy, Culture, and Politics of European Russia, 1800–1921* (Princeton: Princeton UP, 1991), pp. 52–100.

Burger, Werner. 'Minting During the Qianlong Period: Comparing the Actual Coins with the Mint Reports', in Christine Moll-Murata, Song Jianze & Hans Ulrich Vogel (eds), *Chinese Handicraft Regulations of the Qing Dynasty: Theory and Application* (Munich: Iudicium, 2005), pp. 373–94.

Buringh, Eltjo. *Medieval Manuscript Production in the Latin West: Explorations with a Global Database* (Leiden/Boston: Brill, 2011).

Burke, Edward M. 'The Economy of Athens in the Classical Era: Some Adjustments to the Primitivist Model', *Transactions of the American Philological Association*, 122 (1992), pp. 199–226.

Burnett, John. *Idle Hands: The Experience of Unemployment, 1790–1990* (London/New York: Routledge, 1994).

Caland, W. *De Remonstrantie van W. Geleynssen de Jongh* ('s-Gravenhage: Martinus Nijhoff, 1929).

Caminos, Ricardo A. 'Peasants', in Sergio Donadoni (ed.), *The Egyptians* (Chicago/London: University of Chicago Press, 1997), pp. 1–30.

Campbell, Gwyn. 'Slavery in the Indian Ocean World', in Gad Heuman & Trevor Burnard (eds), *The Routledge History of Slavery* (London/New York: Routledge, 2011), pp. 52–63.

Campbell, Gwyn (ed.). *Abolition and its Aftermath in Indian Ocean Africa and Asia* (Abingdon: Routledge, 2012).

Campbell, Gwyn & Alessandro Stanziani (eds). *Bonded Labour and Debt in the Indian Ocean World* (Abingdon: Routledge, 2015).

Campbell, W.P. *Brick: A World History* (London: Thames & Hudson, 2003).

Candido, Mariana P. *An African Slaving Port and the Atlantic World: Benguela and its Hinterland* (Cambridge: CUP, 2013).

Candland, Christopher. 'The Cost of Incorporation: Labor Institutions, Industrial Restructuring, and New Trade Union Strategies in India and Pakistan', in Christopher Candland & Rudra Sil (eds), *The Politics of Labor in a Global Age: Continuity and Change in Late-Industrializing and Post-Socialist Economies* (Oxford: OUP, 2001), pp. 69–94.

Candland, Christopher & Rudra Sil (eds). *The Politics of Labor in a Global Age: Continuity and Change in Late-Industrializing and Post-Socialist Economies* (Oxford: OUP, 2001).

Canuto, Marcello A. et al. 'Ancient Lowland Maya Complexity as Revealed by Airborne Laser Scanning of Northern Guatemala', *Science*, 361 (28 September 2018), pp. 1355–71.

Carlson, Marybeth. 'A Trojan Horse of Worldliness? Maidservants in the Burgher Household in Rotterdam at the End of the Seventeenth Century', in Els Kloek, Nicole Teeuwen & Marijke Huisman (eds), *Women of the Golden Age: An International Debate on Women in Seventeenth-Century Holland, England and Italy* (Hilversum: Verloren, 1994), pp. 87–96.

Casanovas, Joan. 'Slavery, the Labour Movement and Spanish Colonialism in Cuba (1850–1898)', in Tom Brass & Marcel van der Linden (eds), *Free and Unfree Labour: The Debate Continues* (Bern: Peter Lang, 1997), pp. 249–64.

Cashmere, John. 'Sisters Together: Women without Men in Seventeenth-Century French Village Culture', *Journal of Family History*, 21(1) (January 1996), pp. 44–62.

Castel, Robert. *Les métamorphoses de la question sociale: Une chronique du salariat* (Paris: Fayard, 1995).

Chakravarti, Uma. *Everyday Lives, Everyday Histories: Beyond the Kings and Brahmanas of 'Ancient' India* (New Delhi: Tulika, 2006).

Chalcraft, John T. 'Pluralizing Capital, Challenging Eurocentrism: Towards Post-Marxist Historiography', *Radical History Review*, 91 (2005), pp. 13–39.

Chandra, Satish. 'Some Aspects of Urbanisation in Medieval India', in Indu Banga (ed.), *The City in Indian History: Urban Demography, Society and Politics* (New Delhi: Manohar, 2014), pp. 81–6.

Chang, Kai & Fang Lee Cooke. 'Legislating the Right to Strike in China: Historical Development and Prospects', *Journal of Industrial Relations*, 57(3) (2015), pp. 440–55.

Chang, Kwang-Chih. 'China on the Eve of the Historical Period', in Michael Loewe & Edward L. Shaughnessy (eds), *Cambridge History of Ancient China* (Cambridge: CUP, 1999), pp. 37–73.

Chang, Leslie T. *Factory Girls: From Village to City in a Changing China* (New York: Spiegel & Grau, 2009).

Chatterjee, Indrani. *Gender, Slavery and Law in Colonial India* (Delhi: OUP, 1999).

Chatterjee, Indrani & Richard Maxwell Eaton (eds). *Slavery and South Asian History* (Bloomington/ Indianapolis: Indiana UP, 2006).

Chaubey, Gyaneshwer et al. 'Peopling of South Asia: Investigating the Caste-Tribe Continuum in India', *BioEssays*, 29(1) (2006), pp. 91–100.

Chayanov, A.V. *On the Theory of Peasant Economy*, edited by Daniel Thorner, Basile Kerblay & R.E.F. Smith (Homewood: The American Economic Association, 1966).

Chen, Feng. 'Trade Unions and the Quadripartite Interactions in Strike Settlement in China', *The China Quarterly*, 201 (March 2010), pp. 104–24.

Cheng, Tiejun & Mark Selden. 'The Origins and Social Consequences of China's Hukou System', *The China Quarterly*, 139 (1994), pp. 644–68.

Chow, Nelson & Yuebin Xu. *Socialist Welfare in a Market Economy: Social Security Reforms in Guangzhou, China* (Aldershot: Ashgate, 2001).

Christensen, Lars K. 'Institutions in Textile Production: Guilds and Trade Unions', in Lex Heerma van Voss, Els Hiemstra-Kuperus & Elise van Nederveen Meerkerk (eds), *The Ashgate Companion to the History of Textile Workers, 1650–2000* (Farnham: Ashgate, 2010), pp. 749–71.

Clarence-Smith, William (ed.). *The Economics of the Indian Ocean Slave Trade in the Nineteenth Century* (London/New York: Routledge, 2015).

Clark, Andrew E. et al. *The Origins of Happiness: The Science of Well-Being Over the Life Course* (Princeton: Princeton UP, 2018).

Clottes, Jean. 'Paleolithic Cave Art in France', www.bradshawfoundation.com/clottes (visited 15 February 2020; extracted from *Adorant Magazine*, 2002).

Cockshott, Paul. *How the World Works: The Story of Human Labor from Prehistory to the Modern Day* (New York: Monthly Review Press, 2019).

Coe, Michael D. *Angkor and the Khmer Civilization* (London: Thames & Hudson, 2003).

Cohen, Edward E. *Athenian Economy and Society: A Banking Perspective* (Princeton: Princeton UP, 1992).

Cohen, Edward E. 'An Unprofitable Masculinity', in Paul Cartledge, Edward E. Cohen & Lin Foxhall (eds), *Money, Labour and Land: Approaches to the Economies of Ancient Greece* (London/New York: Routledge, 2002), pp. 100–12.

Cohn, Samuel. 'After the Black Death: Labour Legislation and Attitudes Towards Labour in Late-Medieval Western Europe', *EHR*, 60 (2007), pp. 457–85.

Coldham, Peter Wilson. *Emigrants in Chains: A Social History of Forced Emigration to the Americas 1607–1776* (Baltimore: Genealogical Publication Company, 1992).

474

Cole, Jeffrey A. *The Potosí Mita 1573–1700: Compulsory Indian Labor in the Andes* (Stanford: Stanford UP, 1985).

Colebrooke, Henry Thomas. *Remarks on the Husbandry and Internal Commerce of Bengal* (Calcutta: Statesman, 1884; originally 1804).

Conze, Werner. 'Arbeit', in Otto Brunner et al. (eds), *Geschichtliche Grundbegriffe: Historisches Lexikon zur politisch-sozialen Sprache in Deutschland, vol. 1* (Stuttgart: Klett-Cotta, 1972), pp. 154–215.

Cook, Linda J. *The Soviet Social Contract and Why It Failed: Welfare Policy and Workers' Politics from Brezhnev to Yeltsin* (Cambridge, MA/London: Harvard UP, 1993).

Cooney, Gabriel. 'Parallel Worlds or Multi-Stranded Identities? Considering the Process of "Going Over" in Ireland and the Irish Sea Zone', in Alisdair Whittle & Vicki Cummings (eds), *Going Over: The Mesolithic-Neolithic Transition in North-West Europe* (Oxford: OUP, 2007), pp. 544–66.

Cooney, Kathlyn M. 'Labour', in Toby Wilkinson (ed.), *The Egyptian World* (London/New York: Routledge, 2007), pp. 160–74.

Costello, Nancy et al. *Whispering Hope: The True Story of the Magdalene Women* (London: Orion, 2015).

Costin, Cathy Lynn. 'Craft Production Systems', in Gary M. Feinman & T. Douglas Price (eds), *Archaeology at the Millennium: A Sourcebook* (New York: Springer, 2001), pp. 273–326.

Cottereau, Alain. 'Industrial Tribunals and the Establishment of a Kind of Common Law of Labour in Nineteenth-Century France', in Willibald Steinmetz (ed.), *Private Law and Social Inequality in the Industrial Age: Comparing Legal Cultures in Britain, France, Germany and the United States* (Oxford: OUP, 2000), pp. 203–26.

Coxworth, James E. et al. 'Grandmothering Life Stories and Human Pair Bonding', *PNAS*, 112(38) (22 September 2015), pp. 11806–11811.

Cross, Gary S. *Worktime and Industrialization: An International History* (Philadelphia: Temple, 1988).

Cross, Gary S. *A Quest for Time: The Reduction of Work in Britain and France, 1840–1940* (Berkeley: University of California Press, 1989).

Cross, Gary S. 'Work Time', in Peter N. Stearns (ed.), *Encyclopedia of European Social History from 1300 to 2000, Vol. 4* (New York: Scribners, 2001), pp. 501–11.

Crossick, Geoffrey (ed.) *The Artisan and the European Town, 1500–1900* (Aldershot: Scolar Press, 1997a).

Crossick, Geoffrey. 'Past Masters: in Search of the Artisan in European History', in Geoffrey Crossick (ed.), *The Artisan and the European Town, 1500–1900* (Aldershot: Scolar Press, 1997b), pp. 1–40.

Culbertson, Laura (ed.). *Slaves and Households in the Near East* (Chicago: Oriental Institute, 2011a).

Culbertson, Laura. 'Slaves and Households in the Near East', in Laura Culbertson (ed.), *Slaves and Households in the Near East* (Chicago: Oriental Institute, 2011b), pp. 1–17.

Cunningham, Hugh. *Children and Childhood in Western Society since 1500* (London/New York: Longman, 1995).

Cunningham, Hugh. 'The Decline of Child Labour: Labour Markets and Family Economies in Europe and North America since 1830', *EHR*, 53 (2000), pp. 409–28.

Cunningham, Hugh & Pier Paolo Viazzo (eds). *Child Labour in Historical Perspective 1800–1985: Case Studies from Europe, Japan and Colombia* (Florence: UNICEF, 1996).

Dalton, George (ed.). *Primitive, Archaic and Modern Economies: Essays of Karl Polanyi* (Boston: Beacon Press, 1971).

D'Altroy, Terence N. *The Incas* (Malden, MA: Blackwell, 2002).

D'Altroy, Terence N. 'The Inka Empire', in Andrew Monson & Walter Scheidel (eds), *Fiscal Regimes and the Political Economies of Premodern States* (Cambridge: CUP, 2015), pp. 31–70.

Dandamaev, Muhammad A. *Slavery in Babylonia: From Nabopolassar to Alexander the Great (626–331 BC)* (DeKalb: Northern Illinois UP, 2009).

Daniel, Ute. *Arbeiterfrauen in der Kriegsgesellschaft: Beruf, Familie und Politik im Ersten Weltkrieg* (Göttingen: Vandenhoeck & Ruprecht, 1989).

Das Gupta, Monica. 'Lifeboat Versus Corporate Ethic: Social and Demographic Implications of Stem and Joint Families', in Antoinette Fauve-Chamoux & Emiko Ochiai (eds), *House and the Stem Family in Eurasian Perspective* (Proceedings of the C18 Session, Twelfth International Economic History Congress, August 1998), pp. 444–66.

Datta, Rajat. *Society, Economy and Market: Commercialization in Rural Bengal, c. 1760–1800* (New Delhi: Manohar, 2000).

Datta, Satya Brata. *Capital Accumulation and Workers' Struggle in Indian Industrialization: The Case of Tata Iron and Steel Company 1910–1970* (Stockholm: Almqvist & Wiksell, 1986).

Davids, C.A. *Wat lijdt den zeeman al verdriet: Het Nederlandse zeemanslied in de zeiltijd (1600–1900)* (Den Haag: Martinus Nijhoff, 1980).

Davids, Karel. 'Seamen's Organizations and Social Protest in Europe, c. 1300–1825', *IRSH*, 39, Supplement 2 (1994), pp. 145–69.

Davids, Karel. *Religion, Technology, and the Great and Little Divergences: China and Europe Compared c. 700–1800* (Leiden/Boston: Brill, 2013a).

Davids, Karel. 'Moving Machine-Makers: Circulation of Knowledge on Machine-Building in China and Europe Between c. 1400 and the Early Nineteenth Century', in Maarten Prak & Jan Luiten van Zanden (eds), *Technology, Skills and the Pre-Modern Economy in the East and the West. Essays Dedicated to the Memory of S.R. Epstein* (Leiden/Boston: Brill, 2013b), pp. 205–24.

Davids, Karel & Jan Lucassen (eds). *A Miracle Mirrored: The Dutch Republic in European Perspective* (Cambridge: CUP, 1995).

Davies, Margaret Llewelyn (ed.). *Life As We Have Known It by Co-Operative Working Women. With An Introductory Letter by Virginia Woolf. New Introduction by Anna Davin* (London: Virago, 1977).

Deakin, Simon & Frank Wilkinson. *The Law of the Labour Market: Industrialization, Employment and Legal Evolution* (Oxford: OUP, 2005).

Deane, Phyllis. *The First Industrial Revolution* (Cambridge: CUP, 1969).

Dekker, Rudolf. 'Labour Conflicts and Working Class Culture in Early Modern Holland', *IRSH*, 35 (1990), pp. 377–420.

Delêtre, Marc, Doyle B. McKey & Trevor R. Hodkinson. 'Marriage Exchanges, Seed Exchanges, and the Dynamics of Manioc Diversity', *PNAS*, 108(45) (8 November 2011), pp. 18249–54.

Delsalle, Paul. 'Du billet de congé au carnet d'apprentissage: Les archives des livrets d'employés et d'ouvriers (XVIe–XIX siècles)', *Revue du Nord*, 75 (1993), pp. 285–301.

Demarest, Arthur. *Ancient Maya. The Rise and Fall of a Rainforest Civilization* (Cambridge: CUP, 2004).

De Matos, Paulo Teodoro & Jan Lucassen. 'Early Portuguese Data for Wage Developments in India: Kannur (Cananor) 1516–1517', *Ler História*, 75 (2019), pp. 113–31.

Denault, Leigh. 'Partition and the Politics of the Joint Family in Nineteenth-Century North India', *The Indian Economic and Social History Review*, 46(1) (2009), pp. 27–55.

Deng, Kent Gang. 'Why Shipping "Declined" in China from the Middle Ages to the Nineteenth Centuries', in Richard W. Unger (ed.), *Shipping and Economic Growth 1350–1850* (Leiden/Boston: Brill, 2011), pp. 207–21.

Deng, Kent Gang. 'Imperial China under the Song and late Qing', in Andrew Monson & Walter Scheidel (eds), *Fiscal Regimes and the Political Economy of Premodern States* (Cambridge: CUP, 2015), pp. 308–42.

Dennison, Tracy K. *The Institutional Framework of Russian Serfdom* (Cambridge: CUP, 2011).

Dennison, Tracy K. & Sheilagh Ogilvie. 'Serfdom and Social Capital in Bohemia and Russia', *EHR*, 60 (2007), pp. 513–44.

De Vito, Christian G. 'New Perspectives on Global Labour History: Introduction', *Global Labour History* 1(3) (2013), pp. 7–31.

De Vito, Christian G., Juliane Schiel & Matthias van Rossum. 'From Bondage to Precariousness? New Perspectives on Labor and Social History', *Journal of Social History*, 54(2) (2020), pp. 1–19.

Dewar, Robert E. & Alison R. Richard. 'Madagascar: A History of Arrivals, What Happened, and Will Happen Next', *Annual Review of Anthropology*, 41 (2012), pp. 495–517.

Dewulf, Jeroen. *Grijs slavernijverleden? Over zwarte milities en redimoesoegedrag* (Amsterdam: AUP, 2018).

Deyell, John. *Living Without Silver: The Monetary History of Early Medieval North India* (Delhi: OUP, 1990).

Deyell, John. *Treasure, Trade and Tradition: Post-Kidarite Coins of the Gangetic Plains and Punjab Foothills, 590–820 CE* (Delhi: Manohar, 2017).

Diamond, Jared. *The Third Chimpanzee: The Evolution and Future of the Human Animal* (London: Harper Collins, 1992).

Diamond, Jared. *Guns, Germs and Steel: A Short History of Everybody for the Last 13,000 Years* (London: Vintage, 1998).

Dieball, Stefan & Hans-Joachim Rosner. 'Geographic Dimensions of Mining and Transport: Case Studies in Mountainous Yunnan', in Nanny Kim & Keiko Nagase-Reimer (eds), *Mining, Monies, and Culture in Early Modern Societies: East Asian and Global Perspectives* (Leiden/Boston: Brill, 2013), pp. 351–61.

Dikötter, Frank. *Mao's Great Famine: The History of China's Most Devastating Catastrophe, 1958–1962* (London: Bloomsbury, 2010).

Dillon, Nara. *Radical Inequalities: China's Revolutionary Welfare State in Comparative Perspective* (Cambridge, MA: Harvard University Asia Center, 2015).

Dobson, C.R. *Masters and Journeymen: A Prehistory of Industrial Relations 1717–1800* (London: Croom Helm, 1980).

Dommelen, Peter van. 'Colonialism and Migration in the Ancient Mediterranean', *Annual Review of Anthropology*, 41 (2012), pp. 393–409.

Donadoni, Sergio (ed.). *The Egyptians* (Chicago/London: University of Chicago Press, 1997).

Drennan, Robert D., Christian E. Peterson & Jake R. Fox. 'Degrees and Kinds of Inequality', in Douglas T. Price & Brian Hayden (eds), *Pathways to Power: New Perspectives on the Emergence of Social Inequality* (New York: Springer, 2010), pp. 45–76.

476

Drèze, Jean & Amartya Sen. *An Uncertain Glory: India and its Contradictions* (Princeton: Princeton UP, 2013).

Dumolyn, Jan. '"I thought of It at Work, in Ostend": Urban Artisan Labour and Guild Ideology in the Later Medieval Low Countries', *IRSH*, 62 (2017), pp. 389–419.

Dunbar, Robin I.M. 'Why Hominins Had Big Brains', in Wil Roebroeks (ed.), *Guts and Brains: An Integrative Approach to the Hominin Record* (Leiden: Leiden UP, 2007), pp. 91–105.

Dyke, Paul van. *The Canton Trade: Life and Enterprise on the China Coast, 1700–1845* (Hong Kong: Hong Kong UP, 2005).

Dyke, Paul van. 'Operational Efficiencies and the Decline of the Chinese Junk Trade in the Eighteenth and Nineteenth Centuries: The Connection', in Richard W. Unger (ed.), *Shipping and Economic Growth 1350–1850* (Leiden/Boston: Brill, 2011), pp. 224–46.

Earle, Timothy, Clive Gamble & Hendrik Poinar. 'Migration', in Andrew Shyrock & Daniel Lord Smail (eds), *Deep History: The Architecture of Past and Present* (Berkeley: University of California Press, 2011), pp. 191–218.

Earle, Timothy & Michael E. Smith. 'Household Economies Under the Aztec and Inka Empires: A Comparison', in Michael E. Smith (ed.), *The Comparative Archaeology of Complex Societies* (Cambridge: CUP, 2012), pp. 238–84.

Eaton, Richard Maxwell. 'The Rise and Fall of Military Slavery in the Deccan, 1450–1650', in Indrani Chatterjee & Richard Maxwell Eaton (eds), *Slavery and South Asian History* (Bloomington/Indianapolis: Indiana UP, 2006), pp. 115–35.

Eaton, S. Boyd & Stanley B. Eaton III. 'Hunter-Gatherers and Human Health', in Richard B. Lee & Richard Daly (eds), *The Cambridge Encyclopedia of Hunters and Gatherers* (Cambridge: CUP, 2004), pp. 449–56.

Ebeling, Dietrich & Wolfgang Mager (eds). *Protoindustrie in der Region, Europäische Gewerbelandschaften vom 16. bis zum 19. Jahrhundert* (Bielefeld: Verlag für Regionalgeschichte, 1997).

Eckert, Andreas. 'Abolitionist Rhetorics, Colonial Conquest, and the Slow Death of Slavery in Germany's African Empire', in Marcel van der Linden (ed.), *Humanitarian Interventions and Changing Labor Relations: The Long-Term Consequences of the Abolition of the Slave Trade* (Leiden & Boston: Brill, 2011), pp. 351–68.

Eckert, Andreas & Marcel van der Linden. 'New Perspectives on Workers and the History of Work: Global Labor History', in Sven Beckert & Dominic Sachsenmaier (eds), *Global History, Globally: Research and Practice around the World* (London: Bloomsbury, 2018), pp. 145–61.

The Economist. 'Women in India Have Dropped Out of the Workforce. How Can They be Persuaded to Return to it?', *The Economist*, 428(9099) (7–14 July 2018), pp. 14–18.

Eggebrecht, Arne et al. *Geschichte der Arbeit: Vom Alten Ägypten bis zur Gegenwart* (Köln: Kiepenheuer & Witsch, 1980).

Ehlert, Martin. *The Impact of Losing Your Job: Unemployment and Influences from Market, Family, and State on Economic Well-Being in the US and Germany* (Amsterdam: Amsterdam UP, 2016).

Ehmer, Joseph. 'The "Life Stairs": Aging, Generational Relations, and Small Commodity Production in Central Europe', in Tamara K. Hareven (ed.), *Aging and Generational Relations Over the Life Course: A Historical and Cross-Cultural Perspective* (Berlin/New York: De Gruyter, 1996), pp. 53–74.

Ehmer, Joseph. 'Alter, Arbeit, Ruhestand. Zur Dissoziation von Alter und Arbeit in historischer Perspektive', in Ursula Klingenböck, Meta Niederkorn-Bruck & Martin Scheutz (eds), *Alter(n) hat Zukunft. Alterkonzepte* (Innsbruck/Vienna: Studienverlag, 2009a), pp. 114–40.

Ehmer, Joseph. 'Altersbilder im Spannungsfeld von Arbeit und Ruhestand. Historische und aktuelle Perspektive', *Nova Acta Leopoldina*, 99(363) (2009b), pp. 209–34.

Ehmer, Joseph, Helga Grebing & Peter Gutschner (eds.). *"Arbeit": Geschichte – Gegenwart – Zukunft* (Leipzig: Universitätsverlag, 2002).

Ehmer, Joseph & Catharina Lis (eds). *The Idea of Work in Europe from Antiquity to Modern Times* (Farnham: Ashgate, 2009).

Ehret, Christopher. 'Linguistic Testimony and Migration Histories', in Jan Lucassen, Leo Lucassen & Patrick Manning (eds), *Migration History in World History: Multidisciplinary Approaches* (Leiden/Boston: Brill, 2010), pp. 113–54.

Ehret, Christopher. *The Civilizations of Africa: A History to 1800*, 2nd edn (Charlottesville/London: University of Virginia Press, 2016).

Eichengreen, Barry J. & T.J. Hatton. 'Interwar Unemployment in International Perspective: An Overview', in Barry J. Eichengreen & T.J. Hatton (eds), *Interwar Unemployment in International Perspective* (Dordrecht: Kluwer, 1988), pp. 1–59.

Eltis, David. 'Was Abolition of the American and British Slave Trade Significant in the Broader Atlantic Context?', in Marcel van der Linden (ed.), *Humanitarian Interventions and Changing Labor Relations: The Long-Term Consequences of the Abolition of the Slave Trade* (Leiden & Boston: Brill, 2011), pp. 117–39.

Eltis, David & David Richardson. *Atlas of the Transatlantic Slave Trade* (New Haven/London: Yale UP, 2010).

Emmer, P.C. *De Nederlandse slavenhandel 1500–1850* (Amsterdam/Antwerpen: Arbeiderspers, 2000).

Endicott, Karen L. 'Gender Relations in Hunter-Gatherer Societies', in Richard B. Lee & Richard Daly (eds), *The Cambridge Encyclopedia of Hunters and Gatherers* (Cambridge: CUP, 2004), pp. 411–18.

Engelen, Theo. 'Labour Strategies of Families: A Critical Assessment of an Appealing Concept', *IRSH*, 47(3) (2002), pp. 453–64.

Englander, Susan Lyn. 'Rational Womanhood: Lillian M. Gilbreth and the Use of Psychology in Scientific Management, 1914–1935', in Michael C. Wood & John Cunningham Wood (eds), *Frank and Lillian Gilbreth: Critical Evaluations in Business Management, Vol. I* (London: Routledge, 2003), pp. 210–41.

Epstein, Steven A. *Wage Labor and the Guilds in Medieval Europe* (Chapel Hill, NC: University of North Carolina Press, 1991).

Epstein, Steven A. & Maarten Prak (eds). *Guilds, Innovation and the European Economy 1400–1800* (Cambridge: CUP, 2008).

Erdem, Y. Hakan. *Slavery in the Ottoman Empire and its Demise, 1800–1909* (Basingstoke/London: Macmillan, 1996).

Erdkamp, Paul. 'Agriculture, Division of Labour, and the Paths to Economic Growth', in Paul Erdkamp, Koen Verboven & Arjan Zuiderhoek (eds), *Ownership and Exploitation of Land and Natural Resources in the Roman World* (Oxford: OUP, 2015), pp. 18–39.

Erlande-Brandenburg, Alain. *The Cathedral Builders of the Middle Ages* (London: Thames & Hudson, 1995).

Erlandson, Jon M. 'Ancient Immigrants: Archeology and Maritime Migrations', in Jan Lucassen, Leo Lucassen & Patrick Manning (eds), *Migration History in World History: Multidisciplinary Approaches* (Leiden/Boston: Brill, 2010), pp. 191–214.

Espada Lima, Henrique. 'Freedom, Precariousness, and the Law: Freed Persons Contracting out their Labour in Nineteenth-Century Brazil', *IRSH*, 54 (2009), pp. 391–416.

Exell, Karen & Christopher Naunton. 'The Administration', in Toby Wilkinson (ed.), *The Egyptian World* (London/New York: Routledge, 2007), pp. 91–104.

Fahimuddin Pasha, S.M. 'Evolution and Development of the Shipbuilding Industry in Bharati Shipyard Ltd, Maharashtra (India), from the 1970s to 2010', in Raquel Varela, Hugh Murphy & Marcel van der Linden (eds), *Shipbuilding and Ship Repair Workers around the World: Case Studies 1950–2010* (Amsterdam: Amsterdam UP, 2017), pp. 547–62.

Falk, Harry. 'The Tidal Waves of Indian History: Between the Empires and Beyond', in Patrick Olivelle (ed.), *Between the Empires: Society in India 300 BCE to 400 CE* (Oxford: OUP, 2006), pp. 145–66.

Falkenhausen, Lothar von. *Chinese Society in the Age of Confucius (1000–250 BC): The Archaeological Evidence* (Los Angeles: Cotsen Institute of Archaeology, University of California, 2006).

Fauve-Chamoux, Antoinette & Emiko Ochiai (eds). *House and the Stem Family in Eurasian Perspective* (Proceedings of the C18 Session, Twelfth International Economic History Congress, August 1998).

Feinman, Gary M. 'A Dual-Processual Perspective on the Power and Inequality in the Contemporary United States: Framing Political Economy for the Present and the Past', in T. Douglas Price & Gary M. Feinman (eds), *Pathways to Power: New Perspectives on the Emergence of Social Inequality* (New York: Springer, 2012), pp. 255–88.

Feinman, Gary M. & Christopher P. Garraty. 'Preindustrial Markets and Marketing: Archaeological Perspectives', *Annual Review of Anthropology*, 39 (2010), pp. 167–91.

Fellman, Susanna et al. (eds). *Creating Nordic Capitalism: The Business History of a Competitive Economy* (London: Palgrave Macmillan, 2008).

Fernández-Armesto, Felipe, with Daniel Lord Smail. 'Food', in Andrew Shryock & Daniel Lord Smail (eds), *Deep History: The Architecture of Past and Present* (Berkeley: University of California Press, 2011), pp. 131–59.

Fernyhough, Timothy Derek. *Serfs, Slaves and Shifta: Modes of Production and Resistance in Pre-Revolutionary Ethiopia* (Addis Ababa: Shama, 2010).

Feucht, Erika. 'Women', in Sergio Donadoni (ed.), *The Egyptians* (Chicago/London: University of Chicago Press, 1997), pp. 315–46.

Fineman, Martha Albertson & Jonathan W. Fineman (eds). *Vulnerability and the Legal Organization of Work* (London/New York: Routledge, 2018).

Fischer, Josef. 'Freie und unfreie Arbeit in der mykenischen Textilproduktion', in M. Erdem Kabadaye und Tobias Reichardt (eds), *Unfreie Arbeit: Ökonomische und kulturgeschichtliche Perspektiven* (Hildesheim: Olms, 2007), pp. 3–37.

Fitzgerald, Robert. *British Labour Management and Industrial Welfare 1846–1939* (London/Sydney: Croom Helm, 1988).

Fitzpatrick, Tony. *A Green History of the Welfare State* (Abingdon: Routledge, 2017).

Flannery, Kent & Joyce Marcus. *The Creation of Inequality: How Our Prehistoric Ancestors set the Stage for Monarchy, Slavery, and Empire* (Cambridge, MA: Harvard UP, 2012).

Fletcher, Roland. 'Low-Density, Agrarian-Based Urbanism: Scale, Power, and Ecology', in Michael E. Smith (ed.), *The Comparative Archaeology of Complex Societies* (Cambridge: CUP, 2012), pp. 285–320.

Fontana, Giovanni Luigi, Walter Panciera & Giorgio Riello. 'The Italian Textile Industry, 1600–2000: Labour, Sectors and Products', in Lex Heerma van Voss, Els Hiemstra-Kuperus & Elise van Nederveen Meerkerk (eds), *The Ashgate Companion to the History of Textile Workers, 1650–2000* (Farnham: Ashgate, 2010), pp. 275–303.

Fontijn, David. 'Giving Up Weapons', in Mike Parker Pearson & I.J.N. Thorpe (eds), *Warfare, Violence and Slavery: Proceedings of a Prehistoric Society Conference at Sheffield University* (Oxford: BAR Publishing, 2005), pp. 145–54.

Ford, Martin. *The Rise of the Robots: Technology and the Threat of Mass Unemployment* (London: Oneworld, 2017).

Fourshey, Catherine Cymone, Rhonda M. Gonzales & Christine Saidi. *Bantu Africa: 3500 BCE to Present* (New York/Oxford: OUP, 2018).

Frank, Christopher. *Master and Servant Law: Chartists, Trade Unions, Radical Lawyers and the Magistracy in England, 1840–1865* (Farnham: Ashgate, 2010).

Frankopan, Peter. *The New Silk Roads: The Present and Future of the World* (London: Bloomsbury, 2019).

Gabrielsen, Vincent. *Financing the Athenian Fleet: Public Taxation and Social Relations* (Baltimore: Johns Hopkins UP, 1994).

Galenson, David W. *White Servitude in Colonial America: An Economic Analysis* (Cambridge: CUP, 1981).

Galenson, David W. *Traders, Planters, and Slaves: Market Behavior in Early English America* (Cambridge: CUP, 1986).

Galenson, David W. 'Labor Market Behavior in Colonial America: Servitude, Slavery and Free Labor', in David W. Galenson (ed.), *Markets in History: Economic Studies of the Past* (Cambridge: CUP, 1989), pp. 52–96.

Gallant, Thomas W. *Risk and Survival in Ancient Greece: Reconstructing the Rural Domestic Economy* (Cambridge: CUP, 1991).

Garcia-Murillo, Martha & Ian MacInnes. 'The Impact of AI on Employment: A Historical Account of its Evolution', *30th European Conference of the International Telecommunications Society (ITS): Towards a Connected and Automated Society*, Helsinki, 16–19 June 2019.

Garcia-Ventura, Agnès (ed.). *What's in a Name? Terminology Related to the Work Force and Job Categories in the Ancient Near-East* (Münster: Ugarit-Verlag, 2018).

Garlan, Yvon. *Les esclaves en Grèce ancienne: Nouvelle édition revue et complété* (Paris: Éditions la Découverte: 1995).

Garnsey, Peter. *Cities, Peasants, and Food in Classical Antiquity: Essays in Social and Economic History*, edited with addenda by Walter Scheidel (Cambridge: CUP, 1998).

Garon, Sheldon. 'Collective Labor Law in Japan Since 1912', in Marcel van der Linden & Richard Price (eds), *The Rise and Development of Collective Labour Law* (Bern: Peter Lang, 2000), pp. 199–226.

Geary, Dick. *European Labour Protest 1848–1939* (London: Methuen, 1981).

Gelb, Ignace J. 'From Freedom to Slavery', in D.O. Edzard (ed.), *Gesellschaftsklassen im Alten Zweistromland und in den angrenzenden Gebieten. XVIII. Rencontre assyriologique internationale, München, 29. Juni bis 3. Juli 1970* (Munich: Bayerische Akademie der Wissenschaften, 1972), pp. 81–92.

Gelderblom, Oscar. *Cities of Commerce: The Institutional Foundations of International Trade in the Low Countries, 1250–1650* (Princeton: Princeton UP, 2013).

Gentes, Andrew A. *Exile to Siberia 1590–1822* (Basingstoke: Palgrave Macmillan, 2008).

Germonpré, Mietje et al. 'Large Canids at the Gravettian Predmostí Site, the Czech Republic: The Mandible', *Quaternary International*, 359/360 (2014), pp. 261–79.

Gier, Erik de. *Capitalist Workingman's Paradises Revisited: Corporate Welfare Work in Great Britain, the USA, Germany and France in the Golden Age of Capitalism 1880–1930* (Amsterdam: Amsterdam UP, 2016).

Giersch, C. Pat. ' "A Motley Throng": Social Change on Southwest China's Early Modern Frontier, 1700–1800', *The Journal of Asian Studies*, 60(1) (2001), pp. 67–94.

Gifford-Gonzalez, Diane. 'Animal Genetics and African Archaeology: Why it Matters', *African Archaeological Review*, 30 (2013), pp. 1–20.

Gifford-Gonzalez, Diane & Olivier Hanotte. 'Domesticating Animals in Africa: Implications of Genetic and Archaeological Findings', *Journal of World Prehistory*, 24 (2011), pp. 1–23.

Gil Montero, Raquel. 'Free and Unfree Labour in the Colonial Andes in the Sixteenth and Seventeenth Centuries', *IRSH*, 56 (2011), Special Issue, pp. 297–318.

Gilbreth, Frank B. *Motion Study: A Method for Increasing the Efficiency of the Workman* (New York: D. Van Nostrand Company, 1911).

Gillilland, Cora Lee C. *The Stone Money of Yap: A Numismatic Survey* (Washington, DC: Smithsonian Institution, 1975).

Giraldez, Arturo. 'Cacao Beans in Colonial México: Small Change in a Global Economy', in John H. Munro (ed.), *Money in the Pre-Industrial World: Bullion, Debasements and Coin Substitutes* (London: Pickering and Chatto, 2012), pp. 147–61.

Glahn, Richard von. 'Towns and Temples: Urban Growth and Decline in the Yangzi Delta, 1100–1400', in Paul J. Smith & Richard von Glahn (eds), *The Song-Yuan-Ming Transition in Chinese History* (Cambridge, MA: Harvard UP, 2003), pp. 176–211.

Godinho, Vitorino Magelhaes. 'Portuguese Emigration from the Fifteenth to the Twentieth Century: Constants and Changes', in P.C. Emmer & M. Mörner (eds), *European Expansion and Migration: Essays on the Intercontinental Migration from Africa, Asia and Europe* (New York/Oxford: Berg, 1992), pp. 13–48.

Goldin, Claudia. *The Quiet Revolution that Transformed Women's Employment, Education and Family* (Cambridge, MA: National Bureau of Economic Research, 2006).

Goldstone, Jack A. 'Why and Where did Modern Economic Growth Begin?', *TSEG*, 12 (2015), pp. 17–30.

González-Sainz, C. et al. 'Not Only Chauvet: Dating Aurignacien Rock Art in Altxerri B Cave (Northern Spain)', *Journal of Human Evolution*, 65(4) (October 2013), pp. 457–64.

Goodman, Paul. *Growing Up Absurd* (New York: Vintage, 1960).

Goose, Nigel & Katrina Honeyman (eds). *Childhood and Child Labour in Industrial England: Diversity and Agency, 1750–1914* (Farnham: Ashgate, 2012).

Gordon, Matthew S. 'Preliminary Remarks on Slaves and Slave Labor in the Third/Ninth Century 'Abbasid Empire', in Laura Culbertson (ed.), *Slaves and Households in the Near East* (Chicago: Oriental Institute, 2011), pp. 71–84.

Gorshkov, Boris B. 'Serfs on the Move: Peasant Seasonal Migration in Pre-Reform Russia, 1800–61', *Kritika: Explorations in Russian and Eurasian History*, 1(4) (Fall 2000, New Series), pp. 627–56.

Goyal, S.R. *The Coinage of Ancient India* (Jodhpur: Kusumanjali, 1995).

Goyal, Shankar. *Ancient Indian Numismatics: A Historiographical Study* (Jodhpur: Kusumanjali, 1998).

Graeber, David. *Bullshit Jobs: A Theory* (London: Penguin, 2019).

Graham, Laurel D. 'Domesticating Efficiency: Lillian Gilbreth's Scientific Management of Homemakers, 1924–1930', *Signs: Journal of Women in Culture and Society*, 24(3) (1999), pp. 633–75.

Green, Toby. *A Fistful of Shells: West Africa from the Rise of the Slave Trade to the Age of Revolution* (Chicago: University of Chicago Press, 2019).

Greenhouse, Steven. *Beaten Down, Worked Up: The Past, Present, and Future of American Labor* (New York: Anchor Books, 2019).

Greer, Ian et al. *The Marketization of Employment Services: The Dilemmas of Europe's Work-First Welfare States* (Oxford: OUP, 2017).

Greif, Avner, Lynne Kiesling & John V.C. Nye (eds). *Institutions, Innovation, and Industrialization: Essays in Economic History and Development* (Princeton/Oxford: Princeton UP, 2015).

Grewal, J.S. 'Historical Writing on Urbanisation in Medieval India', in Indu Banga (ed.), *The City in Indian History: Urban Demography, Society and Politics* (New Delhi: Manohar, 2014), pp. 69–79.

Griffin, Emma. *A Short History of the British Industrial Revolution* (Basingstoke: Palgrave Macmillan, 2010).

Griffin, P. Bion & Marcus B. Griffin. 'The Agta of Eastern Luzon, Philippines', in Richard B. Lee & Richard Daly (eds), *The Cambridge Encyclopedia of Hunters and Gatherers* (Cambridge: CUP, 2004), pp. 289–93.

Gronenborn, Detlef. 'Beyond the Models: "Neolithisation" in Central Europe', in Alisdair Whittle & Vicki Cummings (eds), *Going Over: The Mesolithic-Neolithic Transition in North-West Europe* (Oxford: OUP, 2007), pp. 73–98.

Grooth, Marjorie de. 'Mijnen in het Krijt: De vuursteenwinning bij Rijckholt', in Leendert P. Louwe Kooijmans (ed.), *Nederland in de prehistorie* (Amsterdam: Bert Bakker, 2005), pp. 243–8.

Guanglin, Liu. 'Market Integration in China, AD 960–1644', in R.J. van der Spek, Bas van Leeuwen & Jan Luiten van Zanden (eds), *A History of Market Performance: From Ancient Babylonia to the Modern World* (London/New York: Routledge, 2015), pp. 308–38.

Guendelsberger, Emily. *On the Clock: What Low-Wage Work Did to Me and How it Drives America Insane* (New York: Little & Brown, 2019).

Guha, Sumit. 'The Population History of South Asia from the Seventeenth to the Twentieth Centuries: An Exploration', in Ts'ui-jung Liu, James Lee et al. (eds), *Asian Population History* (New York: OUP, 2001), pp. 63–78.

Gupta, Bishnupriya. 'Falling Behind and Catching Up: India's Transformation from a Colonial Economy', *Warwick Economic Research Papers*, 1147, January 2018.

Gupta, Ranjan Kumar. *The Economic Life of a Bengal District: Birbhum 1770–1857* (Burdwan: Burdwan University, 1984).

Gurven, Michael & Kim Hill. 'Why Do Men Hunt? A Reevaluation of "Man the Hunter" and the Sexual Division of Labor', *Current Anthropology*, 50(1) (February 2009), pp. 51–74.

Guthrie, R. Dale. 'Haak en Steek – The Tool that Allowed Hominins to Colonize the African Savanna and to Flourish There', in Wil Roebroeks (ed.), *Guts and Brains: An Integrative Approach to the Hominin Record* (Leiden: Leiden UP, 2007), pp. 133–64.

Haas, Randall et al. 'Female Hunters of the Early Americas', *Science Advances*, 6(45) (4 November 2020), eabd0310.

Habib, Irfan. 'The Price-Regulations of 'Ala'uddin Khalji – A Defence of Zia' Barani', in Sanjay Subrahmanyam (ed.), *Money and the Market in India 1100–1700* (Delhi: OUP, 1994), pp. 85–111.

Habib, Irfan. 'The Peasant Protest in Indian History', in Bhairabi Prasad Sahu (ed.), *Land System and Rural Society in Early India* (New Delhi: Manohar, 2004), pp. 205–36.

Hagen, E.H. & H.C. Barrett. 'Perinatal Sadness among Shuar women', *Medical Anthropology Quarterly*, 21 (2007), pp. 22–40.

Haggard, Stephan & Robert Kaufman. *Development, Democracy and Welfare States: Latin America, East Asia, and Eastern Europe* (Princeton/Oxford: Princeton UP, 2008).

Hahn, Sylvia. 'Women in older ages – "old" women?', *History of the Family*, 7 (2002), pp. 33–58.

Hall, Jonathan M. *A History of the Archaic Greek World ca. 1200–479 BCE*, 2nd edn (Chichester: Wiley Blackwell, 2014).

Hall, Kenneth. 'Price-making and Market Hierarchy in Early Medieval South India', in Sanjay Subrahmanyam (ed.), *Money and the Market in India 1100–1700* (Delhi: OUP, 1994), pp. 57–84.

Hansell, Mike. *Built by Animals: The Natural History of Animal Architecture* (Oxford: OUP, 2008).

Harari, Yuval Noah. *Sapiens: A Brief History of Humankind* (London: Vintage, 2014).

Hårde, Andreas. 'The Emergence of Warfare in the Early Bronze Age: The Nitra group in Slovakia and Moravia, 2200–1800 BC', in Mike Parker Pearson & I.J.N. Thorpe (eds), *Warfare, Violence and Slavery: Proceedings of a Prehistoric Society Conference at Sheffield University* (Oxford: BAR Publishing, 2005), pp. 87–105.

Harper, Kyle. *Slavery in the Late Roman World, AD 275–425* (Cambridge: CUP, 2011).

Harper, Kyle. 'Landed Wealth in the Long Term', in Paul Erdkamp, Koen Verboven & Arjan Zuiderhoek (eds), *Ownership and Exploitation of Land and Natural Resources in the Roman World* (Oxford: OUP, 2015), pp. 43–61.

Harris, Edward M. 'Workshop, Marketplace and Household: The Nature of Technical Specialization in Classical Athens and its Influence on Economy and Society', in Paul Cartledge, Edward E. Cohen & Lin Foxhall (eds), *Money, Labour and Land: Approaches to the Economies of Ancient Greece* (London/New York: Routledge, 2002), pp. 67–99.

Harris, W.V. *Rome's Imperial Economy: Twelve Essays* (Oxford: OUP, 2011).

Harvey, John. *Mediaeval Craftsmen* (London/Sydney: Batsford, 1975).

Haselgrove, Colin & Stefan Krmnicek. 'The Archaeology of Money', *Annual Review of Anthropology*, 41 (2012), pp. 235–50.

Hatfield, Gary. 'Introduction: Evolution of Mind, Brain, and Culture', in Gary Hatfield & Holly Pittman (eds), *Evolution of Mind, Brain, and Culture* (Philadelphia: University of Pennsylvania Press, 2013), pp. 1–44.

Hatfield, Gary & Holly Pittman (eds). *Evolution of Mind, Brain, and Culture* (Philadelphia: University of Pennsylvania Press, 2013).

Haupt, Heinz-Gerhard (ed.). *Das Ende der Zünfte: Ein europäischer Vergleich* (Göttingen: Vandenhoeck & Ruprecht, 2002).

Hawke, Kristen. 'How Grandmother Effects plus Individual Variation in Frailty Shape Fertility and Mortality: Guidance from Human-Chimpanzee Comparisons', *PNAS*, 107, Supplement 2 (11 May 2000), pp. 8977–84.

Hay, Douglas & Paul Craven (eds). *Masters, Servants and Magistrates in Britain and the Empire 1562–1955* (Chapel Hill: University of North Carolina Press, 2004).

Hayden, Brian & Suzanne Villeneuve. 'Who Benefits from Complexity? A View from Futuna', in T. Douglas Price & Gary M. Feinman (eds), *Pathways to Power: New Perspectives on the Emergence of Social Inequality* (New York: Springer, 2012), pp. 95–145.

He, Nu. 'The Longshan Period Site of Taosi in Southern Shanxi Province', in Anne P. Underhill (ed.), *A Companion to Chinese Archeology* (Hoboken, NJ: Wiley-Blackwell, 2013), pp. 255–77.

Heald, Henrietta. *Magnificent Women and their Revolutionary Machines* (London: Unbound, 2019).

Heckenberger, Michael & Eduardo Góes Neves. 'Amazonian Archaeology', *Annual Review of Anthropology*, 38 (2009), pp. 251–66.

Heerma van Voss, Lex. 'The International Federation of Trade Unions and the Attempt to Maintain the Eight-Hour Working Day (1919–1929)', in Frits van Holthoon & Marcel van der Linden (eds), *Internationalism in the Labour Movement 1830–1940* (Leiden: Brill, 1988), pp. 518–42.

Heerma van Voss, Lex. *De doodsklok voor den goeden ouden tijd: De achturendag in de jaren twintig* (Amsterdam: Stichting Beheer IISG, 1994).

Heerma van Voss, Lex (ed.). *Petitions in Social History* (Cambridge: CUP, 2002).

Heerma van Vos, Lex & Marcel van der Linden (eds). *Class and Other Identities: Gender, Religion and Ethnicity in the Writing of European Labour History* (New York/Oxford: Berghahn, 2002).

Heerma van Voss, Lex, Patrick Pasture & Jan de Maeyer (eds). *Between Cross and Class: Comparative Histories of Christian Labour in Europe 1840–2000* (Bern: Peter Lang, 2005).

Heesch, Johan van. 'Some Aspects of Wage Payments and Coinage in Ancient Rome, First to Third Centuries CE', in Jan Lucassen (ed.), *Wages and Currency: Global Comparisons from Antiquity to the Twentieth Century* (Bern: Peter Lang, 2007), pp. 77–96.

Heidemann, Stefan. 'The Merger of Two Currency Zones in early Islam: The Byzantine and Sasanian Impact on the Circulation in Former Byzantine Syria and Northern Mesopotamia', *Iran*, 36 (1998), pp. 95–113.

Heidemann, Stefan. 'The History of the Industrial and Commercial Area of 'Abbasid Al-Raqqa, called Al-Raqqa Al-Muhtariqa', *Bulletin of SOAS*, 69(1) (2006), pp. 33–52.

Heidemann, Stefan. 'Entwicklung und Selbstverständnis mittelalterlichen Städte in der Islamischen Welt (7.–15. Jahrhundert)', in Christhard Schrenk (ed.), *Was machte im Mittelalter zur Stadt? Selbstverständnis, Aussensicht, und Erscheinungsbilder mittelalterlicher Städte* (Heilbronn: Stadtarchiv, 2007), pp. 203–43.

Heidemann, Stefan. 'Economic Growth and Currency in Ayyubid Palestine', in Robert Hillenbrand and Sylvia Auld (eds), *Ayyubid Jerusalem: The Holy City in Context 1187–1250* (London: Altjair Trust, 2009a), pp. 276–300.

Heidemann, Stefan. 'Charity and Piety for the Transformation of the Cities: The New Direction in Taxation and Waqf Policy in Mid-Twelfth-Century Syria and Northern Mesopotamia', in Miriam Frenkel & Yaacov Lev (eds), *Charity and Giving in Monotheistic Religions* (Berlin/New York: De Gruyter, 2009b), pp. 153–74.

Heidemann, Stefan. 'Numismatics', in Chase Robinson (ed.), *The Formation of the Islamic World, Sixth to Eleventh Centuries* (Cambridge: CUP, 2010), pp. 648–89.

Heidemann, Stefan. 'The Agricultural Hinterland of Baghdad, Al-Raqqa and Samarra': Settlement Patterns in the Diyar Mudar', in A. Borrut et al. (eds), *Le Proche-Orient de Justinien aux Abbasides: Peuplement et dynamiques spatiales* (Turnhout: Brepols, 2011), pp. 43–57.

Heidemann, Stefan. 'How to Measure Economic Growth in the Middle East? A Framework of Inquiry for the Middle Islamic Period', in Daniella Talmon-Heller & Katia Cytryn-Silverman (eds), *Material Evidence and Narrative Sources: Interdisciplinary Studies of the History of the Muslim Middle East* (Leiden/Boston: Brill, 2015), pp. 30–57.

Heijne, Sander & Hendrik Noten. *Fantoomgroei: Waarom we steeds harder werken voor steeds minder geld* (Amsterdam/Antwerpen: Atlas Contact, 2020).

Hemming, John. 'Indians and the Frontier in Colonial Brazil', in Leslie Bethel (ed.), *The Cambridge History of Latin America, Volume II: Colonial Latin America* (Cambridge: CUP, 1984), pp. 501–45.

Hennock, E.P. *The Origin of the Welfare State in England and Germany, 1850–1914: Social Policies Compared* (Cambridge: CUP, 2007).

Henrich, Joseph, Robert Boyd & Peter J. Richerson. 'The Puzzle of Monogamous Marriage', *Philosophical Transactions of the Royal Society B*, 367 (2012), pp. 657–69.

Herbert, Eugenia W. *Red Gold of Africa: Copper in Precolonial History and Culture* (Madison: University of Wisconsin Press, 1984).

Herbert, Eugenia W. *Iron, Gender, and Power: Rituals of Transformation in African Societies* (Bloomington/Indianapolis: Indiana UP, 1993).

Herbert, U. *A History of Foreign Labor in Germany, 1880–1980: Seasonal Workers/Forced Laborers/Guest Workers* (Ann Arbor: University of Michigan Press, 1990).

Heuman, Gad & Graeme Burnard (eds). *The Routledge History of Slavery* (London/New York: Routledge, 2011).

Heymans, Elon David. 'Argonauts of the Eastern Mediterranean: The Early History of Money in the Eastern Mediterranean Iron Age', PhD diss., University of Tel Aviv, February 2018.

Heywood, Colin. *A History of Childhood: Children and Childhood in the West from Medieval to Modern Times*, 2nd edn (Cambridge: Polity, 2018).

Hingh, Anne E. de. 'Food Production and Food Procurement in the Bronze Age and Early Iron Age (2000–500 BC): The Organization of a Diversified and Intensified Agrarian System in the Meuse-Demer-Scheldt Region (The Netherlands and Belgium) and the Region of the River Moselle (Luxemburg and France)', PhD. diss., Leiden University, 2000.

Hirschman, Albert Otto. *Exit, Voice, and Loyalty: Responses to Decline in Firms, Organizations, and States* (Cambridge, MA: Harvard UP, 1970).

Hirth, Kenneth G. 'Incidental Urbanism: The Structure of the Prehispanic City in Central Mexico', in Joyce Marcus & Jeremy A. Sabloff (eds). *The Ancient City: New Perspectives on Urbanism in the Old and New World* (Santa Fe, NM: School for Advanced Research Press, 2008), pp. 273–97.

Hodges, Richard & John F. Cherry. 'Cost-Control and Coinage: An Archaeological Approach to Anglo-Saxon England', *Research in Economic Anthropology*, 5 (1983), pp. 131–83.

Hoffman, Carl L. 'Punan Foragers in the Trading Networks of Southeast Asia', in Carmel Schrire (ed.), *Past and Present in Hunter Gatherer Studies* (Walnut Creek, CA: Left Coast Press, 2009), pp. 123–49.

Hoffmann, Richard C. 'Frontier Foods for Late Medieval Consumers: Culture, Economy, Ecology', *Environment and History*, 7(2) (2001), pp. 131–67.

Hofmeester, Karin. 'Jewish Ethics and Women's Work in the Late Medieval and Early Modern Arab-Islamic World', *IRSH*, 56, Special Issue 19: The Joy and Pain of Work: Global Attitudes and Valuations, 1500–1650 (21 November 2011), pp. 141–64.

Hofmeester, Karin. 'Attitudes to Work', in Karin Hofmeester & Marcel van der Linden (eds), *Handbook of the Global History of Work* (Berlin/Boston: De Gruyter, 2018), pp. 411–31.

Hofmeester, Karin & Jan Lucassen. 'Ottoman Tax Registers as a Source for Labor Relations in Ottoman Bursa', *International Labor and Working Class History*, 97 (2020), pp. 28–56.

Hofmeester, Karin, Jan Lucassen, Leo Lucassen, Rombert Stapel & Richard Zijdeman. 'The Global Collaboratory on the History of Labour Relations, 1500–2000: Background, Set-Up, Taxonomy, and Applications', IISH Dataverse, V1 (26 October 2015). Available from: http://hdl.handle.net/10622/4OGRAD.

Hofmeester, Karin & Marcel van der Linden (eds). *Handbook of the Global History of Work* (Berlin/Boston: De Gruyter, 2018).

Hogendorn, Jan & Marion Johnson. *The Shell Money of the Slave Trade* (Cambridge: CUP, 1986).

Holderness, B.A. *Pre-Industrial England: Economy and Society from 1500 to 1750* (London/New Jersey: Dent/Rowman & Littlefield, 1976).

Holthoon, Frits van & Marcel van der Linden (eds). *Internationalism in the Labour Movement 1830–1940*, 2 vols (Leiden: Brill, 1988).

Homburg, Heidrun. 'From Unemployment Insurance to Compulsory Labour: The Transformation of the Benefit System in Germany 1927–1933', in Richard J. Evans & Dick Geary (eds), *The German Unemployed: Experiences and Consequences of Mass Unemployment from the Weimar Republic to the Third Reich* (London/Sydney: Croom Helm, 1987), pp. 92–103.

Hommel, Rudolf P. *China at Work: An Illustrated Record of the Primitive Industries of China's Masses, Whose Life is Toil, and thus an Account of Chinese Civilization* (Cambridge, MA/London: MIT, 1969).

Horn, Jeff. 'Avoiding Revolution: The French Path to Industrialization', in Jeff Horn, Leonard N. Rosenband & Merritt Roe Smith (eds), *Reconceptualizing the Industrial Revolution* (Cambridge, MA/London: MIT, 2010), pp. 87–106.

Horn, Jeff, Leonard N. Rosenband & Merritt Roe Smith (eds). *Reconceptualizing the Industrial Revolution* (Cambridge, MA/London: MIT, 2010).

Howgego, Christopher. 'The Supply and Use of Money in the Roman World 200 B.C. to A.D. 300', *The Journal of Roman Studies*, 82 (1992), pp. 1–31.

Hrdy, Sarah Blaffer. *Mothers and Others: The Evolutionary Origins of Mutual Understanding* (Cambridge, MA: Harvard UP, 2009).

Hu, Aiqun & Patrick Manning. 'The Global Social Insurance Movement since the 1880s', *Journal of Global History*, 5 (2010), pp. 125–48.

Huang, Philip C.C. *The Peasant Family and Rural Development in the Yangzi Delta, 1350–1988* (Stanford: Stanford UP, 1990).

Huberman, Michael. *Escape from the Market: Negotiating Work in Lancashire* (Cambridge: CUP, 1996).

Huberman, Michael & Chris Minns. 'The Times They Are Not Changin': Days and Hours of Work in Old and New Worlds, 1870–2000', *Explorations in Economic History*, 44 (2007), pp. 538–76.

Hudson, Pat. 'Proto-Industrialization in England', in Sheilagh C. Ogilvie & Markus Cerman (eds), *European Proto-Industrialization* (Cambridge: CUP, 1996), pp. 49–66.

Humphries, Jane & Jacob Weisdorf. 'Unreal Wages? Real Income and Economic Growth in England, 1260–1850', *Economic Journal*, 129 (2019), pp. 2867–87.

Hurston, Zora Neale. *Barracoon: The Story of the Last 'Black Cargo'* (London: Amistad, 2018).

Hurston, Zora Neale. *Barracoon: Oluale Kossola, overlevende van het laatste slavenschip* (Amsterdam: De Geus, 2019).

Hussain, Syed Ejaz. *The Bengal Sultanate: Politics, Economy and Coins (AD 1205–1576)* (Delhi: Manohar, 2003).

Hussain, Syed Ejaz. *Shiraz-I Hind: A History of Jaunpur Sultanate* (New Delhi: Manohar, 2014).

Huynh, Kim, Bina D'Costa & Katrina Lee-Koo. *Children and Global Conflict* (Cambridge: CUP, 2015).

Ichikawa, Mitsuo. 'The Mbuti of Northern Congo', in Richard B. Lee & Richard Daly (eds), *The Cambridge Encyclopedia of Hunters and Gatherers* (Cambridge: CUP, 2004), pp. 210–14.

Imai Noriko. 'Copper in Edo-Period Japan', in Keiko Nagase-Reimer (ed.), *Copper in the Early-Modern Sino-Japanese Trade* (Leiden/Boston: Brill, 2016), pp. 10–31.

Ingold, Tim. 'On the Social Relations of the Hunter-Gatherer Band', in Richard B. Lee & Richard Daly (eds), *The Cambridge Encyclopedia of Hunters and Gatherers* (Cambridge: CUP, 2004), pp. 399–410.

Izawa, Eiji. 'Developments in Japanese Copper Metallurgy for Coinage and Foreign Trade in the Early Edo Period', in Nanny Kim and Keiko Nagase-Reimer (eds), *Mining, Monies, and Culture in Early Modern Societies: East Asian and Global Perspectives* (Leiden/Boston: Brill, 2013), pp. 13–24.

Jackson, Richard P. 'From Profit-Sailing to Wage Sailing: Mediterranean Owner-Captains and their Crews during the Medieval Commercial Revolution', *Journal of European Economic History*, 18(3) (Winter 1989), pp. 605–28.

Jacobs, Els M. *Koopman in Azië: De handel van de Verenigde Oost-Indische Compagnie tijdens de 18de eeuw* (Zutphen: Walburg Pers, 2000).

Jacoby, Sanford M. *Employing Bureaucracy: Managers, Unions and the Transformation of Work in American Industry, 1900–1945* (New York: Columbia UP, 1985).

Jaffe, Sarah. *Work Won't Love You Back: How Devotion to Our Jobs Keeps Us Exploited, Exhausted, and Alone* (New York: Bold Type Books, 2021).

Jaffer, Aaron. *Lascars and Indian Ocean Seafaring, 1780–1860: Shipboard Life, Unrest and Mutiny* (Woodbridge: The Boydell Press, 2015).

Jain, Rekha. *Ancient Indian Coinage: A Systematic Study of Money Economy from Janapada Period to Early Medieval Period (600 BC to AD 1200)* (New Delhi: Printwork, 1995).

Jameson, Michael H. 'On Paul Cartledge, "The Political Economy of Greek Slavery"', in Paul Cartledge, Edward E. Cohen & Lin Foxhall (eds), *Money, Labour and Land: Approaches to the Economies of Ancient Greece* (London/New York: Routledge, 2002), pp. 167–74.

Jamison, Stephanie W. 'Women "Between the Empires" and "Between the Lines"', in Patrick Olivelle (ed.), *Between the Empires: Society in India 300 BCE to 400 CE* (Oxford: OUP, 2006), pp. 191–214.

Jensen, Carsten & Kees van Kersbergen. *The Politics of Inequality* (London: Palgrave Macmillan, 2017).

Jevons, W. Stanley. *The Theory of Political Economy* (London: Macmillan, 1879).

Jevons, W. Stanley. *The Principles of Economics: A Fragment of a Treatise on the Industrial Mechanisms of Society and Other Papers* (London: Macmillan, 1905).

Jha, D.N. *Ancient India in Historical Outline*, 3rd enlarged edn (New Delhi: Manohar, 2018).

Jha, D.N. *Against the Grain: Notes on Identity, Intolerance and History* (New Delhi: Manohar, 2020).

Jin, Cao & Hans Ulrich Vogel. 'Smoke on the Mountain: The Infamous Counterfeiting Case of Tongzi District, Guizhou province, 1794', in Jane Kate Leonard & Ulrich Theobald (eds), *Money in Asia (1200–1900): Small Currencies in Social and Political Contexts* (Leiden/Boston: Brill, 2015), pp. 188–219.

Jing, Zhichun et al. 'Recent Discoveries and Some Thoughts on Early Urbanization at Anyang', in Anne P. Underhill (ed.), *A Companion to Chinese Archaeology* (Hoboken, NJ: Wiley-Blackwell, 2013), pp. 343–65.

Johnson, Paul. 'Creditors, Debtors, and the Law in Victorian and Edwardian England', in Willibald Steinmetz (ed.), *Private Law and Social Inequality in the Industrial Age: Comparing Legal Cultures in Britain, France, Germany and the United States* (Oxford: OUP, 2000), pp. 485–504.

Jones, Eric. 'The Context of English Industrialization', in Avner Greif, Lynne Kiesling & John V.C. Nye (eds), *Institutions, Innovation, and Industrialization: Essays in Economic History and Development* (Princeton/Oxford: Princeton UP, 2015), pp. 397–409.

Joordens, Josephine C.A. et al. '*Homo erectus* at Trinil on Java Used Shells for Food Production and Engraving', *Nature* (3 December 2014). DOI: 10.1038/nature13962.

Joyce, Arthur A. *Mixtecs, Zapotecs, and Chatinos: Ancient Peoples of Southern Mexico* (Chichester: Wiley-Blackwell, 2010).

Jursa, Michael. *Aspects of the Economic History of Babylonia in the First Millennium BC: Economic Geography, Economic Mentalities, Agriculture, the Use of Money and the Problem of Economic Growth* (Münster: Ugarit Verlag, 2010).

Kaare, Bwire & James Woodburn. 'The Hadza of Tanzania', in Richard B. Lee & Richard Daly (eds), *The Cambridge Encyclopedia of Hunters and Gatherers* (Cambridge: CUP, 2004), pp. 200–4.

Kanigel, Robert. *The One Best Way: Frederick Winslow Taylor and the Enigma of Efficiency* (Cambridge, MA: MIT, 2005).

Kaplan, Hillard S. et al. 'The Evolution of Diet, Brain and Life History among Primates and Humans', in Wil Roebroeks (ed.), *Guts and Brains: An Integrative Approach to the Hominin Record* (Leiden: Leiden UP, 2007), pp. 47–90.

Kaplan, Steven L. & Cynthia Koepp (eds). *Work in France: Representations, Meaning, Organization, and Practice* (Ithaca: Cornell UP, 1986).

Kars, Marjoleine. *Blood on the River: A Chronicle of Mutiny and Freedom on the Wild Coast* (New York: The New Press, 2020).

Karsten, Luchien. *Arbeidstijdverkorting in historisch perspectief, 1817–1919* (Amsterdam: Stichting IISG, 1990).

Katary, Sally L.D. 'Land Tenure and Taxation', in Toby Wilkinson (ed.), *The Egyptian World* (London/New York: Routledge, 2007), pp. 185–201.

Kautilya. *The Arthashastra*. Edited, rearranged, translated and introduced by L.N. Rangarajan (New Delhi: Penguin, 1992).

Kay, Diana & Robert Miles. *Refugees or Migrant Workers? European Volunteer Workers in Britain 1946–1951* (London: Routledge, 1992).

Kearny, Milo. *The Indian Ocean in World History* (New York/London: Routledge, 2004).

Keeley, Lawrence. 'War Before Civilization', in Todd K. Shackelford & Ranald D. Hansen (eds), *The Evolution of Violence* (New York: Springer, 2014), pp. 23–31.

Kehoe, Alice B. 'Blackfoot and Other Hunters of the North American Plains', in Richard B. Lee & Richard Daly (eds), *The Cambridge Encyclopedia of Hunters and Gatherers* (Cambridge: CUP, 2004), pp. 36–40.

Kelder, Jorrit M. *The Kingdom of Mycenae: A Great Kingdom in the Late Bronze Age Aegean* (Bethesda, MD: CDL Press, 2010).

Kelly, Robert L. *The Foraging Spectrum: Diversity in Hunter-Gatherer Lifeways* (Washington, DC/London: Smithsonian Institution Press, 1995).

Kennan, George. *Siberia and the Exile System*, 2 vols (London: Osgood, 1891).

Kennedy, Hugh. 'The Middle East in Islamic Late Antiquity', in Andrew Monson & Walter Scheidel (eds), *Fiscal Regimes and the Political Economy of Premodern States* (Cambridge: CUP, 2015), pp. 390–403.

Kenoyer, Jonathan Mark. 'Indus Urbanism: New Perspectives on its Origin and Character', in Joyce Marcus & Jeremy A. Sabloff (eds), *The Ancient City: New Perspectives on Urbanism in the Old and New World* (Santa Fe, NM: School for Advanced Research Press, 2008), pp. 183–208.

Kessler, Gijs. 'A Population under Pressure: Household Responses to Demographic and Economic Shock in the Interwar Soviet Union', in Donald Filtzer, Wendy Z. Goldman, Gijs Kessler (eds), *A Dream Deferred: New Studies in Russian and Soviet Labour History* (Bern: Peter Lang, 2008), pp. 315–42.

Kessler, Gijs. 'Wage Labor and the Household Economy: A Russian Perspective, 1600–2000', in Marcel van der Linden & Leo Lucassen (eds), *Working on Labor: Essays in Honor of Jan Lucassen* (Leiden/Boston: Brill, 2012), pp. 351–69.

Kessler, Gijs. 'Measuring Migration in Russia: A Perspective of Empire, 1500–1900', in Jan Lucassen & Leo Lucassen (eds), *Globalising Migration History: The Eurasian Experience (16th–21st Centuries)* (Leiden/Boston: Brill, 2014), pp. 71–88.

Kessler, Gijs & Jan Lucassen. 'Labour Relations, Efficiency and the Great Divergence: Comparing Pre-Industrial Brick-Making across Eurasia, 1500–2000', in Maarten Prak & Jan Luiten van Zanden (eds), *Technology, Skills and the Pre-Modern Economy in the East and the West. Essays Dedicated to the Memory of S.R. Epstein* (Leiden/Boston: Brill, 2013), pp. 259–322.

Khazanov, Anatoly M. *Nomads and the Outside World*, 2nd edn (Madison: University of Wisconsin Press, 1994).

Killick, David & Thomas Fenn. 'Archaeometallurgy: The Study of Preindustrial Mining and Metallurgy', *Annual Review of Anthropology*, 41 (2012), pp. 559–75.

Kim, Henry S. 'Archaic Coinage as Evidence for the Use of Money', in Andrew Meadows & Kirsty Shipton (eds), *Money and its Uses in the Ancient Greek World* (Oxford: OUP, 2001), pp. 8–21.

Kim, Henry S. 'Small Change and the Moneyed Economy', in Paul Cartledge, Edward E. Cohen & Lin Foxhall (eds), *Money, Labour and Land: Approaches to the Economies of Ancient Greece* (London/New York: Routledge, 2002), pp. 44–51.

Kim, Nanny. 'Keeping Books and Managing a State Transport: Li Bolong's Copper Convoy of 1807', in Nanny Kim & Keiko Nagase-Reimer (eds). *Mining, Monies, and Culture in Early Modern Societies: East Asian and Global Perspectives* (Leiden/Boston: Brill, 2013), pp. 133–83.

Kim, Nanny & Keiko Nagase-Reimer (eds), *Mining, Monies, and Culture in Early Modern Societies: East Asian and Global Perspectives* (Leiden/Boston: Brill, 2013).

King, Steve A. 'Protoindustrielle Entwicklung in zwei Gemeinden Yorkshires (1660 bis 1830)', in Dietrich Ebeling & Wolfgang Mager (eds), *Protoindustrie in der Region, Europäische Gewerbelandschaften vom 16. bis zum 19. Jahrhundert* (Bielefeld: Verlag für Regionalgeschichte, 1997), pp. 221–54.

Kirch, Patrick V. 'Peopling of the Pacific: A Holistic Anthropological Perspective', *Annual Review of Anthropology*, 39 (2010), pp. 131–48.

Kivelson, Valerie. 'Claiming Siberia: Colonial Possession and Property Holding in the Seventeenth and Early Eighteenth Centuries', in Nicholas B. Breyfogle, Abby Schrader & Willard Sunderland (eds), *Peopling the Russian Periphery: Borderland Colonization in Eurasian History* (London/New York: Routledge, 2007), pp. 21–40.

Klass, Morton. *Caste: The Emergence of the South Asian Social System* (New Delhi: Manohar, 2020).

Kleber, Kristin. 'Dependent Labor and Status in the Neo-Babylonian and Achaemenid Periods', *Alter Orient und Altes Testament: Veröffentlichungen zur Kultur und Geschichte des Alten Orients und des Alten Testaments*, 440 (2018), pp. 441–64.

Klein, Herbert. *African Slavery in Latin America and the Caribbean* (New York/Oxford: OUP, 1986).

Klein, Herbert. *The Atlantic Slave Trade* (Cambridge: CUP, 1999).

Klein, Rüdiger. 'Arbeit und Arbeiteridentitäten in islamischen Gesellschaften: Historische Beispiele', in Jürgen Kocka & Claus Offe (eds), *Geschichte und Zukunft der Arbeit* (Frankfurt/New York: Campus, 2000), pp. 163–74.

Klein Goldewijk, Kees et al. 'The HYDE 3.1 Spatially Explicit Database of Human-Induced Global Land-Use Change Over the Past 12,000 Years', *Global Ecology and Biogeography*, 20(1) (January 2011), pp. 73–86.

Kloosterboer, Willemina. *Involuntary Labour since the Abolition of Slavery: A Survey of Compulsory Labour throughout the World* (Leiden: Brill, 1960).

Knijff, Peter de. 'Population Genetics and the Migration of Modern Humans (*Homo Sapiens*)', in Jan Lucassen, Leo Lucassen & Patrick Manning (eds), *Migration History in World History: Multidisciplinary Approaches* (Leiden/Boston: Brill, 2010), pp. 39–57.

Knotter, Ad. *Transformations of Trade Unionism: Comparative and Transnational Perspectives on Workers Organizing in Europe and the United States, Eighteenth to Twenty-First Centuries* (Amsterdam: AUP, 2018).

Kocka, Jürgen. *White Collar Workers in America 1890–1940: A Social-Political History in International Perspective* (London/Beverly Hills: SAGE, 1980).

Kocka, Jürgen. 'Capitalism and Bureaucracy in German Industrialization before 1914', *EHR*, New Series, 34(3) (1981), pp. 453–68.

Kocka, Jürgen (ed.). *Work in a Modern Society: The German Historical Experience in Comparative Perspective* (New York: Berghahn, 2010).

Kocka, Jürgen. 'Capitalism and its Critics: A Long-Term View', in Ulbe Bosma & Karin Hofmeester (eds), *The Life Work of a Labor Historian: Essays in Honor of Marcel van der Linden* (Leiden/Boston: Brill, 2018), pp. 71–89.

Kocka, Jürgen & Marcel van der Linden (eds). *Capitalism: The Reemergence of a Historical Concept* (London: Bloomsbury, 2016).

Kocka, Jürgen & Claus Offe (eds). *Geschichte und Zukunft der Arbeit* (Frankurt/New York: Campus, 2000).

Kohli, Martin. 'Arbeit im Lebenslauf: alte und neue Paradoxien', in Jürgen Kocka & Claus Offe (eds), *Geschichte und Zukunft der Arbeit* (Frankfurt/New York: Campus, 2000), pp. 362–82.

Kok, Jan (ed.). *Rebellious Families: Household Strategies and Collective Action in the Nineteenth and Twentieth Centuries* (New York/Oxford: Berghahn, 2002).

Kok, Jan. 'The Family Factor in Migration Decisions', in Jan Lucassen, Leo Lucassen & Patrick Manning (eds), *Migration History in World History: Multidisciplinary Approaches* (Leiden/Boston: Brill, 2010), pp. 215–50.

Kolata, Alan L. *The Tiwanaku: Portrait of an Andean Civilization* (Cambridge, MA/Oxford: Blackwell, 1993).

Kolata, Alan L. *Ancient Inca* (Cambridge: CUP, 2013).

Kolchin, Peter. *Unfree Labor: American Slavery and Russian Serfdom* (Cambridge, MA: Harvard UP, 1987).

Kolff, Dirk H.A. *Naukar Rajput and Sepoy: The Ethnohistory of the Military Labour Market in Hindustan, 1440–1850* (Cambridge: CUP, 1990).

Komlosy, Andrea. *Work: The Last 1,000 Years* (London/New York: Verso, 2018).

Kössler, Reinhart. 'Wage Labour and Despoty in Modernity', in Tom Brass & Marcel van der Linden (eds), *Free and Unfree Labour: The Debate Continues* (Bern: Peter Lang, 1997), pp. 91–105.

Kotiswaran, Prabha (ed.). *Revisiting the Law and Governance of Trafficking, Forced Labor and Modern Slavery* (Cambridge: CUP, 2017).

Krishnan, Parameswara. *Glimpses of Indian Historical Demography* (Delhi: B.R. Publishing Corporation, 2014).

Krissman, Fred. 'California's Agricultural Labor Market: Historical Variations in the Use of Unfree Labor, c. 1769–1994', in Tom Brass & Marcel van der Linden (eds), *Free and Unfree Labour: The Debate Continues* (Bern: Peter Lang, 1997), pp. 201–38.

Kristiansen, Kristian. 'Decentralized Complexity: The Case of Bronze Age Northern Europe', in T. Douglas Price & Gary M. Feinman (eds), *Pathways to Power: New Perspectives on the Emergence of Social Inequality* (New York: Springer, 2012), pp. 169–92.

Kulke, Hermann & Dietmar Rothermund. *A History of India* (London/New York: Routledge, 1990).

Kuroda, Akinobu. *A Gobal History of Money* (London/New York: Routledge, 2020).

Kuromiya, Hiroaki. 'Workers' Artels and Soviet Production Relations', in Sheila Fitzpatrick et al. (eds), *Russia in the Era of NEP: Explorations in Soviet Society and Culture* (Bloomington: Indiana UP, 1991), pp. 72–88.

Kusimba, Chapurukha M. 'Early African Cities: Their Role in the Shaping of Urban and Rural Interaction Spheres', in Joyce Marcus & Jeremy A. Sabloff (eds), *The Ancient City: New Perspectives on Urbanism in the Old and New World* (Santa Fe, NM: School for Advanced Research Press, 2008), pp. 229–46.

Kyrtatas, Dimitris J. 'Domination and Exploitation', in Paul Cartledge, Edward E. Cohen & Lin Foxhall (eds), *Money, Labour and Land: Approaches to the Economies of Ancient Greece* (London/New York: Routledge, 2002), pp. 140–55.

Lafargue, Paul. *Le droit à la paresse: Présentation nouvelle de Maurice Dommanget* (Paris: François Maspéro, 1969).

Laila, Russi M. *The Creation of Wealth: A Tata Story* (Bombay: IBH, 1981).

Laiou, Angeliki E. (ed.). *The Economic History of Byzantium: From the Seventh through the Fifteenth Century*, 3 vols (Dumbarton Oaks: Harvard UP, 2002).

La Lone, Darrell. 'The Inca as a Nonmarket Economy: Supply on Command versus Supply and Demand', in Jonathon E. Ericson & Timothy K. Earle (eds), *Contexts for Prehistoric Exchange* (New York: Academic Press, 1982), pp. 291–316.

La Lone, Darrell. 'Rise, Fall, and Semiperipheral Development in the Andean World-System', *Journal of World-Systems Research*, 6(1) (2000), pp. 67–98.

Lambrecht, Thijs. 'Harvest Work and Labor Market Regulation in Old Regime Northern France', in Thomas Max Safley (ed.), *Labor Before the Industrial Revolution: Work, Technology and their Ecologies in an Age of Early Capitalism* (London/New York: Routledge, 2019), pp. 113–31.

Lan, Yong. 'Three Scroll Maps of the Jinshajiang and the Qing State Copper Transport System', in Nanny Kim & Keiko Nagase-Reimer (eds), *Mining, Monies, and Culture in Early Modern Societies: East Asian and Global Perspectives* (Leiden/Boston: Brill, 2013), pp. 329–47.

Lancy, David F. *The Anthropology of Childhood: Cherubs, Chattel, Changelings*, 2nd edn (Cambridge: CUP, 2015).

Langergraber, Kevin E. et al. 'Generation Times in Wild Chimpanzees and Gorillas Suggest Earlier Divergence Times in Great Ape and Human Evolution', *PNAS*, 109(39) (25 September 2012), pp. 15716–21.

Lardinois, Roland. 'Pouvoirs d'État et dénombrements de la population dans le monde indien (fin XVIIe–début XIXe siècle)', *Annales-HSS* (March–April 2002), 2, pp. 407–31.

Lau, George F. *Ancient Alterity in the Andes* (London/New York: Routledge, 2013).

Launaro, Alessandro. 'The Nature of the Village Economy', in Paul Erdkamp, Koen Verboven & Arjan Zuiderhoek (eds), *Ownership and Exploitation of Land and Natural Resources in the Roman World* (Oxford: OUP, 2015), pp. 173–206.

Lawlor, Ellis, Helen Kersley & Susan Steed. *A Bit Rich? Calculating the Real Value to Society of Different Professions* (London: The New Economic Foundation, 2009).

Lazonick, William. *Competitive Advantage on the Shop Floor* (Cambridge, MA: Harvard UP, 1990).

Lee, Cheol-Sung. *When Solidarity Works: Labor-Civic Networks and Welfare States in the Market Reform Era* (Cambridge: CUP, 2016).

Lee, Richard B. & Richard Daly (eds). *The Cambridge Encyclopedia of Hunters and Gatherers* (Cambridge: CUP, 2004).

Leeuwen, Bas van & Jieli van Leeuwen-Li. 'Education since 1820', in Jan Luiten van Zanden et al. (eds), *How Was Life? Global Well-Being Since 1820* (Geneva/Amsterdam: OECD/CLIO INFRA, 2014), pp. 87–100.

Leeuwen, Marco H.D. van. *Mutual Insurance 1550–2015: From Guild Welfare and Friendly Societies to Contemporary Micro-Insurers* (London: Palgrave Macmillan, 2016).

Leick, Gwendolyn. *Mesopotamia: The Invention of the City* (London: Penguin, 2002).

Lenger, Friedrich. 'Beyond Exceptionalism: Notes on the Artisanal Phase of the Labour Movement in France, England, Germany and the United States', *IRSH*, 36 (1991), pp. 1–23.

Leonard, William R., Marcia L. Robertson & J. Josh Snodgrass. 'Energetics and the Evolution of Brain Size in Early *Homo*', in Wil Roebroeks (ed.), *Guts and Brains: An Integrative Approach to the Hominin Record* (Leiden: Leiden UP, 2007), pp. 29–46.

Levi, Scott C. 'Hindus beyond the Hindu Kush: Indians in the Central Asian Slave Trade', *Journal of the Royal Asiatic Society*, Series 3, 12(3) (2002), pp. 277–88.

Lewis, David M. *Greek Slave Systems in their Eastern Mediterranean Context, c. 800–146 BC* (Oxford: OUP, 2018).

Lewis, Mark E. 'Early Imperial China, from the Qin and Han through Tang', in Andrew Monson & Walter Scheidel (eds), *Fiscal Regimes and the Political Economy of Premodern States* (Cambridge: CUP, 2015), pp. 282–307.

Li, Ju. 'Contentious Politics of a Generation of State Workers in China since the 1960s', *IRSH*, 61 (2016), pp. 197–222.

Li, Shi & Hiroshi Sato. *Unemployment, Inequality and Poverty in Urban China* (London/New York: Routledge, 2006).

Li Bozhong. 'Was there a "Fourteenth-Century Turning Point"? Population, Land, Technology, and Farm Management', in Paul J. Smith & Richard von Glahn (eds), *The Song-Yuan-Ming Transition in Chinese History* (Cambridge, MA: Harvard UP, 2003), pp. 135–75.

Liebenberg, Louis. 'Persistence Hunting by Modern Hunter-Gatherers', *Current Anthropology*, 47(6) (December 2006), pp. 1017–26.

Lieberman, Victor. *Strange Parallels: Southeast Asia in Global Context, c. 800–1830, Vol. 1: Integration on the Mainland* (Cambridge, CUP: 2003).

Lin, Man-hough. 'The Devastation of the Qing Mints, 1821–1850', in Jane Kate Leonard & Ulrich Theobald (eds), *Money in Asia (1200–1900): Small Currencies in Social and Political Contexts* (Leiden/Boston: Brill, 2015), pp. 155–87.

Linares, Olga F. 'Robert McC. Netting', in *Biographical Memoirs*, vol. 71 (Washington, DC: The National Academies of Science, Engineering, Medicine, 1997). Available from: https://www.nap.edu/read/5737/chapter/10 (retrieved on 27 July 2020).

Linden, Marcel van der. 'Het westers marxisme en de Sovjetunie: Hoofdlijnen van structurele maatschappijkritiek (1917–1985)', PhD thesis, Universiteit van Amsterdam, 1989.

Linden, Marcel van der (ed.). *Social Security Mutualism: The Comparative History of Mutual Benefit Societies* (Bern: Peter Lang, 1996).

Linden, Marcel van der. 'Forced Labour and Non-Capitalist Industrialization: The Case of Stalinism (c. 1929–c. 1956)', in Tom Brass & Marcel van der Linden (eds), *Free and Unfree Labour: The Debate Continues* (Bern: Peter Lang, 1997a), pp. 351–62.

Linden, Marcel van der. 'The Origins, Spread and Normalization of Free Labour', in Tom Brass & Marcel van der Linden (eds), *Free and Unfree Labour: The Debate Continues* (Bern: Peter Lang, 1997b), pp. 501–23.

Linden, Marcel van der. *Workers of the World: Essays toward a Global Labor History* (Leiden/Boston: Brill, 2008).

Linden, Marcel van der. 'Charles Tilly's Historical Sociology', *IRSH*, 54 (2009), pp. 237–74.

Linden, Marcel van der. 'Re-constructing the Origins of Modern Labor Management', *Labor History*, 51 (2010), pp. 509–22.

Linden, Marcel van der (ed.). *Humanitarian Intervention and Changing Labor Relations: The Long-Term Consequences of the Abolition of the Slave Trade* (Leiden & Boston: Brill, 2011a).

Linden, Marcel van der. 'Studying Attitudes to Work Worldwide, 1500–1650: Concepts, Sources, and Problems of Interpretation', *IRSH*, 56 (2011b, Special Issue), pp. 25–43.

Linden, Marcel van der. 'Dissecting Coerced Labor', in Marcel van der Linden & Magaly Rodríguez García (eds), *On Coerced Labor: Work and Compulsion after Chattel Slavery* (Leiden/Boston: Brill, 2016), pp. 293–322.

Linden, Marcel van der & Jan Lucassen (eds). *Racism and the Labour Market: Historical Studies* (Bern: Peter Lang, 1995).

Linden, Marcel van der & Jan Lucassen. *Prolegomena for a Global Labour History* (Amsterdam: IISH, 1999).

Linden, Marcel van der & Jan Lucassen. *Work Incentives in Historical Perspective: Preliminary Remarks* (Amsterdam: IISH Research Papers 41, 2001).

Linden, Marcel van der & Leo Lucassen (eds). *Working on Labor: Essays in Honor of Jan Lucassen* (Leiden/Boston: Brill, 2012).

Linden, Marcel van der & Richard Price (eds). *The Rise and Development of Collective Labour Law* (Bern: Peter Lang, 2000).

Linden, Marcel van der & Magaly Rodríguez García (eds). *On Coerced Labor: Work and Compulsion after Chattel Slavery* (Leiden/Boston: Brill, 2016).

Linden, Marcel van der & Jürgen Rojahn (eds). *The Formation of Labour Movements 1870–1914: An International Perspective*, 2 vols (Leiden: Brill, 1990).

Linden, Marcel van der & Wayne Thorpe (eds). *Revolutionary Syndicalism: An International Perspective* (Aldershot: Scolar Press, 1990).

Lins, W. 'Arbeitsmarkt und Arbeitsnachweis', in *Handwörterbuch der Staatswissenschaften*, Vol. I (Jena: Fischer, 1923), pp. 824–39.

Lipartito, Kenneth. 'Reassembling the Economic: New Departures in Historical Materialism', *American Historical Review* (February 2016), pp. 101–39.

Lis, Catharina. 'Perceptions of Work in Classical Antiquity: A Polyphonic Heritage', in Joseph Ehmer & Catharina Lis (eds), *The Idea of Work in Europe from Antiquity to Modern Times* (Farnham: Ashgate, 2009), pp. 33–68.

Lis, Catharina, Jan Lucassen & Hugo Soly (eds). *Before the Unions: Wage Earners and Collective Action in Europe, 1300–1850, IRSH*, 39(2) (1994).

Lis, Catharina & Hugo Soly. *Poverty and Capitalism in Pre-Industrial Europe* (Hassocks, Sussex: Harvester Press, 1979).

Lis, Catharina & Hugo Soly. '"An Irresistible Phalanx": Journeymen Associations in Western Europe, 1300–1800', *IRSH*, 39(2) (1994), pp. 11–52.

Lis, Catharina & Hugo Soly. 'Städtische Industrialisierungswege in Brabant und Flandern: De Heyder & Co. in Lier (1750 bis 1815)', in Dietrich Ebeling & Wolfgang Mager (eds), *Protoindustrie in der Region, Europäische Gewerbelandschaften vom 16. bis zum 19. Jahrhundert* (Bielefeld: Verlag für Regionalgeschichte, 1997), pp. 297–319.

Lis, Catharina & Hugo Soly. *Worthy Efforts: Attitudes to Work and Workers in Pre-Industrial Europe* (Leiden/Boston: Brill, 2012).

488

Liu, Le, Shaodong Zhai & Xingcan Chen. 'Production of Ground Stone Tools at Taosi and Huizui: A Comparison', in Anne P. Underhill (ed.), *A Companion to Chinese Archaeology* (Hoboken, NJ: Wiley-Blackwell, 2013).

Livingston, James. *No More Work: Why Full Employment is a Bad Idea* (Chapel Hill: University of North Carolina Press, 2016).

Löbker, Gerard, Hans van den Broek & Hans Morssinkhof. *Bij Stork* (Zwolle: WBooks, 2018).

Looijesteijn, Henk. "Born to the Common Welfare": Pieter Plockhoy's Quest for a Christian Life (c. 1620–1664)', PhD thesis, European University Institute Florence, November 2009.

Looijesteijn, Henk. 'Between Sin and Salvation: The Seventeenth-Century Dutch Artisan Pieter Plockhoy and his Ethics of Work', *IRSH*, 56 (2011), pp. 69–88.

Loomis, William T. *Wages, Welfare Costs and Inflation in Classical Athens* (Ann Arbor: University of Michigan Press, 1998).

Loprieno, Antonio. 'Slaves', in Sergio Donadoni (ed.), *The Egyptians* (Chicago/London: University of Chicago Press, 1997), pp. 185–219.

Lottum, Jelle van, Jan Lucassen & Lex Heerma van Voss. 'Sailors, National and International Labour Markets and National Identity, 1600–1850', in Richard W. Unger (ed.), *Shipping and Economic Growth 1350–1850* (Leiden/Boston: Brill, 2011), pp. 309–51.

Lourens, Piet & Jan Lucassen. 'Marx als Historiker der niederländischen Republik', in Marcel van der Linden (ed.), *Die Rezeption der Marxschen Theorie in den Niederlanden* (Trier: Schriften aus dem Karl-Marx-Haus, 1992), pp. 430–54.

Lourens, Piet & Jan Lucassen. *Arbeitswanderung und berufliche Spezialisierung: Die lippischen Ziegler im 18. und 19. Jahrhundert* (Osnabrück: Rasch, 1999).

Lourens, Piet & Jan Lucassen. 'Labour Mediation among Seasonal Workers, Particularly the Lippe Brickmakers, 1650–1900', in Sigrid Wadauer, Thomas Buchner & Alexander Mejstrik (eds), *History of Labour Intermediation: Institutions and Finding Employment in the Nineteenth and Early Twentieth Centuries* (New York/Oxford: Berghahn, 2015), pp. 335–67.

Lourens, Piet & Jan Lucassen. 'Die lippischen Ziegler um 1800', in Bettina Joergens & Jan Lucassen (eds), *Saisonale Arbeitsmigration in der Geschichte: Die lippischen Ziegler und ihre Herkunftsgesellschaft* (Essen: Klartext, 2017), pp. 73–88.

Lovejoy, Paul. *Transformations in Slavery: A History of Slavery in Africa* (Cambridge: CUP, 2000).

Lovejoy, Paul. *Slavery, Commerce and Production in the Sokoto Caliphate of West Africa* (Trenton/Asmara: Africa World Press, 2005).

Lovejoy, Paul. 'Slavery in Africa', in Gad Heuman & Trevor Burnard (eds), *The Routledge History of Slavery* (London/New York: Routledge, 2011), pp. 35–51.

Lucassen, Jan. *Migrant Labour in Europe 1600–1900: The Drift to the North Sea* (London: Croom Helm, 1987).

Lucassen, Jan. 'Labour and Early Modern Economic Development', in Karel Davids & Jan Lucassen (eds), *A Miracle Mirrored: The Dutch Republic in European Perspective* (Cambridge: CUP, 1995), pp. 367–409.

Lucassen, Jan. 'In Search of Work', Research paper 39 (Amsterdam: IISH, 2000).

Lucassen, Jan. 'Work Incentives in Historical Perspective: Preliminary Remarks on Terminologies and Taxonomies', in Marcel van der Linden & Jan Lucassen, *Work Incentives in Historical Perspective: Preliminary Remarks* (Amsterdam: IISH, 2001).

Lucassen, Jan. 'Coin Production, Coin Circulation, and the Payment of Wages in Europe and China 1200–1900', in Christine Moll-Murata, Song Jianze & Hans Ulrich Vogel (eds), *Chinese Handicraft Regulations of the Qing Dynasty* (Munich: Iudicium, 2005), pp. 423–46.

Lucassen, Jan (ed.). *Global Labour History: A State of the Art* (Bern: Peter Lang 2006a).

Lucassen, Jan. 'Writing Global Labour History c. 1800–1940: A Historiography of Concepts, Periods and Geographical Scope', in *Global Labour History: A State of the Art* (2006b), pp. 39–89.

Lucassen, Jan. 'Brickmakers in Western Europe (1700–1900) and Northern India (1800–2000): Some Comparisons', in *Global Labour History: A State of the Art* (2006c), pp. 513–62.

Lucassen, Jan. 'Leiden: Garenmarkt. Een land van immigranten', in Maarten Prak (ed.), *Plaatsen van herinnering: Nederland in de zeventiende en achttiende eeuw* (Amsterdam: Bert Bakker, 2006d), pp. 63–73.

Lucassen, Jan (ed.). *Wages and Currency: Global Comparisons from Antiquity to the Twentieth Century* (Bern: Peter Lang, 2007a).

Lucassen, Jan. 'The Brickmakers' Strike on the Ganges Canal 1848–1849', in Rana Behal & Marcel van der Linden (eds), *India's Labouring Poor: Historical Studies, c. 1600–c. 2000* (Delhi: Fountain Books, 2007b), pp. 47–83.

Lucassen, Jan. 'Working at the Ichapur Gunpowder Factory in the 1790s', *Indian Historical Review*, 39(1) (2012a), pp. 45–82 (Part 1) and 39(2) (2012b), pp. 251–71 (Part 2).

Lucassen, Jan. 'Outlines of a History of Labour', Research paper 51 (Amsterdam: IISH, 2013).

Lucassen, Jan. 'Deep Monetization: The Case of the Netherlands 1200–1940', *TSEG*, 11 (2014a), pp. 73–121.

Lucassen, Jan. 'Deep Monetization, Commercialization and Proletarianization: Possible Links, India 1200–1900', in Sabyasachi Bhattacharya (ed.), *Towards a New History of Work* (New Delhi: Tulika, 2014b), pp. 17–55.

Lucassen, Jan. 'Workers: New Developments in Labor History since the 1980s', in Ulbe Bosma & Karin Hofmeester (eds), *The Lifework of a Labor Historian* (Leiden/Boston: Brill, 2018a), pp. 22–46.

Lucassen, Jan. 'Wage Labour', in Karin Hofmeester & Marcel van der Linden (eds), *Handbook of the Global History of Work* (Berlin/Boston: De Gruyter, 2018b), pp. 395–409.

Lucassen, Jan. 'Between Self-Employment and Wage Labour: Co-operative Subcontracting Among Manual Brickmakers c. 1600–1900', in Karin Hofmeester (ed.), *Moving In and Out of Self-Employment: A Labour Relation in Historical Perspective* (2021; forthcoming).

Lucassen, Jan & Leo Lucassen. 'The Mobility Transition in Europe Revisited, 1500–1900: Sources and Methods', Research paper 46 (Amsterdam: IISH, 2010).

Lucassen, Jan & Leo Lucassen (eds). *Globalising Migration History: The Eurasian Experience (16th–21st Centuries)* (Leiden/Boston: Brill, 2014).

Lucassen, Jan, Tine de Moor & Jan Luiten van Zanden (eds). 'The Return of the Guilds', *IRSH*, 53 (Supplement, 2008).

Lucassen, Jan & Richard W. Unger. 'Shipping, Productivity and Economic Growth', in Richard W. Unger (ed.), *Shipping and Economic Growth 1350–1850* (Leiden/Boston: Brill, 2011), pp. 3–44.

Lucassen, Leo. 'Beyond the Migration State: Western Europe since World War II', in James Hollifield & Neil Foley (eds), *Globalizing the Nation State* (Stanford: Stanford UP, 2021; forthcoming).

Lucassen, Leo, Osamu Saito & Ryuto Shimada. 'Cross-Cultural Migrations in Japan in a Comparative Perspective, 1600–2000', in Jan Lucassen & Leo Lucassen (eds), *Globalising Migration History: The Eurasian Experience (16th–21st Centuries)* (Leiden/Boston: Brill, 2014), pp. 262–409.

Luzkow, Jack Lawrence. *The Great Forgetting: The Past, Present and Future of Social Democracy and the Welfare State* (Manchester: Manchester UP, 2015).

MacDonald, Katharine. 'Ecological Hypotheses for Human Brain Evolution: Evidence for Skill and Learning Processes in the Ethnographic Literature on Hunting', in Wil Roebroeks (ed.), *Guts and Brains: An Integrative Approach to the Hominin Record* (Leiden: Leiden UP, 2007a), pp. 107–32.

MacDonald, Katharine. 'Cross-cultural Comparison of Learning in Human Hunting: Implications for Life History Evolution', *Human Nature*, 18 (2007b), pp. 386–402.

MacRaild, Donald M. & David E. Martin. *Labour in British Society, 1830–1914* (Basingstoke: Macmillan, 2000).

Madison, Bernice Q. *Social Welfare in the Soviet Union* (Stanford: Stanford UP, 1968).

Magnusson, Lars. *Nation, State and the Industrial Revolution: The Visible Hand* (London/New York: Routledge, 2009).

Majumdar, Susmita Basu. 'Money Matters: Indigenous and Foreign Coins in the Malabar Coast (Second Century BCE–Second Century CE)', in K.S. Mathew (ed.), *Imperial Rome, Indian Ocean Regions and Muziris: New Perspectives on Maritime Trade* (New Delhi: Manohar, 2015), pp. 395–423.

Malevitsj, Kazimir. *Luiheid als levensdoel: Uit het Russisch vertaald door Ineke Mertens* ('s-Hertogenbosch: Voltaire, 2006).

Mamkoottam, Kuriakose. *Trade Unionism: Myth and Reality. Unionism in the Tata Iron and Steel Company* (Delhi: OUP, 1982).

Mandell, Nikki. *The Corporation as Family: The Gendering of Corporate Welfare, 1890–1930* (Chapel Hill: University of North Carolina Press, 2002).

Mangan, Jane E. *Trading Roles: Gender, Ethnicity, and the Urban Economy in Colonial Potosí* (Durham, NC/London: Duke UP, 2005).

Mann, Charles C. *1491: New Revelations of the Americas Before Columbus* (New York: Knopf, 2006).

Manning, Patrick. *Slavery and African Life: Occidental, Oriental, and African Slave Trades* (Cambridge: CUP, 1990).

Manning, Patrick. *Migration in World History*, 2nd edn (London/New York: Routledge, 2013).

Manning, Patrick. *A History of Humanity: The Evolution of the Human System* (Cambridge: CUP, 2020).

Marino, S., J. Roosblad & R. Penninx (eds). *Trade Unions and Migrant Workers: New Contexts and Challenges in Europe* (Cheltenham: Edward Elgar, 2017).

Mason, T.W. 'Labour in the Third Reich, 1933–1939', *Past & Present*, 33 (1966), pp. 112–41.

Mathew, K.S. (ed.). *Imperial Rome, Indian Ocean Regions and Muziris: New Perspectives on Maritime Trade* (New Delhi: Manohar, 2015).

Mathias, Regine. 'Picture Scrolls as a Historical Source on Japanese Mining', in Nanny Kim & Keiko Nagase-Reimer (eds), *Mining, Monies, and Culture in Early Modern Societies: East Asian and Global Perspectives* (Leiden/Boston, Brill, 2013), pp. 311–28.

490

Matsuura, Akira. 'The Import of Chinese Sugar in the Nagasaki Junk Trade and its Impact', in Keiko Nagase-Reimer (ed.), *Copper in the Early Modern Sino-Japanese Trade* (Leiden/Boston: Brill, 2016), pp. 157–74.

Matthews, Roger. *The Archaeology of Mesopotamia: Theory and Approaches* (London/New York: Routledge, 2003).

Maurer, Bill. 'The Anthropology of Money', *Annual Review of Anthropology*, 35 (2006), pp. 15–36.

Mazumdar, B.P. 'New Forms of Specialisation in Industries of Eastern India in the Turko-Afghan Period', *Proceedings of Indian History Congress*, 31 (1969), pp. 226–33.

Mbeki, Linda & Matthias van Rossum. 'Private Slave Trade in the Dutch Indian Ocean World: A Study into the Networks and Backgrounds of the Slavers and the Enslaved in South Asia and South Africa', *Slavery & Abolition*, 38 (2016), pp. 95–116.

McAuley, A. 'The Welfare State in the USSR', in Thomas Wilson & Dorothy Wilson (eds), *The State and Social Welfare: The Objectives of Policy* (London/New York: Routledge, 1991), pp. 191–213.

McBee, Randy. 'Work and Leisure', in Daniel J. Walkowitz (ed.), *A Cultural History of Work in the Modern Age* (London: Bloomsbury, 2019), pp. 157–72.

McConvell, Patrick. 'The Archaeo-Linguistics of Migration', in Jan Lucassen, Leo Lucassen & Patrick Manning (eds), *Migration History in World History: Multidisciplinary Approaches* (Leiden/Boston: Brill, 2010), pp. 155–88.

McCorriston, Joyce. 'Textile Extensification, Alienation, and Social Stratification in Ancient Mesopotamia', *Current Anthropology*, 38(4) (1997), pp. 517–35.

McCreery, David J. 'Wage Labor, Free Labor, and Vagrancy Laws: The Transition to Capitalism in Guatemala, 1920–1945', in Tom Brass & Marcel van der Linden (eds), *Free and Unfree Labour: The Debate Continues* (Bern: Peter Lang, 1997), pp. 303–24.

McCreery, David J. *The Sweat of Their Brow: A History of Work in Latin America* (New York/London: Sharpe, 2000).

McKitterick, Rosamond. *Charlemagne: The Formation of a European Identity* (Cambridge: CUP, 2008).

McNeill, William. *Keeping Together in Time: Dance and Drill in Human History* (Cambridge, MA: Harvard UP, 1995).

Meisenzahl, Ralf R. 'How Britain Lost its Competitive Edge', in Avner Greif, Lynne Kiesling & John V.C. Nye (eds), *Institutions, Innovation, and Industrialization: Essays in Economic History and Development* (Princeton/Oxford: Princeton UP, 2015), pp. 307–35.

Meissner, Martin, Stuart B. Philpott & Diana Philpott. 'The Sign Language of Sawmill Workers in British Columbia', in *Sign Language Studies*, 9 (Winter 1975), pp. 291–308.

Meuwese, Mark. *Brothers in Arms, Partners in Trade: Dutch-Indigenous Alliances in the Atlantic World, 1595–1674* (Leiden & Boston: Brill, 2012).

Meyer, Stephen. 'The Political Culture of Work', in Daniel J. Walkowitz (ed.), *A Cultural History of Work in the Modern Age* (London: Bloomsbury, 2019), pp. 141–56.

Mieroop, Marc van de. *A History of the Ancient Near East ca. 3000–323 BC*, 2nd edn (Malden/Oxford/Carlton: Blackwell, 2007).

Migeotte, Léopold. *The Economy of the Greek Cities: From the Archaic Period to the Early Roman Empire* (Berkeley: University of California Press, 2009).

Milanich, Jerald T. *The Timucua* (Oxford: Blackwell, 1996).

Milanovic, Branko. *Capitalism, Alone: The Future of the System that Rules the World* (Cambridge, MA: Belknap Press, 2019).

Miller, Owen. 'Ties of Labour and Ties of Commerce: Corvée among Seoul Merchants in the Late 19th Century', *JESHO*, 50(1) (2007), pp. 41–71.

Milton, Katherine. 'Civilizations and its Discontents', *Natural History*, 101(3) (1992), pp. 36–43.

Mitch, David, John Brown & Marco H.D. van Leeuwen (eds). *Origins of the Modern Career* (Aldershot: Ashgate, 2004).

Mithen, Steven. *After the Ice: A Global Human History, 20,000–5000 BC* (Cambridge, MA: Harvard UP, 2003).

Mokyr, Joel. *The Gifts of Athena: Historical Origins of the Knowledge Economy* (Princeton: Princeton UP, 2002).

Mokyr, Joel. 'Peer Vries's Great Divergence', *TSEG*, 12 (2015), pp. 93–104.

Molfenter, Christine. 'Forced Labour and Institutional Change in Contemporary India', in Marcel van der Linden & Magaly Rodríguez García (eds), *On Coerced Labor: Work and Compulsion after Chattel Slavery* (Leiden/Boston: Brill, 2016), pp. 50–70.

Moll-Murata, Christine. 'State and Crafts in the Qing Dynasty (1644–1911)', Habilitation thesis, Universität Tübingen, 2008a.

Moll-Murata, Christine. 'Chinese Guilds from the Seventeenth to the Twentieth Centuries: An Overview', in Tine de Moor, Jan Lucassen & Jan Luiten van Zanden (eds), 'The Return of the Guilds', *IRSH*, 53, Supplement 16 (2008b), pp. 5–18.

Moll-Murata, Christine. 'Guilds and Apprenticeship in China and Europe: The Jingdezhen and European Ceramics Industries', in Maarten Prak & Jan Luiten van Zanden (eds), *Technology, Skills and the Pre-Modern Economy in the East and the West. Essays Dedicated to the Memory of S.R. Epstein* (Leiden/Boston: Brill, 2013), pp. 205–57.

Moll-Murata, Christine. 'Legal Conflicts Concerning Wage Payments in Eighteenth- and Nineteenth-Century China: The Baxian Cases', in Jane Kate Leonard & Ulrich Theobald (eds), *Money in Asia (1200–1900): Small Currencies in Social and Political Contexts* (Leiden/Boston: Brill, 2015), pp. 265–308.

Moll-Murata, Christine. *State and Crafts in the Qing Dynasty (1644–1911)* (Amsterdam: Amsterdam UP, 2018).

Moll-Murata, Christine, Song Jianze & Hans Ulrich Vogel (eds). *Chinese Handicraft Regulations of the Qing Dynasty* (Munich: Iudicium, 2005).

Monroe, J. Cameron. 'Power and Agency in Precolonial African States', *Annual Review of Anthropology*, 42 (2013), pp. 17–35.

Monson, Andrew & Walter Scheidel (eds). *Fiscal Regimes and the Political Economy of Premodern States* (Cambridge: CUP, 2015).

Montgomery, David. *The Fall of the House of Labor: The Workplace, the State, and American Labor Activism, 1865–1925* (Cambridge: CUP, 1987).

Montgomery, David. *Citizen Worker: The Experience of Workers in the United States with Democracy and the Free Market in the Nineteenth Century* (Cambridge: CUP, 1993).

Moon, David. 'Peasant Migration, the Abolition of Serfdom, and the Internal Passport System in the Russian Empire c. 1800–1914', in David Eltis (ed.), *Coerced and Free Migration: Global Perspectives* (Stanford: Stanford UP, 2002), pp. 324–57.

Moor, Tine de & Jan Luiten van Zanden. *Vrouwen en de geboorte van het kapitalisme in West-Europa* (Amsterdam: Boom, 2006).

Moor, Tine de, Jan Lucassen & Jan Luiten van Zanden. 'The Return of the Guilds: Towards a Global History of the Guilds in Pre-Industrial Times', *IRSH*, 53, Supplement 16 (2008), pp. 5–18.

Mooring, J.A., Bas van Leeuwen & R.J. van der Spek. 'Introducing Coinage: Comparing the Greek World, the Near East and China', in R.J. van der Spek & Bas van Leeuwen (eds), *Money, Currency and Crisis: In Search of Trust, 2000 BC to AD 2000* (London/New York: Routledge, 2018), pp. 132–48.

Moosvi, Shireen. 'The world of labour in Mughal India (c. 1500–1750)', *IRSH*, 56, Supplement 19 (2011), pp. 245–61.

More, Thomas. *Utopia: Latin Text and English Translation*, edited by George M. Logan, Robert M. Adams & Clarence H. Miller (Cambridge: CUP, 1995).

Moreno García, Juan Carlos. 'La dépendance rurale en Égypte ancienne', *JESHO*, 51 (2008), pp. 99–150.

Morgan, T.J.H. et al. 'Experimental Evidence for the Co-evolution of Hominin Tool-Making Teaching and Language', *Nature Communications*, 6, 6029 (2015).

Morris, Craig. 'Links in the Chain of Inka Cities: Communication, Alliance, and the Cultural Production of Status, Value and Power', in Joyce Marcus & Jeremy A. Sabloff (eds), *The Ancient City: New Perspectives on Urbanism in the Old and New World* (Santa Fe, NM: School for Advanced Research Press, 2008), pp. 299–319.

Morrison, Cécile. 'Byzantine Money: Its Production and Circulation', in Angeliki E. Laiou (ed.), *The Economic History of Byzantium: From the Seventh to the Fifteenth Century* (Washington, DC: Dumbarton Oaks, 2002), pp. 909–66.

Morrison, Cécile & Jean-Claude Cheynet. 'Prices and Wages in the Byzantine World', in Angeliki E. Laiou (ed.), *The Economic History of Byzantium: From the Seventh to the Fifteenth Century* (Washington, DC: Dumbarton Oaks, 2002), pp. 815–77.

Morrison, Kathleen D. & Carla M. Sinopoli. 'Production and Landscape in the Vijayanagara Metropolitan Region: Contributions to the Vijayanagara Metropolitan Survey', in J.M. Fritz, R.P. Brubaker & T.P. Raczek (eds), *Vijayanagara: Archaeological Exploration, 1999–2000* (New Delhi: Manohar, 2006), pp. 423–36.

Moya, Ismaël. *De l'argent aux valeurs: Femmes, économie et société à Dakar* (Paris: Société d'ethnologie, 2017).

Moya Pons, Frank. *History of the Caribbean: Plantations, Trade and War in the Atlantic World* (Princeton: Markus Wiener, 2007).

Muaze, Mariana. 'Ruling the Household: Masters and Domestic Slaves in the Paraíba Valley, Brazil, during the Nineteenth Century', in Dale W. Tomich (ed.), *New Frontiers of Slavery* (New York: SUNY Press, 2016), pp. 203–24.

Mukherjee, Tilottama. *Political Culture and Economy in Eighteenth-Century Bengal: Networks of Exchange, Consumption and Communication* (New Delhi: Orient Black Swan, 2013).

Muldrew, Craig. *Food, Energy and the Creation of Industriousness: Work and Material Culture in Agrarian England, 1550–1780* (Cambridge: CUP, 2011).

Mussi, Margherita. 'Women of the Middle Latitudes: The Earliest Peopling of Europe from a Female Perspective', in Wil Roebroeks (ed.), *Guts and Brains: An Integrative Approach to the Hominin Record* (Leiden: Leiden UP, 2007), pp. 165–83.

Nagase-Reimer, Keiko. 'Water Drainage in the Mines in Tokugawa Japan: Technological Improvements and Economic Limitations', in Nanny Kim & Keiko Nagase-Reimer (eds), *Mining, Monies, and Culture in Early Modern Societies: East Asian and Global Perspectives* (Leiden/Boston: Brill, 2013), pp. 25–42.

Nagase-Reimer, Keiko. 'Introduction', in *Copper in the Early Modern Sino-Japanese Trade* (Leiden/Boston: Brill, 2016), pp. 1–9.

Nagata, Mary Louise. *Labor Contracts and Labor Relations in Early Modern Central Japan* (London/New York: Routledge Curzon, 2005).

Nash, George. 'Assessing Rank and Warfare-Strategy in Prehistoric Hunter-Gatherer Society: A Study of Representational Warrior Figures in Rock-Art from the Spanish Levant, Southeast Spain', in Mike Parker Pearson & I.J.N. Thorpe (eds), *Warfare, Violence and Slavery: Proceedings of a Prehistoric Society Conference at Sheffield University* (Oxford: BAR Publishing, 2005), pp. 75–86.

Nasr, Seyyed Hossein. 'Islamic Work Ethics', in Jaroslav Pellikan, Joseph Kitagawa & Seyyed Hossein Nasr, *Comparative Work Ethics: Judeo-Christian, Islamic, and Eastern* (Washington, DC: Library of Congress, 1985), pp. 51–62.

Nederveen Meerkerk, Elise van. 'Segmentation in the Pre-Industrial Labour Market: Women's Work in the Dutch Textile Industry, 1581–1810', *IRSH*, 51 (2006), pp. 189–216.

Nederveen Meerkerk, Elise van. 'De draad in eigen handen: Vrouwen en loonarbeid in de Nederlandse textielnijverheid, 1581–1810', PhD thesis, Free University Amsterdam, 2007.

Nederveen Meerkerk, Elise van. 'Couples Cooperating? Dutch Textile Workers, Family Labour and the "Industrious Revolution", c. 1600–1800', *Continuity and Change*, 23 (2008), pp. 237–66.

Nederveen Meerkerk, Elise van. 'Market wage or discrimination? The Remuneration of Male and Female Wool Spinners in the Seventeenth-Century Dutch Republic', *EHR*, 63 (2010), pp. 165–86.

Netting, Robert McC. *Smallholders, Householders: Farm Families and the Ecology of Intensive, Sustainable Agriculture* (Stanford: Stanford UP, 1993).

Nieboer, H.J. *Slavery as an Industrial System: Ethnological Researches* (The Hague: Nijhoff, 1910).

Noordegraaf, L. *Hollands welvaren? Levensstandaard in Holland 1450–1650* (Bergen: Octavo,1985).

al-Nubi, Sheikh 'Ibada. 'Soldiers', in Sergio Donadoni (ed.), *The Egyptians* (Chicago/London: University of Chicago Press, 1997), pp. 31–59.

Nunn, Patrick. *The Edge of Memory: Ancient Stories, Oral Tradition and the Post-Glacial World* (London: Bloomsbury Sigma, 2018).

Nystrom, Pia. 'Aggression and Nonhuman Primates', in Mike Parker Pearson & I.J.N. Thorpe (eds), *Warfare, Violence and Slavery: Proceedings of a Prehistoric Society Conference at Sheffield University* (Oxford: BAR Publishing, 2005), pp. 35–40.

O'Brien, Patrick & Kent Deng. 'Can the Debate on the Great Divergence be Located Within the Kuznetsian Paradigm for an Empirical Form of Global Economic History?', *TSEG*, 12 (2015), pp. 63–78.

Ockinga, Boyo G. 'Morality and Ethics', in Toby Wilkinson (ed.), *The Egyptian World* (London/New York: Routledge, 2007), pp. 252–62.

Ogilvie, Sheilagh. '"Whatever is, is right"? Economic institutions in pre-industrial Europe', *EHR*, 60 (2007), pp. 649–84.

Ogilvie, Sheilagh & Markus Cerman (eds). *European Proto-Industrialization* (Cambridge: CUP, 1996).

Ohler, Norman. *Der totale Rausch: Drogen im Dritten Reich* (Cologne: Kiepenheuer & Witsch, 2015).

Oka, Rahul & Chapurukha M. Kusimba. 'The Archaeology of Trade Systems. Part 1: Towards a New Trade Synthesis', *Journal of Archaeological Research*, 16 (2008), pp. 339–95.

Olivelle, Patrick & Donald R. Davis Jr (eds). *Hindu Law: A New History of Dharmasastra* (Oxford: OUP, 2018).

Olsen, Wendy K. 'Marxist and Neo-Classical Approaches to Unfree Labour in India', in Tom Brass & Marcel van der Linden (eds), *Free and Unfree Labour: The Debate Continues* (Bern: Peter Lang, 1997), pp. 379–403.

Olszak, Norbert. 'The Historical Development of Collective Labour Law in France', in Marcel van der Linden & Richard Price (eds), *The Rise and Development of Collective Labour Law* (Bern: Peter Lang, 2000), pp. 141–54.

Ott, Undine. 'Europas Sklavinnen und Sklaven im Mittelalter: Eine Spurensuche in Osten des Kontinents', *WerkstattGeschichte*, 23(1–2) (March 2015), pp. 31–53.

Paesie, Ruud. 'Zeeuwen en de slavenhandel: Een kwantitatieve analyse', *Zeeland*, 19(1) (2010), pp. 2–13.

Paesie, Ruud. *Slavenopstand op de Neptunus: Kroniek van een wanhoopsdaad* (Zutphen: Walburg Pers, 2016).

Pagel, Mark. *Wired for Culture: Origins of the Human Social Mind* (New York/London: W.W. Norton, 2012).

Pahl, R.E. (ed.). *On Work: Historical, Comparative and Theoretical Approaches* (Oxford: Basil Blackwell, 1988).

Pallaver, Karin. 'Population Developments and Labor Relations in Tanzania: Sources, Shifts and Continuities from 1800 to 2000', *History in Africa*, 41 (2014), pp. 307–35.

Palmer, David. 'Foreign Forced Labor at Mitsubishi's Nagasaki and Hiroshima Shipyard: Big Business, Militarized Government, and the Absence of Shipbuilding Workers' Rights in World War II Japan', in Marcel van der Linden & Magaly Rodríguez García (eds), *On Coerced Labor: Work and Compulsion after Chattel Slavery* (Leiden/Boston: Brill, 2016), pp. 159–84.

Pandya, Vishvajit. 'The Andaman Islanders of the Bay of Bengal', in Richard B. Lee & Richard Daly (eds), *The Cambridge Encyclopedia of Hunters and Gatherers* (Cambridge: CUP, 2004), pp. 243–7.

Parasher-Sen, Aloka. 'Naming and Social Exclusion: The Potcast and the Outsider', in Patrick Olivelle (ed.), *Between the Empires: Society in India 300 BCE to 400 CE* (Oxford: OUP, 2006), pp. 415–55.

Parker Pearson, Mike. 'Warfare, Violence and Slavery in Later Prehistory: An Introduction', in Mike Parker Pearson & I.J.N. Thorpe (eds), *Warfare, Violence and Slavery: Proceedings of a Prehistoric Society Conference at Sheffield University* (Oxford: BAR Publishing, 2005), pp. 19–33.

Parker Pearson, Mike & I.J.N. Thorpe (eds). *Warfare, Violence and Slavery: Proceedings of a Prehistoric Society Conference at Sheffield University* (Oxford: BAR Publishing, 2005).

Parthasarathi, Prasannan. *The Transition to a Colonial Economy: Weavers, Merchants and Kings in South India 1720–1800* (Cambridge: CUP, 2001).

Parthasarathi, Prasannan. *Why Europe Grew Rich and Asia Did Not: Global Economic Divergence, 1600–1850* (Cambridge: CUP, 2011).

Patel, Kiran Klaus. *Soldiers of Labor: Labor Service in Nazi Germany and New Deal America, 1933–1945* (Cambridge: CUP, 2005).

Pawley, Andrew. 'Prehistoric Migration and Colonization Processes in Oceania: A View from Historical Linguistics and Archeology', in Jan Lucassen, Leo Lucassen & Patrick Manning (eds), *Migration History in World History: Multidisciplinary Approaches* (Leiden/Boston: Brill, 2010), pp. 77–112.

Pearson, M.N. *Pious Passengers: The Hajj in Earlier Times* (New Delhi: Sterling Publishers, 1994).

Peebles, Gustav. 'The Anthropology of Credit and Debt', *Annual Review of Anthropology*, 39 (2010), pp. 225–40.

Pelling, Henry. *A History of British Trade Unionism* (Harmondsworth: Pelican, 1976).

Pemberton, Trevor J. et al. 'Impact of Restricted Marital Practices on Genetic Variation in an Endogamous Gujarati Group', *American Journal of Physical Anthropology*, 149 (2012), pp. 92–103.

Penninx, Rinus & Judith Roosblad. *Trade Unions, Immigration and Immigrants in Europe 1960–1993* (Oxford: Berghahn, 2000).

Perchard, Andrew. 'Workplace Cultures', in Daniel J. Walkowitz (ed.), *A Cultural History of Work in the Modern Age* (London: Bloomsbury, 2019), pp. 77–92.

Pesante, Maria Luisa. 'Slaves, Servants and Wage Earners: Free and Unfree Labour, from Grotius to Blackstone', *History of European Ideas*, 35 (2009), pp. 289–320.

Peterson, Jane. *Sexual Revolutions: Gender and Labor at the Dawn of Agriculture* (Walnut Creek, CA: Altamira Press, 2002).

Petriglieri, Gianpiero. 'We are all Zoombies now, but it has to stop', *Financial Times*, 14 May 2020.

Phillips, William D. Jr. 'The Old World Background of Slavery in the Americas', in Barbara L. Solow (ed.), *Slavery and the Atlantic System* (Cambridge: CUP, 1991), pp. 43–61.

Pierre, M. 'La Transportation', in J.-G. Petit et al. (eds), *Histoire des galères, bagnes et prisons xii-xxes siècles: Introduction à l'histoire pénale de la France* (Toulouse: Privat, 1991), pp. 231–59.

Piketty, Thomas. *Capital in the Twenty-First Century* (Cambridge, MA: Harvard UP, 2014).

Piketty, Thomas. *Capital and Ideology* (Cambridge, MA: Harvard UP, 2019).

Pimlott, J.A.R. *The Englishman's Holiday* (Hassocks: Harvester, 1976).

Pines, Yuri et al. (eds). *Birth of an Empire: The State of Qin Revisited* (Berkeley: University of California Press, 2014).

Pirngruber, Reinhard Wilfried. 'The Impact of Empire on Market Prices in Babylon in the Late Achaemenid and Seleucid Periods c. 400–140 B.C.', PhD dissertation, Free University Amsterdam, 2012.

Pizzolato, Nicola. 'Workers and Revolutionaries at the Twilight of Fordism: The Breakdown of Industrial Relations in the Automobile Plants of Detroit and Turin, 1967–1973', *Labor History*, 45(4) (November 2004), pp. 419–43.

Pizzolato, Nicola. '"As Much in Bondage as they was Before": Unfree Labor During the New Deal (1935–1952)', in Marcel van der Linden & Magaly Rodríguez García (eds), *On Coerced Labor: Work and Compulsion after Chattel Slavery* (Leiden/Boston: Brill, 2016), pp. 208–24.

Polanyi, Karl. *The Great Transformation* (New York/Toronto: Farrar & Rinehart, 1944).

Polanyi, Karl, Conrad M. Arensberg & Harry W. Pearson. *Trade and Market in the Early Empires: Economies in History and Theory* (Glencoe, IL: The Free Press, 1957).

Pollard, Sidney. *The Genesis of Modern Management: A Study of the Industrial Revolution in Great Britain* (London: Edward Arnold, 1965).

Pollock, Sheldon. *The Ends of Man at the End of Premodernity: 2004 Gonda Lecture* (Amsterdam: Royal Netherlands Academy of Arts and Sciences, 2005).

Pomeranz, Kenneth. *The Great Divergence: China, Europe and the Making of the Modern World Economy* (Princeton: Princeton UP, 2000).

Pomeranz, Kenneth. 'Labour-Intensive Industrialization in the Rural Yangzi Delta: Late Imperial Patterns and their Modern Fates', in Gareth Austin & Kaoru Sugihara (eds), *Labour-Intensive Industrialization in Global History* (London/New York: Routledge, 2013), pp. 122–43.

Powell, Adam, Stephen Shennan & Mark G. Thomas. 'Late Pleistocene Demography and the Appearance of Human Behavior', *Science*, 324(5932) (5 June 2009), pp. 1298–1301.

Prak, Maarten. 'Painters, Guilds, and the Market during the Dutch Golden Age', in S.R. Epstein & Maarten Prak (eds), *Guilds, Innovation, and the European Economy, 1400–1800* (Cambridge: CUP, 2008), pp. 143–71.

Prak, Maarten. 'Mega-Structures of the Middle Ages: The Construction of Religious Buildings in Europe and Asia, c.1000–1500', in Maarten Prak & Jan Luiten van Zanden (eds), *Technology, Skills and the Pre-Modern Economy in the East and the West. Essays Dedicated to the Memory of S.R. Epstein* (Leiden/Boston: Brill, 2013), pp. 131–59.

Prak, Maarten. *Citizens without Nations: Urban Citizenship in Europe and the World c. 1000–1789* (Cambridge: CUP, 2018).

Prak, Maarten, Catharina Lis, Jan Lucassen & Hugo Soly (eds). *Craft Guilds in the Early Modern Low Countries: Work, Power, and Representation* (Aldershot: Ashgate, 2006).

Prak, Maarten & Patrick Wallis (eds). *Apprenticeship in Early Modern Europe* (Cambridge: CUP, 2020).

Prestes Carneiro, Gabriela et al. 'Pre-Hispanic Fishing Practices in Interfluvial Amazonia: Zooarchaeological Evidence from Managed Landscapes on the Llanos de Mojos Savanna', *PLOS ONE*, 14(5) (15 May 2019).

Price, T. Douglas & Ofer Bar-Yosef. 'The Origins of Agriculture: New Data, New Ideas', *Current Anthropology*, 52(S4) (October 2011), pp. S163–74.

Price, T. Douglas & Ofer Bar-Yosef. 'Traces of Inequality and the Origins of Agriculture in the Ancient Near East', in T. Douglas Price & Gary M. Feinman (eds), *Pathways to Power: New Perspectives on the Emergence of Social Inequality* (New York: Springer, 2012), pp. 147–68.

Price, T. Douglas & Gary M. Feinman (eds). *Pathways to Power: New Perspectives on the Emergence of Social Inequality* (New York: Springer, 2012).

Pun, Ngai & Lu Huilin. 'Unfinished Proletarianization: Self, Anger, and Class Action among the Second Generation of Peasant-Workers in Present-Day China', *Modern China*, 36(5) (2010), pp. 493–519.

Pyburn, K. Anne. 'Pomp and Circumstance before Belize: Ancient Maya Commerce and the New River Conurbation', in Joyce Marcus & Jeremy A. Sabloff (eds), *The Ancient City: New Perspectives on Urbanism in the Old and New World* (Santa Fe, NM: School for Advanced Research Press, 2008), pp. 477–95.

Raghavan, T.C.A. *Attendant Lords: Bairam Khan and Abdur Rahim, Courtiers & Poets in Mughal India* (New Delhi: HarperCollins, 2017).

Rahikainen, Marjatta. *Centuries of Child Labour: European Experiences from the Seventeenth to the Twentieth Century* (Aldershot: Ashgate, 2004).

Ramaswami, Shankar. 'Masculinity, Respect, and the Tragic: Themes of Proletarian Humor in Contemporary Industrial Delhi', in Rana Behal & Marcel van der Linden (eds), *India's Labouring Poor: Historical Studies, c. 1600–c. 2000* (Delhi: Fountain Books, 2007), pp. 203–27.

Ramaswamy, Vijaya. 'Vishwakarma Craftsmen in Early Medieval Peninsular India', *JESHO*, 47 (2004), pp. 548–78.

Ramaswamy, Vijaya. 'Gender and the Writing of South Indian History', in Sabyasachi Bhattacharya (ed.), *Approaches to History: Essays in Indian Historiography* (New Delhi: ICHR, 2011), pp. 199–224.

Ramaswamy, Vijaya. 'Mapping Migrations of South Indian Weavers Before, During and After the Vijayanagar Period: Thirteenth to Eighteenth Centuries', in Jan Lucassen & Leo Lucassen (eds), *Globalising Migration History: The Eurasian Experience (16th–21st Centuries)* (Leiden/Boston: Brill, 2014), pp. 91–121.

Rathbone, Dominic. *Economic Rationalism and Rural Society in Third-Century* A.D. *Egypt: The Heroninos Archive and the Appianus Estate* (Cambridge: CUP, 1991).

Ray, Himanshu Prabha. *Monastery and Guild: Commerce under the Satavahanas* (Delhi: OUP, 1986).

Ray, Himanshu Prabha. *The Archaeology of Seafaring in Ancient South Asia* (Cambridge: CUP, 2003).

Ray, Himanshu Prabha. 'Inscribed Pots, Emerging Identities: The Social Milieu of Trade', in Patrick Olivelle (ed.), *Between the Empires: Society in India 300 BCE to 400 CE* (Oxford: OUP, 2006), pp. 130–43.

Ray, Indrajit. *Bengal Industries and the British Industrial Revolution (1757–1857)* (London/New York: Routledge, 2011).

Reden, Sitta von. *Money in Ptolemaic Egypt: From the Macedonian Conquest to the End of the Third Century BC* (Cambridge: CUP, 2007).

Reden, Sitta von. *Money in Classical Antiquity* (Cambridge: CUP, 2010).

Rediker, Marcus. *Between the Devil and the Deep Blue Sea: Merchant Seamen, Pirates and the Anglo-American Maritime World, 1700–1750* (Cambridge: CUP, 1987).

Reich, David. *Who We Are and How We Got There: Ancient DNA and the New Science of the Human Past* (New York: Pantheon, 2018).

Reid, Anthony. *Southeast Asia in the Age of Commerce 1450–1680: Volume One. The Lands below the Winds* (Chiangmai: Silkworm Books, 1998).

Reid, Anthony. *Charting the Shape of Early Modern Southeast Asia* (Chiangmai: Silkworm Books, 1999).

Reinhardt, Max. *Gesellschaftspolitische Ordnungsvorstellungen der SPD-Flügel seit 1945: Zwischen sozialistischer Transformation, linkem Reformismus und Marktideologie* (Baden-Baden: Nomos, 2014).

Reininghaus, Wilfried (ed.). *Zunftlandschaften in Deutschland und den Niederlanden im Vergleich* (Münster: Aschendorf, 2000).

Reith, Reinhold. 'Circulation of Skilled Labour in Late Medieval and Early Modern Central Europe', in S.R. Epstein & Maarten Prak (eds), *Guilds, Innovation, and the European Economy, 1400–1800* (Cambridge: CUP, 2008), pp. 114–42.

Renwick, Chris. *Bread for All: The Origins of the Welfare State* (London: Allen Lane, 2017).

Ribeiro da Silva, Filipa. *Dutch and Portuguese in Western Africa: Empires, Merchants and the Atlantic System, 1580–1674* (Leiden & Boston: Brill, 2012).

Richards, E. 'Migration to Colonial Australia: Paradigms and Disjunctions', in Jan Lucassen & Leo Lucassen (eds), *Migration, Migration History: Old Paradigms and New Perspectives* (Bern: Peter Lang, 1996), pp. 151–76.

Richards, John F. 'The Economic History of the Lodi Period: 1451–1526', in Sanjay Subrahmanyam (ed.), *Money and the Market in India 1100–1700* (Delhi: OUP, 1994), pp. 137–55.

Richards, Michael P. 'Diet Shift in the Middle/Upper Palaeolithic Transition in Europe? The Stable Isotope Evidence', in Wil Roebroeks (ed.), *Guts and Brains: An Integrative Approach to the Hominin Record* (Leiden: Leiden UP, 2007), pp. 223–34.

Rider, Christine & Mícheál Thompson (eds). *The Industrial Revolution in Comparative Perspective* (Malabar, FL: Krieger, 2000).

Rieksen, Evert Jan. 'Voetstappen zonder echo: Het oud-Hollandse 2ᵉ/3ᵉ/1ᵉ regiment jagers – 33ᵉ regiment lichte infanterie aan het werk in de Franse Tijd 1806–1814', PhD thesis, Free University Amsterdam, 2020.

Riello, Giorgio & Tirthankar Roy (eds). *How India Clothed the World: The World of South Asian Textiles, 1500–1850* (Leiden/Boston: Brill, 2009).

Rihll, Tracey. 'The Origin and Establishment of Ancient Greek Slavery', in M.L. Bush (ed.), *Serfdom and Slavery: Studies in Legal Bondage* (London/New York: Longman, 1996), pp. 89–111.

Rimlinger, Gaston V. *Welfare Policy and Industrialization in Europe, America and Russia* (New York: Wiley, 1971).

Rio, Alice. *Slavery after Rome, 500–1100* (Oxford: OUP, 2020).

Rival, Laura M. 'Introduction: South America', in Richard B. Lee & Richard Daly (eds), *The Cambridge Encyclopedia of Hunters and Gatherers* (Cambridge: CUP, 2004a), pp. 77–85.

Rival, Laura M. 'The Huaorani', in Richard B. Lee & Richard Daly (eds), *The Cambridge Encyclopedia of Hunters and Gatherers* (Cambridge: CUP, 2004b), pp. 100–4.

Roebroeks, Wil (ed.). *Guts and Brains: An Integrative Approach to the Hominin Record* (Leiden: Leiden UP, 2007).

Roebroeks, Wil. *The Neandertal Experiment* (Leiden: tweeëndertigste Kroon-voordracht, 2010).

Roebroeks, Wil. 'Art on the move', *Nature*, 514 (9 October 2014), pp. 170–1.

Roessingh, H.K. *Inlandse tabak: Expansie en contractie van een handelsgewas in de 17ᵈᵉ en 18ᵈᵉ eeuw in Nederland* (Wageningen: A.A.G. Bijdragen 20, 1976).

Romer, John. *A History of Ancient Egypt: From the First Farmers to the Great Pyramid* (London: Penguin, 2012).

Romer, John. *A History of Ancient Egypt: From the Great Pyramid to the Fall of the Middle Kingdom* (London: Penguin, 2017).

Roosevelt, Anna C. 'Archeology of South American Hunters and Gatherers', in Richard B. Lee & Richard Daly (eds), *The Cambridge Encyclopedia of Hunters and Gatherers* (Cambridge: CUP, 2004), pp. 86–91.

Röschenthaler, Ute & Alessandro Jedlowski (eds). *Mobility between Africa, Asia and Latin America: Economic Networks and Cultural Interaction* (London: Bloomsbury, 2017).

Rose, Clare. 'Working Lads in Late-Victorian London', in Nigel Goose & Katrina Honeyman (eds), *Childhood and Child Labour in Industrial England: Diversity and Agency, 1750–1914* (Farnham: Ashgate, 2012), pp. 297–313.

Rosefielde, Steven & Jonathan Leightner. *China's Market Communism: Challenges, Dilemmas, Solutions* (London/New York: Routledge, 2018).

Rosenblatt, Paul C. *Two in a Bed: The Social System of Couple Bed Sharing* (New York: SUNY Press, 2006).

Ross, Michale L. 'Oil, Islam and Women', *American Political Science Review*, 102(1) (February 2008), pp. 107–23.

Rossum, Matthias van. *Werkers van de wereld: Globalisering, arbeid en interculturele ontmoetingen tussen Aziatische en Europese zeelieden in dienst van de VOC, 1600–1800* (Hilversum: Verloren, 2014).

Rossum, Matthias van. *Kleurrijke tragiek: De geschiedenis van slavernij in Azië onder de VOC* (Hilversum: Verloren, 2015a).

Rossum, Matthias van. ' "Vervloekte goudzucht": De VOC, slavenhandel en slavernij in Azië', *TSEG*, 12 (2015b), pp. 29–57.

Rossum, Matthias van. 'Towards a Global Perspective on Early Modern Slave Trade: Prices of the Enslaved in the Indian Ocean, Indonesian Archipelago and Atlantic Worlds', *Journal of Global History* (2021a; forthcoming).

Rossum, Matthias van. 'Slavery and its Transformations: Prolegomena for a Global and Comparative Research Agenda', *Comparative Studies in Society and History* (2021b; forthcoming).

Rossum, Matthias van & Karwan Fatah-Black. 'Wat is winst? De economische impact van de Nederlandse trans-Atlantische slavenhandel', *TSEG*, 9 (2012), pp. 3–29.

Rossum, Matthias van & Merve Tosun. 'Corvée Capitalism: The Dutch East India Company, Labour Regimes and (Merchant) Capitalism', *Journal of Asian Studies* (2021; forthcoming).

Rossum, Matthias van et al. *Testimonies of Enslavement: Sources on Slavery from the Indian Ocean World* (London: Bloomsbury Academic, 2020).

Roth, Karl-Heinz. 'Unfree Labour in the Area under German Hegemony, 1930–1945: Some Historical and Methodological Questions', in Tom Brass & Marcel van der Linden (eds), *Free and Unfree Labour: The Debate Continues* (Bern: Peter Lang, 1997), pp. 127–43.

Rotman, Youval. *Byzantine Slavery and the Mediterranean World* (Cambridge, MA: Harvard UP, 2009).

Roullier, Caroline et al. 'Historical Collections Reveal Patterns of Diffusion of Sweet Potato in Oceania Obscured by Modern Plant Movements and Recombination', *PNAS*, 110(6) (2013), pp. 2205–10.

Rowlandson, Jane. 'Money Use among the Peasantry of Ptolomaic and Roman Egypt', in Andrew Meadows & Kirsty Shipton (eds), *Money and its Uses in the Ancient Greek World* (Oxford, OUP 2001), pp. 145–55.

Roy, Tirthankar. 'Labour-Intensity and Industrialization in Colonial India', in Gareth Austin & Kaoru Sugihara (eds), *Labour-Intensive Industrialization in Global History* (London/New York: Routledge, 2013), pp. 107–21.

Roy, Tirthankar & Giorgio Riello (eds). *Global Economic History* (London: Bloomsbury Academic, 2019).

Rubin, Beth A. 'Shifting Social Contracts and the Sociological Imagination', *Social Forces*, 91(2) (December 2012), pp. 327–46.

Rubin, Gerry R. 'The Historical Development of Collective Labour Law: The United Kingdom', in Marcel van der Linden & Richard Price (eds), *The Rise and Development of Collective Labour Law* (Bern: Peter Lang, 2000), pp. 291–341.

Rule, John (ed.). *British Trade Unionism 1750–1850: The Formative Years* (London/New York: Longman, 1988).

Russell, J.C. 'Population in Europe 500–1500', in Carlo M. Cipolla (ed.), *The Fontana Economic History of Europe: The Middle Ages, Vol. 1* (Glasgow: Collins/Fontana, 1972).

Saeger, James Schofield. *The Chaco Mission Frontier: The Guaycuruan Experience* (Tucson: University of Arizona Press, 2000).

Safley, Thomas Max (ed.). *Labor Before the Industrial Revolution: Work, Technology and their Ecologies in an Age of Early Capitalism* (London & New York: Routledge, 2019).

Safley, Thomas Max & Leonard N. Rosenband. 'Introduction', in Thomas Max Safley (ed.), *Labor Before the Industrial Revolution: Work, Technology and their Ecologies in an Age of Early Capitalism* (London & New York: Routledge, 2019), pp. 1–19.

Sahlins, Marshall. *Stone Age Economics* (Chicago: Aldine Publishing Company, 1972).

Santen, H.W. van. *VOC-dienaar in India: Geleynssen de Jongh in het land van de Groot-Mogol* (Franeker: Van Wijnen, 2001).

Santiago-Valles, Kelvin. 'Forced Labor in Colonial Penal Institutions across the Spanish, U.S., British, French Atlantic, 1860s–1920s', in Marcel van der Linden & Magaly Rodríguez García (eds), *On Coerced Labor: Work and Compulsion after Chattel Slavery* (Leiden/Boston: Brill, 2016), pp. 73–97.

Saradamoni, K. 'Agrestic Slavery in Kerala in the Nineteenth Century', *The Indian Economic and Social History Review* 10(4) (1973), pp. 371–85.

Saradamoni, K. 'How Agrestic Slavery was Abolished in Kerala', *The Indian Economic and Social History Review* 11(2/3) (1974), pp. 291–308.

Sarasúa, Carmen. 'The Role of the State in Shaping Women's and Men's Entrance into the Labour Market: Spain in the Eighteenth and Nineteenth Centuries', *Continuity and Change*, 12(3) (1997), pp. 347–71.

Scammell, Geoffrey Vaughn. *The World Encompassed: The First European Maritime Empires c. 800–1650* (Berkeley: University of California Press, 1981).

Schaps, David M. *The Invention of Coinage and the Monetization of Ancient Greece* (Ann Arbor: University of Michigan Press, 2004).

Scheidel, Walter. 'The Monetary Systems of the Han and Roman Empires', in *Rome and China: Comparative Perspectives on Ancient World Empires* (Oxford: OUP, 2009), pp. 137–207.

Scheidel, Walter. 'Real Wages in Early Economies: Evidence for Living Standards from 1800 BCE to 1300 CE', *JESHO*, 53 (2010), pp. 425–62.

Scheidel, Walter. 'Building for the State: A World-Historical Perspective', *Princeton/Stanford Working Papers in Classics*, Version 1.0 (May 2015a).

Scheidel, Walter (ed.). *State Power in Ancient China and Rome* (New York: OUP, 2015b).

Scheidel, Walter. *The Great Leveler: Violence and the History of Inequality from the Stone Age to the Twenty-First Century* (Princeton: Princeton UP, 2017).

Schendel, Willem van (ed.). *Francis Buchanan in Southeast Bengal* (New Delhi: Manohar, 1992).

Schendel, Willem van. 'Green Plants into Blue Cakes: Working for Wages in Colonial Bengal's Indigo Industry', in Marcel van der Linden & Leo Lucassen (eds), *Working on Labor: Essays in Honor of Jan Lucassen* (Leiden/Boston: Brill, 2012), pp. 47–73.

Schendel, Willem van. 'Beyond Labor History's Comfort Zone? Labor Regimes in Northeast India, from the Nineteenth to the Twenty-First Century', in Ulbe Bosma & Karin Hofmeester (eds), *The Life Work of a Labor Historian: Essays in Honor of Marcel van der Linden* (Leiden/Boston: Brill, 2018), pp. 174–207.

Scherjon, Fulco, Corrie Bakels, Katharine MacDonald & Wil Roebroeks. 'Burning the Land: An Ethnographic Study of Off-Site Fire Use by Current and Historically Documented Foragers and Implications for the Interpretation of Past Fire Practices in the Landscape', *Current Anthropology*, 56(3) (June 2015), pp. 299–326.

Schiavone, Aldo. *Spartacus* (Cambridge, MA: Harvard UP, 2013).

Schloss, David. *Methods of Industrial Remuneration*, 3rd edn, revised and enlarged (London: Williams & Norgate, 1898).

Schloss, David. *Les modes de rémunération du travail: Traduit sur la 3e édition, précédé d'une introduction, et augmenté de notes et d'appendices par Charles Rist* (Paris: Giard & Brière, 1902).

Schmandt-Besserat, Denise. *Before Writing, Vol. I: From Counting to Cuneiform; Vol II: A Catalogue of Near Eastern Tokens* (Austin: University of Texas Press, 1992).

Schmidt, Ariadne. 'Women and Guilds: Corporations and Female Labour Market Participation in Early Modern Holland', *Gender & History*, 21(1) (2009), pp. 170–89.

Schmidt, Peter R. *Iron Technology in East Africa: Symbolism, Science and Archaeology* (Bloomington: Indiana UP, 1997).

Schneider, William H. 'The Scientific Study of Labor in Interwar France', in Michael C. Wood & John Cunningham Wood (eds), *Frank and Lillian Gilbreth: Critical Evaluations in Business Management, Vol. II* (London: Routledge, 2003), pp. 196–229.

Scholliers, Peter. *Wages, Manufacturers and Workers in the Nineteenth-Century Factory: The Voortman Cotton Mill in Ghent* (Oxford: OUP, 1996).

Schrire, Carmel (ed.). *Past and Present in Hunter Gatherer Studies* (Walnut Creek, CA: Left Coast Press, 2009).

Schumpeter, Joseph A. *History of Economic Analysis* (London: Allen & Unwin, 1972).

Seaford, Richard. *The Origins of Philosophy in Ancient Greece and Ancient India: A Historical Comparison* (Cambridge: CUP, 2020).

Sebeta, Judith Lynn. 'Women's Costume and Feminine Civic Morality in Augustan Rome', *Gender & History*, 9(3) (1997), pp. 529–41.

Segal, Paul. 'Inequality as Entitlements over Labour', Working Paper 43 (London: LSE Inequalities Institute, 2020).

Segalen, Martine. *Love and Power in the Peasant Family: Rural France in the Nineteenth Century* (Chicago: Chicago UP, 1983).

Seibert, Julia. 'More Continuity than Change? New Forms of Unfree Labor in the Belgian Congo 1908–1930', in Marcel van der Linden (ed.), *Humanitarian Interventions and Changing Labor Relations: The Long-Term Consequences of the Abolition of the Slave Trade* (Leiden & Boston: Brill, 2011), pp. 369–86.

Seland, Eivind Heldaas. 'Archaeology of Trade in the Western Indian Ocean, 200 BC–AD 700', *Journal of Archaeological Research*, 22 (2014), pp. 367–402.

Semo, Enrique. *The History of Capitalism in Mexico: Its Origins, 1521–1763* (Austin: University of Texas Press, 1993).

Sen, A.K. 'Cooperation, Inequality and the Family', *Population and Development Review*, 15, Supplement (1989), pp. 61–76.

Sennett, Richard. *The Craftsman* (New Haven/London: Yale UP, 2008).

Sharma, R.S. 'Urbanism in Early Historical India', in Indu Banga (ed.), *The City in Indian History: Urban Demography, Society and Politics* (New Delhi: Manohar, 2014), pp. 9–18.

Shatzmiller, Maya. *Labour in the Medieval Islamic World* (Leiden: Brill, 1994).

Shatzmiller, Maya. *Her Day in Court: Women's Property Rights in Fifteenth-Century Granada* (Cambridge MA: Harvard UP, 2007).

Shelach-Lavi, Gideon. *The Archaeology of Early China: From Prehistory to the Han Dynasty* (Cambridge: CUP, 2015).

Shen, Jianfa. 'From Mao to the Present: Migration in China since the Second World War', in Jan Lucassen & Leo Lucassen (eds), *Globalising Migration History: The Eurasian Experience (16th–21st Centuries)* (Leiden/Boston: Brill, 2014), pp. 335–61.

Shieh, G.S. 'Cultivation, Control and Dissolution: The Historical Transformation of the Labour Union Act of Taiwan, 1911–1990', in Marcel van der Linden & Richard Price (eds), *The Rise and Development of Collective Labour Law* (Bern: Peter Lang, 2000), pp. 265–90.

Shimada, Ryuto. *The Intra-Asian Trade in Japanese Copper by the Dutch East-India Company during the Eighteenth Century* (Leiden: Brill, 2006).

Shin, Wonchul. 'The Evolution of Labour Relations in the South Korean Shipbuilding Industry: A Case Study of Hanjin Heavy Industries, 1950–2014', in Raquel Varela, Hugh Murphy & Marcel van der Linden (eds), *Shipbuilding and Ship Repair Workers around the World: Case Studies 1950–2010* (Amsterdam: Amsterdam UP, 2017), pp. 615–36.

Shiuh-Feng, Liu. 'Copper Administration Reform and Copper Imports from Japan in the Qianlong Reign of the Qing Dynasty', in Keiko Nagase-Reimer (ed.), *Copper in the Early Modern Sino-Japanese Trade* (Leiden/Boston: Brill, 2016), pp. 72–117.

Shlomowitz, Ralph. 'Team Work and Incentives: The Origins and Development of the Butty Gang System in Queensland's Sugar Industry, 1891–1913', *Journal of Comparative Economics*, 3 (1979), pp. 41–55.

Shlomowitz, Ralph. 'The Transition from Slave to Freedmen Labor in the Cape Colony, the British West Indies, and the Postbellum American South: Comparative Perspectives', in Tom Brass & Marcel van der Linden (eds), *Free and Unfree Labour: The Debate Continues* (Bern: Peter Lang, 1997), pp. 239–48.

Shnirelman, Victor A. 'Archeology of North Eurasian Hunters and Gatherers', in Richard B. Lee & Richard Daly (eds), *The Cambridge Encyclopedia of Hunters and Gatherers* (Cambridge: CUP, 2004a), pp. 127–31.

Shnirelman, Victor A. 'The Itenm'i', in Richard B. Lee & Richard Daly (eds), *The Cambridge Encyclopedia of Hunters and Gatherers* (Cambridge: CUP, 2004b), pp. 147–51.

Shrimali, Krishna Mohan. 'Money, Market and Indian Feudalism: AD 60–1200)', in Amiya Kumar Bagchi (ed.), *Money & Credit in Indian History: From Early Medieval Times* (New Delhi: Tulika, 2002), pp. 1–39.

Shrimali, Krishna Mohan. 'The Monetary History of Early India: Distinctive Landmarks', in Susmita Basu Majumdar & S.K. Bose (eds), *Money and Money Matters in Pre-Modern South Asia. Nicholas G. Rhodes Commemoration Volume* (New Delhi: Manohar, 2019), pp. 173–220.

Shryock, Andrew & Daniel Lord Smail (eds). *Deep History: The Architecture of Past and Present* (Berkeley: University of California Press, 2011).

Shryock, Andrew, Thomas R. Trautmann & Clive Gamble. 'Imagining the Human in Deep Time', in Andrew Shryock and Daniel Lord Smail (eds), *Deep History: The Architecture of Past and Present* (Berkeley: University of California Press, 2011), pp. 21–52.

Siegelbaum, Lewis H. *Stakhanovism and the Politics of Productivity in the USSR, 1935–1941* (Cambridge: CUP, 1988).

Simitis, Spiros. 'The Case of the Employment Relationship: Elements of a Comparison', in Willibald Steinmetz (ed.), *Private Law and Social Inequality in the Industrial Age: Comparing Legal Cultures in Britain, France, Germany and the United States* (Oxford: OUP, 2000), pp. 181–202.

Simonton, Deborah & Anne Montenach (eds). *A Cultural History of Work*, 6 vols (London: Bloomington 2019).

Singh, Anankoha Narayan. 'Regulating Slavery in Colonial India', *Labour & Development*, 21 (2014), pp. 102–20.

Singha, Radhika. *A Despotism of Law: Crime and Justice in Early Colonial India* (Delhi: OUP, 1998).

Sinha, Nitin & Nitin Varma (eds). *Servants' Pasts, 18th–20th Centuries, Vol. 2* (New Delhi: Orient Blackswan, 2019).

Sinha, Nitin, Nitin Varma & Pankaj Jha (eds). *Servants' Pasts, 16th–18th Centuries, Vol. 1* (New Delhi: Orient Blackswan, 2019).

Sinopoli, Carla M. 'Empires', in Gary M. Feinman & T. Douglas Price (eds), *Archaeology at the Millennium: A Sourcebook* (New York: Springer, 2001), pp. 439–71.

Sinopoli, Carla M. & Kathleen D. Morrison. 'Dimensions of Imperial Control: The Vijayanagara Capital', *American Anthropologist*, 97 (1995), pp. 83–96.

Skipp, Victor. *Crisis and Development: An Ecological Case Study of the Forest of Arden 1570–1674* (Cambridge: CUP, 1978).

Slicher van Bath, Bernhard H. *The Agrarian History of Western Europe A.D. 500–1850* (London: Arnold, 1963a).

Slicher van Bath, Bernhard H. 'De oogstopbrengsten van verschillende gewassen, voornamelijk granen, in verhouding tot het zaaizaad', *A.A.G. Bijdragen*, 9 (1963b), pp. 29–125.

Slicher van Bath, Bernhard H. 'Yield Ratios, 810–1820', *A.A.G. Bijdragen*, 10 (1963c), pp. 1–264.

Sloman, Peter. *Transfer State: The Idea of a Guaranteed Income and the Politics of Redistribution in Modern Britain* (Oxford: OUP, 2019).

Smith, Adam. *An Inquiry into the Nature and the Wealth of Nations. A careful reprint of edition (3 volumes) 1812 with notes by J.R. McCulloch* (London: Ward, Lock & Co, n.d.).

Smith, Andrew B. 'Archeology and Evolution of Hunters and Gatherers', in Richard B. Lee & Richard Daly (eds), *The Cambridge Encyclopedia of Hunters and Gatherers* (Cambridge: CUP, 2004), pp. 384–90.

Smith, Eric Alden et al. 'Wealth Transmission and Inequality Among Hunter-Gatherers', *Current Anthropology*, 51(1) (February 2010), pp. 19–34.

Smith, Mark B. 'Social Rights in the Soviet Dictatorship: The Constitutional Right to Welfare from Stalin to Brezhnev', *Humanity*, 3(3) (Winter 2012), pp. 385–406.

Smith, Mark B. 'The Withering Away of the Danger Society: The Pensions Reform 1956 and 1964 in the Soviet Union', *Social Science History*, 39(1) (March 2015a), pp. 129–48.

Smith, Mark B. 'Faded Red Paradise: Welfare and the Soviet City after 1953', *Contemporary European History*, 24(4) (October 2015b), pp. 597–615.

Smith, Michael E. (ed.). *The Comparative Archaeology of Complex Societies* (Cambridge: CUP, 2012a).

Smith, Michael E. *The Aztecs*, 3rd edn (Oxford: Wiley-Blackwell, 2012b).

Smith, Michael E. 'The Aztec Empire', in Andrew Monson & Walter Scheidel (eds), *Fiscal Regimes and the Political Economies of Premodern States* (Cambridge: CUP, 2015), pp. 71–114.

Snell, K.D.M. *Annals of the Labouring Poor: Social Change and Agrarian England 1660–1900* (Cambridge: CUP, 1985).

Sonenscher, Michael. *Work and Wages: Natural Law, Politics and the Eighteenth-Century French Trades* (Cambridge: CUP, 1989).

Song, Jesook. *South Koreans in the Debt Crisis: The Creation of a Neoliberal Welfare Society* (Durham, NC/London: Duke UP, 2009).

Spalinger, Anthony. 'The Army', in Toby Wilkinson (ed.), *The Egyptian World* (London/New York: Routledge, 2007), pp. 118–28.

Spek, R.J. van der. 'Cuneiform Documents on the Parthian History: The Rahimesu Archive. Materials for the Study of the Standard of Living', in Josef Wiesehöfer (ed.), *Das Partherreich und seine Zeugnisse* (Stuttgart: Steiner, 1998), pp. 205–58.

Spek, R.J. van der. 'Palace, Temple and Market in Seleucid Babylonia', in V. Chankowski et F. Duyrat (eds), *Le roi et l'économie: Autonomies locales et structures royales dans l'économie de l'empire séleucide. Topoi, Orient-Occident*, Supplement 6 (2004), pp. 303–32.

Spek, R.J. van der. 'Feeding Hellenistic Seleucia on the Tigris and Babylon', in Richard Alston & Otto M. van Nijf (eds), *Feeding the Ancient Greek City* (Leuven: Peeters, 2008), pp. 33–45.

Spek, R.J. van der, Bas van Leeuwen & Jan Luiten van Zanden (eds), *A History of Market Performance: From Ancient Babylonia to the Modern World* (London/New York: Routledge, 2015).

Spek, R.J. van der et al. 'Money, Silver and Trust in Mesopotamia', in R.J. van der Spek & Bas van Leeuwen (eds), *Money, Currency and Crisis: In Search of Trust, 2000 BC to AD 2000* (London/New York: Routledge, 2018), pp. 102–31.

Spittler, Gerd. 'Beginnings of the Anthropology of Work: Nineteenth-Century Social Scientists and their Influence on Ethnography', in Jürgen Kocka (ed.), *Work in a Modern Society: The German Historical Experience in Comparative Perspective* (New York: Berghahn, 2010), pp. 37–54.

Spufford, Margaret. *The Great Reclothing of Rural England: Petty Chapmen and their Wares in the Seventeenth Century* (London: The Hambleton Press, 1984).

Spufford, Margaret. 'Literacy, Trade and Religion in the Commercial Centres of Europe', in Karel Davids & Jan Lucassen (eds), *A Miracle Mirrored: The Dutch Republic in European Perspective* (Cambridge: CUP, 1995), pp. 229–83.

Spufford, Margaret. 'The Cost of Apparel in Seventeenth-Century England, and the Accuracy of Gregory King', *EHR*, 53 (2000), pp. 677–705.

Spufford, Peter. *Money and its Use in Medieval Europe* (Cambridge: CUP, 1988).

Spufford, Peter. 'How Rarely did Medieval Merchants Use Coin?', Van Gelder lecture 5, Stichting Nederlandse Penningkabinetten, Utrecht, 2008.

Stabel, Peter. 'Labour Time, Guild Time? Working Hours in the Cloth Industry of Medieval Flanders and Artois (Thirteenth–Fourteenth Centuries)', *TSEG*, 11 (2014), pp. 27–53.

Standing, Guy. *The Precariat: The New Dangerous Class* (London: Bloomsbury, 2016).

Stanziani, Alessandro. 'Serfs, Slaves, or Wage Earners? The Legal Status of Labour in Russia from a Comparative Perspective, from the Sixteenth to the Nineteenth Century', *Journal of Global History*, 3 (2008), pp. 183–202.

Stanziani, Alessandro. 'The Legal Status of Labour from the Seventeenth to the Nineteenth Century: Russia in a Comparative European Perspective', *IRSH*, 54 (2009a), pp. 359–89.

Stanziani, Alessandro. 'The Travelling Panopticon: Labor Institutions and Labor Practices in Russia and Britain in the Eighteenth and Nineteenth Centuries', *Comparative Studies in Society and History*, 51(4) (October 2009b), pp. 715–41.

Stanziani, Alessandro. *After Oriental Despotism: Eurasian Growth in a Global Perspective* (London: Bloomsbury, 2014).

Stanziani, Alessandro. 'Labour Regimes and Labour Mobility from the Seventeenth to the Nineteenth Century', in Tirthankar Roy & Giorgio Riello (eds), *Global Economic History* (London: Bloomsbury Academic, 2019), pp. 175–94.

Stearns, Peter. *Debating the Industrial Revolution* (London: Bloomsbury, 2015).

Stein, Burton. *A History of India*, 2nd edn, edited by David Arnold (Chichester: Wiley-Blackwell, 2010).

Steinfeld, Robert J. *The Invention of Free Labor: The Employment Relation in English and American Law and Culture, 1350–1870* (Chapel Hill/London: University of North Carolina Press, 1991).

Steinfeld, Robert J. *Coercion, Contract and Free Labor in the Nineteenth Century* (Cambridge: CUP, 2001).

Steinfeld, Robert J. 'Suffrage and the Terms of Labor', in David Eltis, Frank D. Lewis & Kenneth L. Sokoloff (eds), *Human Capital and Institutions: A Long Run View* (Cambridge: CUP, 2009), pp. 267–84.

Steinmetz, Willibald (ed.). *Private Law and Social Inequality in the Industrial Age: Comparing Legal Cultures in Britain, France, Germany and the United States* (Oxford: OUP, 2000).

Sterelny, Kim. 'Human Behavioral Ecology, Optimality, and Human Action', in Gary Hatfield & Holly Pittman (eds), *Evolution of Mind, Brain, and Culture* (Philadelphia: University of Pennsylvania Press, 2013), pp. 303–24.

Stevens, Anne & Mark Eccleston. 'Craft Production and Technology', in Toby Wilkinson (ed.), *The Egyptian World* (London/New York: Routledge, 2007), pp. 146–59.

Stillman, Norman A. 'The Eleventh Century Merchant House of Ibn 'Akwal (A Geniza Study)', *JESHO*, 16 (1973), pp. 15–88.

Stiner, Mary C. et al. 'Scale', in Andrew Shryock & Daniel Lord Smail (eds), *Deep History: The Architecture of Past and Present* (Berkeley: University of California Press, 2011), pp. 242–72.

Stone, Glenn Davis, Robert McC. Netting & M. Priscilla Stone. 'Seasonality, Labor Scheduling, and Agricultural Intensification in the Nigerian Savanna', *American Anthropologist*, New Series, 92(1) (1990), pp. 7–23.

Studer, Roman. *The Great Divergence Reconsidered. Europe, India, and the Rise of Global Economic Power* (Cambridge: CUP, 2015).

Subbarayalu, Y. 'Trade Guilds in South India up to the Tenth Century', *Studies in People's History*, 2(1) (2015), pp. 21–6.

Subrahmanyam, Sanjay. 'Introduction' in Sanjay Subrahmanyam (ed.), *Money and the Market in India 1100–1700* (Delhi: OUP, 1994), pp. 1–56.

Subramanian, Lakshmi. 'The Political Economy of Textiles in Western India: Weavers, Merchants and the Transition to a Colonial Economy', in Giorgio Riello & Tirthankar Roy (eds), *How India Clothed the World: The World of South Asian Textiles, 1500–1850* (Leiden/Boston: Brill, 2009), pp. 253–80.

Sugihara, Kaoru. 'Labour-Intensive Industrialization in Global History: An Interpretation of East Asian Experiences', in Gareth Austin & Kaoru Sugihara (eds), *Labour-Intensive Industrialization in Global History* (London/New York: Routledge, 2013), pp. 20–64.

Sunderland, Willard. 'Catherine's Dilemma: Resettlement and Power in Russia: 1500s–1914', in Jan Lucassen & Leo Lucassen (eds), *Globalising Migration History: The Eurasian Experience (16th–21st Centuries)* (Leiden/Boston: Brill, 2014), pp. 55–70.

Suzman, James. *Affluence without Abundance: The Disappearing World of the Bushmen* (London: Bloomsbury, 2017).

Suzman, James. *Work: A History of How We Spend Our Time* (London: Bloomsbury, 2020).

Taylor, Frederick Winslow. *The Principles of Scientific Management* (New York: Harper, 1911).

Taylor, Tim. 'Ambushed by a Grotesque: Archeology, Slavery and the Third Paradigm', in Mike Parker Pearson & I.J.N. Thorpe (eds), *Warfare, Violence and Slavery: Proceedings of a Prehistoric Society Conference at Sheffield University* (Oxford: BAR Publishing, 2005), pp. 225–33.

Temin, Peter. *The Roman Market Economy* (Princeton/Oxford: Princeton UP, 2012).

Tenney, Jonathan S. 'Household Structure and Population Dynamics in the Middle Babylonian Provincial "Slave" Population', in Laura Culbertson (ed.), *Slaves and Households in the Near East* (Chicago: Oriental Institute, 2011), pp. 135–46.

Teulings, Chris. *Gildepenningen: hun rol binnen de ambachtsgilden van de Noordelijke Nederlanden* (Woudrichem: Pictures Publishers, 2019).

Thapar, Romila. *The Penguin History of Early India: From the Origins to* AD *1300* (London: Penguin, 2002).

Tharoor, Shashi. *Why I am a Hindu* (New Delhi: Aleph, 2018).

Thierry, François. *Monnaies chinoises. I. L'antiquité préimpériale* (Paris: BNF, 1997).

Thierry, François. 'Archéologie et Numismatique. Les cinq découvertes qui ont bouleversé l'histoire monétaire du Chin', in Wolfgant Szaivert et al. (eds). *TOYTO APECHTH XΩPA: Festschrift für Wolfgang Hahn zum 70. Geburtstag* (Vienna: VIN, 2015), pp. 433–51.

Thomas, Keith (ed.). *The Oxford Book of Work* (Oxford: OUP, 1999).

Thomas, Keith. *The Ends of Life: Roads to Fulfilment in Early Modern England* (Oxford: OUP, 2009).

Thomaz, Luís Filipe F.R. *Oranjemund Coins: Shipwreck of the Portuguese Carrack "Bom Jesus" (1533)* (Lisbon/Windhoek: IISTP/National Museum of Namibia, 2014).

Thompson, Edward. *The Making of the English Working Class* (Harmondsworth: Penguin, 1968).

Thorpe, I.J.N. 'The Ancient Origins of Warfare and Violence', in Mike Parker Pearson & I.J.N. Thorpe (eds), *Warfare, Violence and Slavery: Proceedings of a Prehistoric Society Conference at Sheffield University* (Oxford: BAR Publishing, 2005), pp. 1–18.

Thorpe, Wayne. *'The workers themselves': Revolutionary Syndicalism and International Labour, 1913–1923* (Dordrecht: Kluwer, 1989).

Tilgher, Adriano. *Work: What it Has Meant to Men Through the Ages* (New York: Harcourt, Brace & Co., 1930; Arno Press, 1977).

Tilly, Charles. *As Sociology Meets History* (New York: Academic Press, 1981).

Tilly, Chris & Charles Tilly. *Work under Capitalism* (Boulder, CO: Westview Press, 1998).

Toledano, Ehud. 'An Empire of Many Households: The Case of Ottoman Enslavement', in Laura Culbertson (ed.), *Slaves and Households in the Near East* (Chicago: Oriental Institute, 2011), pp. 85–97.

Tomber, Roberta. *Indo-Roman Trade: From Pots to Pepper* (London: Duckworth, 2008).

Tomka, Béla. *Welfare in East and West: Hungarian Social Security in an International Comparison 1918–1990* (Berlin: Akademie Verlag, 2004).

Tomlins, Christopher. 'Early British America, 1585–1830: Freedom Bound', in Douglas Hay & Paul Craven (eds), *Masters, Servants and Magistrates in Britain and the Empire 1562–1955* (Chapel Hill: University of North Carolina Press, 2004), pp. 117–52.

Tomlinson, Jim. *Employment Policy: The Crucial Years 1939–1955* (Oxford: Clarendon Press, 1987).

Tonioli, Gianni & Francesco Piva. 'Unemployment in the 1930s: The Case of Italy', in Barry J. Eichengreen & T.J. Hatton (eds), *Interwar Unemployment in International Perspective* (Dordrecht: Kluwer, 1988), pp. 221–45.

Tonkinson, Robert. 'The Ngarrindjeri of Southeastern Australia', in Richard B. Lee & Richard Daly (eds), *The Cambridge Encyclopedia of Hunters and Gatherers* (Cambridge: CUP, 2004), pp. 343–7.

Toussaint, Sandy. 'Kimberley Peoples of Fitzroy Valley, Western Australia', in Richard B. Lee & Richard Daly (eds), *The Cambridge Encyclopedia of Hunters and Gatherers* (Cambridge: CUP, 2004), pp. 339–42.

Trappenburg, Margot, Wouter Scholten & Thijs Jansen (eds). *Loonfatsoen: Eerlijk verdienen of graaicultuur* (Amsterdam: Boom, 2014).

Trautmann, Thomas R., Gilliam Feeley-Harnik & John C. Mitani. 'Deep Kinship', in Andrew Shryock & Daniel Lord Smail (eds), *Deep History: The Architecture of Past and Present* (Berkeley: University of California Press, 2011), pp. 160–88.

Trevett, Jeremy. 'Coinage and Democracy at Athens', in Andrew Meadows & Kirsty Shipton (eds), *Money and its Uses in the Ancient Greek World* (Oxford: OUP, 2001), pp. 25–34.

Truant, Cynthia Maria. *The Rites of Labor: Brotherhoods of Compagnonnage in Old and New Regime France* (Ithaca: Cornell UP, 1994).

Tsurumi, E. Patricia. *Factory Girls: Women in the Thread Mills of Meiji Japan* (Princeton: Princeton UP, 1990).

Turrell, Robert Vicat. *Capital and Labour on the Kimberley Diamond Fields 1871–1890* (Cambridge: CUP, 1987).

Udovitch, Abraham L. 'Labor Partnerships in Early Islamic Law', *JESHO*, 10 (1961), pp. 64–80.

Ulin, Robert C. 'Work as Cultural Production: Labour and Self-Identity among Southwest French Wine-Growers', *Journal of the Royal Anthropological Institute (N.S.)*, 8 (2002), pp. 691–702.

Underhill, Anne P. (ed.). *A Companion to Chinese Archaeology* (Hoboken, NJ: Wiley-Blackwell, 2013).

Vaesen, Krist, Mark Collard, Richard Cosgrove & Will Roebroeks. 'Population Size Does Not Explain Past Changes in Cultural Complexity', *PNAS* (4 April 2016), pp. E2241–7.

Valbelle, Dominique. 'Craftsmen', in Sergio Donadoni (ed.), *The Egyptians* (Chicago/London: University of Chicago Press, 1997), pp. 31–59.

Vandenbroeke, Christiaan. 'Proto-Industry in Flanders: A Critical Review', in Sheilagh C. Ogilvie & Markus Cerman (eds), *European Proto-Industrialization* (Cambridge: CUP, 1996), pp. 102–17.

Vanhaute, Eric. *Peasants in World History* (New York/Abingdon: Routledge, 2021; forthcoming).

Vanhaute, Eric & Hanne Cottyn. 'Into their Lands and Labours: A Comparative and Global Analysis of Trajectories of Peasant Transformation', *ICAS Review Paper Series No. 8* (February 2017) https://biblio.ugent.be/publication/8512518/file/8512519 (retrieved on 24 April 2018).

Vanina, Eugenia. *Urban Crafts and Craftsmen in Medieval India (Thirteenth–Eighteenth Centuries)* (New Delhi: Munshiram Manoharlal, 2004).

Veblen Thorstein V. *The Instinct of Workmanship and the State of the Industrial Arts* (New York: Augustus M. Kelly, originally 1914).

Vélissaroupolos-Karakostas, Julie. 'Merchants, Prostitutes and the "New Poor": Forms of Contract and Social Status', in Paul Cartledge, Edward E. Cohen & Lin Foxhall (eds), *Money, Labour and Land: Approaches to the Economies of Ancient Greece* (London/New York: Routledge, 2002), pp. 130–9.

Veraghtert, Karel & Brigitte Widdershoven. *Twee eeuwen solidariteit: De Nederlandse, Belgische en Duitse ziekenfondsen tijdens de negentiende en twintigste eeuw* (Amsterdam/Zeist: Aksant, 2002).

Verboven, Koenraad. 'Currency, Bullion and Accounts: Monetary Modes in the Roman World', *Revue Belge de Numismatique et de Sigillographie*, 140 (2009), pp. 91–124.

Verboven, Koenraad. 'Introduction: Professional Collegia: Guilds or Social Clubs?', *Ancient Society*, 41 (2011), pp. 187–95.

Verhulst, Adriaan. *The Rise of Cities in North-West Europe* (Cambridge: CUP, 1999).

Verlinden, Charles. *L'esclavage dans l'Europe médiévale. I: Péninsule Ibérique-France; II: Italie, Colonies italiennes du levant, Levant latin, Empire byzantine* (Ghent: Faculté de Philosophie et Lettres, 1955, 1977).

Verlinden, Charles. 'Le retour de l'esclavage aux XVe et XVIe siècles', in Annalisa Guarducci (ed.), *Forme ed evoluzione del lavoro in Europa: XIII–XVIII secc.*, *Serie II Atti delle 'Settimane di Studi' e altri Convegni No. 13* (Prato: Instituto F. Datini, 1991), pp. 65–92.

Versieren, Jelle & Bert de Munck. 'The Commodity Form of Labor: Discursive and Cultural Traditions to Capitalism(s) and Labor in the Low Countries' Ceramic Industries (1500–1900)', in Thomas Max Safley (ed.), *Labor Before the Industrial Revolution: Work, Technology and their Ecologies in an Age of Early Capitalism* (London & New York: Routledge, 2019), pp. 70–95.

Victor, Sandrine. ' "Quand le Bâtiment Va, Tout Va": The Building Trade in the Latin West in the Middle Ages', in Thomas Max Safley (ed.), *Labor Before the Industrial Revolution: Work, Technology and their Ecologies in an Age of Early Capitalism* (London & New York: Routledge, 2019), pp. 132–49.

Vidal, Hern N.J. 'The Yamana of Tierra del Fuego', in Richard B. Lee & Richard Daly (eds), *The Cambridge Encyclopedia of Hunters and Gatherers* (Cambridge: CUP, 2004), pp. 114–18.

Villa, Paola & Wil Roebroeks. 'Neanderthal Demise: An Archaeological Analysis of the Modern Human Superiority Complex', *PLOS ONE*, 9(4) (April 2014), pp. 1–10.

Villotte, Sébastien & Christopher J. Knüsel. ' "I Sing of Arms and of a Man . . .": Medial Epicondylosis and the Sexual Division of Labour in Prehistoric Europe', *Journal of Archaeological Science*, 43 (March 2014), pp. 168–74.

Vink, Markus. ' "The World's Oldest Trade": Dutch Slavery and Slave Trade in the Indian Ocean in the Seventeenth Century', *Journal of World History*, 14 (2003), pp. 131–77.

Vleuten, Lotte van der. 'Empowerment and Education: A Historical Study into the Determinants of Global Educational Participation of Women, ca. 1850–2010', PhD thesis, Radboud Universiteit Nijmegen, 2016.

Vogel, Hans Ulrich. 'Unrest and Strikes at the Metropolitan Mints in 1741 and 1816 and their Economic and Social Background', in Christine Moll-Murata, Song Jianze & Hans Ulrich Vogel (eds), *Chinese Handicraft Regulations of the Qing Dynasty: Theory and Application* (Munich: Iudicium, 2005), pp. 395–422.

Vogel, Hans Ulrich. *Marco Polo Was in China, New Evidence from Currencies, Salt and Revenues* (Leiden/Boston: Brill, 2013).

Voth, Hans-Joachim. *Time and Work in England 1750–1830* (Oxford: Clarendon Press, 2000).

Vries, Jan de. *The Dutch Rural Economy in the Golden Age 1500–1700* (New Haven/London: Yale UP, 1974).

Vries, Jan de. *European Urbanization 1500–1800* (London: Methuen, 1984).

Vries, Jan de. 'The Industrial Revolution and the Industrious Revolution', *The Journal of Economic History*, 54 (1994), pp. 249–70.

Vries, Jan de. *The Industrious Revolution: Consumer Behavior and the Household Economy, 1650 to the Present* (Cambridge: CUP, 2008).

Vries, Jan de. 'The Industrious Revolutions in East and West', in Gareth Austin & Kaoru Sugihara (eds), *Labour-Intensive Industrialization in Global History* (London/New York: Routledge, 2013), pp. 65–84.

Vries, Jan de & Ad van der Woude. *The First Modern Economy: Success, Failure, and Perseverance of the Dutch Economy, 1500–1815* (Cambridge: CUP, 1997).

Vries, Peer. *Escaping Poverty: The Origins of Modern Economic Growth* (Goettingen/Vienna: Vienna UP, 2013).

503

Vries, Peer. 'Replies to my Commentators', *TSEG*, 12 (2015), pp. 105–20.

Waal, Frans de. *Good Natured: The Origins of Right and Wrong in Humans and Other Animals* (Cambridge, MA: Harvard UP, 1996).

Waal, Frans de. *Our Inner Ape: The Best and Worst of Human Nature* (London: Granta Books, 2005).

Waal, Frans de. *The Age of Empathy: Nature's Lessons for a Kinder Society* (New York: Harmony Books, 2009).

Wadauer, Sigrid, Thomas Buchner & Alexander Mejstrik (eds). *History of Labour Intermediation: Institutions and Finding Employment in the Nineteenth and Early Twentieth Centuries* (New York/Oxford: Berghahn, 2015).

Wade, Lizzie. 'Unearthing Democracy's Rules', *Science*, 355 (17 March 2017), pp. 1114–18.

Wagner-Hasel, Beate. 'Egoistic Exchange and Altruistic Gift', in Gadi Algazi, Valentin Groebner & Bernhard Jussen (eds), *Negotiating the Gift: Pre-Modern Figurations of Exchange* (Göttingen: Vandenhoeck & Ruprecht, 2003), pp. 141–71.

Wagner-Hasel, Beate. *Die Arbeit des Gelehrten: Der Nationalökonom Karl Bücher (1847–1930)* (Frankfurt: Campus, 2011).

Wallerstein, Immanuel. *The Modern World System*, vols I–III (New York/London: Academic Press, 1974–1989).

Walvin, James. *Atlas of Slavery* (Harlow: Pearson/Longman, 2006).

Wang, Helen. *Money on the Silk Road: The Evidence from Eastern Central Asia to c. AD 800* (London: British Museum, 2004).

Wang, Helen. 'Official Salaries and Local Wages at Juyan, North-West China, First Century BCE to First Century CE', in Jan Lucassen, *Wages and Currency: Global Comparisons from Antiquity to the Twentieth Century* (Bern: Peter Lang, 2007), pp. 59–76.

Wang, Helen et al. (eds). *Metallurgical Analysis of Chinese Coins at the British Museum* (London: British Museum, 2005).

Weber, Max. 'Agrarverhältnisse im Altertum', in *Handwörterbuch der Staatswissenschaften* (Jena: Gustav Fischer, 1909), pp. 52–188.

Weber, Max. *Wirtschaft und Gesellschaft*, edited by Johannes Winckelman (Tübingen: Mohr, 1976).

Weeks, Kathi. *The Problem with Work: Feminism, Marxism, Antiwork Politics, and Postwork Imaginaries* (Durham, NC/London: Duke UP, 2011).

Weil, David. *The Fissured Workplace: Why Work Became So Bad for So Many and What Can be Done to Improve it* (Cambridge, MA: Harvard UP, 2014).

Weill, Claudie. *L'Internationale et l'Autre: Les Relations interethniques dans la IIe Internationale (discussions et débats)* (Paris: Arcantère, 1987).

Wells, H.G. *An Englishman Looks at the World, Being a Series of Unrestrained Remarks upon Contemporary Matters* (London: Cassel, 1914).

Wendt, Ian C. 'Four Centuries of Decline? Understanding the Changing Structure of the South Indian Textile Industry', in Giorgio Riello & Tirthankar Roy (eds), *How India Clothed the World: The World of South Asian Textiles, 1500–1850* (Leiden/Boston: Brill, 2009), pp. 193–215.

Wengrow, David. *The Archaeology of Early Egypt: Social Transformations in North-East Africa, 10,000 to 2650 BC* (Cambridge: CUP, 2006).

Westerhoff, Christian. *Zwangsarbeit im Ersten Weltkrieg: Deutsche Arbeitskräftepolitik im besetzten Polen und Litauen 1914–1918* (Paderborn: Schöningh, 2012).

Wezel Stone, Katherine van. 'Labor and the American State: The Evolution of Labor Law in the United States', in Marcel van der Linden & Richard Price (eds), *The Rise and Development of Collective Labour Law* (Bern: Peter Lang, 2000), pp. 351–76.

Whatley, Christopher A. 'Scottish "Collier Serfs" in the 17th and 18th Centuries: A New Perspective', *VSWG-Beiheft*, 115 (1995a), pp. 239–55.

Whatley, Christopher A. 'Collier Serfdom in Mid-Eighteenth-Century Scotland: New Light from the Rothes MSS', *Archives*, 22(93) (1995b), pp. 25–33.

White, Jerry. *Mansions of Misery: A Biography of the Marshalsea Debtors' Prison* (London: Bodley Head, 2016).

Whitehouse, Nicki J. & Wiebke Kirleis. 'The World Reshaped: Practices and Impacts of Early Agrarian Societies', *Journal of Archaeological Science*, 51 (2014), pp. 1–11.

Whittle, Alasdair & Vicki Cummings (eds). *Going Over: The Mesolithic-Neolithic Transition in North-West Europe* (Oxford: OUP, 2007).

Wicks, Robert S. *Money, Markets, and Trade in Early Southeast Asia: The Development of Indigenous Monetary Systems to AD 1400* (Ithaca, NY: Cornell UP, 1992).

Wierling, Dorothee. *Mädchen für alles: Arbeitsalltag und Lebensgeschichte städtischer Dienstmädchen um die Jahrhundertwende* (Berlin: Dietz, 1987).

Wilkinson, Toby (ed.). *The Egyptian World* (London/New York: Routledge, 2010).

Williams, Colin C. *The Informal Economy* (Newcastle upon Tyne: Agenda, 2019).

Witwer, David. *Shadow of the Racketeer: Scandal in Organized Labor* (Urbana, IL/Chicago: University of Illinois Press, 2009).

Witzel, Michael. 'Brahmanical Reactions to Foreign Influences and to Social and Religious Change', in Patrick Olivelle (ed.), *Between the Empires: Society in India 300 BCE to 400 CE* (Oxford: OUP, 2006), pp. 457–99.

Wong, R. Bin. 'Divergence Displaced: Patterns of Economic and Political Change in Early Modern and Modern History', lecture, Utrecht University, 26 May 2016.

Wood, Michael C. & John Cunningham Wood (eds). *Frank and Lillian Gilbreth: Critical Evaluations in Business Management*, 2 vols (London: Routledge, 2003).

Wright, Rita P. *The Ancient Indus: Urbanism, Economy, and Society* (Cambridge: CUP, 2010).

Wright, Thomas. *Some Habits and Customs of the Working Classes by a Journeyman Engineer* (1867; reprint New York: Kelley, 1967).

Wulff, Birgit. 'The Third Reich and the Unemployed: The National-Socialist Work-Creation Schemes in Hamburg 1933–1934', in Richard J. Evans & Dick Geary (eds), *The German Unemployed: Experiences and Consequences of Mass-Unemployment from the Weimar Republic to the Third Reich* (London/Sydney: Croom Helm, 1987), pp. 281–302.

Wyatt, David. *Slaves and Warriors in Medieval Britain and Ireland, 800–1200* (Leiden/Boston: Brill, 2011).

Wylie, Alex. *Labour, Leisure and Luxury: A Contribution to Present Practical Political Economy* (London: Longmans, Green and Co., 1884).

Xiang, Biao. *Global 'Body Shopping': An Indian Labor System in the Informal Technology Industry* (Princeton/Oxford: Princeton UP, 2007).

Xiang, Hai et al. 'Early Holocene Chicken Domestication in Northern China', *PNAS*, 111(49) (December 9, 2014), pp. 17564–9.

Xu, Hong. 'The Erlitou Culture', in Anne P. Underhill (ed.), *A Companion to Chinese Archaeology* (Hoboken, NJ: Wiley-Blackwell, 2013), pp. 300–22.

Yamauchi, Takashi et al. 'Overwork-Related Disorders in Japan: Recent Trends and Development of a National Policy to Promote Preventive Measures', *Industrial Health*, 55(3) (2017), pp. 293–302.

Yang, Bin. *Cowrie Shells and Cowrie Money: A Global History* (London/New York: Routledge, 2019).

Yang, Yuda. 'Silver Mines in Frontier Zones: Chinese Mining Communities along the Southwestern Borders of the Qing Empire', in Nanny Kim & Keiko Nagase-Reimer (eds), *Mining, Monies, and Culture in Early Modern Societies: East Asian and Global Perspectives* (Leiden/Boston: Brill, 2013), pp. 87–114.

Yetish, Gandhi et al. 'Natural Sleep and its Seasonal Variations in Three Pre-Industrial Societies', *Current Biology*, 25 (2 November 2015), pp. 2862–8.

Yuan, Guangkuo. 'The Discovery and Study of the Early Shang Culture', in Anne P. Underhill (ed.), *A Companion to Chinese Archaeology* (Hoboken, NJ: Wiley-Blackwell, 2013), pp. 323–42.

Zanden, Jan Luiten van. 'The Road to the Industrial Revolution: Hypotheses and Conjectures about the Medieval Origins of the "European Miracle"', *Journal of Global History*, 3 (2008), pp. 337–59.

Zanden, Jan Luiten van. *The Long Road to the Industrial Revolution: The European Economy in a Global Perspective, 1000–1800* (Leiden/Boston: Brill, 2009).

Zanden, Jan Luiten van. 'Explaining the Global Distribution of Book Production before 1800', in Maarten Prak & Jan Luiten van Zanden (eds), *Technology, Skills and the Pre-Modern Economy in the East and the West. Essays dedicated to the memory of S.R. Epstein* (London/Boston: Brill, 2013), pp. 323–40.

Zanden, Jan Luiten van, Tine de Moor & Sarah Carmichael. *Capital Women: The European Marriage Pattern, Female Empowerment, and Economic Development in Western Europe, 1300–1800* (Oxford: OUP, 2019).

Zanden, Jan Luiten van et al. (eds). *How Was Life? Global Well-Being Since 1820* (Geneva/Amsterdam: OECD/CLIO INFRA, 2014).

Zeder, Melinda A. 'The Origins of Agriculture in the Near East', *Current Anthropology*, 52(S4) (October 2011), pp. S221–35.

Zeder, Melinda A. 'The Domestication of Animals', *Journal of Anthropological Research*, 68(2) (Summer 2012), pp. 161–89.

Zietlow, Rebecca E. 'The Constitutional Right to Organize', in Martha Albertson & Jonathan W. Fineman (eds), *Vulnerability and the Legal Organization of Work* (London/New York: Routledge, 2018), pp. 13–33.

Zijdeman, Richard L. 'Status Attainment in the Netherlands 1811–1941: Spatial and Temporal Variation before and after Industrialization', PhD thesis, Utrecht University, 2010.

Zijdeman, Richard L. & Filipa Ribeiro da Silva. 'Life Expectancy since 1820', in Jan Luiten van Zanden et al. (eds), *How Was Life? Global Well-Being Since 1820* (Geneva/Amsterdam: OECD/CLIO INFRA, 2014), pp. 101–16.

Zilfi, Madeline C. *Women and Slavery in the Late Ottoman Empire: The Design of Difference* (Cambridge: CUP, 2010).

Zimmermann, Susan. 'The Long-Term Trajectory of Anti-Slavery in International Politics: From the Expansion of the European International System to Unequal International Development', in Marcel van der Linden (ed.), *Humanitarian Interventions and Changing Labor Relations: The Long-Term Consequences of the Abolition of the Slave Trade* (Leiden & Boston: Brill, 2011), pp. 435–97.

Znamenski, Andrei A. ' "The Ethic of Empire" on the Siberian Borderland: The Peculiar Case of the "Rock People", 1791–1878', in Nicholas B. Breyfogle, Abby Schrader & Willard Sunderland (eds), *Peopling the Russian Periphery: Borderland Colonization in Eurasian History* (London/New York: Routledge, 2007), pp. 106–27.

Zuiderhoek, Arjan. 'Introduction: Land and Natural Resources in the Roman World in Historiographical and Theoretical Perspective', in Paul Erdkamp, Koen Verboven & Arjan Zuiderhoek (eds), *Ownership and Exploitation of Land and Natural Resources in the Roman World* (Oxford: OUP, 2015), pp. 1–17.

Zurbach, Julien. 'La Formation des Cités Grecques: Statuts, Classes et Systèmes Fonciers', *Annales-HSS*, 68(4) (October–December 2014), pp. 957–98.

Zürcher, Erik-Jan (ed.). *Fighting for a Living: A Comparative History of Military Labour 1500–2000* (Amsterdam: Amsterdam UP, 2013).

Zwart, Pim de & Jan Lucassen. 'Poverty or Prosperity in Northern India? New Evidence on Real Wages, 1590s–1870s', *EHR*, 73 (2020), pp. 644–67.

Zwart, Pim de & Jan Luiten van Zanden. *The Origins of Globalization, World Trade in the Making of the Global Economy, 1500–1800* (Cambridge: CUP, 2018).

INDEX

507